CW01572625

AFQR 2011

Airline Fleets
Quick Reference

Compiled by Pete Webber

Copyright © Air-Britain (Historians) Ltd 2011

Published by: Air-Britain (Historians) Ltd

Sales Department: 41 Penshurst Road, Leigh,
Tonbridge, Kent TN11 8HL

Membership Enquiries: 1 Rose Cottages, 179 Penn Road,
Hazlemere, Buckinghamshire HP15 7NE

ISBN: 978-0-85130-432-8

PHOTO CAPTIONS:
Front: East African Express DC-9-14 5Y-XXA together with FLY540 DHC-8-102 5Y-BXB beneath a dramatic tropical
sky at Nairobi International on 6.10.10. (Rod Simpson)
Back: Top: Jetstream 41 VH-TAH of Bringabella seen at Tamworth, NSW on 18.7.10. (Stewart Kedar)
Centre: Airbus A380-861 A6-EDG of Emirates on approach at Heathrow on 8.4.10. (Roger Birchall)
Bottom: Turkuaz Airbus A321-211 TC-TCE was visiting Glasgow on 13.7.10. (Charlie Stewart)

Printed by Bell & Bain Ltd, Glasgow

Air-Britain supports the fight against terrorism and the efforts of the Police and other Authorities in protecting airports and airfields from criminal activity.
If you see anything suspicious do not hesitate to call the
Anti-Terrorist Hotline 0800 789321
or alert a Police Officer.

AFQR 2011

Airline Fleets Quick Reference 2011

Welcome to the eleventh edition of Airline Fleets Quick Reference. The comments received from members (and other users) are very much appreciated and some slight changes have been incorporated this year as a result. Please contact us if you can offer any further improvements for future editions.

Coverage is, as always, worldwide. For European operations, fleets are included for airlines operating aircraft with more than 19 seats (i.e. Jetstream / Beech 1900 size); this means that any airliner above that size likely to be seen at a European airport should be included (unless it is out of service or stored). Again the fleets of the American majors and other operators using jets or large turboprop aircraft are included with the same cut-off size as European airlines. The major national and international carriers from the rest of the world are included but for these the smallest aircraft listed are usually ATR 42s.

The fleets are ordered as follows: first each fleet is listed alphabetically within the country of registration. For the larger fleets the aircraft are then listed in type and registration order. Small fleets are listed in registration order regardless of type. As with any rule you will find some entries that do not follow precisely, I also have to consider that fully laying out any fleet will take up more room than listing in registration order. This whole area is subject to ongoing review and entries may change for airlines as they add aircraft. I hope that what you will see is the best compromise that results in a good combination of space-saving and ease of use.

Information is provided in four columns for each entry - namely registration; type (abridged); constructor's number (and line number for Boeing and McDonnell-Douglas aircraft) plus a column for notes. This last column contains details of fleet number, (where appropriate), aircraft in temporary storage, details of leases between airlines and aircraft on order (where possible this is restricted to those due in the next 12 months). The types used in AFQR are the marketing names, rather than the name on the type certificate (e.g. CRJ-200 instead of CL-600-2B19). Extra data on the airlines and aircraft listed in this book, plus hundreds of other operators, as well as a full decode of airline three letter codes appear in *Airline Fleets 2011*.

New this year is the listing of corporate and VIP aircraft whose size falls within the scope of this book, the listing is at the end of the book after the fleets listings.

Thanks, as always, go to Chris Chatfield, Terry Smith, Barrie Towey and Tony Pither for reading the first draft and offering suggestions and changes, and to Dave Partington for preparing the finished article.

Data is believed correct up to 8th February 2011 so there are some updates from the main book. Obviously members will have comments to make on the content and concept of this publication and constructive criticism is welcome at the editorial address below. Please remember, however, that this book (in common with all Air-Britain publications) has been produced entirely in our own time. Of course, don't forget that AFQR 2011, like Airline Fleets 2011, can be kept up-to-date through the Commercial Scene section of our flagship magazine, *Air-Britain News*.

Please contact us at
airlinefleets@air-britain.co.uk

Abbreviations:
♦	New or changed entry in this edition
>	Leased to
<	Leased from
o/o	on order (aircraft believed for delivery within the next twelve months)
[xxx]	Storage location

AP - PAKISTAN

AIRBLUE   ED / ABQ

☐	AP-BIE	A319-112	3385
☐	AP-BIF	A319-112	3388
☐	AP-EDB	A319-111	3364 ♦
☐	AP-EDC	A319-111	3403 ♦
☐	AP-BGW	A320-232	0760
☐	AP-EDA	A320-214	3974 ♦
☐	AP-BJA	A321-231	1199
☐	AP-BRJ	A321-231	1008

JS FOCUS AIR   JSJ

☐	AP-BHZ	F.27 Friendship 500	10686

PAKISTAN INTERNATIONAL AL   PK / PIA

☐	AP-BDZ	A310-308	585
☐	AP-BEB	A310-308	587
☐	AP-BEC	A310-308	590
☐	AP-BEG	A310-308	653
☐	AP-BEQ	A310-308	656
☐	AP-BEU	A310-308	691
☐	AP-BGN	A310-324ET	676
☐	AP-BGO	A310-324ET	678
☐	AP-BGP	A310-324ET	682
☐	AP-BGQ	A310-325ET	660
☐	AP-BGR	A310-325ET	687
☐	AP-BGS	A310-325ET	689
☐	AP-BHH	ATR 42-500	645
☐	AP-BHI	ATR 42-500	653
☐	AP-BHJ	ATR 42-500	657
☐	AP-BHM	ATR 42-500	659
☐	AP-BHN	ATR 42-500	661
☐	AP-BHO	ATR 42-500	663
☐	AP-BHP	ATR 42-500	665
☐	AP-BCA	B737-340	23294/1114
☐	AP-BCB	B737-340	23295/1116
☐	AP-BCC	B737-340	23296/1121
☐	AP-BCD	B737-340	23297/1122
☐	AP-BCF	B737-340	23299/1235
☐	AP-BEH	B737-33A	25504/2341
☐	AP-BFT	B737-340	23298/1123
☐	AP-BAK	B747-240M	21825/383
☐	AP-BAT	B747-240M	22077/429
☐	AP-BFU	B747-367	23392/634
☐	AP-BFV	B747-367	23534/659
☐	AP-BFW	B747-367	23221/615
☐	AP-BFX	B747-367	23709/671
☐	AP-BFY	B747-367	23920/690
☐	AP-BGG	B747-367	24215/709
☐	AP-BGJ	B777-240ER	33775/467
☐	AP-BGK	B777-240ER	33776/469
☐	AP-BGL	B777-240ER	33777/473
☐	AP-BGY	B777-240LR	33781/504
☐	AP-BGZ	B777-240LR	33782/519
☐	AP-BHV	B777-340ER	33778/601
☐	AP-BHW	B777-340ER	33779/611
☐	AP-BHX	B777-240ER	35296/613
☐	AP-BID	B777-340ER	33780/705

RAYYAN AIR

☐	AP-BIB	B747-21AC	23652/669

SHAHEEN AIR INTERNATIONAL   SAI

☐	AP-BHA	B737-277	22645/768
☐	AP-BHB	B737-277	22655/872
☐	AP-BHC	B737-291	21509/521
☐	AP-BHG	B737-201	21666/547
☐	AP-BIK	B737-2B7	23114/997
☐	AP-BIP	B737-230	22634/840
☐	AP-BIQ	B737-258	22857/919
☐	AP-BIR	B737-228	23006/944
☐	AP-BIS	B737-228	23008/952 ♦
☐	AP-BIT	B737-236	21803/677
☐	AP-BIU	B737-236	21807/710
☐	AP-BJI	B737-201	22444/800

STAR AIR AVIATION   6S / URJ

☐	AP-URJ	B727-224F	20660/985

VISION AIR INTERNATIONAL   VIS

☐	AP-BIA	B737-2H3	22625/776

A2 - BOTSWANA

AIR BOTSWANA   BP / BOT

☐	A2-ABD	BAe146 Srs.100	E1101
☐	A2-ABN	ATR 42-500	507
☐	A2-ABO	ATR 42-500	511
☐	A2-ABP	ATR 42-500	512
☐	A2-ABR	ATR 72-212A	786
☐	A2-ABS	ATR 72-212A	788

A4O - OMAN

OMANAIR   WY / OMA

☐	A4O-DA	A330-243	1038
☐	A4O-DB	A330-343X	1044
☐	A4O-DC	A330-243	1049
☐	A4O-DD	A330-343X	1063
☐	A4O-DE	A330-343X	1093 ♦
☐	A4O-DF	A330-243	1120 ♦
☐	A4O-	A330-243	o/o ♦
☐	A4O-BA	B737-8BK/W	29685/2457
☐	A4O-BB	B737-8Q8/W	30721/2255
☐	A4O-BC	B737-81M/W	35284/2738
☐	A4O-BD	B737-81M/W	35287/2804
☐	A4O-BE	B737-81M/W	37161/2919
☐	A4O-BF	B737-8FZ/W	29637/3051
☐	A4O-BG	B737-8FZ/W	29664/3060
☐	A4O-BJ	B737-81M/W	34242/1674
☐	A4O-BM	B737-8FZ/W	29682/2853
☐	A4O-BN	B737-8Q8/W	30652/1018
☐	A4O-BO	B737-71M	33103/1154
☐	A4O-BP	B737-8Q8/W	35272/2537
☐	A4O-BR	B737-81M/W	33104/1337
☐	A4O-BS	B737-7Q8	30649/1048
☐	A4O-BU	B737-81M/W	35108/2554
☐	A4O-	B737-8	o/o ♦
☐	A4O-	B737-8	o/o ♦
☐	A4O-AS	ATR 42-500	574
☐	A4O-AT	ATR 42-500	576 >DKN
☐	A4O-	ERJ-175LR	o/o ♦
☐	A4O-	ERJ-175LR	o/o ♦
☐	A4O-	ERJ-175LR	o/o ♦

A5 - BHUTAN

DRUKAIR — KB / DRK

☐	A5-RGF	A319-115	2306
☐	A5-RGG	A319-115	2346

A6 - UNITED ARAB EMIRATES

ABU DHABI AVIATION

☐	A6-ADA	DHC-8Q-202	471
☐	A6-ADB	DHC-8Q-315	650
☐	A6-ADC	DHC-8Q-202	473
☐	A6-ADD	DHC-8Q-315	627
☐	A6-ADE	DHC-8Q-315	628
☐	A6-ADF	DHC-8Q-315	610
☐	A6-ADG	DHC-8Q-315	624
☐	A6-ADK	DHC-8-402Q	4222

AIR ARABIA — G9 / ABY

☐	A6-ABA	A320-214	2158	
☐	A6-ABB	A320-214	2166	
☐	A6-ABC	A320-214	2278	
☐	A6-ABD	A320-214	2349	
☐	A6-ABE	A320-214	2712	
☐	A6-ABG	A320-214	2930	
☐	A6-ABH	A320-214	2964	
☐	A6-ABI	A320-214	3044	
☐	A6-ABJ	A320-214	3218	
☐	A6-ABK	A320-214	3444	
☐	A6-ABL	A320-214	3476	
☐	A6-ABO	A320-214	3626	
☐	A6-ABP	A320-214	3802	
☐	A6-ABQ	A320-214	3840	
☐	A6-ABR	A320-214	3925	
☐	A6-ABS	A320-214	4061	
☐	A6-ABT	A320-214	4243	♦
☐	A6-ANA	A320-214	4468	♦
☐	A6-ANB	A320-214	4524	♦
☐	A6-ANC	A320-214	4539	♦
☐	A6-AND	A320-214	4568	♦
☐	A6-	A320-214	o/o	♦
☐	A6-	A320-214	o/o	♦
☐	A6-	A320-214	o/o	♦
☐	A6-	A320-214	o/o	♦
☐	A6-	A320-214	o/o	♦
☐	A6-	A320-214	o/o	♦

AVE.COM — 2E / PHW

☐	A6-PHA	B737-2T4	23444/1154
☐	A6-PHC	B737-33A	23626/1284
☐	A6-PHD	B737-2T5	22395/729
☐	A6-PHF	B737-219	21645/535
☐	A6-PHG	B737-3Q8	24986/2192
☐	A6-PHH	B737-3Q8	26314/2707
☐	EX-077	B737-268	21277/469

DOLPHIN AIR — ZD / FDN

☐	A6-ZYA	B737-2S2C	21926/597	[RKT]
☐	A6-ZYC	B737-2X2	22679/807	[RKT]

EASTERN SKYJETS — ESJ

☐	A6-ESA	DC-9-51	48136/993	
☐	A6-ESC	DC-9-32	48150/1014	
☐	A6-ESF	B737-4Y0	25177/2176	♦
☐	A6-ESK	BAeJetstream 41	41090	

EASTOK AVIA — EAA

☐	EY-621	A320-232	0386	♦
☐	EX-532	B737-247	23605/1371	
☐	EX-734	B737-25A	23791/1486	

EMIRATES — EK / UAE

☐	A6-EAA	A330-243	348	
☐	A6-EAD	A330-243	382	
☐	A6-EAE	A330-243	384	
☐	A6-EAF	A330-243	392	
☐	A6-EAG	A330-243	396	
☐	A6-EAH	A330-243	409	
☐	A6-EAI	A330-243	437	
☐	A6-EAJ	A330-243	451	
☐	A6-EAK	A330-243	452	
☐	A6-EAL	A330-243	462	
☐	A6-EAM	A330-243	491	
☐	A6-EAN	A330-243	494	
☐	A6-EAO	A330-243	509	
☐	A6-EAP	A330-243	525	
☐	A6-EAQ	A330-243	518	
☐	A6-EAR	A330-243	536	
☐	A6-EAS	A330-243	455	
☐	A6-EKQ	A330-243	248	
☐	A6-EKR	A330-243	251	
☐	A6-EKS	A330-243	283	
☐	A6-EKT	A330-243	293	
☐	A6-EKU	A330-243	295	
☐	A6-EKV	A330-243	314	
☐	A6-EKW	A330-243	316	
☐	A6-EKX	A330-243	326	
☐	A6-EKY	A330-243	328	
☐	A6-EKZ	A330-243	345	
☐	A6-ERA	A340-541	457	
☐	A6-ERB	A340-541	471	
☐	A6-ERC	A340-541	485	
☐	A6-ERD	A340-541	520	
☐	A6-ERE	A340-541	572	
☐	A6-ERF	A340-541	394	
☐	A6-ERG	A340-541	608	
☐	A6-ERH	A340-541	611	
☐	A6-ERI	A340-541	685	
☐	A6-ERJ	A340-541	694	
☐	A6-ERM	A340-313X	236	
☐	A6-ERN	A340-313X	166	
☐	A6-ERO	A340-313X	163	
☐	A6-ERP	A340-313X	185	
☐	A6-ERQ	A340-313X	190	
☐	A6-ERR	A340-313X	202	
☐	A6-ERS	A340-313X	139	
☐	A6-ERT	A340-313X	149	
☐	A6-EDA	A380-861	011	
☐	A6-EDB	A380-861	013	
☐	A6-EDC	A380-861	016	
☐	A6-EDD	A380-861	020	
☐	A6-EDE	A380-861	017	
☐	A6-EDF	A380-861	007	
☐	A6-EDG	A380-861	023	
☐	A6-EDH	A380-861	025	
☐	A6-EDI	A380-861	028	♦
☐	A6-EDJ	A380-861	009	♦
☐	A6-EDK	A380-861	030	♦
☐	A6-EDL	A380-861	046	♦
☐	A6-EDM	A380-861	042	♦
☐	A6-EDN	A380-861	056	♦
☐	A6-EDO	A380-861	057	♦
☐	A6-EDP	A380-861	o/o	♦
☐	A6-EDQ	A380-861	o/o	♦
☐	A6-EDR	A380-861	o/o	♦
☐	A6-EDS	A380-861	o/o	♦
☐	A6-EDT	A380-861	o/o	♦

A6-EBA	B777-31HER	32706/506
A6-EBB	B777-36NER	32789/508
A6-EBC	B777-36NER	32790/512
A6-EBD	B777-31HER	33501/516
A6-EBE	B777-36NER	32788/532
A6-EBF	B777-31HER	32708/536
A6-EBG	B777-36NER	33862/535
A6-EBH	B777-31HER	32707/539
A6-EBI	B777-36NER	32785/540
A6-EBJ	B777-36NER	32787/542
A6-EBK	B777-31HER	34481/549
A6-EBL	B777-31HER	32709/551
A6-EBM	B777-31HER	34482/556
A6-EBN	B777-36NER	32791/560
A6-EBO	B777-36NER	32792/568
A6-EBP	B777-31HER	32710/569
A6-EBQ	B777-36NER	33863/576
A6-EBR	B777-31HER	34483/578
A6-EBS	B777-31HER	32715/582
A6-EBT	B777-31HER	32730/585
A6-EBU	B777-31HER	34484/590
A6-EBV	B777-31HER	32728/594
A6-EBW	B777-36NER	32793/598
A6-EBX	B777-31HER	32729/619
A6-EBY	B777-36NER	33864/622
A6-EBZ	B777-31HER	32713/628
A6-ECA	B777-36NER	32794/632
A6-ECB	B777-31HER	32714/641
A6-ECC	B777-36NER	33865/664
A6-ECD	B777-36NER	32795/669
A6-ECE	B777-31HER	35575/681
A6-ECF	B777-31HER	35574/690
A6-ECG	B777-31HER	35579/709
A6-ECH	B777-31HER	35581/714
A6-ECI	B777-31HER	35580/728
A6-ECJ	B777-31HER	35583/734
A6-ECK	B777-31HER	35584/743
A6-ECL	B777-31HER	37704/748
A6-ECM	B777-31HER	37703/755
A6-ECN	B777-31HER	37705/761
A6-ECO	B777-31HER	37706/765
A6-ECP	B777-31HER	37707/768
A6-ECQ	B777-31HER	35588/779
A6-ECR	B777-31HER	35592/794
A6-ECS	B777-31HER	38980/803
A6-ECT	B777-31HER	35591/808
A6-ECU	B777-31HER	35593/817
A6-ECV	B777-31HER	35594/824
A6-ECW	B777-31HER	38981/828
A6-ECX	B777-31HER	38982/830
A6-ECY	B777-31HER	35595/840
A6-ECZ	B777-31HER	38983/847 ♦
A6-EFD	B777-F1H	35606/766
A6-EFE	B777-F1H	35607/788
A6-	B777-F1H	o/o♦
A6-EGA	B777-31HER	38984/861 ♦
A6-	B777-31HER	o/o♦
A6-	B777-31HER	o/o♦
A6-	B777-31HER	o/o♦
A6-	B777-31HER	o/o♦
A6-	B777-31HER	o/o♦
A6-	B777-31HER	o/o♦
A6-EMD	B777-21H	27247/30
A6-EME	B777-21H	27248/33
A6-EMF	B777-21H	27249/42
A6-EMG	B777-21HER	27252/63
A6-EMH	B777-21HER	27251/54
A6-EMI	B777-21HER	27250/47
A6-EMJ	B777-21HER	27253/91
A6-EMK	B777-21HER	29324/171
A6-EML	B777-21HER	29325/176
A6-EMM	B777-31H	29062/256
A6-EMN	B777-31H	29063/262
A6-EMO	B777-31H	28680/300
A6-EMP	B777-31H	29395/326

A6-EMQ	B777-31H	32697/396	
A6-EMR	B777-31H	29396/402	
A6-EMS	B777-31H	29067/408	
A6-EMT	B777-31H	32699/414	
A6-EMU	B777-31H	29064/418	
A6-EMV	B777-31H	28687/432	
A6-EMW	B777-31H	32700/434	
A6-EMX	B777-31H	32702/444	
A6-EWA	B777-21HLR	35572/654	
A6-EWB	B777-21HLR	35573/662	
A6-EWC	B777-21HLR	35576/677	
A6-EWD	B777-21HLR	35577/688	
A6-EWE	B777-21HLR	35582/725	
A6-EWF	B777-21HLR	35586/739	
A6-EWG	B777-21HLR	35578/741	
A6-EWH	B777-21HLR	35587/747	
A6-EWI	B777-21HLR	35589/757	
A6-EWJ	B777-21HLR	35590/775	
A6-EFI	B747-81HF	37451/ .	o/o
A6-	B747-81HF		o/o
N408MC	B747-47UF	29261/1192	<GTI
N415MC	B747-47UF	32837/1304	<GTI
N497MC	B747-47UF	29258/1220	<GTI
OO-THC	B747-4HAERF	35235/1389	<TAY
OO-THD	B747-4HAERF	35236/1399	<TAY

ETIHAD AIRWAYS EY / ETD

A6-EID	A319-132	1947	
A6-EIE	A319-132	1955	
A6-EIA	A320-232	1944	
A6-EIB	A320-232	1945	
A6-EIC	A320-232	2167	
A6-EIF	A320-232	3004	
A6-EIG	A320-232	3050	
A6-EIH	A320-232	3693	
A6-EII	A320-232	3713	
A6-EIJ	A320-232	3902	
A6-EIK	A320-232	3676	
A6-EIL	A320-232	4066	
A6-EIM	A320-232	4077	
A6-EIN	A320-232	4124	
A6-EIZ	A320-211	0350	
A6-AFA	A330-343X	1071	
A6-AFB	A330-343X	1081	
A6-AFC	A330-343X	1167	♦
A6-	A330-343X	o/o♦	
A6-	A330-343X	o/o♦	
A6-	A330-343X	o/o♦	
A6-EYD	A330-243	658	
A6-EYE	A330-243	688	
A6-EYF	A330-243	717	
A6-EYG	A330-243	724	
A6-EYH	A330-243	729	
A6-EYI	A330-243	730	
A6-EYJ	A330-243	737	
A6-EYK	A330-243	788	
A6-EYL	A330-243	809	
A6-EYM	A330-243	824	
A6-EYN	A330-243	832	
A6-EYO	A330-243	852	
A6-EYP	A330-243	854	
A6-EYQ	A330-243	868	
A6-EYR	A330-243	975	
A6-EYS	A330-243	991	
A6-DCA	A330-243F	1032	♦
A6-DCB	A330-243F	1070	♦
A6-EHA	A340-541	748	
A6-EHB	A340-541	757	
A6-EHC	A340-541	761	
A6-EHD	A340-541	783	
A6-EHE	A340-642HGW	829	
A6-EHF	A340-642HGW	837	

☐ A6-EHH	A340-642HGW	870	
☐ A6-EHI	A340-642HGW	929	
☐ A6-EHJ	A340-642HGW	933	
☐ A6-EHK	A340-642HGW	1030	
☐ A6-EHL	A340-642HGW	1040	
☐ A6-ETA	B777-3FXER	34597/538	
☐ A6-ETB	B777-3FXER	34598/543	
☐ A6-ETC	B777-3FXER	34599/544	
☐ A6-ETD	B777-3FXER	34600/547	
☐ A6-ETE	B777-3FXER	34601/548	
☐ A6-ETF	B777-3FXER	39700/832	♦
☐ A6-ETG	B777-3FXER		o/o♦
☐ A6-ETH	B777-3FXER		o/o♦
☐ A6-EYZ	B767-341ER	30341/768	<AUH
☐ TF-ELK	A300B4-622RF	557	<ABD

FALCON EXPRESS CARGO AL   FC / FVS

☐ A6-FCA	Beech 1900C-1	UC-57	
☐ A6-FCB	Beech 1900C-1	UC-66	
☐ A6-FCC	Beech 1900C-1	UC-68	
☐ A6-FCD	Beech 1900C-1	UC-71	
☐ A6-FCY	F.27 Friendship 500	10370	♦
☐ A6-FCZ	F.27 Friendship 500	10448	

FLYDUBAI   FZ / FDB

☐ A6-FDA	B737-8KN/W	35794/2794	
☐ A6-FDB	B737-8KN/W	35795/2829	
☐ A6-FDC	B737-8KN/W	40233/2952	
☐ A6-FDD	B737-8KN/W	40234/2966	
☐ A6-FDE	B737-8KN/W	40235/3053	
☐ A6-FDF	B737-8KN/W	40236/3110	
☐ A6-FDG	B737-8KN/W	29636/3197	♦
☐ A6-FDH	B737-8KN/W	31716/3270	♦
☐ A6-FDI	B737-8KN/W	31765/3302	♦
☐ A6-FDJ	B737-8KN/W	40237/3356	♦
☐ A6-FDK	B737-8KN/W	40238/3391	♦
☐ A6-FDL	B737-8KN/W	40239/3460	♦
☐ A6-FDM	B737-8KN/W	40240/3485	♦
☐ A6-FDN	B737-8KN/W	40241/3517	♦
☐ A6-FDO	B737-8KN/W	40242/3540	o/o♦
☐ A6-	B737-8KN/W		o/o♦
☐ A6-	B737-8KN/W		o/o♦
☐ A6-	B737-8KN/W		o/o♦
☐ A6-	B737-8KN/W		o/o♦
☐ A6-	B737-8KN/W		o/o♦
☐ A6-	B737-8KN/W		o/o♦
☐ A6-	B737-8KN/W		o/o♦

HEAVYLIFT INTERNATIONAL   HVL

☐ A6-HLC	DC-8-63AF	46126/524	
☐ A6-HLG	B737-3G7F	24710/1825	
☐ A6-HLH	B737-3G7F	24711/1843	

MAXIMUS AIR CARGO   MXU

☐ A6-MAC	L-382G-44K-30 Hercules	5024	
☐ A6-MAX	L-382G-44K-30 Hercules	4895	
☐ A6-MXA	A300B4-622RF	788	<ABD
☐ A6-MXB	A300B4-622RF	767	<ABD
☐ UR-ZYD	An-124	19530502843	<UAK
☐ UR-BXQ	Il-76TD	1023410360	<UKL
☐ UR-BXR	Il-76TD	1023411384	<UKL
☐ UR-BXS	Il-76TD	1023411368	<UKL

MIDEX AIRLINES   MG / MIX

☐ A6-MDA	A300B4-203F	157	Midex 1
☐ A6-MDB	A300B4-203F	196	Midex 2
☐ A6-MDC	A300B4-203F	218	Midex 3
☐ A6-MDD	A300B4-203F	203	
☐ A6-MDE	A300B4-203F	125	

☐ A6-MDF	A300B4-203F	134	
☐ A6-MDG	B747-228F	25266/878	
☐ A6-MDH	B747-228F	24735/772	♦
☐ A6-MDI	B747-228F	24879/822	♦

RAK AIRWAYS   RT / RKM

☐ A6-AAM	A318-112	1599	
☐ A6-RKA	B757-256	29311/940	

SILVER AIR

☐ A6-JUD	B737-306	23541/1309	

SKYLINK ARABIA

☐ ER-AVB	An-26B-100	57303204	♦
☐ ER-AZN	An-24RV	037308801	
☐ RDPL-34157	Il-76TD	093418556	
☐ UP-I7611	Il-76T	093418548	
☐ UP-I7630	Il-76T	023441189	
☐ UP-AN203	An-12AP	347408	
☐ ZS-MAD	F.28 Fellowship 4000	11225	
☐ 4L-GLT	An-12BK	7345305	

A7 - QATAR

QATAR AIRWAYS   QR / QTR

☐ A7-ABX	A300B4-622RF	554	
☐ A7-ABY	A300B4-622RF	560	
☐ A7-AFB	A300B4-622RF	614	
☐ A7-CJA	A319-133LR	1656	
☐ A7-CJB	A319-133LR	2341	
☐ A7-MED	A319-133LR	4114	♦
☐ A7-ADA	A320-232	1566	
☐ A7-ADB	A320-232	1648	
☐ A7-ADC	A320-232	1773	
☐ A7-ADD	A320-232	1895	
☐ A7-ADE	A320-232	1957	
☐ A7-ADF	A320-232	2097	
☐ A7-ADG	A320-232	2121	
☐ A7-ADH	A320-232	2138	
☐ A7-ADI	A320-232	2161	
☐ A7-ADJ	A320-232	2288	
☐ A7-ADU	A320-232	3071	
☐ A7-AHA	A320-232	4110	
☐ A7-AHB	A320-232	4130	
☐ A7-AHC	A320-232	4183	
☐ A7-AHD	A320-232	4436	♦
☐ A7-AHE	A320-232	4479	♦
☐ A7-AHF	A320-232	4496	♦
☐ A7-	A320-232		o/o♦
☐ A7-	A320-232		o/o♦
☐ A7-	A320-232		o/o♦
☐ A7-	A320-232		o/o♦
☐ A7-	A320-232		o/o♦
☐ A7-	A320-232		o/o♦
☐ A7-	A320-232		o/o♦
☐ A7-	A320-232		o/o♦
☐ A7-ADK	A321-231	1487	
☐ A7-ADS	A321-231	1928	
☐ A7-ADT	A321-231	2107	
☐ A7-ADV	A321-231	3274	
☐ A7-ADW	A321-231	3369	
☐ A7-ADX	A321-231	3397	
☐ A7-ADY	A321-231	3636	
☐ A7-ADZ	A321-231	3669	
☐ A7-AIA	A321-231	4173	♦
☐ A7-AIB	A321-231	4382	♦
☐ A7-AIC	A321-231	4406	♦
☐ A7-ACA	A330-202	473	

☐ A7-ACB	A330-202	489		
☐ A7-ACC	A330-202	511		
☐ A7-ACD	A330-202	521		
☐ A7-ACE	A330-202	571		
☐ A7-ACF	A330-202	638		
☐ A7-ACG	A330-202	743		
☐ A7-ACH	A330-202	441		
☐ A7-ACI	A330-202	746		
☐ A7-ACJ	A330-202	760		
☐ A7-ACK	A330-202	792		
☐ A7-ACL	A330-202	820		
☐ A7-ACM	A330-202	849		
☐ A7-ACN	A330-202	893		
☐ A7-AFL	A330-202	612		
☐ A7-AFM	A330-202	616		
☐ A7-AFP	A330-202	684		
☐ A7-AEA	A330-302	623		
☐ A7-AEB	A330-302	637		
☐ A7-AEC	A330-302	659		
☐ A7-AED	A330-302	680		
☐ A7-AEE	A330-302	711		
☐ A7-AEF	A330-302	721		
☐ A7-AEG	A330-302	734		
☐ A7-AEH	A330-302	789		
☐ A7-AEI	A330-302	813		
☐ A7-AEJ	A330-302	826		
☐ A7-AEM	A330-302	893		
☐ A7-AEN	A330-302	907		
☐ A7-AEO	A330-302	918		
☐ A7-AGA	A340-642HGW	740		
☐ A7-AGB	A340-642HGW	715		
☐ A7-AGC	A340-642HGW	766		
☐ A7-AGD	A340-642HGW	798		
☐ A7-BBA	B777-2DZLR	36012/753		
☐ A7-BBB	B777-2DZLR	36013/762		
☐ A7-BBC	B777-2DZLR	36015/825		
☐ A7-BBD	B777-2DZLR	36016/831		
☐ A7-BBE	B777-2DZLR	36017/837		
☐ A7-BBF	B777-2DZLR	36018/842		
☐ A7-BBG	B777-2DZLR	36101/883	♦	
☐ A7-BBH	B777-2DZLR	36102/885	♦	
☐ A7-	B777-2DZLR		o/o♦	
☐ A7-BFA	B777-FDZ	36098/865	♦	
☐ A7-BFB	B777-FDZ	36100/874	♦	
☐ A7-BAA	B777-3DZER	36009/676		
☐ A7-BAB	B777-3DZER	36103/686		
☐ A7-BAC	B777-3DZER	36010/731		
☐ A7-BAE	B777-3DZER	36104/769		
☐ A7-BAF	B777-3DZER	37661/815		
☐ A7-BAG	B777-3DZER	36014/819		
☐ A7-BAH	B777-3DZER	37662/849	♦	
☐ A7-BAI	B777-3DZER	36095/742		
☐ A7-BAJ	B777-3DZER	36096/851	♦	
☐ A7-BAK	B777-3DZER	36097/859	♦	
☐ A7-BAL	B777-3DZER	38244/893	♦	
☐ A7-BAM	B777-3DZER	38245/922	o/o♦	
☐ A7-BAN	B777-3DZER		o/o♦	
☐ A7-BAO	B777-3DZER	36011/750		
☐ A7-BAP	B777-3DZER		o/o♦	
☐ A7-BAQ	B777-3DZER	38247/910	♦	
☐ A7-	B787-8		o/o♦	
☐ A7-	B787-8		o/o♦	
☐ A7-	B787-8		o/o♦	
☐ A7-	B787-8		o/o♦	

A9C - Bahrain

BAHRAIN AIR — 2B / BAB

☐ A9C-BAO	A320-214	4600	♦	
☐ A9C-BAU	A320-214	4055		
☐ A9C-BAV	A320-214	3861		
☐ A9C-BAW	A319-111	2763		
☐ A9C-BAX	A319-111	2700		
☐ A9C-BAY	A320-212	0579		

DHL INTERNATIONAL AVIATION — ES / DHX

☐ HZ-SNA	B727-264F	20896/1051	
☐ HZ-SNB	B727-223F	21084/1199	
☐ HZ-SNC	B727-230F	20905/1091	
☐ HZ-SND	B727-223F	20994/1190	
☐ HZ-SNF	B727-277F	22643/1762	

GULF AIR — GF / GFA

☐ A9C-AA	A320-214	3706		
☐ A9C-AB	A320-214	4030		
☐ A9C-AC	A320-214	4059		
☐ A9C-AD	A320-214	4083		
☐ A9C-AE	A320-214	4146		
☐ A9C-AF	A320-214	4158		
☐ A9C-AG	A320-214	4188		
☐ A9C-AH	A320-214	4218		♦
☐ A9C-AI	A320-214	4255		♦
☐ A9C-AJ	A320-214	4502		♦
☐ A9C-AK	A320-214	4541		♦
☐ A9C-	A320-214			o/o♦
☐ A9C-	A320-214			o/o♦
☐ A9C-	A320-214			o/o♦
☐ A9C-	A320-214			o/o♦
☐ A9C-	A320-214			o/o♦
☐ A9C-EE	A320-212	0419	805	
☐ A9C-EL	A320-212	0497	812	
☐ A9C-EN	A320-212	0537	814	
☐ A9C-ES	A321-211	0675		
☐ A9C-ET	A321-211	0761		
☐ A9C-EU	A319-112	1884		
☐ A9C-EV	A319-112	1901		
☐ A9C-KA	A330-243	276	501	
☐ A9C-KB	A330-243	281	502	
☐ A9C-KC	A330-243	286	503	
☐ A9C-KD	A330-243	287	504	
☐ A9C-KE	A330-243	334	505	
☐ A9C-KF	A330-243	340	506	
☐ A9C-KG	A330-243	527		
☐ A9C-KH	A330-243	529		
☐ A9C-KI	A330-243	532		
☐ A9C-KJ	A330-243	992		
☐ A9C-LF	A340-312	133	406	
☐ A9C-LG	A340-313X	212	407	
☐ A9C-LH	A340-313X	215	408	
☐ A9C-LI	A340-313X	554	409	
☐ A9C-LJ	A340-313X	282	410	
☐ A9C-MA	ERJ-170LR	17000293		♦
☐ A9C-MB	ERJ-170LR	17000278		♦
☐ A9C-MC	ERJ-190AR	19000372		♦
☐ A9C-MD	ERJ-190AR	19000373		♦

B - CHINA

AIR CHINA — CA / CCA

☐ B-2223	A319-111	1679	
☐ B-2225	A319-111	1654	
☐ B-2339	A319-111	1753	
☐ B-2364	A319-115	2499	
☐ B-2404	A319-131	2454	
☐ B-6004	A319-115	2508	
☐ B-6014	A319-115	2525	
☐ B-6022	A319-131	2000	
☐ B-6023	A319-131	2007	
☐ B-6024	A319-131	2015	

	Reg	Type	Serial	Marks
☐	B-6031	A319-131	2172	
☐	B-6032	A319-131	2202	
☐	B-6033	A319-131	2205	
☐	B-6034	A319-115	2237	
☐	B-6035	A319-115	2269	
☐	B-6036	A319-115	2285	
☐	B-6037	A319-115	2293	
☐	B-6038	A319-115	2298	
☐	B-6044	A319-115	2532	
☐	B-6046	A319-115	2545	
☐	B-6047	A319-115	2551	
☐	B-6048	A319-131	2559	
☐	B-6213	A319-131	2614	
☐	B-6216	A319-131	2643	
☐	B-6223	A319-115	2805	
☐	B-6225	A319-115	2819	
☐	B-6226	A319-115	2839	
☐	B-6227	A319-115	2847	
☐	B-6228	A319-115	2890	
☐	B-6235	A319-131	3195	
☐	B-6236	A319-131	3200	
☐	B-6237	A319-131	3226	
☐	B-6238	A319-115	3250	
☐	B-2210	A320-214	1296	
☐	B-2354	A320-214	0707	
☐	B-2355	A320-214	0724	
☐	B-2376	A320-214	0876	
☐	B-2377	A320-214	0921	
☐	B-6606	A320-214	3337	
☐	B-6607	A320-214	3461	
☐	B-6608	A320-214	3601	
☐	B-6676	A320-232	4317	♦
☐	B-6677	A320-232	4348	♦
☐	B-	A320-232		o/o♦
☐	B-	A320-232		o/o♦
☐	B-	A320-232		o/o♦
☐	B-	A320-232		o/o♦
☐	B-	A320-232		o/o♦
☐	B-	A320-232		o/o♦
☐	B-	A320-232		o/o♦
☐	B-6326	A321-213	3329	
☐	B-6327	A321-213	3307	
☐	B-6361	A321-213	3523	
☐	B-6362	A321-213	3623	
☐	B-6363	A321-213	3653	
☐	B-6365	A321-213	3655	
☐	B-6382	A321-213	3665	
☐	B-6383	A321-213	3678	
☐	B-6385	A321-213	3722	
☐	B-6386	A321-213	3725	
☐	B-6555	A321-213	3766	
☐	B-6556	A321-213	3806	
☐	B-6593	A321-213	3973	
☐	B-6595	A321-213	4022	
☐	B-6596	A321-213	4031	
☐	B-6597	A321-213	4062	
☐	B-6599	A321-213	3940	
☐	B-6603	A321-213	4131	
☐	B-6605	A321-213	4091	
☐	B-6631	A321-213	4180	
☐	B-6632	A321-213	4221	♦
☐	B-6633	A321-213	4283	♦
☐	B-6665	A321-213	4318	♦
☐	B-6675	A321-213	4377	♦
☐	B-6701	A321-213	4472	♦
☐	B-6711	A321-213	4494	♦
☐	B-	A321-213		o/o♦
☐	B-	A321-213		o/o♦
☐	B-	A321-213		o/o♦
☐	B-	A321-213		o/o♦
☐	B-	A321-213		o/o♦
☐	B-	A321-213		o/o♦
☐	B-	A321-213		o/o♦
☐	B-	A321-213		o/o♦
☐	B-6070	A330-243	750	
☐	B-6071	A330-243	756	
☐	B-6072	A330-243	759	
☐	B-6073	A330-243	780	
☐	B-6075	A330-243	785	
☐	B-6076	A330-243	797	
☐	B-6079	A330-243	810	
☐	B-6080	A330-243	815	
☐	B-6081	A330-243	839	
☐	B-6090	A330-243	860	
☐	B-6091	A330-243	867	
☐	B-6092	A330-243	873	
☐	B-6093	A330-243	884	
☐	B-6113	A330-243	890	
☐	B-6115	A330-243	909	
☐	B-6117	A330-243	903	
☐	B-6130	A330-243	930	
☐	B-6131	A330-243	941	
☐	B-6132	A330-243	944	
☐	B-6505	A330-243	957	
☐	B-6511	A330-243	1110	♦
☐	B-6512	A330-243	1087	♦
☐	B-6513	A330-243	1130	♦
☐	B-6523	A330-243	1187	♦
☐	B-6525	A330-243	1199	o/o♦
☐	B-	A330-243		o/o♦
☐	B-	A330-343		o/o♦
☐	B-	A330-343		o/o♦
☐	B-	A330-343		o/o♦
☐	B-2385	A340-313X	192	
☐	B-2386	A340-313X	199	
☐	B-2387	A340-313X	201	
☐	B-2388	A340-313X	242	
☐	B-2389	A340-313X	243	
☐	B-2390	A340-313X	264	
☐	B-2522	B737-3Z0	23451/1240	
☐	B-2530	B737-3Z0	27046/2252	
☐	B-2533	B737-3Z0	27138/2436	
☐	B-2535	B737-3J6	25078/2002	
☐	B-2580	B737-3J6	25080/2254	
☐	B-2581	B737-3J6	25081/2263	
☐	B-2584	B737-3J6	25891/2385	
☐	B-2585	B737-3J6	27045/2384	
☐	B-2586	B737-3Z0	27047/2357	
☐	B-2587	B737-3J6	25892/2396	
☐	B-2588	B737-3J6	25893/2489	
☐	B-2590	B737-3Z0	27126/2370	
☐	B-2597	B737-3Z0	27176/2495	
☐	B-2598	B737-3J6	27128/2493	
☐	B-2599	B737-3Z0	25896/2558	
☐	B-2600	B737-36N	28554/2835	
☐	B-2627	B737-36E	26315/2706	
☐	B-2630	B737-36E	26317/2719	
☐	B-2905	B737-33A	25506/2360	
☐	B-2906	B737-33A	25507/2373	
☐	B-2907	B737-33A	25508/2414	
☐	B-2947	B737-33A	25511/2599	
☐	B-2948	B737-3J6	27361/2631	
☐	B-2949	B737-3J6	27372/2650	
☐	B-2950	B737-3Z0	27374/2647	
☐	B-2951	B737-3Z0	27373/2658	
☐	B-2953	B737-3J6	27523/2710	
☐	B-2954	B737-3J6	27518/2768	
☐	B-2957	B737-3Z0	27521/2738	
☐	B-5035	B737-36N	28672/2976	
☐	B-5036	B737-36N	28673/2995	
☐	B-2612	B737-79L	33411/1538	
☐	B-2613	B737-79L	33412/1544	
☐	B-2700	B737-79L	33413/1560	
☐	B-5043	B737-79L	33408/1331	
☐	B-5044	B737-79L	33409/1351	

☐ B-5045	B737-79L	33410/1354	
☐ B-5063	B737-7BX	30736/658	
☐ B-5064	B737-7BX	30737/687	
☐ B-5201	B737-79L/W	34023/1795	
☐ B-5202	B737-79L/W	34537/1837	
☐ B-5203	B737-79L/W	34538/1853	
☐ B-5211	B737-79L	34019/1749	
☐ B-5213	B737-79L/W	34020/1769	
☐ B-5214	B737-79L/W	34021/1774	
☐ B-5217	B737-79L/W	34022/1786	
☐ B-5220	B737-79L/W	34539/1856	
☐ B-5226	B737-79L/W	34540/1877	
☐ B-5227	B737-79L/W	34541/1937	
☐ B-5228	B737-79L/W	34542/1993	
☐ B-5229	B737-79L/W	34543/2006	
☐ B-2161	B737-86N	28655/965	
☐ B-2509	B737-8Z0	30072/466	
☐ B-2510	B737-8Z0	30071/381	
☐ B-2511	B737-8Z0	30073/487	
☐ B-2641	B737-89L	29876/337	
☐ B-2642	B737-89L	29877/359	
☐ B-2643	B737-89L	29878/379	
☐ B-2645	B737-89L	29879/427	
☐ B-2648	B737-89L	29880/511	
☐ B-2649	B737-89L	30159/572	
☐ B-2650	B737-89L	30160/594	
☐ B-2657	B737-89L	30517/1224	
☐ B-2670	B737-89L	30514/1055	
☐ B-2671	B737-89L	30515/1165	
☐ B-2672	B737-89L	30516/1168	
☐ B-2673	B737-86N	29888/1133	
☐ B-2690	B737-86N	29889/1153	
☐ B-5167	B737-808	34701/1887	
☐ B-5168	B737-808	34702/1917	
☐ B-5169	B737-808	34703/1941	
☐ B-5170	B737-808	34705/1998	
☐ B-5171	B737-808	34706/2014	
☐ B-5172	B737-8Q8	30704/1985	
☐ B-5173	B737-8Q8	30705/2001	
☐ B-5175	B737-86N	35209/2067	
☐ B-5176	B737-86N	34258/2096	
☐ B-5177	B737-86N	35210/2127	
☐ B-5178	B737-86N	32682/2117	
☐ B-5179	B737-86N	35211/2146	
☐ B-5196	B737-86N	36810/2699	
☐ B-5197	B737-86N/W	36811/2777	
☐ B-5198	B737-89L/W	36491/2759	
☐ B-5311	B737-8Q8	29373/2171	
☐ B-5312	B737-8Q8	29374/2203	
☐ B-5313	B737-8Q8	30716/2210	
☐ B-5325	B737-86N	32692/2275	
☐ B-5326	B737-86N	35214/2308	
☐ B-5327	B737-86N	35219/2371	
☐ B-5328	B737-86N	35221/2444	
☐ B-5329	B737-86N	35222/2463	
☐ B-5341	B737-89L/W	36483/2403	
☐ B-5342	B737-89L/W	36484/2441	
☐ B-5343	B737-89L/W	36485/2470	
☐ B-5387	B737-89L/W	36492/2828	
☐ B-5390	B737-89L/W	36486/2606	
☐ B-5391	B737-89L/W	36487/2664	
☐ B-5392	B737-89L/W	36488/2674	
☐ B-5397	B737-89L/W	36489/2704	
☐ B-5398	B737-89L/W	36490/2715	
☐ B-5422	B737-89L/W	36741/2845	
☐ B-5423	B737-89L/W	36742/2877	
☐ B-5425	B737-89L/W	36743/2896	
☐ B-5426	B737-89L/W	36744/2969	
☐ B-5431	B737-86N	36812/2918	
☐ B-5436	B737-86N	36813/2976	
☐ B-5437	B737-86N/W	36815/3020	
☐ B-5438	B737-86N/W	36816/3032	
☐ B-5442	B737-86N/W	36745/3049	
☐ B-5443	B737-86N/W	36746/3072	

☐ B-5447	B737-89L/W	40015/3509	♦
☐ B-5455	B737-86N/W	36774/2944	
☐ B-5457	B737-86N/W	36775/2951	
☐ B-5477	B737-89L/W	36755/3387	♦
☐ B-5485	B737-89L/W	36747/3124	
☐ B-5486	B737-89L/W	36748/3127	
☐ B-5495	B737-89L/W	36749/3145	
☐ B-5496	B737-89L/W	36750/3155	
☐ B-5497	B737-89L/W	36751/3167	♦
☐ B-5500	B737-89L/W	36752/3188	♦
☐ B-5507	B737-89L/W	36753/3247	♦
☐ B-5508	B737-89L/W	36545/3275	♦
☐ B-5509	B737-89L/W	36547/3300	♦
☐ B-5510	B737-89L/W	36548/3312	♦
☐ B-5518	B737-89L/W	36754/3336	♦
☐ B-5519	B737-86N	36802/3350	♦
☐ B-5525	B737-86N	37886/3436	♦
☐ B-5547	B737-88N/W	36806/3509	♦
☐ B-	B737-8		o/o♦
☐ B-	B737-8		o/o♦
☐ B-	B737-8		o/o♦
☐ B-	B737-8		o/o♦
☐ B-	B737-8		o/o♦
☐ B-	B737-8		o/o♦
☐ B-	B737-8		o/o♦
☐ B-	B737-8		o/o♦
☐ B-2443	B747-4J6	25881/957	
☐ B-2445	B747-4J6	25882/1021	
☐ B-2447	B747-4J6	25883/1054	
☐ B-2460	B747-4J6M	24348/792	
☐ B-2467	B747-4J6M	28754/1119	
☐ B-2468	B747-4J6M	28755/1128	
☐ B-2469	B747-4J6M	28756/1175	
☐ B-2470	B747-4J6M	29070/1181	
☐ B-2471	B747-4J6M	29071/1229	
☐ B-2472	B747-4J6	30158/1243	
☐ B-2820	B757-2Z0	25885/476	
☐ B-2821	B757-2Z0	25886/480	
☐ B-2826	B757-2Y0	26155/495	
☐ B-2832	B757-2Z0	25887/554	
☐ B-2836	B757-2Z0	27258/595	
☐ B-2837	B757-2Z0	27259/609	
☐ B-2839	B757-2Z0	27269/615	
☐ B-2840	B757-2Z0	27270/622	
☐ B-2841	B757-2Z0	27367/624	
☐ B-2844	B757-2Z0	27511/669	
☐ B-2845	B757-2Z0	27512/674	
☐ B-2855	B757-2Z0	29792/822	
☐ B-2856	B757-2Z0	29793/833	
☐ B-2499	B767-332ER	30597/797	
☐ B-2553	B767-2J6ER	23744/155	
☐ B-2557	B767-3J6	25875/429	
☐ B-2558	B767-3J6	25876/478	
☐ B-2559	B767-3J6	25877/530	
☐ B-2560	B767-3J6	25878/569	
☐ B-2059	B777-2J6	29153/168	
☐ B-2060	B777-2J6	29154/173	
☐ B-2061	B777-2J6	29155/179	
☐ B-2063	B777-2J6	29156/214	
☐ B-2064	B777-2J6	29157/240	
☐ B-2065	B777-2J6	29744/280	
☐ B-2066	B777-2J6	29745/290	
☐ B-2067	B777-2J6	29746/338	
☐ B-2068	B777-2J6	29747/344	
☐ B-2069	B777-2J6	29748/349	
☐ B-	B777-3J6		o/o♦
☐ B-	B777-3J6		o/o♦
☐ B-	B777-3J6		o/o♦
☐ B-	B777-3J6		o/o♦

AIR CHINA CARGO — CA / CCO

	Reg	Type	MSN/Line	Note
☐	B-2409	B747-412 (SF)	26560/1052	<SQC
☐	B-2455	B747-412BCF	27070/1049	♦
☐	B-2456	B747-4J6BCF	24346/743	
☐	B-2458	B747-4J6BCF	24347/775	
☐	B-2462	B747-2J6F	24960/814	
☐	B-2475	B747-4FTF	34239/1367	
☐	B-2476	B747-4FTF	34240/1373	
☐	B-2477	B747-433BCF	24998/840	
☐	B-2478	B747-433BCF	25075/868	
☐	B-2871	Tu-204-120SE	64030	
☐	B-2872	Tu-204-120SE	64031	o/o♦
☐	B-2873	Tu-204-120SE	64034	o/o♦
☐	B-	Tu-204-120SE		o/o♦
☐	B-	Tu-204-120SE		o/o♦

CAPITAL AIRLINES — JD / DRA

	Reg	Type	MSN	Note
☐	B-6156	A319-112	2849	<CHH
☐	B-6157	A319-112	2891	<CHH
☐	B-6169	A319-112	2985	<CHH
☐	B-6177	A319-112	3285	<CHH
☐	B-6178	A319-132	3548	<CHH
☐	B-6179	A319-132	3561	<CHH
☐	B-6180	A319-132	3578	
☐	B-6181	A319-132	3580	
☐	B-6182	A319-132	3520	
☐	B-6192	A319-132	3768	<CHH
☐	B-6193	A319-133	3849	
☐	B-6198	A319-112	2617	
☐	B-6199	A319-112	2644	
☐	B-6212	A319-115	2581	<CGN
☐	B-6215	A319-112	2611	<CGN
☐	B-6221	A319-112	2746	
☐	B-6222	A319-112	2733	
☐	B-6245	A319-133	3851	
☐	B-6400	A319-132	3638	
☐	B-6401	A319-133	3842	
☐	B-6402	A319-132	3914	
☐	B-6403	A319-132	3958	
☐	B-6405	A319-132	3982	
☐	B-6417	A319-133	4522	<CHH♦
☐	B-	A319-133X	4042	o/o
☐	B-6709	A320-232	4412	<CHH♦
☐	B-6710	A320-232	4440	<CHH♦
☐	B-6723	A320-232	4483	<CHH♦
☐	B-6726	A320-232	4505	<CHH♦
☐	B-2112	B737-36N	28599/3115	<CHH
☐	B-2113	B737-36N	28602/3118	<CHH
☐	B-2115	B737-36N	28606/3124	<CHH
☐	B-2608	B737-36Q	28662/2914	<CHH
☐	B-3000	B737-36Q	29326/3020	<CHH

CHANG AN AIRLINES — HU / CGN

	Reg	Type	MSN	Note
☐	B-3444	AVIC I Y7-100C	9701	
☐	B-3445	AVIC I Y7-100C	9705	
☐	B-3475	AVIC I Y7-100C	6703	
☐	B-3707	AVIC I Y7-100C	12701	
☐	B-3708	AVIC I Y7-100C	11705	
☐	B-5092	B737-705	29092/260	<CHH
☐	B-5115	B737-8FH/W	29640/1649	<CHH
☐	B-5116	B737-8FH/W	29672/1745	<CHH
☐	B-5180	B737-8FH/W	35089/2042	<CHH
☐	B-5181	B737-8FH/W	35090/2073	<CHH
☐	B-6210	A319-115	2557	<CHH
☐	B-6211	A319-115	2561	<CHH
☐	B-6212	A319-115	2581	>DRA
☐	B-6215	A319-112	2611	>DRA

CHENGDU AIRLINES — EU

	Reg	Type	MSN	Note
☐	B-6151	A319-112	1263	
☐	B-6152	A319-112	0946	
☐	B-6155	A319-112	0949	
☐	B-6163	A319-112	3024	
☐	B-6229	A319-112	2762	♦
☐	B-6230	A319-112	2774	
☐	B-	A320-214	2820	o/o♦

CHINA CARGO AIRLINES — CK / CKK

	Reg	Type	MSN/Line	Note
☐	B-2076	B777-F6N	37711/846	♦
☐	B-2077	B777-F6N	37713/856	♦
☐	B-2078	B777-F6N	37714/869	♦
☐	B-2079	B777-F6N	37715/876	♦
☐	B-2082	B777-F6N		o/o♦
☐	B-2083	B777-F6N		o/o♦
☐	B-2170	MD-11F	48461/475	
☐	B-2171	MD-11F	48495/461	
☐	B-2172	MD-11F	48496/496	
☐	B-2174	MD-11F	48498/522	
☐	B-2175	MD-11F	48520/541	
☐	B-2308	A300B4-605RF	532	
☐	B-2425	B747-40BERF	35207/1377	
☐	B-2426	B747-40BERF	35208/1392	
☐	B-	Tu-204-120SE	64041	o/o

CHINA EASTERN AIRLINES — MU / CES

	Reg	Type	MSN	Note
☐	B-2306	A300B4-605RF	521	
☐	B-2307	A300B4-605RF	525	
☐	B-2317	A300B4-605R	741	
☐	B-2318	A300B4-605R	707	
☐	B-2319	A300B4-605R	732	
☐	B-2324	A300B4-622R	725	
☐	B-2325	A300B4-605R	746	
☐	B-2326	A300B4-605R	754	
☐	B-2330	A300B4-605R	763	
☐	B-2215	A319-112	1541	
☐	B-2216	A319-112	1551	
☐	B-2217	A319-112	1601	
☐	B-2222	A319-112	1603	
☐	B-2226	A319-112	1786	
☐	B-2227	A319-112	1778	
☐	B-2331	A319-112	1285	
☐	B-2332	A319-112	1303	
☐	B-2333	A319-112	1377	
☐	B-2334	A319-112	1386	
☐	B-6167	A319-115	3168	
☐	B-6172	A319-115	3186	
☐	B-6217	A319-115	2693	
☐	B-6218	A319-115	2757	
☐	B-6231	A319-115	2825	
☐	B-6332	A319-115	3262	
☐	B-2201	A320-214	0914	
☐	B-2202	A320-214	0925	
☐	B-2203	A320-214	1005	
☐	B-2205	A320-214	0984	
☐	B-2206	A320-214	0986	
☐	B-2207	A320-214	1028	
☐	B-2208	A320-214	1070	
☐	B-2209	A320-214	1030	
☐	B-2211	A320-214	1041	
☐	B-2212	A320-214	1316	
☐	B-2213	A320-214	1345	
☐	B-2219	A320-214	1532	
☐	B-2220	A320-214	1542	
☐	B-2221	A320-214	1639	
☐	B-2228	A320-214	1906	
☐	B-2229	A320-214	1911	
☐	B-2230	A320-214	1964	

Reg	Type	MSN	Notes
☐ B-2335	A320-214	1312	
☐ B-2336	A320-214	1330	
☐ B-2337	A320-214	1357	
☐ B-2338	A320-214	1361	
☐ B-2356	A320-214	0665	
☐ B-2357	A320-214	0754	
☐ B-2358	A320-214	0838	
☐ B-2359	A320-214	0854	
☐ B-2362	A320-214	0828	
☐ B-2363	A320-214	0883	
☐ B-2372	A320-214	0897	
☐ B-2375	A320-214	0909	
☐ B-2378	A320-214	0939	
☐ B-2379	A320-214	0967	
☐ B-2398	A320-214	1108	
☐ B-2399	A320-214	1093	
☐ B-2400	A320-214	1072	
☐ B-2410	A320-214	2437	
☐ B-2411	A320-214	2451	
☐ B-2412	A320-214	2478	
☐ B-2413	A320-214	2493	
☐ B-2415	A320-214	2498	
☐ B-6001	A320-214	1981	
☐ B-6002	A320-214	2022	
☐ B-6003	A320-214	2034	
☐ B-6005	A320-214	2036	
☐ B-6006	A320-214	2068	
☐ B-6007	A320-214	2056	
☐ B-6008	A320-214	2049	
☐ B-6009	A320-214	2219	
☐ B-6010	A320-214	2221	
☐ B-6011	A320-214	2235	
☐ B-6012	A320-214	2239	
☐ B-6013	A320-214	2244	
☐ B-6015	A320-214	2212	
☐ B-6016	A320-214	2155	
☐ B-6017	A320-214	2274	
☐ B-6028	A320-214	2171	
☐ B-6029	A320-214	2182	
☐ B-6030	A320-214	2199	
☐ B-6259	A320-214	2562	
☐ B-6260	A320-214	2591	
☐ B-6261	A320-214	2606	
☐ B-6262	A320-214	2627	
☐ B-6333	A320-214	3170	
☐ B-6335	A320-214	3197	
☐ B-6346	A320-232	3481	
☐ B-6370	A320-214	3559	
☐ B-6371	A320-214	3611	
☐ B-6372	A320-232	3613	
☐ B-6373	A320-232	3650	
☐ B-6375	A320-232	3677	
☐ B-6376	A320-232	3692	
☐ B-6399	A320-232	3716	
☐ B-6558	A320-232	3793	
☐ B-6559	A320-232	3904	
☐ B-6560	A320-232	3937	
☐ B-6585	A320-232	3965	
☐ B-6586	A320-232	3775	
☐ B-6587	A320-232	3797	
☐ B-6600	A320-232	3870	
☐ B-6601	A320-232	4037	
☐ B-6616	A320-232	3929	
☐ B-6617	A320-232	4144	
☐ B-6635	A320-232	4027	♦
☐ B-6638	A320-232	4240	♦
☐ B-6639	A320-232	4252	♦
☐ B-6653	A320-232	4232	o/o
☐ B-6671	A320-232	4186	♦
☐ B-6672	A320-232	4220	o/o
☐ B-6673	A320-232	4340	♦
☐ B-6695	A320-232	4297	♦
☐ B-6715	A320-232	4355	♦
☐ B-	A320-232		o/o♦
☐ B-	A320-232		o/o♦
☐ B-	A320-232		o/o♦
☐ B-	A320-232		o/o♦
☐ B-	A320-232		o/o♦
☐ B-	A320-232		o/o♦
☐ B-	A320-232		o/o♦
☐ B-	A320-232		o/o♦
☐ B-	A320-232		o/o♦
☐ B-	A320-232		o/o♦
☐ B-	A320-232		o/o♦
☐ B-	A320-232		o/o♦
☐ B-2289	A321-211	2309	
☐ B-2290	A321-211	2315	
☐ B-2291	A321-211	2543	
☐ B-2292	A321-211	2549	
☐ B-2419	A321-211	2882	
☐ B-2420	A321-211	2895	
☐ B-6329	A321-211	3233	
☐ B-6330	A321-211	3247	
☐ B-6331	A321-211	3249	
☐ B-6332	A321-211	3262	
☐ B-6345	A321-211	3471	
☐ B-6366	A321-211	3593	
☐ B-6367	A321-211	3612	
☐ B-6368	A321-211	3639	
☐ B-6369	A321-211	3682	
☐ B-	A321-211		o/o♦
☐ B-	A321-211		o/o♦
☐ B-6082	A330-243	821	
☐ B-6083	A330-343E	830	
☐ B-6085	A330-343E	836	
☐ B-6095	A330-343E	851	
☐ B-6096	A330-343E	862	
☐ B-6097	A330-343E	866	
☐ B-6099	A330-243	916	
☐ B-6100	A330-343E	928	
☐ B-6119	A330-343	713	
☐ B-6120	A330-343	720	
☐ B-6121	A330-243	728	
☐ B-6122	A330-243	732	
☐ B-6123	A330-243	735	
☐ B-6125	A330-343	773	
☐ B-6126	A330-343	777	
☐ B-6127	A330-343	781	
☐ B-6128	A330-343	782	
☐ B-6129	A330-343	791	
☐ B-6506	A330-343E	936	
☐ B-6507	A330-343E	942	
☐ B-	A330-343E		o/o♦
☐ B-	A330-343E		o/o♦
☐ B-	A330-343E		o/o♦
☐ B-2380	A340-313X	129	
☐ B-2381	A340-313X	131	
☐ B-2382	A340-313X	141	
☐ B-2383	A340-313X	161	
☐ B-2384	A340-313X	182	
☐ B-6050	A340-642	468	
☐ B-6051	A340-642	488	
☐ B-6052	A340-642	514	
☐ B-6053	A340-642	577	
☐ B-6055	A340-642	586	
☐ B-2538	B737-3W0	25090/2040	
☐ B-2571	B737-39P	29410/3053	
☐ B-2572	B737-39P	29411/3071	
☐ B-2573	B737-39P	29412/3080	
☐ B-2589	B737-3W0	27127/2377	
☐ B-2594	B737-341	26853/2275	
☐ B-2955	B737-33A	27453/2687	
☐ B-2956	B737-33A	27907/2690	
☐ B-2958	B737-3W0	27522/2727	
☐ B-2966	B737-33A	27462/2765	
☐ B-2969	B737-36R	30102/3108	
☐ B-2981	B737-3W0	28972/2919	
☐ B-2983	B737-3W0	28973/2941	

	Reg	Type	c/n
☐	B-2985	B737-3W0	29068/2945
☐	B-2986	B737-3W0	29069/2951
☐	B-2988	B737-36R	29087/2970
☐	B-2502	B737-7W0	30075/311
☐	B-2503	B737-7W0	30074/292
☐	B-2639	B737-7W0	29912/140
☐	B-2640	B737-7W0	29913/148
☐	B-2665	B737-86R	30495/876
☐	B-2680	B737-76Q	30282/1143
☐	B-2681	B737-79P	33037/1198
☐	B-2682	B737-79P	33038/1219
☐	B-2683	B737-79P	28253/1247
☐	B-2684	B737-79P	33039/1227
☐	B-2685	B737-79P	33040/1244
☐	B-5030	B737-79P	30651/1267
☐	B-5031	B737-79P	28255/1284
☐	B-5032	B737-79P	30035/1288
☐	B-5033	B737-79P	30657/1319
☐	B-5034	B737-79P	30036/1336
☐	B-5054	B737-79P	29365/1841
☐	B-5074	B737-79P	33008/1718
☐	B-5084	B737-79P	33009/1728
☐	B-5085	B737-89P/W	30691/1702
☐	B-5086	B737-89P/W	32800/1681
☐	B-5087	B737-89P/W	32802/1725
☐	B-5093	B737-79P/W	29357/1630
☐	B-5094	B737-79P/W	29358/1651
☐	B-5095	B737-79P/W	29361/1694
☐	B-5096	B737-79P/W	29362/1713
☐	B-5097	B737-79P	29364/1823
☐	B-5100	B737-89P/W	30681/1645
☐	B-5101	B737-89P/W	30682/1673
☐	B-5199	B737-89P/W	36272/2753
☐	B-5208	B737-79P/W	33041/1902
☐	B-5209	B737-79P/W	33042/1947
☐	B-5210	B737-79P/W	33043/1976
☐	B-5223	B737-79P/W	33044/1987
☐	B-5225	B737-79P/W	33045/1999
☐	B-5231	B737-79P/W	33046/2034
☐	B-5242	B737-79P/W	36269/2357
☐	B-5243	B737-79P/W	36270/2398
☐	B-5245	B737-79P/W	36271/2697
☐	B-5255	B737-79P/W	36757/2902
☐	B-5256	B737-79P/W	36758/2949
☐	B-5257	B737-79P/W	36760/2968
☐	B-5258	B737-79P/W	36760/3009
☐	B-5259	B737-79P/W	36762/3046
☐	B-5262	B737-79P/W	36764/3067
☐	B-5263	B737-79P/W	36766/3086
☐	B-5265	B737-79P/W	36767/3239 ♦
☐	B-5267	B737-79P/W	36768/3269 ♦
☐	B-5271	B737-79P/W	36772/3444 ♦
☐	B-5376	B737-86N/W	35226/2641
☐	B-5472	B737-89P/W	36761/3001
☐	B-5473	B737-89P/W	36763/3036
☐	B-5475	B737-89P/W	36765/3065
☐	B-5492	B737-89P/W	29661/3083
☐	B-5493	B737-89P/W	29652/3121
☐	B-5501	B737-89P/W	39388/3203 ♦
☐	B-5515	B737-89P/W	36769/3311 ♦
☐	B-5516	B737-89P/W	39389/3304 ♦
☐	B-5517	B737-89P/W	29653/3294 ♦
☐	B-5527	B737-89P/W	36771/3343 ♦
☐	B-5530	B737-89P/W	29655/3351 ♦
☐	B-2568	B767-3W0ER	28148/620
☐	B-2569	B767-3W0ER	28149/627
☐	B-5001	B767-3W0ER	28264/644
☐	B-3013	CRJ-200LR	7571
☐	B-3019	CRJ-200LR	7581
☐	B-3021	CRJ-200LR	7596
☐	B-3070	CRJ-200LR	7647
☐	B-3071	CRJ-200LR	7684

	Reg	Type	c/n	
☐	B-3049	ERJ-145LI	14500839	
☐	B-3050	ERJ-145LI	14500848	
☐	B-3051	ERJ-145LI	14500898	
☐	B-3052	ERJ-145LI	14500905	
☐	B-3053	ERJ-145LI	14500882	
☐	B-3055	ERJ-145LI	14500921	
☐	B-3056	ERJ-145LI	14500928	
☐	B-3057	ERJ-145LI	14500932	
☐	B-3058	ERJ-145LI	14500958	
☐	B-3059	ERJ-145LI	14500949	

CHINA EXPRESS AIRLINES G5 / HXA

	Reg	Type	c/n	
☐	B-3001	CRJ-200LR	7565	<CDG
☐	B-3012	CRJ-200LR	7557	<CDG
☐	B-3016	CRJ-200LR	7614	
☐	B-7700	CRJ-200LR	7704	♦

CHINA POSTAL AIRLINES 8Y / CYZ

	Reg	Type	c/n	
☐	B-3101	AVIC II Y-8F-100	10(08)01	
☐	B-3102	AVIC II Y-8F-100	10(08)02	
☐	B-3103	AVIC II Y-8F-100	10(08)05	
☐	B-3109	AVIC II Y-8F-100	13(08)03	
☐	B-3110	AVIC II Y-8F-100	13(08)04	
☐	B-2135	B737-45R(SF)	29035/3046	
☐	B-2513	B737-45R(SF)	29034/3015	♦
☐	B-2526	B737-3Y0(SF)	25172/2089	
☐	B-2527	B737-3Y0(SF)	25173/2097	
☐	B-2528	B737-3Y0(SF)	25174/2168	
☐	B-2656	B737-3Q8(SF)	26292/2519	
☐	B-2661	B737-3Q8(SF)	26284/2418	
☐	B-2662	B737-3Q8(SF)	24988/2466	
☐	B-2881	B737-45R(SF)	29032/2943	
☐	B-2882	B737-45R(SF)	29033/2963	
☐	B-2891	B737-46J(SF)	28334/2802	
☐	B-2892	B737-46J(SF)	28271/2801	
☐	B-5046	B737-341(SF)	24276/1645	
☐	B-5047	B737-341(SF)	24278/1660	
☐	B-5071	B737-341(QC)	24277/1658	
☐	B-5072	B737-341(QC)	24279/1673	

CHINA SOUTHERN AIRLINES CZ / CSN

	Reg	Type	c/n
☐	B-2315	A300B4-622RF	733
☐	B-2316	A300B4-622R	734
☐	B-2323	A300B4-622R	739
☐	B-2328	A300B4-622RF	756
☐	B-2294	A319-132	2371
☐	B-2295	A319-132	2408
☐	B-2296	A319-132	2426
☐	B-2297	A319-132	2435
☐	B-6018	A319-132	1971
☐	B-6019	A319-132	1986
☐	B-6020	A319-133	2004
☐	B-6021	A319-133	2008
☐	B-6039	A319-132	2200
☐	B-6040	A319-132	2203
☐	B-6041	A319-132	2232
☐	B-6042	A319-132	2273
☐	B-6158	A319-132	2901
☐	B-6160	A319-132	2940
☐	B-6161	A319-132	2948
☐	B-6162	A319-132	2969
☐	B-6168	A319-132	3020
☐	B-6183	A319-115	3828
☐	B-6187	A319-115	3903
☐	B-6190	A319-132	3860
☐	B-6191	A319-132	3890
☐	B-6195	A319-112	3983
☐	B-6200	A319-115	2519
☐	B-6201	A319-115	2541
☐	B-6202	A319-115	2546
☐	B-6203	A319-112	2554

	Reg	Type	c/n	
☐	B-6205	A319-132	2505	
☐	B-6206	A319-132	2574	
☐	B-6207	A319-132	2579	
☐	B-6208	A319-112	2555	
☐	B-6209	A319-112	2558	
☐	B-6219	A319-132	2667	
☐	B-6220	A319-132	2815	
☐	B-6239	A319-132	3144	
☐	B-6240	A319-132	3258	
☐	B-6241	A319-132	3269	
☐	B-6242	A319-132	3311	
☐	B-6243	A319-132	3342	
☐	B-6407	A319-132	4036	
☐	B-6408	A319-112	4038	
☐	B-6409	A319-112	4071	
☐	B-2347	A320-233	0705	
☐	B-2350	A320-232	0712	
☐	B-2351	A320-233	0718	
☐	B-2352	A320-232	0720	
☐	B-2353	A320-232	0722	
☐	B-2365	A320-232	0849	
☐	B-2366	A320-232	0859	
☐	B-2367	A320-232	0881	
☐	B-2368	A320-232	0895	
☐	B-2369	A320-232	0900	
☐	B-2374	A320-232	2345	
☐	B-2391	A320-232	0950	
☐	B-2392	A320-232	0966	
☐	B-2393	A320-232	1035	
☐	B-2395	A320-232	1039	
☐	B-2396	A320-232	1057	
☐	B-2405	A320-232	2343	
☐	B-2406	A320-214	2354	
☐	B-2407	A320-232	2334	
☐	B-2408	A320-214	2361	
☐	B-2459	A320-214	0709	
☐	B-6251	A320-214	2484	
☐	B-6252	A320-214	2506	
☐	B-6253	A320-214	2511	
☐	B-6255	A320-214	2637	
☐	B-6263	A320-214	2708	
☐	B-6269	A320-232	2743	
☐	B-6272	A320-214	2770	
☐	B-6275	A320-232	2680	
☐	B-6276	A320-232	2689	
☐	B-6277	A320-232	2701	
☐	B-6278	A320-232	2714	
☐	B-6279	A320-232	2772	
☐	B-6281	A320-214	2796	
☐	B-6282	A320-214	2824	
☐	B-6283	A320-214	2834	
☐	B-6287	A320-214	2899	
☐	B-6288	A320-214	2855	
☐	B-6289	A320-214	2861	
☐	B-6290	A320-214	2877	
☐	B-6291	A320-214	2915	
☐	B-6292	A320-214	2960	
☐	B-6293	A320-214	2986	
☐	B-6303	A320-214	2950	
☐	B-6575	A320-232	3910	
☐	B-6576	A320-232	3941	
☐	B-6577	A320-232	3959	
☐	B-6582	A320-232	3999	
☐	B-6583	A320-232	4003	
☐	B-6588	A320-232	4017	
☐	B-6620	A320-214	4172	
☐	B-6623	A320-214	4205	♦
☐	B-6627	A320-232	4225	♦
☐	B-6641	A320-232	4140	♦
☐	B-6651	A320-232	4260	♦
☐	B-6652	A320-232	4290	♦
☐	B-6655	A320-214	4350	♦
☐	B-6656	A320-214	4322	♦
☐	B-6681	A320-214	4365	♦
☐	B-6703	A320-214	4396	♦
☐	B-	A320-214		o/o♦
☐	B-	A320-214		o/o♦
☐	B-	A320-214		o/o♦
☐	B-	A320-214		o/o♦
☐	B-2280	A321-231	1596	
☐	B-2281	A321-231	1614	
☐	B-2282	A321-231	1776	
☐	B-2283	A321-231	1788	
☐	B-2284	A321-231	1974	
☐	B-2285	A321-231	1995	
☐	B-2287	A321-231	2080	
☐	B-2288	A321-231	2067	
☐	B-2417	A321-231	2521	
☐	B-2418	A321-231	2530	
☐	B-6265	A321-231	2713	
☐	B-6267	A321-231	2741	
☐	B-6270	A321-231	2759	
☐	B-6271	A321-231	2767	
☐	B-6273	A321-231	2809	
☐	B-6302	A321-231	2936	
☐	B-6305	A321-231	2971	
☐	B-6306	A321-231	3067	
☐	B-6307	A321-231	3075	
☐	B-6308	A321-231	3112	
☐	B-6317	A321-231	3217	
☐	B-6318	A321-231	3251	
☐	B-6319	A321-231	3241	
☐	B-6339	A321-231	3507	
☐	B-6342	A321-231	3459	
☐	B-6343	A321-231	3493	
☐	B-6345	A321-231	3471	
☐	B-6353	A321-231	3552	
☐	B-6355	A321-231	3566	
☐	B-6356	A321-231	3587	
☐	B-6378	A321-231	3645	
☐	B-6379	A321-231	3681	
☐	B-6389	A321-231	3764	
☐	B-6397	A321-231	3784	
☐	B-6398	A321-231	3847	
☐	B-6552	A321-231	3867	
☐	B-6553	A321-231	3920	
☐	B-6578	A321-231	3934	
☐	B-6579	A321-231	3938	
☐	B-6580	A321-231	3951	
☐	B-6581	A321-231	3981	
☐	B-6622	A321-231	4194	♦
☐	B-6625	A321-231	4184	♦
☐	B-6626	A321-231	4189	♦
☐	B-6628	A321-231	4217	♦
☐	B-6629	A321-231	4224	♦
☐	B-6630	A321-231	4230	♦
☐	B-6657	A321-231	4266	♦
☐	B-6659	A321-231	4292	♦
☐	B-6660	A321-231	4299	♦
☐	B-6661	A321-231	4341	♦
☐	B-6663	A321-231	4338	♦
☐	B-6683	A321-231	4369	♦
☐	B-6685	A321-231	4416	♦
☐	B-6686	A321-231	4387	♦
☐	B-6687	A321-231	4430	♦
☐	B-6056	A330-243	649	
☐	B-6057	A330-243	652	
☐	B-6058	A330-243	656	
☐	B-6059	A330-243	664	
☐	B-6077	A330-243	818	
☐	B-6078	A330-243	840	
☐	B-6086	A330-343E	879	
☐	B-6087	A330-343E	889	
☐	B-6098	A330-343E	908	
☐	B-6111	A330-343E	935	
☐	B-6112	A330-343E	937	
☐	B-6135	A330-343E	1096	♦
☐	B-6500	A330-343E	954	
☐	B-6501	A330-343E	964	

	Reg	Type	c/n	Notes
☐	B-6502	A330-343E	958	
☐	B-6515	A330-343E	1115	♦
☐	B-6516	A330-343E	1129	♦
☐	B-	A330-343E		o/o♦
☐	B-	A330-343E		o/o♦
☐	B-	A330-343E		o/o♦
☐	B-	A330-343E		o/o♦
☐	B-	A380-841	54	o/o♦
☐	B-3022	ATR 72-212A	521	
☐	B-3023	ATR 72-212A	531	
☐	B-3025	ATR 72-212A	547	
☐	B-3026	ATR 72-212A	552	
☐	B-3027	ATR 72-212A	555	
☐	B-2539	B737-3Y0	26068/2306	
☐	B-2574	B737-37K	29407/3100	
☐	B-2575	B737-37K	29408/3104	
☐	B-2582	B737-31B	25895/2499	
☐	B-2583	B737-31B	25897/2554	
☐	B-2596	B737-31B	27151/2437	
☐	B-2909	B737-3Y0	26082/2456	
☐	B-2910	B737-3Y0	26083/2459	
☐	B-2911	B737-3Y0	26084/2460	
☐	B-2920	B737-3Q8	27271/2523	
☐	B-2921	B737-3Q8	27286/2528	
☐	B-2922	B737-31B	27272/2555	
☐	B-2923	B737-31B	27275/2565	
☐	B-2924	B737-31B	27287/2575	
☐	B-2926	B737-31B	27289/2593	
☐	B-2927	B737-31B	27290/2595	
☐	B-2929	B737-31B	27343/2619	
☐	B-2930	B737-31L	27273/2556	
☐	B-2931	B737-31L	27276/2567	
☐	B-2935	B737-37K	27283/2547	
☐	B-2936	B737-37K	27335/2609	
☐	B-2941	B737-31B	27344/2622	
☐	B-2946	B737-37K	27375/2655	
☐	B-2952	B737-31B	27519/2678	
☐	B-2959	B737-31B	27520/2775	
☐	B-2162	B737-7K9	30041/909	
☐	B-2163	B737-7K9	30042/931	
☐	B-2169	B737-71B	32936/1531	
☐	B-2620	B737-71B	32937/1569	
☐	B-2622	B737-71B	32938/1603	
☐	B-2698	B737-76N	32583/994	
☐	B-2699	B737-76N	32596/1028	
☐	B-2916	B737-71B	32939/1607	
☐	B-2917	B737-71B	32940/1624	
☐	B-5068	B737-71B	32933/1430	
☐	B-5069	B737-71B	32934/1465	
☐	B-5070	B737-71B	32935/1507	
☐	B-5107	B737-7K9	34320/1763	
☐	B-5108	B737-7K9	34321/1802	
☐	B-5221	B737-71B	29366/1872	
☐	B-5222	B737-71B	29367/1896	
☐	B-5230	B737-71B	29371/2064	
☐	B-5232	B737-71B	35360/2051	
☐	B-5233	B737-71B	35361/2077	
☐	B-5235	B737-71B	29370/2137	
☐	B-5236	B737-71B	35362/2102	
☐	B-5237	B737-71B	29372/2131	
☐	B-5238	B737-71B	35363/2066	
☐	B-5239	B737-71B	35364/2156	
☐	B-5240	B737-71B	35368/2264	
☐	B-5241	B737-71B	35372/2291	
☐	B-5247	B737-71B	35377/2980	
☐	B-5250	B737-71B	35378/2346	
☐	B-5251	B737-71B	35384/2446	
☐	B-5252	B737-71B	35382/3034	
☐	B-5253	B737-71B	35383/3005	
☐	B-	B737-71B		o/o♦
☐	B-	B737-71B		o/o♦
☐	B-	B737-71B		o/o♦
☐	B-	B737-71B		o/o♦
☐	B-	B737-71B		o/o♦
☐	B-2693	B737-81B	32921/1187	
☐	B-2694	B737-81B	32922/1199	
☐	B-2695	B737-81B	32923/1213	
☐	B-2696	B737-81B	32924/1230	
☐	B-2697	B737-81B	32925/1250	
☐	B-5020	B737-81B	32926/1268	
☐	B-5021	B737-81B	32927/1290	
☐	B-5022	B737-81B	32928/1323	
☐	B-5040	B737-81B	32929/1348	
☐	B-5041	B737-81B	32930/1355	
☐	B-5042	B737-81B	32931/1362	
☐	B-5067	B737-81B	32932/1395	
☐	B-5112	B737-86N	34248/1806	
☐	B-5113	B737-81B	34250/1784	
☐	B-5120	B737-83N/W	32580/1024	
☐	B-5121	B737-83N/W	32609/1059	
☐	B-5122	B737-83N/W	32610/1110	
☐	B-5123	B737-83N/W	32611/1135	
☐	B-5125	B737-83N/W	32612/1184	
☐	B-5126	B737-83N/W	32613/1197	
☐	B-5127	B737-83N/W	32615/1207	
☐	B-5128	B737-83N/W	32882/1163	
☐	B-5129	B737-83N/W	32884/1181	
☐	B-5133	B737-86N	34252/1851	
☐	B-5147	B737-81B	30697/1915	
☐	B-5149	B737-81B	30699/1933	
☐	B-5155	B737-8K5/W	30783/804	
☐	B-5156	B737-81Q/W	30786/1138	
☐	B-5157	B737-81Q/W	30787/1234	
☐	B-5163	B737-81B	30708/2087	
☐	B-5165	B737-81B	30709/1961	
☐	B-5166	B737-81B	33006/1983	
☐	B-5189	B737-81B	35365/2191	
☐	B-5190	B737-81B	35366/2223	
☐	B-5191	B737-81B	35367/2237	
☐	B-5192	B737-81B	35369/2272	
☐	B-5193	B737-81B	35370/2299	
☐	B-5195	B737-81B	35371/2302	
☐	B-5300	B737-81B	35375/2314	
☐	B-5310	B737-81B	35376/2329	
☐	B-5339	B737-81B	35380/2372	
☐	B-5340	B737-81B	35381/2402	
☐	B-5356	B737-81B	35385/2486	
☐	B-5419	B737-81B	35379/2957	
☐	B-5420	B737-81B	35374/2940	
☐	D-5421	D737-01D	35373/2001	
☐	B-5445	B737-81B	35388/3154	
☐	B-5446	B737-81B	35389/3144	
☐	B-5468	B737-81B	35386/3068	
☐	B-5469	B737-81B	35387/3041	
☐	B-	B737-8Q8		o/o♦
☐	B-	B737-8Q8		o/o♦
☐	B-	B737-8Q8		o/o♦
☐	B-2461	B747-41BF	32804/1312	
☐	B-2473	B747-41BF	32803/1306	
☐	B-2812	B757-28S	32341/961	
☐	B-2813	B757-28S	32342/966	
☐	B-2816	B757-21B	25083/359	
☐	B-2817	B757-21B	25258/389	
☐	B-2818	B757-21B	25259/392	
☐	B-2822	B757-21B	25884/461	
☐	B-2823	B757-21B	25888/575	
☐	B-2824	B757-21B	25889/583	
☐	B-2825	B757-21B	25890/585	
☐	B-2827	B757-2Y0	26156/503	
☐	B-2830	B757-28S	32343/1015	
☐	B-2831	B757-2Y0	26153/482	
☐	B-2835	B757-236	25598/445	
☐	B-2838	B757-2Z0	27260/613	
☐	B-2851	B757-28S	29215/797	
☐	B-2853	B757-28S	29216/811	

	Reg	Type	C/n	Notes
☐	B-2859	B757-28S	29217/868	
☐	B-2860	B757-236	29945/873	
☐	B-2051	B777-21B	27357/20	
☐	B-2052	B777-21B	27358/24	
☐	B-2053	B777-21B	27359/46	
☐	B-2054	B777-21B	27360/48	
☐	B-2055	B777-21BER	27524/55	
☐	B-2056	B777-21BER	27525/66	
☐	B-2057	B777-21BER	27604/106	
☐	B-2058	B777-21BER	27605/110	
☐	B-2062	B777-21BER	27606/121	
☐	B-2070	B777-21BER	32703/472	
☐	B-2071	B777-F1B	37309/760	♦
☐	B-2072	B777-F1B	37310/770	♦
☐	B-2073	B777-F1B	37311/811	
☐	B-2075	B777-F1B	37312/820	
☐	B-2081	B777-F1B	37313/888	♦
☐	B-	B777-F1B		o/o♦
☐	B-	B787-8		o/o♦
☐	B-	B787-8		o/o♦
☐	B-	B787-8		o/o♦
☐	B-3060	ERJ-145LI	145701	
☐	B-3061	ERJ-145LI	145755	
☐	B-3062	ERJ-145LI	145781	
☐	B-3063	ERJ-145LI	14500804	
☐	B-3065	ERJ-145LI	14500815	
☐	B-3066	ERJ-145LI	14500823	
☐	B-2132	MD-82	49516/1622	
☐	B-2136	MD-82	49520/1671	
☐	B-2143	MD-82	49851/1807	
☐	B-2145	MD-82	49853/1981	
☐	B-2152	MD-82	53164/2041	
☐	B-2100	MD-90-30	60001/4001	
☐	B-2103	MD-90-30	60002/4002	
☐	B-2251	MD-90-30	53524/2146	
☐	B-2252	MD-90-30	53525/2150	
☐	B-2254	MD-90-30	53527/2175	
☐	B-2255	MD-90-30	53528/2177	
☐	B-2259	MD-90-30	53529/2220	
☐	B-2260	MD-90-30	53530/2222	
☐	B-2261	MD-90-30	53531/2228	
☐	B-2266	MD-90-30	53532/2253	
☐	B-2267	MD-90-30	53533/2258	

CHINA UNITED AIRLINES　　　　KN / CUA

	Reg	Type	C/n	Notes
☐	B-4008	B737-3T0	23839/1507	Opf Govt
☐	B-4009	B737-3T0	23840/1516	Opf Govt
☐	B-4018	B737-33A	25502/2310	Opf Govt
☐	B-4019	B737-33A	25503/2313	Opf Govt
☐	B-4020	B737-34N	28081/2746	Opf Govt
☐	B-4021	B737-34N	28082/2747	Opf Govt
☐	B-4052	B737-3Q8	24701/1957	Opf Govt
☐	B-4053	B737-3Q8	24702/1994	Opf Govt
☐	B-2663	B737-7AD	28437/72	<CSH
☐	B-2997	B737-7Q8	28223/272	<CSH
☐	B-4025	B737-76D	33470/1334	Opf Govt
☐	B-4026	B737-76D	33472/1343	Opf Govt
☐	B-5183	B737-8Q8/W	30711/2159	<CSH
☐	B-5323	B737-8Q8/W	30725/2292	<CSH
☐	B-5399	B737-86N/W	35224/2617	<CSH
☐	B-5547	B737-86N/W	36806/3448	♦
☐	B-4005	CRJ-200LR	7138	Opf Govt
☐	B-4006	CRJ-200LR	7149	Opf Govt
☐	B-4007	CRJ-200LR	7180	Opf Govt
☐	B-4010	CRJ-200LR	7189	Opf Govt
☐	B-4011	CRJ-200LR	7193	Opf Govt
☐	B-4701	CRJ-200LR	7639	
☐	B-4702	CRJ-200LR	7455	
☐	B-4060	CRJ-701ER	10164	

	Reg	Type	C/n	Notes
☐	B-4061	CRJ-701ER	10183	
☐	B-4062	CRJ-701ER	10187	
☐	B-4063	CRJ-701ER	10204	
☐	B-4064	CRJ-701ER	10206	
☐	B-4016	Tu-154M	91A872	
☐	B-4017	Tu-154M	91A873	
☐	B-4028	Tu-154M	93A967	VIP

CHINA XINHUA AIRLINES　　　　HU / CXH

	Reg	Type	C/n	Notes
☐	B-2908	B737-341	26854/2303	<CHH
☐	B-2934	B737-39K	27274/2559	<CHH
☐	B-2942	B737-332	25997/2506	<CHH
☐	B-2943	B737-332	25998/2510	<CHH
☐	B-2945	B737-39K	27362/2639	<CHH
☐	B-2982	B737-36Q	28657/2859	
☐	B-2987	B737-46Q	28663/2922	<CHH
☐	B-2989	B737-46Q	28758/2939	<CHH
☐	B-2993	B737-46Q	28759/2981	<CHH
☐	B-5080	B737-86N	28614/477	<CHH
☐	B-5081	B737-86N	30231/515	<CHH
☐	B-5138	B737-84P/W	32607/1832	<CHH
☐	B-5139	B737-84P/W	32608/1855	<CHH
☐	B-5141	B737-84P/W	34030/1800	<CHH
☐	B-5153	B737-84P/W	34029/1921	<CHH

CHONGQING AIRLINES　　　　OQ / CQN

	Reg	Type	C/n	Notes
☐	B-2343	A320-233	0696	<CSN
☐	B-2345	A320-233	0698	<CSN
☐	B-2346	A320-233	0704	<CSN
☐	B-6246	A319-133	3836	
☐	B-6247	A319-133	3876	
☐	B-6248	A319-133	3901	

DONGHAI AIRLINES　　　　J5 / EPA

	Reg	Type	C/n	Notes
☐	B-2517	B737-3W0(SF)	23396/1166	
☐	B-2518	B737-3W0(SF)	23397/1193	
☐	B-2897	B737-3B7F	24902/1973	
☐	B-2898	B737-3Y0F	24916/2066	

GRAND CHINA AIRLINES　　　　CN / GDC

	Reg	Type	C/n	Notes
☐	B-2637	B737-86N	28576/103	
☐	B-2652	B737-84P	30475/731	
☐	B-5337	B737-84P/W	35747/2433	<CHH

GRANDSTAR CARGO INTL　　　　GD / GSC

	Reg	Type	C/n	Notes
☐	B-2427	B747-4B5F	26401/1087	

GREAT WALL AIRLINES　　　　IJ / GWL

	Reg	Type	C/n	Notes
☐	B-2428	B747-412F	28263/1094	
☐	B-2430	B747-412BCF	27137/990	
☐	B-2433	B747-412F	28027/1256	

HAINAN AIRLINES　　　　HU / CHH

	Reg	Type	C/n	Notes
☐	B-6156	A319-112	2849	>DRA
☐	B-6157	A319-112	2891	>DRA
☐	B-6169	A319-112	2985	>DRA
☐	B-6177	A319-112	3285	>DRA
☐	B-6178	A319-132	3548	>DRA
☐	B-6179	A319-132	3561	>DRA
☐	B-6192	A319-132	3768	Lst DRA
☐	B-6210	A319-115	2557	Opb CGN
☐	B-6211	A319-115	2561	Opb CGN
☐	B-6212	A319-115	2581	Opb CGN
☐	B-6215	A319-112	2611	
☐	B-6221	A319-112	2746	
☐	B-6222	A319-112	2733	
☐	B-6412	A319-132	4292	>CHB♦
☐	B-6413	A319-132	4452	>CHB♦

	Reg	Type	c/n	Notes
☐	B-6417	A319-133	4522	>DRA♦
☐	B-	A319-133		o/o♦
☐	B-6709	A320-232	4412	>DRA♦
☐	B-6710	A320-232	4440	>DRA♦
☐	B-6723	A320-232	4483	>DRA♦
☐	B-6726	A320-232	4505	>DRA♦
☐	B-6743	A320-232	4569	<CHB♦
☐	B-	A320-232		o/o♦
☐	B-	A320-232		o/o♦
☐	B-	A320-232		o/o♦
☐	B-	A320-232		o/o♦
☐	B-	A320-232		o/o♦
☐	B-	A320-232		o/o♦
☐	B-	A320-232		o/o♦
☐	B-	A320-232		o/o♦
☐	B-	A320-232		o/o♦
☐	B-6088	A330-243	906	
☐	B-6089	A330-243	919	
☐	B-6116	A330-243	875	
☐	B-6118	A330-243	881	
☐	B-6133	A330-243	982	
☐	B-6519	A330-243	1159	♦
☐	B-6520	A330-343X	1168	♦
☐	B-6527	A330-343X	1178	♦
☐	B-6529	A330-343X	1190	♦
☐	B-6508	A340-642	436	
☐	B-6509	A340-642	453	
☐	B-6510	A340-642	475	
☐	B-2112	B737-36N	28599/3115	>DRA
☐	B-2113	B737-36N	28602/3118	>DRA
☐	B-2115	B737-36N	28606/3124	>DRA
☐	B-2501	B737-44P	29914/3067	
☐	B-2576	B737-44P	29915/3106	
☐	B-2578	B737-33A	25603/2333	
☐	B-2579	B737-33A	25505/2342	
☐	B-2608	B737-36Q	28662/2914	>DRA
☐	B-2934	B737-39K	27274/2559	>CXH
☐	B-2942	B737-332	25997/2506	>CXH
☐	B-2943	B737-332	25998/2510	>CXH
☐	B-2945	B737-39K	27362/2639	>CXH
☐	B-2960	B737-4Q8	24332/1866	
☐	B-2963	B737-3Q8	26325/2772	
☐	B-2965	B737-4Q8	26334/2782	
☐	B-2967	B737-4Q8	26335/2793	
☐	B-2970	B737-4Q8	26337/2811	
☐	B-2987	B737-46Q	28663/2922	>CXH
☐	B-2989	B737-46Q	28758/2939	>CXH
☐	B-2993	B737-46Q	28759/2981	>CXH
☐	B-3000	B737-36Q	29326/3020	>DRA
☐	B-5053	B737-322F	24378/1704	>YZR
☐	B-5055	B737-330(QC)	24283/1677	>YZR
☐	B-5056	B737-330(QC)	23836/1508	>YZR
☐	B-5057	B737-330(QC)	23837/1514	>YZR
☐	B-5058	B737-330(QC)	23835/1465	>YZR
☐	B-5059	B737-322F	24362/1696	>YZR
☐	B-5060	B737-76N	28582/154	>CXI
☐	B-5061	B737-76N	28583/163	>CXI
☐	B-5062	B737-76N	28585/173	>CXI
☐	B-5091	B737-705	29091/230	>LKE
☐	B-5092	B737-705	29092/260	>CGN
☐	B-5248	B737-790/W	30626/1273	>LKE
☐	B-5249	B737-790	33011/1291	>LKE
☐	B-2157	B737-84P/W	32600/1015	
☐	B-2158	B737-84P/W	32601/1033	
☐	B-2159	B737-84P/W	32599/972	
☐	B-2636	B737-86N	28574/67	
☐	B-2638	B737-8Q8	28220/212	
☐	B-2646	B737-8Q8	28056/273	
☐	B-2647	B737-84P	29947/345	
☐	B-2651	B737-84P	30474/607	
☐	B-2675	B737-86Q/W	32885/1147	
☐	B-2676	B737-84P/W	32602/1170	
☐	B-2677	B737-84P/W	32604/1191	
☐	B-5080	B737-86N	28614/477	>CXH
☐	B-5081	B737-86N	30231/515	>CXH
☐	B-5082	B737-883	30193/587	>CXH
☐	B-5083	B737-883	28319/548	
☐	B-5089	B737-883	28320/551	
☐	B-5090	B737-883	28321/577	
☐	B-5115	B737-8FH/W	29640/1649	>CGN
☐	B-5116	B737-8FH/W	29672/1745	>CGN
☐	B-5135	B737-84P/W	32603/1766	
☐	B-5136	B737-84P/W	32605/1796	
☐	B-5137	B737-84P/W	32606/1805	
☐	B-5138	B737-84P/W	32607/1832	>CXH
☐	B-5139	B737-84P/W	32608/1855	>CXH
☐	B-5141	B737-84P/W	34030/1800	>CXH
☐	B-5153	B737-84P/W	34029/1921	>CXH
☐	B-5180	B737-8FH/W	35089/2042	>CGN
☐	B-5181	B737-8FH/W	35090/2073	>CGN
☐	B-5182	B737-808/W	34708/2097	
☐	B-5337	B737-84P/W	35747/2433	>GDC
☐	B-5338	B737-84P/W	35749/2330	
☐	B-5346	B737-8BK/W	29673/2373	
☐	B-5358	B737-84P/W	35077/2419	
☐	B-5359	B737-8FH/W	35101/2459	
☐	B-5371	B737-84P/W	35752/2556	
☐	B-5372	B737-84P/W	35758/2593	
☐	B-5373	B737-84P/W	35754/2618	
☐	B-5375	B737-84P/W	35762/2648	
☐	B-5403	B737-84P/W	35756/2691	
☐	B-5405	B737-84P/W	35759/2668	
☐	B-5406	B737-84P/W	35760/2678	
☐	B-5407	B737-808/W	34967/2239	
☐	B-5408	B737-84P/W	35764/2778	
☐	B-5409	B737-808/W	34968/2265	
☐	B-5416	B737-84P/W	34031/2801	
☐	B-5417	B737-86N/W	35639/2821	
☐	B-5418	B737-86N/W	36541/2769	
☐	B-5427	B737-8Q8/W	35285/2772	
☐	B-5428	B737-86N/W	36542/2806	
☐	B-5429	B737-86N/W	36543/2831	
☐	B-5430	B737-84P/W	34032/2827	
☐	B-5439	B737-808/W	34707/2046	
☐	B-5449	B737-808/W	34971/2400	
☐	B-5462	B737-84P/W	36780/3095	
☐	B-5465	B737-84P/W	34033/2854	
☐	B-5466	B737-84P/W	34034/2912	
☐	B-5467	B737-84P/W	36779/2885	
☐	B-5478	B737-84P/W	35751/3038	
☐	B-5479	B737-84P/W	35753/3066	
☐	B-5480	B737-86N/W	35648/2973	
☐	B-5481	B737-86N/W	25649/2981	
☐	B-5482	B737-84P/W	35748/2938	
☐	B-5483	B737-84P/W	35750/3007	
☐	B-5502	B737-84P/W	35757/3192	♦
☐	B-5503	B737-84P/W	36782/3186	♦
☐	B-5520	B737-84P/W	35765/3344	♦
☐	B-5521	B737-84P/W	35766/3313	♦
☐	B-5522	B737-84P/W	36781/3278	♦
☐	B-5538	B737-84P/W	36783/3382	♦
☐	B-5539	B737-84P/W	35763/3378	♦
☐	B-	B737-84P/W		o/o
☐	B-	B737-84P/W		o/o
☐	B-	B737-84P/W		o/o
☐	B-	B737-84P/W		o/o
☐	B-KBI	B737-808/W	34709/2121	>CRK
☐	B-KBK	B737-84P/W	35072/2155	>CRK
☐	B-KBM	B737-84P/W	35076/2380	>CRK
☐	B-KBQ	B737-84P/W	35274/2570	>HKE
☐	B-KBR	B737-84P/W	35276/2611	>HKE
☐	B-KBT	B737-84P/W	37422/3241	>CRK♦
☐	B-KXE	B737-808/W	34710/2144	>HKE
☐	B-2490	B767-34PER	33047/889	
☐	B-2491	B767-34PER	33048/891	
☐	B-2492	B767-34PER	33049/893	

HEBEI AIRLINES — NS / DBH

☐ B-3040	ERJ-145LR	145317	<CSC
☐ B-3041	ERJ-145LR	145349	<CSC
☐ B-6170	A319-132	2396	<CSC

HENAN AIRLINES — VD / KPA

☐ B-7691	CRJ-200LR	7218	
☐ B-3126	190-100LR	19000201	
☐ B-3131	190-100LR	19000230	
☐ B-3132	190-100LR	19000263	
☐ B-3133	190-100LR	19000264	

JADE CARGO — JI / JAE

☐ B-2421	B747-4EVERF	35169/1391
☐ B-2422	B747-4EVERF	35173/1387
☐ B-2423	B747-4EVERF	35174/1398
☐ B-2439	B747-4EVERF	35170/1376
☐ B-2440	B747-4EVERF	35171/1380
☐ B-2441	B747-4EVERF	35172/1383

JUNEYAO AIRLINES — HO / DKH

☐ B-6232	A319-112	2879	
☐ B-6233	A319-112	2913	
☐ B-6298	A320-214	2975	
☐ B-6311	A320-214	3027	
☐ B-6338	A320-214	3368	
☐ B-6340	A320-214	3234	
☐ B-6341	A320-214	3268	
☐ B-6381	A320-214	3485	
☐ B-6395	A320-214	3596	
☐ B-6396	A320-214	3605	
☐ B-6572	A320-214	3967	
☐ B-6602	A320-214	3984	
☐ B-6618	A320-214	4102	
☐ B-6619	A320-214	4154	
☐ B-6640	A320-214	4064	
☐ B-6670	A320-214	4276	♦
☐ B-6717	A320-214	4401	♦
☐ B-6735	A320-214	4429	♦
☐ B-	A320-214		o/o♦
☐ B-	A320-214		o/o♦
☐ B-	A320-214		o/o♦
☐ B-	A320-214		o/o♦
☐ B-	A320-214		o/o♦

KUNMING AIRLINES — KY / KNA

☐ B-2635	B737-79K	29191/127	<CSZ♦
☐ B-2668	B737-78S	30171/681	<CSZ♦
☐ B-2678	B737-76N	32244/895	
☐ B-2679	B737-76N	29893/710	

LUCKY AIRLINES — 8L / LKE

☐ B-5060	B737-76N	28582/154	<CXI
☐ B-5061	B737-76N	28583/163	<CXI
☐ B-5091	B737-705	29091/230	<CHH
☐ B-5246	B737-7Q8/W	30674/1511	
☐ B-5248	B737-790/W	30626/1273	<CHH
☐ B-5249	B737-790	33011/1291	<CHH
☐ B-5268	B737-790/W	30662/1382	♦
☐ B-5272	B737-790/W	30663/1386	♦

OK AIRWAYS — BK / OKA

☐ B-2117	B737-3Q8(SF)	24961/2133	
☐ B-2863	B737-83N/W	30673/1500	
☐ B-2865	B737-83N/W	30679/1404	
☐ B-5367	B737-8Q8/W	30733/2452	
☐ B-5562	B737-8HO/W	37934/3491	♦

☐ B-5571	B737-86N/W	35643/2884	♦
☐ B-5573	B737-8HO/W	37932/3498	♦
☐ B-5575	B737-8AS/W	33554/1418	♦
☐ B-5577	B737-8AS/W	33557/1438	♦
☐ B-	B737-8HO/W		o/o♦
☐ B-	B737-8HO/W		o/o♦
☐ B-	B737-8HO/W		o/o♦
☐ B-	B737-8HO/W		o/o♦

SF AIRLINES

☐ B-2899	B757-21B(SF)	24401/232

SHAN XI AIRLINES — CXI

☐ B-5060	B737-76N	28582/154	>LKE
☐ B-5061	B737-76N	28583/163	>LKE
☐ B-5062	B737-76N	28585/173	<CHH

SHANDONG AIRLINES — SC / CDG

☐ B-2111	B737-36Q	29405/3047	
☐ B-2877	B737-33V	29331/3062	
☐ B-2878	B737-36Q	28760/2989	
☐ B-2961	B737-35N	28156/2774	
☐ B-2962	B737-35N	28157/2778	
☐ B-2968	B737-35N	28158/2818	
☐ B-2995	B737-35N	29315/3054	
☐ B-2996	B737-35N	29316/3065	
☐ B-5065	B737-36Q	28664/2940	
☐ B-5066	B737-36Q	28761/3011	
☐ B-5098	B737-36Q	29140/3013	
☐ B-5099	B737-36Q	29189/3057	
☐ B-5205	B737-75N/W	33654/1790	
☐ B-5206	B737-75N/W	33666/1742	
☐ B-5207	B737-75N/W	33663/1838	
☐ B-5111	B737-85N/W	33660/1752	
☐ B-5117	B737-85N/W	33661/1770	
☐ B-5118	B737-85N/W	33664/1726	
☐ B-5119	B737-85N/W	33665/1775	
☐ B-5321	B737-8AL/W	35073/2197	
☐ B-5331	B737-8AL/W	35075/2287	
☐ B-5332	B737-8FH/W	35095/2295	
☐ B-5333	B737-8FH/W	35096/2336	
☐ B-5335	B737-8FH/W	35097/2345	
☐ B-5336	B737-8FH/W	35098/2361	
☐ B-5347	B737-85N/W	36190/2429	
☐ B-5348	B737-85N/W	36191/2453	
☐ B-5349	B737-85N/W	36192/2642	
☐ B-5350	B737-85N/W	36193/2669	
☐ B-5351	B737-85N/W	36194/2684	
☐ B-5352	B737-85N/W	36195/2823	
☐ B-5450	B737-85N/W	36773/2874	
☐ B-5451	B737-85N/W	36776/2998	
☐ B-5452	B737-85N/W	36777/3045	
☐ B-5453	B737-85N/W	36778/3277	♦
☐ B-5513	B737-86N/W	36546/3293	♦
☐ B-5526	B737-8FZ/W	31717/3237	♦
☐ B-5536	B737-8AL/W	37424/3342	♦
☐ B-5541	B737-85N/W	40882/3368	♦
☐ B-5542	B737-85N/W	40883/3383	♦
☐ B-5543	B737-86N/W	39392/3447	♦
☐ B-5560	B737-86N/W	38013/3560	♦
☐ B-3001	CRJ-200LR	7565	>HXA
☐ B-3005	CRJ-200LR	7435	
☐ B-3006	CRJ-200LR	7443	
☐ B-3007	CRJ-200LR	7498	
☐ B-3008	CRJ-200LR	7512	
☐ B-3009	CRJ-200LR	7522	
☐ B-3012	CRJ-200LR	7557	>HXA
☐ B-3079	CRJ-701ER	10118	
☐ B-3080	CRJ-701ER	10120	

SHANGHAI AIRLINES — F4 / CSH

	Reg	Type	Serial	
☐	B-6591	A321-231	3969	
☐	B-6592	A321-231	4045	
☐	B-6622	A321-231	4198	♦
☐	B-6643	A321-231	4209	♦
☐	B-6668	A321-231	4378	♦
☐	B-2577	B737-76D	30168/600	
☐	B-2631	B737-7Q8	28212/35	
☐	B-2632	B737-7Q8	28216/122	
☐	B-2663	B737-7AD	28437/72	>CUA
☐	B-2913	B737-76D	30167/550	
☐	B-2997	B737-7Q8	28223/272	>CUA
☐	B-5260	B737-76D/W	35777/3037	
☐	B-5261	B737-76D/W	35778/3064	
☐	B-2153	B737-8Q8	28242/942	
☐	B-2167	B737-8Q8	30631/1047	
☐	B-2168	B737-8Q8	30632/1086	
☐	B-2686	B737-8Q8	28251/1200	
☐	B-2688	B737-86D/W	33471/1192	
☐	B-5076	B737-86N	32739/1434	
☐	B-5077	B737-86N	32742/1464	
☐	B-5088	B737-82R	30666/1460	
☐	B-5130	B737-8Q8	32801/1666	
☐	B-5131	B737-8Q8	30686/1704	
☐	B-5132	B737-8Q8	30685/1789	
☐	B-5140	B737-8Q8	30698/1911	
☐	B-5142	B737-8Q8	30700/1942	
☐	B-5143	B737-86N/W	32691/2033	
☐	B-5145	B737-8Q8	33007/1986	
☐	B-5148	B737-86N/W	34254/1897	
☐	B-5183	B737-8Q8/W	30711/2159	>CUA
☐	B-5185	B737-8Q8/W	30715/2230	
☐	B-5315	B737-86D	35767/2316	
☐	B-5316	B737-86D	35768/2362	
☐	B-5320	B737-8Q8/W	30718/2251	
☐	B-5323	B737-8Q8/W	30725/2292	>CUA
☐	B-5330	B737-86N/W	35212/2277	
☐	B-5353	B737-8Q8	30728/2386	
☐	B-5368	B737-8Q8	35273/2567	
☐	B-5369	B737-8Q8/W	35281/2709	
☐	B-5370	B737-8Q8/W	35271/2551	
☐	B-5393	B737-86D/W	35769/3632	
☐	B-5395	B737-86D/W	35770/2698	
☐	B-5396	B737-86D/W	35771/2740	
☐	B-5399	B737-86D/W	35224/2617	>CUA
☐	B-5160	B737 86D/W	35772/3047	
☐	B-5461	B737-86D/W	35773/2939	
☐	B-5470	B737-86D/W	35774/3010	
☐	B-5471	B737-86D/W	35775/3098	
☐	B-5523	B737-86D/W	35776/3360	♦
☐	B-5545	B737-86N/W	36803/3376	♦
☐	B-5546	B737-86N/W	39391/3431	♦
☐	B-5548	B737-86N/W	36807/3479	♦
☐	B-5549	B737-86N/W	37888/3470	♦
☐	B-5550	B737-86N/W	39393/3483	♦
☐	B-5576	B737-86N/W	38011/3531	♦
☐	B-2833	B757-26D	27152/560	
☐	B-2834	B757-26D	27183/576	
☐	B-2842	B757-26D	27342/626	
☐	B-2843	B757-26D	27681/684	
☐	B-2850	B757-231	30338/891	
☐	B-2857	B757-26D	33959/1044	
☐	B-2858	B757-26D	33960/1045	
☐	B-2875	B757-26D	33966/1049	
☐	B-2876	B757-26D	33967/1050	
☐	B-2880	B757-26D	33961/1046	
☐	B-2498	B767-36D	27684/849	
☐	B-2500	B767-36DER	35155/946	
☐	B-2563	B767-36D	27309/546	
☐	B-2566	B767-36DER	35156/950	
☐	B-2567	B767-36D	27685/686	
☐	B-2570	B767-36D	27941/770	
☐	B-5018	B767-3Q8ER	28207/695	
☐	B-3011	CRJ-200ER	7556	
☐	B-3018	CRJ-200ER	7453	
☐	B-3020	CRJ-200ER	7459	
☐	B-3075	CRJ-200ER	7226	
☐	B-7698	CRJ-200ER	7247	

SHANGHAI CARGO — F4 / SHQ

	Reg	Type	Serial
☐	B-2176	MD-11F	48415/576
☐	B-2177	MD-11F	48544/580
☐	B-2178	MD-11F	48543/572
☐	B-2179	MD-11F	48545/587
☐	B-2808	B757-26D (PCF)	24471/231
☐	B-2809	B757-26D (PCF)	24472/235

SHENZHEN AIRLINES — ZH / CSZ

	Reg	Type	Serial	
☐	B-6153	A319-115	2841	
☐	B-6159	A319-115	2905	
☐	B-6165	A319-115X	2935 VIP [CJ]	
☐	B-6196	A319-115	2672	
☐	B-6197	A319-115	2684	
☐	B-	A319-115		o/o
☐	B-2416	A320-214	0994	
☐	B-6286	A320-214	2909	
☐	B-6296	A320-214	2973	
☐	B-6297	A320-214	2980	
☐	B-6312	A320-214	3131	
☐	B-6313	A320-214	3132	
☐	B-6315	A320-214	3153	
☐	B-6316	A320-214	3206	
☐	B-6351	A320-214	3366	
☐	B-6352	A320-214	3383	
☐	B-6357	A320-214	3440	
☐	B-6358	A320-214	3435	
☐	B-6359	A320-214	3456	
☐	B-6360	A320-214	3528	
☐	B-6377	A320-214	3599	
☐	B-6392	A320-214	3696	
☐	B-6550	A320-214	3756	
☐	B-6563	A320-214	3698	
☐	B-6565	A320-214	3971	
☐	B-6566	A320-214	3855	
☐	B-6567	A320-214	3887	
☐	B-6568	A320-214	3898	
☐	B-6569	A320-214	3848	
☐	B-6570	A320-214	4010	
☐	B-6571	A320-232	3935	
☐	B-6589	A320-214	4028	
☐	B-6613	A320-232	4176	
☐	B-6615	A320-232	4214	
☐	B-6647	A320-214	4226	♦
☐	B-6648	A320-214	4159	♦
☐	B-6650	A320-232	4300	♦
☐	B-6690	A320-232	4359	♦
☐	B-6691	A320-232	4409	♦
☐	B-6720	A320-214	4474	♦
☐	B-6721	A320-214	4515	♦
☐	B-6722	A320-214	4531	♦
☐	B-	A320-214		o/o ♦
☐	B-	A320-214		o/o ♦
☐	B-	A320-214		o/o ♦
☐	B-	A320-214		o/o ♦
☐	B-	A320-214		o/o ♦
☐	B-	A320-214		o/o ♦
☐	B-	A320-214		o/o ♦
☐	B-	A320-214		o/o ♦
☐	B-	A320-214		o/o ♦
☐	B-	A320-214		o/o ♦
☐	B-2601	B737-36N	28559/2882	
☐	B-2602	B737-36N	28573/3041	

☐ B-2687	B737-36N	28555/2846	
☐ B-2932	B737-3K9	25787/2302	
☐ B-2933	B737-3K9	25788/2331	
☐ B-2939	B737-31L	27345/2625	
☐ B-2940	B737-31L	27346/2636	
☐ B-2971	B737-3Q8	25373/2290	
☐ B-2972	B737-33A	27463/2831	
☐ B-2633	B737-79K	29190/110	
☐ B-2635	B737-79K	29191/127	>KMG
☐ B-2666	B737-78S	30169/631	
☐ B-2667	B737-78S	30170/654	
☐ B-2668	B737-78S	30171/681	>KMG
☐ B-2669	B737-77L	32722/1023	
☐ B-2691	B737-8Q8	30628/808	
☐ B-2692	B737-8Q8	28241/841	
☐ B-5025	B737-7BX	30742/864	
☐ B-5026	B737-7BX	30741/823	
☐ B-5049	B737-86N	28639/772	
☐ B-5050	B737-86N	28643/828	
☐ B-5073	B737-8Q8/W	30680/1402	
☐ B-5075	B737-8Q8	30692/1410	
☐ B-5078	B737-8Q8	30690/1414	
☐ B-5079	B737-8Q8	30693/1422	
☐ B-5102	B737-97L	33644/1750	
☐ B-5103	B737-97L	33645/1760	
☐ B-5105	B737-97L	33646/1764	
☐ B-5106	B737-97L	33648/1722	
☐ B-5109	B737-97L	33649/1755	
☐ B-5186	B737-8BK	33020/2103	
☐ B-5187	B737-8BK	33828/2124	
☐ B-5317	B737-86N/W	32686/2175	
☐ B-5322	B737-86N/W	32688/2218	
☐ B-5345	B737-86N/W	35215/2306	
☐ B-5357	B737-8AL/W	35081/2519	
☐ B-5360	B737-86J/W	30062/485	<BER
☐ B-5361	B737-86J/W	30063/517	<BER
☐ B-5362	B737-86J/W	30499/567	<BER
☐ B-5363	B737-86J/W	30500/593	<BER
☐ B-5365	B737-86J/W	30501/619	<BER
☐ B-5377	B737-8AL/W	35079/2555	
☐ B-5378	B737-8AL/W	35085/2563	
☐ B-5379	B737-8AL/W	35087/2605	
☐ B-5380	B737-87L/W	35527/2616	
☐ B-5381	B737-87L/W	35528/2631	
☐ B-5400	B737-87L/W	35529/2677	
☐ B-5401	B737-87L/W	35530/2703	
☐ B-5402	B737-87L/W	35531/2726	
☐ B-5410	B737-8AL/W	35088/2771	
☐ B-5411	B737-87L/W	35532/2851	
☐ B-5412	B737-87L/W	35533/2900	
☐ B-5413	B737-87L/W	35535/2895	
☐ B-5440	B737-87L/W	35534/3003	
☐ B-5441	B737-87L/W	35536/3019	

SICHUAN AIRLINES   3U / CSC

☐ B-2298	A319-133	2534	
☐ B-2299	A319-133	2597	
☐ B-2300	A319-133	2639	
☐ B-6043	A319-133	2313	
☐ B-6045	A319-133	2348	
☐ B-6054	A319-133	2510	
☐ B-6170	A319-132	2396	>DBH
☐ B-6171	A319-132	2431	<ACG
☐ B-6173	A319-133	3114	
☐ B-6175	A319-133	3116	
☐ B-6176	A319-133	3124	
☐ B-6185	A319-133	3680	
☐ B-6406	A319-133	3962	
☐ B-6410	A319-133	4018	
☐ B-	A319-133		o/o♦
☐ B-2340	A320-233	0540	
☐ B-2341	A320-232	0551	
☐ B-2342	A320-232	0556	

☐ B-2348	A320-233	0912	
☐ B-2373	A320-233	0919	
☐ B-2397	A320-233	1013	
☐ B-6025	A320-232	0573	
☐ B-6026	A320-232	0582	
☐ B-6027	A320-233	1007	
☐ B-6049	A320-233	0902	
☐ B-6256	A320-232	0872	
☐ B-6257	A320-233	0874	
☐ B-6295	A320-233	1500	
☐ B-6321	A320-232	3210	
☐ B-6322	A320-232	3158	
☐ B-6323	A320-232	3167	
☐ B-6325	A320-232	3196	
☐ B-6347	A320-232	3386	
☐ B-6348	A320-232	3449	
☐ B-6388	A320-232	3591	
☐ B-6621	A320-232	4068	
☐ B-6697	A320-232	4288	♦
☐ B-6700	A320-232	4326	♦
☐ B-6718	A320-232	4420	♦
☐ B-6719	A320-232	4424	♦
☐ B-	A320-232		o/o♦
☐ B-	A320-232		o/o♦
☐ B-	A320-232		o/o♦
☐ B-	A320-232		o/o♦
☐ B-	A320-232		o/o♦
☐ B-	A320-232		o/o♦
☐ B-2286	A321-131	550	
☐ B-2293	A321-131	591	
☐ B-2370	A321-231	878	
☐ B-2371	A321-231	915	
☐ B-6285	A321-231	1060	
☐ B-6300	A321-231	1293	
☐ B-6387	A321-231	3583	
☐ B-6551	A321-231	3730	
☐ B-6590	A321-231	3893	
☐ B-6598	A321-231	3996	
☐ B-	A321-231		o/o♦
☐ B-	A321-231		o/o♦
☐ B-	A321-231		o/o♦
☐ B-6517	A330-240	1138	♦
☐ B-6518	A330-240	1082	♦
☐ B-	A330-240		o/o♦
☐ B-3040	ERJ-145LR	145317	>DBH
☐ B-3041	ERJ-145LR	145349	>DBH
☐ B-3042	ERJ-145LR	145352	
☐ B-3043	ERJ-145LR	145377	
☐ B-3045	ERJ-145LR	145470	

SPRING AIRLINES   9S / CQH

☐ B-6250	A320-214	1372	
☐ B-6280	A320-214	1286	
☐ B-6301	A320-214	2939	
☐ B-6309	A320-214	3014	
☐ B-6310	A320-214	3023	
☐ B-6320	A320-214	1686	
☐ B-6328	A320-214	0978	
☐ B-6349	A320-214	1852	
☐ B-6380	A320-214	1769	
☐ B-6561	A320-214	3819	
☐ B-6562	A320-214	3747	
☐ B-6573	A320-214	1920	
☐ B-6612	A320-214	4072	
☐ B-6645	A320-214	4168	
☐ B-6646	A320-214	4093	
☐ B-6667	A320-214	4244	♦
☐ B-6705	A320-214	4331	♦
☐ B-6706	A320-214	4366	♦
☐ B-6707	A320-214	4373	♦
☐ B-6708	A320-214	4375	♦
☐ B-	A320-214		o/o♦

☐	B-	A320-214		o/o♦
☐	B-	A320-214		o/o♦
☐	B-	A320-214		o/o♦
☐	B-	A320-214		o/o♦
☐	B-	A320-214		o/o♦
☐	B-	A320-214		o/o♦

TIANJIN AIRLINES — GS / GCR

☐	B-3873	Do 328 Jet	3201	
☐	B-3892	Do 328 Jet	3212	
☐	B-3946	Do 328 Jet	3208	
☐	B-3947	Do 328 Jet	3203	
☐	B-3948	Do 328 Jet	3204	
☐	B-3949	Do 328 Jet	3198	
☐	B-3960	Do 328 Jet	3123	
☐	B-3961	Do 328 Jet	3128	
☐	B-3962	Do 328 Jet	3143	
☐	B-3963	Do 328 Jet	3138	
☐	B-3965	Do 328 Jet	3140	
☐	B-3966	Do 328 Jet	3135	
☐	B-3967	Do 328 Jet	3144	
☐	B-3968	Do 328 Jet	3148	
☐	B-3969	Do 328 Jet	3153	
☐	B-3970	Do 328 Jet	3154	
☐	B-3971	Do 328 Jet	3172	
☐	B-3972	Do 328 Jet	3175	
☐	B-3973	Do 328 Jet	3158	
☐	B-3975	Do 328 Jet	3159	
☐	B-3976	Do 328 Jet	3177	
☐	B-3977	Do 328 Jet	3182	
☐	B-3978	Do 328 Jet	3187	
☐	B-3979	Do 328 Jet	3191	
☐	B-3982	Do 328 Jet	3195	
☐	B-3983	Do 328 Jet	3211	
☐	B-3985	Do 328 Jet	3215	
☐	B-3986	Do 328 Jet	3217	
☐	B-3987	Do 328 Jet	3218	
☐	B-3030	ERJ-145LI	14501009	
☐	B-3031	ERJ-145LI	14501013	
☐	B-3032	ERJ-145LI	14501019	
☐	B-3033	ERJ-145LI	14501022	
☐	B-3035	ERJ-145LI	14500996	
☐	B-3036	ERJ-145LI	14501000	
☐	B-3037	ERJ-145LI	14501005	
☐	B-3038	ERJ-145LI	14501024	
☐	B-3039	ERJ-145LI	14500992	
☐	B-3067	ERJ-145LI	14501036	
☐	B-3068	ERJ-145LI	14501040	
☐	B-3069	ERJ-145LI	14501043	
☐	B-3081	ERJ-145LI	14501027	
☐	B-3082	ERJ-145LI	14501030	
☐	B-3083	ERJ-145LI	14501033	
☐	B-3085	ERJ-145LI	14501043	
☐	B-3086	ERJ-145LI	14501050	♦
☐	B-3087	ERJ-145LI	14501053	♦
☐	B-3088	ERJ-145LI	14501056	♦
☐	B-3089	ERJ-145LI	14501063	♦
☐	B-3091	ERJ-145LI	14501065	♦
☐	B-3092	ERJ-145LI	14501068	♦
☐	B-	ERJ-145LI	14501028	o/o♦
☐	B-	ERJ-145LI	14501059	o/o♦
☐	B-	ERJ-145LI	14501068	o/o♦
☐	B-	ERJ-145LI	14501070	o/o♦
☐	B-	ERJ-145LI	14501073	o/o♦
☐	B-3120	ERJ-190LR	19000171	
☐	B-3121	ERJ-190LR	19000181	
☐	B-3122	ERJ-190LR	19000186	
☐	B-3123	ERJ-190LR	19000192	
☐	B-3125	ERJ-190LR	19000194	
☐	B-3127	ERJ-190LR	19000207	
☐	B-3128	ERJ-190LR	19000229	
☐	B-3129	ERJ-190LR	19000246	
☐	B-3150	ERJ-190LR	19000253	
☐	B-3151	ERJ-190LR	19000268	
☐	B-3152	ERJ-190LR	19000274	
☐	B-3153	ERJ-190LR	19000284	
☐	B-3155	ERJ-190LR	19000293	
☐	B-3156	ERJ-190LR	19000299	
☐	B-3157	ERJ-190LR	19000306	
☐	B-3158	ERJ-190LR	19000313	
☐	B-3159	ERJ-190LR	19000318	
☐	B-3160	ERJ-190LR	19000325	
☐	B-3161	ERJ-190LR	19000328	
☐	B-3162	ERJ-190LR	19000331	
☐	B-3163	ERJ-190LR	19000335	♦
☐	B-3165	ERJ-190LR	19000340	♦
☐	B-3166	ERJ-190LR	19000348	♦
☐	B-3167	ERJ-190LR	19000352	♦
☐	B-3168	ERJ-190LR	19000355	♦
☐	B-3169	ERJ-190LR	19000369	♦
☐	B-3170	ERJ-190LR	19000371	♦
☐	B-3171	ERJ-190LR	19000379	♦
☐	B-3172	ERJ-190LR	19000385	♦
☐	B-3173	ERJ-190LR	19000394	♦
☐	B-3175	ERJ-190LR	19000405	♦
☐	B-3176	ERJ-190LR	19000406	♦
☐	B-	ERJ-190LR		o/o♦
☐	B-	ERJ-190LR		o/o♦
☐	B-	ERJ-190LR		o/o♦
☐	B-	ERJ-190LR		o/o♦
☐	B-	ERJ-190LR		o/o♦
☐	B-	ERJ-190LR		o/o♦

UNI-TOP AIRLINES — UW

☐	B-2448	B747-2J6B (SF)	23461/628	[WUH]
☐	B-2450	B747-2J6B (SF)	23746/670	[PEK]

WEST AIR — PN / CHB

☐	B-6412	A319-132	4292	<CHH♦
☐	B-6413	A319-132	4452	<CHH♦
☐	B-6743	A320-232	4569	<CHH♦
☐	B-2963	B737-3Q8	26325/2772	<CHH

XIAMEN AIRLINES — MF / CXA

☐	B-2658	B737-75C	30512/637
☐	B-2659	B737-75C	30513/676
☐	B-2991	B737-75C	29085/90
☐	B-2992	B737-75C	29086/108
☐	B-2998	B737-75C	29042/73
☐	B-2999	B737-75C	29084/86
☐	B-5028	B737-75C	30034/1275
☐	B-5029	B737-75C	30634/1229
☐	B-5038	B737-7Q8	30656/1304
☐	B-5039	B737-75C	28258/1315
☐	B-5212	B737-75C	34024/1703
☐	B-5215	B737-75C	34025/1724
☐	B-5216	B737-75C	34026/1733
☐	B-5218	B737-75C	34027/1767
☐	B-5219	B737-75C	34028/1771
☐	B-5146	B737-86N/W	34253/1866
☐	B-5151	B737-86N/W	34255/1975
☐	B-5152	B737-86N/W	34256/1990
☐	B-5159	B737-85C/W	35044/2018
☐	B-5160	B737-85C/W	35045/2050
☐	B-5161	B737-85C/W	35046/2105
☐	B-5162	B737-85C/W	35047/2130
☐	B-5301	B737-85C/W	35048/2194
☐	B-5302	B737-85C/W	35049/2271
☐	B-5303	B737-85C/W	35050/2305
☐	B-5305	B737-85C/W	35051/2364
☐	B-5306	B737-85C/W	35052/2418
☐	B-5307	B737-85C/W	35053/2447
☐	B-5308	B737-86N/W	32687/2229
☐	B-5309	B737-86N/W	32689/2254
☐	B-5318	B737-85C/W	30723/2283
☐	B-5319	B737-8FH/W	35102/2471

☐ B-5355	B737-8FH/W	35104/2495	
☐ B-5382	B737-86N/W	36540/2681	
☐ B-5383	B737-86N/W	35631/2693	
☐ B-5385	B737-86N/W	35633/2741	
☐ B-5386	B737-86N/W	35634/2732	
☐ B-5388	B737-86N/W	35635/2764	
☐ B-5389	B737-86N/W	35636/2775	
☐ B-5432	B737-86N/W	35641/2852	
☐ B-5433	B737-86N/W	35642/2855	
☐ B-5435	B737-86N/W	35644/2922	
☐ B-5456	B737-85C/W	35054/2914	
☐ B-5458	B737-85C/W	35055/3016	
☐ B-5459	B737-85C/W	35057/2992	
☐ B-5476	B737-85C/W	35056/3091	
☐ B-5487	B737-85C/W	35058/3150	
☐ B-5488	B737-85C/W	37148/3104	
☐ B-5489	B737-85C/W	37149/3142	
☐ B-5498	B737-85C/W	37574/3160	
☐ B-5499	B737-85C/W	37575/3190	♦
☐ B-5511	B737-85C/W	37576/3245	♦
☐ B-5512	B737-85C/W	37577/3255	♦
☐ B-5529	B737-85C/W	37150/3386	♦
☐ B-5532	B737-85C/W	37151/3397	♦
☐ B-5535	B737-85C/W	37579/3424	♦
☐ B-5551	B737-84P/W	36697/3443	♦
☐ B-5552	B737-84P/W	37425/3408	♦
☐ B-5563	B737-86N	38012/3550	o/o♦
☐ B-5565	B737-86N	38015/3566	o/o♦
☐ B-	B737-		o/o♦
☐ B-	B737-		o/o♦
☐ B-	B737-		o/o♦
☐ B-	B737-		o/o♦
☐ B-	B737-		o/o♦
☐ B-	B737-		o/o♦
☐ B-	B737-		o/o♦
☐ B-	B737-		o/o♦
☐ B-	B737-		o/o♦
☐ B-	B737-		o/o♦
☐ B-	B737-		o/o♦
☐ B-	B737-		o/o♦

☐ B-2828	B757-25C	25899/565	
☐ B-2829	B757-25C	25900/574	
☐ B-2848	B757-25C	27513/685	
☐ B-2849	B757-25C	27517/698	
☐ B-2862	B757-25C	34008/1047	
☐ B-2866	B757-25C	34009/1048	
☐ B-2868	B757-25C	32941/993	
☐ B-2869	B757-25C	32942/1009	

YANGTZE RIVER EXPRESS — Y8 / YZR

☐ B-5053	B737-322F	24378/1704	<CHH
☐ B-5055	B737-330(QC)	24283/1677	<CHH
☐ B-5056	B737-330(QC)	23836/1508	<CHH
☐ B-5057	B737-330(QC)	23837/1514	<CHH
☐ B-5058	B737-330(QC)	23835/1465	<CHH
☐ B-5059	B737-322F	24362/1696	<CHH
☐ B-2431	B747-409F	30761/1254	<CAL
☐ B-2432	B747-481(SF)	28283/1142	
☐ B-2435	B747-481(SF)	28282/1133	

B-H/K/L CHINA - HONG KONG

AIR HONG KONG — LD / AHK

☐ B-LDA	A300F4-605R	855
☐ B-LDB	A300F4-605R	856
☐ B-LDC	A300F4-605R	857
☐ B-LDD	A300F4-605R	858
☐ B-LDE	A300F4-605R	859
☐ B-LDF	A300F4-605R	860
☐ B-LDG	A300F4-605R	870
☐ B-LDH	A300F4-605R	871	
☐ TC-AGK	A300B4-203F	117	<KZU
☐ TC-KZU	A300B4-203	173	<KZU

CATHAY PACIFIC AIRWAYS — CX / CPA

☐ B-HLA	A330-342	071	
☐ B-HLB	A330-342	083	
☐ B-HLC	A330-342	099	
☐ B-HLD	A330-342	102	
☐ B-HLE	A330-342	109	
☐ B-HLF	A330-342	113	
☐ B-HLG	A330-342	118	
☐ B-HLH	A330-342	121	
☐ B-HLI	A330-342	155	
☐ B-HLJ	A330-342	012	
☐ B-HLK	A330-342	017	
☐ B-HLL	A330-342	244	
☐ B-HLM	A330-343X	386	
☐ B-HLN	A330-343X	389	
☐ B-HLO	A330-343X	393	
☐ B-HLP	A330-343X	418	
☐ B-HLQ	A330-343X	420	
☐ B-HLR	A330-343X	421	
☐ B-HLS	A330-343X	423	
☐ B-HLT	A330-343X	439	
☐ B-HLU	A330-343X	539	
☐ B-HLV	A330-343X	548	
☐ B-HLW	A330-343X	565	
☐ B-LAA	A330-342E	669	
☐ B-LAB	A330-342E	673	
☐ B-LAC	A330-342E	679	
☐ B-LAD	A330-342E	776	
☐ B-LAE	A330-342E	850	
☐ B-LAF	A330-342E	855	
☐ B-LAG	A330-342E	895	
☐ B-LAH	A330-342E	915	
☐ B-LAI	A330-342E	959	
☐ B-LAJ	A330-343X	1163	♦
☐ B-	A330-343X		o/o♦
☐ B-	A330-343X		o/o♦
☐ B-	A330-343X		o/o♦
☐ B-HXA	A340-313X	136	
☐ B-HXB	A340-313X	137	
☐ B-HXC	A340-313X	142	
☐ B-HXD	A340-313X	147	
☐ B-HXE	A340-313X	157	
☐ B-HXF	A340-313X	160	
☐ B-HXG	A340-313X	208	
☐ B-HXH	A340-313X	218	
☐ B-HXI	A340-313X	220	
☐ B-HXJ	A340-313X	227	
☐ B-HXK	A340-313X	228	
☐ B-HXM	A340-313X	123	[VCV]
☐ B-HXN	A340-313X	126	[VCV]
☐ B-HXO	A340-313X	128	[VCV]
☐ B-HKE	B747-412	25127/859	
☐ B-HKF	B747-412	25128/860	
☐ B-HKH	B747-412BCF	24227/831	
☐ B-HKJ	B747-412BCF	27133/962	
☐ B-HKT	B747-412	27132/955	
☐ B-HKU	B747-412	27069/1010	
☐ B-HKV	B747-412	26552/1056	
☐ B-HKX	B747-412BCF	26557/1101	
☐ B-HMD	B747-2L5B(SF)	22105/435	[VCV]
☐ B-HME	B747-2L5B(SF)	22106/443	[VCV]
☐ B-HOP	B747-467	23815/728	
☐ B-HOR	B747-467	24631/771	
☐ B-HOS	B747-467	24850/788	
☐ B-HOT	B747-467	24851/813	
☐ B-HOU	B747-467BCF	24925/834	♦
☐ B-HOV	B747-467	25082/849	
☐ B-HOW	B747-467	25211/873	
☐ B-HOX	B747-467	24955/877	

	Reg	Type	MSN	Notes
☐	B-HOY	B747-467	25351/887	
☐	B-HOZ	B747-467BCF	25871/925	
☐	B-HUA	B747-467	25872/930	
☐	B-HUB	B747-467	25873/937	
☐	B-HUD	B747-467	25874/949	
☐	B-HUE	B747-467	27117/970	
☐	B-HUF	B747-467	25869/993	
☐	B-HUG	B747-467	25870/1007	
☐	B-HUH	B747-467F	27175/1020	
☐	B-HUI	B747-467	27230/1033	
☐	B-HUJ	B747-467	27595/1061	
☐	B-HUK	B747-467F	27503/1065	
☐	B-HUL	B747-467F	30804/1255	
☐	B-HUO	B747-467F	32571/1271	
☐	B-HUP	B747-467F	30805/1282	
☐	B-HUQ	B747-467F	34150/1356	
☐	B-HUR	B747-444BCF	24976/827	♦
☐	B-HUS	B747-444BCF	25152/861	♦
☐	B-HVX	B747-267F	24568/776	[VCV]
☐	B-HVZ	B747-267F	23864/687	[VCV]
☐	B-KAA	B747-312M	23769/666	Ftr
☐	B-KAB	B747-312M	23409/637	[VCV]
☐	B-KAC	B747-3H6M	23600/650	[VCV]
☐	B-KAD	B747-209F	24308/752	[VCV]
☐	B-KAE	B747-412BCF	25068/852	[VCV]
☐	B-KAF	B747-412BCF	26547/921	[VCV]
☐	B-KAG	B747-412BCF	27067/953	
☐	B-KAH	B747-412BCF	27134/981	
☐	B-KAI	B747-412BCF	27217/1023	♦
☐	B-LIA	B747-467ERF	37299/1404	
☐	B-LIB	B747-467ERF	36867/1409	
☐	B-LIC	B747-467ERF	36868/1413	
☐	B-LID	B747-467ERF	36869/1414	
☐	B-LIE	B747-467ERF	36870/1514	
☐	B-LIF	B747-467ERF	36871/1417	
☐	B-LJA	B747-867F	39238/1427	o/o♦
☐	B-LJB	B747-867F	39239/1428	o/o♦
☐	B-LJC	B747-867F	39240/1433	o/o♦
☐	B-	B747-867F		o/o♦
☐	B-	B747-867F		o/o♦
☐	B-	B747-867F		o/o♦
☐	B-HNA	B777-267	27265/14	
☐	B-HNB	B777-267	27266/18	
☐	B-HNC	B777-267	27263/28	
☐	B-HND	B777-267	27264/31	
☐	B-HNE	B777-267	27507/94	
☐	B-HNF	B777-367	27506/102	
☐	B-HNG	B777-367	27505/118	
☐	B-HNH	B777-367	27504/136	
☐	B-HNI	B777-367	27508/204	
☐	B-HNJ	B777-367	27509/224	
☐	B-HNK	B777-367	27510/248	
☐	B-HNL	B777-267	27116/1	
☐	B-HNM	B777-367	33702/456	
☐	B-HNN	B777-367	33703/462	
☐	B-HNO	B777-367	33704/470	
☐	B-HNP	B777-367	34243/513	
☐	B-HNQ	B777-367	34244/567	
☐	B-KPA	B777-367ER	36154/661	
☐	B-KPB	B777-367ER	35299/670	
☐	B-KPC	B777-367ER	34432/674	
☐	B-KPD	B777-367ER	36155/680	
☐	B-KPE	B777-367ER	36156/685	
☐	B-KPF	B777-367ER	36832/692	
☐	B-KPG	B777-367ER	35300/700	
☐	B-KPH	B777-367ER	35301/720	
☐	B-KPI	B777-367ER	36833/746	
☐	B-KPJ	B777-367ER	36157/754	
☐	B-KPK	B777-367ER	36158/783	
☐	B-KPL	B777-367ER	36161/818	
☐	B-KPM	B777-367ER	36159/835	
☐	B-KPN	B777-367ER	36165/839	
☐	B-KPO	B777-367ER	36160/843	
☐	B-KPP	B777-367ER	36164/845	♦
☐	B-KPQ	B777-367ER	36162/860	♦
☐	B-KPR	B777-367ER	36163/877	♦
☐	B-KPS	B777-367ER	39232/921	o/o♦
☐	B-	B777-367ER		o/o♦
☐	B-	B777-367ER		o/o♦
☐	B-	B777-367ER		o/o♦
☐	B-	B777-367ER		o/o♦
☐	B-	B777-367ER		o/o♦
☐	B-	B777-367ER		o/o♦

DRAGONAIR — KA / HDA

	Reg	Type	MSN	Notes
☐	B-HSD	A320-232	0756	
☐	B-HSE	A320-232	0784	
☐	B-HSG	A320-232	0812	
☐	B-HSI	A320-232	0930	
☐	B-HSJ	A320-232	1253	
☐	B-HSK	A320-232	1721	
☐	B-HSL	A320-232	2229	
☐	B-HSM	A320-232	2238	
☐	B-HSN	A320-232	2428	
☐	B-HSO	A320-232	4023	
☐	B-HSP	A320-232	4247	♦
☐	B-HTD	A321-231	0993	
☐	B-HTE	A321-231	1024	
☐	B-HTF	A321-231	0633	
☐	B-HTG	A321-231	1695	
☐	B-HTH	A321-231	1984	
☐	B-HTI	A321-231	2021	
☐	B-HWF	A330-343	654	
☐	B-HWG	A330-343	662	
☐	B-HWH	A330-343	692	
☐	B-HWI	A330-343	716	
☐	B-HWJ	A330-343	741	
☐	B-HWK	A330-343	786	
☐	B-HYB	A330-342	106	
☐	B-HYD	A330-342	132	
☐	B-HYF	A330-342	234	
☐	B-HYG	A330-343	405	
☐	B-HYI	A330-343	479	
☐	B-HYJ	A330-343	512	
☐	B-HYQ	A330-343	581	

HONG KONG AIRLINES — HX / CRK

	Reg	Type	MSN	Notes
☐	B-LNC	A330-223	1031	♦
☐	B-LND	A330-223	1042	♦
☐	B-LNE	A330-223	1039	♦
☐	B-LNF	A330-223	1059	♦
☐	B-LNG	A330-223	1054	♦
☐	B-	A330-223		o/o♦
☐	B-	A330-223		o/o♦
☐	B-	A330-223		o/o♦
☐	B-LNY	A330-243F	1062	♦
☐	B-LNZ	A330-243F	1051	♦
☐	B-KBI	B737-808/W	34709/2121	<CHH
☐	B-KBK	B737-84P/W	35072/2155	<CHH
☐	B-KBM	B737-84P/W	35076/2380	<CHH
☐	B-KBT	B737-84P/W	37422/3241	<CHH♦
☐	B-KBU	B737-84P/W	35953/3299	<CHH♦

HONG KONG EXPRESS — UO / HKE

	Reg	Type	MSN	Notes
☐	B-KBQ	B737-84P/W	35274/2570	<CHH
☐	B-KBR	B737-84P/W	35276/2611	<CHH
☐	B-KXE	B737-808/W	34710/2144	<CHH

B-M CHINA - MACAU

AIR MACAU — NX / AMU

	Reg	Type	MSN	Notes
☐	B-MAS	A300B4-622RF	743	
☐	B-MBJ	A300B4-622RF	677	
☐	B-MAK	A319-132	1758	

☐ B-MAL	A319-132	1790	
☐ B-MAM	A319-112	1893	
☐ B-MAN	A319-132	1912	
☐ B-MAO	A319-132	1962	
☐ B-MAH	A320-232	0805	
☐ B-MAX	A320-232	0928	
☐ B-MAB	A321-131	0557	
☐ B-MAF	A321-131	0620	
☐ B-MAG	A321-131	0631	
☐ B-MAJ	A321-231	0908	
☐ B-MAP	A321-231	1850	
☐ B-MAQ	A321-231	1926	
☐ B-MAR	A321-131	0597	

B- CHINA - TAIWAN

CHINA AIRLINES — CI / CAL

☐ B-18301	A330-302	602	
☐ B-18302	A330-302	607	
☐ B-18303	A330-302	641	
☐ B-18305	A330-302	671	
☐ B-18306	A330-302	675	
☐ B-18307	A330-302	691	
☐ B-18308	A330-302	699	
☐ B-18309	A330-302	707	
☐ B-18310	A330-302	714	
☐ B-18311	A330-302	752	
☐ B-18312	A330-302	769	
☐ B-18315	A330-302	823	
☐ B-18316	A330-302	838	
☐ B-18317	A330-302	861	
☐ B-18351	A330-302	725	
☐ B-18352	A330-302	805	
☐ B-18353	A330-302	920	
☐ B-18355	A330-302	1177	♦
☐ B-18801	A340-313X	402	
☐ B-18802	A340-313X	406	
☐ B-18803	A340-313X	411	
☐ B-18805	A340-313X	415	
☐ B-18806	A340-313X	433	
☐ B-18807	A340-313X	541	
☐ B-18601	B737-809/W	28402/113	
☐ B-18605	B737-809/W	28404/130	
☐ B-18606	B737-809/W	28405/132	
☐ B-18607	B737-809/W	29104/139	
☐ B-18608	B737-809/W	28406/141	
☐ B-18609	B737-809/W	28407/161	
☐ B-18610	B737-809/W	29105/295	
☐ B-18612	B737-809/W	30173/695	
☐ B-18615	B737-809/W	30174/1175	
☐ B-16817	B737-809/W	29106/302	
☐ B-18201	B747-409	28709/1114	
☐ B-18202	B747-409	28710/1132	
☐ B-18203	B747-409	28711/1136	
☐ B-18205	B747-409	28712/1137	
☐ B-18206	B747-409	29030/1145	
☐ B-18207	B747-409	29219/1176	
☐ B-18208	B747-409	29031/1186	
☐ B-18210	B747-409	33734/1353	
☐ B-18211	B747-409	33735/1354	
☐ B-18212	B747-409	33736/1357	
☐ B-18215	B747-409	33737/1358	
☐ B-18251	B747-409	27965/1063	
☐ B-18701	B747-409F	30759/1249	
☐ B-18702	B747-409F	30760/1252	
☐ B-18705	B747-409F	30762/1263	
☐ B-18706	B747-409F	30763/1267	
☐ B-18707	B747-409F	30764/1269	
☐ B-18708	B747-409F	30765/1288	
☐ B-18709	B747-409F	30766/1294	

☐ B-18710	B747-409F	30767/1300	
☐ B-18711	B747-409F	30768/1314	
☐ B-18712	B747-409F	33729/1332	
☐ B-18715	B747-409F	33731/1334	
☐ B-18716	B747-409F	33732/1339	
☐ B-18717	B747-409F	30769/1346	
☐ B-18718	B747-409F	30770/1348	
☐ B-18719	B747-409F	33739/1355	
☐ B-18720	B747-409F	33733/1359	
☐ B-18721	B747-409F	33738/1362	
☐ B-18722	B747-409F	34265/1372	
☐ B-18723	B747-409F	34266/1379	
☐ B-18725	B747-409F	30771/1385	
☐ N168CL	B747-409	29906/1219	

EVA AIRWAYS — BR / EVA

☐ B-16301	A330-203	530	
☐ B-16302	A330-203	535	
☐ B-16303	A330-203	555	
☐ B-16305	A330-203	573	
☐ B-16306	A330-203	587	
☐ B-16307	A330-203	634	
☐ B-16308	A330-203	655	
☐ B-16309	A330-203	661	
☐ B-16310	A330-203	678	
☐ B-16311	A330-203	693	
☐ B-16312	A330-203	755	
☑ B-16401	B747-45E	27062/942	23/3.
☐ B-16402	B747-45ESF	27063/947	
☐ B-16403	B747-45EM	27141/976	
☐ B-16405	B747-45EM	27142/982	
☐ B-16406	B747-45EMSF	27898/1051	
☐ B-16407	B747-45EMSF	27899/1053	
☐ B-16408	B747-45EM	28092/1076	
☐ B-16409	B747-45EM	28093/1077	
☐ B-16410	B747-45E	29061/1140	
☐ B-16411	B747-45E	29111/1151	
☐ B-16412	B747-45E	29112/1159	
☐ B-16462	B747-45EMSF	27173/998	
☐ B-16463	B747-45EMSF	27174/1004	
☐ B-16481	B747-45EF	30607/1251	
☐ B-16482	B747-45EF	30608/1279	
☐ B-16483	B747-45EF	30609/1309	
☐ B-16701	B777-35EER	32639/524	
☐ B-16702	B777-35EER	32640/531	
☐ B-16703	B777-35EER	32643/572	
☐ B-16705	B777-35EER	32645/597	
☐ B-16706	B777-35EER	33750/612	
☐ B-16707	B777-35EER	33751/634	
☐ B-16708	B777-35EER	33752/658	
☐ B-16709	B777-35EER	33753/683	
☐ B-16710	B777-35EER	32641/707	
☐ B-16711	B777-35EER	33754/721	
☐ B-16712	B777-35EER	33755/735	
☐ B-16713	B777-35EER	33756/758	
☐ B-16715	B777-35EER	33757/810	♦
☐ B-16716	B777-35EER	32642/822	♦
☐ B-16717	B777-35EER	32644/863	♦
☐ B-16101	MD-11F	48542/570	
☐ B-16107	MD-11F	48546/589	
☐ B-16108	MD-11F	48778/619	
☐ B-16109	MD-11F	48779/620	
☐ B-16110	MD-11F	48786/630	
☐ B-16111	MD-11F	48787/631	
☐ B-16112	MD-11F	48789/633	
☐ B-16113	MD-11F	48790/634	
☐ B-17913	MD-90-30	53537/2162	<UIA
☐ B-17917	MD-90-30ER	53572/2217	<UIA
☐ B-17923	MD-90-30ER	53534/2153	<UIA
☐ B-17925	MD-90-30ER	53568/2171	<UIA
☐ B-17926	MD-90-30ER	53567/2169	<UIA

MANDARIN AIRLINES — AE / MDA

	Reg	Type	MSN
☐	B-16821	190-100AR	19000087
☐	B-16822	190-100AR	19000091
☐	B-16823	190-100AR	19000099
☐	B-16825	190-100AR	19000167
☐	B-16826	190-100AR	19000175
☐	B-16827	190-100AR	19000182
☐	B-16828	190-100AR	19000190
☐	B-16829	190-100AR	19000302

TRANSASIA AIRWAYS — GE / TNA

	Reg	Type	MSN
☐	B-22310	A320-232	0791
☐	B-22311	A320-232	0822
☐	B-22601	A321-131	0538
☐	B-22602	A321-131	0555
☐	B-22605	A321-131	0606
☐	B-22606	A321-131	0731
☐	B-22607	A321-131	0746
☐	B-22801	ATR 72-212A	517
☐	B-22802	ATR 72-212A	525
☐	B-22803	ATR 72-212A	527
☐	B-22805	ATR 72-212A	558
☐	B-22806	ATR 72-212A	560
☐	B-22807	ATR 72-212A	567
☐	B-22810	ATR 72-212A	642
☐	B-22811	ATR 72-212A	749
☐	B-22812	ATR 72-212A	774

UNI AIR — B7 / UIA

	Reg	Type	MSN	
☐	B-15217	DHC-8-311A	379	
☐	B-15219	DHC-8-311A	381	
☐	B-15225	DHC-8-311B	405	
☐	B-15231	DHC-8-311B	414	
☐	B-15233	DHC-8-311B	402	
☐	B-15235	DHC-8Q-311B	443	
☐	B-15237	DHC-8Q-311B	467	
☐	B-15239	DHC-8Q-311B	571	
☐	B-17911	MD-90-30	53535/2158	
☐	B-17913	MD-90-30	53537/2162	>EVA
☐	B-17917	MD-90-30ER	53572/2217	>EVA
☐	B-17918	MD-90-30ER	53571/2193	
☐	B-17919	MD-90-30	53569/2173	
☐	B-17920	MD-90-30	53574/2186	
☐	B-17921	MD-90-30	53554/2166	
☐	B-17922	MD-90-30	53601/2243	
☐	B-17923	MD-90-30ER	53534/2153	>EVA
☐	B-17925	MD-90-30ER	53568/2171	>EVA
☐	B-17926	MD-90-30ER	53567/2169	>EVA

C - CANADA

ADLAIR AVIATION

	Reg	Type	MSN
☐	C-GFYN	DHC-6 Twin Otter 200	209

AIR CANADA — AC / ACA

	Reg	Type	MSN	
☐	C-FBLJ	A319-112	1630	♦
☐	C-FYIY	A319-114	0634	252
☐	C-FYJE	A319-114	0656	255
☐	C-FYJG	A319-114	0670	256
☐	C-FYJH	A319-114	0672	257
☐	C-FYJI	A319-114	0682	258
☐	C-FYJP	A319-114	0688	259
☐	C-FYKC	A319-114	0691	260
☐	C-FYKR	A319-114	0693	261
☐	C-FYKW	A319-114	0695	262
☐	C-FYNS	A319-114	0572	251
☐	C-FZUG	A319-114	0697	263
☐	C-FZUH	A319-114	0711	264
☐	C-FZUJ	A319-114	0719	265
☐	C-FZUL	A319-114	0721	266
☐	C-GAPY	A319-114	0728	267
☐	C-GAQL	A319-114	0732	268
☐	C-GAQX	A319-114	0736	269
☐	C-GAQZ	A319-114	0740	270
☐	C-GARG	A319-114	0742	271
☐	C-GARJ	A319-114	0752	272
☐	C-GARO	A319-114	0757	273
☐	C-GBHM	A319-114	0769	274
☐	C-GBHN	A319-114	0773	275
☐	C-GBHO	A319-114	0779	276
☐	C-GBHR	A319-114	0785	277
☐	C-GBHY	A319-114	0800	278
☐	C-GBHZ	A319-114	0813	279
☐	C-GBIA	A319-114	0817	280
☐	C-GBIJ	A319-114	0829	281
☐	C-GBIK	A319-114	0831	282
☐	C-GBIM	A319-114	0840	283
☐	C-GBIN	A319-114	0845	284
☐	C-GBIP	A319-114	0546	285
☐	C-GITP	A319-112	1562	286
☐	C-GITR	A319-112	1577	287
☐	C-GKNW	A319-112	1805	♦
☐	C-GKOB	A319-112	1853	296♦
☐	C-FDCA	A320-211	0232	405
☐	C-FDQQ	A320-211	0059	201
☐	C-FDQV	A320-211	0068	202
☐	C-FDRH	A320-211	0073	203
☐	C-FDRK	A320-211	0084	204
☐	C-FDRP	A320-211	0122	205
☐	C-FDSN	A320-211	0126	206
☐	C-FDST	A320-211	0127	207
☐	C-FDSU	A320-211	0141	208
☐	C-FFWI	A320-211	0149	209
☐	C-FFWJ	A320-211	0150	210
☐	C-FFWM	A320-211	0154	211
☐	C-FFWN	A320-211	0159	212
☐	C-FGYL	A320-211	0254	218
☐	C-FGYS	A320-211	0255	219
☐	C-FKCK	A320-211	0265	220
☐	C-FKCO	A320-211	0277	221
☐	C-FKCR	A320-211	0290	222
☐	C-FKOJ	A320-211	0330	226
☐	C-FKPT	A320-211	0324	225
☐	C-FLSS	A320-211	0284	408
☐	C-FLSU	A320-211	0309	411
☐	C-FMSX	A320-211	0378	232
☐	C-FNVU	A320-211	0403	415
☐	C-FNVV	A320-211	0404	416
☐	C-FPDN	A320-211	0341	228
☐	C-FPWD	A320-211	0231	404
☐	C-FPWE	A320-211	0175	402
☐	C-FTJO	A320-211	0183	213
☐	C-FTJP	A320-211	0233	214
☐	C-FTJQ	A320-211	0242	215
☐	C-FTJR	A320-211	0248	216
☐	C-FTJS	A320-211	0253	217
☐	C-FXCD	A320-214	2018	239
☐	C-FZQS	A320-214	2145	240
☐	C-FZUB	A320-214	1940	238
☐	C-GJVT	A320-214	1719	235
☐	C-GKOD	A320-214	1864	236
☐	C-GKOE	A320-214	1874	237
☐	C-GPWG	A320-211	0174	401
☐	C-GQCA	A320-211	0210	403
☐	C-GITU	A321-211	1602	451
☐	C-GITY	A321-211	1611	452
☐	C-GIUB	A321-211	1623	453
☐	C-GIUE	A321-211	1632	454
☐	C-GIUF	A321-211	1638	455
☐	C-GJVX	A321-211	1726	456
☐	C-GJWD	A321-211	1748	457
☐	C-GJWI	A321-211	1772	458

	Reg	Type	c/n	Fleet
☐	C-GJWN	A321-211	1783	459
☐	C-GJWO	A321-211	1811	460
☐	C-GFAF	A330-343X	277	931
☐	C-GFAH	A330-343X	279	932
☐	C-GFAJ	A330-343X	284	933
☐	C-GFUR	A330-343X	344	934
☐	C-GHKR	A330-343X	400	935
☐	C-GHKW	A330-343X	408	936
☐	C-GHKX	A330-343X	412	937
☐	C-GHLM	A330-343X	419	938
☐	C-FBEF	B767-233ER	24323/250	[ROW]
☐	C-FBEG	B767-233ER	24324/252	[ROW]
☐	C-FBEM	B767-233ER	24325/254	[ROW]
☐	C-FCAB	B767-375ER	24082/213	681
☐	C-FCAE	B767-375ER	24083/215	682
☐	C-FCAF	B767-375ER	24084/219	683
☐	C-FCAG	B767-375ER	24085/220	684
☐	C-FMWP	B767-333ER	25583/508	631
☐	C-FMWQ	B767-333ER	25584/596	632
☐	C-FMWU	B767-333ER	25585/597	633
☐	C-FMWV	B767-333ER	25586/599	634
☐	C-FMWY	B767-333ER	25587/604	635
☐	C-FMXC	B767-333ER	25588/606	636
☐	C-FOCA	B767-375ER	24575/311	640
☐	C-FPCA	B767-375ER	24306/258	637
☐	C-FTCA	B767-375ER	24307/259	638
☐	C-FVNM	B767-209ER	22681/18	[ROW]
☐	C-FXCA	B767-375ER	24574/302	639
☐	C-GAUE	B767-233	22518/22	[MZJ]
☐	C-GAUW	B767-233	22524/88	[MHV]
☐	C-GAVC	B767-233ER	22527/102	[ROW]
☐	C-GBZR	B767-38EER	25404/411	645
☐	C-GDSP	B767-233ER	24142/229	[ROW]
☐	C-GDSS	B767-233ER	24143/233	[MHV]
☐	C-GDSU	B767-233ER	24144/234	[ROW]
☐	C-GDSY	B767-233ER	24145/236	[ROW]
☐	C-GDUZ	B767-38EER	25347/399	646
☐	C-GEOQ	B767-375ER	30112/765	647
☐	C-GEOU	B767-375ER	30108/771	648
☐	C-GHLA	B767-35HER	26387/445	656
☐	C-GHLK	B767-35HER	26388/456	657
☐	C-GHLQ	B767-333ER	30846/832	658
☐	C-GHLT	B767-333ER	30850/835	659
☐	C-GHLU	B767-333ER	30851/836	660
☐	C-GHLV	B767-333ER	30852/843	661
☐	C-GHOZ	B767-375ER	24087/249	685
☐	C-GHPD	B767-3Y0ER	24999/354	687
☐	C-GHPF	B767-3Y0ER	26206/487	689
☐	C-GHPH	B767-3Y0ER	26207/503	690
☐	C-GLCA	B767-375ER	25120/361	641
☐	C-GSCA	B767-375ER	25121/372	642
☐	C-FIUA	B777-233LR	35239/640	701
☐	C-FIUF	B777-233LR	35243/651	702
☐	C-FIUJ	B777-233LR	35244/679	703
☐	C-FIVK	B777-233LR	35245/689	704
☐	C-FNND	B777-233LR	35246/695	705
☐	C-FNNH	B777-233LR	35247/699	706
☐	C-FITL	B777-333ER	35256/620	731
☐	C-FITU	B777-333ER	35254/626	732
☐	C-FITW	B777-333ER	35298/638	733
☐	C-FIUL	B777-333ER	35255/642	734
☐	C-FIUR	B777-333ER	35242/649	735
☐	C-FIUV	B777-333ER	35248/702	736
☐	C-FIUW	B777-333ER	35249/712	737
☐	C-FIVM	B777-333ER	35251/717	738
☐	C-FIVQ	B777-333ER	35240/749	740
☐	C-FIVR	B777-333ER	35241/763	741
☐	C-FIVS	B777-333ER	35784/797	742
☐	C-FRAM	B777-333ER	35250/726	739
☐	C-FEIQ	170-200SU	17000083	371
☐	C-FEIX	170-200SU	17000085	372
☐	C-FEJB	170-200SU	17000086	373
☐	C-FEJC	170-200SU	17000089	374
☐	C-FEJD	170-200SU	17000090	375
☐	C-FEJF	170-200SU	17000091	376
☐	C-FEJL	170-200SU	17000095	377
☐	C-FEJP	170-200SU	17000096	378
☐	C-FEJY	170-200SU	17000097	379
☐	C-FEKD	170-200SU	17000101	380
☐	C-FEKH	170-200SU	17000102	381
☐	C-FEKI	170-200SU	17000103	382
☐	C-FEKJ	170-200SU	17000109	383
☐	C-FEKS	170-200SU	17000110	384
☐	C-FFYG	170-200SU	17000116	385
☐	C-FFYJ	190-100IGW	19000013	302
☐	C-FFYM	190-100IGW	19000015	303
☐	C-FFYT	190-100IGW	19000018	304
☐	C-FGLW	190-100IGW	19000022	306
☐	C-FGLX	190-100IGW	19000024	307
☐	C-FGLY	190-100IGW	19000028	308
☐	C-FGMF	190-100IGW	19000019	305
☐	C-FHIQ	190-100IGW	19000031	309
☐	C-FHIS	190-100IGW	19000036	310
☐	C-FHIU	190-100IGW	19000037	311
☐	C-FHJJ	190-100IGW	19000041	312
☐	C-FHJT	190-100IGW	19000043	313
☐	C-FHJU	190-100IGW	19000044	314
☐	C-FHKA	190-100IGW	19000046	315
☐	C-FHKE	190-100IGW	19000048	316
☐	C-FHKI	190-100IGW	19000052	317
☐	C-FHKP	190-100IGW	19000055	318
☐	C-FHKS	190-100IGW	19000064	319
☐	C-FHLH	190-100IGW	19000068	320
☐	C-FHNL	190-100IGW	19000070	321
☐	C-FHNP	190-100IGW	19000071	322
☐	C-FHNV	190-100IGW	19000075	323
☐	C-FHNW	190-100IGW	19000077	324
☐	C-FHNX	190-100IGW	19000083	325
☐	C-FHNY	190-100IGW	19000085	326
☐	C-FHON	190-100IGW	19000097	330
☐	C-FHOS	190-100IGW	19000101	331
☐	C-FHOY	190-100IGW	19000105	332
☐	C-FLWE	190-100IGW	19000092	327
☐	C-FLWH	190-100IGW	19000094	328
☐	C-FLWK	190-100IGW	19000096	329
☐	C-FMYV	190-100IGW	19000108	333
☐	C-FMZB	190-100IGW	19000111	334
☐	C-FMZD	190-100IGW	19000115	335
☐	C-FMZR	190-100IGW	19000116	336
☐	C-FMZU	190-100IGW	19000118	337
☐	C-FMZW	190-100IGW	19000124	338
☐	C-FNAI	190-100IGW	19000132	339
☐	C-FNAJ	190-100IGW	19000134	340
☐	C-FNAN	190-100IGW	19000136	341
☐	C-FNAP	190-100IGW	19000142	342
☐	C-FNAQ	190-100IGW	19000146	343
☐	C-FNAW	190-100IGW	19000149	344
☐	C-FNAX	190-100IGW	19000151	345
☐	C-GWEN	190-100IGW	19000010	301

AIR CANADA JAZZ — QK / JZA

	Reg	Type	c/n	Fleet
☐	C-GJZB	B757-28AER	28203/802	♦
☐	C-GJZD	B757-2G5	26278/671	♦
☐	C-GJZH	B757-25F	30758/932	♦
☐	C-GJZS	B757-21K	28674/746	♦
☐	C-GJZT	B757-28A	28835/858	♦
☐	C-FDJA	CRJ-200ER	7979	162
☐	C-FEJA	CRJ-200ER	7983	163
☐	C-FFJA	CRJ-200ER	7985	164
☐	C-FIJA	CRJ-200ER	7987	165
☐	C-FRIA	CRJ-100ER	7045	101
☐	C-FRIB	CRJ-100ER	7047	102
☐	C-FRID	CRJ-100ER	7049	103
☐	C-FSJF	CRJ-100ER	7054	105

	Reg	Type	c/n	Fleet
☐	C-FSJJ	CRJ-100ER	7058	106
☐	C-FSJU	CRJ-100ER	7060	107
☐	C-FSKE	CRJ-100ER	7065	108
☐	C-FSKM	CRJ-100ER	7071	110
☐	C-FVKM	CRJ-100ER	7074	111
☐	C-FVKN	CRJ-100ER	7078	112
☐	C-FVKR	CRJ-100ER	7083	114
☐	C-FVMD	CRJ-100ER	7082	113
☐	C-FWJB	CRJ-100ER	7087	115
☐	C-FWJF	CRJ-100ER	7095	116
☐	C-FWJI	CRJ-100ER	7096	117
☐	C-FWJS	CRJ-100ER	7097	118
☐	C-FWJT	CRJ-100ER	7098	119
☐	C-FWRR	CRJ-100ER	7107	120
☐	C-FWRS	CRJ-100ER	7112	121
☐	C-FWRT	CRJ-100ER	7118	122
☐	C-FWSC	CRJ-100ER	7120	123
☐	C-FXMY	CRJ-100ER	7124	124
☐	C-FZJA	CRJ-200ER	7988	166
☐	C-GGJA	CRJ-200ER	8002	167
☐	C-GJZD	CRJ-200ER	7544	155
☐	C-GJZJ	CRJ-200ER	7553	157
☐	C-GJZZ	CRJ-200ER	7978	161
☐	C-GKEJ	CRJ-200ER	7269	180
☐	C-GKEK	CRJ-200ER	7270	181
☐	C-GKEM	CRJ-200ER	7277	182
☐	C-GKEP	CRJ-200ER	7303	183
☐	C-GKER	CRJ-200ER	7368	184
☐	C-GKEU	CRJ-200ER	7376	185
☐	C-GKEW	CRJ-200ER	7385	186
☐	C-GKEZ	CRJ-200ER	7327	187
☐	C-GKFR	CRJ-200ER	7330	188
☐	C-GKGC	CRJ-200ER	7334	189
☐	C-GMJA	CRJ-200ER	8003	168
☐	C-GNJA	CRJ-200ER	8004	169
☐	C-GOJA	CRJ-200ER	8009	170
☐	C-GQJA	CRJ-200ER	7963	171
☐	C-GTJA	CRJ-200ER	7966	172
☐	C-GUJA	CRJ-200ER	8011	173
☐	C-GXJA	CRJ-200ER	8017	174
☐	C-GZJA	CRJ-200ER	8018	175
☐	C-FBJZ	CRJ-705ER	15037	702
☐	C-FCJZ	CRJ-705ER	15040	703
☐	C-FDJZ	CRJ-705ER	15041	704
☐	C-FJJZ	CRJ-705ER	15043	705
☐	C-FKJZ	CRJ-705ER	15044	706
☐	C-FLJZ	CRJ-705ER	15045	707
☐	C-FNJZ	CRJ-705ER	15046	708
☐	C-FTJZ	CRJ-705ER	15047	709
☐	C-FUJZ	CRJ-705ER	15048	710
☐	C-GDJZ	CRJ-705ER	15049	711
☐	C-GFJZ	CRJ-705ER	15050	712
☐	C-GJAZ	CRJ-705ER	15036	701
☐	C-GLJZ	CRJ-705ER	15051	713
☐	C-GNJZ	CRJ-705ER	15052	714
☐	C-GOJZ	CRJ-705ER	15053	715
☐	C-GPJZ	CRJ-705ER	15055	716
☐	C-FABA	DHC-8-102	92	805
☐	C-FABN	DHC-8-102	44	803
☐	C-FABT	DHC-8-102	49	848
☐	C-FABW	DHC-8-102	97	806
☐	C-FACD	DHC-8-102	150	808
☐	C-FACF	DHC-8-311A	259	308
☐	C-FACT	DHC-8-311A	262	309
☐	C-FACV	DHC-8-311A	278	311
☐	C-FADF	DHC-8-311A	272	310
☐	C-FGQK	DHC-8-102	193	819
☐	C-FGRC	DHC-8-102	195	821
☐	C-FGRM	DHC-8-102	199	820
☐	C-FGRP	DHC-8-102	207	822
☐	C-FGRY	DHC-8-102	212	844
☐	C-FJFM	DHC-8-311A	240	324
☐	C-FJMG	DHC-8-102A	255	824
☐	C-FJVV	DHC-8-311A	271	306

	Reg	Type	c/n	Fleet
☐	C-FJXZ	DHC-8-311A	264	326
☐	C-FMDW	DHC-8-311A	269	305
☐	C-FPON	DHC-8-102	171	836
☐	C-FRUZ	DHC-8-311	293	327
☐	C-FSOU	DHC-8-311A	342	328
☐	C-FTAK	DHC-8-311A	246	323
☐	C-GABF	DHC-8-102	25	816
☐	C-GABO	DHC-8-311A	248	312
☐	C-GABP	DHC-8-311A	257	307
☐	C-GANF	DHC-8-102	42	802
☐	C-GANI	DHC-8-102	64	830
☐	C-GANK	DHC-8-102	87	831
☐	C-GANQ	DHC-8-102	96	833
☐	C-GANS	DHC-8-102	57	828
☐	C-GCTC	DHC-8-102	65	846
☐	C-GETA	DHC-8-301	186	321
☐	C-GEWQ	DHC-8-311A	202	325
☐	C-GHTA	DHC-8-301	198	316
☐	C-GION	DHC-8-102	127	832
☐	C-GJIG	DHC-8-102	68	826
☐	C-GJMI	DHC-8-102	77	825
☐	C-GJMO	DHC-8-102	79	834
☐	C-GJSV	DHC-8-102	85	814
☐	C-GJSX	DHC-8-102	88	835
☐	C-GKON	DHC-8-102	130	815
☐	C-GKTA	DHC-8-301	124	317
☐	C-GLTA	DHC-8-301	154	318
☐	C-GMON	DHC-8-301	131	301
☐	C-GMTA	DHC-8-301	174	319
☐	C-GNON	DHC-8-301	137	302
☐	C-GOND	DHC-8-102	90	840
☐	C-GONJ	DHC-8-102	95	839
☐	C-GONN	DHC-8-102	101	898
☐	C-GONO	DHC-8-102	102	807
☐	C-GONR	DHC-8-102	109	841
☐	C-GONW	DHC-8-102	112	843
☐	C-GONX	DHC-8-102	118	829
☐	C-GONY	DHC-8-102	115	827
☐	C-GSTA	DHC-8-301	182	320
☐	C-GTAG	DHC-8-301	200	315
☐	C-GTAI	DHC-8-102	78	853
☐	C-GTAQ	DHC-8-301	180	313
☐	C-GTAT	DHC-8-301	188	314
☐	C-GTBP	DHC-8-102	66	855
☐	C-GUON	DHC-8-301	143	303
☐	C-GVON	DHC-8-301	149	304
☐	C-GVTA	DHC-8-301	190	322
☐	C-	DHC-8-402Q		o/o♦
☐	C-	DHC-8-402Q		o/o♦
☐	C-	DHC-8-402Q		o/o♦
☐	C-	DHC-8-402Q		o/o♦
☐	C-	DHC-8-402Q		o/o♦

AIR CREEBEC   YN / CRQ

	Reg	Type	c/n	
☐	C-FTQR	Beech 1900D	UE-129	
☐	C-FCLS	DHC-8-102	249	
☐	C-FCSK	DHC-8-102	122	
☐	C-FDWO	DHC-8-106	277	
☐	C-GAIS	DHC-8-102	138	
☐	C-GJOP	DHC-8-102	121	
☐	C-GTCO	DHC-8-102	119	
☐	C-GYWX	DHC-8-102	175	
☐	C-GZEW	DHC-8-314	393	
☐	C-FPCM	EMB.110P1	110340	
☐	C-FPCU	EMB.110P1	110445	
☐	C-FYRH	EMB.110P1	110259	
☐	C-FLIY	HS.748 Srs.2A/244	1723	
☐	C-FPJR	HS.748 Srs.2A/244	1725	

AIR GEORGIAN   ZX / GGN

	Reg	Type	c/n	
☐	C-GAAR	Beech 1900D	UE-207	964
☐	C-GAAS	Beech 1900D	UE-209	965

☐	C-GAAU	Beech 1900D	UE-232	904
☐	C-GAAV	Beech 1900D	UE-235	967
☐	C-GGGA	Beech 1900D	UE-291	951
☐	C-GHGA	Beech 1900D	UE-293	953
☐	C-GMGA	Beech 1900D	UE-315	956
☐	C-GORA	Beech 1900D	UE-326	957
☐	C-GORC	Beech 1900D	UE-320	959
☐	C-GORF	Beech 1900D	UE-330	958
☐	C-GORI	Beech 1900D	UE-47	970
☐	C-GORZ	Beech 1900D	UE-134	973
☐	C-GVGA	Beech 1900D	UE-292	952
☐	C-GWGA	Beech 1900D	UE-309	955
☐	C-GZGA	Beech 1900D	UE-306	954

AIR INUIT   3H / AIE

☐	C-FAIY	DHC-6 Twin Otter 300	362
☐	C-FJFR	DHC-6 Twin Otter 300	784
☐	C-FNBL	DHC-6 Twin Otter 300	625
☐	C-FTJJ	DHC-6 Twin Otter 300	325
☐	C-GKCJ	DHC-6 Twin Otter 300	698
☐	C-GMDC	DHC-6 Twin Otter 300	763
☐	C-GNDO	DHC-6 Twin Otter 300	430
☐	C-GTYX	DHC-6 Twin Otter 300	631
☐	C-FAIV	DHC-8-102	235
☐	C-FCJD	DHC-8-102	158
☐	C-FDAO	DHC-8-102	123
☐	C-FDND	DHC-8-102	129
☐	C-GAII	DHC-8-102	160
☐	C-GAIW	DHC-8-102	155
☐	C-GRAI	DHC-8Q-314	483
☐	C-GUAI	DHC-8Q-314	423
☐	C-FDOX	HS.748 Srs.2A/310LFD	1749
☐	C-FGET	HS.748 Srs.2A/244	1724
☐	C-GAIG	B737-2S2C	21928/603
☐	C-GCUK	HS.748 Srs.2A/343LFD	1762
☐	C-GEGJ	HS.748 Srs.2A/244	1711
☐	C-GMAI	B737-2Q2C	21467/515 ♦

AIR LABRADOR   WJ / LAL

☐	C-FGON	DHC-6 Twin Otter 300	369
☐	C-GLAI	DHC-6 Twin Otter 300	296
☐	C-GNQY	DHC-6 Twin Otter 300	450
☐	C-FXON	DHC-8-102	183
☐	C-GLHO	Beech 1900D	UE-266
☐	C-GLON	DHC-8-102	133
☐	C-GTMB	Beech 1900D	UE-345

AIR MIKISEW   V8

☐	C-FKAM	BAeJetstream 31	724
☐	C-FMCM	Beech 1900D	UE-20
☐	C-FUAM	BAeJetstream 31	746

AIR NORTH   4N / ANT

☐	C-FANB	B737-48E	25764/2314 ♦
☐	C-FJLB	B737-201	22273/680
☐	C-GANH	B737-505/W	27153/2516 ♦
☐	C-GANV	B737-2X6C	23122/1036
☐	C-GNAU	B737-201	21817/602
☐	C-FAID	DHC-8Q-314	400
☐	C-FAGI	HS.748 Srs.2A/276	1699
☐	C-FCSE	HS.748 Srs 2A/269	1679
☐	C-FYDU	HS.748 Srs.2A/273	1694
☐	C-FYDY	HS.748 Srs.2A/233	1661

AIR TINDI   8T

☐	C-GHUE	Beech 1900D	UE-52 ♦
☐	C-FASG	DHC-6 Twin Otter 300	373

☐	C-FATM	DHC-6 Twin Otter 300	265
☐	C-FATN	DHC-6 Twin Otter 300	226
☐	C-FATO	DHC-6 Twin Otter 310	674
☐	C-FATW	DHC-6 Twin Otter 300	525
☐	C-FGOG	DHC-6 Twin Otter 300	348
☐	C-GMAS	DHC-6 Twin Otter 300	438
☐	C-GNPS	DHC-6 Twin Otter 300	558
☐	C-FWZV	DHC-7-103	81
☐	C-GCEV	DHC-7-102	63
☐	C-GFFL	DHC-7-102	74

AIR TRANSAT   TS / TSC

☐	C-FDAT	A310-308	658	305
☐	C-GFAT	A310-304	545	301
☐	C-GLAT	A310-308	588	302
☐	C-GPAT	A310-308	597	303
☐	C-GSAT	A310-308	600	304
☐	C-GTSF	A310-308	472	345
☐	C-GTSH	A310-308	599	343
☐	C-GTSK	A310-304	541	
☐	C-GTSW	A310-304	483	
☐	C-GTSX	A310-304	527	346
☐	C-GTSY	A310-304	447	344
☐	C-GVAT	A310-304	485	321
☐	C-GCTS	A330-342	177	
☒	C-GGTS	A330-243	250	101 3/3
☒	C-GITS	A330-243	271	102
☐	C-GKTS	A330-342	111	100
☐	C-GPTS	A330-243	480	103
☐	C-GTSN	A330-243	369	♦
☐	C-	A330-243		o/o ♦
☐	C-	A330-243		o/o ♦

AIRCO AIRCRAFT CHARTERS

☐	C-FTOW	Beech 1900D	UE-130

ALBERTA CENTRAL AIRWAYS

☐	C-FTSU	DHC-6 Twin Otter 300	451
☐	C-FTWU	DHC-6 Twin Otter 300	372

ALBERTA CITYLINK   ABK

☐	C-FBID	BAeJetstream 31	802
☐	C-FZVY	BAeJetstream 31	833
☐	C-GZOS	BAeJetstream 31	796

ALKAN AIR   AKN

☐	C-FTBI	Short SC.7 Skyvan	SH1847

ALTA FLIGHTS   ALZ

☐	C-FAFI	SA.227DC Metro 23	DC-868B
☐	C-GAAF	SA.227DC Metro 23	DC-891B
☐	C-GSAF	SA.227DC Metro 23	DC-866B

ARCTIC SUNWEST CHARTERS

☐	C-FASC	DHC-8-102	38
☐	C-FASQ	DHC-6 Twin Otter 100	78
☐	C-FASV	DHC-5A Buffalo	95A
☐	C-FASY	DHC-5A Buffalo	107A
☐	C-FTFX	DHC-6 Twin Otter 300	340
☐	C-FTXQ	DHC-6 Twin Otter 300	308
☐	C-GARW	DHC-6 Twin Otter 300	367
☐	C-GASB	DHC-8-102	13

BEARSKIN AIRLINES   JV / BLS

☐	C-FAMC	SA.227AC Metro III	AC-719B
☐	C-FFZN	SA.227AC Metro III	AC-785B

☐ C-FXUS	SA.227CC Metro 23	CC-841B	
☐ C-FYAG	SA.227AC Metro III	AC-670B	
☐ C-FYWG	SA.227AC Metro III	AC-782B	
☐ C-GAFQ	SA.227DC Metro 23	DC-890B	
☐ C-GJVB	SA.227DC Metro 23	DC-902B	
☐ C-GJVC	SA.227DC Metro 23	DC-885B	
☐ C-GJVH	SA.227DC Metro 23	DC-898B	
☐ C-GYHD	SA.227AC Metro III	AC-739B	
☐ C-GYQT	SA.227AC Metro III	AC-644B	
☐ C-GYRL	SA.227AC Metro III	AC-706B	
☐ C-GYTL	SA.227CC Metro 23	CC-829B	
☐ C-GYXL	SA.227AC Metro III	AC-752B	

BUFFALO AIRWAYS — J4 / BFL

☐ C-FTXB	CL-215	1007	298
☐ C-GBPD	CL-215	1084	291
☐ C-GBYU	CL-215	1083	290
☐ C-GCSX	CL-215	1088	295
☐ C-GDHN	CL-215	1089	296
☐ C-GFNF	CL-215	1027	299
☐ C-FCUE	DC-3	12983	
☐ C-FDTB	DC-3	12597	[YQF]
☐ C-FDTH	DC-3	12591	[YQF]
☐ C-FFAY	DC-3	4785	[YQF]
☐ C-FLFR	DC-3	13155	
☐ C-GJKM	DC-3	13580	
☐ C-GPNR	DC-3	13333	
☐ C-GWIR	DC-3	9371	
☐ C-GWZS	DC-3	12327	
☐ C-FBAA	C-54D-DC	10653	[YZF]
☐ C-FBAJ	C-54A-DC	3088	[YHY]
☐ C-FBAK	C-54D-DC	10613	[YHY]
☐ C-FBAM	C-54G-DC	36009	[YHY]
☐ C-FBAP	C-54A-DC	36089	[YHY]
☐ C-FIQM	C-54G-DC	36088	57
☐ C-GBAJ	C-54A-DC	27328	
☐ C-GBNV	C-54G-DC	35988	56
☐ C-GBPA	C-54D-DC	10673	[YZF]
☐ C-GCTF	C-54E-DC	27281	58
☐ C-GPSH	C-54A-DC	7458	1
☐ C-FAVO	Curtiss C-46D Commando	33242	
☐ C-FBAQ	L-188AF Electra	1039	
☐ C-FIJX	L-188CF Electra	2010	♦
☐ C-GLBA	L-188AF Electra	1145	

CALM AIR — MO / CAV

☐ C-FCIJ	ATR 42-300	139	
☐ C-FECI	ATR 42-320	203	♦
☐ C-FJYV	ATR 42-300	216	421
☐ C-FJYW	ATR 42-300	235	422
☐ C-FMAK	ATR 42-300	142	
☐ C-FCRZ	ATR 72-202	357	♦
☐ C-FULE	ATR 72-212	215	
☐ C-FAMO	HS.748 Srs.2A/258LFD	1669	746
☐ C-GDOP	HS.748 Srs.2A/283	1745	[YTH]
☐ C-GEPB	HS.748 Srs.2A/254	1686	[YTH]
☐ C-GHSC	HS.748 Srs.2B/FAALFD	1790	745
☐ C-GSBF	HS.748 Srs.2A/210	1662	
☐ C-FSPB	SAAB SF.340B	340B-351	345
☐ C-FTJV	SAAB SF.340B	340B-366	341
☐ C-FTJW	SAAB SF.340B	340B-377	342
☐ C-FTLW	SAAB SF.340B	340B-336	346
☐ C-GMNM	SAAB SF.340B	340B-364	344
☐ C-GTJY	SAAB SF.340B	340B-166	343

CANADIAN NORTH — 5T / ANX

☐ C-GCNO	B737-25A	23790/1422
☐ C-GCNS	B737-275	23283/1109
☐ C-GCNV	B737-232	23074/993	586
☐ C-GDPA	B737-2T2C	22056/655	584
☐ C-GFPW	B737-275C	21294/481	552
☐ C-GKCP	B737-217	22729/915	523
☐ C-GNDU	B737-242C	22877/880	562
☐ C-GOPW	B737-275C	22160/688	582
☐ C-GSPW	B737-275C	22618/813	583
☐ C-FTAY	F.28 Fellowship 1000	11084	158
☐ C-GECN	DHC-8-106	324	
☐ C-GRGI	DHC-8-106	304	
☐ C-GRGO	DHC-8-106	258	
☐ C-GXCN	DHC-8-106	345	

CANJET — C6 / CJA

☐ C-FTCX	B737-8AS/W	29921/560	801
☐ C-FTCZ	B737-8AS/W	29923/576	802
☐ C-FXGG	B737-81Q/W	29051/479	
☐ C-FYQN	B737-8AS/W	29933/1038	
☐ C-FYQO	B737-8AS/W	29934/1050	
☐ C-GDGQ	B737-8FH/W	35093/2176	♦
☐ C-GDGY	B737-8Q8/W	28218/160	♦

CARGOJET AIRWAYS — W8 / CJT

☐ C-FCJF	B727-223F	22011/1653	
☐ C-FCJI	B727-225F	22435/1674	[YHM]
☐ C-FCJP	B727-223F	22012/1655	
☐ C-FCJU	B727-260F	22759/1789	
☐ C-GCJB	B727-225F	21855/1535	
☐ C-GCJD	B727-231F	21988/1586	
☐ C-GCJN	B727-225F	21451/1310	
☐ C-GCJQ	B727-225F	22437/1682	
☐ C-GCJY	B727-223F/W	22460/1746	
☐ C-GCJZ	B727-225F	21854/1532	
☐ C-GUJC	B727-260F	21979/1534	
☐ C-FKCJ	B757-236F	24792/279	
☐ C-FGAJ	B767-223F	22319/112	
☐ C-FMCJ	B767-223F	22316/95	

CARSON AIR

☐ C-FAFR	SA.227AC Metro III	AC-684	
☐ C-FBWQ	SA.226TC Metro II	TC-379	
☐ C-FJKK	SA.227AC Metro III	AC-713B	
☐ C-FKKR	SA.226TC Metro II	TC-308	
☐ C-FTJC	SA.226TC Metro II	TC-274	
☐ C-FTSK	SA.227AC Metro III	AC-674B	
☐ C-GAMI	SA.227AC Metro III	AC-587	
☐ C-GCAU	SA.226TC Metro II	TC-331E	
☐ C-GCAW	SA.226TC Metro II	TC-358	
☐ C-GDLK	SA.226TC Metro II	TC-302	
☐ C-GKKC	SA.226TC Metro II	TC-370	
☐ C-GKLK	SA.227AC Metro III	AC-741B	♦
☐ C-GKLJ	SA.226TC Metro II	TC-380	
☐ C-GKLN	SA.226TC Metro II	TC-253	
☐ C-GLSC	SA.226TC Metro II	TC-325	
☐ C-GSKC	SA.226TC Metro II	TC-235	

CENTRAL MOUNTAIN AIR — 9M / GLR

☐ C-FCMB	Beech 1900D	UE-278	916
☐ C-FCME	Beech 1900D	UE-277	915
☐ C-FCMN	Beech 1900D	UE-276	914
☐ C-FCMO	Beech 1900D	UE-281	917
☐ C-FCMP	Beech 1900D	UE-271	912
☐ C-FCMR	Beech 1900D	UE-283	918
☐ C-FCMU	Beech 1900D	UE-285	919
☐ C-FCMV	Beech 1900D	UE-272	913
☐ C-FDTR	Beech 1900D	UE-76	
☐ C-GCMA	Beech 1900D	UE-289	920
☐ C-GCML	Beech 1900D	UE-243	925
☐ C-GCMY	Beech 1900D	UE-287	921
☐ C-GFSV	Beech 1900D	UE-346	922

☐ C-GGBY	Beech 1900D	UE-351	923
☐ C-GGCA	Beech 1900D	UE-359	924
☐ C-FDYN	Do328-110	3096	

CONAIR AVIATION — CRC

☐ C-FEKF	Convair 580	80	445
☐ C-FFKF	Convair 580	179	444
☐ C-FHKF	Convair 580	374	455
☐ C-FJVD	Convair 580	478	
☐ C-FKFA	Convair 580	100	452
☐ C-FKFB	Convair 580	57	447
☐ C-FKFL	Convair 580	465	449
☐ C-FKFM	Convair 580	70	454
☐ C-GKFO	Convair 580	78	453
☐ C-GYXC	Convair 580	507	
☐ C-GYXS	Convair 580	501	
☐ C-GFSK	CL-215	1085	201
☐ C-GFSL	CL-215	1086	202
☐ C-GFSM	CL-215	1098	203
☐ C-GFSN	CL-215	1099	204
☐ C-GHLY	DC-6B	45501/953	446
☐ C-GIBS	DC-6A/C	45531/1015	451
☐ C-GKUG	DC-6A/B	45177/859	450
☐ C-FYYJ	L-188AC Electra	1143	♦
☐ C-GYCG	L-188PF Electra	1138	♦

CORPORATE EXPRESS AIRLINE — CPB

☐ C-GEXI	CRJ-200	7186
☐ C-GEXM	CRJ-200	7187
☐ C-GXPS	SAAB SF.340A	340A-075

COULSON AIRCRANE

☐ C-FLYK	Martin JRM-3 Mars	76820
☐ C-FLYL	Martin JRM-3 Mars	76823

COURTESY AIR

☐ C-FJDF	Beech 1900C	UB-68

ENERJET — ENJ

☐ C-GOEJ	B737-7BD/W	33920/1753

EXPLOITS VALLEY AIR SERVICES

☐ C-FEVA	Beech 1900D	UE-126	♦
☐ C-GAAT	Beech 1900D	UE-217	963

EXPRESS AIR — WEW

☐ C-FKAZ	Cessna 208 Caravan I	20800236

FIRST AIR — 7F / FAB

☐ C-FIQR	ATR 42-300(QC)	133
☐ C-FIQU	ATR 42-300(QC)	138
☐ C-FTCP	ATR 42-300(QC)	143
☐ C-FTJB	ATR 42-300(QC)	119
☐ C-GHCP	ATR 42-300(QC)	123
☐ C-GKLB	ATR 42-310	331
☐ C-GSRR	ATR 42-300(QC)	125
☐ C-GULU	ATR 42-310	155
☐ C-GUNO	ATR 42-310	132
☐ C-FUFA	B727-233F	20941/1128
☐ C-GXFA	B727-233F	20938/1105
☐ C-FACP	B737-2L9	22072/623
☐ C-FNVK	B737-2R4C	23130/1040
☐ C-FNVT	B737-248C	21011/411
☐ C-GCPT	B737-217	22258/770

☐ C-GNDC	B737-242C	21728/580	
☐ C-GNWN	B737-210C	21067/414	
☐ C-GKLY	B767-223 (SCD)	22314/73	
☐ C-GFNW	HS.748 Srs.2A /335LFD	1758	405
☐ C-GHPW	L-382G-42C Hercules	4799	
☐ C-GUSI	L-328G-31C Hercules	4600	

FLAIR AIRLINES — FLE

☐ C-FLEJ	B737-4B3	24751/2107
☐ C-FLEN	B737-4K5	24769/1839
☐ C-FLER	B737-46B	24573/1844

FUGRO AVIATION CANADA

☐ C-FDKM	CASA 212 Srs 200	CC40-2-196
☐ C-GDPP	CASA 212 Srs 200	CC50-3-265

GOVERNMENT OF QUEBEC — QUE

☐ C-FASE	CL-215T	1114	238
☐ C-FAWQ	CL-215T	1115	239
☐ C-FTXG	CL-215	1014	228
☐ C-FTXJ	CL-215	1017	230
☐ C-FTXK	CL-215	1018	231
☐ C-GFQB	CL-215	1092	237
☐ C-GQBA	CL-415	2005	240
☐ C-GQBC	CL-415	2012	241
☐ C-GQBD	CL-415	2016	242
☐ C-GQBE	CL-415	2017	243
☐ C-GQBF	CL-415	2019	244
☐ C-GQBG	CL-415	2022	245
☐ C-GQBI	CL-415	2023	246
☐ C-GQBK	CL-415	2026	247
☐ C-GQBT	DHC-8Q-202	470EMS/VIP	

HAWKAIR AVIATION SERVICE — BH

☐ C-FABG	DHC-8-102	147
☐ C-FCJE	DHC-8-102	165
☐ C-FDNG	DHC-8-102	166
☐ C-FIDL	DHC-8-311	305

HYDRO-QUEBEC — HYD

☐ C-GHQL	DHC-8-402Q	4115
☐ C-GHQP	DHC-8-402Q	4004
☐ C-GJNL	DHC-8-311	422

INTEGRAAIR

☐ C-FFIA	BAeJetstream 31	779
☐ C-GGIA	BAeJetstream 31	778

KEEWATIN AIR — FK

☐ C-FBPK	Beech 1900D	UE-128
☐ C-FJXO	Beech 1900C	UC-124

KELOWNA FLIGHTCRAFT — KW / KFA

☐ C-GACU	B727-225F/W	20152/775	710
☐ C-GGKF	B727-223F	21523/1467	718
☐ C-GIKF	B727-227F	20772/982	721
☐ C-GJKF	B727-227F	21042/1106	722
☐ C-GKFJ	B727-281F	21455/1316	715
☐ C-GKKF	B727-227F	21043/1113	723
☐ C-GLKF	B727-227F	21118/1167	724
☐ C-GMKF	B727-227F	21119/1175	725
☐ C-GNKF	B727-227F	20839/1031	726
☐ C-GQKF	B727-243F	21265/1226	720
☐ C-GTKF	B727-225F	21580/1435	728
☐ C-GWKF	B727-243F/W	21270/1231	719
☐ C-GXKF	B727-243F/W	21663/1438	716

☐	C-FKFZ	Convair 580F	151	510
☐	C-GKFF	Convair 580F	160	511
☐	C-GKFG	Convair 580F	22	[YLW]
☐	C-GKFU	Convair 580F	82	501
☐	C-GKFA	DC-10-30F	46921/214	101
☐	C-GKFB	DC-10-30F	46949/179	102
☐	C-GKFD	DC-10-30F	47928/192	103◆
☐	C-	DC-10-30F	46917/211	[YHM]◆

KENN BOREK AIR   4K / KBA

☐	C-FMKB	Basler BT-67TP	47/19560
☐	C-GAWI	Basler BT-67	19227
☐	C-GEAI	Basler BT-67	16305/33053
☐	C-GJKB	Basler BT-67	13383
☐	C-GVKB	Basler BT-67	12300
☐	C-FAKB	DHC-6 Twin Otter 300	273
☐	C-FBBA	DHC-6 Twin Otter 300	276
☐	C-FBBV	DHC-6 Twin Otter 300	311
☐	C-FBBW	DHC-6 Twin Otter 300	588
☐	C-FDHB	DHC-6 Twin Otter 300	338
☐	C-FHKB	DHC-6 Twin Otter 300	402 ◆
☐	C-FWKX	DHC-6 Twin Otter 300	755
☐	C-GBPE	DHC-6 Twin Otter 100	021
☐	C-GCKB	DHC-6 Twin Otter 300	312
☐	C-GDHC	DHC-6 Twin Otter 300	494
☐	C-GIKB	DHC-6 Twin Otter 300	064
☐	C-GKBC	DHC-6 Twin Otter 300	650
☐	C-GKBG	DHC-6 Twin Otter 300	733
☐	C-GKBH	DHC-6 Twin Otter 300	732
☐	C-GKBO	DHC-6 Twin Otter 300	725
☐	C-GSKB	DHC-6 Twin Otter 300	099
☐	C-GTKB	DHC-6 Twin Otter 300	060
☐	C-GXXB	DHC-6 Twin Otter 300	426
☐	C-FLKB	EMB.110P1	110397
☐	C-GANR	EMB.110P1	110373
☐	C-GBBR	EMB.110P1	110444
☐	C-GFKB	EMB.110P1	110400

KIVALLIQ AIR   FK

☐	C-FJXL	Beech 1900C	UC-102

MANITOBA GOVERNMENT AIR SERVICES

☐	C-FTUV	CL-215	1020	256
☐	C-FTXI	CL-215	1016	255
☐	C-GBOW	CL-215	1087	253
☐	C-GMAF	CL-215	1044	250
☐	C-GMAK	CL-215	1107	254
☐	C-GUMW	CL-215	1065	251
☐	C-GYJB	CL-215	1068	252
☐	C-FWAH	DHC-6 Twin Otter 300	240	

MORNINGSTAR AIR EXPRESS   MAL

☐	C-GATK	ATR 42-310F	135Opf FDX
☐	C-FMES	B727-225F	22548/1734Opf FDX
☐	C-FMEY	B727-247F	21328/1251Opf FDX
☐	C-FMEI	B757-2B7SF	27199/586Opf FDX◆
☐	C-FMEK	B757-2B7SF	27123/534Opf FDX◆
☐	C-FMEP	B757-2B7SF	27144/544Opf FDX◆
☐	C-FMEU	B757-2B7	27200/589Opf FDX◆
☐	C-FMFG	B757-2B7	27198/584Opf FDX◆
☐	C-FEXB	C208B Caravan	208B0539Opf FDX
☐	C-FEXE	C208B Caravan	208B0244Opf FDX
☐	C-FEXF	C208B Caravan	208B0508Opf FDX
☐	C-FEXV	C208B Caravan	208B0482Opf FDX
☐	C-FEXX	C208B Caravan	208B0209Opf FDX
☐	C-FEXY	C208B Caravan	208B0226Opf FDX

NAKINA CAMPS OUTPOST & AIR SVC   T2

☐	C-FDGV	DHC-6 Twin Otter 200	154

NEWFOUNDLAND & LABRADOR A/S

☐	C-FAYN	CL-215	1105	282
☐	C-FAYU	CL-215	1106	283
☐	C-FTXA	CL-215	1006	284
☐	C-FYWP	CL-215	1002	285
☐	C-GDKW	CL-215	1095	280
☐	C-GDKY	CL-215	1096	281
☐	C-FIZU	CL-415	2075	◆
☐	C-FNJC	CL-415	2076	◆
☐	C-GMFY	CL-415	2077	◆

NOLINOR AVIATION   NRL

☐	C-GNLN	B737-2B6C	23050/975	
☐	C-GTUK	B737-2B6C	23049/951	
☐	C-FAWV	Convair 580F	154	
☐	C-FHNM	Convair 580F	454	Lst GV
☐	C-FTAP	Convair 580	334	
☐	C-GKFP	Convair 580	446	
☐	C-GNRL	Convair 580F	375	
☐	C-GQHB	Convair 580	376	
☐	C-GRLQ	Convair 580	347	

NORTH CARIBOO AIR   NCB

☐	C-FCWP	DHC-8-102	111	
☐	C-FLSX	DHC-8-102	285	
☐	C-FNCG	DHC-8-102	211	
☐	C-FNCL	Beech 1900D	UE-11	
☐	C-FNCP	Beech 1900D	UE-58	
☐	C-FODL	DHC-8-102	294	
☐	C-GAQN	DHC-8-311	548	
☐	C-GZTU	Beech 1900C-1	UC-103	
☐	C-GIGK	DHC-6 Twin Otter 300	492	
☐	C-GNCF	DHC-8-311A	244	◆

NORTH WRIGHT AIRWAYS   HW / NWL

☐	C-FNWL	DHC-6 Twin Otter 300	596
☐	C-GRDD	DHC-6 Twin Otter 100	54

NORTHWESTERN AIR   J3 / PLR

☐	C-FCPE	BAeJetstream 31	825
☐	C-FNAE	BAeJetstream 31	881
☐	C-FNAF	BAeJetstream 31	789
☐	C-FNAM	BAeJetstream 31	767
☐	C-FNAY	BAeJetstream 31	768
☐	C-FNAZ	BAeJetstream 32	843
☐	C-GNAQ	BAeJetstream 32EP	837
☐	C-GNGI	BAeJetstream 31	739

NT AIR   NTA

☐	C-FCPV	DHC-6 Twin Otter 300	371	
☐	C-FHVX	Do328-100	3094	
☐	C-GCMT	Beech 1900C-1	UC-120	
☐	C-GCMY	Beech 1900D	UE-287	921
☐	C-GCMZ	Beech 1900C-1	UC-61	929
☐	C-GEFA	Beech 1900C-1	UC-94	927

ONTARIO MINISTRY OF NATURAL RES'CES

☐	C-GOGD	CL-415	2028	270
☐	C-GOGE	CL-415	2031	271
☐	C-GOGF	CL-415	2032	272
☐	C-GOGG	CL-415	2033	273
☐	C-GOGH	CL-415	2034	274
☐	C-GOGW	CL-415	2037	275

☐	C-GOGX	CL-415	2038	276
☐	C-GOGY	CL-415	2040	277
☐	C-GOGZ	CL-415	2043	278
☐	C-FOPG	DHC-6 Twin Otter 300	232	
☐	C-FOPI	DHC-6 Twin Otter 300	243	
☐	C-FOPJ	DHC-6 Twin Otter 300	344	
☐	C-GOGA	DHC-6 Twin Otter 300	739	
☐	C-GOGB	DHC-6 Twin Otter 300	761	
☐	C-GOGC	DHC-6 Twin Otter 300	750	

OSPREY WINGS

☐	C-FLXP	DHC-6 Twin Otter 200	217	
☐	C-FVEG	DHC-6 Twin Otter 300	260	
☐	C-GQOQ	DHC-6 Twin Otter 200	155	

PACIFIC COASTAL AIRLINES — 8P / PCO

☐	C-FPCO	Beech 1900C	UB-52	
☐	C-FPCV	Beech 1900C	UB-9	302
☐	C-FPCX	Beech 1900C	UB-66	
☐	C-GBPC	Beech 1900C	UB-43	
☐	C-GCPZ	Beech 1900C	UB-71	♦
☐	C-GIPC	Beech 1900C-1	UC-110	
☐	C-GPCY	Beech 1900C	UB-45	301
☐	C-GCPU	SAAB SF.340A	340A-140	
☐	C-GPCE	SAAB SF.340A	340A-004	
☐	C-GPCG	SAAB SF.340A	340A-094	
☐	C-GPCJ	SAAB SF.340A	340A-006	
☐	C-GPCN	SAAB SF.340A	340A-027	
☐	C-GPCQ	SAAB SF.340A	340A-043	
☐	C-GPCF	Short SD.3-60	SH3620	706
☐	C-GPCW	Short SD.3-60	SH3622	703

PASCAN AVIATION — PSC

☐	C-FHQA	BAeJetstream 32	876	
☐	C-FKQA	BAeJetstream 32	877	
☐	C-GQJT	BAeJetstream 32EP	886	
☐	C-GUSC	BAeJetstream 32	902	

PERIMETER AVIATION — 4B / PAG

☐	C-FBTL	SA.226TC Metro II	TC-385	
☐	C-FFJM	SA.227AC Metro III	AC-700	
☐	C-FFDB	SA.226TC Metro II	TC-249	
☐	C-FIHB	SA.226TC Metro II	TC-361	
☐	C-FIHE	SA.226TC Metro II	TC-373	
☐	C-FIIA	SA.226TC Metro II	TC-329	
☐	C-FJNW	SA.226TC Metro IIA	TC-352	
☐	C-FMAV	SA.227AC Metro III	AC-616	
☐	C-FSLZ	SA.226TC Metro II	TC-222EE	
☐	C-FSWT	SA.226TC Metro II	TC-382	
☐	C-FUZY	SA.226TC Metro II	TC-343	
☐	C-GFWX	SA.227AC Metro III	AC-650B	
☐	C-GIQF	SA.226TC Metro II	TC-279	
☐	C-GIQG	SA.226TC Metro II	TC-285	
☐	C-GIQK	SA.226TC Metro II	TC-288	
☐	C-GPCL	SA.226AT Merlin IV	AT-017	
☐	C-GQAJ	SA.226TC Metro II	TC-295	
☐	C-GQAP	SA.226TC Metro II	TC-263	
☐	C-GWVH	SA.227AC Metro IIIA	AC-714	
☐	C-GYRD	SA.226TC Metro II	TC-278	
☐	C-FOFR	DHC-8-106	317	
☐	C-FPPW	DHC-8-102A	390	♦
☐	C-GWPS	DHC-8-102	120	

PORTER AIRLINES — PD / POE

☐	C-FLQY	DHC-8-402Q	4306	♦
☐	C-GLQB	DHC-8-402Q	4130	
☐	C-GLQC	DHC-8-402Q	4134	
☐	C-GLQD	DHC-8-402Q	4138	
☐	C-GLQE	DHC-8-402Q	4140	
☐	C-GLQF	DHC-8-402Q	4193	
☐	C-GLQG	DHC-8-402Q	4194	
☐	C-GLQH	DHC-8-402Q	4225	
☐	C-GLQJ	DHC-8-402Q	4228	
☐	C-GLQK	DHC-8-402Q	4247	
☐	C-GLQL	DHC-8-402Q	4249	
☐	C-GLQM	DHC-8-402Q	4252	
☐	C-GLQN	DHC-8-402Q	4254	
☐	C-GLQO	DHC-8-402Q	4270	
☐	C-GLQP	DHC-8-402Q	4271	
☐	C-GLQQ	DHC-8-402Q	4272	
☐	C-GLQR	DHC-8-402Q	4278	
☐	C-GLQV	DHC-8-402Q	4279	
☐	C-GLQX	DHC-8-402Q	4282	
☐	C-GLQZ	DHC-8-402Q	4308	♦
☐	C-	DHC-8-402Q	4357	o/o ♦
☐	C-	DHC-8-402Q		o/o ♦
☐	C-	DHC-8-402Q		o/o ♦
☐	C-	DHC-8-402Q		o/o ♦

PRINCE EDWARD AIR — CME

☐	C-FKAX	Beech 1900C	UB-67	
☐	C-GKGA	Beech 1900C-1	UC-117	
☐	C-GSKA	Beech 1900C	UB-32	
☐	C-GSKG	Beech 1900C-1	UC-22	
☐	C-GSKM	Beech 1900C	UB-21	
☐	C-GSKN	Beech 1900C-1	UC-54	
☐	C-GSKU	Beech 1900C	UB-35	
☐	C-GSKW	Beech 1900C	UB-33	
☐	C-GTGA	Beech 1900C-1	UC-62	
☐	N340AQ	SAAB SF.340AF	340A-019	

PROVINCE OF ALBERTA — GOA

☐	C-GFSJ	DHC-8-103	17	

PROVINCIAL AIRLINES — PB / SPR

☐	C-FUMY	DHC-6 Twin Otter 300	675	
☐	C-FWLG	DHC-6 Twin Otter 300	731	
☐	C-GHVV	DHC-6 Twin Otter 300	391	
☐	C-GIED	DHC-6 Twin Otter 300	600	
☐	C-GJDE	DHC-6 Twin Otter 300	471	
☐	C-FHRC	DHC-8-102	209	
☐	C-GPAB	DHC-8-106MPA	275	
☐	C-GPAL	DHC-8-102	157	
☐	C-GPAU	DHC-8-106	282	
☐	C-GRNN	DHC-8-106MPA	314	
☐	C-FPAG	SAAB SF.340A	340A-028	
☐	C-FPAI	SAAB SF.340A	340A-047	
☐	C-GMEW	SA.227AC Metro III	AC-668B	

REGIONAL 1 AIRLINES — TSH

☐	C-FJFW	DHC-8-311	315	
☐	C-FYDH	DHC-8-102	083	
☐	C-GRGK	DHC-8Q-202	522	
☐	C-GZKH	DHC-8-103	117	

SASKATCHEWAN GOVT AIR OPS — SGS

☐	C-FAFN	CL-215	1093	216
☐	C-FAFO	CL-215	1094	217
☐	C-FAFP	CL-215	1100	218
☐	C-FAFQ	CL-215	1101	219
☐	C-FYWO	CL-215	1003	214
☐	C-FYXG	CL-215	1009	215
☐	C-GSKJ	Convair 580	202	
☐	C-GSKR	Convair 580	509	471
☐	C-GSKQ	Convair 580	217	
☐	C-GVSK	Convair 580	238	
☐	C-GYSK	Convair 580	234	

SKY REGIONAL AIRLINES

☐	C-FSRJ	DHC-8-402Q	4165 ♦
☐	C-FSRN	DHC-8-402Q	4170 ♦
☐	C-FSRW	DHC-8-402Q	4172 ♦
☐	C-	DHC-8-402Q	4174 ♦
☐	C-	DHC-8-402Q	4181 ♦
☐	C-	DHC-8-402Q	4182 ♦
☐	C-	DHC-8-402Q	4184 ♦

STARLINK AVIATION   ANU

☐	C-GCCN	BAeJetstream 31	704
☐	C-GCCZ	BAeJetstream 31	712
☐	C-GDFW	BAeJetstream 31	720
☐	C-GEMQ	BAeJetstream 31	747
☐	C-GNRG	BAeJetstream 31	791
☐	C-GOAD	EMB.120ER	120086

SUMMIT AIR CHARTERS

☐	C-FEQV	Do228-202	8126 [OBF]
☐	C-FEQX	Do228-202	8101
☐	C-FPSA	Do228-202	8122
☐	C-FPSH	Do228-202	8071
☐	C-FUCN	Do228-202	8109
☐	C-GJPY	Do228-202	8088
☐	C-GSAX	Do228-202	8153
☐	C-FYSQ	Short SC.7 Skyvan	SH1968
☐	C-GJGS	Short SC.7 Skyvan	SH1909
☐	C-GKOA	Short SC.7 Skyvan	SH1905

SUNWEST AVIATION   CNK

☐	C-FGEW	SA.226TC Metro II	TC-347
☐	C-GMWW	SA.227DC Metro 23	DC-852B
☐	C-GSHV	SA.227DC Metro 23	DC-900B
☐	C-GSHY	SA.227DC Metro 23	DC-897B
☐	C-GSHZ	SA.227DC Metro 23	DC-887B
☐	C-GSLX	Beech 1900D	UE-264
☐	C-GSWB	Beech 1900D	UE-386
☐	C-GSWK	SA.226TC Metro II	TC-368
☐	C-GSWV	Beech 1900D	UE-141
☐	C-GSWX	Beech 1900D	UE-63
☐	C-GSWZ	Beech 1900D	UE-337

SUNWING AIRLINES   WG / SWG

☐	C-ГCAK	B737-86Q/W	30292/1451
☐	C-FLSW	B737-8HX/W	36552/2658
☐	C-FRZG	B737-8K5/W	35139/2538
☐	C-FTAE	B737-8Q8/W	30637/800
☐	C-FTAH	B737-8Q8/W	29351/1471
☐	C-FTDW	B737-808/W	34704/1958
☐	C-FTJH	B737-8BK	29642/2247
☐	C-FTOH	B737-8HX/W	29647/2865
☐	C-FYLC	B737-8BK/W	33029/1945
☐	C-GLBW	B737-8Q8/W	30671/1307 <ECA
☐	C-GTVG	B737-8Q8/W	30719/2257 ♦

SUSTUT AIR

☐	C-FUMC	Short SC.7 Skyvan	SH1844

SWANBERG AIR

☐	C-GPSN	BAeJetstream 31	783
☐	C-GPSO	BAeJetstream 31	756
☐	C-GPSV	BAeJetstream 31	816
☐	C-GPSW	BAeJetstream 31	735

TLI CHO AIR

☐	C-FATN	DHC-6 Twin Otter 300	226

TRANS CAPITALAIR

☐	C-FJHQ	DHC-7-103	11 Opf UN
☐	C-FWYU	DHC-7-103	12 Opf UN
☐	C-GCPP	DHC-7-102	87 [YTZ]
☐	C-GGXS	DHC-7-102	64
☐	C-GVPP	DHC-7-102	72 Opf UN
☐	C-GVWD	DHC-7-102	108 Opf UN

TRANSWEST AIR   9T / ABS

☐	C-FCCE	DHC-6 Twin Otter 100	8
☐	C-FGLF	DHC-6 Twin Otter 200	138
☐	C-FPGE	DHC-6 Twin Otter 200	197
☐	C-FSCA	DHC-6 Twin Otter 100	17
☐	C-FVOG	DHC-6 Twin Otter 100	35
☐	C-FSEW	BAeJetstream 31	764
☐	C-GTJX	SAAB SF.340B	340B-165
☐	C-GTWG	Beech 1900D	UE-79
☐	C-GTWK	SAAB SF.340B	340B-190

TRIUMPH AIRWAYS

☐	C-FOOW	DC-3	13342

VOYAGEUR AIRWAYS   VC / VAL

☐	C-FMCY	CRJ-200	7064
☐	C-FMUV	CRJ-200	7073
☐	C-FTYS	CRJ-200LR	7039
☐	C-FWWU	CRJ-200LR	7299
☐	C-FXHC	CRJ-200ER	7329
☐	C-FXLH	CRJ-200LR	7283
☐	C-FZKM	DHC-7-102	61
☐	C-GFOF	DHC-7-102	37
☐	C-GGUL	DHC-7-102	70
☐	C-GGUN	DHC-7-110	66
☐	C-GJPI	DHC-7-102	36
☐	C-GLOL	DHC-7-102	39
☐	C-FEYG	DHC-8-311	320
☐	C-FEXZ	DHC-8-314	319
☐	C-FEZD	DHC-8-314	385
☐	C-FIQT	DHC-8-314	395
☐	C-FNCU	DHC-8-314	517
☐	C-GHQZ	DHC-8-314	370

WASAYA AIRWAYS   WT / WSG

☐	C-FQWA	Beech 1900D	UE-75	
☐	C-FWAU	Beech 1900D	UE-164	
☐	C-FWAX	Beech 1900D	UE-297	
☐	C-FZWK	Beech 1900D	UE-8	
☐	C-GSWA	Beech 1900D	UE-34	
☐	C-GZVJ	Beech 1900D	UE-223	
☐	C-FFFS	HS.748 Srs.2A/209LFD	1663	806
☐	C-FTTW	HS.748 Srs.2A/264	1681	805
☐	C-GLTC	HS.748 Srs.2A/244LFD	1656	801
☐	C-GMAA	HS.748 Srs.2A/214LFD	1576	807

WEST COAST AIR   8O

☐	C-FGQE	DHC-6 Twin Otter 100	40	609
☐	C-FGQH	DHC-6 Twin Otter 100	106	604
☐	C-FMHR	DHC-6 Twin Otter 100	51	605
☐	C-FWTE	DHC-6 Twin Otter 100	96	603
☐	C-GJAW	DHC-6 Twin Otter 200	176	607
☐	C-GQKN	DHC-6 Twin Otter 100	94	606

WESTWIND AVIATION   WEW

☐	C-FCPD	BAeJetstream 31	822
☐	C-GHGK	BAeJetstream 31	786

☐	C-GPRT	Beech 1900C	UC-140	
☐	C-GPRZ	Beech 1900C-1	UC-76	
☐	C-GWWC	ATR 42-300	209	
☐	C-GWWD	ATR 42-300	211	
☐	C-GWWR	ATR 42-300	238	
☐	C-GWWX	Beech 1900C-1	UC-44	
☐	C-GWWY	Beech 1900C-1	UC-63	

WESTJET   WS / WJA

☐	C-FAWJ	B737-8CT/W	35502/2323	807
☐	C-FBWJ	B737-7CT/W	32767/1629	230
☐	C-FBWS	B737-7CT/W	37088/3080	255
☐	C-FCWJ	B737-7CT/W	35086/2613	250
☐	C-FEWJ	B737-7CT/W	32769/1665	232
☐	C-FGWJ	B737-7CT/W	32764/1553	226
☐	C-FIWJ	B737-7CT/W	30712/2185	240
☐	C-FIWS	B737-76N/W	32404/851	001
☐	C-FJWS	B737-76N/W	28651/872	002
☐	C-FKWJ	B737-8CT/W	36435/3469	815♦
☐	C-FKWS	B737-76N/W	30134/905	003
☐	C-FLWJ	B737-7CT/W	38096/3520	262♦
☐	C-FMWJ	B737-7CT/W	32771/1754	233
☐	C-FTWJ	B737-7CT/W	30713/2220	241
☐	C-FUWS	B737-7CT/W	32765/1574	228
☐	C-FWAD	B737-7CT/W	32753/1222	201
☐	C-FWAF	B737-7CT/W	32747/1239	202
☐	C-FWAI	B737-7CT/W	33656/1246	203
☐	C-FWAO	B737-7CT/W	33657/1254	205
☐	C-FWAQ	B737-7CT/W	32748/1266	206
☐	C-FWBG	B737-7CT/W	32749/1281	207
☐	C-FWBL	B737-7CT/W	32750/1286	208
☐	C-FWBW	B737-7CT/W	33697/1303	209
☐	C-FWBX	B737-7CT/W	32751/1333	210
☐	C-FWCC	B737-7CT/W	32752/1339	211
☐	C-FWCN	B737-7CT/W	33698/1346	212
☐	C-FWSE	B737-8CT/W	36690/2987	811
☐	C-FWSF	B737-7CT/W	32758/1431	218
☐	C-FWSI	B737-7CT/W	36691/2983	253
☐	C-FWSK	B737-7CT/W	36420/2671	251
☐	C-FWSO	B737-7CT/W	32759/1445	219
☐	C-FWSV	B737-7CT/W	32760/1472	220
☐	C-FWSX	B737-7CT/W	32761/1493	221
☐	C-FWSY	B737-7CT/W	32762/1501	222
☐	C-FXWJ	B737-7CT/W	32768/1648	231
☐	C-FZWS	B737-76N/W	32731/1044	006
☐	C-GBWS	B737-6CT	34288/1931	608
☐	C-GCWJ	B737-7CT/W	33970/1556	227
☐	C-GEWJ	B737-6CT	35571/2045	615
☐	C-GGWJ	B737-7CT/W	35503/2334	242
☐	C-GJWS	B737-8CT/W	34152/1714	802
☐	C-GKWJ	B737-8CT/W	34151/1684	801
☐	C-GLWS	B737-76N/W	32581/1009	005
☐	C-GMWJ	B737-7CT/W	35985/2135	239
☐	C-GPWS	B737-6CT	34284/1759	601
☐	C-GQWJ	B737-7CT/W	35505/2436	246
☐	C-GRWS	B737-76N/W	32881/1155	007
☐	C-GSWJ	B737-7CT/W	37423/3347	261♦
☐	C-GTWS	B737-76N/W	32883/1179	008
☐	C-GUWJ	B737-7CT/W	36422/2497	248
☐	C-GUWS	B737-76N/W	33378/1206	009
☐	C-GVWJ	B737-7CT/W	36421/2484	247
☐	C-GWAZ	B737-7CT/W	32763/1522	223
☐	C-GWBF	B737-7CT/W	32757/1370	213
☐	C-GWBJ	B737-7CT/W	32754/1385	215
☐	C-GWBL	B737-8CT	34154/1734	806
☐	C-GWBN	B737-7CT/W	34155/1772	235
☐	C-GWBT	B737-7CT/W	32755/1396	216
☐	C-GWBX	B737-7CT/W	34156/1793	236
☐	C-GWCM	B737-7CT/W	32756/1413	217
☐	C-GWCN	B737-7CT/W	34157/1818	237
☐	C-GWCQ	B737-6CT	35111/2004	610
☐	C-GWCT	B737-6CT	35112/2016	611
☐	C-GWCY	B737-6CT	35113/2022	612
☐	C-GWJE	B737-7CT/W	35078/2431	245

☐	C-GWJF	B737-7CT/W	32766/1599	229
☐	C-GWJG	B737-7CT/W	35504/2366	243
☐	C-GWJK	B737-7CT/W	35084/2564	249
☐	C-GWJO	B737-7CT/W	33969/1527	225
☐	C-GWJT	B737-7CT/W	40338/3529	♦
☐	C-GWJU	B737-6CT	34289/1956	609
☐	C-GWSA	B737-8CT/W	34153/1731	805
☐	C-GWSB	B737-6CT	34285/1797	602
☐	C-GWSE	B737-76N/W	33379/1216	010
☐	C-GWSH	B737-76N/W	29886/1258	011
☐	C-GWSI	B737-6CT	34286/1816	603
☐	C-GWSJ	B737-6CT	34621/1862	605
☐	C-GWSK	B737-6CT	34287/1912	607
☐	C-GWSL	B737-6CT	34633/1884	606
☐	C-GWSN	B737-7CT/W	37089/3090	256♦
☐	C-GWSO	B737-7CT/W	37090/3092	257
☐	C-GWSP	B737-7CT/W	36693/3108	258
☐	C-GWSQ	B737-7CT/W	37091/3134	259
☐	C-GWSR	B737-8CT/W	35288/2802	809
☐	C-GWSU	B737-7CT/W	36689/2860	252
☐	C-GWSV	B737-8CT/W	37158/2841	810
☐	C-GWSX	B737-8CT/W	366963314	813♦
☐	C-GWSY	B737-7CT/W	37421/3184	260♦
☐	C-GWSZ	B737-8CT/W	37092/3164	812
☐	C-GWWJ	B737-8CT/W	35080/2524	808
☐	C-GXWJ	B737-6CT	35570/2032	613
☐	C-GYWJ	B737-7CT/W	32772/1879	238
☐	C-GZWS	B737-8CT/W	32770/1719	803
☐	C-	B737-		o/o♦
☐	C-	B737-		o/o♦
☐	C-	B737-		o/o♦
☐	C-	B737-		o/o♦
☐	C-	B737-		o/o♦
☐	C-	B737-		o/o♦

CC - CHILE

AEROCARDAL

☐	CC-ACG	Do328-110	3063	♦

AEROLINEA PRINCIPAL CHILE   PCP

☐	CC-ACD	B737-2K9	23404/1176	♦
☐	CC-ACE	B737-322	24669/1907	♦
☐	CC-CZK	B737-236	21804/686	
☐	CC-CZO	B737-236	22030/693	

AEROVIAS DAP   DAP

☐	CC-ACO	BAe146 Srs.200	E2094	♦
☐	CC-CHV	DHC-6 Twin Otter 300	709	
☐	CC-CZP	BAe146 Srs.200	E2042	

LAN AIRLINES   LA / LAN

☐	CC-CVA	A318-121	3001	
☐	CC-CVB	A318-121	3030	
☐	CC-CVF	A318-121	3062	
☐	CC-CVH	A318-121	3214	
☐	CC-CVN	A318-121	3216	
☐	CC-CVP	A318-121	3371	
☐	CC-CVR	A318-121	3390	
☐	CC-CVS	A318-121	3438	
☐	CC-CVU	A318-121	3469	
☐	CC-CVV	A318-121	3509	
☐	CC-CZJ	A318-121	3585	
☐	CC-CZN	A318-121	3602	
☐	CC-CZQ	A318-121	3606	
☐	CC-CZR	A318-121	3635	
☐	CC-CZS	A318-121	3642	
☐	CC-BCA	A319-132	4563	♦
☐	CC-BCB	A319-132	4598	o/o♦
☐	CC-	A319-132		o/o♦
☐	CC-	A319-132		o/o♦

☐	CC-COU	A319-132	2089	>LPE
☐	CC-COX	A319-132	2096	>LPE
☐	CC-COY	A319-132	2295	>LPE
☐	CC-COZ	A319-132	2304	>LPE
☐	CC-CPE	A319-132	2321	>LPE
☐	CC-CPF	A319-132	2572	>LPE
☐	CC-CPI	A319-132	2585	>LPE
☐	CC-CPJ	A319-132	2845	
☐	CC-CPL	A319-132	2858	
☐	CC-CPM	A319-132	2864	>LPE
☐	CC-CPO	A319-132	2872	>LPE
☐	CC-CPQ	A319-132	2886	>LPE
☐	CC-CPX	A319-132	2887	>LPE
☐	CC-CQK	A319-132	2892	>LPE
☐	CC-CQL	A319-132	2894	>LPE
☐	CC-CYE	A319-132	3663	
☐	CC-CYF	A319-132	3671	
☐	CC-CYI	A319-132	3770	
☐	CC-CYJ	A319-132	3772	
☐	CC-CYL	A319-132	3779	
☐	CC-BAA	A320-233	4383	♦
☐	CC-BAB	A320-233	4400	♦
☐	CC-BAC	A320-233	4439	♦
☐	CC-BAD	A320-233	4476	♦
☐	CC-BAE	A320-233	4509	♦
☐	CC-BAF	A320-233	4516	♦
☐	CC-BAG	A320-233	4546	♦
☐	CC-BAH	A320-233	4549	♦
☐	CC-BAI	A320-233	4543	♦
☐	CC-BAJ	A320-233	4576	o/o♦
☐	CC-BAK	A320-233	4597	o/o♦
☐	CC-	A320-2		o/o♦
☐	CC-	A320-2		o/o♦
☐	CC-	A320-2		o/o♦
☐	CC-	A320-2		o/o♦
☐	CC-	A320-2		o/o♦
☐	CC-	A320-2		o/o♦
☐	CC-BJB	A320-232	3264	♦
☐	CC-BJC	A320-232	3330	♦
☐	CC-COF	A320-233	1355	
☐	CC-COI	A320-233	1526	
☐	CC-COL	A320-233	1568	
☐	CC-COM	A320-233	1626	
☐	CC-CQM	A320-233	3280	>LPE
☐	CC-CQN	A320-233	3319	
☐	CC-CQO	A320-233	3535	
☐	CC-CQP	A320-233	3556	
☐	CC-CQA	A340-313X	359	
☐	CC-CQC	A340-313X	363	
☐	CC-CQE	A340-313X	429	
☐	CC-CQF	A340-313X	442	
☐	CC-CQG	A340-313X	167	
☐	CC-BJA	B767-316ER/W	26329/641	♦
☐	CC-CDM	B767-352ER	26261/575	
☐	CC-CDP	B767-316ER/W	27597/602	
☐	CC-CEB	B767-316ER/W	26327/621	
☐	CC-CRG	B767-375ER	25865/430	♦
☐	CC-CRH	B767-375ER	25864/426	
☐	CC-CRV	B767-316ER/W	27615/681	
☐	CC-CWF	B767-316ER/W	34626/940	
☐	CC-CWG	B767-316ER/W	34629/944	
☐	CC-CWH	B767-316ER/W	34628/945	
☐	CC-CWV	B767-316ER/W	35230/955	
☐	CC-CWY	B767-316ER/W	35231/961	
☐	CC-CXC	B767-316ER/W	36710/962	
☐	CC-CXE	B767-316ER/W	35696/968	
☐	CC-CXG	B767-316ER/W	36712/972	
☐	CC-CXI	B767-316ER/W	37800/984	
☐	CC-CXJ	B767-316ER/W	37801/985	
☐	CC-CXK	B767-316ER/W	37802/987	♦
☐	CC-CXL	B767-31BER	26265/570	
☐	CC-CZT	B767-316ER/W	29228/699	
☐	CC-CZU	B767-316ER/W	29229/729	

☐	CC-CZW	B767-316ER/W	29227/698	
☐	CC-	B767-316ER/W		o/o♦
☐	CC-	B767-316ER/W		o/o♦
☐	CC-	B787-816	38464/10	o/o♦
☐	CC-	B787-816	38475/16	o/o♦

LAN CARGO — UC / LCO

☐	CC-CSD	B737-204F	20417/255	<LAN
☐	CC-CZZ	B767-316F/W	25756/712	
☐	N314LA	B767-316F/W	32573/848opb	MAA
☐	N316LA	B767-316F/W	30842/860opb	FWL
☐	N420LA	B767-316F/W	34627/948	>MAA
☐	N524LA	B767-346F	35816/956	♦
☐	PR-ABD	B767-316F/W	34245/935	>TUS
☐	N772LA	B777-F6N	37708/774	
☐	N774LA	B777-F6N	37710/782	

SKY AIRLINES — H2 / SKU

☐	CC-ABW	A320-233	1523	♦
☐	CC-ADP	A320-231	0406	♦
☐	CC-AAG	B737-247	23608/1399	♦
☐	CC-CAP	B737-236	22027/654	
☐	CC-CDB	B737-230	22120/715	
☐	CC-CTB	B737-2Q3	23481/1241	
☐	CC-CTD	B737-2Q3	23117/1033	
☐	CC-CTF	B737-230	22122/721	
☐	CC-CTH	B737-230	22636/808	
☐	CC-CTK	B737-230	22402/744	
☐	CC-CTM	B737-230	22139/791	
☐	CC-CTO	B737-230	22114/657	
☐	CC-CTX	B737-2T4	22698/823	

CN - MOROCCO

AIR ARABIA MAROC — 3O / MAC

☐	CN-NMA	A320-214	3809	
☐	CN-NMB	A320-214	3833	
☐	CN-NMC	A320-214	3246	
☐	CN-NMD	A320-214	4310	♦

ATLAS BLUE — 8A / BMM

☐	CN-RMF	B737-4B6	24807/1880	<RAM
☐	CN-RMG	B737-4B6	24808/1888	<RAM
☐	CN-RMX	B737-4B6	26526/2219	<RAM
☐	CN-RNC	B737-4B6	26529/2584	<RAM
☐	CN-RND	B737-4B6	26530/2588	<RAM
☐	CN-RNX	A321-211	2064	<RAM
☐	CN-RNY	A321-211	2076	<RAM
☐	CN-ROF	A321-211	2726	<RAM
☐	CN-ROM	A321-211	3070	<RAM

JET4YOU — 8J / JFU

☐	CN-RPA	B737-4B3	24750/1916	<CRL
☐	CN-RPC	B737-4K5	24125/1687	
☐	CN-RPE	B737-8K5/W	27990/246	<HLF
☐	CN-RPF	B737-8K5/W	34691/2246	
☐	CN-RPG	B737-8K5/W	34692/2249	
☐	CN-RPH	B737-46J	28867/2879	

REGIONAL AIR LINES — FN / RGL

☐	CN-CDU	ATR 42-300	134	[NTE]♦
☐	CN-CDV	ATR 42-300	137	[CMN]♦
☐	CN-RLA	Beech 1900D	UE-259	
☐	CN-RLD	Beech 1900D	UE-267	
☐	CN-RLF	ATR 42-320	208	
☐	CN-RLG	ATR 42-320	366	

ROYAL AIR MAROC			AT / RAM
☐ CN-RNX	A321-211	2064	>BMM
☐ CN-RNY	A321-211	2076	>BMM
☐ CN-ROF	A321-211	2726	>BMM
☐ CN-ROM	A321-211	3070	>BMM
☐ CN-CDU	ATR 42-300	134	>RGL
☐ CN-CDV	ATR 42-300	137	>RGL
☐ CN-COA	ATR 72-201	441	
☐ CN-COB	ATR 72-202	444	
☐ CN-COC	ATR 72-201	470	
☐ CN-COD	ATR 72-202	483	
☐ CN-RMF	B737-4B6	24807/1880Lsd	BMM
☐ CN-RMG	B737-4B6	24808/1888Lsd	BMM
☐ CN-RMI	B737-2B6	21214/449	[CAS]
☐ CN-RMJ	B737-2B6	21215/452	[CAS]
☐ CN-RMK	B737-2B6	21216/456	[CAS]
☐ CN-RML	B737-2B6	22767/851	[CMN]
☐ CN-RMV	B737-5B6	25317/2157	
☐ CN-RMW	B737-5B6	25364/2166	
☐ CN-RMX	B737-4B6	26526/2219	>BMM
☐ CN-RMY	B737-5B6	26525/2209	
☐ CN-RNB	B737-5B6	26527/2472	
☐ CN-RNC	B737-4B6	26529/2584	>BMM
☐ CN-RND	B737-4B6	26530/2588	>BMM
☐ CN-RNG	B737-5B6	27679/2734	
☐ CN-RNH	B737-5B6	27680/2855	
☐ CN-ROX	B737-3M8F	24020/1614	
☐ CN-RNL	B737-7B6/W	28982/236	
☐ CN-RNM	B737-7B6/W	28984/294	
☐ CN-RNQ	B737-7B6/W	28985/501	
☐ CN-RNR	B737-7B6/W	28986/519	
☐ CN-RNV	B737-7B6/W	28988/1261	
☐ CN-RNJ	B737-8B6/W	28980/55	
☐ CN-RNK	B737-8B6/W	28981/60	
☐ CN-RNP	B737-8B6/W	28983/492	
☐ CN-RNU	B737-8B6/W	28987/1095	
☐ CN-RNW	B737-8B6/W	33057/1347	
☐ CN-RNZ	B737-8B6/W	33058/1432	
☐ CN-ROA	B737-8B6/W	33059/1457	
☐ CN-ROB	B737-8B6/W	33060/1646	
☐ CN-ROC	B737-8B6/W	33061/1661	
☐ CN-ROD	B737-7B6/W	33062/1883	
☐ CN-ROE	B737-8B6/W	33063/1913	
☐ CN-ROH	B737-85P	33978/1957	
☐ CN-ROJ	B737-85P	33979/1963	
☐ CN-ROK	B737-8B6/W	33064/2180	
☐ CN-ROL	B737-8B6/W	33065/2206	
☐ CN-ROP	B737-8B6/W	33066/2506	
☐ CN-ROR	B737-8B6/W	33067/2527	
☐ CN-ROS	B737-8B6/W	37718/2773	
☐ CN-ROT	B737-8B6/W	33068/2883	
☐ CN-ROU	B737-8B6/W	33069/2911	
☐ CN-ROY	B737-8B6/W	33070/3233	♦
☐ CN-ROZ	B737-8B6/W	33071/3258	♦
☐ CN-	B737-8B6/W		o/o♦
☐ CN-	B737-8B6/W		o/o♦
☐ CN-	B737-8B6/W		o/o♦
☐ CN-	B737-8B6/W		o/o♦
☐ CN-	B737-8B6/W		o/o♦
☐ CN-	B737-8B6/W		o/o♦
☐ CN-	B737-8B6/W		o/o♦
☐ CN-RGA	B747-428	25629/956	
☐ CN-RMT	B757-2B6	23686/103	
☐ CN-RMZ	B757-2B6	23687/106	
☐ CN-RNS	B767-36NER	30115/863	
☐ CN-RNT	B767-36NER	30843/867	
☐ CN-ROG	B767-328ER	27212/531	
☐ CN-ROV	B767-3Q8ER	27686/793	
☐ CN-ROW	B767-343ER	30008/743	

☐ CN-	B787-8B6	35507/17	o/o♦
☐ CN-	B787-8B6	35508/19	o/o♦

CP - BOLIVIA

AEROLINEAS SUD AMERICANAS

☐ CP-2499	B727-224	22449/1756

AEROSUR			5L / RSU
☐ CP-2377	B727-23	20044/592	[VVI]
☐ CP-2422	B727-264	21617/1416	
☐ CP-2423	B727-264	21638/1457	
☐ CP-2424	B727-264	22156/1607	[CBB]
☐ CP-2431	B727-264	22411/1696	[VVI]
☐ CP-2447	B727-264	22409/1676	
☐ CP-2455	B727-287	22606/1812	
☐ CP-2462	B727-264	22158/1642	
☐ CP-2498	B727-223	22463/1755	
☐ CP-2515	B727-222	21904/1528	
☐ CP-2438	B737-201	21815/589	
☐ CP-2476	B737-281	21771/594	
☐ CP-2484	B737-281	21768/586	
☐ CP-2486	B737-281	21769/587	
☐ CP-2561	B737-281	21613/530	
☐ CP-2595	B737-33A	24790/1955	
☐ CP-2603	B747-443	32339/1275	
☐ CP-2521	B767-260ER	23107/93	
☐ CP-2659	B767-284ER	24742/303	♦

ALAS DEL SUR

☐ CP-2479	Fairchild F-27	99

BOLIVIANA DE AVIACION

☐ CP-2550	B737-33A	25118/2065
☐ CP-2551	B737-382	24449/1857
☐ CP-2552	B737-3M8	25041/2024
☐ CP-2553	B737-382	24450/1873 ♦

LAB AIRLINES			LB / LLB
☐ CP-1366	B727-2K3/W	21494/1373	
☐ CP-1367	B727-2K3/W	21495/1403	
☐ CP-	B727-2S7	22492/1729	[CBB]

TAB CARGO			BOL
☐ CP-1376	L.382C-72D Hercules	4759	
☐ CP-2184	L.182A-2A Hercules	3228	
☐ CP-2489	DC-10-10F	46903/43	
☐ CP-2555	DC-10-30F	46937/152	

TAM - TRANSPORTES AEREO MILITAR

☐ FAB-61	282-1B Hercules	3549	
☐ FAB-65	282-1B Hercules	3588	
☐ FAB-66	282-1B Hercules	3560	
☐ FAB-90	Fokker F.27M Troopship	400M10578	
☐ FAB-93	Fokker F.27M Troopship	400M10599	
☐ FAB-96	CAIC MA60	411	
☐ FAB-97	CAIC MA60	412	
☐ FAB-99	BAe146 Srs.100	E1081	
☐ FAB-100	BAe146 Srs.200	E2080	
☐ FAB-101	BAe146 Srs.200	E2041	
☐ FAB-102	BAe146 Srs.200	E2023	
☐ FAB-103	BAe146 Srs.200	E2040	
☐ FAB-104	BAe146 Srs.200	E2024	[CBB]

CS - PORTUGAL

AEROVIP

☐	CS-AYT	Do228-200	8084
☐	CS-TGG	Do228-202K	8160
☐	CS-TLJ	Short SD.3-60	SH3692

EURO ATLANTIC AIRWAYS — MM / MMZ

☐	CS-TEB	L-1011-500 Tristar	293A-1240	[AMM]
☐	CS-TFK	B757-2G5	23983/161	
☐	CS-TFM	B777-212ER	28513/144	>BBG
☐	CS-TFS	B767-3Y0ER	25411/408	
■	CS-TFT	B767-3Y0ER	26208/505	9/7
☐	CS-TLO	B767-383ER	24318/257	
☐	CS-TLX	B757-2G5	24176/173	
☐	CS-TLZ	B767-375ERF	24086/248	

HI FLY — 5K / HFY

☐	CS-TEI	A310-304	495	>PFL♦
☐	CS-TEX	A310-304	565	
☐	CS-TFZ	A330-243	1008	
☐	CS-TMT	A330-322	096	
☐	CS-TQM	A340-313X	117	
☐	OY-KBM	A340-313X	450	♦

LUZAIR — LUZ

☐	CS-TFY	A320-232	1868
☐	CS-TMP	L-1011-500 Tristar	293A-1248
☐	CS-TMR	L-1011-500 Tristar	293B-1241 [VCV]
☐	CS-TQI	B767-3S1ER	25221/384

ORBEST — ORB

☐	CS-TRA	A330-243	461 >NVR

PGA EXPRESS

☐	CS-TMU	Beech 1900D	UE-335Opb OAV
☐	CS-TMV	Beech 1900D	UE-341Opb OAV

PORTUGALIA AIRLINES — NI / PGA

☐	CS-TPG	ERJ-145EP	145014
☐	CS-TPH	ERJ-145EP	145017
☐	CS-TPI	ERJ-145EP	145031
☐	CS-TPJ	ERJ-145EP	145036
☐	CS-TPK	ERJ-145EP	145041
☐	CS-TPL	ERJ-145EP	145051
☐	CS-TPM	ERJ-145EP	145095
☐	CS-TPN	ERJ-145EP	145099
☐	CS-TPA	Fokker 100	11257
☐	CS-TPB	Fokker 100	11262
☐	CS-TPC	Fokker 100	11287
☐	CS-TPD	Fokker 100	11317
☐	CS-TPE	Fokker 100	11342
☐	CS-TPF	Fokker 100	11258

SATA AIR ACORES — SP / SAT

☐	CS-TRB	DHC-8Q-202	476
☐	CS-TRC	DHC-8Q-202	480
☐	CS-TRD	DHC-8-402Q	4291
☐	CS-TRE	DHC-8-402Q	4295
☐	CS-TRF	DHC-8-402Q	4297
☐	CS-TRG	DHC-8-402Q	4298
☐	CS-TGO	Do228	8119

SATA INTERNATIONAL — S4 / RZO

☐	CS-TGU	A310-304	0571

☐	CS-TGV	A310-304	0651
☐	CS-TKJ	A320-212	0795
☐	CS-TKK	A320-214	2390
☐	CS-TKL	A320-214	2425
☐	CS-TKM	A310-304	661
☐	CS-TKN	A310-325ET	624 <AUA
☐	CS-TKO	A320-214	3891

TAP AIR PORTUGAL — TP / TAP

☐	CS-TTA	A319-111	0750
☐	CS-TTB	A319-111	0755
☐	CS-TTC	A319-111	0763
☐	CS-TTD	A319-111	0790
☐	CS-TTE	A319-111	0821
☐	CS-TTF	A319-111	0837
☐	CS-TTG	A319-111	0906
☐	CS-TTH	A319-111	0917
☐	CS-TTI	A319-111	0933
☐	CS-TTJ	A319-111	0979
☐	CS-TTK	A319-111	1034
☐	CS-TTL	A319-111	1100
☐	CS-TTM	A319-111	1106
☐	CS-TTN	A319-111	1120
☐	CS-TTO	A319-111	1127
☐	CS-TTP	A319-111	1165
☐	CS-TTQ	A319-112	0629
☐	CS-TTR	A319-112	1756
☐	CS-TTS	A319-112	1765
☐	CS-TMW	A320-214	1667
☐	CS-TNB	A320-211	0191
☐	CS-TNG	A320-214	0945
☐	CS-TNH	A320-214	0960
☐	CS-TNI	A320-214	0982
☐	CS-TNJ	A320-214	1181
☐	CS-TNK	A320-214	1206
☐	CS-TNL	A320-214	1231
☐	CS-TNM	A320-214	1799
☐	CS-TNN	A320-214	1816
☐	CS-TNP	A320-214	2178
☐	CS-TNQ	A320-214	3769
☐	CS-TNR	A320-214	3883
☐	CS-TNS	A320-214	4021
☐	CS-TNT	A320-214	4095
☐	CS-TNU	A320-214	4106
☐	CS-TNV	A320-214	4145
☐	CS-TQD	A320-214	0870
☐	CS TJE	A321-211	1307
☐	CS-TJF	A321-211	1399
☐	CS-TJG	A321-211	1713
☐	CS-TOE	A330-223	305
☐	CS-TOF	A330-223	308
☐	CS-TOG	A330-223	312
☐	CS-TOH	A330-223	181
☐	CS-TOI	A330-223	195
☐	CS-TOJ	A330-223	223
☐	CS-TOK	A330-223	317
☐	CS-TOL	A330-223	877
☐	CS-TOM	A330-202	899
☐	CS-TON	A330-202	904
☐	CS-TOO	A330-202	914
☐	CS-TOP	A330-202	934
☐	CS-TOA	A340-312	041
☐	CS-TOB	A340-312	044
☐	CS-TOC	A340-312	079
☐	CS-TOD	A340-312	091

WHITE — WHT

☐	CS-TDI	A310-308	573	
☐	CS-TKI	A310-304	448	
☐	CS-TQK	A320-232	2204	
☐	CS-TQO	A320-214	0548	♦

CU - CUBA

AEROCARIBBEAN   7L / CRN

☐	CU-T1509	ATR 42-300	9
☐	CU-T1512	ATR 42-300	136
☐	CU-T1544	ATR 72-212	472
☐	CU-T1545	ATR 72-212	473
☐	CU-T1547	ATR 72-212	485
☐	CU-T1550	ATR 42-300	14
☐	CU-T1506	An-26	87306710
☐	CU-C1515	Il-18GrM	188010805
☐	CU-T1532	Il-18D	188010904
☐	CU-T1534	Yak-40	9731754
☐	CU-T1537	Yak-40	9021360
☐	CU-T1538	Yak-40	9021260

AEROGAVIOTA   KG / GTV

☐	CU-T1402	An-26B	12605
☐	CU-T1403	An-26B	12905
☐	CU-T1404	An-26B	12906
☐	CU-T1406	An-26B	13502
☐	CU-T1408	An-26	6903
☐	CU-T1417	An-26	
☐	CU-T1420	An-26	87306607
☐	CU-T1421	An-26	6610
☐	CU-T1425	An-26	6904
☐	CU-T1426	An-26	5603
☐	CU-T1428	An-26B	11303
☐	CU-T1429	An-26	7006
☐	CU-T1432	An-26	7306
☐	CU-T1433	An-26	7309
☐	CU-T1434	An-26	7701
☐	CU-T1435	An-26	7702
☐	CU-T1240	ATR 42-500	617
☐	CU-T1454	ATR 42-500	616
☐	CU-T1455	ATR 42-500	618
☐	CU-T1456	ATR 42-500	619

CUBANA DE AVIACION   CU / CUB

☐	CU-T1214	An-24RV	47309404	
☐	CU-T1223	An-24RV	47309405	
☐	CU-T1244	An-24RV	57310301	
☐	CU-T1257	An-24RV	37309104	
☐	CU-T1260	An-24RV	57310307	
☐	CU-T1263	An-24RV	47309610	
☐	CU-T1267	An-24RV	47309907	
☐	CU-T1228	An-26B	12604	
☐	CU-T1229	An-26B	13501	
☐	CU-T1240	ATR 42-500	617	VIP
☐	CU-T1280	Il-62M	3749648	
☐	CU-T1282	Il-62M	2052456	[HAV]
☐	CU-T1284	Il-62M	4053732	
☐	CU-T1250	Il-96-300	74393202015	
☐	CU-T1251	Il-96-300	74393202016	
☐	CU-T1254	Il-96-300	74393202017	
☐	CU-	Il-96-300		o/o
☐	CU-C1700	Tu-204-100SE	64036	
☐	CU-T1701	Tu-204-100E	64035	
☐	CU-T1702	Tu-204-100E	64042	
☐	CU-C1703	Tu-204-100SE	64037	
☐	CU-T1247	Yak-42D	3303016	
☐	CU-T1255	Yak-42D	4309017	<AKT
☐	CU-T1704	Yak-42D	2014549	
☐	CU-T1707	Yak-42D	23016269	♦
☐	CU-T1708	Yak-42D	23606265	♦
☐	CU-T1709	Yak-42D	4520424811442	♦

CX - URUGUAY

BQB LINEAS AEREAS

☐	CX-JCL	ATR 72-212A	805	♦
☐	CX-JPL	ATR 72-212A	816	♦

PLUNA   PU / PUA

☐	CX-BON	B737-2A3	22737/830	[MVD]
☐	CX-BOO	B737-2A3	22738/834	[MVD]
☐	CX-BOP	B737-2A3	22739/844	[MVD]
☐	CX-PUF	B737-230	22135/781	
☐	CX-CRA	CRJ-900	15165	
☐	CX-CRB	CRJ-900	15169	
☐	CX-CRC	CRJ-900	15175	
☐	CX-CRD	CRJ-900	15180	
☐	CX-CRE	CRJ-900	15185	
☐	CX-CRF	CRJ-900	15204	
☐	CX-CRH	CRJ-900	15233	♦
☐	CX-CRI	CRJ-900	15234	♦
☐	CX-CRK	CRJ-900	15239	♦

C2 - NAURU

OUR AIRLINE   ON / RON

☐	VH-INU	B737-3Y0	23684/1353

C5 - GAMBIA

SLOK AIR INTERNATIONAL   S0 / OKS

☐	C5-EUN	B737-201	22798/924	
☐	C5-IFY	B737-201	22797/916	
☐	C5-NYA	B737-201	22799/932	[PGF]
☐	C5-OBJ	B737-201	22795/912	
☐	C5-OUK	B737-201	22796/914	
☐	C5-ZNA	B737-201	22806/938	

C6 - BAHAMAS

BAHAMASAIR   UP / BHS

☐	C6-BFG	DHC-8-311A	288
☐	C6-BFH	DHC-8-311A	291
☐	C6-BFJ	DHC-8Q-311	323
☐	C6-BFO	DHC-8-301	164
☐	C6-BFP	DHC-8Q-311	309
☐	C6-BFM	B737-2K5	22596/763
☐	C6-BFW	B737-2K5	22601/833
☐	C6-BGK	B737-275	22086/667
☐	C6-BGL	B737-275	22087/673

CAT ISLAND AIR

☐	C6-CAA	SAAB SF.340A	340A-122	
☐	C6-CAH	EMB.110P1	110249	[NAS]
☐	C6-CAP	EMB.110P1	110304	

LEAIR CHARTER SERVICES

☐	C6-CAB	EMB.110P1	110198	
☐	C6-PDX	EMB.110P1	110288	[NAS]

PINEAPPLEAIR   PNP

☐	N60MJ	Beech 1900D	UE-60
☐	N157PA	Beech 1900C	UB-56
☐	N381CR	Beech 1900C	UB-69

SKY BAHAMAS — SBM

☐	C6-SBB	SAAB SF.340A	340A-149
☐	C6-SBC	SAAB SF.340A	340A-023
☐	C6-SBD	SAAB SF.340A	340A-021
☐	C6-SBG	SAAB SF.340A	340A-110 ♦

SOUTHERN AIR CHARTER — PL / SOA

☐	N376SA	Beech 1900C	UB-72
☐	N378SA	Beech 1900C	UB-31

VISION AIR

☐	N888MX	Beech 1900C	UB-39

WESTERN AIR — WST

☐	C6-FPO	SA.227AC Metro III	AC-652
☐	C6-JER	SA.227AC Metro III	AC-588
☐	C6-KER	SA.227AC Metro III	AC-595
☐	C6-REX	SA.227AC Metro III	AC-649 [REX]
☐	C6-SAD	SA.227AC Metro III	AC-746B
☐	C6-SAR	SA.227AC Metro III	AC-598
☐	C6-HBW	SAAB SF.340A	340A-067
☐	C6-JAY	SAAB SF.340A	340A-120
☐	C6-RMW	SAAB SF.340A	340A-120
☐	C6-SLR	SAAB SF.340B	340B-248 ♦
☐	C6-VIP	SAAB SF.340A	340A-098
☐	N900MX	Beech 1900C	UB-55

C9 - MOZAMBIQUE

LAM — TM / LAM

☐	C9-AUL	DHC-8-402Q	4019
☐	C9-AUM	DHC-8-402Q	4020
☐	C9-BAJ	B737-205	23464/1223
☐	C9-BAO	B737-205	23467/1245
☐	C9-EMA	ERJ-190AR	19000301
☐	C9-EMB	ERJ-190AR	19000309

MOCAMBIQUE EXPRESS — MXE

☐	C9-AUK	BAeJetstream 41	41044
☐	ZS-AAB	EMB.120RT	120208

D - GERMANY

ADVANCED AVIATION

☐	D-CAAL	Do228-202K	8152
☐	D-ISIS	Do228-200	8007
☐	D4-CBK	Do228-212	8222

AEROLOGIC — BOX

☐	D-AALA	B777-FZN	36001/780
☐	D-AALB	B777-FZN	36002/799
☐	D-AALC	B777-FZN	36003/836
☐	D-AALD	B777-FZN	36004/838
☐	D-AALE	B777-FZN	36198/872
☐	D-AALF	B777-FZN	36201/881 ♦
■	D-AALG	B777-FZN	36199/894 ♦
☐	D-AALH	B777-FZN	36200/904 ♦

AIR CARGO GERMANY — 6U / ACX

☐	D-ACGA	B747-409(BDSF)	24311/869
☐	D-ACGB	B747-409(BDSF)	24312/954
☐	D-ACGC	B747-412BCF	24975/838 ♦

AIR BERLIN — AB / BER

☐	D-ABGA	A319-132	2383	
☐	D-ABGC	A319-132	2468	
☐	D-ABGH	A319-112	3245	
☐	D-ABGI	A319-112	3346	
☐	D-ABGJ	A319-112	3415	
☐	D-ABGK	A319-112	3447	
☐	D-ABGL	A319-112	3586	
☐	D-ABGN	A319-112	3661	
☐	D-ABGO	A319-112	3689	
☐	D-ABGP	A319-112	3728	
☐	D-ABGQ	A319-112	3700	
☐	D-ABGR	A319-112	3704	
☐	D-ABGS	A319-112	3865	
☐	D-ABDA	A320-214	2539	
☐	D-ABDB	A320-214	2619	
☐	D-ABDC	A320-214	2654	
☐	D-ABDD	A320-214	2685	
☐	D-ABDE	A320-214	2696	
☐	D-ABDG	A320-214	2835	
☐	D-ABDP	A320-214	3093	
☐	D-ABDQ	A320-214	3121	
☐	D-ABDR	A320-214	3242	
☐	D-ABDS	A320-214	3289	
☐	D-ABDU	A320-214	3516	
☐	D-ABDW	A320-214	3945	
☐	D-ABDX	A320-214	3995	
☐	D-ABDY	A320-214	4013	
☐	D-ABFA	A320-214	4101	
☐	D-ABFB	A320-214	4128	
☐	D-ABFC	A320-214	4161	
☐	D-ABFD	A320-214	4187	
☐	D-ABFE	A320-214	4269	♦
☐	D-ABFF	A320-214	4329	♦
☐	D-ABFG	A320-214	4291	♦
☐	D-ABFK	A320-214	4433	♦
☐	D-ABFL	A320-214	4463	♦
☐	D-ABFM	A320-214	4478	♦
☐	D-ABFN	A320-214	4510	♦
☐	D-ABFO	A320-214	4565	♦
☐	D-ABFP	A320-214	4606	o/o♦
☐	D-	A320-214		o/o♦
☐	D-	A320-214		o/o♦
☐	D-	A320-214		o/o♦
☐	D-	A320-214		o/o♦
☐	D-	A320-214		o/o♦
☐	D-ALTB	A320-214	1385	[DUS]♦
☐	D-ALTC	A320-214	1441	[DUB]♦
☐	D-ALTD	A320-214	1493	
☐	D-ALTE	A320-214	1504	
☐	D-ALTF	A320-214	1553	
☐	D-ALTH	A320-214	1797	
☐	D-ALTJ	A320-214	1838	
☐	D-ALTK	A320-214	1931	
☐	D-ALTL	A320-214	2009	
☐	D-ABCA	A321-211	3708	
☐	D-ABCB	A321-211	3749	
☐	D-ABCF	A321-211	1966	
☐	D-ABCG	A321-211	1988	
☐	D-ALSA	A321-211	1629	
☐	D-ALSB	A321-211	1994	
☐	D-ALSC	A321-211	2005	
☐	D-ALSD	A321-211	1607	
☐	D-AERK	A330-322	120	
☐	D-AERQ	A330-322	127	
☐	D-AERS	A330-322	171	
☐	D-ALPA	A330-223	403	
■	D-ALPB	A330-223	432	
■	D-ALPC	A330-223	444	
☐	D-ALPD	A330-223	454	
☐	D-ALPE	A330-223	469	
☐	D-ALPF	A330-223	476	

	Reg	Type	c/n	Notes
☐	D-ALPG	A330-223	493	
☐	D-ALPH	A330-223	739	
☐	D-ALPI	A330-223	828	
■	D-ALPJ	A330-223	911	12/3
☐	D-ADIH	B737-3Y0	23921/1513	
☐	D-AGEB	B737-322	24320/1670	[TXL]
☐	D-ABAA	B737-76Q	30271/740	
☐	D-ABAB	B737-76Q	30277/947	
☐	D-ABBS	B737-76N/W	28654/986	
☐	D-ABBT	B737-76N/W	32582/1013	
☐	D-ABBV	B737-7Q8	30629/1011	
☐	D-ABBW	B737-7Q8	30642/1097	
☐	D-ABLA	B737-76J/W	36114/2421	
☐	D-ABLB	B737-76J/W	36115/2692	
☐	D-ABLC	B737-76J/W	36116/2730	
☐	D-ABLD	B737-76J/W	36117/2776	
☐	D-ABLE	B737-76J/W	36873/3496	♦
☐	D-ABLF	B737-76J/W	36874/3488	o/o♦
☐	D-	B737-76J/W		o/o♦
☐	D-	B737-76J/W		o/o♦
☐	D-	B737-76J/W		o/o♦
☐	D-	B737-76J/W		o/o♦
☐	D-	B737-76J/W		o/o♦
☐	D-AGEC	B737-76J/W	36118/2832	
☐	D-AGEL	B737-75B	28110/5	<GMI
☐	D-AGEN	B737-75B	28100/16	<GMI
☐	D-AGEP	B737-75B	28102/18	<GMI
☐	D-AGER	B737-75B	28107/27	<GMI
☐	D-AGES	B737-75B	28108/28	<GMI
☐	D-AGEU	B737-75B	28104/39	<GMI
☐	D-AHIA	B737-73S	29082/229	<HLX
☐	D-AHXA	B737-7K5/W	30714/2202	<TUI
☐	D-AHXB	B737-7K5/W	30717/2228	♦
☐	D-AHXC	B737-7K5/W	34693/2260	♦
☐	D-AHXD	B737-7K5/W	30726/2298	<TUI
☐	D-AHXE	B737-7K5/W	35135/2451	<TUI
☐	D-AHXF	B737-7K5/W	35136/2465	<TUI
☐	D-AHXH	B737-7K5/W	35282/2585	<TUI
☐	D-AHXG	B737-7K5/W	35140/2575	♦
☐	D-AHXJ	B737-7K5/W	35277/2609	♦
☐	D-ABAF	B737-86J/W	30878/844	
☐	D-ABAG	B737-86J/W	30879/871	
☐	D-ABAP	B737-86J/W	28070/106	
☐	D-ABAQ	B737-86J/W	28071/133	
☐	D-ABAR	B737-86J/W	28072/147	
☐	D-ABAS	B737-86J/W	28073/200	
☐	D-ABAV	B737-86J/W	30498/450	
☐	D-ABBA	B737-86J/W	30570/879	
☐	D-ABBB	B737-86J/W	32624/961	
☐	D-ABBC	B737-86J/W	32625/995	
☐	D-ABBD	B737-86J/W	30880/1043	
☐	D-ABBE	B737-86J/W	30881/1067	
☐	D-ABBF	B737-86J/W	32917/1210	
☐	D-ABBG	B737-86J/W	32918/1255	
☐	D-ABBH	B737-86J/W	32919/1279	
☐	D-ABBI	B737-86J/W	32920/1293	
☐	D-ABBJ	B737-86Q/W	30286/1280	
☐	D-ABBK	B737-8BK/W	33013/1317	
☐	D-ABBU	B737-8Q8	30627/752	
☐	D-ABBX	B737-808	34969/2293	
☐	D-ABBY	B737-808	34970/2379	
☐	D-ABBZ	B737-85F	30478/997	
☐	D-ABKA	B737-82R	29329/224	
☐	D-ABKD	B737-86J/W	37742/2796	
☐	D-ABKE	B737-86J/W	37743/2834	
☐	D-ABKF	B737-86J/W	37745/3044	
☐	D-ABKG	B737-86J/W	37746/3109	
☐	D-ABKH	B737-86J/W	37747/3120	
☐	D-ABKI	B737-86J/W	37748/3157	
☐	D-ABKJ	B737-86J/W	37749/3176	♦
☐	D-ABKK	B737-86J/W	37753/3261	♦
☐	D-ABKL	B737-86J/W	37754/3306	♦
☐	D-ABKM	B737-86J/W	37755/3349	♦
☐	D-ABKN	B737-86J/W	37756/3371	♦
☐	D-ABKO	B737-86J/W	37757/3377	♦
☐	D-ABKP	B737-86J/W	37758/3439	♦
☐	D-ABKQ	B737-86J/W	37760/3545	o/o♦
☐	D-	B737-86J/W		o/o♦
☐	D-	B737-86J/W		o/o♦
☐	D-	B737-86J/W		o/o♦
☐	D-	B737-86J/W		o/o♦
☐	D-	B737-86J/W		o/o♦
☐	D-	B737-86J/W		o/o♦
☐	D-	B737-86J/W		o/o♦
☐	D-ABQA	DHC-8-402Q	4223	
☐	D-ABQB	DHC-8-402Q	4226	
☐	D-ABQC	DHC-8-402Q	4231	
☐	D-ABQD	DHC-8-402Q	4234	
☐	D-ABQE	DHC-8-402Q	4239	
☐	D-ABQF	DHC-8-402Q	4245	
☐	D-ABQG	DHC-8-402Q	4250	
☐	D-ABQH	DHC-8-402Q	4256	
☐	D-ABQI	DHC-8-402Q	4264	
☐	D-ABQJ	DHC-8-402Q	4274	

ARCUS AIR — ZE / AZE

	Reg	Type	c/n	Notes
☐	D-CAAM	Do228-212	8205	
☐	D-CAAR	Do228-212	8211	
☐	D-CAAZ	Do228-212	8212	
☐	D-CUTT	Do228-212	8200	

AUGSBURG AIRWAYS — IQ / AUB

	Reg	Type	c/n	Notes
☐	D-ADHA	DHC-8-402Q	4028	
☐	D-ADHB	DHC-8-402Q	4029	
☐	D-ADHC	DHC-8-402Q	4045	
☐	D-ADHD	DHC-8-402Q	4056	
☐	D-ADHE	DHC-8-402Q	4066	
☐	D-ADHP	DHC-8-402Q	4003	
☐	D-ADHQ	DHC-8-402Q	4016	
☐	D-ADHR	DHC-8-402Q	4041	
☐	D-ADHS	DHC-8-402Q	4044	
☐	D-ADHT	DHC-8-402Q	4281	
☐	D-AEMA	ERJ-190LR	19000290	
☐	D-AEMB	ERJ-190LR	19000297	
☐	D-AEMC	ERJ-190LR	19000300	
☐	D-AEMD	ERJ-190LR	19000305	
☐	D-AEME	ERJ-190LR	19000308	
☐	D-AEMF	ERJ-190LR	19000310	
☐	D-AEMG	ERJ-190LR	19000404	♦

AVANTI AIR — EEX

	Reg	Type	c/n	Notes
☐	D-ANFC	ATR 72-202	237	
☐	D-BCRN	ATR 42-300	329	
☐	D-BCRP	ATR 42-300(QC)	158	

BINAIR — BID

	Reg	Type	c/n
☐	D-CBIN	SA.226AT Expediter	IVAT-440B
☐	D-CCCC	SA.227AT Merlin IVC	AT-511
☐	D-CKPP	SA.227DC Metro 23	DC-805B
☐	D-CPSW	SA.227AC Metro III	AC-757B
☐	D-IBIN	SA.226TC Metro II	TC-252
☐	D-ICRK	SA.226TC Metro II	TC-333

BREMENFLY

	Reg	Type	c/n	Notes
☐	D-ABRF	B737-4Q8	26281/2380	[SXF]♦

BUSINESSWINGS

	Reg	Type	c/n
☐	D-CULT	Do228-212	8192
☐	D-IROL	Do228-100	7003
☐	D-IVER	DHC-6 Twin Otter 300	411

CIRRUS AIRLINES — C9 / RUS

	Reg	Type	Serial	
☐	D-BGAE	Do 328 Jet	3146	
☐	D-BGAL	Do 328 Jet	3131	
☐	D-BGAQ	Do 328 Jet	3130	
☐	D-CCIR	Do328-130	3100	
☐	D-CIRA	Do328-120	3077	
☐	D-CIRB	Do328-110	3017	
☐	D-CIRC	Do328-100	3041	
☐	D-CIRD	Do328-110	3011	
☐	D-CIRG	Do328-110	3040	o/o
☐	D-CIRI	Do328-110	3005	
☐	D-CIRJ	Do328-110	3035	o/o
☐	D-CIRK	Do328-110	3050	
☐	D-CIRL	Do328-110	3075	
☐	D-CIRM	Do328-110	3068	o/o
☐	D-CIRO	Do328-110	3025	o/o
☐	D-CIRP	Do328-110	3006	
☐	D-CIRT	Do328-110	3093	
☐	D-CIRU	Do328-110	3033	o/o
☐	D-CIRW	Do328-110	3044	o/o
☐	D-COSA	Do328-110	3085	
☐	D-CPRP	Do328-110	3066	
☐	D-CPRW	Do328-110	3097	
☐	D-ALIA	ERJ-170LR	17000006	
☐	D-ALIE	ERJ-170LR	17000059	

CONDOR — DE / CFG

	Reg	Type	Serial	
☐	D-ABOA	B757-330/W	29016/804	
☐	D-ABOB	B757-330/W	29017/810	
☐	D-ABOC	B757-330/W	29015/818	
☐	D-ABOE	B757-330/W	29012/839	
☐	D-ABOF	B757-330/W	29013/846	
☐	D-ABOG	B757-330/W	29014/849	
☐	D-ABOH	B757-330/W	30030/855	
☐	D-ABOI	B757-330/W	29018/909	
☐	D-ABOJ	B757-330/W	29019/915	
☐	D-ABOK	B757-330/W	29020/918	♦
☐	D-ABOL	B757-330/W	29021/923	♦
☐	D-ABOM	B757-330/W	29022/926	
☐	D-ABON	B757-330/W	29023/929	
☐	D-ABUA	B767-330ER/W	26991/455	
☐	D-ABUB	B767-330ER/W	26987/466	
☐	D-ABUC	B767-330ER/W	26992/470	
☐	D-ABUD	B767-330ER/W	26983/471	
☐	D-ABUE	B767-330ER/W	26984/518	
☐	D-ABUF	B767-330ER/W	26985/537	
☐	D-ABUH	B767-330ER/W	26986/553	
☐	D-ABUI	B767-330ER/W	26988/562	
☐	D-ABUZ	B767-330ER/W	25209/382	

CONDOR BERLIN — CIB

	Reg	Type	Serial
☐	D-AICA	A320-212	0774
☐	D-AICC	A320-212	0809
☐	D-AICD	A320-212	0884
☐	D-AICE	A320-212	0894
☐	D-AICF	A320-212	0905
☐	D-AICG	A320-212	0957
☐	D-AICH	A320-212	0971
☐	D-AICI	A320-212	1381
☐	D-AICJ	A320-212	1402
☐	D-AICK	A320-212	1416
☐	D-AICL	A320-212	1437
☐	D-AICN	A320-214	1968

CONTACT AIR — KIS

	Reg	Type	Serial	
☐	D-BMMM	ATR 42-500	546	<EWG
☐	D-BPPP	ATR 42-500	581	<EWG
☐	D-BQQQ	ATR 42-500	584	[SCN]♦
☐	D-BSSS	ATR 42-500	602	<EWG
☐	D-BTTT	ATR 42-500	603	<EWG

	Reg	Type	Serial	
☐	D-AFKA	Fokker 100	11517	
☐	D-AFKB	Fokker 100	11527	
☐	D-AFKC	Fokker 100	11496	
☐	D-AFKD	Fokker 100	11500	
☐	D-AFKE	Fokker 100	11505	
☐	D-AFKF	Fokker 100	11470	
☐	D-AGPH	Fokker 100	11308	
☐	D-AGPK	Fokker 100	11313	>SWR

EAT LEIPZIG — BCS

	Reg	Type	Serial	
☐	D-ALEA	B757-236(SF)	22172/9	♦
☐	D-ALEB	B757-236(SF)	22173/10	♦
☐	D-ALEC	B757-236(SF)	22175/13	♦
☐	D-ALED	B757-236(SF)	22179/24	♦
☐	D-ALEE	B757-236(SF)	22183/32	♦
☐	D-ALEF	B757-236(SF)	22189/58	♦
☐	D-ALEG	B757-236(SF)	23398/77	♦
☐	D-ALEH	B757-236(SF)	23492/89	♦
☐	D-ALEI	B757-236(SF)	23493/90	♦
☐	D-AELJ	B757-23APF	24971/340	♦
☐	D-ALEK	B757-236(SF)	23533/93	♦

EUROWINGS — EW / EWG

	Reg	Type	Serial	
☐	D-BMMM	ATR 42-500	546	>KIS
☐	D-BPPP	ATR 42-500	581	>KIS
☐	D-BQQQ	ATR 42-500	584	[SCN]♦
☐	D-BSSS	ATR 42-500	602	>KIS
☐	D-BTTT	ATR 42-500	603	>KIS
☐	D-ACRA	CRJ-200LR	7567	
☐	D-ACRB	CRJ-200LR	7570	
☐	D-ACRC	CRJ-200LR	7573	
☐	D-ACRD	CRJ-200LR	7583	
☐	D-ACRE	CRJ-200LR	7607	
☐	D-ACRF	CRJ-200LR	7619	
☐	D-ACRG	CRJ-200LR	7630	
☐	D-ACRH	CRJ-200LR	7738	
☐	D-ACRI	CRJ-200ER	7862	
☐	D-ACRJ	CRJ-200LR	7864	
☐	D-ACRK	CRJ-200LR	7901	
☐	D-ACRL	CRJ-200LR	7902	
☐	D-ACRM	CRJ-200LR	7478	
☐	D-ACRN	CRJ-200LR	7486	
☐	D-ACRO	CRJ-200LR	7494	
☐	D-ACRP	CRJ-200LR	7625	
☐	D-ACRQ	CRJ-200LR	7629	
☐	D-ACNA	CRJ-900NG	15229	
☐	D-ACNB	CRJ-900NG	15230	
☐	D-ACNC	CRJ-900NG	15236	
☐	D-ACND	CRJ-900NG	15238	
☐	D-ACNE	CRJ-900NG	15241	
☐	D-ACNF	CRJ-900NG	15243	
☐	D-ACNG	CRJ-900NG	15245	
☐	D-ACNH	CRJ-900NG	15247	
☐	D-ACNI	CRJ-900NG	15248	
☐	D-ACNJ	CRJ-900NG	15249	
☐	D-ACNK	CRJ-900NG	15251	
☐	D-ACNL	CRJ-900NG	15252	
☐	D-ACNM	CRJ-900NG	15253	
☐	D-ACNN	CRJ-900NG	15254	♦
☐	D-ACNO	CRJ-900NG	15255	♦
☐	D-ACNP	CRJ-900NG	15259	♦
☐	D-ACNQ	CRJ-900NG	15260	♦

FLM AVIATION — FKI

	Reg	Type	Serial
☐	D-CNAG	SA.227DC Metro 23	DC-893B
☐	D-CSAL	SA.227AC Metro III	AC-601

GERMANIA — ST / GMI

	Reg	Type		
☐	D-	A319-1		o/o♦
☐	D-	A319-1		o/o♦

☐ D-	A319-1		o/o♦
☐ D-	A319-1		o/o♦
☐ D-	A319-1		o/o♦
☐ D-ADII	B737-329	23775/1412	
☐ D-AGEE	B737-35B	24238/1626	
☐ D-AGEG	B737-35B	24237/1624	
☐ D-AGEJ	B737-3L9	24221/1604	
☐ D-AGEK	B737-3M8	25015/1991	
☐ D-AGEL	B737-75B	28110/5	>BER
☐ D-AGEN	B737-75B	28100/16	>BER
☐ D-AGEP	B737-75B	28102/18	>BER
☐ D-AGEQ	B737-75B	28103/23	
☐ D-AGER	B737-75B	28107/27	>BER
☐ D-AGES	B737-75B	28108/28	>BER
☐ D-AGET	B737-75B	28109/31	
☐ D-AGEU	B737-75B	28104/39	>BER
☐ D-AGPC	Fokker 100	11280	[WOE]
☐ D-AGPD	Fokker 100	11281	[WOE]

GERMANWINGS 4U / GWI

☐ D-AGWA	A319-132	2813	
☐ D-AGWB	A319-132	2833	
☐ D-AGWC	A319-132	2976	
☐ D-AGWD	A319-132	3011	
☐ D-AGWE	A319-132	3128	
☐ D-AGWF	A319-132	3172	
☐ D-AGWG	A319-132	3193	
☐ D-AGWH	A319-132	3352	
☐ D-AGWI	A319-132	3358	
☐ D-AGWJ	A319-132	3375	
☐ D-AGWK	A319-132	3500	
☐ D-AGWL	A319-132	3534	
☐ D-AGWM	A319-132	3839	
☐ D-AGWN	A319-132	3841	
☐ D-AGWO	A319-132	4166	
☐ D-AGWP	A319-132	4227	♦
☐ D-AGWQ	A319-132	4256	♦
☐ D-AGWR	A319-132	4285	♦
☐ D-AKNK	A319-112	1077	
☐ D-AKNL	A319-112	1084	
☐ D-AKNM	A319-112	1089	
☐ D-AKNN	A319-112	1136	
☐ D-AKNO	A319-112	1147	
☐ D-AKNP	A319-112	1155	
☐ D-AKNQ	A319-112	1170	
☐ D-AKNR	A319-112	1209	
☐ D-AKNS	A319-112	1277	
☐ D-AKNT	A319-112	2607	
☐ D-AKNU	A319-112	2628	
☐ D-AKNV	A319-112	2632	

GERMAN SKY AIRLINES GHY

☐ D-AGSA	B737-883	28323/625	♦

LGW HE / LGW

☐ D-IKBA	Do228-200	8066
☐ D-ILWB	Do228-200	8035
☐ D-ILWD	Do228-200	8069
☐ D-ILWS	Do228-200	8002
☐ D-IMIK	Do228-200	8058

LUFTHANSA LH / DLH

☐ D-AIBA	A319-114	4141	
☐ D-AIBB	A319-112	4182	
☐ D-AIBC	A319-112	4332	♦
☐ D-AIBD	A319-112	4455	♦
☐ D-AIBE	A319-112	4511	♦
☐ D-	A319-112		o/o♦
☐ D-	A319-112		o/o♦

☐ D-AILA	A319-114	0609	
☐ D-AILB	A319-114	0610	
☐ D-AILC	A319-114	0616	
☐ D-AILD	A319-114	0623	
☐ D-AILE	A319-114	0627	
☐ D-AILF	A319-114	0636	
☐ D-AILH	A319-114	0641	
☐ D-AILK	A319-114	0679	
☐ D-AILL	A319-114	0689	
☐ D-AILM	A319-114	0694	
☐ D-AILN	A319-114	0700	
☐ D-AILP	A319-114	0717	
☐ D-AILR	A319-114	0723	
☐ D-AILS	A319-114	0729	
☐ D-AILT	A319-114	0738	
☐ D-AILU	A319-114	0744	
☐ D-AILW	A319-114	0853	
☐ D-AILX	A319-114	0860	
☐ D-AILY	A319-114	0875	
☐ D-AIPA	A320-211	0069	
☐ D-AIPB	A320-211	0070	
☐ D-AIPC	A320-211	0071	
☐ D-AIPD	A320-211	0072	
☐ D-AIPE	A320-211	0078	
☐ D-AIPF	A320-211	0083	
☐ D-AIPH	A320-211	0086	
☐ D-AIPK	A320-211	0093	
☐ D-AIPL	A320-211	0094	
☐ D-AIPM	A320-211	0104	
☐ D-AIPP	A320-211	0110	
☐ D-AIPR	A320-211	0111	
☐ D-AIPS	A320-211	0116	
☐ D-AIPT	A320-211	0117	
☐ D-AIPU	A320-211	0135	
☐ D-AIPW	A320-211	0137	
☐ D-AIPX	A320-211	0147	
☐ D-AIPY	A320-211	0161	
☐ D-AIPZ	A320-211	0162	
☐ D-AIQA	A320-211	0172	
☐ D-AIQB	A320-211	0200	
☐ D-AIQC	A320-211	0201	
☐ D-AIQD	A320-211	0202	
☐ D-AIQE	A320-211	0209	
☐ D-AIQF	A320-211	0216	
☐ D-AIQH	A320-211	0217	
☐ D-AIQK	A320-211	0218	
☐ D-AIQL	A320-211	0267	
☐ D-AIQM	A320-211	0268	
☐ D-AIQN	A320-211	0269	
☐ D-AIQP	A320-211	0346	
☐ D-AIQR	A320-211	0382	
☐ D-AIQS	A320-211	0401	
☐ D-AIQT	A320-211	1337	
☐ D-AIQU	A320-211	1365	
☐ D-AIQW	A320-211	1367	
☐ D-AIZA	A320-214	4097	
☐ D-AIZB	A320-214	4120	
☐ D-AIZC	A320-214	4153	
☐ D-AIZD	A320-214	4191	♦
☐ D-AIZE	A320-214	4261	♦
☐ D-AIZF	A320-214	4289	♦
☐ D-AIZG	A320-214	4324	♦
☐ D-AIZH	A320-214	4363	♦
☐ D-AIZI	A320-214	4398	♦
☐ D-AIZJ	A320-214	4449	♦
☐ D-AIZK	A320-214		o/o♦
☐ D-AIDA	A321-231	4360	♦
☐ D-AIDB	A321-231	4545	♦
☐ D-AIDC	A321-231	4560	♦
☐ D-AIDD	A321-231	4585	o/o♦
☐ D-AIDE	A321-231	4607	o/o♦
☐ D-AIDF	A321-231	4626	o/o♦
☐ D-AIDG	A321-231	4672	o/o♦
☐ D-AIDH	A321-231	4710	o/o♦

Reg	Type	c/n	Notes
☐ D-	A321-231		o/o♦
☐ D-	A321-231		o/o♦
☐ D-	A321-231		o/o♦
☐ D-	A321-231		o/o♦
☐ D-	A321-231		o/o♦
☐ D-AIRA	A321-131	0458	
☐ D-AIRB	A321-131	0468	
☐ D-AIRC	A321-131	0473	
☐ D-AIRD	A321-131	0474	
☐ D-AIRE	A321-131	0484	
☐ D-AIRF	A321-131	0493	
☐ D-AIRH	A321-131	0412	
☐ D-AIRK	A321-131	0502	
☐ D-AIRL	A321-131	0505	
☐ D-AIRM	A321-131	0518	
☐ D-AIRN	A321-131	0560	
☐ D-AIRO	A321-131	0563	
☐ D-AIRP	A321-131	0564	
☐ D-AIRR	A321-131	0567	
☐ D-AIRS	A321-131	0595	
☐ D-AIRT	A321-131	0652	
☐ D-AIRU	A321-131	0692	
☐ D-AIRW	A321-131	0699	
☐ D-AIRX	A321-131	0887	
☐ D-AIRY	A321-131	0901	
☐ D-AISB	A321-231	1080	
☐ D-AISC	A321-231	1161	
☐ D-AISD	A321-231	1188	
☐ D-AISE	A321-231	1214	
☐ D-AISF	A321-231	1260	
☐ D-AISG	A321-231	1273	
☐ D-AISH	A321-231	3265	
☐ D-AISI	A321-231	3339	
☐ D-AISJ	A321-231	3360	
☐ D-AISK	A321-231	3387	
☐ D-AISL	A321-231	3434	
☐ D-AISN	A321-231	3592	
☐ D-AISO	A321-231	3625	
☐ D-AISP	A321-231	3864	
☐ D-AISQ	A321-231	3936	
☐ D-AISR	A321-231	3987	
☐ D-AIST	A321-231	4005	
☐ D-AISU	A321-231	4016	
☐ D-AISV	A321-231	4047	
☐ D-AISW	A321-231	4054	
☐ D-AISX	A321-231	4073	
☐ D-AISZ	A321-231	4085	
☐ D-AIKA	A330-343X	570	
☐ D-AIKB	A330-343X	576	
☐ D-AIKC	A330-343X	579	
☐ D-AIKD	A330-343X	629	
☐ D-AIKE	A330-343X	636	
☐ D-AIKF	A330-343X	642	
☐ D-AIKG	A330-343X	645	
☐ D-AIKH	A330-343X	648	
☐ D-AIKI	A330-343X	687	
☐ D-AIKJ	A330-343X	701	
☐ D-AIKK	A330-343X	896	
☐ D-AIKL	A330-343X	905	
☐ D-AIKM	A330-343X	913	
☐ D-AIKN	A330-343X	922	
☐ D-AIKO	A330-343X	989	
☐ D-AIFA	A340-313X	352	
☐ D-AIFB	A340-313X	355	
☐ D-AIFC	A340-313X	379	
☐ D-AIFD	A340-313X	390	
☐ D-AIFE	A340-313X	434	
☐ D-AIFF	A340-313X	447	
☐ D-AIGA	A340-311	020	
☐ D-AIGB	A340-311	024	
☐ D-AIGC	A340-311	027	
☐ D-AIGD	A340-311	028	
☐ D-AIGF	A340-311	035	
☐ D-AIGH	A340-311	052	
☐ D-AIGI	A340-311	053	
☐ D-AIGK	A340-311	056	
☐ D-AIGL	A340-313X	135	
☐ D-AIGM	A340-313X	158	
☐ D-AIGN	A340-313X	213	
☐ D-AIGO	A340-313X	233	
☐ D-AIGP	A340-313X	252	
☐ D-AIGS	A340-313X	297	
☐ D-AIGT	A340-313X	304	
☐ D-AIGU	A340-313X	321	
☐ D-AIGV	A340-313X	325	
☐ D-AIGW	A340-313X	327	
☐ D-AIGX	A340-313X	354	
☐ D-AIGY	A340-313X	335	
☐ D-AIGZ	A340-313X	347	
☐ D-AIHA	A340-642	482	M/s.
☐ D-AIHB	A340-642	517	
☐ D-AIHC	A340-642	523	
☐ D-AIHD	A340-642	537	
☐ D-AIHE	A340-642	540	
☐ D-AIHF	A340-642	543	25/3
☐ D-AIHH	A340-642	566	
☐ D-AIHI	A340-642	569	
☐ D-AIHK	A340-642	580	
☐ D-AIHL	A340-642	583	
☐ D-AIHM	A340-642	762	
☐ D-AIHN	A340-642	763	
☐ D-AIHO	A340-642	767	
☐ D-AIHP	A340-642	771	
☐ D-AIHQ	A340-642	790	
☐ D-AIHR	A340-642	794	
☐ D-AIHS	A340-642	812	
☐ D-AIHT	A340-642	846	
☐ D-AIHU	A340-642	848	
☐ D-AIHV	A340-642	897	
☐ D-AIHW	A340-642	972	
☐ D-AIHX	A340-642	981	
☐ D-AIHY	A340-642	987	
☐ D-AIHZ	A340-642	1005	
☐ D-AIMA	A380-841	038	♦
☐ D-AIMB	A380-841	041	♦
☐ D-AIMC	A380-841	044	♦
☐ D-AIMD	A380-841	048	♦
☐ D-AIME	A380-841	061	o/o♦
☐ D-AIMF	A380-841	066	o/o♦
☐ D-AIMG	A380-841	069	o/o♦
☐ D-AIMH	A380-841	070	o/o♦
☐ D-	A380-841		o/o♦
☐ D-	A380-841		o/o♦
☐ D-ABEA	B737-330	24565/1818	
☐ D-ABEB	B737-330	25148/2077	
☐ D-ABEC	B737-330	25149/2081	
☐ D-ABED	B737-330	25215/2082	
☐ D-ABEE	B737-330	25216/2084	
☐ D-ABEF	B737-330	25217/2094	
☐ D-ABEH	B737-330	25242/2102	
☐ D-ABEI	B737-330	25359/2158	
☐ D-ABEK	B737-330	25414/2164	
☐ D-ABEL	B737-330	25415/2175	
☐ D-ABEM	B737-330	25416/2182	
☐ D-ABEN	B737-330	26428/2196	
☐ D-ABEO	B737-330	26429/2207	
☐ D-ABEP	B737-330	26430/2216	
☐ D-ABER	B737-330	26431/2242	
☐ D-ABES	B737-330	26432/2247	
☐ D-ABET	B737-330	27903/2682	
☐ D-ABEU	B737-330	27904/2691	
☐ D-ABEW	B737-330	27905/2705	
☐ D-ABIA	B737-530	24815/1933	
☐ D-ABIB	B737-530	24816/1958	
☐ D-ABIC	B737-530	24817/1967	
☐ D-ABID	B737-530	24818/1974	
☐ D-ABIE	B737-530	24819/1979	
☐ D-ABIF	B737-530	24820/1985	

☐ D-ABIH	B737-530	24821/1993
☐ D-ABII	B737-530	24822/1997
☐ D-ABIK	B737-530	24823/2000
☐ D-ABIL	B737-530	24824/2006
☐ D-ABIM	B737-530	24937/2011
☐ D-ABIN	B737-530	24938/2023
☐ D-ABIO	B737-530	24939/2031
☐ D-ABIP	B737-530	24940/2034
☐ D-ABIR	B737-530	24941/2042
☐ D-ABIS	B737-530	24942/2048
☐ D-ABIT	B737-530	24943/2049
☐ D-ABIU	B737-530	24944/2051
☐ D-ABIW	B737-530	24945/2063
☐ D-ABIX	B737-530	24946/2070
☐ D-ABIY	B737-530	25243/2086
☐ D-ABIZ	B737-530	25244/2098
☐ D-ABJA	B737-530	25270/2116
☐ D-ABJB	B737-530	25271/2117
☐ D-ABJC	B737-530	25272/2118
☐ D-ABJD	B737-530	25309/2122
☐ D-ABJE	B737-530	25310/2126
☐ D-ABJF	B737-530	25311/2128
☐ D-ABJH	B737-530	25357/2141
☐ D-ABJI	B737-530	25358/2151
☐ D-ABWH	B737-330(QC)	24284/1685
☐ D-ABXL	B737-330	23531/1307
☐ D-ABXM	B737-330	23871/1433
☐ D-ABXN	B737-330	23872/1447
☐ D-ABXO	B737-330	23873/1489
☐ D-ABXP	B737-330	23874/1495
☐ D-ABXR	B737-330	23875/1500
☐ D-ABXS	B737-330	24280/1656
☐ D-ABXT	B737-330	24281/1664
☐ D-ABXU	B737-330	24282/1671
☐ D-ABXW	B737-330	24561/1785
☐ D-ABXX	B737-330	24562/1787
☐ D-ABXY	B737-330	24563/1801
☐ D-ABXZ	B737-330	24564/1807
☐ D-ABTA	B747-430M	24285/747 [HAM]
☐ D-ABTB	B747-430M	24286/749
☐ D-ABTC	B747-430M	24287/754
☐ D-ABTD	B747-430M	24715/785
☐ D-ABTE	B747-430M	24966/846
■ D-ABTF	B747-430M	24967/848 >5/3
☐ D-ABTH	B747-430M	25047/856
☐ D-ABTK	B747-430	29871/1293
☐ D-ABTL	B747-430	29872/1299
☐ D-ABVA	B747-430	23816/723
☐ D-ABVB	B747-430	23817/700
■ D-ABVC	B747-430	24288/757 >5/3
☐ D-ABVD	B747-430	24740/786
☐ D-ABVE	B747-430	24741/787
☐ D-ABVF	B747-430	24761/796
☐ D-ABVH	B747-430	25045/845
☐ D-ABVK	B747-430	25046/847
☐ D-ABVL	B747-430	26425/898
☐ D-ABVM	B747-430	29101/1143
☐ D-ABVN	B747-430	26427/915
☐ D-ABVO	B747-430	28086/1080
☐ D-ABVP	B747-430	28284/1103
☐ D-ABVR	B747-430	28285/1106
☐ D-ABVS	B747-430	28286/1109
☐ D-ABVT	B747-430	28287/1110
☐ D-ABVU	B747-430	29492/1191
■ D-ABVW	B747-430	29493/1205 14/7
☐ D-ABVX	B747-430	29868/1237
☐ D-ABVY	B747-430	29869/1261
■ D-ABVZ	B747-430	29870/1264 >7/5

LUFTHANSA CARGO　　　　LH / GEC

☐ D-ALCA	MD-11F	48781/625
☐ D-ALCB	MD-11F	48782/626
☐ D-ALCC	MD-11F	48783/627
☐ D-ALCD	MD-11F	48784/628

☐ D-ALCE	MD-11F	48785/629
☐ D-ALCF	MD-11F	48798/637
☐ D-ALCG	MD-11F	48799/639
☐ D-ALCH	MD-11F	48801/640
☐ D-ALCI	MD-11F	48800/641
☐ D-ALCJ	MD-11F	48802/642
☐ D-ALCK	MD-11F	48803/643
☐ D-ALCL	MD-11F	48804/644
☐ D-ALCM	MD-11F	48805/645
☐ D-ALCN	MD-11F	48806/646
☐ D-ALCO	MD-11F	48413/488
■ D-ALCP	MD-11F	48414/491 >3/3 ♦
☐ D-ALCR	MD-11F	48581/565 ♦
☐ D-ALCS	MD-11F	48630/567 ♦

LUFTHANSA CITYLINE　　　　CL / CLH

☐ D-AVRA	Avro 146-RJ85	E2256
☐ D-AVRB	Avro 146-RJ85	E2253
☐ D-AVRG	Avro 146-RJ85	E2266
☐ D-AVRH	Avro 146-RJ85	E2268
☐ D-AVRI	Avro 146-RJ85	E2270
☐ D-AVRJ	Avro 146-RJ85	E2277
☐ D-AVRK	Avro 146-RJ85	E2278
☐ D-AVRM	Avro 146-RJ85	E2288
☐ D-AVRN	Avro 146-RJ85	E2293
☐ D-AVRO	Avro 146-RJ85	E2246
☐ D-AVRP	Avro 146-RJ85	E2303
☐ D-AVRQ	Avro 146-RJ85	E2304
☐ D-AVRR	Avro 146-RJ85	E2317
☐ D-ACHA	CRJ-200LR	7378
☐ D-ACHD	CRJ-200LR	7403
☐ D-ACHE	CRJ-200LR	7407 [CGN]♦
☐ D-ACHF	CRJ-200LR	7431
☐ D-ACHI	CRJ-200LR	7464 [CGN]♦
☐ D-ACHK	CRJ-200LR	7499
☐ D-ACJB	CRJ-200LR	7128
☐ D-ACJC	CRJ-200LR	7130
☐ D-ACJF	CRJ-200LR	7200
☐ D-ACLY	CRJ-200LR	7119
☐ D-ACLZ	CRJ-200LR	7121
☐ D-ACPA	CRJ-701ER	10012
☐ D-ACPB	CRJ-701ER	10013
☐ D-ACPC	CRJ-701ER	10014
☐ D-ACPD	CRJ-701ER	10015
☐ D-ACPE	CRJ-701ER	10027
☐ D-ACPF	CRJ-701ER	10030
☐ D-ACPG	CRJ-701ER	10034
☐ D-ACPH	CRJ-701ER	10043
☐ D-ACPI	CRJ-701ER	10046
☐ D-ACPJ	CRJ-701ER	10040
☐ D-ACPK	CRJ-701ER	10063
☐ D-ACPL	CRJ-701ER	10076
☐ D-ACPM	CRJ-701ER	10080
☐ D-ACPN	CRJ-701ER	10083
☐ D-ACPO	CRJ-701ER	10085
☐ D-ACPP	CRJ-701ER	10086
☐ D-ACPQ	CRJ-701ER	10091
☐ D-ACPR	CRJ-701ER	10098
☐ D-ACPS	CRJ-701ER	10100
☐ D-ACPT	CRJ-701ER	10103
☐ D-ACKA	CRJ-900LR	15072
☐ D-ACKB	CRJ-900LR	15073
☐ D-ACKC	CRJ-900LR	15078
☐ D-ACKD	CRJ-900LR	15080
☐ D-ACKE	CRJ-900LR	15081
☐ D-ACKF	CRJ-900LR	15083
☐ D-ACKG	CRJ-900LR	15084
☐ D-ACKH	CRJ-900LR	15085
☐ D-ACKI	CRJ-900LR	15088
☐ D-ACKJ	CRJ-900LR	15089
☐ D-ACKK	CRJ-900LR	15094
☐ D-ACKL	CRJ-900LR	15095

D-	CRJ-900LR		o/o♦
D-	CRJ-900LR		o/o♦
D-	CRJ-900LR		o/o♦
D-	CRJ-900LR		o/o♦
D-AEBA	ERJ-195LR	19000314	
D-AEBB	ERJ-195LR	19000316	
D-AEBC	ERJ-195LR	19000320	
D-AEBD	ERJ-195LR	19000324	
D-AEBE	ERJ-195LR	19000350	♦
D-	ERJ-195LR		o/o♦
D-	ERJ-195LR		o/o♦
D-	ERJ-195LR		o/o♦
D-AECA	ERJ-190LR	19000327	
D-AECB	ERJ-190LR	19000332	
D-AECC	ERJ-190LR	19000333	
D-AECD	ERJ-190LR	19000337	♦
D-AECE	ERJ-190LR	19000341	♦
D-AECF	ERJ-190LR	19000359	♦
D-AECG	ERJ-190LR	19000368	♦
D-AECH	ERJ-190LR	19000376	♦
D-AECI	ERJ-190LR	19000381	♦

NIGHTEXPRESS — EXT

D-CCAS	Short SD.3-60	SH3737
D-CRAS	Short SD.3-60	SH3744

OCA INTERNATIONAL

D-COPS	SAAB SF.340A	340A-087	<CCB

OLT — OL / OLT

D-AOLG	Fokker 100	11452
D-AOLH	Fokker 100	11265
D-AOLB	SAAB 2000	2000-005
D-AOLC	SAAB 2000	2000-016
D-AOLT	SAAB 2000	2000-037
D-CASB	SAAB SF.340B	340B-223
D-COLE	SAAB SF.340A	340A-144
D-COLB	SA.227AC Metro III	AC-754B
D-COLD	SA.227AC Metro III	AC-421B
D-COLT	SA.227AC Metro III	AC-690
D-CSWF	SA.227DC Metro III	DC-896B

PRIVATAIR — PTG

D-APBB	B737-8Q8/W	35278/2625
D-APBC	B737-8BK/W	33016/1588
D-APBD	B737-8BK/W	33021/1667

PRIVATE WINGS — 8W / PWF

D-BIRD	Do 328 Jet	3180	
D-BJET	Do 328 Jet	3207	
D-CATZ	Do328-110	3090	
D-COCA	Beech 1900D	UE-224	
D-CPWF	Do328-110	3112	
D-CREW	Do328-110	3113	>SUS

REGIO-AIR — RAG

D-IESS	SA.226TC Metro II	TC-338

TUIFLY — X3 / HLX

D-AGEQ	B737-75B	28103/23	<GMI
D-AGET	B737-75B	28109/31	<GMI
D-AHIA	B737-73S	29082/229	>BER
D-AHXA	B737-7K5/W	30714/2202	>BER
D-AHXD	B737-7K5/W	30726/2298	>BER
D-AHXE	B737-7K5/W	35135/2451	>BER
D-AHXF	B737-7K5/W	35136/2465	>BER

D-AHXH	B737-7K5/W	35282/2585	>BER
D-AHFA	B737-8K5/W	27981/7	
D-AHFB	B737-8K5/W	27982/8	
D-AHFH	B737-8K5/W	27983/218	
D-AHFI	B737-8K5/W	27984/220	
D-AHFK	B737-8K5/W	27991/248	
D-AHFL	B737-8K5/W	27985/470	
D-AHFM	B737-8K5/W	27986/474	
D-AHFO	B737-8K5/W	27987/499	
D-AHFP	B737-8K5/W	27988/508	
D-AHFR	B737-8K5/W	30593/528	
D-AHFS	B737-8K5/W	28623/556	
D-AHFT	B737-8K5/W	30413/636	
D-AHFU	B737-8K5/W	30414/703	
D-AHFV	B737-8K5/W	30415/719	
D-AHFW	B737-8K5/W	30882/760	
D-AHFX	B737-8K5/W	30416/778	
D-AHFY	B737-8K5/W	30417/781	
D-AHFZ	B737-8K5/W	30883/783	
D-AHLK	B737-8K5/W	35143/2763	
D-ATUA	B737-8K5/W	37245/3486	♦
D-ATUB	B737-8K5/W	35247/3497	♦
D-ATUC	B737-8K5/W	34684/1870	
D-ATUD	B737-8K5/W	34685/1901	
D-ATUE	B737-8K5/W	34686/1903	
D-ATUF	B737-8K5/W	34687/1907	
D-ATUG	B737-8K5/W	34688/1909	
D-ATUH	B737-8K5/W	34689/1935	
D-ATUI	B737-8K5/W	37252/3554	o/o♦
D-	B737-8K5/W		o/o♦
D-	B737-8K5/W		o/o♦
D-	B737-8K5/W		o/o♦

WDL AVIATION — WE / WDL

D-ALIN	BAe146 Srs.300	E3142	[CGN]
D-AMAJ	BAe146 Srs.200	E2028	
D-AMAX	BAe146 Srs.300	E3157	[CGN]
D-AMGL	BAe146 Srs.200	E2055	
D-AWBA	BAe146 Srs.300A	E3134	
D-AWUE	BAe146 Srs.200	E2050	
D-ADEP	F.27 Friendship 600	10318	
D-ADOP	F.27 Friendship 600	10316	[CGN]
D-AELG	F.27 Friendship 600	10338	[CGN]
D-AELH	F.27 Friendship 400	10340	
D-AELJ	F.27 Friendship 600	10342	[CGN]
D-AELK	F.27 Friendship 600	10361	
D-AELM	F.27 Friendship 600	10450	[CGN]
D-AISY	F.27 Friendship 600	10391	[CGN]
D-BAKB	F.27 Friendship 600	10261	
D-BAKC	F.27 Friendship 600	10195	[CGN]
D-BAKD	F.27 Friendship 600	10179	[CGN]

XL AIRWAYS GERMANY — GV / GXL

D-AXLD	B737-8FH/W	35093/2176
D-AXLE	B737-8Q8/W	30724/2286
D-AXLF	B737-8Q8/W	28218/160
D-AXLG	B737-8Q8	28226/77

DQ - FIJI

AIR PACIFIC — PC / FJI

DQ-FJC	B767-3X2ER	26260/552	
DQ-FJF	B737-7X2/W	28878/96	
DQ-FJG	B737-8X2/W	29968/275	
DQ-FJH	B737-8X2/W	29969/339	
DQ-FJK	B747-412	24064/755	<SIA
DQ-FJL	B747-412	24062/722	<SIA

D2 - ANGOLA

AEROJET — MBC

☐ D2-FER	Yak-40	9541844

AIR GEMINI — GLL

☐ D2-ERJ	DC-9-32	47765/900	
☐ D2-ERL	DC-9-32	47788/901	
☐ D2-ERN	B727-25C	19358/367	
☐ D2-ERS	DC-9-32	47110/167	
☐ D2-ERU	B727-2S7	22020/1592	
☐ S9-BAR	B727-22C	19098/318	[LAD]
☐ S9-BOE	B727-22C	19192/388	[LAD]

ALADA — RAD

☐ D2-FAX	An-32A	1510
☐ D2-FFR	Il-18D	393607150
☐ D2-FRB	An-32	2208

ANGOLA AIR CHARTER — AGO

☐ D2-FCO	Il-76MD	43454615
☐ D2-FCP	B727-77C	20370/821
☐ D2-MBV	An-12BP	5343208

DIEXIM EXPRESS

☐ D2-FFW	ERJ-145MP	145360

GIRA GLOBO — GGL

☐ D2-FCN	Il-76TD	53462872
☐ D2-FDG	An-32B	2201
☐ D2-FEM	Il-76TD	63469062
☐ D2-FEW	Il-76TD	73475239

HM AIRWAYS

☐ D2-EUO	DHC-8-402NG	4312	♦
☐ D2-EUP	DHC-8-402NG	4315	♦
☐ D2-	DHC-8-402NG	4322	o/o♦
☐ D2-	DHC-8-402NG	4325	o/o♦
☐ D2-EYL	DHC-8-315	613	
☐ D2-EYM	DHC-8-315	614	
☐ D2-EYU	DHC-8-315	645	

SERVISAIR

☐ D2-FGJ	MD-82	53220/2073	♦

SONAIR — SOR

☐ D2-ESN	F.27 Friendship 500	10610	
☐ D2-ESR	Fokker 50	20240	
☐ D2-ESU	B727-23F	19431/372	
☐ D2-ESW	Fokker 50	20241	
☐ D2-EVD	B727-29C	19403/435	
☐ D2-EVG	B727-29C	19402/415	
☐ D2-EVW	B737-7HB	35954/2310	
☐ D2-EVZ	B737-7HBC/W	35955/2531	
☐ D2-EWS	B737-7HBC/W	35956/2536	
☐ D2-FSA	B727-29C	19987/634	
☐ D2-	DHC-8-315	563	
☐ N262SG	B747-481	29262/1199	[KUL]
☐ N263SG	B747-481	29263/1204	[HKG]
☐ N322SG	B747-481	30322/1250	[HKG]

TAAG ANGOLA AIRLINES — DT / DTA

☐ D2-TBC	B737-2M2C	21173/447
☐ D2-TBF	B737-7M2/W	34559/2013
☐ D2-TBG	B737-7M2/W	34560/2036
☐ D2-TBH	B737-7M2/W	34561/2043
☐ D2-TBJ	B737-7M2/W	34562/2149
☐ D2-TBO	B737-2M2	22776/891 [BBU]
☐ D2-TBX	B737-2M2	23351/1117
☐ D2-TEA	B747-312M	23410/653
☐ D2-TEB	B747-357M	23751/686
☐ D2-TED	B777-2M2ER	34565/581
☐ D2-TEE	B777-2M2ER	34566/587
☐ D2-TEF	B777-2M2ER	34567/687
☐ D2-	B777-3M2ER	o/o♦
☐ D2-	B777-3M2ER	o/o♦

D4 - CAPE VERDE ISLANDS

HALCYON AIR

☐ D4-CBQ	ATR 42-320	296	
☐ D4-CBW	ATR 42-500	532	♦

TACV — VR / TCV

☐ D4-CBP	B757-2Q8	30045/957
☐ D4-CBT	ATR 72-212A	747
☐ D4-CBU	ATR 72-212A	755
☐ D4-CBV	ATR 42-512	669

D6 - COMORES

COMORES AVIATION

☐ ZS-AAY	BAe146 Srs.200	E2044	♦

COMORO ISLAND AIRWAYS

☐ D6-CAS	A320-214	3040	>SUD

EC - SPAIN

AERONOVA — OVA

☐ EC-GVE	SA.227AC Metro III	AC-669B
☐ EC-HCH	SA.227AC Metro III	AC-658B
☐ EC-HZH	SA.227AC Metro III	AC-720
☐ EC-IXL	SA.227AC Metro III	AC-689B
☐ EC-JCU	SA.227AC Metro III	AC-679B

AIR EUROPA — UX / AEA

☐ EC-JPF	A330-202	733
☐ EC-JQG	A330-202	745
☐ EC-JQQ	A330-202	749
☐ EC-JZL	A330-202	814
☐ EC-KOM	A330-202	931
☐ EC-KTG	A330-202	950
☐ EC-HBL	B737-85P	28381/250
☐ EC-HBM	B737-85P	28382/256
☐ EC-HGO	B737-85P	28384/420
☐ EC-HGP	B737-85P	28385/421
☐ EC-HGQ	B737-85P	28386/426
☐ EC-HJP	B737-85P	28535/480
☐ EC-HJQ	B737-85P	28387/522
☐ EC-HKQ	B737-85P/W	28388/533
☐ EC-HKR	B737-85P/W	28536/540
☐ EC-HZS	B737-86Q/W	30276/920
☐ EC-IDA	B737-86Q/W	32773/1051
☐ EC-IDT	B737-86Q/W	30281/1076
☐ EC-III	B737-86Q/W	30284/1233
☐ EC-ISE	B737-86Q/W	30290/1406
☐ EC-ISN	B737-86Q/W	30291/1435
☐ EC-JAP	B737-85P/W	33971/1580
☐ EC-JBJ	B737-85P/W	33972/1598
☐ EC-JBK	B737-85P/W	33973/1606

	Reg	Type	MSN	Notes
☐	EC-JBL	B737-85P/W	33974/1610	
☐	EC-JHK	B737-85P/W	33975/1716	
☐	EC-JHL	B737-85P/W	33976/1740	
☐	EC-JNF	B737-85P/W	33977/1878	
☐	EC-KBV	B737-85P/W	33980/2245	
☐	EC-KCG	B737-85P/W	33981/2269	
☐	EC-KEO	B737-85P/W	33982/2338	
☐	EC-	B737-85P		o/o
☐	EC-	B737-85P		o/o
☐	EC-	B737-85P		o/o
☐	EC-HPU	B767-3Q8ER	30048/828	
☐	EC-HSV	B767-3Q8ER	29387/840	
☐	SP-LPF	B767-319ER	24876/413	<LOT
☐	EC-KRJ	ERJ-195LR	19000196	
☐	EC-KXD	ERJ-195LR	19000244	
☐	EC-KYO	ERJ-195LR	19000276	
☐	EC-KYP	ERJ-195LR	19000281	
☐	EC-LCQ	ERJ-195LR	19000303	♦
☐	EC-LEK	ERJ-195LR	19000344	♦
☐	EC-LFZ	ERJ-195LR	19000357	♦
☐	EC-LIN	ERJ-195LR	19000401	♦
☐	EC-	ERJ-195LR		o/o♦
☐	EC-	ERJ-195LR		o/o♦

AIR NOSTRUM YW / ANE

	Reg	Type	MSN	Notes
☐	EC-HBY	ATR 72-212A	578	
☐	EC-HCG	ATR 72-212A	580	
☐	EC-HEI	ATR 72-212A	570	
☐	EC-HEJ	ATR 72-212A	565	
☐	EC-HJI	ATR 72-212A	562	
☐	EC-	ATR 72-600		o/o♦
☐	EC-	ATR 72-600		o/o♦
☐	EC-	ATR 72-600		o/o♦
☐	EC-	ATR 72-600		o/o♦
☐	EC-GYI	CRJ-200ER	7249	
☐	EC-GZA	CRJ-200ER	7252	
☐	EC-HEK	CRJ-200ER	7320	
☐	EC-HHI	CRJ-200ER	7343	
☐	EC-HHV	CRJ-200ER	7350	
☐	EC-HPR	CRJ-200ER	7430	
☐	EC-HSH	CRJ-200ER	7466	
☐	EC-HTZ	CRJ-200ER	7493	
☐	EC-HXM	CRJ-200ER	7514	
☐	EC-HYG	CRJ-200ER	7529	
☐	EC-HZR	CRJ-200ER	7547	
☐	EC-IAA	CRJ-200ER	7563	
☐	EC-IBM	CRJ-200ER	7591	
☐	EC-IDC	CRJ-200ER	7622	
☐	EC-IGO	CRJ-200ER	7661	
☐	EC-IJE	CRJ-200ER	7700	
☐	EC-IJF	CRJ-200ER	7705	
☐	EC-IJS	CRJ-200ER	7706	
☐	EC-IKZ	CRJ-200ER	7732	
☐	EC-ILF	CRJ-200ER	7746	
☐	EC-INF	CRJ-200ER	7785	
☐	EC-IRI	CRJ-200ER	7851	
☐	EC-ITU	CRJ-200ER	7866	
☐	EC-IVH	CRJ-200ER	7915	
☐	EC-IZP	CRJ-200ER	7950	
☐	EC-JCG	CRJ-200ER	7973	
☐	EC-JCL	CRJ-200ER	7975	
☐	EC-JCM	CRJ-200ER	7981	
☐	EC-JCO	CRJ-200ER	7984	
☐	EC-JEE	CRJ-200ER	7989	
☐	EC-JEF	CRJ-200ER	8008	
☐	EC-JEN	CRJ-200ER	7958	
☐	EC-JNX	CRJ-200ER	8058	
☐	EC-JOD	CRJ-200ER	8061	
☐	EC-JOY	CRJ-200ER	8064	
🖼	EC-JNB	CRJ-900ER	15057	23/3
☐	EC-JTS	CRJ-900ER	15071	

	Reg	Type	MSN	Notes
☐	EC-JTT	CRJ-900ER	15074	
☐	EC-JTU	CRJ-900ER	15079	
☐	EC-JXZ	CRJ-900ER	15087	
☐	EC-JYA	CRJ-900ER	15090	
☐	EC-JYV	CRJ-900ER	15106	
☐	EC-JZS	CRJ-900ER	15111	
☐	EC-JZT	CRJ-900ER	15113	
☐	EC-JZU	CRJ-900ER	15115	
☐	EC-JZV	CRJ-900ER	15117	
☐	EC-LJR	CRJ-1000	19002	♦
☐	EC-LJS	CRJ-1000	19003	♦
☐	EC-LJT	CRJ-1000	19005	♦
☐	EC-LJX	CRJ-1000	19008	♦
☐	EC-LKF	CRJ-1000	19011	♦
☐		CRJ-1000		o/o♦
☐		CRJ-1000		o/o♦
☐		CRJ-1000		o/o♦
☐		CRJ-1000		o/o♦
☐		CRJ-1000		o/o♦
☐		CRJ-1000		o/o♦
☐	EC-IBS	DHC-8Q-315	560	
☐	EC-IGE	DHC-8Q-315	576	
☐	EC-IIA	DHC-8Q-315	587	
☐	EC-IIB	DHC-8Q-315	588	
☐	EC-IOV	DHC-8Q-315	581	
☐	EC-LFE	DHC-8Q-315	589	♦
☐	EC-LFG	DHC-8Q-315	582	♦
☐	EC-LFH	DHC-8Q-315	586	♦
☐	EC-LFU	DHC-8Q-315	574	♦

ALBA STAR LAV

	Reg	Type	MSN	Notes
☐	EC-LAV	B737-408	24352/1705	♦

ANDALUS LINEAS AEREAS

	Reg	Type	MSN
☐	EC-LCP	ERJ-145MP	145408

AUDELI ADI

	Reg	Type	MSN
☐	EC-IDF	A340-313X	474
☐	EC-IIH	A340-313X	483
☐	EC-KCL	A340-311	005

BINTER CANARIAS NT / IBB

	Reg	Type	MSN	Notes
☐	EC-GQF	ATR 72-202	489	<NAY
☐	EC-GRP	ATR 72-202	488	<NAY
☐	EC-GRU	ATR 72-202	493	<NAY
☐	EC-HEZ	ATR 72-212A	582	<NAY
☐	EC-IYC	ATR 72-212A	709	
☐	EC-IZO	ATR 72-212A	711	
☐	EC-JAH	ATR 72-212A	712	
☐	EC-JBI	ATR 72-212A	713	
☐	EC-JEH	ATR 72-212A	716	
☐	EC-JEV	ATR 72-212A	717	
☐	EC-JQL	ATR 72-212A	726	
☐	EC-KGI	ATR 72-212A	752	<NAY
☐	EC-KGJ	ATR 72-212A	753	<NAY
☐	EC-KRY	ATR 72-212A	795	<NAY
☐	EC-KSG	ATR 72-212A	796	<NAY
☐	EC-KYI	ATR 72-212A	850	<NAY
☐	EC-LAD	ATR 72-212A	864	<NAY
☐	EC-LFA	ATR 72-212A	902	♦
☐	EC-LGF	ATR 72-212A	907	♦
☐	EC-IJO	Beech 1900D	UE-300	<NAY

CALIMA AVIACION

	Reg	Type	MSN	Notes
☐	EC-LDN	B737-448	24474/1742	♦
☐	EC-LKO	B737-85F	28821/151	♦

CEGISA

☐	EC-GBP	CL-215	1031	Tanker
☐	EC-GBQ	CL-215	1033	Tanker
☐	EC-GBR	CL-215	1051	Tanker
☐	EC-GBS	CL-215	1052	Tanker
☐	EC-GBT	CL-215	1054	Tanker
☐	EC-HET	CL-215	1034	Tanker
☐	EC-HEU	CL-215	1038	Tanker

EURO CONTINENTAL AIR   ECN

☐	EC-GPS	SA.227AC Metro III	AC-722	>EAL
☐	EC-JIP	SA.226TC Metro II	TC-301	
☐	EC-JQC	SA.226AC Merlin IVA	AT-066	

FLIGHTLINE   FTL

☐	EC-GFK	SA.226AT Merlin IVA	AT-062	
☐	EC-HBF	SA.226AT Merlin IVA	AT-074	
☐	EC-HHN	EMB.120RT	120103	
☐	EC-LFT	EMB.120RT	120014	♦

GESTAIR CARGO   RGN

☐	EC-FTR	B757-256 (PCF)	26239/553	
☐	EC-KLD	B757-256 (PCF)	24121/183	
☐	EC-LKI	B767-383ERBDSF	26544/412	♦
☐	EC-	B767-383ERBDSF	24729/358	o/o♦

IBERIA   IB / IBE

☐	EC-HGR	A319-111	1154	
☐	EC-HGS	A319-111	1180	
☐	EC-HGT	A319-111	1247	
☐	EC-HKO	A319-111	1362	
☐	EC-JAZ	A319-111	2264	
☐	EC-JDL	A319-111	2365	
☐	EC-JEI	A319-111	2311	
☐	EC-JVE	A319-111	2843	
☐	EC-JXA	A319-111	2870	
☐	EC-JXJ	A319-111	2889	
☐	EC-JXV	A319-111	2897	
☐	EC-KBJ	A319-111	3054	
☐	EC-KBX	A319-111	3078	
☐	EC-KDI	A319-111	3102	
☐	EC-KEV	A319-111	3169	
☐	EC-KFT	A319-111	3179	
☐	EC-KHM	A319-111	3209	
☐	EC-KJC	A319-111	3255	
☐	EC-KKS	A319-111	3320	
☐	EC-KMD	A319-111	3380	
☐	EC-KME	A319-111	3377	
☐	EC-KOY	A319-111	3443	
☐	EC-KUB	A319-111	3651	
☐	EC-LEI	A319-111	3744	
☐	EC-FDA	A320-211	0176	
☐	EC-FDB	A320-211	0173	
☐	EC-FGR	A320-211	0224	[MAD]
☐	EC-FGV	A320-211	0207	[MAD]
☐	EC-FLP	A320-211	0266	[MAD]
☐	EC-FLQ	A320-211	0274	[MAD]
☐	EC-FNR	A320-211	0323	
☐	EC-FQY	A320-211	0356	
☐	EC-HAG	A320-214	1059	
☐	EC-HDK	A320-214	1067	
☐	EC-HDT	A320-214	1119	
☐	EC-HGZ	A320-214	1208	
☐	EC-HQG	A320-214	1379	[MAD]
☐	EC-HSF	A320-214	1255	
☐	EC-HTA	A320-214	1516	
☐	EC-HTB	A320-214	1530	
☐	EC-HTC	A320-214	1540	
☐	EC-HUJ	A320-214	1292	
☐	EC-HUK	A320-214	1318	
☐	EC-HUL	A320-214	1347	
☐	EC-HYC	A320-214	1262	
☐	EC-HYD	A320-214	1288	
☐	EC-IEF	A320-214	1655	
☐	EC-IEG	A320-214	1674	
☐	EC-IEI	A320-214	1694	
☐	EC-ILQ	A320-214	1736	
☐	EC-ILR	A320-214	1793	
☐	EC-ILS	A320-214	1809	
☐	EC-IZH	A320-214	2225	
☐	EC-IZR	A320-214	2242	
☐	EC-JFG	A320-214	2143	
☐	EC-JFH	A320-214	2104	
☐	EC-JFN	A320-214	2391	
☐	EC-JSB	A320-214	2776	
☐	EC-JSK	A320-214	2807	
☐	EC-KHJ	A320-214	2347	
☐	EC-KNM	A320-214	1229	
☐	EC-KOH	A320-214	2248	
☐	EC-LEA	A320-214	1099	♦
☐	EC-LKG	A320-214	1047	♦
☐	EC-LKH	A320-214	1101	♦
☐	EC-	A320-214		o/o♦
☐	EC-	A320-214		o/o♦
☐	EC-	A320-214		o/o♦
☐	EC-HUH	A321-211	1021	
☐	EC-HUI	A321-211	1027	
☐	EC-IGK	A321-211	1572	
☐	EC-IIG	A321-211	1554	
☐	EC-IJN	A321-211	1836	
☐	EC-ILO	A321-211	1681	
☐	EC-ILP	A321-211	1716	
☐	EC-ITN	A321-211	2115	
☐	EC-IXD	A321-211	2220	
☐	EC-JDM	A321-211	2357	
☐	EC-JDR	A321-211	2488	
☐	EC-JEJ	A321-211	2381	
☐	EC-JGS	A321-211	2472	
☐	EC-JLI	A321-211	2563	
☐	EC-JMR	A321-211	2599	
☐	EC-JNI	A321-211	2270	
☐	EC-JQZ	A321-211	2736	
☐	EC-JRE	A321-211	2756	
☐	EC-JZM	A321-211	2996	
☐	EC-GGS	A340-313	125	
☐	EC-GHX	A340-313	134	
☐	EC-GJT	A340-313	145	
☐	EC-GLE	A340-313	146	
☐	EC-GPB	A340-313X	193	
☐	EC-GQK	A340-313X	197	[CHR]♦
☐	EC-GUP	A340-313X	217	
☐	EC-GUQ	A340-313X	221	
☐	EC-HDQ	A340-313X	302	
☐	EC-HGU	A340-313X	318	
☐	EC-HGV	A340-313X	329	
☐	EC-HGX	A340-313X	332	
☐	EC-HQN	A340-313X	414	
☐	EC-ICF	A340-313X	459	
☐	EC-IDF	A340-313X	474	
☐	EC-IIH	A340-313X	483	
☐	EC-KCL	A340-311	005	
☐	EC-KOU	A340-313	088	
☐	EC-KSE	A340-313X	170	
☐	EC-LHM	A340-313X	387	♦
☐	EC-INO	A340-642	431	
☐	EC-IOB	A340-642	440	
☐	EC-IQR	A340-642	460	
☐	EC-IZX	A340-642	601	
☐	EC-IZY	A340-642	604	
☐	EC-JBA	A340-642	606	
☐	EC-JCY	A340-642	617	
☐	EC-JCZ	A340-642	619	
☐	EC-JFX	A340-642	672	

☐	EC-JLE	A340-642	702	
☐	EC-JNQ	A340-642	727	
☐	EC-JPU	A340-642	744	
☐	EC-KZI	A340-642	1017	♦
☐	EC-LCZ	A340-642	993	[MAD]♦
☐	EC-LEU	A340-642	960	♦
☐	EC-LEV	A340-642	1079	♦
☐	EC-LFS	A340-642	1122	o/o♦
☐	EC-EXG	MD-87	49833/1706	
☐	EC-EXM	MD-87	49835/1717	[MAD]
☐	EC-FHD	MD-87	53212/1877	
☐	EC-FIG	MD-88	53195/1929	[MAD]
☐	EC-FJE	MD-88	53197/1940	[MAD]
☐	EC-FLN	MD-88	53303/1974	
☐	EC-FOF	MD-88	53307/2015	
☐	EC-FOZ	MD-88	53308/2022	
☐	EC-FPD	MD-88	53309/2023	[MAD]

IBERWORLD AIRLINES — TY / IWD

☐	EC-INZ	A320-214	2011	
☐	EC-JQP	A320-214	2745	
☐	EC-KYZ	A320-214	3758	
☐	EC-KZG	A320-214	3868	
☐	EC-LAJ	A320-214	3889	
☐	EC-LAQ	A320-214	3933	
☐	EC-IJH	A330-322	072	
☐	EC-JHP	A330-343X	670	
☐	EC-KCP	A330-343E	833	
☐	EC-LEQ	A330-343E	1097	>XLF♦

ISLAS AIRWAYS — IF / ISW

☐	EC-IKQ	ATR 72-202	477	
☐	EC-JCD	ATR 72-202	452	
☐	EC-KKZ	ATR 72-212	766	
☐	EC-KNO	ATR 72-212	770	
☐	EC-KUR	ATR 72-212A	808	
☐	EC-LKK	ATR 72-212	461	♦
☐	EC-	ATR 72-500		o/o♦
☐	EC-	ATR 72-500		o/o♦
☐	EC-	ATR 72-500		o/o♦

MINT AIRWAYS

☐	EC-LBC	B757-28A	26276/704	
☐	EC-LHL	B757-28A	24544/280	♦

NAYSA AEROTAXIS — ZN / NAY

☐	EC-GQF	ATR 72-202	489	>IBB
☐	EC-GRP	ATR 72-202	488	>IBB
☐	EC-GRU	ATR 72-202	493	>IBB
☐	EC-IPJ	ATR 72-202	307	>IBB
☐	EC-KGI	ATR 72-212A	752	>IBB
☐	EC-KGJ	ATR 72-212A	753	>IBB
☐	EC-KRY	ATR 72-212A	795	>IBB
☐	EC-KSG	ATR 72-212A	796	>IBB
☐	EC-KYI	ATR 72-212A	850	>IBB
☐	EC-LAD	ATR 72-212A	864	>IBB
☐	EC-IJO	Beech 1900D	UE-300	

PANAIR LINEAS AEREAS — PV / PNR

☐	EC-ELT	BAe146 Srs.200QT	E2102	
☐	EC-FVY	BAe146 Srs.200QT	E2117	
☐	EC-FZE	BAe146 Srs.200QT	E2105	
☐	EC-GQO	BAe146 Srs.200QT	E2086	
☐	EC-HDH	BAe146 Srs.200QT	E2056	
☐	EC-HJH	BAe146 Srs.200QT	E2112	
☐	EC-HQT	A300B4-103F	124	[MHV]

PIRINAIR EXPRESS — PRN

☐	EC-FZB	SA.226TC Metro II	TC-221	
☐	EC-JCV	SA.226AT Merlin IVA	AT-038	

PRIVILEGE STYLE — PVG

☐	EC-HDS	B757-256	26252/900
☐	EC-ISY	B757-256	26241/572

PRONAIR AIRLINES

☐	EC-KJI	MD-87	49836/1721
☐	EC-KRP	B747-245F	20826/242
☐	EC-KRV	MD-87	49843/1771

PULLMANTUR AIR

☐	EC-KQC	B747-412	26549/1030	
☐	EC-KSM	B747-412	27178/1015	
☐	EC-KXN	B747-4H6	25703/1025	
☐	EC-LGL	B747-412	26555/1075	♦

RYJET

☐	EC-JHE	SAAB SF.340A	340A-018

SAICUS AIR — FYA

☐	EC-JUV	B737-301(SF)	23741/1498	
☐	EC-KKJ	B737-4B7(SF)	24559/1847	[PMI]

SERAIR — SEV

☐	EC-GTM	Beech 1900C	UB-30
☐	EC-GUD	Beech 1900C-1	UC-156
☐	EC-GZG	Beech 1900C-1	UC-161
☐	EC-JDY	Beech 1900C-1	UC-91

SPANAIR — JK / JKK

☐	EC-HPM	A321-231	1276	
☐	EC-HQZ	A321-231	1333	
☐	EC-HRG	A321-231	1366	
☐	EC-HRP	A320-232	1349	
☐	EC-HXA	A320-232	1497	
☐	EC-IAZ	A320-232	1631	
☐	EC-ICL	A320-232	1682	
☐	EC-IEJ	A320-232	1749	
☐	EC-IIZ	A320-232	1862	
☐	EC-IJU	A321-231	1843	
☐	EC-ILH	A320-232	1914	
☐	EC-IMB	A320-232	1933	
☐	EC-INB	A321-231	1946	
☐	EC-INM	A320-232	1979	
☐	EC-IOH	A320-232	1998	
☐	EC-IPI	A320-232	2027	
☐	EC-IVG	A320-232	2168	
☐	EC-IYG	A320-232	2210	
☐	EC-IZK	A320-232	2223	
☐	EC-JJD	A320-232	2479	
☐	EC-JNC	A320-232	2589	
☐	EC-KEC	A320-232	1183	
☐	EC-KOX	A320-232	1383	
☐	EC-KPX	A320-232	1407	
☐	EC-FTS	MD-83	49621/1495	
☐	EC-GCV	MD-82	53165/2042	
☐	EC-GNY	MD-83	49396/1305	
☐	EC-GQG	MD-83	49577/1454	
☐	EC-GVO	MD-83	49642/1421	
☐	EC-GXU	MD-83	49622/1498	
☐	EC-KAZ	MD-87	49614/1556	<SAS
☐	EC-KCZ	MD-87	49609/1517	<SAS
☐	EC-KHA	MD-87	49611/1522	<SAS
☐	EC-KJE	MD-87	49606/1569	<SAS

☐	EC-KVA	MD-87	53208/1865	[MAD]

SWIFTAIR　　　　　　　　　　　　　SWT

☐	EC-INV	ATR 72-201	274	
☐	EC-ISX	ATR 42-320	242	
☐	EC-IVP	ATR 42-300	231	
☐	EC-IYH	ATR 72-212	330	
☐	EC-JAD	ATR 42-300	321	
☐	EC-JBN	ATR 42-300(QC)	218	
☐	EC-JBX	ATR 42-300	254	
☐	EC-JDX	ATR 72-201	234	
☐	EC-JQF	ATR 72-201F	147	
☐	EC-JRP	ATR 72-212	446	
☐	EC-JXF	ATR 72-201F	150	
☐	EC-KAD	ATR 72-202F	171	
☐	EC-KAE	ATR 72-202F	192	
☐	EC-KAI	ATR 42-300F	141	
☐	EC-KIZ	ATR 72-202F	204	<FPO
☐	EC-KJA	ATR 72-202F	207	<FPO
☐	EC-KKQ	ATR 72-212A	763	
☐	EC-KUL	ATR 72-212A	809	
☐	EC-KVI	ATR 72-212A	824	>AEE
☐	EC-IMY	B727-225	21293/1241	
☐	EC-JHU	B727-230F	21442/1326	
☐	EC-KDY	B737-3S3F	23811/1445	
☐	EC-KLR	B737-3Q8(SF)	23766/1375	
☐	EC-KRA	B737-3Y0F	24679/1897	
☐	EC-KTZ	B737-375F	23708/1395	
☐	EC-KVD	B737-306F	23538/1288	
☐	EC-LAC	B737-3M8F	24022/1662	
☐	EC-LJI	B737-301(SF)	23512/1291	♦
☐	EC-GQA	EMB-120ER	120027	
☐	EC-HAK	EMB-120ER	120008	
☐	EC-HCF	EMB.120ER	120007	
☐	EC-HFK	EMB.120ER	120063	
☐	EC-HMY	EMB.120ER	120009	
☐	EC-HTS	EMB.120ER	120168	
☐	EC-IMX	EMB.120ER	120158	
☐	EC-JBD	EMB.120ER	120012	
☐	EC-JBE	EMB.120ER	120013	
☐	EC-JKH	EMB.120ER	120092	
☐	EC-JJS	MD-83	49793/1656	
☐	EC-JQV	MD-83	49526/1342	
☐	EC-JUF	MD-83	53168/2061	Opf UN
☐	EC-JUG	MD-83	49847/1585	
☐	EC-KCX	MD-83	49619/1483	
☐	EC-LEY	MD-83	53182/2068	♦

TAS TRANSPORTES AEREOS DEL SUR

☐	EC-KEK	CASA CN-235-300MPA	C166
☐	EC-KEL	CASA CN-235-300MPA	169
☐	EC-KEM	CASA CN-235-300MPA	171

TOP-FLY　　　　　　　　　　　　　　TLY

☐	EC-GJM	SA.227AC Metro III	BC-772B
☐	EC-IDG	ATR 42-320	3
☐	EC-IRS	SA.227BC Metro III	BC-786B
☐	EC-ITP	SA.227BC Metro III	BC-789B

VUELING AIRLINES　　　　　　　　VY / VLG

☐	EC-FCB	A320-211	0158	♦
☐	EC-GRG	A320-211	0143	
☐	EC-GRH	A320-211	0146	
☐	EC-GRI	A320-211	0177	
☐	EC-HHA	A320-214	1221	
☐	EC-HQI	A320-214	1396	
☐	EC-HQJ	A320-214	1430	
☐	EC-HQL	A320-214	1461	

☐	EC-HTD	A320-214	1550	
☐	EC-ICQ	A320-211	0199	
☐	EC-ICR	A320-211	0240	
☐	EC-ICS	A320-211	0241	
☐	EC-ICT	A320-211	0264	
☐	EC-IZD	A320-214	2207	
☐	EC-JFF	A320-214	2388	
☐	EC-JGM	A320-214	2407	
☐	EC-JSY	A320-214	2785	
☐	EC-JTQ	A320-214	2794	
☐	EC-JTR	A320-214	2798	
☐	EC-JYX	A320-214	2962	
☐	EC-JZI	A320-214	2988	
☐	EC-JZQ	A320-214	0992	
☐	EC-KBU	A320-214	1413	
☐	EC-KCU	A320-216	3109	
☐	EC-KDG	A320-214	3095	
☐	EC-KDH	A320-214	3083	
☐	EC-KDT	A320-216	3145	
☐	EC-KDX	A320-216	3151	
☐	EC-KFI	A320-216	3174	
☐	EC-KHN	A320-216	3203	
☐	EC-KJD	A320-216	3237	
☐	EC-KKT	A320-214	3293	
☐	EC-KLB	A320-214	3321	
☐	EC-KLT	A320-214	3376	
☐	EC-KMI	A320-216	3400	
☐	EC-KRH	A320-214	3529	
☐	EC-LAA	A320-214	2678	
☐	EC-LAB	A320-214	2761	
☐	EC-	A320-214		o/o♦
☐	EC-	A320-214		o/o♦
☐	EC-	A320-214		o/o♦
☐	EC-	A320-214		o/o♦
☐	EC-	A320-214		o/o♦
☐	EC-	A320-214		o/o♦

VUELOS MEDITERRANEO　　　　　　VMM

☐	EC-HCU	SA.226TC Metro II	TC-390

ZOREX　　　　　　　　　　　　　　　ORZ

☐	EC-HJC	SA.226TC Metro II	TC-318
☐	EC-JYC	SA.226TC Metro II	TC-303

EI - EIRE

AER ARANN　　　　　　　　　　　RE / REA

☐	EI-BYO	ATR 42-310	161	
☐	EI-CBK	ATR 42-310	199	
☐	EI-CPT	ATR 42-300	191	
☐	EI-CVR	ATR 42-310	022	
☐	EI-EHH	ATR 42-300	196	
☐	EI-REH	ATR 72-202	260	
☐	EI-REI	ATR 72-202	267	
☐	EI-REL	ATR 72-212A	748	
☐	EI-REM	ATR 72-212A	760	
☐	EI-REO	ATR 72-212A	787	
☐	EI-REP	ATR 72-212A	797	
☐	EI-RES	ATR 72-212A		o/o
☐	EI-RET	ATR 72-212A		o/o
☐	EI-REU	ATR 72-212A		o/o
☐	EI-REV	ATR 72-212A		o/o

AER LINGUS　　　　　　　　　　EI / EIN

☐	EI-CVA	A320-214	1242	
■	EI-CVB	A320-214	1394	14.VI.2014
☐	EI-CVC	A320-214	1443	
☐	EI-CVD	A320-214	1467	
☐	EI-DEA	A320-214	2191	
☐	EI-DEB	A320-214	2206	

	Reg	Type	c/n	
■	EI-DEC	A320-214	2217	
□	EI-DEE	A320-214	2250	
□	EI-DEF	A320-214	2256	
■	EI-DEG	A320-214	2272	
■	EI-DEH	A320-214	2294	
□	EI-DEI	A320-214	2374	
■	EI-DEJ	A320-214	2364	
■	EI-DEK	A320-214	2399	
□	EI-DEL	A320-214	2409	
□	EI-DEM	A320-214	2411	
□	EI-DEN	A320-214	2432	
□	EI-DEO	A320-214	2486	
□	EI-DEP	A320-214	2542	
■	EI-DER	A320-214	2583	
■	EI-DES	A320-214	2635	
■	EI-DET	A320-214	2810	
■	EI-DVE	A320-214	3129	
□	EI-DVF	A320-214	3136	
■	EI-DVG	A320-214	3318	
■	EI-DVH	A320-214	3345	
□	EI-DVI	A320-214	3501	
■	EI-DVJ	A320-214	3857	
□	EI-DVK	A320-214	4572	♦
■	EI-DYK	A320-214		o/o♦
■	EI-DVN	A320-214		o/o♦
□	EI-	A320-214		o/o♦
□	EI-EDP	A320-214	3781	
□	EI-EDS	A320-214	3755	
□	EI-CPC	A321-211	0815	
□	EI-CPD	A321-211	0841	
□	EI-CPE	A321-211	0926	
□	EI-CPF	A321-211	0991	
□	EI-CPG	A321-211	1023	
■	EI-CPH	A321-211	1094	
□	EI-DAA	A330-202	397	
□	EI-DUO	A330-202	841	
■	EI-DUZ	A330-302	847	
■	EI-EAV	A330-302	985	
■	EI-EDY	A330-302	1025	
□	EI-ELA	A330-302X	1106	♦
□	EI-LAX	A330-202	269	
□	EI-ORD	A330-301	059	

AIR CONTRACTORS AG / ABR

	Reg	Type	c/n	
□	EI-DHL	A300B4-203F	274	
□	EI-EAB	A300B4-203F	199	♦
□	EI-EAC	A300B4-203F	250	
□	EI-EAD	A300B4-203F	289	
□	EI-OZB	A300B4-103F	184	
□	EI-OZC	A300B4-103F	189	
□	EI-OZD	A300B4-203F	236	
□	EI-OZE	A300B4-203F	152	
□	EI-OZF	A300B4-203F	259	
□	EI-OZG	A300B4-203F	208	
□	EI-OZH	A300B4-203F	234	
□	EI-OZI	A300B4-203F	219	♦
□	EI-SAF	A300B4-203F	220	
□	EI-FXA	ATR 42-320F	282	Opf FDX
□	EI-FXB	ATR 42-320F	243	Opf FDX
□	EI-FXC	ATR 42-320F	310	Opf FDX
□	EI-FXD	ATR 42-300F	273	Opf FDX
□	EI-FXE	ATR 42-320F	327	Opf FDX
□	EI-FXG	ATR 72-202F	224	Opf FDX
□	EI-FXH	ATR 72-202F	229	Opf FDX
□	EI-FXI	ATR 72-202F	294	Opf FDX
□	EI-FXJ	ATR 72-202F	292	Opf FDX
□	EI-FXK	ATR 72-202F	256	Opf FDX
□	EI-REJ	ATR 72-202F	126	Opf FDX
□	EI-SLA	ATR 42-300F	149	>MSA
□	EI-SLC	ATR 42-300F	082	>MSA
□	EI-SLF	ATR 72-202F	210	
□	EI-SLG	ATR 72-202F	183	

	Reg	Type	c/n	
□	EI-SLH	ATR 72-202F	157	
□	EI-SLI	ATR 42-320	115	
□	EI-SLJ	ATR 72-201	324	
□	EI-SLK	ATR 72-212	395	
□	EI-SLL	ATR 72-212	387	
□	EI-SLM	ATR 72-212	413	
□	EI-SLN	ATR 72-212	405	♦
□	EI-JIV	L-382G-35C Hercules	4673	<SFR

CITYJET WX / BCY

	Reg	Type	c/n	
□	EI-RJA	Avro 146-RJ85	E2329	
□	EI-RJB	Avro 146-RJ85	E2330	
□	EI-RJC	Avro 146-RJ85	E2333	
□	EI-RJD	Avro 146-RJ85	E2334	
□	EI-RJE	Avro 146-RJ85	E2335	
□	EI-RJF	Avro 146-RJ85	E2337	
□	EI-RJG	Avro 146-RJ85	E2344	
□	EI-RJH	Avro 146-RJ85	E2345	
□	EI-RJI	Avro 146-RJ85	E2346	
□	EI-RJJ	Avro 146-RJ85	E2347	
□	EI-RJK	Avro 146-RJ85	E2348	[NWI]
□	EI-RJL	Avro 146-RJ85	E2349	[NWI]♦
□	EI-RJM	Avro 146-RJ85	E2350	[NWI]♦
□	EI-RJN	Avro 146-RJ85	E2351	
□	EI-RJO	Avro 146-RJ85	E2352	
□	EI-RJP	Avro 146-RJ85	E2363	
□	EI-RJR	Avro 146-RJ85	E2364	
□	EI-RJS	Avro 146-RJ85	E2365	
□	EI-RJT	Avro 146-RJ85	E2366	
□	EI-RJU	Avro 146-RJ85	E2367	
□	EI-RJV	Avro 146-RJ85	E2370	
□	EI-RJW	Avro 146-RJ85	E2371	
□	EI-RJX	Avro 146-RJ85	E2372	
□	EI-RJY	Avro 146-RJ85	E2307	
□	EI-RJZ	Avro 146-RJ85	E2326	
□	EI-WXA	Avro 146-RJ85	E2310	
□	EI-WXB	Avro 146-RJ85	E2311	[NWI]

RYANAIR FR / RYR

	Reg	Type	c/n	
■	EI-DAC	B737-8AS/W	29938/1240	
□	EI-DAD	B737-8AS/W	33544/1249	
□	EI-DAE	B737-8AS/W	33545/1252	
□	EI-DAF	B737-8AS/W	29939/1262	
□	EI-DAG	B737-8AS/W	29940/1265	
□	EI-DAH	B737-8AS/W	33546/1269	
□	EI-DAI	B737-8AS/W	33547/1271	
□	EI-DAJ	B737-8AS/W	33548/1274	
□	EI-DAK	B737-8AS/W	33717/1310	
■	EI-DAL	B737-8AS/W	33718/1311	
□	EI-DAM	B737-8AS/W	33719/1312	
□	EI-DAN	B737-8AS/W	33549/1361	
□	EI-DAO	B737-8AS/W	33550/1366	
□	EI-DAP	B737-8AS/W	33551/1368	
□	EI-DAR	B737-8AS/W	33552/1371	
■	EI-DAS	B737-8AS/W	33553/1372	
□	EI-DAY	B737-8AS/W	33558/1441	
□	EI-DAZ	B737-8AS/W	33559/1443	
□	EI-DCB	B737-8AS/W	33560/1447	
□	EI-DCC	B737-8AS/W	33561/1463	
□	EI-DCD	B737-8AS/W	33562/1466	
□	EI-DCE	B737-8AS/W	33563/1473	
■	EI-DCF	B737-8AS/W	33804/1529	
□	EI-DCG	B737-8AS/W	33806/1530	
□	EI-DCH	B737-8AS/W	33566/1546	
□	EI-DCI	B737-8AS/W	33567/1547	
□	EI-DCJ	B737-8AS/W	33564/1562	
■	EI-DCK	B737-8AS/W	33565/1563	
□	EI-DCL	B737-8AS/W	33806/1576	
□	EI-DCM	B737-8AS/W	33807/1578	
□	EI-DCN	B737-8AS/W	33808/1590	
□	EI-DCO	B737-8AS/W	33809/1592	
■	EI-DCP	B737-8AS/W	33810/1595	
□	EI-DCR	B737-8AS/W	33811/1613	

	Reg	Type	C/n		Reg	Type	C/n
☐	EI-DCS	B737-8AS/W	33812/1615	☐	EI-DPZ	B737-8AS/W	33616/2376
☐	EI-DCT	B737-8AS/W	33813/1617	☐	EI-DWA	B737-8AS/W	33617/2377
☐	EI-DCV	B737-8AS/W	33814/1618	☐	EI-DWB	B737-8AS/W	36075/2382
☐	EI-DCW	B737-8AS/W	33568/1631	☐	EI-DWC	B737-8AS/W	36076/2384
☐	EI-DCX	B737-8AS/W	33569/1635	☑	EI-DWD	B737-8AS/W	33642/2389
☐	EI-DCY	B737-8AS/W	33670/1637	☑	EI-DWE	B737-8AS/W	36074/2391
☐	EI-DCZ	B737-8AS/W	33815/1638	☐	EI-DWF	B737-8AS/W	33619/2396
☑	EI-DHA	B737-8AS/W	33571/1642	☑	EI-DWG	B737-8AS/W	33620/2397
☐	EI-DHB	B737-8AS/W	33572/1652	☐	EI-DWH	B737-8AS/W	33637/2408
☐	EI-DHC	B737-8AS/W	33573/1655	☐	EI-DWI	B737-8AS/W	33643/2410
☐	EI-DHD	B737-8AS/W	33816/1657	☑	EI-DWJ	B737-8AS/W	36077/2411
☐	EI-DHE	B737-8AS/W	33574/1658	☐	EI-DWK	B737-8AS/W	36078/2415
☐	EI-DHF	B737-8AS/W	33575/1660	☐	EI-DWL	B737-8AS/W	33618/2416
☐	EI-DHG	B737-8AS/W	33576/1670	☐	EI-DWM	B737-8AS/W	36080/2430
☐	EI-DHH	B737-8AS/W	33817/1677	☐	EI-DWO	B737-8AS/W	36079/2440
☐	EI-DHI	B737-8AS/W	33818/1685	☐	EI-DWP	B737-8AS/W	36082/2443
☐	EI-DHJ	B737-8AS/W	33819/1691	☐	EI-DWR	B737-8AS/W	36081/2448
☐	EI-DHK	B737-8AS/W	33820/1696	☐	EI-DWS	B737-8AS/W	33625/2472
☑	EI-DHM	B737-8AS/W	33821/1698	☑	EI-DWT	B737-8AS/W	33626/2489
☐	EI-DHN	B737-8AS/W	33577/1782	☐	EI-DWV	B737-8AS/W	33627/2492
☐	EI-DHO	B737-8AS/W	33578/1792	☐	EI-DWW	B737-8AS/W	33629/2507
☐	EI-DHP	B737-8AS/W	33579/1794	☐	EI-DWX	B737-8AS/W	33630/2508
☐	EI-DHR	B737-8AS/W	33822/1798	☐	EI-DWY	B737-8AS/W	33638/2518
☐	EI-DHS	B737-8AS/W	33580/1807	☐	EI-DWZ	B737-8AS/W	33628/2520
☐	EI-DHT	B737-8AS/W	33581/1809	☐	EI-DYA	B737-8AS/W	33631/2529
☐	EI-DHV	B737-8AS/W	33582/1811	☐	EI-DYB	B737-8AS/W	33633/2542
☐	EI-DHW	B737-8AS/W	33823/1819	☐	EI-DYC	B737-8AS/W	36567/2543
☐	EI-DHX	B737-8AS/W	33585/1824	☐	EI-DYD	B737-8AS/W	33632/2544
☑	EI-DHY	B737-8AS/W	33824/1826	☑	EI-DYE	B737-8AS/W	36568/2548
☐	EI-DHZ	B737-8AS/W	33583/1834	☐	EI-DYF	B737-8AS/W	36569/2549
☑	EI-DLB	B737-8AS/W	33584/1836	☐	EI-DYH	B737-8AS/W	36570/2573
☐	EI-DLC	B737-8AS/W	33586/1844	☐	EI-DYI	B737-8AS/W	36571/2574
☐	EI-DLD	B737-8AS/W	33825/1847	☐	EI-DYJ	B737-8AS/W	36572/2580
☐	EI-DLE	B737-8AS/W	33587/1864	☐	EI-DYK	B737-8AS/W	36573/2581
☐	EI-DLF	B737-8AS/W	33588/1867	☐	EI-DYL	B737-8AS/W	36574/2635
☐	EI-DLG	B737-8AS/W	33589/1869	☐	EI-DYM	B737-8AS/W	36575/2636
☑	EI-DLH	B737-8AS/W	33590/1886	☐	EI-DYN	B737-8AS/W	36576/2367
☐	EI-DLI	B737-8AS/W	33591/1894	☐	EI-DYO	B737-8AS/W	33636/2728
☐	EI-DLJ	B737-8AS/W	34177/1899	☑	EI-DYP	B737-8AS/W	37515/2729
☐	EI-DLK	B737-8AS/W	33592/1904	☐	EI-DYR	B737-8AS/W	37513/2734
☐	EI-DLL	B737-8AS/W	33593/1914	☑	EI-DYS	B737-8AS/W	37514/2735
☐	EI-DLM	B737-8AS/W	33694/1923	☐	EI-DYT	B737-8AS/W	33634/2745
☐	EI-DLN	B737-8AS/W	33595/1926	☐	EI-DYV	B737-8AS/W	37512/2746
☐	EI-DLO	B737-8AS/W	34178/1929	☐	EI-DYW	B737-8AS/W	33635/2747
☐	EI-DLR	B737-8AS/W	33596/2057	☐	EI-DYX	B737-8AS/W	33517/2754
☐	EI-DLS	B737-8AS/W	33621/2058	☐	EI-DYY	B737-8AS/W	37521/2755
☐	EI-DLT	B737-8AS/W	33597/2060	☐	EI-DYZ	B737-8AS/W	37518/2760
☐	EI-DLV	B737-8AS/W	33598/2063	☐	EI-EBA	B737-8AS/W	37516/2761
☐	EI-DLW	B737-8AS/W	33599/2078	☐	EI-EBB	B737-8AS/W	37519/2779
☐	EI-DLX	B737-8AS/W	33600/2082	☐	EI-EBC	B737-8AS/W	37520/2780
☐	EI-DLY	B737-8AS/W	33601/2088	☐	EI-EBD	B737-8AS/W	37522/2781
☐	EI-DLZ	B737-8AS/W	33622/2101	☑	EI-EBE	B737-8AS/W	37523/2788
☑	EI-DPA	B737-8AS/W	33602/2109	☐	EI-EBF	B737-8AS/W	37524/2791
☐	EI-DPB	B737-8AS/W	33603/2112	☑	EI-EBG	B737-8AS/W	37525/2792
☐	EI-DPC	B737-8AS/W	33604/2120	☐	EI-EBH	B737-8AS/W	37526/2797
☑	EI-DPD	B737-8AS/W	33623/2123	☐	EI-EBI	B737-8AS/W	37527/2798
☐	EI-DPE	B737-8AS/W	33605/2140	☐	EI-EBK	B737-8AS/W	37528/2807
☐	EI-DPF	B737-8AS/W	33606/2158	☐	EI-EBL	B737-8AS/W	37529/2808
☐	EI-DPG	B737-8AS/W	33607/2163	☐	EI-EBM	B737-8AS/W	35002/2839
☐	EI-DPH	B737-8AS/W	33624/2168	☐	EI-EBN	B737-8AS/W	35003/2840
☐	EI-DPI	B737-8AS/W	33608/2173	☐	EI-EBO	B737-8AS/W	35004/2843
☐	EI-DPJ	B737-8AS/W	33609/2179	☐	EI-EBP	B737-8AS/W	37531/2844
☐	EI-DPK	B737-8AS/W	33610/2183	☑	EI-EBR	B737-8AS/W	37530/2856
☑	EI-DPL	B737-8AS/W	33611/2189	☐	EI-EBS	B737-8AS/W	35001/2857
☐	EI-DPM	B737-8AS/W	33640/2198	☑	EI-EBT	B737-8AS/W	35000/2858
☐	EI-DPN	B737-8AS/W	33549/2200	☐	EI-EBV	B737-8AS/W	35009/2872
☑	EI-DPO	B737-8AS/W	33612/2207	☐	EI-EBW	B737-8AS/W	35010/2873
☐	EI-DPP	B737-8AS/W	33613/2213	☐	EI-EBX	B737-8AS/W	35007/2882
☐	EI-DPR	B737-8AS/W	33614/2219	☐	EI-EBY	B737-8AS/W	35006/2886
☐	EI-DPS	B737-8AS/W	33641/2222	☐	EI-EBZ	B737-8AS/W	35008/2887
☐	EI-DPT	B737-8AS/W	35550/2227	☐	EI-EFA	B737-8AS/W	35005/2892
☐	EI-DPV	B737-8AS/W	35551/2236	☐	EI-EFB	B737-8AS/W	37532/2893
☐	EI-DPW	B737-8AS/W	35552/2263	☑	EI-EFC	B737-8AS/W	35015/2901
☐	EI-DPX	B737-8AS/W	35553/2279	☐	EI-EFD	B737-8AS/W	35011/2903
☐	EI-DPY	B737-8AS/W	33615/2375	☐	EI-EFE	B737-8AS/W	37533/2905

	Reg	Type	C/n	Notes
■	EI-EFF	B737-8AS/W	35016/2917	*25/2.*
□	EI-EFG	B737-8AS/W	35014/2921	
□	EI-EFH	B737-8AS/W	35012/2923	
□	EI-EFI	B737-8AS/W	35013/2924	
□	EI-EFJ	B737-8AS/W	37536/2936	
□	EI-EFK	B737-8AS/W	37537/2948	
□	EI-EFL	B737-8AS/W	37534/2958	
□	EI-EFM	B737-8AS/W	37535/2960	
□	EI-EFN	B737-8AS/W	37538/2967	
□	EI-EFO	B737-8AS/W	37539/2978	
□	EI-EFP	B737-8AS/W	37540/2979	
□	EI-EFR	B737-8AS/W	37541/3012	
□	EI-EFS	B737-8AS/W	37542/3021	
□	EI-EFT	B737-8AS/W	37543/3023	
□	EI-EFV	B737-8AS/W	35017/3052	
□	EI-EFW	B737-8AS/W	35018/3078	
□	EI-EFX	B737-8AS/W	35019/3079	
■	EI-EFY	B737-8AS/W	35020/3084	*18/2.*
□	EI-EFZ	B737-8AS/W	38489/3089	
□	EI-EGA	B737-8AS/W	38490/3096	
□	EI-EGB	B737-8AS/W	38491/3097	
□	EI-EGC	B737-8AS/W	38492/3099	
□	EI-EGD	B737-8AS/W	34981/3420	♦
□	EI-EKA	B737-8AS/W	35022/3139	
□	EI-EKB	B737-8AS/W	38494/3141	
□	EI-EKC	B737-8AS/W	38495/3143	
□	EI-EKD	B737-8AS/W	35024/3146	
■	EI-EKE	B737-8AS/W	35023/3148	*1/3.*
□	EI-EKF	B737-8AS/W	35025/3152	
□	EI-EKG	B737-8AS/W	35021/3161	
□	EI-EKH	B737-8AS/W	38493/3162	
□	EI-EKI	B737-8AS/W	38496/3168	♦
□	EI-EKJ	B737-8AS/W	38497/3173	♦
□	EI-EKK	B737-8AS/W	38500/3174	♦
□	EI-EKL	B737-8AS/W	38498/3179	♦
■	EI-EKM	B737-8AS/W	38499/3181	*6/9*
■	EI-EKN	B737-8AS/W	35026/3187	♦
□	EI-EKO	B737-8AS/W	35027/3198	♦
□	EI-EKP	B737-8AS/W	35028/3199	♦
■	EI-EKR	B737-8AS/W	38503/3202	*17/3* ♦
□	EI-EKS	B737-8AS/W	38504/3203	♦
□	EI-EKT	B737-8AS/W	38505/3206	♦
□	EI-EKV	B737-8AS/W	38507/3211	♦
□	EI-EKW	B737-8AS/W	38506/3220	♦
□	EI-EKX	B737-8AS/W	35030/3221	♦
□	EI-EKY	B737-8AS/W	35031/3230	♦
□	EI-EKZ	B737-8AS/W	38508/3234	♦
□	EI-EMA	B737-8AS/W	35032/3240	♦
□	EI-EMB	B737-8AS/W	35811/3241	♦
□	EI-EMC	B737-8AS/W	35810/3246	♦
□	EI-EMD	B737-8AS/W	35809/3248	♦
□	EI-EME	B737-8AS/W	35029/3254	♦
■	EI-EMF	B737-8AS/W	34978/3256	*18. of. 14f* ♦
□	EI-EMH	B737-8AS/W	34974/3262	♦
□	EI-EMI	B737-8AS/W	34979/3263	♦
□	EI-EMJ	B737-8AS/W	34975/3271	♦
□	EI-EMK	B737-8AS/W	38512/3272	♦
□	EI-EML	B737-8AS/W	38513/3283	♦
□	EI-EMM	B737-8AS/W	38514/3284	♦
□	EI-EMN	B737-8AS/W	38515/3285	♦
□	EI-EMO	B737-8AS/W	40283/3318	♦
□	EI-EMP	B737-8AS/W	40285/3322	♦
■	EI-EMR	B737-8AS/W	40284/3323	*30/1* ♦
□	EI-ENA	B737-8AS/W	34983/3416	♦
□	EI-ENB	B737-8AS/W	40289/3418	♦
□	EI-ENC	B737-8AS/W	34980/3419	♦
□	EI-ENE	B737-8AS/W	34976/3428	♦
□	EI-ENF	B737-8AS/W	35034/3451	♦
□	EI-ENG	B737-8AS/W	34977/3453	♦
□	EI-ENH	B737-8AS/W	35033/3454	♦
□	EI-ENI	B737-8AS/W	40300/3514	♦
□	EI-ENJ	B737-8AS/W	40301/3516	♦
□	EI-ENK	B737-8AS/W	40303/3524	♦
■	EI-ENL	B737-8AS/W	35037/3527	♦
□	EI-ENM	B737-8AS/W	35038/3528	♦

	Reg	Type	C/n	Notes
□	EI-ENN	B737-8AS/W	35036/3533	♦
■	EI-ENO	B737-8AS/W	40302/3534	♦
□	EI-ENP	B737-8AS/W	40304/3535	♦
□	EI-ENR	B737-8AS/W	35041/3538	♦
□	EI-ENS	B737-8AS/W	40307/3541	♦
□	EI-ENT	B737-8AS/W	35040/3544	o/o♦
□	EI-ENV	B737-8AS/W	35039/3546	o/o♦
□	EI-ENW	B737-8AS/W	40306/3551	o/o♦
□	EI-ENX	B737-8AS/W	40305/3556	o/o♦
□	EI-ENY	B737-8AS/W	35042/3559	o/o♦
□	EI-ENZ	B737-8AS/W	40308/3561	o/o♦
□	EI-EPA	B737-8AS/W	34987/3568	o/o♦
■	EI-EPB	B737-8AS/W	34986/3570	o/o♦ *2/9*
□	EI-EPC	B737-8AS/W	40312/3574	o/o♦
□	EI-EPD	B737-8AS/W		o/o♦
□	EI-EPE	B737-8AS/W		o/o♦
□	EI-EPF	B737-8AS/W		o/o♦
□	EI-EPG	B737-8AS/W		o/o♦
□	EI-EPH	B737-8AS/W		o/o♦
■	EI-*ESR.*	B737-8AS/W	*9/7.*	o/o♦
■	EI-*ESL.*	B737-8AS/W	*23/3*	o/o♦
■	EI-*ESM.*	B737-8AS/W	*15/3*	o/o♦
■	EI-*ESY*	B737-8AS/W	*25/3*	o/o♦
■	EI-*EVL.*	B737-8AS/W	*27/3*	o/o♦

EK - ARMENIA

AIR ARMENIA — QN / ARR

	Reg	Type	C/n	Notes
□	EK-11001	An-12TBK	8346107	
□	EK-12104	An-12BK	8346104	

AIR ARMENIA CARGO

	Reg	Type	C/n	Notes
□	EK-11810	An-12BP	5342908	

AIR HIGHNESSES — HNS

	Reg	Type	C/n	Notes
□	EK-12006	An-12B	1348006	
□	EK-12908	An-12B	7344908	
□	EK-76300	Il-76TD	083410300	
□	EK-76310	Il-76T	1013409310	♦

ARARAT INTERNATIONAL AIRLINES

	Reg	Type	C/n	Notes
□	EK-82224	MD-82	53224/2084	>IRK♦
□	EK-85852	MD-82	49852/1959	

ARK AIRWAYS

	Reg	Type	C/n	Notes
□	EK-76555	Il-76TD	1033416515	♦

ARMAVIA — U8 / RNV

	Reg	Type	C/n	Notes
□	EK-RA01	A319-132	0913	Opf Govt
□	EK-32007	A319-111	3834	
□	EK-32011	A319-132	2277	
□	EK-32012	A319-132	2362	
□	EK-32005	A320-211	3492	
□	EK-32006	A320-214	0772	♦
□	EK-32008	A320-211	0229	
□	EK-20014	CRJ-200LR	7282	
□	EK-86118	Il-86	51483209086	
□	EK-95015	Sukhoi Superjet 100	95007	o/o♦
□	EK-	Sukhoi Superjet 100	95008	o/o♦
□	EK-65072	Tu-134A-3	49972	Opf Govt
□	EK-42362	Yak-42D	48111431	
□	EK-42417	Yak-42D	3219110	
□	EK-42470	Yak-42D	4520424116677	♦

AYKAVIA

	Reg	Type	C/n	Notes
□	EK-32410	An-32	2416	

☐ EK-74027	An-74-200	36547096920	
☐ EK-74043	An-74-200	36547096923	

BLUE SKY   BLM

☐ EK-30044	A300B2K-3C	244	>IRM
☐ EK-30060	A300B2K-3C	160	>IRM
☐ EK-74763	B747-422	24363/740	
☐ EP-MNC	B747-422	26879/973	>IRM

CENTRAL AIRWAYS

☐ EK-26443	An-26	17311705	

MIAPET AVIA   MPT

☐ EK-11660	An-12BP	5343209	

NAVIGATOR AIRLINES

☐ EK-26440	An-26	57303504	

PHOENIX AVIA   PHY

☐ EK-11007	An-12	5343506	
☐ EK-12148	An-12BK	4341906	
☐ EK-12803	An-12B	1347803	
☐ EK-46419	An-24B	87303704	
☐ EK-46741	An-12BK	8345408	
☐ EK-46839	An-24T	7910201	
☐ EK-76464	Il-76TD	0023437090	♦

SOUTH AIRLINES   STH

☐ EK-11112	An-12BP	5343307	
☐ EK-11779	An-12BP	5343402	
☐ EK-12122	An-12BP	5343507	
☐ EK-12305	An-12BP	347305	
☐ EK-26441	An-26	57303009	
☐ EK-46507	An-24RV	37308403	
☐ EK-46656	An-24RV	47309302	
☐ EK-47828	An-24B	17307209	
☐ EK-72101	An-72-100	36572040548	
☐ EK-74045	An-74-200	36547098966	
☐ EK-76707	Il-76TD	0073410292	
☐ EK-76717	Il-76TD	0043450484	
☐ EK-76727	Il-76TD	0063467021	
☐ EK-76737	Il-76MD	0083483502	

TARON AVIA   TRV

☐ EK-12005	An-12BP	5343005	
☐ EK-12129	An-12BP	5342903	
☐ EK-76643	Il-76TD	0083488643	♦

VERTIR   VRZ

☐ EK-31095	A310-304	595	
☐ EK-74711	B747-SR81	22711/559	♦

VETERAN AIRLINE   RVT

☐ EK-46513	An-24RV	37308409	
☐ EK-74798	B747-281BSF	23698/667	♦
☐ EK-76381	Il-76MD	1033418596	♦

EP - IRAN

ARIA AIR   IRX

☐ EP-EAF	Fokker 50	20235	
☐ EP-EAH	Fokker 50	20234	

ATA AIR

☐ UR-CDN	MD-83	53520/2137	<KHO♦
☐ UR-CHM	MD-83	53465/2093	<KHO♦
☐ UR-CHP	MD-83	53466/2101	<KHO♦
☐ UR-CHQ	MD-83	53488/2134	<KHO♦

CASPIAN AIRLINES   RV / CPN

☐ EP-CPN	Tu-154M	91A898	
☐ EP-CPO	Tu-154M	91A899	
☐ EP-CPS	Tu-154M	93A957	
☐ UR-BHJ	MD-83	53184/2088	<UKM
☐ UR-CHN	MD-83	49938/1785	<UKM♦

CHABAHAR AIR   IRU

☐ EP-CFM	Fokker 100	11394	>IRA
☐ EP-CFN	Fokker 100	11423	>IRA
☐ EP-CFO	Fokker 100	11389	>IRA
☐ EP-CFP	Fokker 100	11409	>IRA
☐ EP-CFQ	Fokker 100	11429	>IRA
☐ EP-CFR	Fokker 100	11383	>IRA

ERAM AIR   YE / IRY

☐ EP-EKA	Tu-154M	92A912	<OMS
☐ EP-EKB	Tu-154M	92A946	<OMS
☐ EP-EKC	Tu-154M	89A799	
☐ EP-EKE	Tu-154M	92A940	<NKZ

FARS AIR   QFZ

☐ EP-QFA	Yak-42D	2007108	
☐ EP-QFB	Yak-42D	2003109	

IRAN AIR   IR / IRA

☐ EP-IBA	A300B4-605R	723	
☐ EP-IBB	A300B4-605R	727	
☐ EP-IBC	A300B4-605R	632	
☐ EP-IBD	A300B4-605R	696	
☐ EP-IBG	A300B4-203F	299	
☐ EP-IBH	A300B4-203F	302	
☐ EP-IBI	A300B4-2C	151	
☐ EP-IBJ	A300B4-2C	256	
☐ EP-IBS	A300B2-203	080	
☐ EP-IBT	A300B2-203	185	
☐ EP-IBV	A300B2-203	187	
☐ EP-IBZ	A300B2-203	226	
☐ EP-ICE	A300B4-203F	139	
☐ EP-IBK	A310-304	671	
☐ EP-IBL	A310-304	436	
☐ EP-IBM	A310-203	338	
☐ EP-IBN	A310-203	375	
☐ EP-IBP	A310-203	370	
☐ EP-IBQ	A310-203	389	[THR]
☐ EP-IBX	A310-203	390	[THR]
☐ EP-IEA	A320-232	0530	
☐ EP-IEB	A320-232	0575	
☐ EP-IEC	A320-232	0857	
☐ EP-IED	A320-212	0345	
☐ EP-IEE	A320-211	0303	
☐ EP-IEF	A320-211	0312	
☐ EP-IEG	A320-211	2054	
☐ EP-IRR	B727-286	20946/1052	
☐ EP-IRS	B727-286	20947/1070	
☐ EP-IRT	B727-286	21078/1114	
☐ EP-IAA	B747SP-86	20998/275	
☐ EP-IAB	B747SP-86	20999/278	
☐ EP-IAC	B747SP-86	21093/307	
☐ EP-IAD	B747SP-86	21758/371	

☐ EP-IAG	B747-286M	21217/291	
☐ EP-IAH	B747-286M	21218/300	
☐ EP-IAI	B747-230M	22670/550	
☐ EP-IAM	B747-186B	21759/381	
☐ EP-ICD	B747-21AC	24134/712	
☐ EP-AWZ	Fokker 100	11497	
☐ EP-CFD	Fokker 100	11442	
☐ EP-CFE	Fokker 100	11422	
☐ EP-CFH	Fokker 100	11443	
☐ EP-CFI	Fokker 100	11511	
☐ EP-CFJ	Fokker 100	11516	
☐ EP-CFK	Fokker 100	11518	
☐ EP-CFL	Fokker 100	11343	
☐ EP-CFM	Fokker 100	11394	<IRU
☐ EP-CFN	Fokker 100	11423	<IRU
☐ EP-CFO	Fokker 100	11389	<IRU
☐ EP-CFP	Fokker 100	11409	<IRU
☐ EP-CFQ	Fokker 100	11429	<IRU
☐ EP-IDA	Fokker 100	11292	
☐ EP-IDD	Fokker 100	11294	
☐ EP-IDF	Fokker 100	11298	
☐ EP-IDG	Fokker 100	11302	
☐ UR-CHW	MD-82	49510/1514	
☐ UR-CHX	MD-82	53162/2010	[THR]

IRAN AIR TOUR AIRLINE — B9 / IRB

☐ UR-BXM	MD-82	49505/1381	♦
☐ EP-MBQ	Tu-154M	92A931	<NKZ
☐ EP-MBT	Tu-154M	92A930	<NKZ
☐ EP-MCJ	Tu-154M	89A800	
☐ EP-MCL	Tu-154M	91A880	
☐ EP-MCM	Tu-154M	90A855	
☐ EP-MCN	Tu-154M	88A792	
☐ EP-MCO	Tu-154M	88A774	
☐ EP-MCP	Tu-154M	85A724	
☐ EP-MCS	Tu-154M	88A795	
☐ EP-MCT	Tu-154M	90A860	
☐ EP-MCU	Tu-154M	93A977	
☐ EP-MCV	Tu-154M	85A706	
☐ EP-MCX	Tu-154M	85A707	
☐ EP-	Tu-204-100		o/o
☐ EP-	Tu-204-100		o/o

IRAN ASEMAN AIRLINES — EP / IRC

☐ EP-ATA	ATR 72-212	334	
☐ EP-ATI	ATR 72-212	339	
☐ EP-ATS	ATR 72-212	391	
☐ EP-ATU	ATR 72-212A	697	
☐ EP-ATX	ATR 72-212A	573	
☐ EP-ATZ	ATR 72-212	398	
☐ EP-ASA	B727-228	22081/1594	
☐ EP-ASB	B727-228	22082/1603	
☐ EP-ASC	B727-228	22084/1638	
☐ EP-ASD	B727-228	22085/1665	
☐ EP-ASG	Fokker 100	11438	[DNR]
☐ EP-ASI	Fokker 100	11519	
☐ EP-ASJ	Fokker 100	11378	
☐ EP-ASK	Fokker 100	11388	
☐ EP-ASM	Fokker 100	11433	
☐ EP-ASO	Fokker 100	11454	
☐ EP-ASP	Fokker 100	11504	
☐ EP-ASQ	Fokker 100	11513	
☐ EP-ASR	Fokker 100	11522	
☐ EP-AST	Fokker 100	11523	
☐ EP-ASU	Fokker 100	11430	
☐ EP-ASX	Fokker 100	11431	>IRK
☐ EP-ASZ	Fokker 100	11421	
☐ EP-ATB	Fokker 100	11401	
☐ EP-ATC	Fokker 100	11296	♦

☐ EP-ATD	Fokker 100	11387	♦
☐ EP-ATF	Fokker 100	11476	♦
☐ EP-ATG	Fokker 100	11329	♦

KISH AIR — Y9 / IRK

☐ EP-LBV	Fokker 50	20158	
☐ EP-LCB	Fokker 50	20274	
☐ EP-LCC	Fokker 50	20275	
☐ EP-LCE	Fokker 50	20265	
☐ EP-LCF	Fokker 50	20263	
☐ EP-LCG	Fokker 50	20236	
☐ EP-ASX	Fokker 100	11431	<IRC
☐ EK-82224	MD-82	53224/2084	♦
☐ EP-LCI	MD-83	49844/1579	<KHO
☐ UR-BXN	MD-83	49569/1405	<KHO
☐ UR-CHS	MD-83	49572/1468	<KHO
☐ EP-LBR	Tu-154M	90A838	
☐ EP-LBS	Tu-154M	91A901	

MAHAN AIR — W5 / IRM

☐ EK-30044	A300B2K-3C	244	
☐ EK-30060	A300B2K-3C	160	
☐ EP-MHF	A300B4-103	55	
☐ EP-MHG	A300B4-203	204	
☐ EP-MHL	A300B4-203	175	
☐ EP-MHM	A300B2K-3C	90	<SGX
☐ EP-MNG	A300B4-603	401	♦
☐ EP-MNI	A300B4-603	405	♦
☐ EP-MNJ	A300B4-603	380	♦
☐ EP-MNK	A300B4-603	618	♦
☐ EP-MNM	A300B4-605R	773	♦
☐ EP-MNN	A300B4-605R	701	♦
☐ EP-MNQ	A300B4-603	553	
☐ EP-MNR	A300B4-603	411	
☐ EP-MNS	A300B4-603	414	
☐ EP-MNT	A300B4-603	546	
☐ EP-MNU	A300B4-605R	608	
☐ EP-	A300B4-601	368	o/o ♦
☐ EP-MHO	A310-304	488	
☐ EP-MNX	A310-304	564	
☐ EX-301	A310-304	524	<KTC
☐ EX-35003	A310-304	567	<KTC
☐ EX-35004	A310-308	620	<KTC
☐ F-OJHH	A310-304ER	586	
☐ F-OJHI	A310-304ER	537	
☐ EP-MNA	B747-422	24383/811	
☐ EP-MNB	B747-422	24363/740	
☐ EP-MNC	B747-422	26879/973	
☐ EP-MND	B747-3B3 (SCD)	23413/632	
☐ EP-MNE	B747-3B3 (SCD)	23480/641	
☐ EX-27000	BAe146 Srs.300	E3216	
☐ EX-27001	BAe146 Srs.300	E3212	

NAFT AIR — IRG

☐ EP-GAS	Fokker 50	20224	
☐ EP-MIS	Fokker 100	11503	
☐ EP-NFT	Fokker 50	20220	
☐ EP-OIL	Fokker 50	20222	
☐ EP-OPI	Fokker 100	11509	
☐ EP-PET	Fokker 50	20283	
☐ EP-SUS	Fokker 100	11487	

PAYAM INTERNATIONAL AIR — 2F / IRP

☐ EP-	B727-222F	21920/1634	
☐ EP-	B727-222F	21917/1616	

QESHM AIR — IRQ

☐ JY-JRF	B767-233	22526/92	

SAFAT AIRLINES			IRV
☐ EP-SAJ	An-26	57314002	
☐ EP-SAK	An-26	57314001	

SAFIRAN AIRLINES			SFN
☐ EP-SFD	Ir.An-140	9001	
☐ EP-SFE	Ir.An-140	9002	
☐ EP-SFF	Ir.An-140	9003	
☐ EP-	Ir.An-140		o/o

SAHA AIRLINE			IRZ
☐ EP-SIF	A300B4-622R	762	♦
☐ EP-SIG	A300B4-622R	750	♦
☐ EP-SHG	B707-3J9C	20830/876	
☐ EP-SHK	B707-3J9C	21128/917	
☐ EP-SHU	B707-3J9C	21126/914	[THR]
☐ EP-SHV	B707-3J9C	21125/912	

TABAN AIR			TBM
☐ LZ-HBD	BAe146 Srs.300	E3141	<HMS
☐ LZ-HBZ	BAe146 Srs.200	E2103	<HMS
☐ EK-82523	MD-82	49523/1724	♦
☐ EK-82524	MD-82	49524/1746	♦
☐ EP-TBA	Tu-154M	97A1008	
☐ RA-85761	Tu-154M	93A944	<KGL

YAS AIR			
☐ EP-GOL	Il-76	1013409297	
☐ EP-GOM	Il-76TD	1023409321	
☐ EP-GOQ	An-74-200	365470991021	

ZAGROS AIRLINES			IZG
☐ SX-BTM	MD-83	49627/1580	
☐ UR-CDQ	MD-82	49372/1252	<KHO

ER - MOLDOVA

AERIANTUR-M AIRLINES			MBV
☐ ER-AXI	An-12B	6344310	

AIR MOLDOVA			9U / MLD
☐ ER-AXP	A320-233	0741	
☐ ER-AXV	A320-211	0622	
☐ ER-YGD	Yak-40D	9831458Opf Govt	
☐ ER-65140	Tu-134A-3	60932Opf Govt	

AIRLINK ARABIA			
☐ ER-AZX	An-24RV	47309804	

GRIXONA			
☐ ER-ICS	IL-18D	187009903	

MOLDOVIAN AIRLINES			2M / MDV
☐ ER-FZA	Fokker 100	11395	
☐ ER-SFA	SAAB 2000	2000-056	<SWR
☐ ER-SFB	SAAB 2000	2000-022	

TEPAVIA TRANS AIRLINE			TET
☐ ER-AJC	WSK-PZL/An-28	1AJ003-12	
☐ ER-AWM	An-32B	3009	
☐ ER-AZW	An-32A	2109	
☐ ER-LIC	LET L-410UVP	820904	

☐ ER-LID	LET L-410UVP-E	902437	

ES - ESTONIA

AIREST			AIT
☐ ES-LLB	LET L-410UVP-E20C	912608	
☐ ES-LLC	LET L-410UVP-E20C	912609	

AVIES AIR COMPANY			U3 / AIA
☐ ES-PJG	BAeJetstream 31	701	
☐ ES-PJR	BAeJetstream 32EP	949	
☐ ES-PLB	LET L-410UVP	851413	
☐ LY-PCL	LET L-410UVP-E	892335	

ENIMEX			ENI
☐ ES-NOB	An-72-100	36572070695	
☐ ES-NOH	An-72-100	36572095909	
☐ ES-NOI	An-72-100	36572096914	
☐ ES-NOK	An-72-100	36572090780	

ESTONIAN AIR			OV / ELL
☐ ES-ABJ	B737-33R	28873/2975	
☐ ES-ABK	B737-36N	28572/3031	
☐ ES-ABL	B737-5L9	28997/3008	
☐ ES-ABO	B737-505	24646/2138	♦
☐ ES-ABP	B737-5L9	27425/2730	♦
☐ ES-ACB	CRJ-900ER	15261	♦
☐ ES-ACC	CRJ-900ER	15262	♦

ESTONIAN AIR REGIONAL			OV / ELL
☐ ES-ASM	SAAB SF.340A	340A-132	
☐ ES-ASN	SAAB SF.340A	340A-151	

FLYLAL CHARTERS EESTI			
☐ ES-LBD	B737-35B	25069/2053	

JP AIR CARGO			
☐ ES-JFA	SA.227AC Metro III	AC-657	

ET - ETHIOPIA

ETHIOPIAN AIRLINES			ET / ETH
☐ ET-ALK	B737-760/W	33764/1408	
☐ ET-ALM	B737-760/W	33765/1539	
☐ ET-ALN	B737-760/W	33766/1757	
☐ ET-ALQ	B737-76N/W	33420/1459	
☐ ET-ALU	B737-76N/W	32741/1487	
☐ ET-AMZ	B737-8BK/W	29646/2282	
☐ ET-ANA	B737-86R/W	30494/786	
☐ ET-ANG	B737-7K9/W	34401/2216	>SKK♦
☐ ET-ANH	B737-7K9/W	34402/2270	>SKK♦
☐ ET-ANZ	B737-8HO/W	37933/3437	♦
☐ ET-AOA	B737-8HO/W	37936/3459	♦
☐ ET-AOB	B737-8HO/W	37937/3467	♦
☐ ET-	B737-8HO/W		o/o♦
☐ ET-AOK	B737-790/W	33012/1206	>SKK♦
☐ ET-AJS	B757-260PF	24845/300	
☐ ET-AJX	B757-260 (PCF)	25014/348	
☐ ET-AKC	B757-260	25353/408	
☐ ET-AKE	B757-260ER	26057/444	
☐ ET-AKF	B757-260ER	26058/496	
☐ ET-ALY	B757-231	28480/750	
☐ ET-ALZ	B757-231	30319/883	
☐ ET-AMK	B757-23N	32449/974	
☐ ET-AMT	B757-23N	27976/814	
☐ ET-AMU	B757-23N	27975/779	

☐	ET-ALC	B767-33AER	28043/734
☐	ET-ALH	B767-3BGER	30565/802
☐	ET-ALJ	B767-360ER	33767/918
☐	ET-ALL	B767-3BGER	30564/798
☐	ET-ALO	B767-360ER	33768/922
☐	ET-ALP	B767-360ER	33769/933
☐	ET-AME	B767-306ER	27611/633
☐	ET-AMF	B767-3BGER	30563/786
☐	ET-AMG	B767-3BGER	30566/817
☐	ET-AMQ	B767-33AER	27909/591
☐	ET-ANN	B777-260LR	40770/900 ♦
☐	ET-ANO	B777-260LR	40771/908 ♦
☐	ET-ANP	B777-260LR	40772/914 ♦
☐	ET-	B777-260LR	o/o♦
☐	ET-	B777-260LR	o/o♦
☐	ET-	B787-860	o/o♦
☐	ET-	B787-860	o/o♦
☐	ET-	B787-860	o/o♦
☐	ET-	B787-860	o/o♦
☐	ET-AIT	DHC-6 Twin Otter 310	820
☐	ET-AIX	DHC-6 Twin Otter 300	835
☐	ET-ANI	DHC-8-402Q	4299 ♦
☐	ET-ANJ	DHC-8-402Q	4303 ♦
☐	ET-ANK	DHC-8-402Q	4304 ♦
☐	ET-ANL	DHC-8-402Q	4307 ♦
☐	ET-ANV	DHC-8-402Q	4317 ♦
☐	ET-ANW	DHC-8-402Q	4320 >SKK♦
☐	ET-ANX	DHC-8-402Q	4330 ♦
☐	ET-AKR	Fokker 50	20313
☐	ET-AKS	Fokker 50	20328
☐	ET-AKT	Fokker 50	20331
☐	ET-AKU	Fokker 50	20333
☐	ET-AKV	Fokker 50	20335
☐	ET-AML	MD-11ERF	48758/615
☐	ET-AND	MD-11BCF	48780/624

TRANS NATION AIRWAYS   TNW

☐	ET-AKZ	DHC-8-202	469	>ETC
☐	ET-ALX	DHC-8-202	475	>RWD

EW - BELARUS

BELAVIA BELARUSSIAN AIRLINES   B2 / BRU

☐	EW-250PA	B737-524	26319/2748	
☐	EW-251PA	B737-5Q8	27634/2889	
☐	EW-252PA	B737-524	26340/2777	
☐	EW-253PA	B737-524	26339/2771	
☐	EW-254PA	B737-3Q8	26294/2550	
☐	EW-282PA	B737-3Q8	26321/2764	
☐	EW-283PA	B737-3Q8	26333/2786	
☐	EW-290PA	B737-522	27629/2834	
☐	EW-294PA	B737-505	26338/2822 ♦	
☐	EW-001PA	B737-8EV/W	33079/1075	BBJ2
☐	EW-100PJ	CRJ-200LR	7309	
☐	EW-276PJ	CRJ-200ER	7799	
☐	EW-277PJ	CRJ-200ER	7852	
☐	EW-85703	Tu-154M	91A878	
☐	EW-85706	Tu-154M	91A881	
☐	EW-85741	Tu-154M	91A896	
☐	EW-85748	Tu-154M	92A924	
☐	EW-85815	Tu-154M	95A1010	VIP
☐	EW-88187	Yak-40	9620748	Opf Govt

GENEX

☐	EW-246TG	An-26B	67314403

☐	EW-259TG	An-26B	27312706
☐	EW-278TG	An-26	13306

GOMELAVIA   YD / GOM

☐	EW-245TI	An-12BP	06344608	
☐	EW-46250	An-24B	77303208	[GME]
☐	EW-46304	An-24B	97305304	[GME]
☐	EW-46631	An-24RV	37308810	
☐	EW-47697	An-24RV	27307604	

RUBYSTAR   RSB

☐	EW-275TI	An-12BK	347210
☐	EW-47808	An-24RV	17306910

TRANS AVIA EXPORT CARGO AL   AL / TXC

☐	EW-269TI	An-12BP	1340106	
☐	EW-76710	Il-76TD	63473182	
☐	EW-76711	Il-76TD	63473187	
☐	EW-76712	Il-76TD	63473190	
☐	EW-76735	Il-76TD	73476314	
☐	EW-76737	Il-76TD	73477323	>AYZ
☐	EW-78769	Il-76MD	83487607	
☐	EW-78779	Il-76TD	83489662	>AYZ
☐	EW-78787	Il-76MD	83490698	
☐	EW-78792	Il-76TD	93490718	all-white
☐	EW-78799	Il-76TD	93491754	
☐	EW-78801	Il-76TD	93492763	
☐	EW-78808	Il-76TD	93493794	
☐	EW-78819	Il-76TD	93495883	
☐	EW-78827	Il-76TD	1003499997	
☐	EW-78828	Il-76TD	1003401004	
☐	EW-78836	Il-76TD	93499986	
☐	EW-78839	Il-76TD	1003402047	
☐	EW-78848	Il-76TD	1003405159	

EX - KYRGYZSTAN

AEROVISTA AIRLINES   AAP

☐	EX-007	Yak-40	9640152	all-white
☐	EX-87250	Yak-40	9310726	<TLR
☐	EX-87412	Yak-40	9420434	>TLR
☐	EX-87426	Yak-40	9420235	>TLR
☐	EX-87664	Yak-40	9240825	>TLR
☐	EX-88207	Yak-40K	9631149	>TLR
☐	EX-88270	Yak-40	9720853	>TLR

AIR MANAS   MBB

☐	EX-00002	Tu-154M	91A904

ANIKAYAIR   AKF

☐	EX-405	Il-18D	184007405
☐	EX-601	Il-18E	185008601

AVIA TRAFFIC COMPANY   AVJ

☐	EX-051	An-24RV	57310105	
☐	EX-076	B737-268	20882/356	<ESD
☐	EX-777	B737-268	21654/532	<ESD
☐	EX-27002	BAe146 Srs.200	E2172	♦
☐	EX-27007	BAe146 Srs.200	E2180	♦

BOTIR-AVIA   B8 / BTR

☐	EX-89616	Il-76T	23438120	[SHJ]

BRITISH GULF INTERNATIONAL AL   BGK

☐	S9-SAE	An-12B	402408
☐	S9-SAH	An-12B	5343703

☐ S9-SAJ	An-12TB	401901	
☐ S9-SAM	An-12BP	3341408	[SHJ]
☐ S9-SAP	An-12BP	5343305	
☐ S9-SAR	An-12TA	2340801	
☐ S9-SAV	An-12AP	2340602	

CLICK AIRWAYS — 4C / CGK

☐ EK-11418	An-12BP	7344705	
☐ EX-029	An-12BP	8345607	
☐ EX-169	An-12BP	01348005	
☐ EX-401	An-12		
☐ EX-402	An-12		
☐ EX-403	An-12		
☐ EY-402	An-12B	8346006	
☐ EK-76400	Il-76TD	1023413438	
☐ EX-033	Il-76TD	33446235	
☐ EX-035	Il-76TD	93498962	
☐ EX-036	Il-76TD	93495863	
☐ EY-604	Il-76TD	1023410355	

ESEN AIR — ESD

☐ EX-076	B737-268	20882/356	>AVJ
☐ EX-777	B737-268	21654/532	>AVJ

GALAXY AIRLINES — GAL

☐ EX-786	Il-18V	188011201	
☐ EX-75466	Il-18	187010403	

GARINCO AIRWAYS

☐ EX-87820	Yak-40	9231224	

INTAL AIR — INL

☐ EX-050	B737-229C	21139/437	
☐ EX-061	B737-2S2C	21927/600	
☐ EX-081	B737-268	21283/477	
☐ EX-201	Il-18D	188011201	

ITEK AIR — GI / IKA

☐ EX-127	B737-275	21819/627	
☐ EX-25003	B737-2T5	22632/847	

KYRGYZSTAN — QH / LYN

☐ EX-014	An-24RV	77310807	
☐ EX-020	Tu-134A-3	61042	
☐ EX-24805	An-24RV	77310805	
☐ EX-85718	Tu-154M	91A900	

KYRGHYZSTAN AIRLINES — R8 / KGA

☐ EX-25004	B737-247	23516/1257	
☐ EX-85257	Tu-154B-2	78A257	
☐ EX-85590	Tu-154B-2	84A590	
☐ EX-85762	Tu-154M	92A945	
☐ EX-87538	Yak-40	9530342	
☐ EX-87571	Yak-40	9221521	
☐ EX-87589	Yak-40	9220123	

KYRGYZ AIRWAYS — EAV

☐ EX-736	B737-247	23517/1261	♦
☐ EX-32001	A320-212	0445	♦
☐ EX-37001	B737-301	23937/1587	♦
☐ EX-	ATR42-320	213	o/o♦

KYRGYZ TRANS AIR — KTC

☐ EX-301	A310-304	524	>IRM

☐ EX-35003	A310-304	567	>IRM
☐ EX-35004	A310-308	620	>IRM

SKYWAY AIR — SAB

☐ EX-016	An-26	17311207	
☐ EX-126	An-26	11508	

TENIR AIRLINES — TEB

☐ EK-11032	An-12V	7345004	
☐ EX-075	Il-76TD	0053463908	

TRANS AIR

☐ EX-24103	An-24B	7306103	

TRAST AERO — S5 / TSJ

☐ EK-46581	An-24B	97304910	
☐ EX-103	ROMBAC 1-11 561RC	403	
☐ TN-AGB	An-26B-100	87307210	
☐ 3X-GET	An-26B	67304104	
☐ 4L-BKA	An-26B	87306407	
☐ 4L-GAS	B707-379C	19821/718	
☐ 4L-OVA	An-32	1408	

EY - TAJIKSTAN

EAST AIR — EG

☐ EY-321	ATR 42-320	213	♦
☐ EY-532	B737-25A	23791/1486	
☐ EY-538	B737-4Y0	23980/1667	

RUS AVIATION

☐ EY-403	An-12BP	347107	

SOMON AIR

☐ EY-777	B737-8GJ/W	34960/2765	
☐ EY-787	B737-8GJ/W	34955/2512	
☐ OK-TVH	B737-8Q8/W	35275/2604	<TVS♦

TAJIK AIR — 7J / TJK

☐ EY-46365	An-24B	7305906	
☐ EY-45595	An-24B	97305105	
☐ EY-47693	An-24RV	27307510	>DAO
☐ EY-47802	An-24RV	17306901	
☐ EY-65763	Tu-134A-3	62299	
☐ EY-65788	Tu-134A-3	62835	
☐ EY-85651	Tu-154M	88A793	
☐ EY-85691	Tu-154M	90A864	>IRX
☐ EY-85692	Tu-154M	90A865	
☐ EY-85717	Tu-154M	91A897	
☐ EY-87214	Yak-40K	9640851	
☐ EY-87217	Yak-40	9510340	
☐ EY-87434	Yak-40	9431035	
☐ EY-87922	Yak-40K	9731355	
☐ EY-87963	Yak-40K	9831058	>KMF
☐ EY-87967	Yak-40K	9831158	
☐ EY-88267	Yak-40K	9720553	
☐ EY-536	B737-3B7	23700/1461	
☐ LY-AWF	B737-522	26707/2512	
☐ LY-AWG	B737-522	26700/2490	
☐ EY-751	B757-2Q8	24964/424	
☐ EY-26205	An-26B	14107	
☐ EY-26658	An-26	7904	

EZ - TURKMENISTAN

TURKMENISTAN AIRLINES — T5 / ASB

	Reg	Type	C/n
☐	EZ-A101	B717-22K	55153/5072
☐	EZ-A102	B717-22K	55154/5078
☐	EZ-A103	B717-22K	55155/5086
☐	EZ-A104	B717-22K	55195/5130
☐	EZ-A105	B717-22K	55196/5133
☐	EZ-A106	B717-22K	55186/5146
☐	EZ-A107	B717-22K	55187/5147
☐	EZ-A001	B737-341	26855/2305
☐	EZ-A002	B737-332	25994/2439
☐	EZ-A003	B737-332	25995/2455
☐	EZ-A004	B737-82K	36088/2181
☐	EZ-A005	B737-82K	36089/2233
☐	EZ-A006	B737-7GL/W	37236/2986
☐	EZ-A007	B737-7GL/W	37234/2682
☐	EZ-A008	B737-7GL/W	37237/2988
☐	EZ-A009	B737-7GL/W	372352993
☐	EZ-	B737-9	o/o♦
☐	EZ-	B737-9	o/o♦
☐	EZ-A010	B757-23A	25345/412
☐	EZ-A011	B757-22K	28336/725
☐	EZ-A012	B757-22K	28337/726
☐	EZ-A014	B757-22K	30863/952
☐	EZ-A700	B767-32KER	33968/926Opf Govt
☐	EZ-A777	B777-22KLR	39548/889Opf Govt
☐	EZ-F423	Il-76TD	1033418608
☐	EZ-F426	Il-76TD	1033418609
☐	EZ-F427	Il-76TD	1033418620
☐	EZ-F428	Il-76TD	1043418624

E3 - ERITREA

ERITREAN AIRLINES — B8 / ERT

☐	E3-AAQ	B767-238ER	23309/129

NAS AIR

☐	E3-NAD	B737-268	21276/468
☐	E3-NAS	B737-2T5	21960/642

E5 - COOK ISLANDS

AIR RAROTONGA

☐	E5-EFS	SAAB SF.340A	340A-049

E7 - BOSNIA-HERZEGOVINA

BH AIRLINES — JA / BON

☐	E7-AAD	ATR 72-212	464Sarajevo
☐	E7-AAE	ATR 72-212	465 Mostar
☐	TC-JLR	A319-132	3142 <THY♦

ICAR

☐	E7-AAK	LET L410-UVP-E	892321

F - FRANCE

AIGLE AZUR — ZI / AAF

☐	F-GXAH	A319-112	1846
☐	F-HBMI	A319-114	0639
☐	F-GJVF	A320-211	0244

☐	F-HBAC	A320-214	0888
☐	F-HBII	A320-233	3852
☐	F-	A320-214	o/o♦
☐	F-GUAA	A321-211	0808
☐	F-HBAB	A321-211	0823
☐	F-HBAF	A321-211	1006
☐	F-HCAI	A321-211	1451

AIR CORSICA — XK / CCM

☐	F-GYFK	A320-214	0533
☐	F-GYFM	A319-112	1068
☐	F-GYJM	A319-112	1145
☐	F-HBEV	A320-216	3952
☐	F-HBSA	A320-216	3882
☐	F-GRPI	ATR 42-500	722
☐	F-GRPJ	ATR 42-500	724
☐	F-GRPK	ATR 72-212A	727
☐	F-GRPX	ATR 72-212A	734
☐	F-GRPY	ATR 72-212A	742
☐	F-GRPZ	ATR 72-212A	745
☐	F-HAPL	ATR 72-212A	654

AIR FRANCE — AF / AFR

☐	F-GUGA	A318-111	2035
☐	F-GUGB	A318-111	2059
☐	F-GUGC	A318-111	2071
☐	F-GUGD	A318-111	2081
☐	F-GUGE	A318-111	2100
☐	F-GUGF	A318-111	2109
☐	F-GUGG	A318-111	2317
☐	F-GUGH	A318-111	2344
☐	F-GUGI	A318-111	2350
☐	F-GUGJ	A318-111	2582
☐	F-GUGK	A318-111	2601
☐	F-GUGL	A318-111	2686
☐	F-GUGM	A318-111	2750
☐	F-GUGN	A318-111	2918
☐	F-GUGO	A318-111	2951
☐	F-GUGP	A318-111	2967
☐	F-GUGQ	A318-111	2972
☐	F-GUGR	A318-111	3009
☐	F-GPMA	A319-113	0598
☐	F-GPMB	A319-113	0600
☐	F-GPMC	A319-113	0608
☐	F-GPMD	A319-113	0618
☐	F-GPME	A319-113	0625
☐	F-GPMF	A319-113	0637
☐	F-GRHA	A319-111	0938
☐	F-GRHB	A319-111	0985
☐	F-GRHC	A319-111	0998
☐	F-GRHD	A319-111	1000
☐	F-GRHE	A319-111	1020
☐	F-GRHF	A319-111	1025
☐	F-GRHG	A319-111	1036
☐	F-GRHH	A319-111	1151
☐	F-GRHI	A319-111	1169
☐	F-GRHJ	A319-111	1176
☐	F-GRHK	A319-111	1190
☐	F-GRHL	A319-111	1201
☐	F-GRHM	A319-111	1216
☐	F-GRHN	A319-111	1267
☐	F-GRHO	A319-111	1271
☐	F-GRHP	A319-111	1344
☐	F-GRHQ	A319-111	1404
☐	F-GRHR	A319-111	1415
☐	F-GRHS	A319-111	1444
☐	F-GRHT	A319-111	1449
☐	F-GRHU	A319-111	1471
☐	F-GRHV	A319-111	1505
☐	F-GRHX	A319-111	1524
☐	F-GRHY	A319-111	1616

Reg	Type	c/n	Notes
☐ F-GRHZ	A319-111	1622	
☐ F-GRXA	A319-111	1640	
☐ F-GRXB	A319-111	1645	
☐ F-GRXC	A319-111	1677	
☐ F-GRXD	A319-111	1699	
☐ F-GRXE	A319-111	1733	
☐ F-GRXF	A319-111	1938	
☐ F-GRXG	A319-115LR	2213	
☐ F-GRXH	A319-115LR	2228	
☐ F-GRXI	A319-115LR	2279	
☐ F-GRXJ	A319-115LR	2456	
☐ F-GRXK	A319-115LR	2716	
☐ F-GRXL	A319-111	2938	
☐ F-GRXM	A319-111	2961	
☐ F-GRXN	A319-115LR	3065	
☐ F-GFKH	A320-211	0061	
☐ F-GFKJ	A320-211	0063	
☐ F-GFKM	A320-211	0102	
☐ F-GFKR	A320-211	0186	
☐ F-GFKS	A320-211	0187	
☐ F-GFKV	A320-211	0227	
☐ F-GFKX	A320-211	0228	
☐ F-GFKY	A320-211	0285	
☐ F-GFKZ	A320-211	0286	
☐ F-GHQC	A320-211	0044	
☐ F-GHQE	A320-211	0115	
☐ F-GHQG	A320-211	0155	
☐ F-GHQH	A320-211	0156	
☐ F-GHQJ	A320-211	0214	
☐ F-GHQK	A320-211	0236	
☐ F-GHQL	A320-211	0239	
☐ F-GHQM	A320-211	0237	
☐ F-GHQO	A320-211	0278	
☐ F-GHQP	A320-211	0337	
☐ F-GHQQ	A320-211	0352	
☐ F-GHQR	A320-211	0377	
☐ F-GJVA	A320-211	0144	
☐ F-GJVB	A320-211	0145	
☐ F-GJVG	A320-211	0270	
☐ F-GJVW	A320-211	0491	
☐ F-GKXA	A320-211	0287	
☐ F-GKXC	A320-214	1502	
☐ F-GKXD	A320-214	1873	
☐ F-GKXE	A320-214	1879	
☐ F-GKXF	A320-214	1885	
☐ F-GKXG	A320-214	1894	
☐ F-GKXH	A320-214	1924	
☐ F-GKXI	A320-214	1949	
☐ F-GKXJ	A320-214	1900	
☐ F-GKXK	A320-214	2140	
☐ F-GKXL	A320-214	2705	
☐ F-GKXM	A320-214	2721	
☐ F-GKXN	A320-214	3008	
☐ F-GKXO	A320-214	3420	
☐ F-GKXP	A320-214	3470	
☐ F-GKXQ	A320-214	3777	
☐ F-GKXR	A320-214	3795	
☐ F-GKXS	A320-214	3825	
☐ F-GKXT	A320-214	3859	
☐ F-GKXU	A320-214	4063	
☐ F-GKXV	A320-214	4084	
☐ F-GKXY	A320-214	4105	
☐ F-GKXZ	A320-214	4137	
☐ F-HBNA	A320-214	4335	♦
☐ F-HEPA	A320-214	4139	
☐ F-HEPB	A320-214	4241	♦
☐ F-HEPC	A320-214	4267	♦
☐ F-HEPD	A320-214	4295	♦
☐ F-HEPE	A320-214	4298	♦
☐ F-	A320-214		o/o♦
☐ F-	A320-214		o/o♦
☐ F-	A320-214		o/o♦
☐ F-	A320-214		o/o♦
☐ F-	A320-214		o/o♦
☐ F-	A320-214		o/o♦
☐ F-	A320-214		o/o♦
☐ F-	A320-214		o/o♦
☐ F-	A320-214		o/o♦
☐ F-	A320-214		o/o♦
☐ F-	A320-214		o/o♦
☐ F-	A320-214		o/o♦
☐ F-GMZA	A321-111	0498	
☐ F-GMZB	A321-111	0509	
☐ F-GMZC	A321-111	0521	
☐ F-GMZD	A321-111	0529	
☐ F-GMZE	A321-111	0544	
☐ F-GTAD	A321-212	0777	
☐ F-GTAE	A321-212	0796	
☐ F-GTAH	A321-212	1133	
☐ F-GTAI	A321-212	1299	
☐ F-GTAJ	A321-212	1476	
☐ F-GTAK	A321-212	1658	
☐ F-GTAL	A321-212	1691	
☐ F-GTAM	A321-212	1859	
☐ F-GTAN	A321-212	3051	
☐ F-GTAO	A321-212	3098	
☐ F-GTAP	A321-212	3372	
☐ F-GTAQ	A321-212	3399	
☐ F-GTAR	A321-212	3401	
☐ F-GTAS	A321-212	3419	
☐ F-GTAT	A321-212	3441	
☐ F-GTAU	A321-212	3814	
☐ F-GTAV	A321-212	3884	
☐ F-GTAX	A321-212	3930	
☐ F-GTAY	A321-212	4251	♦
☐ F-	A321-212		o/o♦
☐ F-GZCA	A330-203	422	
☐ F-GZCB	A330-203	443	
☐ F-GZCC	A330-203	448	
☐ F-GZCD	A330-203	458	
☐ F-GZCE	A330-203	465	
☐ F-GZCF	A330-203	481	
☐ F-GZCG	A330-203	498	
☐ F-GZCH	A330-203	500	
☐ F-GZCI	A330-203	502	
☐ F-GZCJ	A330-203	503	
☐ F-GZCK	A330-203	516	
☐ F-GZCL	A330-203	519	
☐ F-GZCM	A330-203	567	
☐ F-GZCN	A330-203	584	
☐ F-GZCO	A330-203	657	
☐ F-GLZC	A340-311	029	
☐ F-GLZH	A340-311	078	
☐ F-GLZI	A340-311	084	
☐ F-GLZJ	A340-313X	186	
☐ F-GLZK	A340-313X	207	
☐ F-GLZL	A340-313X	210	
☐ F-GLZM	A340-313X	237	
☐ F-GLZN	A340-313X	245	
☐ F-GLZO	A340-313X	246	
☐ F-GLZP	A340-313X	260	
☐ F-GLZR	A340-313X	307	
☐ F-GLZS	A340-313X	310	
☐ F-GLZT	A340-313X	319	
☐ F-GLZU	A340-313X	377	
☐ F-GNIH	A340-313X	373	
☐ F-GNII	A340-313X	399	
☐ F-HPJA	A380-861	033	
☐ F-HPJB	A380-861	040	
☐ F-HPJC	A380-861	043	♦
☐ F-HPJD	A380-861	049	♦
☐ F-HPJE	A380-861	052	♦
☐ F-HPJF	A380-861	064	o/o♦
☐ F-HPJG	A380-861	067	o/o♦
☐ F-HPJH	A380-861	077	o/o♦
☐ F-GCBG	B747-228F	22939/569	[XCR]

☐	F-GEXA	B747-4B3	24154/741	
☐	F-GEXB	B747-4B3M	24155/864	
☐	F-GISB	B747-428MBCF	25302/884	[XCR]
☐	F-GISC	B747-428M	25599/899	[XCR]
☐	F-GISD	B747-428M	25628/934	
☐	F-GISE	B747-428BCF	25630/960	[XCR]
☐	F-GITD	B747-428	25600/901	
☐	F-GITE	B747-428	25601/906	
☐	F-GITF	B747-428	25602/909	
☐	F-GITH	B747-428	32868/1325	
☐	F-GITI	B747-428	32869/1327	
☐	F-GITJ	B747-428	32871/1343	
☐	F-GIUA	B747-428ERF	32866/1315	
☐	F-GIUC	B747-428ERF	32867/1318	
☐	F-GIUD	B747-428ERF	32870/1344	
☐	F-GSPA	B777-228ER	29002/129	
☐	F-GSPB	B777-228ER	29003/133	
☐	F-GSPC	B777-228ER	29004/138	
☐	F-GSPD	B777-228ER	29005/187	
☐	F-GSPE	B777-228ER	29006/189	
☐	F-GSPF	B777-228ER	29007/201	
☐	F-GSPG	B777-228ER	27609/195	
☐	F-GSPH	B777-228ER	28675/210	
☐	F-GSPI	B777-228ER	29008/258	
☐	F-GSPJ	B777-228ER	29009/263	
☐	F-GSPK	B777-228ER	29010/267	
☐	F-GSPL	B777-228ER	30457/284	
☐	F-GSPM	B777-228ER	30456/307	
☐	F-GSPN	B777-228ER	29011/314	
☐	F-GSPO	B777-228ER	30614/320	
☐	F-GSPP	B777-228ER	30615/327	
☐	F-GSPQ	B777-228ER	28682/331	
☐	F-GSPR	B777-228ER	28683/367	
☐	F-GSPS	B777-228ER	32306/370	
☐	F-GSPT	B777-228ER	32308/382	
☐	F-GSPU	B777-228ER	32309/383	
☐	F-GSPV	B777-228ER	28684/385	
☐	F-GSPX	B777-228ER	32698/392	
☐	F-GSPY	B777-228ER	32305/395	
☐	F-GSPZ	B777-228ER	32310/401	
☐	F-GSQA	B777-328ER	32723/466	
☐	F-GSQB	B777-328ER	32724/478	
☐	F-GSQC	B777-328ER	32727/480	
☐	F-GSQD	B777-328ER	32726/490	
☐	F-GSQE	B777-328ER	32851/492	
☐	F-GSQF	B777-328ER	32849/494	
☐	F-GSQG	B777-328ER	32850/500	
☐	F-GSQH	B777-328ER	32711/501	
☐	F-GSQI	B777-328ER	32725/502	
☐	F-GSQJ	B777-328ER	32852/510	
☐	F-GSQK	B777-328ER	32845/530	
☐	F-GSQL	B777-328ER	32853/545	
☐	F-GSQM	B777-328ER	32848/558	
☐	F-GSQN	B777-328ER	32960/565	
☐	F-GSQO	B777-328ER	32961/570	
☐	F-GSQP	B777-328ER	35676/573	
☐	F-GSQR	B777-328ER	35677/579	
☐	F-GSQS	B777-328ER	32962/608	
☐	F-GSQT	B777-328ER	32846/616	
☐	F-GSQU	B777-328ER	32847/624	
☐	F-GSQV	B777-328ER	32854/636	
☐	F-GSQX	B777-328ER	32963/645	
☐	F-GSQY	B777-328ER	35678/647	
☐	F-GUOB	B777-F28	32965/732	
☐	F-GUOC	B777-F28	32966/752	
☐	F-GZNA	B777-328ER	35297/671	
☐	F-GZNB	B777-328ER	32964/715	
☐	F-GZNC	B777-328ER	35542/723	
☐	F-GZND	B777-328ER	35543/777	
☐	F-GZNE	B777-328ER	37432/790	
☐	F-GZNF	B777-328ER	37433/792	
☐	F-GZNG	B777-328ER	32968/795	
☐	F-GZNH	B777-328ER	35544/905	♦
☐	F-	B777-328ER	o/o	♦
☐	F-	B777-328ER	o/o	♦

☐	F-	B777-328ER	o/o	♦
☐	F-	B777-328ER	o/o	♦
☐	F-	B777-328ER	o/o	♦

AIR MEDITERRANEE — BIE

☐	F-GYAI	A320-211	0293
☐	F-GYAJ	A321-211	2707
☐	F-GYAN	A321-111	0535
☐	F-GYAO	A321-111	0642
☐	F-GYAP	A321-111	0517
☐	F-GYAQ	A321-211	0827
☐	F-GYAR	A321-211	0891
☐	F-GYAZ	A321-111	0519
☐	F-HCOA	B737-5L9	28084/2788	♦

AIRBUS TRANSPORT INTL — 4Y / BGA

☐	F-GSTA	A300B4-608ST	Beluga655/001
☐	F-GSTB	A300B4-608ST	Beluga751/002
☐	F-GSTC	A300B4-608ST	Beluga765/003
☐	F-GSTD	A300B4-608ST	Beluga776/004
☐	F-GSTF	A300B4-608ST	Beluga796/005

AIRLINAIR — A5 / RLA

☐	F-GKNB	ATR 42-300	226	
☐	F-GKNC	ATR 42-300	230	
☐	F-GKYN	ATR 42-300	95	
☐	F-GPYA	ATR 42-500	457	
☐	F-GPYB	ATR 42-500	480	
☐	F-GPYC	ATR 42-500	484	
☐	F-GPYD	ATR 42-500	490	
☐	F-GPYF	ATR 42-500	495Opf AFR	
☐	F-GPYK	ATR 42-500	537Opf AFR	
☐	F-GPYL	ATR 42-500	542Opf AFR	
☐	F-GPYM	ATR 42-500	520Opf AFR	
☐	F-GPYN	ATR 42-500	539Opf AFR	
☐	F-GPYO	ATR 42-500	544	
☐	F-GVZB	ATR 42-500	524	
☐	F-GVZJ	ATR 42-320	093	
☐	F-GVZO	ATR 42-300	080	♦
☐	F-GVZZ	ATR 42-300	055	
☐	F-GKPD	ATR 72-202	177	
☐	F-GPOC	ATR 72-202(QC)	311Opf AFR	
☐	F-GPOD	ATR 72-202(QC)	361Opf AFR	
☐	F-GVZG	ATR 72-201	145	
☐	F-GVZL	ATR 72-212A	553	
☐	F-GVZM	ATR 72-212A	590	
☐	F-GVZN	ATR 72-212A	563	

ATLANTIQUE AIR ASSISTANCE — TLB

☐	F-GNBR	Beech 1900D	UE-327
☐	F-GPYY	Beech 1900C-1	UC-115
☐	F-GTVA	EMB.120ER	120253
☐	F-HAAV	ATR 42-320	19
☐	F-HBSO	ATR 42-320	66

BLUE LINE — BLE

☐	F-GMLI	MD-83	53014/1740	VIP
☐	F-GMLK	MD-83	49672/1494	
☐	F-GMLX	MD-83	49823/1540	
☐	F-HBOS	A310-325ET	674	♦

BRIT' AIR — DB / BZH

☐	F-GRJE	CRJ-100ER	7106
☐	F-GRJF	CRJ-100ER	7108
☐	F-GRJG	CRJ-100ER	7143
☐	F-GRJI	CRJ-100ER	7147
☐	F-GRJJ	CRJ-100ER	7190
☐	F-GRJK	CRJ-100ER	7219

☐	F-GRJL	CRJ-100ER	7221
☐	F-GRJM	CRJ-100ER	7222
☐	F-GRJN	CRJ-100ER	7262
☐	F-GRJO	CRJ-100ER	7296
☐	F-GRJP	CRJ-100ER	7301
☐	F-GRJQ	CRJ-100ER	7321
☐	F-GRJR	CRJ-100ER	7375
☐	F-GRJT	CRJ-100ER	7389
☐	F-GRZA	CRJ-701	10006
☐	F-GRZB	CRJ-701	10007
☐	F-GRZC	CRJ-701	10008
☐	F-GRZD	CRJ-701	10016
☐	F-GRZE	CRJ-701	10032
☐	F-GRZF	CRJ-701	10036
☐	F-GRZG	CRJ-701	10037
☐	F-GRZH	CRJ-701	10089
☐	F-GRZI	CRJ-701	10093
☐	F-GRZJ	CRJ-701	10096
☐	F-GRZK	CRJ-701	10198
☐	F-GRZL	CRJ-701	10245
☐	F-GRZM	CRJ-701	10263
☐	F-GRZN	CRJ-701	10264
☐	F-GRZO	CRJ-701	10265
☐	F-HDTA	CRJ-900ER	15001 ◆
☐	F-HMLA	CRJ-1000	19004 ◆
☐	F-HMLC	CRJ-1000	19006 ◆
☐	F-HMLD	CRJ-1000	19007 ◆
☐	F-HMLE	CRJ-1000	19009 ◆
☐	F-	CRJ-1000	o/o◆
☐	F-	CRJ-1000	o/o◆
☐	F-	CRJ-1000	o/o◆
☐	F-GKHD	Fokker 100	11381
☐	F-GKHE	Fokker 100	11386
☐	F-GPXB	Fokker 100	11492
☐	F-GPXC	Fokker 100	11493
☐	F-GPXD	Fokker 100	11494
☐	F-GPXE	Fokker 100	11495
☐	F-GPXF	Fokker 100	11330
☐	F-GPXJ	Fokker 100	11323

CHALAIR AVIATION — CLG

☐	F-GOOB	Beech 1900C-1	UC-153
☐	F-HBCA	Beech 1900D	UE-188
☐	F-HBCB	Beech 1900D	UE-390
☐	F-HBCC	Beech 1900D	UE-350

CORSAIR — SS / CRL

☐	F-GTUI	B747-422	26875/931
☐	F-HKIS	B747-422	25380/913
☐	F-HSEA	B747-422	26877/944
☐	F-HSEX	B747-422	26878/966
☐	F-HSUN	B747-422	26880/984
☐	F-HLOV	B747-422	25379/911
☐	F-HBIL	A330-243	320
☑	F-HCAT	A330-243	285

EUROPE AIRPOST — 5O / FPO

☐	F-GPOA	ATR 72-202(QC)	204
☐	F-GPOB	ATR 72-202(QC)	207
☐	F-GPOC	ATR 72-202(QC)	311 >RLA
☐	F-GPOD	ATR 72-202(QC)	361 >RLA
☐	EI-STA	B737-31S	29057/2942 ◆
☐	F-GFUE	B737-3B3(QC)	24387/1693
☐	F-GFUF	B737-3B3(QC)	24388/1725
☐	F-GIXB	B737-33A(QC)	24789/1953
☐	F-GIXC	B737-38B(QC)	25124/2047
☐	F-GIXD	B737-33A(QC)	25744/2198
☐	F-GIXE	B737-3B3(QC)	26850/2235
☐	F-GIXF	B737-3B3(QC)	26851/2267
☐	F-GIXH	B737-3S3(QC)	23788/1393
☐	F-GIXI	B737-348(QC)	23809/1458
☐	F-GIXJ	B737-3Y0(QC)	23685/1357
☐	F-GIXL	B737-348(QC)	23810/1474
☐	F-GIXO	B737-3Q8(QC)	24132/1555
☐	F-GIXR	B737-3H6(SF)	27125/2415
☐	F-GIXS	B737-3H6(SF)	27347/2615
☐	F-GIXT	B737-39M(QC)	28898/2906
☐	F-GZTA	B737-33V(QC)	29333/3084
☐	F-GZTB	B737-33VF	29336/3102
☐	F-GZTC	B737-73V	32414/1214
☐	F-GZTD	B737-73V	32418/1300 ◆

HEX'AIR — UD / HER

☐	F-GOPE	Beech 1900D	UE-103
☐	F-GUPE	Beech 1900D	UE-248

OPENSKIES — BOS

☐	F-GPEJ	B757-236/W	25807/610 ◆
☐	F-GPEK	B757-236/W	25808/665 ◆
☑	F-HAVI	B757-26D/W	24473/301
☐	F-HAVN	B757-230/W	25140/382

PAN EUROPEENE AIR SERVICE — PEA

☐	F-GYPE	ERJ-135LR	145492
☐	F-HAPE	Beech 1900D	UE-367
☐	F-HBPE	ERJ-145LR	145106

REGIONAL — YS / RAE

☐	F-GOHA	ERJ-135ER	145189
☐	F-GOHC	ERJ-135ER	145243
☐	F-GOHD	ERJ-135ER	145252
☐	F-GOHE	ERJ-135ER	145335
☐	F-GOHF	ERJ-135ER	145347
☐	F-GRGP	ERJ-135ER	145188
☐	F-GRGQ	ERJ-135ER	145233
☐	F-GRGR	ERJ-135ER	145236
☐	F-GRGA	ERJ-145EP	145008
☐	F-GRGB	ERJ-145EP	145010
☐	F-GRGC	ERJ-145EP	145012
☐	F-GRGD	ERJ-145EP	145043
☐	F-GRGE	ERJ-145EP	145047
☐	F-GRGF	ERJ-145EP	145050
☐	F-GRGG	ERJ-145EP	145118
☐	F-GRGH	ERJ-145EP	145120
☐	F-GRGI	ERJ-145EP	145152
☐	F-GRGJ	ERJ-145EP	145297
☐	F-GRGK	ERJ-145EP	145324
☐	F-GRGL	ERJ-145EP	145375
☐	F-GRGM	ERJ-145EP	145418
☐	F-GUAM	ERJ-145MP	145266
☐	F-GUBA	ERJ-145MP	145398
☐	F-GUBB	ERJ-145MP	145419
☐	F-GUBC	ERJ-145MP	145556
☐	F-GUBD	ERJ-145MP	145333
☐	F-GUBE	ERJ-145MP	145668
☐	F-GUBF	ERJ-145MP	145669
☐	F-GUBG	ERJ-145MP	14500890
☐	F-GUEA	ERJ-145MP	145342
☐	F-GUFD	ERJ-145MP	145197
☐	F-GUMA	ERJ-145MP	145405
☐	F-GUPT	ERJ-145MP	145294
☐	F-GVGS	ERJ-145MP	145385
☐	F-GVHD	ERJ-145MP	145178
☐	F-HBXA	ERJ-170STD	17000237
☐	F-HBXB	ERJ-170STD	17000250
☐	F-HBXC	ERJ-170STD	17000263
☐	F-HBXD	ERJ-170STD	17000281
☐	F-HBXE	ERJ-170STD	17000286
☐	F-HBXF	ERJ-170STD	17000292

☐ F-HBXG	ERJ-170STD	17000301	♦
☐ F-HBXH	ERJ-170STD	17000307	♦
☐ F-HBXI	ERJ-170STD	17000310	♦
☐ F-HBXJ	ERJ-170STD	17000312	♦
☐ F-HBLA	ERJ-190LR	19000051	
☐ F-HBLB	ERJ-190LR	19000060	
☐ F-HBLC	ERJ-190LR	19000080	
☐ F-HBLD	ERJ-190LR	19000113	
☐ F-HBLE	ERJ-190LR	19000123	
☐ F-HBLF	ERJ-190LR	19000158	
☐ F-HBLG	ERJ-190LR	19000254	
☐ F-HBLH	ERJ-190LR	19000266	
☐ F-HBLI	ERJ-190STD	19000298	
☐ F-HBLJ	ERJ-190STD	19000311	

REGOURD AVIATION

☐ F-GTSK	EMB.120RT	120213

SECURITE CIVIL

☐ F-ZBEU	CL-415	2024	42
☐ F-ZBFN	CL-415	2006	33
☐ F-ZBFP	CL-415	2002	31
☐ F-ZBFS	CL-415	2001	32
☐ F-ZBFV	CL-415	2013	37
☐ F-ZBFW	CL-415	2014	38
☐ F-ZBFX	CL-415	2007	34
☐ F-ZBFY	CL-415	2010	35
☐ F-ZBME	CL-415	2057	44
☐ F-ZBMF	CL-415	2063	45
☐ F-ZBMG	CL-415	2065	48
☐ F-ZBMC	DHC-8-402QMRT	4040	73
☐ F-ZBMD	DHC-8-402QMRT	4043	74

TRANSAVIA FRANCE   TO / TVF

☐ F-GZHA	B737-8GJ/W	34901/2267
☐ F-GZHB	B737-8GJ/W	34902/2309
☐ F-GZHC	B737-8K2/W	29651/2534
☐ F-GZHD	B737-8K2/W	29650/2583
☐ F-GZHE	B737-8K2/W	29678/2615
☐ F-GZHF	B737-8HX/W	29677/2946 ♦
☐ F-GZHN	B737-85H/W	29445/186
☐ F-GZHV	B737-85H/W	29444/178

TWIN JET   T7 / TJT

☐ F-GLND	Beech 1900D	UE-196
☐ F-GLNE	Beech 1900D	UE-197
☐ F-GLNF	Beech 1900D	UE-69
☐ F-GLNH	Beech 1900D	UE-73
☐ F-GLNK	Beech 1900D	UE-269
☐ F-GLPL	Beech 1900C-1	UC-92
☐ F-GRYL	Beech 1900D	UE-301
☐ F-GTKJ	Beech 1900D	UE-348
☐ F-GTVC	Beech 1900D	UE-349

XL AIRWAYS FRANCE   SE / XLF

☐ F-GKHK	A320-211	0343	
☐ F-GRSI	A320-214	0973	
☐ F-GTHL	A320-212	0189	
☐ F-GRSQ	A330-243	0501	
☐ F-GSEU	A330-243	0635	
☐ EC-LEQ	A330-343E	1097	<IWD♦
☐ F-HAXL	B737-8Q8/W	35279/2626	
☐ F-HJUL	B737-8Q8/W	38819/3519	♦

F-O - PACIFIC TERRITORIES

AIR CALEDONIE   TY / TPC

☐ F-OIPI	ATR 42-500	647
☐ F-OIPN	ATR 72-212A	735
☐ F-OIPS	ATR 72-212A	764

AIR TAHITI   VT / VTA

☐ F-OIQB	ATR 42-500	621	
☐ F-OIQC	ATR 42-500	627	
☐ F-OIQD	ATR 42-500	631	
☐ F-O	ATR 42-500		o/o♦
☐ F-OHJS	ATR 72-212A	696	
☐ F-OIQN	ATR 72-212A	719	
☐ F-OIQO	ATR 72-212A	731	
☐ F-OIQR	ATR 72-212A	862	
☐ F-OIQU	ATR 72-212A	751	
☐ F-OIQT	ATR 72-212A	829	
☐ F-OIQV	ATR 72-212A	806	

AIR TAHITI NUI   TN / THT

☐ F-OJGF	A340-313X	385
☐ F-OJTN	A340-313X	395
☐ F-OLOV	A340-313E	668
☐ F-OSEA	A340-313X	438
☐ F-OSUN	A340-313X	446

AIRCALIN   SB / ACI

☐ F-OHSD	A330-202	507
☐ F-OJSB	A320-232	2152
☐ F-OJSE	A330-202	510

F-O - ATLANTIC / INDIAN OCEAN

AIR AUSTRAL   UU / REU

☐ F-OHSF	ATR 72-212A	650	
☐ F-OMRU	ATR 72-212A	855	
☐ F-OZSE	ATR 72-212A	813	
☐ F-ODZJ	B737-53A	24877/1943	[DNR]♦
☐ F-ODZY	B737-33A	27452/2679	[DNR]♦
☐ F-ONGA	B737-89M/W	40910/3484	♦
☐ F-ONGB	B737-89M/W	40911/3504	♦
☐ F-OMAY	B777-2Q8ER	29402/517	
☐ F-ONOU	B777-3Q8ER	35783/786	
☐ F-OPAR	B777-2Q8ER	29908/229	
☐ F-OREU	B777-39MER	37434/912	♦
☐ F-ORUN	B777-2Q8ER	28676/246	
☐ F-OSYD	B777-3Q8ER	35782/778	
☐ F-	B777-2		o/o♦

AIR ST PIERRE   PJ / SPM

☐ F-OFSP	ATR 42-500	801

F-O - FRENCH CARIBBEAN

AIR ANTILLES EXPRESS   3S

☐ F-OIJB	ATR 42-500	579	<GUY
☐ F-OIXD	ATR 42-500	695	
☐ F-OIXE	ATR 42-500	807	
☐ F-OIXH	ATR 42-500	831	♦

AIR CARAIBES   TX / FWI

☐ F-OIJH	ATR 72-212A	682
☐ F-OIJK	ATR 72-212A	736

| ☐ | F-OIXL | ATR 72-212A | 888 |
| ☐ | F-OSUD | ERJ-190LR | 19000130 |

AIR CARAIBES ATLANTIQUE   TX / CAJ

☐	F-GOTO	A330-323E	1021	
☐	F-OFDF	A330-223	253	
☐	F-OONE	A330-323E	965	
☐	F-ORLY	A330-323X	758	
☐	F-	A330-323X		o/o♦

AIR GUYANE EXPRESS   3S / GUY

| ☐ | F-OIJB | ATR 42-500 | 579 |

G - UNITED KINGDOM

AIR ATLANTIQUE   7M / AAG

| ☐ | G-APSA | DC-6A | 45497/995 |

AIR SOUTHWEST   WOW

☐	G-WOWA	DHC-8-311	296
☐	G-WOWB	DHC-8-311	334
☐	G-WOWC	DHC-8-311	311
☐	G-WOWD	DHC-8-311	286
☐	G-WOWE	DHC-8-311	256

ASTRAEUS   5W / AEU

☐	G-STRP	A320-211	0136	
☐	G-PJPJ	B737-5H6	27355/2646	
☐	G-STRF	B737-76N/W	29885/1120	
☐	G-STRI	B737-33A	25011/2012	
☐	G-STRJ	B737-33A	25119/2069	
☐	G-STRN	B737-7L9/W	28007/136	
☐	G-OJIB	B757-23AER	24292/219	
☐	G-STRW	B757-28A	24543/286	
☐	G-STRX	B757-2Q8	25621/457	
☐	G-STRY	B757-2Q8	28161/723	>BMA
☐	G-STRZ	B757-258	27622/745	

AURIGNY AIR SERVICES   GR / AUR

☐	G-BDTO	BN Trislander	1027
☐	G-BEVT	BN Trislander	1057
☐	G-FTSE	BN Trislander	1053
☐	G-JOEY	BN Trislander	1016
☐	G-RBCI	BN Trislander	1035
☐	G-RLON	BN Trislander	1008
☐	G-XTOR	BN Trislander	359
☐	G-BWDB	ATR 72-202	449
☐	G-COBO	ATR 72-212A	852
☐	G-VZON	ATR 72-212A	853

BA CITYFLYER   CJ / CFE

☐	G-LCYD	ERJ-170STD	17000294	
☐	G-LCYE	ERJ-170STD	17000296	
☐	G-LCYF	ERJ-170STD	17000298	
☐	G-LCYG	ERJ-170STD	17000300	
☐	G-LCYH	ERJ-170STD	17000302	
☐	G-LCYI	ERJ-170STD	17000305	
☐	G-LCYJ	ERJ-190SR	19000339	♦
☐	G-LCYK	ERJ-190SR	19000343	♦
☐	G-LCYL	ERJ-190SR	19000346	♦
☐	G-LCYM	ERJ-190SR	19000351	♦
☐	G-LCYN	ERJ-190SR	19000392	♦
☐	G-	ERJ-190SR		o/o♦
☐	G-	ERJ-190SR		o/o♦

BLUE ISLANDS   XA / BCI

☐	G-BEDP	BN Trislander	1039	
☐	G-DRFC	ATR 42-320	007	
☐	G-ISLB	BAeJetstream 32	871	
☐	G-ISLC	BAeJetstream 32	873	
☐	G-ISLD	BAeJetstream 32EP	915	
☐	G-LCOC	BN Trislander	366	
☐	G-XAXA	BN Islander	530	
☐	LN-FAN	BAeJetstream 32	864	<HTA

BMI BRITISH MIDLAND INTL   BD / BMA

☐	G-DBCA	A319-131	2098	
☐	G-DBCB	A319-131	2188	
☐	G-DBCC	A319-131	2194	
☐	G-DBCD	A319-131	2389	
☐	G-DBCE	A319-131	2429	
☐	G-DBCF	A319-131	2466	
☐	G-DBCG	A319-131	2694	
☐	G-DBCH	A319-131	2697	
☐	G-DBCI	A319-131	2720	
☐	G-DBCJ	A319-131	2981	
☐	G-DBCK	A319-131	3049	
☐	G-MEDH	A320-232	1922	
☐	G-MEDK	A320-232	2441	
☐	G-MIDO	A320-232	1987	
☐	G-MIDP	A320-232	1732	
☐	G-MIDS	A320-232	1424	
☐	G-MIDT	A320-232	1418	
☐	G-MIDX	A320-232	1177	
☐	G-MIDY	A320-232	1014	
☐	G-MEDF	A321-231	1690	
☐	G-MEDG	A321-231	1711	
☐	G-MEDJ	A321-231	2190	
☐	G-MEDL	A321-231	2653	
☐	G-MEDM	A321-231	2799	
☐	G-MEDN	A321-231	3512	
☐	G-MEDU	A321-231	3926	
☐	G-WWBD	A330-243	401	
☐	G-WWBM	A330-243	398	>THY
☐	G-STRY	B757-2Q8	28161/723	<AEU

BMI REGIONAL   BD / BMR

☐	G-EMBI	ERJ-145EP	145126	
☐	G-EMBJ	ERJ-145EP	145134	
☐	G-EMBN	ERJ-145EP	145201	
☐	G-EMBP	ERJ-145EP	145300	♦
☐	G-RJXA	ERJ-145EP	145136	
☐	G-RJXB	ERJ-145EP	145142	
☐	G-RJXC	ERJ-145EP	145153	
☐	G-RJXD	ERJ-145EP	145207	
☐	G-RJXE	ERJ-145EP	145245	
☐	G-RJXF	ERJ-145EP	145280	
☐	G-RJXG	ERJ-145EP	145390	
☐	G-RJXH	ERJ-145EP	145442	
☐	G-RJXI	ERJ-145EP	145454	
☐	G-RJXJ	ERJ-135ER	145473	
☐	G-RJXK	ERJ-135ER	145494	
☐	G-RJXL	ERJ-135ER	145376	
☐	G-RJXM	ERJ-145MP	145216	
☐	G-RJXN	ERJ-145MP	145336	
☐	G-RJXP	ERJ-135ER	145431	
☐	G-RJXR	ERJ-145EP	145070	

BMIBABY   WW / BMI

☐	G-BVKB	B737-59D	27268/2592
☐	G-BVKD	B737-59D	26421/2279
☐	G-BVZE	B737-59D	26422/2412
☐	G-OBMP	B737-3Q8	24963/2193

	Registration	Type	Serial	Notes
☐	G-ODSK	B737-37Q	28537/2904	
■	G-OGBD	B737-3L9	27833/2688	
☐	G-TOYA	B737-3Q8	26310/2680	
☐	G-TOYD	B737-3Q8	26307/2664	
☐	G-TOYF	B737-36N	28557/2862	
☐	G-TOYG	B737-36N	28872/3082	
☐	G-TOYH	B737-36N	28570/3010	
☐	G-TOYI	B737-3Q8	28054/3016	
☐	G-TOYJ	B737-36M	28332/2809	
☐	G-TOYK	B737-33R	28870/2899	
☐	G-TOYM	B737-36Q	29141/3035	

BRITISH AIRWAYS BA / BAW

	Registration	Type	Serial	Notes
☐	G-EUNA	A318-112	4007	
☐	G-EUNB	A318-112	4039	
☐	G-EUOA	A319-131	1513	
☐	G-EUOB	A319-131	1529	
☐	G-EUOC	A319-131	1537	
☐	G-EUOD	A319-131	1558	
☐	G-EUOE	A319-131	1574	
☐	G-EUOF	A319-131	1590	
☐	G-EUOG	A319-131	1594	
☐	G-EUOH	A319-131	1604	
☐	G-EUOI	A319-131	1606	
☐	G-EUPA	A319-131	1082	
☐	G-EUPB	A319-131	1115	
☐	G-EUPC	A319-131	1118	
☐	G-EUPD	A319-131	1142	
☐	G-EUPE	A319-131	1193	
☐	G-EUPF	A319-131	1197	
☐	G-EUPG	A319-131	1222	
☐	G-EUPH	A319-131	1225	
☐	G-EUPJ	A319-131	1232	
☐	G-EUPK	A319-131	1236	
☐	G-EUPL	A319-131	1239	
☐	G-EUPM	A319-131	1258	
☐	G-EUPN	A319-131	1261	
☐	G-EUPO	A319-131	1279	
☐	G-EUPP	A319-131	1295	
☐	G-EUPR	A319-131	1329	
☐	G-EUPS	A319-131	1338	
☐	G-EUPT	A319-131	1380	
☐	G-EUPU	A319-131	1384	
☐	G-EUPV	A319-131	1423	
☐	G-EUPW	A319-131	1440	
☐	G-EUPX	A319-131	1445	
☐	G-EUPY	A319-131	1466	
☐	G-EUPZ	A319-131	1510	
☐	G-BUSI	A320-211	0103	[LDE]♦
☐	G-BUSJ	A320-211	0109	
☐	G-BUSK	A320-211	0120	
☐	G-EUUA	A320-232	1661	
☐	G-EUUB	A320-232	1689	
☐	G-EUUC	A320-232	1696	
☐	G-EUUD	A320-232	1760	
☐	G-EUUE	A320-232	1782	
☐	G-EUUF	A320-232	1814	
☐	G-EUUG	A320-232	1829	
☐	G-EUUH	A320-232	1665	
☐	G-EUUI	A320-232	1871	
☐	G-EUUJ	A320-232	1883	
☐	G-EUUK	A320-232	1899	
☐	G-EUUL	A320-232	1708	
☐	G-EUUM	A320-232	1907	
☐	G-EUUN	A320-232	1910	
☐	G-EUUO	A320-232	1958	
☐	G-EUUP	A320-232	2038	
☐	G-EUUR	A320-232	2040	
☐	G-EUUS	A320-232	3301	
☐	G-EUUT	A320-232	3314	
☐	G-EUUU	A320-232	3351	
☐	G-EUUV	A320-232	3468	
☐	G-EUUW	A320-232	3499	
☐	G-EUUX	A320-232	3550	
☐	G-EUUY	A320-232	3607	
☐	G-EUUZ	A320-232	3649	
☐	G-EUYA	A320-232	3697	
☐	G-EUYB	A320-232	3703	
☐	G-EUYC	A320-232	3721	
☐	G-EUYD	A320-232	3726	
☐	G-EUYE	A320-232	3912	
☐	G-EUYF	A320-232	4185	
☐	G-EUYG	A320-232	4238	♦
☐	G-EUYH	A320-232	4265	♦
☐	G-EUYI	A320-232	4306	♦
☐	G-EUYJ	A320-232	4464	♦
☐	G-EUYK	A320-232	4551	♦
☐	G-EUYL	A320-232		o/o♦
☐	G-EUYM	A320-232		o/o♦
☐	G-EUYN	A320-232		o/o♦
☐	G-TTOB	A320-232	1687	
☐	G-TTOE	A320-232	1754	
☐	G-EUXC	A321-231	2305	
☐	G-EUXD	A321-231	2320	
☐	G-EUXE	A321-231	2323	
☐	G-EUXF	A321-231	2324	
☐	G-EUXG	A321-231	2351	
☐	G-EUXH	A321-231	2363	
☐	G-EUXI	A321-231	2536	
☐	G-EUXJ	A321-231	3081	
☐	G-EUXK	A321-231	3235	
☐	G-EUXL	A321-231	3254	
☐	G-EUXM	A321-231	3290	
☐	G-DOCA	B737-436	25267/2131	
☐	G-DOCB	B737-436	25304/2144	
☐	G-DOCE	B737-436	25350/2167	
☐	G-DOCF	B737-436	25407/2178	
☐	G-DOCG	B737-436	25408/2183	
☐	G-DOCH	B737-436	25428/2185	
☐	G-DOCL	B737-436	25842/2228	
☐	G-DOCN	B737-436	25848/2379	
☐	G-DOCO	B737-436	25849/2381	
☐	G-DOCS	B737-436	25852/2390	
☐	G-DOCT	B737-436	25853/2409	
☐	G-DOCU	B737-436	25854/2417	
☐	G-DOCV	B737-436	25855/2420	
☐	G-DOCW	B737-436	25856/2422	
☐	G-DOCX	B737-436	25857/2451	
☐	G-DOCY	B737-436	25844/2514	
☐	G-DOCZ	B737-436	25858/2522	
☐	G-GBTA	B737-436	25859/2532	
☐	G-GBTB	B737-436	25860/2545	
☐	G-BNLA	B747-436	23908/727	[VCV]
☐	G-BNLB	B747-436	23909/730	[CWL]
☐	G-BNLC	B747-436	23910/734	[CWL]
☐	G-BNLD	B747-436	23911/744	[VCV]♦
☐	G-BNLE	B747-436	24047/753	
☐	G-BNLF	B747-436	24048/773	
☐	G-BNLG	B747-436	24049/774	[VCV]
☐	G-BNLH	B747-436	24050/779	[VCV]
☐	G-BNLI	B747-436	24051/784	
☐	G-BNLJ	B747-436	24052/789	
☐	G-BNLK	B747-436	24053/790	
☐	G-BNLL	B747-436	24054/794	
☐	G-BNLM	B747-436	24055/795	
☐	G-BNLN	B747-436	24056/802	
☐	G-BNLO	B747-436	24057/817	
☐	G-BNLP	B747-436	24058/828	
☐	G-BNLR	B747-436	24447/829	
■	G-BNLS	B747-436	24629/841	
☐	G-BNLT	B747-436	24630/842	
☐	G-BNLU	B747-436	25406/895	[VCV]
☐	G-BNLV	B747-436	25427/900	
☐	G-BNLW	B747-436	25432/903	
☐	G-BNLX	B747-436	25435/908	
☐	G-BNLY	B747-436	27090/959	

□	G-BNLZ	B747-436	27091/964
□	G-BYGA	B747-436	28855/1190
□	G-BYGB	B747-436	28856/1194
□	G-BYGC	B747-436	25823/1195
□	G-BYGD	B747-436	28857/1196
□	G-BYGE	B747-436	28858/1198
□	G-BYGF	B747-436	25824/1200
□	G-BYGG	B747-436	28859/1212
□	G-CIVA	B747-436	27092/967
□	G-CIVB	B747-436	25811/1018
□	G-CIVC	B747-436	25812/1022
□	G-CIVD	B747-436	27349/1048
■	G-CIVE	B747-436	27350/1050
□	G-CIVF	B747-436	25434/1058
□	G-CIVG	B747-436	25813/1059
□	G-CIVH	B747-436	25809/1078
□	G-CIVI	B747-436	25814/1079
□	G-CIVJ	B747-436	25817/1102
□	G-CIVK	B747-436	25818/1104
■	G-CIVL	B747-436	27478/1108
□	G-CIVM	B747-436	28700/1116
□	G-CIVN	B747-436	28848/1129
□	G-CIVO	B747-436	28849/1135
□	G-CIVP	B747-436	28850/1144
□	G-CIVR	B747-436	25820/1146
■	G-CIVS	B747-436	28851/1148
□	G-CIVT	B747-436	25821/1149
□	G-CIVU	B747-436	25810/1154
□	G-CIVV	B747-436	25819/1156
□	G-CIVW	B747-436	25822/1157
□	G-CIVX	B747-436	28852/1172
□	G-CIVY	B747-436	28853/1178
□	G-CIVZ	B747-436	28854/1183
□	G-CPEM	B757-236	28665/747
□	G-CPEN	B757-236	28666/751
□	G-CPEO	B757-236	28667/762
□	G-CPET	B757-236	29115/798
□	G-BNWA	B767-336ER	24333/265
□	G-BNWB	B767-336ER	24334/281
□	G-BNWC	B767-336ER	24335/284
□	G-BNWH	B767-336ER	24340/335
□	G-BNWI	B767-336ER	24341/342
□	G-BNWM	B767-336ER	25204/376
□	G-BNWN	B767-336ER	25444/398
□	G-BNWO	B767-336ER	25442/418
□	G-BNWR	B767-336ER	25732/421
□	G-BNWS	B767-336ER	25826/473
□	G-BNWT	B767-336ER	25828/476
□	G-BNWU	B767-336ER	25829/483
□	G-BNWV	B767-336ER	27140/490
□	G-BNWW	B767-336ER	25831/526
□	G-BNWX	B767-336ER	25832/529
□	G-BNWY	B767-336ER	25834/608
□	G-BNWZ	B767-336ER	25733/648
□	G-BZHA	B767-336ER	29230/702
□	G-BZHB	B767-336ER	29231/704
□	G-BZHC	B767-336ER	29232/708
□	G-RAES	B777-236ER	27491/76
■	G-VIIA	B777-236ER	27483/41
■	G-VIIB	B777-236ER	27484/49
□	G-VIIC	B777-236ER	27485/53
□	G-VIID	B777-236ER	27486/56
□	G-VIIE	B777-236ER	27487/58
■	G-VIIF	B777-236ER	27488/61
□	G-VIIG	B777-236ER	27489/65
□	G-VIIH	B777-236ER	27490/70
□	G-VIIJ	B777-236ER	27492/111
□	G-VIIK	B777-236ER	28840/117
□	G-VIIL	B777-236ER	27493/127
□	G-VIIM	B777-236ER	28841/130
□	G-VIIN	B777-236ER	29319/157
■	G-VIIO	B777-236ER	29320/182

□	G-VIIP	B777-236ER	29321/193
■	G-VIIR	B777-236ER	29322/203
□	G-VIIS	B777-236ER	29323/206
■	G-VIIT	B777-236ER	29962/217
□	G-VIIU	B777-236ER	29963/221
□	G-VIIV	B777-236ER	29964/228
□	G-VIIW	B777-236ER	29965/233
□	G-VIIX	B777-236ER	29966/236
□	G-VIIY	B777-236ER	29967/251
□	G-YMMA	B777-236ER	30302/242
□	G-YMMB	B777-236ER	30303/265
□	G-YMMC	B777-236ER	30304/268
□	G-YMMD	B777-236ER	30305/269
□	G-YMME	B777-236ER	30306/275
■	G-YMMF	B777-236ER	30307/281
□	G-YMMG	B777-236ER	30308/301
□	G-YMMH	B777-236ER	30309/303
□	G-YMMI	B777-236ER	30310/308
□	G-YMMJ	B777-236ER	30311/311
□	G-YMMK	B777-236ER	30312/312
□	G-YMML	B777-236ER	30313/334
□	G-YMMN	B777-236ER	30316/346
□	G-YMMO	B777-236ER	30317/361
□	G-YMMP	B777-236ER	30315/369
□	G-YMMR	B777-236ER	36516/771
■	G-YMMS	B777-236ER	36517/784
□	G-YMMT	B777-236ER	36518/791
□	G-YMMU	B777-236ER	36519/796
□	G-ZZZA	B777-236	27105/6
□	G-ZZZB	B777-236	27106/10
□	G-ZZZC	B777-236	27107/15
□	G-STBA	B777-336ER	40542/879 ♦
□	G-STBB	B777-336ER	39286/887 ♦
□	G-STBC	B777-336ER	39287/901 ♦
□	G-STBD	B777-336ER	o/o♦
□	G-STBE	B777-336ER	o/o♦

DHLAIR — D0 / DHK

□	G-BIKC	B757-236(SF)	22174/11
□	G-BIKF	B757-236(SF)	22177/16
□	G-BIKG	B757-236(SF)	22178/23
□	G-BIKI	B757-236(SF)	22180/25
□	G-BIKJ	B757-236(SF)	22181/29
□	G-BIKK	B757-236(SF)	22182/30
□	G-BIKM	B757-236(SF)	22184/33
□	G-BIKN	B757-236(SF)	22186/50
□	G-BIKO	B757-236(SF)	22187/52
□	G-BIKP	B757-236(SF)	22188/54
□	G-BIKS	B757-236(SF)	22190/63
□	G-BIKU	B757-236(SF)	23399/78
□	G-BIKV	B757-236(SF)	23400/81
□	G-BIKZ	B757-236(SF)	23532/98
□	G-BMRA	B757-236(SF)	23710/123
□	G-BMRB	B757-236(SF)	23975/145
□	G-BMRC	B757-236(SF)	24072/160
□	G-BMRD	B757-236(SF)	24073/166
□	G-BMRE	B757-236(SF)	24074/168
□	G-BMRF	B757-236(SF)	24101/175
□	G-BMRH	B757-236(SF)	24266/210
□	G-BMRJ	B757-236(SF)	24268/214 >AXF♦
□	G-DHLE	B767-3JHF/W	37805/980
□	G-DHLF	B767-3JHF/W	37806/981
□	G-DHLG	B767-3JHF/W	37807/982

DIRECTFLIGHT — DCT

□	G-LUXE	BAe146 Srs.301	E3001

EASTERN AIRWAYS — T3 / EZE

□	G-CDYI	BAeJetstream 41	41019
□	G-MAJA	BAeJetstream 41	41032
□	G-MAJB	BAeJetstream 41	41018

☐	G-MAJC	BAeJetstream 41	41005
☐	G-MAJD	BAeJetstream 41	41006
☐	G-MAJE	BAeJetstream 41	41007
☐	G-MAJF	BAeJetstream 41	41008
☐	G-MAJG	BAeJetstream 41	41009
☐	G-MAJH	BAeJetstream 41	41010
☐	G-MAJI	BAeJetstream 41	41011
☐	G-MAJJ	BAeJetstream 41	41024
☐	G-MAJL	BAeJetstream 41	41087
☐	G-MAJP	BAeJetstream 41	41039
☐	G-MAJU	BAeJetstream 41	41071
☐	G-MAJW	BAeJetstream 41	41015
☐	G-MAJX	BAeJetstream 41	41098
☐	G-MAJY	BAeJetstream 41	41099
☐	G-MAJZ	BAeJetstream 41	41100
☐	G-CGMC	ERJ-135ER	145198 ◆
☐	G-CDEA	SAAB 2000	2000-009
☐	G-CDEB	SAAB 2000	2000-036
☐	G-CDKA	SAAB 2000	2000-006
☐	G-CDKB	SAAB 2000	2000-032
☐	G-CERY	SAAB 2000	2000-008
☐	G-CERZ	SAAB 2000	2000-042
☐	G-CFLU	SAAB 2000	2000-055
☐	G-CFLV	SAAB 2000	2000-023

EASYJET AIRLINES — U2 / EZY

☐	G-EJAR	A319-111	2412
☐	G-EJJB	A319-111	2380
☐	G-EZAA	A319-111	2677
☐	G-EZAB	A319-111	2681
■	G-EZAC	A319-111	2691
■	G-EZAD	A319-111	2702
☐	G-EZAF	A319-111	2715
■	G-EZAG	A319-111	2727
☐	G-EZAI	A319-111	2735
■	G-EZAJ	A319-111	2742
☐	G-EZAK	A319-111	2744
☐	G-EZAL	A319-111	2754
☐	G-EZAM	A319-111	2037
☐	G-EZAN	A319-111	2765
☐	G-EZAO	A319-111	2769
☐	G-EZAP	A319-111	2777
☐	G-EZAS	A319-111	2779
☐	G-EZAT	A319-111	2782
☐	G-EZAU	A319-111	2795
☐	G-EZAV	A319-111	2803
☐	G-EZAW	A319-111	2812
☐	G-EZAX	A319-111	2818
☐	G-EZAY	A319-111	2827
■	G-EZAZ	A319-111	2829
☐	G-EZBA	A319-111	2860
☐	G-EZBB	A319-111	2854
☐	G-EZBC	A319-111	2866
☐	G-EZBD	A319-111	2873
☐	G-EZBE	A319-111	2884
☐	G-EZBF	A319-111	2923
☐	G-EZBG	A319-111	2946
■	G-EZBH	A319-111	2959
☐	G-EZBI	A319-111	3003
☐	G-EZBJ	A319-111	3036
☐	G-EZBK	A319-111	3041
☐	G-EZBL	A319-111	3053
☐	G-EZBM	A319-111	3059
☐	G-EZBN	A319-111	3061
☐	G-EZBO	A319-111	3082
☐	G-EZBR	A319-111	3088
☐	G-EZBT	A319-111	3090
☐	G-EZBU	A319-111	3118
☐	G-EZBV	A319-111	3122
☐	G-EZBW	A319-111	3134
☐	G-EZBX	A319-111	3137
☐	G-EZBY	A319-111	3176
☐	G-EZBZ	A319-111	3184

☐	G-EZDA	A319-111	3413
☐	G-EZDB	A319-111	3411
☐	G-EZDC	A319-111	2043
☐	G-EZDD	A319-111	3442
☐	G-EZDE	A319-111	3426
☐	G-EZDF	A319-111	3432
☐	G-EZDH	A319-111	3466
☐	G-EZDI	A319-111	3537
☐	G-EZDJ	A319-111	3544
☐	G-EZDK	A319-111	3555
☐	G-EZDL	A319-111	3569
☐	G-EZDM	A319-111	3571
☐	G-EZDN	A319-111	3608
☐	G-EZDO	A319-111	3634
☐	G-EZDP	A319-111	3675
☐	G-EZDR	A319-111	3683
☐	G-EZDS	A319-111	3702
☐	G-EZDT	A319-111	3720
☐	G-EZDU	A319-111	3735
☐	G-EZDV	A319-111	3742
☐	G-EZDW	A319-111	3746
☐	G-EZDX	A319-111	3754
☐	G-EZDY	A319-111	3763
☐	G-EZDZ	A319-111	3774
☐	G-EZEA	A319-111	2119
☐	G-EZEB	A319-111	2120
☐	G-EZEC	A319-111	2129
☐	G-EZED	A319-111	2170
☐	G-EZEF	A319-111	2176
☐	G-EZEG	A319-111	2181
☐	G-EZEJ	A319-111	2214
☐	G-EZEK	A319-111	2224
☐	G-EZEO	A319-111	2249
■	G-EZEP	A319-111	2251
☐	G-EZET	A319-111	2271
☐	G-EZEU	A319-111	2283
☐	G-EZEV	A319-111	2289
☐	G-EZEW	A319-111	2300
☐	G-EZEZ	A319-111	2360
☐	G-EZFA	A319-111	3788
☐	G-EZFB	A319-111	3799
☐	G-EZFC	A319-111	3808
☐	G-EZFD	A319-111	3810
☐	G-EZFE	A319-111	3824
☐	G-EZFF	A319-111	3844
■	G-EZFG	A319-111	3845
■	G-EZFH	A319-111	3854
■	G-EZFI	A319-111	3888
☐	G-EZFJ	A319-111	4040
☐	G-EZFK	A319-111	4048
☐	G-EZFL	A319-111	4056
☐	G-EZFM	A319-111	4069
■	G-EZFN	A319-111	4076
☐	G-EZFO	A319-111	4080
☐	G-EZFP	A319-111	4087
☐	G-EZFR	A319-111	4125
■	G-EZFS	A319-111	4129
☐	G-EZFT	A319-111	4132
☐	G-EZFU	A319-111	4313 ◆
☐	G-EZFV	A319-111	4327 ◆
☐	G-EZFW	A319-111	4380 ◆
■	G-EZFX	A319-111	4385 ◆
☐	G-EZFY	A319-111	4418 ◆
☐	G-EZFZ	A319-111	4425 ◆
☐	G-EZGA	A319-111	4427 ◆
☐	G-EZGB	A319-111	4437 ◆
■	G-EZGC	A319-111	4444 ◆
☐	G-EZGD	A319-111	4451 ◆
■	G-EZGE	A319-111	o/o ◆
☐	G-	A319-111	o/o ◆
☐	G-	A319-111	o/o ◆
☐	G-	A319-111	o/o ◆
☐	G-	A319-111	o/o ◆
☐	G-	A319-111	o/o ◆

	Reg	Type	Serial	
☐	G-	A319-111		o/o♦
☐	G-	A319-111		o/o♦
☐	G-	A319-111		o/o♦
☐	G-	A319-111		o/o♦
☐	G-	A319-111		o/o♦
☐	G-EZIA	A319-111	2420	
☐	G-EZIC	A319-111	2436	
☐	G-EZID	A319-111	2442	
☐	G-EZIE	A319-111	2446	
☐	G-EZIG	A319-111	2460	
☐	G-EZIH	A319-111	2463	
☐	G-EZII	A319-111	2471	
☐	G-EZIJ	A319-111	2477	
☐	G-EZIK	A319-111	2481	
☐	G-EZIL	A319-111	2492	
☐	G-EZIM	A319-111	2495	
☐	G-EZIN	A319-111	2503	
☐	G-EZIO	A319-111	2512	
☐	G-EZIP	A319-111	2514	
☐	G-EZIR	A319-111	2527	
☐	G-EZIS	A319-111	2528	
☐	G-EZIT	A319-111	2538	
☐	G-EZIU	A319-111	2548	
☐	G-EZIV	A319-111	2565	
☐	G-EZIW	A319-111	2578	
☐	G-EZIX	A319-111	2605	
☐	G-EZIY	A319-111	2636	
☐	G-EZIZ	A319-111	2646	
☐	G-EZMH	A319-111	2053	
☐	G-EZMS	A319-111	2378	
☐	G-EZNC	A319-111	2050	
☐	G-EZPG	A319-111	2385	
☐	G-EZSM	A319-111	2062	
☐	G-EZTA	A320-214	3805	
☐	G-EZTB	A320-214	3843	
☐	G-EZTC	A320-214	3871	
☐	G-EZTD	A320-214	3909	
☐	G-EZTE	A320-214	3913	
☐	G-EZTF	A320-214	3922	
☐	G-EZTG	A320-214	3946	
☐	G-EZTH	A320-214	3953	
☐	G-EZTI	A320-214	3975	
☐	G-EZTJ	A320-214	3979	
☐	G-EZTK	A320-214	3991	
☐	G-EZTL	A320-214	4012	
☐	G-EZTM	A320-214	4014	
☐	G-EZTN	A320-214	4006	
☐	G-EZTP	A320-214	4157	
☐	G-EZTR	A320-214	4179	
☐	G-EZTS	A320-214	4196	
☐	G-EZTT	A320-214	4219	♦
☐	G-EZTU	A320-214	4233	♦
☐	G-EZTV	A320-214	4234	♦
☐	G-EZTW	A320-214	4250	♦
☐	G-EZTX	A320-214	4286	♦
☐	G-EZTY	A320-214	4543	♦
☐	G-EZTZ	A320-214	4556	♦
☐	G-EZUA	A320-214	4588	♦
☐	G-EZUC	A320-214	4591	♦
☐	G-EZUD	A320-214	4636	o/o♦
☐	G-EZUE	A320-214		o/o♦
☐	G-EZUF	A320-214		o/o♦
☐	G-EZUG	A320-214		o/o♦
☐	G-EZUH	A320-214		o/o♦
☐	G-	A320-214		o/o♦
☐	G-	A320-214		o/o♦
☐	G-	A320-214		o/o♦
☐	G-	A320-214		o/o♦
☐	G-TTOG	A320-232	1969	
☐	G-TTOJ	A320-232	2157	
☐	G-EZJZ	B737-73V	32421/1357	
☐	G-EZKA	B737-73V	32422/1363	
☐	G-EZKC	B737-73V	32424/1450	
☐	G-EZKD	B737-73V	32425/1453	
☐	G-EZKE	B737-73V	32426/1474	
☐	G-EZKF	B737-73V	32427/1489	
☐	G-EZKG	B737-73V	32428/1495	

FLYBE — BE / BEE

	Reg	Type	Serial	
☐	G-ECOA	DHC-8-402Q	4180	
☐	G-ECOB	DHC-8-402Q	4185	
☐	G-ECOC	DHC-8-402Q	4197	
☐	G-ECOD	DHC-8-402Q	4206	
☐	G-ECOE	DHC-8-402Q	4212	♦
☐	G-ECOF	DHC-8-402Q	4216	♦
☐	G-ECOG	DHC-8-402Q	4220	
☐	G-ECOH	DHC-8-402Q	4221	
☐	G-ECOI	DHC-8-402Q	4224	
☐	G-ECOJ	DHC-8-402Q	4229	
☐	G-ECOK	DHC-8-402Q	4230	
☐	G-ECOM	DHC-8-402Q	4233	
☐	G-ECOO	DHC-8-402Q	4237	
☐	G-ECOP	DHC-8-402Q	4242	
☐	G-ECOR	DHC-8-402Q	4248	
☐	G-ECOT	DHC-8-402Q	4251	
☐	G-ECOV	DHC-8-402Q	4033	
☐	G-ECOY	DHC-8-402Q	4022	
☐	G-ECOZ	DHC-8-402Q	4034	
☐	G-FLBA	DHC-8-402Q	4253	
☐	G-FLBB	DHC-8-402Q	4255	
☐	G-FLBC	DHC-8-402Q	4257	
☐	G-FLBD	DHC-8-402Q	4259	♦
☐	G-FLBE	DHC-8-402Q	4261	♦
☐	G-FLBF	DHC-8-402Q	4344	♦
☐	G-FLBG	DHC-8-402Q	4350	o/o♦
☐	G-FLBH	DHC-8-402Q	4366	o/o♦
☐	G-FLBI	DHC-8-402Q	4370	o/o♦
☐	G-JECE	DHC-8-402Q	4094	
☐	G-JECF	DHC-8-402Q	4095	
☐	G-JECG	DHC-8-402Q	4098	
☐	G-JECH	DHC-8-402Q	4103	
☐	G-JECI	DHC-8-402Q	4105	
☐	G-JECJ	DHC-8-402Q	4110	
☐	G-JECK	DHC-8-402Q	4113	
☐	G-JECL	DHC-8-402Q	4114	
☐	G-JECM	DHC-8-402Q	4118	
☐	G-JECN	DHC-8-402Q	4120	
☐	G-JECO	DHC-8-402Q	4126	
☐	G-JECP	DHC-8-402Q	4136	
☐	G-JECR	DHC-8-402Q	4139	
☐	G-JECS	DHC-8-402Q	4142	
☐	G-JECT	DHC-8-402Q	4144	
☐	G-JECU	DHC-8-402Q	4146	
☐	G-JECX	DHC-8-402Q	4155	
☐	G-JECY	DHC-8-402Q	4157	
☐	G-JECZ	DHC-8-402Q	4179	
☐	G-JEDI	DHC-8-402Q	4052	
☐	G-JEDJ	DHC-8-402Q	4058	
☐	G-JEDK	DHC-8-402Q	4065	
☐	G-JEDL	DHC-8-402Q	4067	
☐	G-JEDM	DHC-8-402Q	4077	
☐	G-JEDN	DHC-8-402Q	4078	
☐	G-JEDO	DHC-8-402Q	4079	
☐	G-JEDP	DHC-8-402Q	4085	
☐	G-JEDR	DHC-8-402Q	4087	
☐	G-JEDT	DHC-8-402Q	4088	
☐	G-JEDU	DHC-8-402Q	4089	
☐	G-JEDV	DHC-8-402Q	4090	
☐	G-JEDW	DHC-8-402Q	4093	
☐	G-KKEV	DHC-8-402Q	4201	
☐	G-	ERJ-175LR		o/o♦
☐	G-	ERJ-175LR		o/o♦
☐	G-	ERJ-175LR		o/o♦
☐	G-	ERJ-175LR		o/o♦
☐	G-FBEA	ERJ-195LR	19000029	
☐	G-FBEB	ERJ-195LR	19000057	
☐	G-FBEC	ERJ-195LR	19000069	

☐	G-FBED	ERJ-195LR	19000084
☐	G-FBEE	ERJ-195LR	19000093
☐	G-FBEF	ERJ-195LR	19000104
☐	G-FBEG	ERJ-195LR	19000120
☐	G-FBEH	ERJ-195LR	19000128
☐	G-FBEI	ERJ-195LR	19000143
☐	G-FBEJ	ERJ-195LR	19000155
☐	G-FBEK	ERJ-195LR	19000168
☐	G-FBEL	ERJ-195LR	19000184
☐	G-FBEM	ERJ-195LR	19000204
☐	G-FBEN	ERJ-195LR	19000213

GLOBAL SUPPLY SYSTEMS — GSS

☐	G-GSSA	B747-47UF	29256/1213	<GTI
☐	G-GSSB	B747-47UF	29252/1165	<GTI
☐	G-GSSC	B747-47UF	29255/1184	<GTI
☐	G-GSSD	B747-87UF	37562/1429	o/o♦
☐	G-GSSE	B747-87UF	37563/1432	o/o♦

HD AIR — RPX

☐	G-CLAS	Short SD.3-60	SH3635

ISLES OF SCILLY SKYBUS — 5Y / IOS

☐	G-BIHO	DHC-6 Twin Otter 310	738
☐	G-CBML	DHC-6 Twin Otter 310	695
☐	G-CEWM	DHC-6 Twin Otter 300	656

JANES AVIATION

☐	G-AYIM	HS.748 Srs.2A/270	1687	[SEN]
☐	G-OSOE	HS.748 Srs.2A/270	1697	[SEN]

JET2 — LS / EXS

☐	G-CELA	B737-377	23663/1323	
☐	G-CELB	B737-377	23664/1326	
☐	G-CELC	B737-33A	23831/1471	
☐	G-CELD	B737-33A	23832/1473	
■	G-CELE	B737-33A	24029/1601	19/3
☐	G-CELF	B737-377	24302/1618	
☐	G-CELG	B737-377	24303/1620	
☐	G-CELH	B737-330(QC)	23525/1278	
☐	G-CELI	B737-330	23526/1282	
☐	G-CELJ	B737-330	23529/1293	
☐	G-CELK	B737-330	23530/1297	
■	G-CELO	B737-33A(QC)	24028/1599	9/7.
☐	G-CELP	B737-330(QC)	23522/1246	
☐	G-CELR	B737-330(QC)	23523/1271	
■	G-CELS	B737-377	23660/1294	23/3.
☐	G-CELU	B737-377	23657/1280	
■	G-CELV	B737-377	23661/1314	19/3
☐	G-CELW	B737-377F	23659/1292	
☐	G-CELX	B737-377	23654/1273	
☐	G-CELY	B737-377F	23662/1316	
■	G-CELZ	B737-377F	23658/1281	>A/3
☐	G-CGET	B737-33A	27455/2709	
☐	G-GDFA	B737-3G7	24011/1608	
☐	G-GDFB	B737-33A	25743/2206	♦
☐	G-GDFC	B737-8K2/W	28375/85	♦
☐	G-LSAA	B757-236	24122/187	
☐	G-LSAB	B757-27B/W	24136/169	
☐	G-LSAC	B757-23A/W	25488/471	
■	G-LSAD	B757-236	24397/221	
☐	G-LSAE	B757-27B/W	24135/165	
■	G-LSAG	B757-21B	24014/144	11/3
☐	G-LSAH	B757-21B	24015/148	
☐	G-LSAI	B757-21B	24016/150	
☐	G-LSAJ	B757-236	24793/292	
☐	G-LSAK	B757-23N	27973/735	

LOGANAIR — LOG

☐	G-GNTB	SAAB SF.340A(QC)	340A-082
☐	G-GNTF	SAAB SF.340A(QC)	340A-113
☐	G-LGNA	SAAB SF.340B	340B-199
☐	G-LGNB	SAAB SF.340B	340B-216
☐	G-LGNC	SAAB SF.340B	340B-318
☐	G-LGND	SAAB SF.340B	340B-169
☐	G-LGNE	SAAB SF.340B	340B-172
☐	G-LGNF	SAAB SF.340B	340B-192
☐	G-LGNG	SAAB SF.340B	340B-327
☐	G-LGNH	SAAB SF.340B	340B-333
☐	G-LGNI	SAAB SF.340B	340B-160
☐	G-LGNJ	SAAB SF.340B	340B-173
☐	G-LGNK	SAAB SF.340B	340B-185
☐	G-LGNL	SAAB SF.340B	340B-246
☐	G-LGNM	SAAB SF.340B	340B-187
☐	G-LGNN	SAAB SF.340B	340B-197
☐	G-BJOP	BN Islander	2132
☐	G-BLDV	BN Islander	2179
☐	G-BPCA	BN Islander	2198
☐	G-BVVK	DHC-6 Twin Otter 310	666
☐	G-BZFP	DHC-6 Twin Otter 310	696

LYDD AIR — LYD

☐	G-OJAV	BN Trislander	1024

MANX2 AIRLINES

☐	D-CMNX	Do228-202K	8065
☐	D-IFLM	Do228-201	8046
☐	D-ILKA	Do228-100	7005
☐	OK-ASA	LET L-410UVP-E	902439
☐	OK-TCA	LET L-410UVP-E	902431
☐	OK-UBA	LET L-410UVP-E	892319

MONARCH AIRLINES — ZB / MON

☐	G-MAJS	A300B4-605R	604
☐	G-MONR	A300B4-605R	540
☐	G-MONS	A300B4-605R	556
☐	G-OJMR	A300B4-605R	605
☐	G-MONX	A320-212	0392
☐	G-MPCD	A320-212	0379
☐	G-MRJK	A320-214	1081
☐	G-OZBD	A320-212	0389
☐	G-OZBK	A320-214	1370
☐	G-MARA	A321-231	0983
☐	G-OJEG	A321-231	1015
☐	G-OZBE	A321-231	1707
☐	G-OZBF	A321-231	1763
☐	G-OZBG	A321-231	1941
☐	G-OZBH	A321-231	2105
☐	G-OZBI	A321-231	2234
☐	G-OZBL	A321-231	0864
☐	G-OZBM	A321-231	1045
■	G-OZBN	A321-231	1153	19/3
■	G-OZBO	A321-231	1207
☐	G-OZBP	A321-231	1433
☐	G-OZBR	A321-231	1794
☐	G-OZBS	A321-231	1428
☐	G-OZBT	A321-231	3546
☐	G-OZBU	A321-231	3575
☐	G-EOMA	A330-243	265
☐	G-SMAN	A330-243	261
☐	G-DAJB	B757-2T7ER	23770/125
☐	G-MONJ	B757-2T7ER	24104/170
☐	G-MONK	B757-2T7ER	24105/172

SCOTAIRWAYS — CB / SAY

	Type	Serial
☐ G-BWIR	Do328-100	3023
☐ G-BWWT	Do328-110	3022
☐ G-BYHG	Do328-110	3098
☐ G-BYMK	Do328-110	3062
☐ G-BZOG	Do328-110	3088
☐ G-CCGS	Do328-110	3101

SKYSOUTH — SDL

	Type	Serial	
☐ G-TABS	EMB.110P1	110212	[SEN]

THOMAS COOK AIRLINES — MT / TCX

	Type	Serial	
☐ G-CRPH	A320-231	0424	
☐ G-DHJZ	A320-214	1965	
☐ G-DHRG	A320-214	1942	>SSV
☐ G-FTDF	A320-231	0437	<SSV
☐ G-GTDL	A320-231	0476	
☐ G-KKAZ	A320-214	2003	
☐ G-OMYA	A320-214	0716	
☐ G-SUEW	A320-214	1961	19/2
☐ G-TCAC	A320-232	1411	
☐ G-TCAD	A320-214	2114	
☐ G-DHJH	A321-211	1238	
☐ G-NIKO	A321-211	1250	
☐ G-OMYJ	A321-211	0677	
☐ G-TCDA	A321-211	2060	
☐ G-MDBD	A330-243	266	
☐ G-MLJL	A330-243	254	
☐ G-OJMB	A330-243	427	
☐ G-OJMC	A330-243	456	
☐ G-OMYT	A330-243	301	
☐ G-TCXA	A330-243	795	
☐ G-FCLA	B757-28A	27621/738	
☐ G-FCLB	B757-28A	28164/749	
☐ G-FCLC	B757-28A	28166/756	
☐ G-FCLD	B757-25F	28718/752	
☐ G-FCLE	B757-28A	28171/805	17/3
☐ G-FCLF	B757-28A	28835/858	
☐ G-FCLH	B757-28A	26274/676	
☐ G-FCLI	B757-28A	26275/672	
☐ G-FCLJ	B757-2Y0	26160/555	
☐ G-FCLK	B757-2Y0	26161/557	
☐ G-JMAA	B757-3CQ	32241/960	
☐ G-JMAB	B757-3CQ	32242/963	
☐ G-JMCD	B757-25F	30757/928	
☐ G-JMCE	B757-25F	30758/932	
☐ G-JMCG	B757-2G5	26278/671	
☐ G-TCBA	B757-28AER	28203/802	
☐ G-TCBB	B757-236	29945/873	♦
☐ G-TCBC	B757-236	29946/877	♦
☐ G-WJAN	B757-21K	28674/746	
☐ G-DAJC	B767-31KER/W	27206/533	19/2
☐ G-TCCA	B767-31KER/W	27205/528	
☐ G-TCCB	B767-31KER/W	28865/657	♦

THOMSONFLY.COM — BY / TOM

	Type	Serial	
☐ G-OOAR	A320-214	1320	19/3
☐ G-OOPP	A320-214	1571	
☐ G-OOPT	A320-214	1605	
☐ G-OOPU	A320-214	1637	
☐ G-OOPX	A320-214	2180	
☐ G-OOPE	A321-211	0852	
☐ G-OOPH	A321-211	0781	
☐ G-THOL	B737-36N	28594/3107	
☐ G-THON	B737-36N	28596/3112	
☐ G-THOO	B737-33V	29335/3094	
☐ G-THOP	B737-3U3	28740/3003	

	Type	Serial	
☐ G-CDZH	B737-804	28227/452	
☐ G-CDZI	B737-804	28229/478	
☐ G-CDZL	B737-804	30465/502	
☐ G-CDZM	B737-804	30466/505	
☐ G-FDZA	B737-8K5/W	35134/2152	
☐ G-FDZB	B737-8K5/W	35131/2242	
☐ G-FDZD	B737-8K5/W	35132/2276	
☐ G-FDZE	B737-8K5/W	35137/2482	
☐ G-FDZF	B737-8K5/W	35138/2499	
☐ G-FDZG	B737-8K5/W	35139/2538	
☐ G-FDZJ	B737-8K5/W	34690/2184	<HLX
☐ G-FDZR	B737-8K5/W	35145/2849	
☐ G-FDZS	B737-8K5/W	35147/2866	
☐ G-FDZT	B737-8K5/W	37248/3532	♦
☐ G-FDZU	B737-8K5/W	37253/3562	o/o♦
☐ G-FDZW	B737-8K5/W		o/o♦
☐ G-FDZX	B737-8K5/W		o/o♦
☐ G-FDZY	B737-8K5/W		o/o♦
☐ G-FDZZ	B737-8K5/W		o/o♦
☐ G-BYAI	B757-204	26967/522	
☐ G-BYAL	B757-204	25626/549	
☐ G-BYAO	B757-204	27235/598	
☐ G-BYAP	B757-204	27236/600	
☐ G-BYAT	B757-204	27208/606	
☐ G-BYAU	B757-204	27220/618	
☐ G-BYAW	B757-204	27234/663	
☐ G-BYAX	B757-204/W	28834/850	
☐ G-BYAY	B757-204/W	28836/861	
☐ G-CPEP	B757-2Y0	25268/400	
☐ G-CPEU	B757-236/W	29941/864	
☐ G-CPEV	B757-236/W	29943/871	
☐ G-OOBA	B757-28A/W	32446/950	
☐ G-OOBB	B757-28A/W	32447/951	
☐ G-OOBC	B757-28A/W	33098/1026	♦
☐ G-OOBD	B757-28A	33099/1028	
☐ G-OOBE	B757-28A	33100/1029	
☐ G-OOBF	B757-28A/W	33101/1041	
☐ G-OOBG	B757-236/W	29942/867	
☐ G-OOBH	B757-236/W	29944/872	19/2
☐ G-OOBI	B757-2B7	27146/551	
☐ G-OOBJ	B757-2B7	27147/552	
☐ G-OOBN	B757-2Q8ER	29379/919	♦
☐ G-OOBP	B757-2Q8ER	30394/922	♦
☐ G-OOOX	B757-2Y0ER	26158/526	
☐ G-DBLA	B767-35EER/W	26063/434	
☐ G-OOAN	B767-39HER/W	26256/484	♦
☐ G-OOBK	B767-324ER/W	27392/568	>/6
☐ G-OOBL	B767-324ER/W	27393/571	13/2
☐ G-OOBM	B767-324ER/W	27568/593	
☐ G-OBYD	B767-304ER/W	28042/649	
☐ G-OBYE	B767-304ER/W	28979/691	
☐ G-OBYF	B767-304ER/W	28208/705	
☐ G-OBYG	B767-304ER/W	29137/733	
☐ G-OBYH	B767-304ER/W	28883/737	
☐ G-OBYJ	B767-304ER/W	29384/784	
☐ G-PJLO	B767-35EER	26064/438	

TITAN AIRWAYS — ZT / AWC

	Type	Serial	
☐ G-POWF	Avro 146-RJ100	E3373	♦
☐ G-ZAPK	BAe146 Srs.200(QC)	E2148	
☐ G-ZAPN	BAe146 Srs.200(QC)	E2119	
☐ G-ZAPO	BAe146 Srs.200(QC)	E2176	
☐ G-ZAPR	BAe146 Srs.200QT	E2114	
☐ G-POWC	B737-33A(QC)	25402/2159	
☐ G-ZAPV	B737-3Y0(SF)	24546/1811	
☐ G-ZAPW	B737-3L9(QC)	24219/1600	
☐ G-ZAPZ	B737-33A(QC)	25401/2067	
☐ G-ZAPX	B757-256	29309/936	
☐ G-POWD	B767-36NER	30847/902	

VIRGIN ATLANTIC AIRWAYS — VS / VIR

	Reg	Type	Serial	Notes
☐	G-VGEM	A330-3	1215	o/o ♦
☐	G-VINE	A330-3	1231	o/o ♦
■	G-VKSS	A330-3	1201	o/o ♦
☐	G-VLUV	A330-3	1206	o/o ♦
☐	G-VSXY	A330-3	1195	o/o ♦
☐	G-VAIR	A340-313X	164	
☐	G-VELD	A340-313X	214	
☐	G-VFAR	A340-313X	225	
☐	G-VHOL	A340-311	002	
☐	G-VSEA	A340-311	003	
☐	G-VSUN	A340-313	114	
☐	G-VATL	A340-642	376	
☐	G-VBLU	A340-642	723	
☐	G-VBUG	A340-642HGW	804	
☐	G-VEIL	A340-642	575	
☐	G-VFIT	A340-642	753	
☐	G-VFIZ	A340-642	764	
☐	G-VFOX	A340-642	449	
☐	G-VGAS	A340-642	639	
☐	G-VGOA	A340-642	371	[LDE]
☐	G-VMEG	A340-642	391	
☐	G-VNAP	A340-642	622	
☐	G-VOGE	A340-642	416	
■	G-VRED	A340-642	768	
☐	G-VSHY	A340-642	383	
☐	G-VSSH	A340-642	615	
☐	G-VWEB	A340-642	787	
☐	G-VWIN	A340-642	736	
☐	G-VWKD	A340-642	706	
☐	G-VYOU	A340-642	765	
■	G-VAST	B747-41R	28757/1117	
☐	G-VBIG	B747-4Q8	26255/1081	
☐	G-VFAB	B747-4Q8	24958/1028	
■	G-VGAL	B747-443	32337/1272	
☐	G-VHOT	B747-4Q8	26326/1043	
☐	G-VLIP	B747-443	32338/1274	
■	G-VROC	B747-41R	32746/1336	
■	G-VROS	B747-443	30885/1268	
■	G-VROY	B747-443	32340/1277	
■	G-VTOP	B747-4Q8	28194/1100	
☐	G-VWOW	B747-41R	32745/1287	
■	G-VXLG	B747-41R	29406/1177	

WEST ATLANTIC — NPT

	Reg	Type	Serial	Notes
☐	G-BTPA	BAeATP (LFD)	2007	
☐	G-BTPE	BAeATP (LFD)	2012	
☐	G-BTPF	BAeATP (LFD)	2013	
☐	G-BTPG	BAeATP (LFD)	2014	[CVT]
☐	G-BTPH	BAeATP (LFD)	2015	
☐	G-BTPJ	BAeATP (LFD)	2016	[CVT]
☐	G-BTPL	BAeATP (LFD)	2042	[CVT]
☐	G-BTTO	BAeATP (LFD)	2033	
☐	G-BUUP	BAeATP (LFD)	2008	
☐	G-BUUR	BAeATP (LFD)	2024	
☐	G-MANC	BAeATP (LFD)	2054	[CVT]
☐	G-MANH	BAeATP (LFD)	2017	
☐	G-OAAF	BAeATP	2029	
☐	G-OBWP	BAeATP (LFD)	2051	[CVT]
☐	G-JMCL	B737-322F	23951/1532	
☐	G-FIZU	L-188CF Electra	2014	
☐	G-LOFC	L-188CF Electra	1100	
☐	G-LOFE	L-188CF Electra	1144	

HA - HUNGARY

ABC AIR HUNGARY — AHU

	Reg	Type	Serial	Notes
☐	HA-LAD	LET L-410UVP-E	902516	
☐	HA-LAE	LET L-410UVP-E	902517	
☐	HA-LAS	LET L-410UVP-E4	871924	
☐	HA-LAV	LET L-410UVP-E	892215	<BPS
☐	HA-LAZ	LET L-410UVP-E	902504	<BPS

ATLANT HUNGARY — ATU

	Reg	Type	Serial	Notes
☐	HA-TCK	Il-76TD	1023409280	

BUDAPEST AIR SERVICES — BPS

	Reg	Type	Serial	Notes
☐	HA-FAI	EMB.120ER	120123	
☐	HA-FAL	EMB.120RT	120176	
☐	HA-FAN	EMB.120ER	120104	
☐	HA-LAF	LET L-410UVP-E8A	902518	
☐	HA-LAV	LET L-410UVP-E	892215	>AHU
☐	HA-LAZ	LET L-410UVP-E	902504	>AHU
☐	HA-TCT	An-26B	13505	
☐	HA-TCY	An-26B	97308205	<MJL
☐	HA-YFD	LET L-410UVP-E17	892324	

CITYLINE HUNGARY — ZM / CNB

	Reg	Type	Serial	Notes
☐	HA-TCM	An-26	14009	
☐	HA-TCN	An-26	7705	
☐	HA-TCO	An-26	2208	

FARNAIR HUNGARY — FAH

	Reg	Type	Serial	Notes
☐	HA-FAD	F.27 Friendship 500	10449	
☐	HA-FAF	F.27 Friendship 500F	10632	
☐	HA-FAH	F.27 Friendship 500F	10634	
☐	HA-FAJ	Beech 1900C-1	UC-79	
☐	HA-FAM	Beech 1900D	UE-16	
☐	HA-LAQ	LET L-410UVP-E4	841332	
☐	HA-YFC	LET L-410FG	851528	

FLEET AIR INTERNATIONAL

	Reg	Type	Serial	Notes
☐	HA-TAB	SAAB SF.340A	340A-083	
☐	HA-TAD	SAAB SF.340A	340A-126	

HEGEDUS

	Reg	Type	Serial	Notes
☐	HA-TCO	An-26	2208	>CNB

MALEV - HUNGARIAN AIRLINES — MA / MAH

	Reg	Type	Serial	Notes
☐	HA-LOA	B737-7Q8	28254/1283	
☐	HA-LOB	B737-7Q8	29346/1264	
☐	HA-LOC	B737-8Q8	32797/1287	
☐	HA-LOD	B737-6Q8	28259/1378	
☐	HA-LOE	B737-6Q8	28260/1400	
☐	HA-LOF	B737-6Q8	29348/1415	
☐	HA-LOG	B737-6Q8	28261/1437	
☐	HA-LOH	B737-7Q8	30667/1448	
☐	HA-LOI	B737-7Q8	29350/1452	
☐	HA-LOJ	B737-6Q8	29349/1455	
☐	HA-LOK	B737-8Q8	30669/1479	
☐	HA-LOL	B737-7Q8	29352/1491	
☐	HA-LOM	B737-8Q8	30672/1497	
☐	HA-LON	B737-6Q8	29353/1508	
☐	HA-LOP	B737-7Q8	29354/1581	
☐	HA-LOR	B737-7Q8	29355/1609	
☐	HA-LOS	B737-7Q8	29359/1659	
☐	HA-LOU	B737-8Q8	30684/1689	
☐	HA-LQA	DHC-8-402Q	4054	
☐	HA-LQB	DHC-8-402Q	4057	
☐	HA-LQC	DHC-8-402Q	4062	
☐	HA-LQD	DHC-8-402Q	4063	
☐	HA-LHB	B767-27GER	27049/482	[BUD]
☐	HA-LNA	CRJ-200ER	7676	[BUD]

TRAVEL SERVICE HUNGARY — TVL

☐	HA-LKB	B737-86Q/W	30294/1469
☐	HA-LKE	B737-86Q/W	30278/963 ♦

WIZZ AIR — W6 / WZZ

☐	HA-LPA	A320-233	0839
☐	HA-LPB	A320-233	1635
☐	HA-LPC	A320-233	0892
☐	HA-LPD	A320-233	1902
☐	HA-LPE	A320-233	1892
☐	HA-LPF	A320-233	1834
☐	HA-LPH	A320-232	2688
☐	HA-LPI	A320-232	2752
☐	HA-LPJ	A320-232	3127
☐	HA-LPK	A320-232	3143
☐	HA-LPL	A320-232	3166
☐	HA-LPM	A320-232	3177
☐	HA-LPN	A320-232	3354
☐	HA-LPO	A320-232	3384
☐	HA-LPQ	A320-232	3409
☐	HA-LPR	A320-232	3430
☐	HA-LPS	A320-232	3771
☐	HA-LPT	A320-232	3807
☐	HA-LPU	A320-232	3877
☐	HA-LPV	A320-232	3927
☐	HA-LPW	A320-232	3947
☐	HA-LPX	A320-232	3968
☐	HA-LPY	A320-232	4109
☐	HA-LPZ	A320-232	4174
☐	HA-LWA	A320-232	4223 ♦
☐	HA-LWB	A320-232	4246 ♦
☐	HA-LWC	A320-232	4323 ♦
☐	HA-LWD	A320-232	4351 ♦
☐	HA-LWE	A320-232	4372 ♦
☐	HA-	A320-232	o/o♦
☐	HA-	A320-232	o/o♦
☐	HA-	A320-232	o/o♦
☐	HA-	A320-232	o/o♦
☐	HA-	A320-232	o/o♦
☐	HA-	A320-232	o/o♦

HB - SWITZERLAND

AIR ENGIADINA

☐	HB-AEU	Do 328 Jet	3199

BELAIR AIRLINES — 4T / BHP

☐	HB-IOX	A319-112	3604
☐	HB-IOY	A319-112	3202 ♦
☐	HB-IOP	A320-214	4187 ♦
☐	HB-IOQ	A320-214	3422 ♦
☐	HB-IOR	A320-214	4033
☐	HB-IOS	A320-214	2968
☐	HB-IOU	A320-214	3006
☐	HB-IOW	A320-214	3055
☐	HB-IOZ	A320-214	4294 ♦

BABOO — F7 / BBO

☐	HB-JQA	DHC-8-402Q	4017
☐	HB-JQB	DHC-8-402Q	4175

DARWIN AIRLINE — 0D / DWT

☐	HB-IYD	SAAB 2000	2000-059
☐	HB-IZG	SAAB 2000	2000-012
☐	HB-IZH	SAAB 2000	2000-011
☐	HB-IZJ	SAAB 2000	2000-015
☐	HB-IZZ	SAAB 2000	2000-048

EASYJET SWITZERLAND — DS / EZS

☐	HB-JZF	A319-111	2184	<EZY
☐	HB-JZG	A319-111	2196	<EZY
☐	HB-JZH	A319-111	2230	<EZY
☐	HB-JZI	A319-111	2245	<EZY
☐	HB-JZJ	A319-111	2265	<EZY
☐	HB-JZK	A319-111	2319	<EZY
☐	HB-JZL	A319-111	2353	<EZY
☐	HB-JZM	A319-111	2370	<EZY
☐	HB-JZN	A319-111	2387	<EZY
☐	HB-JZO	A319-111	2398	<EZY
☐	HB-JZP	A319-111	2427	<EZY
☐	HB-JZQ	A319-111	2450	<EZY
☐	HB-JZR	A320-214	4034	<EZY
☐	HB-JZS	A319-111	3084	<EZY
☐	HB-JZU	A319-111	2402	<EZY♦
☐	HB-JZV	A319-111	2709	<EZY♦
☐	HB-JZW	A319-111	2729	<EZY♦

EDELWEISS AIR — WK / EDW

☐	HB-IHX	A320-214	942	<Alp Air
☐	HB-IHY	A320-214	947	<Alp Air
☐	HB-IHZ	A320-214	1026	

FARNAIR SWITZERLAND — FAT

☐	HB-AFC	ATR 42-320F	87
☐	HB-AFD	ATR 42-320	121
☐	HB-AFF	ATR 42-320	264
☐	HB-AFG	ATR 72-201F	108
☐	HB-AFH	ATR 72-202F	313
☐	HB-AFJ	ATR 72-202F	154
☐	HB-AFK	ATR 72-202F	232
☐	HB-AFL	ATR 72-202F	222
☐	HB-AFM	ATR 72-202F	364
☐	HB-AFN	ATR 72-202F	389
☐	HB-AFP	ATR 72-201F	381
☐	HB-AFR	ATR 72-201F	195
☐	HB-AFS	ATR 72-201F	198
☐	HB-AFV	ATR 72-201F	341 ♦
☐	HB-AFW	ATR 72-201F	419 ♦

HELLO — HW / FHE

☐	HB-JIY	A320-214	1171 ♦
☐	HB-JIZ	A320-214	0936 ♦
☐	HB-JID	MD-90-30	53460/2142
☐	HB-JIE	MD-90-30	53461/2147
☐	HB-JIF	MD-90-30	53462/2149

HELVETIC AIRWAYS — 2L / OAW

☐	HB-JVC	Fokker 100	11501
☐	HB-JVE	Fokker 100	11459
☐	HB-JVF	Fokker 100	11466
☐	HB-JVG	Fokker 100	11478
☐	HB-JVH	Fokker 100	11324 ♦
☐	HB-JVI	Fokker 100	11325 ♦

PRIVATAIR — PTI

☐	D-APBB	B737-8Q8/W	35278/2625	
☐	HB-IEE	B757-23A/W	24527/249	
☐	HB-IIQ	B737-7CN/W	30752/451	[AMM]
☐	HB-IIR	B737-86Q/W	30295/1600	
☐	HB-JJA	B737-7AK/W	34303/1758	>KLM
☐	HB-JJG	B767-306ER	30393/781	

SKYWORK AIRLINES — SRK

☐	HB-AES	Do328-110	3021
☐	HB-JGA	DHC-8-402Q	4198

SWISS EUROPEAN AIR LINES — SWU

☐	HB-IXN	Avro 146-RJ100	E3286
☐	HB-IXO	Avro 146-RJ100	E3284
☐	HB-IXP	Avro 146-RJ100	E3283
☐	HB-IXQ	Avro 146-RJ100	E3282
☐	HB-IXR	Avro 146-RJ100	E3281
☐	HB-IXS	Avro 146-RJ100	E3280
☐	HB-IXT	Avro 146-RJ100	E3259
☐	HB-IXU	Avro 146-RJ100	E3276
☐	HB-IXV	Avro 146-RJ100	E3274
☐	HB-IXW	Avro 146-RJ100	E3272
☐	HB-IXX	Avro 146-RJ100	E3262
☐	HB-IYQ	Avro 146-RJ100	E3384
☐	HB-IYR	Avro 146-RJ100	E3382
☐	HB-IYS	Avro 146-RJ100	E3381
☐	HB-IYT	Avro 146-RJ100	E3380
☐	HB-IYU	Avro 146-RJ100	E3379
☐	HB-IYV	Avro 146-RJ100	E3377
☐	HB-IYW	Avro 146-RJ100	E3359
☐	HB-IYY	Avro 146-RJ100	E3339
☐	HB-IYZ	Avro 146-RJ100	E3338

SWISS INTERNATIONAL AIRLINES — LX / SWR

☐	HB-IPR	A319-112	1018	
☐	HB-IPS	A319-112	0734	
☐	HB-IPT	A319-112	0727	
☐	HB-IPU	A319-112	0713	
☐	HB-IPV	A319-112	0578	
☐	HB-IPX	A319-112	0612	
☐	HB-IPY	A319-112	0621	
☐	HB-IJB	A320-214	0545	
☐	HB-IJD	A320-214	0553	
☐	HB-IJE	A320-214	0559	
☐	HB-IJF	A320-214	0562	
☐	HB-IJH	A320-214	0574	
☐	HB-IJI	A320-214	0577	
☐	HB-IJJ	A320-214	0585	
☐	HB-IJK	A320-214	0596	
☐	HB-IJL	A320-214	0603	
☐	HB-IJM	A320-214	0635	
☐	HB-IJN	A320-214	0643	
☐	HB-IJO	A320-214	0673	
☐	HB-IJP	A320-214	0681	
☐	HB-IJQ	A320-214	0701	
☐	HB-IJR	A320-214	0703	
☐	HB-IJS	A320-214	0782	
☐	HB-IJU	A320-214	1951	
☐	HB-IJV	A320-214	2024	
☐	HB-IJW	A320-214	2134	
☐	HB-IJX	A320-214	1762	
☐	HB-	A320-214		o/o♦
☐	HB-	A320-214		o/o♦
☐	HB-IOC	A321-111	0520	
☐	HB-IOD	A321-111	0522	
☐	HB-IOF	A321-111	0541	
☐	HB-IOH	A321-111	0664	
☐	HB-IOK	A321-111	0987	
☐	HB-IOL	A321-111	1144	
☐	HB-IOM	A321-212	4534	♦
☐	HB-IQA	A330-223	229	
☐	HB-IQC	A330-223	249	
☐	HB-IQH	A330-223	288	
☐	HB-IQI	A330-223	291	
☐	HB-IQQ	A330-223	322	
☐	HB-JHA	A330-343E	1000	
☐	HB-JHB	A330-343E	1018	
☐	HB-JHC	A330-343E	1026	
☐	HB-JHD	A330-343E	1029	
☐	HB-JHE	A330-343E	1084	
☐	HB-JHF	A330-343E	1089	♦
☐	HB-JHG	A330-343E	1101	♦
☐	HB-JHH	A330-343E	1145	♦
☐	HB-JHI	A330-343E	1181	♦
☐	HB-JHJ	A330-343E	1188	♦
☐	HB-	A330-343E		o/o♦
☐	HB-JMA	A340-313X	538	
☐	HB-JMB	A340-313X	545	
☐	HB-JMC	A340-313X	546	
☐	HB-JMD	A340-313X	556	
☐	HB-JME	A340-313X	559	
☐	HB-JMF	A340-313X	561	
☐	HB-JMG	A340-313X	562	
☐	HB-JMH	A340-313E	585	
☐	HB-JMI	A340-313E	598	
☐	HB-JMJ	A340-313X	150	
☐	HB-JMK	A340-313X	169	
☐	HB-JML	A340-313X	263	<AUA
☐	HB-JMM	A340-313X	154	
☐	HB-JMN	A340-313X	175	
☐	HB-JMO	A340-313X	179	
☐	HB-IIR	B737-86Q/W	1600/30295	<PTI
☐	D-AGPK	Fokker 100	11313	<KI

ZIMEX AVIATION — C4 / IMX

☐	HB-LOK	DHC-6 Twin Otter 300	658	
☐	HB-LQV	DHC-6 Twin Otter 300	643	
☐	HB-LRO	DHC-6 Twin Otter 300	523	
☐	HB-LRR	DHC-6 Twin Otter 300	505	
☐	HB-LTG	DHC-6 Twin Otter 300	628	
☐	HB-LTR	DHC-6 Twin Otter 300	238	
☐	HB-LUC	DHC-6 Twin Otter 300	351	
☐	HB-LUE	DHC-6 Twin Otter 300	233	
☐	HB-LUM	DHC-6 Twin Otter 300	420	
☐	ST-LRN	DHC-6 Twin Otter 310	636	
☐	HB-AEK	Beech 1900D	UE-296	
☐	HB-AEL	Beech 1900D	UE-385	
☐	HB-AEM	Beech 1900D	UE-379	

HC - ECUADOR

AEROGAL — 2K / GLG

☐	HC-CKL	A319-112	1866	♦
☐	HC-CKM	A319-112	1872	♦
☐	HC-	A319-112		o/o♦
☐	HC-	A319-112		o/o♦
☐	HC-	A319-112		o/o♦
☐	HC-CJM	A320-214	4379	♦
☐	HC-CJV	A320-214	4547	♦
☐	HC-CJW	A320-214	4489	♦
☐	HC-CDJ	B727-227	21246/1216	
☐	HC-CED	B737-2B7	22887/976	
☐	HC-CEQ	B737-2Y5	23848/1418	
☐	HC-CER	B737-2Y5	23847/1414	
☐	HC-CFG	B737-281	21770/588	
☐	HC-CFH	B737-2T5	22979/950	
☐	HC-CFM	B737-244	22589/843	
☐	HC-CFO	B737-2E3	22703/811	
☐	HC-CFR	B737-244	22581/796	
☐	HC-CGS	B737-3S3	23787/1374	
☐	HC-CHC	B757-236	25592/453	
☐	HC-CIY	B757-2K2/W	26635/608	♦
☐	HC-CIJ	B767-322ER	25287/449	

AIR CUENCA

☐	HC-CJB	B737-548	26287/2427	♦

ICARO EXPRESS — X8 / ICD

☐	HC-CFD	B737-236	21801/669 <SFR
☐	HC-CFL	B737-236	22026/644 <SFR
☐	HC-CFY	B737-290QC	22577/760
☐	HC-CJI	B737-205	22022/616 ♦

LAN ECUADOR — XL / LNE

☐	HC-CGZ	B767-3Q8ER/W	28206/694
☐	HC-CHA	B767-316ER/W	27613/652
☐	HC-CIZ	B767-316ER/W	36711/970 ♦
☐	HC-CJA	B767-316ER/W	35698/973 ♦
☐	HC-CJX	B767-316ER/W	35697/967 ♦

TAME — EQ / TAE

☐	HC-CGT	A319-132	2659
☐	HC-CGW	A320-233	2084
☐	HC-CDY	A320-233	2014
☐	HC-CGJ	A320-214	0657
☐	HC-CID	A320-232	0934
☐	HC-BHM	B727-2T3	22078/1644
☐	HC-BLE	B727-134	19691/487
☐	HC-BZS	B727-230	21620/1419
☐	HC-CEX	ERJ-170LR	17000087
☐	HC-CEY	ERJ-170LR	17000092
☐	HC-CEZ	ERJ-190LR	19000027
☐	HC-CGF	ERJ-190LR	19000137
☐	HC-CGG	ERJ-190LR	19000141
☐	HC-BZU	F.28 Fellowship 4000	11112
☐	HC-CEH	F.28 Fellowship 4000	11228

TRANS AM — 7T / TRM

☐	HC-CDX	ATR 42-300F	81Opf DHL

VIP -VUELOS INTERNOS PRIVADOS V6 / VUR

☐	HC-CFC	Do328-110	3018
☐	HC-CFI	Do328-110	3084
☐	HC-CFS	Do328-110	3039

HI - DOMINICAN REPUBLIC

AIR SANTO DOMINGO — EX / SDO

☐	HI657CT	Short SD.3-60	SH3672

CARIBAIR — CBC

☐	HI848	SAAB SF.340A	340A-128
☐	HI866	SAAB SF.340A	340A-138 o/o

PAN AM DOMINICA

☐	HI869	DC-9-32	47566/691
☐	HI876	DC-9-32	47046/168

HK - COLOMBIA

AERCARIBE

☐	HK-4427	An-32	1909
☐	HK-4257	An-32B	3203

AEROREPUBLICA COLOMBIA — P5 / RPB

☐	HK-3928X	DC-9-32	47311/398
☐	HK-3963	DC-9-32	47437/544
☐	HK-4155	DC-9-32	47524/632

☐	HK-4453X	ERJ-190LR	19000063
☐	HK-4454X	ERJ-190LR	19000061
☐	HK-4455X	ERJ-190LR	19000076
☐	HK-4456X	ERJ-190LR	19000074
☐	HK-4505X	ERJ-190LR	19000114
☐	HK-4506X	ERJ-190LR	19000110
☐	HK-4507X	ERJ-190LR	19000122
☐	HK-4508X	ERJ-190LR	19000138
☐	HK-4559X	ERJ-190LR	19000200
☐	HK-4560X	ERJ-190LR	19000208
☐	HK-4599	ERJ-190LR	19000269
☐	HK-4601	ERJ-190LR	19000251
☐	HP-1562CMP	ERJ-190AR	19000095 <CMP
☐	HK-4238X	MD-81	48009/985 [BOG]
☐	HK-4259	MD-81	48005/957
☐	HK-4265	MD-81	48002/938
☐	HK-4408X	MD-83	53124/1991 [VCV]♦

AEROSUCRE — 6N / KRE

☐	HK-727	B727-59F	19127/243
☐	HK-3985	B727-224F	20465/814
☐	HK-4216	B737-230C	20253/223
☐	HK-4253X	B737-2H6C	21109/436
☐	HK-4328	B737-2S5C	22148/663
☐	HK-4465	B727-222F	19915/681
☐	HK-4504	B727-2J0F	21108/1174
☐	HK-4544	B727-2J0F	21105/1158

AIRES — 4C / ARE

☐	HK-3951	DHC-8-301	184
☐	HK-3952	DHC-8-301	169
☐	HK-4030	DHC-8-301	100
☐	HK-4107X	DHC-8Q-311	224
☐	HK-4345	DHC-8-102	63
☐	HK-4432X	DHC-8-201	428
☐	HK-4473	DHC-8Q-201	479
☐	HK-4480	DHC-8Q-201	509
☐	HK-4491	DHC-8Q-201	478
☐	HK-4495	DHC-8Q-201	497
☐	HK-4509	DHC-8Q-201	507
☐	HK-4513X	DHC-8Q-201	468
☐	HK-4520	DHC-8Q-201	465
☐	HK-4539	DHC-8Q-201	452
☐	HK-4554X	DHC-8Q-201	450
☐	HK-4618	DHC-8-201	432
☐	HK-4724X	DHC-8-402Q	4137 ♦
☐	HK-4725X	DHC-8-402Q	4124 ♦
☐	HK-4726	DHC-8-402Q	4119 ♦
☐	HK-4727X	DHC-8-402Q	4129 ♦
☐	HK-4608	B737-73S/W	29080/211
☐	HK-4623	B737-73S/W	29081/215
☐	HK-4627	B737-73S/W	29078/187
☐	HK-4635	B737-73V/W	30249/1128
☐	HK-4641	B737-73V/W	30244/1148
☐	HK-4660X	B737-752/W	34296/1783
☐	HK-4675X	B737-73V/W	32415/1260
☐	HK-4694	B737-7Q8/W	30687/2252 ♦
☐	HK-4695	B737-7Q8/W	30710/2188 ♦

ARKAS

☐	HK-4492X	ATR 42-300	15
☐	HK-4493X	ATR 42-300F	18

AVIANCA — AV / AVA

☐	N590EL	A318-111	2328 ♦
☐	N591EL	A318-111	2333 ♦
☐	N592EL	A318-111	2358 ♦
☐	N593EL	A318-111	2367 ♦
☐	N594EL	A318-111	2377 ♦
☐	N595EL	A318-111	2394 ♦

☐	N596EL	A318-111	2523	♦
☐	N597EL	A318-111	2544	♦
☐	N598EL	A318-111	2552	♦
☐	N599EL	A318-111	2575	♦
☐	HK-4553	A319-112	3467	
☐	HK-4552	A319-112	3518	
☐	N422AV	A319-115	4200	♦
☐	N647AV	A319-115	3647	
☐	N691AV	A319-115	3691	
☐		A319-115		o/o♦
☐		A319-115		o/o♦
☐		A319-115		o/o♦
☐	HK-4549	A320-214	3408	
☐	HK-4659	A320-214	4100	
☐	N281AV	A320-214	4281	♦
☐	N284AV	A320-214	4284	♦
☐	N345AV	A320-214	4345	♦
☐	N398AV	A320-214	3988	
☐	N401AV	A320-214	4001	
☐	N411AV	A320-214	4011	
☐	N416AV	A320-214	4167	
☐	N417AV	A320-214	4175	♦
☐	N426AV	A320-214	4026	
☐	N446AV	A320-214	4046	
☐	N451AV	A320-214	4051	
☐	N481AV	A320-214	4381	♦
☐	N664AV	A320-214	3664	
☐	N961AV	A320-214	3961	
☐	N980AV	A320-214	3980	
☐	N992AV	A320-214	3992	
☐		A320-214		o/o♦
☐		A320-214		o/o♦
☐		A320-214		o/o♦
☐		A320-214		o/o♦
☐	N948AC	A330-243	948	
☐	N967CG	A330-243	967	
☐	N968AV	A330-243	1009	
☐	N969AV	A330-243	1016	
☐	N973AV	A330-243	1073	
☐		A330-243		o/o♦
☐	N421AV	B767-2B1ER	25421/407	
☐	N728CG	B767-283ER	24728/305	
☐	N984AN	B767-383ER	24357/262	
☐	N986AN	B767-259ER	24835/321	
☐	HK-4467	Fokker 50	20301	
☐	HK-4468X	Fokker 50	20300	>SAM
☐	HK-4469X	Fokker 50	20285	>SAM
☐	HK-4470	Fokker 50	20297	
☐	HK-4487X	Fokker 50	20266	>SAM
☐	HK-4496X	Fokker 50	20278	
☐	HK-4497X	Fokker 50	20288	>SAM
☐	HK-4501X	Fokker 50	20299	
☐	HK-4580	Fokker 50	20296	
☐	HK-4581	Fokker 50	20281	
☐	EI-CBY	MD-83	49944/1888	
☐	EI-CBZ	MD-83	49945/1889	
☐	EI-CCE	MD-83	49947/1900	
☐	EI-CEQ	MD-83	53123/1987	
☐	HK-4590X	MD-83	49942/1799	♦
☐	HK-4592X	MD-83	53122/1984	♦
☐	N632CT	MD-83	49632/1603	

COSMOS AIR CARGO

☐	HK-4386X	B727-82C/W	19968/660
☐	HK-4407X	B727-30C/W	19011/387

EASYFLY

☐	HK-4502	BAeJetstream 4101	41091
☐	HK-4503	BAeJetstream 4101	41093
☐	HK-4521	BAeJetstream 4101	41092
☐	HK-4522	BAeJetstream 4101	41086
☐	HK-4551	BAeJetstream 4101	41089
☐	HK-4568	BAeJetstream 4101	41057
☐	HK-4584X	BAeJetstream 4101	41073 [BOG]
☐	HK-4585X	BAeJetstream 4101	41067
☐	HK-4596X	BAeJetstream 4101	41079
☐	HK-	BAeJetstream 41	41074 ♦

HELICOL — HEL

☐	HK-3340W	DHC-7-102	108

LAN CARGO COLOMBIA

☐	N312LA	B767-316F/W	32572/846
☐	N418LA	B767-316F/W	34246/936

LINEAS AEREAS SURAMERICANAS — LAU

☐	HK-1271	B727-24C	19524/428
☐	HK-1273	B727-24C	19526/442
☐	HK-3814X	B727-25F	18270/79
☐	HK-4154	B727-51F	18804/162
☐	HK-4261	B727-251F	21156/1170
☐	HK-4262	B727-2F9F/W	21427/1291
☐	HK-4354	B727-2X3F	22608/1727
☐	HK-4401	B727-2X3F	22609/1731
☐	HK-4607	B727-259F	22476/1747
☐	HK-4636	B727-2S2F	22927/1821
☐	HK-4637	B727-2S2F	22928/1822

SADELCA — SDK

☐	HK-4136X	An-32B	2509

SAEP — KSP

☐	HK-4296X	An-32A	1704

SAM — MM / SAM

☐	HK-4469X	Fokker 50	20285
☐	HK-4487X	Fokker 50	20266
☐	HK-4497X	Fokker 50	20288
☐	HK-4419	Fokker 100	11457
☐	HK-4420	Fokker 100	11482
☐	HK-4430	Fokker 100	11465
☐	HK-4431	Fokker 100	11506
☐	HK-4437	Fokker 100	11469
☐	HK-4438	Fokker 100	11514
☐	HK-4443	Fokker 100	11479
☐	HK-4444	Fokker 100	11458
☐	HK-4445	Fokker 100	11449
☐	HK-4451	Fokker 100	11464
☐	HK-4486	Fokker 100	11414
☐	HK-4488	Fokker 100	11376
☐	HK-4489	Fokker 100	11377
☐	HK-4578	Fokker 100	11413
☐	HK-4579	Fokker 100	11419

SATENA — 9N / NSE

☐	FAC-1182	ATR 42-500	526	♦
☐	FAC-1183	ATR 42-500	522	♦
☐	FAC-1160	Do328-120	3079	
☐	FAC-1161	Do328-120	3080	
☐	FAC-1162	Do328-120	3082	
☐	FAC-1163	Do328-120	3081	
☐	FAC-1164	Do328-120	3092	
☐	FAC-1165	Do328-120	3103	
☐	FAC-1171	ERJ-145LR	145774	
☐	FAC-1172	ERJ-145LR	145776	
☐	FAC-1176	ERJ-145EP	145165	

☐ FAC-1177	ERJ-145EP	145227	
☐ FAC-1180	ERJ-170LR	17000151	

SELVA

☐ HK-4052	An-32	1805	
☐ HK-4240	An-32B	3204	
☐ HK-4295	An-26	67304702	
☐ HK-4356	An-26B-100	77305109	
☐ HK-4369	An-32	2510	
☐ HK-4388	An-26B-100	27312402	
☐ HK-4706	An-26B-100	27312203	♦

TAMPA AIRLINES · QT / TPA

☐ N767QT	B767-241ER(SF)	23804/178
☐ N768QT	B767-241ER(SF)	23803/161
☐ N769QT	B767-241ER(SF)	23801/170
☐ N770QT	B767-241ER(SF)	23802/172

TAP LINEAS AEREAS

☐ HK-	B727-151C	19868/529

HL - SOUTH KOREA

AIR BUSAN · BX / ABL

☐ HL8213	A321-231	1970	♦
☐ HL8236	A321-231	1174	♦
☐ HL7232	B737-58E	25767/2614	
☐ HL7233	B737-58E	25768/2724	
☐ HL7250	B737-58E	25769/2737	
☐ HL7510	B737-48E	25771/2816	
☐ HL7517	B737-48E	25774/2909	

ASIANA AIRLINES · OZ / AAR

☐ HL7737	A320-232	2397	
☐ HL7738	A320-232	2459	
☐ HL7744	A320-232	2808	
☐ HL7745	A320-232	2840	
☐ HL7753	A320-232	2943	
☐ HL7762	A320-232	3244	
☐ HL7769	A320-232	3437	
☐ HL7772	A320-232	3483	
☐ HL7773	A320-232	3496	
☐ HL7776	A320-232	3641	
☐ HL7788	A320-232	3873	
☐ HL7594	A321-231	1356	
☐ HL7703	A321-231	1511	
☐ HL7711	A321-231	1636	
☐ HL7713	A321-231	1734	
☐ HL7722	A321-231	2041	
☐ HL7723	A321-231	2045	
☐ HL7729	A321-231	2110	
☐ HL7730	A321-231	2226	
☐ HL7731	A321-231	2247	
☐ HL7735	A321-231	2290	
☐ HL7761	A321-231	1227	
☐ HL7763	A321-231	3297	
☐ HL7767	A321-231	0802	
☐ HL7789	A321-231	4112	
☐ HL7790	A321-231	4142	
☐ HL7736	A330-323X	640	
☐ HL7740	A330-323X	676	
☐ HL7741	A330-323X	708	
☐ HL7746	A330-323X	772	
☐ HL7747	A330-323X	803	
☐ HL7754	A330-323X	845	
☐ HL7792	A330-323X	1001	
☐ HL7793	A330-323X	1055	
☐ HL7794	A330-323X	1151	♦
☐ HL	A330-323X		o/o♦

☐ HL7508	B737-48E	25772/2791	
☐ HL7511	B737-48E	27630/2848	
☐ HL7513	B737-48E	25776/2860	
☐ HL7413	B747-48EM(SF)	25405/880	
☐ HL7414	B747-48EM(SF)	25452/892	
☐ HL7415	B747-48EM(SF)	25777/946	
☐ HL7616	B747-446F	37483/1351	♦
☐ HL7417	B747-48EM	25779/1006	
☐ HL7418	B747-48E	25780/1035	
☐ HL7419	B747-48EF	25781/1044	
☐ HL7420	B747-48EF	25783/1064	
☐ HL7421	B747-48EM	25784/1086	
☐ HL7423	B747-48EM	25782/1115	
☐ HL7428	B747-48E	28552/1160	
☐ HL7436	B747-48EF	29170/1305	
☐ HL7604	B747-48EF	29907/1370	
☐ HL7247	B767-38E	25757/523	
☐ HL7248	B767-38E	25758/582	
☐ HL7506	B767-38E	25760/639	
☐ HL7507	B767-38EF	25761/616	
☐ HL7514	B767-38E	25763/656	
☐ HL7515	B767-38E	25762/658	
☐ HL7516	B767-38E	25759/668	
☐ HL7528	B767-38E	29129/693	
☐ HL7500	B777-28EER	28685/400	
☐ HL7596	B777-28EER	28681/322	
☐ HL7597	B777-28EER	28686/359	
☐ HL7700	B777-28EER	30859/403	
☐ HL7732	B777-28EER	29174/481	
☐ HL7739	B777-28EER	29175/526	
☐ HL7742	B777-28EER	29171/553	
☐ HL7755	B777-28EER	30861/646	
☐ HL7756	B777-28EER	30860/659	
☐ HL7775	B777-28EER	30862/738	
☐ HL7791	B777-28EER	35525/853	♦

EASTARJET · ZE / ESR

☐ HL7781	B737-683	28302/243	
☐ HL7797	B737-73V	30240/974	
☐ HL8204	B737-73V	30248/1118	
☐ HL8205	B737-73V	32412/1151	
☐ HL8207	B737-73V	32413/1202	
☐ HL8215	B737-73V	32417/1285	♦

JEJU AIR · 7C / JJA

☐ HL7779	B737-85F	28824/180	
☐ HL7780	B737-85F	28827/467	
☐ HL7796	B737-86N/W	28628/573	
☐ HL8206	B737-86J/W	30877/782	
☐ HL8214	B737-86N/W	28608/410	♦
☐ HL8232	B737-8K5/W	27979/44	♦
☐ HL8233	B737-85P/W	28383/266	♦
☐ HL8234	B737-86Q/W	30285/1237	♦

JIN AIR · LJ / JNA

☐ HL7555	B737-86N	30230/460
☐ HL7558	B737-86N	28625/590
☐ HL7564	B737-86N	28638/765
☐ HL7798	B737-809/W	28236/739

KOREAN AIR · KE / KAL

☐ HL7239	A300B4-622R	627
☐ HL7240	A300B4-622R	631
☐ HL7241	A300B4-622R	662
☐ HL7242	A300B4-622R	685
☐ HL7243	A300B4-622R	692
☐ HL7245	A300B4-622R	731
☐ HL7295	A300B4-622R	582
☐ HL7297	A300B4-622R	609

☐	HL7524	A330-322	206	
☐	HL7525	A330-322	219	
☐	HL7538	A330-223	222	
☐	HL7539	A330-223	226	
☐	HL7540	A330-322	241	
☐	HL7550	A330-322	162	
☐	HL7551	A330-322	172	
☐	HL7552	A330-223	258	
☐	HL7553	A330-323X	267	
☐	HL7554	A330-323X	256	
☐	HL7584	A330-323X	338	
☐	HL7585	A330-323X	350	
☐	HL7586	A330-323X	351	
☐	HL7587	A330-323X	368	
☐	HL7701	A330-323	425	
☐	HL7702	A330-323	428	
☐	HL7709	A330-323	484	
☐	HL7710	A330-323	490	
☐	HL7720	A330-323	550	
☐	HL8211	A330-223	1133	♦
☐	HL8212	A330-223	1155	♦
☐	HL	A330-223		o/o♦
☐	HL	A330-223		o/o♦
☐	HL7611	A380-861	035	o/o♦
☐	HL	A380-861		o/o♦
☐	HL	A380-861		o/o♦
☐	HL	A380-861		o/o♦
☐	HL	A380-861		o/o♦
☐	HL7556	B737-86N	28615/482	
☐	HL7557	B737-86N	28622/562	
☐	HL7559	B737-86N	28626/611	
☐	HL7560	B737-8B5/W	29981/622	
☐	HL7561	B737-8B5/W	29982/663	
☐	HL7562	B737-8B5	29983/678	
☐	HL7563	B737-86N	28636/756	
☐	HL7565	B737-8B5/W	29984/848	
☐	HL7566	B737-8B5/W	29985/852	
☐	HL7567	B737-86N	28647/878	
☐	HL7568	B737-8B5/W	29986/891	
☐	HL7757	B737-8GQ/W	35790/2119	
☐	HL7758	B737-8GQ/W	35791/2150	
☐	HL7785	B737-8GQ/W	37162/2906	
☐	HL7786	B737-8GQ/W	37163/2955	
☐	HL	B737-8GQ/W		o/o♦
☐	HL	B737-8GQ/W		o/o♦
☐	HL	B737-8GQ/W		o/o♦
☐	HL	B737-8GQ/W		o/o♦
☐	HL7569	B737-9B5	29987/999	
☐	HL7599	B737-9B5	29988/1026	
☐	HL7704	B737-9B5	29989/1082	
☐	HL7705	B737-9B5	29990/1162	
☐	HL7706	B737-9B5	29991/1188	
☐	HL7707	B737-9B5	29992/1190	
☐	HL7708	B737-9B5	29993/1208	
☐	HL7716	B737-9B5	29994/1320	
☐	HL7717	B737-9B5	29995/1332	
☐	HL7718	B737-9B5	29996/1338	
☐	HL7719	B737-9B5	29997/1416	
☐	HL7724	B737-9B5	29998/1494	
☐	HL7725	B737-9B5	29999/1512	
☐	HL7726	B737-9B5	30001/1729	
☐	HL7727	B737-9B5	30000/1536	
☐	HL7728	B737-9B5	30002/1620	
☐	HL	B737-9B5		o/o♦
☐	HL	B737-9B5		o/o♦
☐	HL7400	B747-4B5F	26414/1295	
☐	HL7402	B747-4B5	26407/1155	
☐	HL7403	B747-4B5F	26408/1163	
☐	HL7404	B747-4B5	26409/1170	
☐	HL7434	B747-4B5F	32809/1316	
☐	HL7437	B747-4B5F	32808/1323	
☐	HL7438	B747-4B5ERF	33515/1329	

☐	HL7439	B747-4B5ERF	33516/1338	
☐	HL7443	B747-2B5B	21772/363	
☐	HL7448	B747-4B5F	26416/1246	
☐	HL7449	B747-4B5F	26411/1248	
☐	HL7460	B747-4B5	26404/1107	
☐	HL7461	B747-4B5	26405/1118	
☐	HL7462	B747-4B5F	26406/1123	
☐	HL7465	B747-4B5	26412/1284	
☐	HL7466	B747-4B5F	26413/1286	
☐	HL7467	B747-4B5F	27073/1291	
☐	HL7472	B747-4B5	26403/1095	
☐	HL7473	B747-4B5	28335/1098	
☐	HL7480	B747-4B5M	24619/793	
☐	HL7482	B747-4B5BCF	25205/853	
☐	HL7483	B747-4B5BCF	25275/874	
☐	HL7484	B747-4B5	26392/893	
☐	HL7485	B747-4B5	26395/922	
☐	HL7486	B747-4B5	26396/951	
☐	HL7487	B747-4B5	26393/958	
☐	HL7488	B747-4B5	26394/986	
☐	HL7489	B747-4B5	27072/1013	
☐	HL7490	B747-4B5	27177/1019	
☐	HL7491	B747-4B5	27341/1037	
☐	HL7492	B747-4B5	26397/1055	
☐	HL7493	B747-4B5	26398/1057	
☐	HL7494	B747-4B5	27662/1067	
☐	HL7495	B747-4B5	28096/1073	
☐	HL7498	B747-4B5	26402/1092	
☐	HL7499	B747-4B5ERF	33517/1340	
☐	HL7600	B747-4B5ERF	33945/1347	
☐	HL7601	B747-4B5ERF	33946/1350	
☐	HL7602	B747-4B5ERF	34301/1365	
☐	HL7603	B747-4B5ERF	34302/1368	
☐	HL7605	B747-4B5ERF	35526/1375	
☐	HL7606	B747-4B5BCF	24199/739	
☐	HL7607	B747-4B5	24198/729	
☐	HL7608	B747-4B5BCF	24621/830	
☐	HL7609	B747-8HTF	37132/1425	o/o♦
☐	HL7610	B747-8HTF	37133/1426	o/o♦
☐	HL7526	B777-2B5ER	27947/148	
☐	HL7530	B777-2B5ER	27945/59	
☐	HL7531	B777-2B5ER	27946/62	
☐	HL7574	B777-2B5ER	28444/305	
☐	HL7575	B777-2B5ER	28445/309	
☐	HL7598	B777-2B5ER	27949/356	
☐	HL7714	B777-2B5ER	27951/411	
☐	HL7715	B777-2B5ER	28372/416	
☐	HL7721	B777-2B5ER	33727/452	
☐	HL7733	B777-2B5ER	34206/520	
☐	HL7734	B777-2B5ER	34207/528	
☐	HL7743	B777-2B5ER	34208/584	
☐	HL7750	B777-2B5ER	34209/633	
☐	HL7751	B777-2B5ER	34210/657	
☐	HL7752	B777-2B5ER	34211/682	
☐	HL7764	B777-2B5ER	34214/684	
☐	HL7765	B777-2B5ER	34212/711	
☐	HL7766	B777-2B5ER	34213/730	
☐	HL7532	B777-3B5	28371/162	
☐	HL7533	B777-3B5	27948/178	
☐	HL7534	B777-3B5	27950/120	
☐	HL7573	B777-3B5	27952/288	
☐	HL7782	B777-3B5ER	37643/785	
☐	HL7783	B777-3B5ER	37644/808	
☐	HL7784	B777-3B5ER	37136/823	
☐	HL8208	B777-3B5ER	37645/867	♦
☐	HL8209	B777-3B5ER	37646/875	♦
☐	HL8210	B777-3B5ER	40377/882	♦
☐	HL	B777-3B5ER		o/o♦
☐	HL	B777-3B5ER		o/o♦
☐	HL	B777-3B5ER		o/o♦

T'Way Air

☐	HL8232	B737-8K5/W	27979/44	♦

☐ HL8235	B737-8KG/W	39448/3262	♦
☐ HL8237	B737-8Q8/W	30654/1295	♦

YEONGNAM AIR

☐ HL7774	Fokker 100	11293

HP - PANAMA

AEROPERLAS · WL / APP

☐ HP-1251APP	Short SD.3-60	SH3610	
☐ HP-1315APP	Short SD.3-60	SH3614	[PAC]
☐ HP-1319APP	Short SD.3-60	SH3607	
☐ HP-1326APP	Short SD.3-60	SH3631	[BLB]
☐ HP-004APP	ATR 42-300	4	<ISV
☐ HP-1445APP	CL-66B	CL66B-7	
☐ TG-MYH	ATR 42-300	113	<TSP

AIR PANAMA · PST

☐ HP-1625PST	DHC-8-311A	519
☐ HP-1542PST	F.27 Friendship 500F	10560
☐ HP-1543PST	F.27 Friendship 400	10268
☐ HP-1604PST	F.27 Friendship 500F	10471
☐ HP-1631PST	F.27 Friendship 500	10658
☐ HP-1670PST	SAAB SF.340B	340B-299
☐ HP-1671PST	SAAB SF.340B	340B-294

ARROW PANAMA · 8A / WAP

☐ HP-441WAP	DC-8-63CF	45988/416

COPA AIRLINES · CM / CMP

☐ HP-1369CMP	B737-71Q/W	29047/235	669
☐ HP-1370CMP	B737-71Q/W	29048/288	670
☐ HP-1371CMP	B737-7V3/W	30049/388	671
☐ HP-1372CMP	B737-7V3/W	28607/399	672
☐ HP-1373CMP	B737-7V3/W	30458/459	673
☐ HP-1374CMP	B737-7V3/W	30459/494	674
☐ HP-1375CMP	B737-7V3/W	30460/558	675
☐ HP-1376CMP	B737-7V3/W	30497/574	676
☐ HP-1377CMP	B737-7V3/W	30462/1161	677
☐ HP-1378CMP	B737-7V3/W	30461/1173	678
☐ HP-1379CMP	B737-7V3/W	30463/1221	679
☐ HP-1380CMP	B737-7V3/W	30464/1241	680
☐ HP-1520CMP	B737-7V3/W	33707/1376	681
☐ HP-1521CMP	B737-7V3/W	33708/1379	682
☐ HP-1524CMP	B737-7V3/W	33705/1505	683
☐ HP-1525CMP	B737-7V3/W	33706/1518	684
☐ HP-1527CMP	B737-7V3/W	30676/1619	685
☐ HP-1528CMP	B737-7V3/W	29360/1644	686
☐ HP-1530CMP	B737-7V3/W	34535/1962	687
☐ HP-1531CMP	B737-7V3/W	34536/1995	688
☐ HP-1522CMP	B737-8V3/W	33709/1387	480
☐ HP-1523CMP	B737-8V3/W	33710/1397	481
☐ HP-1526CMP	B737-8V3/W	34006/1585	482
☐ HP-1529CMP	B737-8V3/W	29670/1711	483
☐ HP-1532CMP	B737-8V3/W	35068/2343	484
☐ HP-1533CMP	B737-8V3/W	35067/2423	485
☐ HP-1534CMP	B737-8V3/W	35125/2624	486
☐ HP-1535CMP	B737-8V3/W	35126/2805	487
☐ HP-1536CMP	B737-8V3/W	35127/2963	488
☐ HP-1537CMP	B737-8V3/W	36550/3114	489
☐ HP-1538CMP	B737-8V3/W	36554/3130	490
☐ HP-1539CMP	B737-8V3/W	29667/3151	491
☐ HP-1711CMP	B737-8V3/W	40663/3265	492♦
☐ HP-1712CMP	B737-8V3/W	40664/3267	493♦
☐ HP-1713CMP	B737-8V3/W	40890/3455	494♦
☐ HP-1714CMP	B737-8V3/W	40891/3476	495♦
☐ HP-1715CMP	B737-8V3/W	40361/3500	496♦

☐ HP-1716CMP	B737-8V3/W	40666/3567	o/o♦
☐ HP-	B737-8V3/W		o/o♦
☐ HP-	B737-8V3/W		o/o♦
☐ HP-	B737-8V3/W		o/o♦
☐ HP-	B737-8V3/W		o/o♦
☐ HP-	B737-8V3/W		o/o♦
☐ HP-	B737-8V3/W		o/o♦
☐ HP-	B737-8V3/W		o/o♦
☐ HP-	B737-8V3/W		o/o♦
☐ HP-	B737-8V3/W		o/o♦
☐ HP-1540CMP	ERJ-190AR	19000012	
☐ HP-1556CMP	ERJ-190AR	19000016	
☐ HP-1557CMP	ERJ-190AR	19000034	
☐ HP-1558CMP	ERJ-190AR	19000038	
☐ HP-1559CMP	ERJ-190AR	19000053	
☐ HP-1560CMP	ERJ-190AR	19000056	
☐ HP-1561CMP	ERJ-190AR	19000089	
☐ HP-1562CMP	ERJ-190AR	19000095	>RMB
☐ HP-1563CMP	ERJ-190AR	19000098	
☐ HP-1564CMP	ERJ-190AR	19000100	
☐ HP-1565CMP	ERJ-190AR	19000126	
☐ HP-1566CMP	ERJ-190AR	19000165	
☐ HP-1567CMP	ERJ-190AR	19000174	
☐ HP-1568CMP	ERJ-190AR	19000212	
☐ HP-1569CMP	ERJ-190AR	19000222	

DHLAERO EXPRESSO · D5 / DAE

☐ HP-1510DAE	B727-264F	20709/950	[ROW]
☐ HP-1610DAE	B727-264F	20780/986	
☐ HP-1710DAE	B727-2Q4F	22424/1683	
☐ HP-1810DAE	B757-27A	29611/910	♦
☐ HP-1910DAE	B757-27A	29607/832	♦
☐ HP-	B757-27A	29610/904	♦

PANAIR CARGO

☐ HP-1653CTW	B727-277F	21695/1481

PANAVIA CARGO AIRLINES · 6Z / PVI

☐ HP-1261PVI	B727-25F/W	18965/205	[PTY]
☐ HP-1585PVI	B727-224F	20662/1072	

HR - HONDURAS

AEROLINEAS SOSA · P4 / VSO

☐ HR-ARJ	Nord 262A-14	15
☐ HR-ARP	Nord 262A-27	33
☐ HR-ARU	Nord 262A-21	21
☐ HR-ASR	Fairchild F-27F	84

ATLANTIC AIRLINES · ZF / HHA

☐ HR-ATC	HS.748 Srs 2B/424	1801
☐ HR-ATI	Fairchild F-27F	95
☐ HR-ATL	F.27 Friendship 500F	10522
☐ HR-ATN	B737-2Y5	23040/955

ISLENA AIRLINES · WC / ISV

☐ HR-AUX	ATR 42-320(QC)	394
☐ HR-AVA	ATR 42-320	388
☐ HR-IAP	Short SD.3-60	SH3616
☐ HR-IAW	Short SD.3-60	SH3669
☐ HR-IAY	ATR 42-300	120

HS - THAILAND

BANGKOK AIRWAYS · PG / BKP

☐ HS-PGN	A319-132	3759

☐	HS-PGT	A319-132	3421
☐	HS-PGX	A319-132	3424
☐	HS-PGY	A319-132	3454
☐	HS-PGZ	A319-132	3694
☐	HS-PPA	A319-132	3911
☐	HS-PGU	A320-232	2254
☐	HS-PGV	A320-232	2310
☐	HS-PGW	A320-232	2509
☐	HS-PGA	ATR 72-212A	710
☐	HS-PGB	ATR 72-212A	708
☐	HS-PGC	ATR 72-212A	715
☐	HS-PGD	ATR 72-212A	833
☐	HS-PGF	ATR 72-212A	700
☐	HS-PGG	ATR 72-212A	692
☐	HS-PGK	ATR 72-212A	680
☐	HS-PGM	ATR 72-212A	704
☐	HS-	ATR 72-600	o/o♦
☐	HS-	ATR 72-600	o/o♦

BUSINESS AIR

☐	HS-BIA	B767-222ER	21868/10	
☐	HS-BIB	B767-341ER	24753/291	♦
☐	HS-BIC	B767-341ER	24752/289	♦

K-MILE AIR   8K / KMI

☐	HS-SCH	B727-247F	21700/1489	<TSE
☐	HS-SCJ	B727-247F	21392/1305	<TSE

NOK AIR   DD / NOK

☐	HS-DDL	B737-4Y0	24917/2071	
☐	HS-DDM	B737-4Y0	26065/2284	
☐	HS-DDN	B737-4Q8	24707/2057	♦
☐	HS-DDO	B737-4Y0	26081/2442	♦
☐	HS-DDP	B737-406	25355/2132	♦
☐	HS-DDQ	B737-4M0	29204/3051	♦
☐	HS-TDA	B737-4D7	24830/1899	
☐	HS-TDB	B737-4D7	24831/1922	
☐	HS-TDE	B737-4D7	26612/2330	
☐	HS-	B737-800		o/o
☐	HS-	B737-800		o/o

ONE-TWO GO   OG / QTG

☐	HS-OMA	MD-82	49439/1318	[DMK]
☐	HS-OMB	MD-82	49441/1322	
☐	HS OMC	MD-82	49479/1297	[DMK]
☐	HS-OMD	MD-82	49485/1316	
☐	HS-OME	MD-82	49182/1128	
☐	HS-OMI	MD-87	49464/1476	[DMK]
☐	HS-OMJ	MD-87	49465/1604	[DMK]
☐		MD-87	53040/1897	o/o
☐		MD-81	53297/2040	o/o
☐		MD-81	53298/2045	o/o
☐	HS-UTN	B747-346	23149/599	

ORIENT THAI AIRLINES   OX / OEA

☐	HS-	B737-324/W	23374/1204	o/o♦
☐	HS-STC	B747-412	26548/923	♦
☐	HS-UTD	B747-146A	21029/259	>QTG
☐	HS-UTM	B747-346SR	23637/655	
☐	HS-UTO	B747-346	23639/664	
☐	HS-UTV	B747-346	23151/607	
☐	HS-UTW	B747-346	23067/588	

PHUKET AIRLINES

☐	HS-AGN	B747-422	26474/988	♦
☐	HS-AKS	B747-422	26881/889	♦
☐	HS-VAC	B747-306	23056/587	
☐	HS-VAN	B747-312	23245/626	

SKY EYES AVIATION   I6 / SEQ

☐	HS-SEC	L-1011-200F Tristar	193N-1212	[FJR]

SKYSTAR AIRWAYS   XT / SKT

☐	HS-SSA	B767-222ER	21871/15	[ICN]
☐	HS-SSB	B767-222ER	21872/20	[ICN]
☐	HS-SSD	B767-222	21880/50	[CAN]

SUVARNABHUMI AIRLINES

☐	HS-AKU	B737-2B7	23115/998

THAI AIRASIA   FD / AIQ

☐	HS-ABA	A320-216	3277	
☐	HS-ABB	A320-216	3299	
☐	HS-ABC	A320-216	3338	
☐	HS-ABD	A320-216	3394	
☐	HS-ABE	A320-216	3489	
☐	HS-ABF	A320-216	3505	
☐	HS-ABG	A320-216	3576	
☐	HS-ABH	A320-216	3679	
☐	HS-ABI	A320-216	3729	
☐	HS-ABJ	A320-216	4019	
☐	HS-ABK	A320-216	4088	
☐	HS-ABL	A320-216	4126	
☐	HS-ABM	A320-216	4278	♦
☐	HS-ABN	A320-216	4302	♦
☐	HS-ABO	A320-216	4333	♦
☐	HS-ABP	A320-216	4367	♦
☐	HS-ABQ	A320-216	4386	♦
☐	HS-ABR	A320-216	4390	♦
☐	HS-ABS	A320-216	4426	♦
☐	HS-ABT	A320-216	4557	♦
☐	HS-	A320-216		o/o♦

THAI AIRWAYS INTERNATIONAL   TG / THA

☐	HS-TAF	A300B4-601	398	
☐	HS-TAG	A300B4-605R	464	
☐	HS-TAH	A300B4-605R	518	
☐	HS-TAK	A300B4-622R	566	
☐	HS-TAL	A300B4-622R	569	
☐	HS-TAM	A300B4-622R	577	
☐	HS-TAN	A300B4-622R	628	
☐	HS-TAO	A300B4-622R	629	
☐	HS-TAP	A300B4-622R	635	
☐	HS-TAR	A300B4-622R	681	
☐	HS-TAS	A300B4-622R	705	
☐	HS-TAT	A300B4-622R	782	
☐	HS-TAW	A300B4-622R	784	
☐	HS-TAX	A300B4-622R	785	
☐	HS-TAY	A300B4-622R	786	
☐	HS-TAZ	A300B4-622R	787	
☐	HS-TEA	A330-321	50	
☐	HS-TEB	A330-321	60	
☐	HS-TEC	A330-321	62	
☐	HS-TED	A330-321	64	
☐	HS-TEE	A330-321	65	
☐	HS-TEF	A330-321	66	
☐	HS-TEG	A330-321	112	
☐	HS-TEH	A330-321	122	
☐	HS-TEJ	A330-322	209	
☐	HS-TEK	A330-322	224	
☐	HS-TEL	A330-322	231	
☐	HS-TEM	A330-323X	346	
☐	HS-TEN	A330-343E	990	
☐	HS-TEO	A330-343E	1003	
☐	HS-TEP	A330-343E	1035	
☐	HS-TEQ	A330-343E	1037	[BOD]
☐	HS-TER	A330-343E	1060	[BOD]
☐	HS-TES	A330-343E	1074	[BOD]
☐	HS-TET	A330-343E	1086	[BOD]♦

☐	HS-TEU	A330-343E	1090	[BOD]♦
☐	HS-TLA	A340-541	624	
☐	HS-TLB	A340-541	628	
☐	HS-TLC	A340-541	698	
☐	HS-TLD	A340-541	775	
☐	HS-TNA	A340-642	677	
☐	HS-TNB	A340-642	681	
☐	HS-TNC	A340-642	689	
☐	HS-TND	A340-642	710	
☐	HS-TNE	A340-642	719	
☐	HS-TNF	A340-642	953	
☐	HS-	A380-841	70	o/o
☐	HS-	A380-841	75	o/o
☐	HS-TDF	B737-4D7	26613/2338	
☐	HS-TDG	B737-4D7	26614/2481	
☐	HS-TDH	B737-4D7	28703/2962	
☐	HS-TDJ	B737-4D7	28704/2968	
☐	HS-TDK	B737-4D7	28701/2977	
☐	HS-TYS	B737-8Z6/W	35478/1955	BBJ2
☐	HS-TGA	B747-4D7	32369/1273	
☐	HS-TGB	B747-4D7	32370/1278	
☐	HS-TGF	B747-4D7	33770/1335	
☐	HS-TGG	B747-4D7	33771/1337	
☐	HS-TGH	B747-4D7	24458/769	
☐	HS-TGJ	B747-4D7	24459/777	
☐	HS-TGK	B747-4D7	24993/833	
☐	HS-TGL	B747-4D7	25366/890	
☐	HS-TGM	B747-4D7	27093/945	
☐	HS-TGN	B747-4D7	26615/950	
☐	HS-TGO	B747-4D7	26609/1001	
☐	HS-TGP	B747-4D7	26610/1047	
☐	HS-TGR	B747-4D7	27723/1071	
☐	HS-TGT	B747-4D7	26616/1097	
☐	HS-TGW	B747-4D7	27724/1111	
☐	HS-TGX	B747-4D7	27725/1134	
☐	HS-TGY	B747-4D7	28705/1164	
☐	HS-TGZ	B747-4D7	28706/1214	
☐	HS-TJA	B777-2D7	27726/25	
☐	HS-TJB	B777-2D7	27727/32	
☐	HS-TJC	B777-2D7	27728/44	
☐	HS-TJD	B777-2D7	27729/51	
☐	HS-TJE	B777-2D7	27730/89	
☐	HS-TJF	B777-2D7	27731/95	
☐	HS-TJG	B777-2D7	27732/100	
☐	HS-TJH	B777-2D7	27733/113	
☐	HS-TJR	B777-2D7ER	34586/588	
☐	HS-TJS	B777-2D7ER	34587/595	
☐	HS-TJT	B777-2D7ER	34588/596	
☐	HS-TJU	B777-2D7ER	34589/599	
☐	HS-TJV	B777-2D7ER	34590/665	
☐	HS-TJW	B777-2D7ER	34591/672	
☐	HS-TKA	B777-3D7	29150/156	
☐	HS-TKB	B777-3D7	29151/170	
☐	HS-TKC	B777-3D7	29211/250	
☐	HS-TKD	B777-3D7	29212/260	
☐	HS-TKE	B777-3D7	29213/304	
☐	HS-TKF	B777-3D7	29214/310	
☐	N774SA	B777-FZB	37986/844	Lf SOO
☐	N775SA	B777-FZB	37987/852	Lf SOO
☐	HS-TRA	ATR 72-201	164	
☐	HS-TRB	ATR 72-201	167	

HZ - SAUDI ARABIA

ALWAFEER AIR　　　　　　　　　　　　　WFR

☐	HZ-AWA1	B747-4H6	27672/1091
☐	HZ-AWA2	B747-4H6	28426/1130
☐	HZ-AWA3	B747-4H6	25701/997

NAS AIR　　　　　　　　　　　　　　2N / KNE

☐	VP-CAN	A319-112	1886	
☐	HZ-XY7	A320-214	2165	
☐	VP-CXR	A320-214	3894	
☐	VP-CXS	A320-214	3787	
☐	VP-CXT	A320-214	3817	
☐	VP-CXW	A320-214	3475	
☐	VP-CXX	A320-214	3425	
☐	VP-CXY	A320-214	3396	
☐	VP-CXZ	A320-214	3361	
☐	VP-CQV	ERJ-190LR	19000367	♦
☐	VP-CQW	ERJ-190LR	19000232	
☐	VP-CQX	ERJ-190LR	19000233	
☐	VP-CQY	ERJ-190LR	19000227	
☐	VP-CQZ	ERJ-190LR	19000217	
☐		ERJ-190LR		o/o♦
☐		ERJ-190LR		o/o♦
☐		ERJ-190LR		o/o♦
☐		ERJ-190LR		o/o♦
☐		ERJ-190LR		o/o♦
☐		ERJ-190LR		o/o♦
☐		ERJ-190LR		o/o♦
☐		ERJ-190LR		o/o♦

SAUDI ARABIAN AIRLINES　　　　　　SV / SVA

☐	HZ-ASA	A320-214	4081	
☐	HZ-ASB	A320-214	4090	
☐	HZ-ASC	A320-214	4337	♦
☐	HZ-ASD	A320-214	4364	♦
☐	HZ-ASE	A320-214	4408	♦
☐	HZ-AS11	A320-214	4015	
☐	HZ-AS12	A320-214	4057	
☐	HZ-AS13	A320-214	4104	
☐	HZ-AS14	A320-214	4115	
☐	HZ-AS15	A320-214	4122	
☐	HZ-AS16	A320-214	4135	
☐	HZ-AS17	A320-214	4349	♦
☐	HZ-AS18	A320-214	4357	♦
☐	HZ-AS19	A320-214	4376	♦
☐	HZ-AS20	A320-214	4392	♦
☐	HZ-AS21	A320-214	4414	♦
☐	HZ-AS22	A320-214	4484	♦
☐	HZ-AS23	A320-214	4519	♦
☐	HZ-AS31	A320-214	4092	
☐	HZ-AS32	A320-214	4273	♦
☐	HZ-AS33	A320-214	4313	♦
☐	HZ-AS34	A320-214	4397	♦
☐	HZ-AS35	A320-214	4391	♦
☐	HZ-AS36	A320-214	4393	♦
☐	HZ-AS37	A320-214	4394	♦
☐	HZ-AS38	A320-214	4432	♦
☐	HZ-AS39	A320-214	4442	♦
☐	HZ-AS40	A320-214	4419	♦
☐	HZ-AS41	A320-214	4454	♦
☐	HZ-AS42	A320-214	4501	♦
☐	HZ-AS43	A320-214	4517	♦
☐	HZ-AS44	A320-214	4564	♦
☐	HZ-	A320-214		o/o♦
☐	HZ-	A320-214		o/o♦
☐	HZ-	A320-214		o/o♦
☐	HZ-	A320-214		o/o♦
☐	HZ-	A320-214		o/o♦
☐	HZ-	A320-214		o/o♦
☐	HZ-ASH	A321-211	4467	♦
☐	HZ-ASI	A321-211	4542	♦
☐	HZ-ASJ	A321-211	4577	♦
☐	HZ-ASK	A321-211	4590	o/o♦
☐	HZ-AQA	A330-343X	1108	♦
☐	HZ-AQB	A330-343X	1127	♦
☐	HZ-AQC	A330-343X	1137	♦

□	HZ-AQD	A330-343	1141	♦
□	HZ-AQE	A330-343	1147	♦
□	HZ-AQF	A330-343	1153	♦
□	HZ-AQG	A330-343	1192	♦
□	HZ-AQH	A330-343	1189	♦
□	TC-ETK	A330-223	358 Lsf KKK	
□	TC-ETL	A330-223	364 Lsf KKK	
□	HZ-AIB	B747-168B	22499/517	[JED]
□	HZ-AIC	B747-168B	22500/522	
□	HZ-AID	B747-168B	22501/525	
□	HZ-AIE	B747-168B	22502/530	
□	HZ-AII	B747-168B	22749/557	
□	HZ-AIK	B747-368	23262/616	
□	HZ-AIL	B747-368	23263/619	
□	HZ-AIM	B747-368	23264/620	
□	HZ-AIN	B747-368	23265/622	
□	HZ-AIP	B747-368	23267/630	
□	HZ-AIQ	B747-368	23268/631	
□	HZ-AIR	B747-368	23269/643	
□	HZ-AIS	B747-368	23270/645	
□	HZ-AIT	B747-368	23271/652	
□	HZ-AIU	B747-268F	24359/724	
□	HZ-AIV	B747-468	28339/1122	
□	HZ-AIW	B747-468	28340/1138	
□	HZ-AIX	B747-468	28341/1182	
□	HZ-AIY	B747-468	28342/1216	
□	TF-AMI	B747-412(SF)	27066/940	<ABD
□	TF-AMS	B747-481	24920/832 Lsf ABD	
□	TF-AMT	B747-481	25135/863	<ABD
□	TF-AMU	B747-48EF	27603/1210 Lsf ABD	
□	TF-AMV	B747-412	28022/1082	<ABD
□	TF-ARU	B747-344	22970/577	<ABD
□	HZ-AKA	B777-268ER	28344/98	
□	HZ-AKB	B777-268ER	28345/99	
□	HZ-AKC	B777-268ER	28346/101	
□	HZ-AKD	B777-268ER	28347/103	
□	HZ-AKE	B777-268ER	28348/109	
□	HZ-AKF	B777-268ER	28349/114	
□	HZ-AKG	B777-268ER	28350/119	
□	HZ-AKH	B777-268ER	28351/124	
□	HZ-AKI	B777-268ER	28352/143	
□	HZ-AKJ	B777-268ER	28353/147	
□	HZ-AKK	B777-268ER	28354/154	
□	HZ-AKL	B777-268ER	28355/166	
□	HZ-AKM	B777-268ER	28356/175	
□	HZ-AKN	B777-268ER	28357/181	
□	HZ-AKO	B777-268ER	28358/186	
□	HZ-AKP	B777-268ER	28359/194	
□	HZ-AKQ	B777-268ER	28360/219	
□	HZ-AKR	B777-268ER	28361/230	
□	HZ-AKS	B777-268ER	28362/255	
□	HZ-AKT	B777-268ER	28363/298	
□	HZ-AKU	B777-268ER	28364/306	
□	HZ-AKV	B777-268ER	28365/323	
□	HZ-AKW	B777-268ER	28366/351	
□	HZ-	B777-368		o/o♦
□	HZ-	B777-368		o/o♦
□	HZ-AEA	ERJ-170LR	17000108	
□	HZ-AEB	ERJ-170LR	17000114	
□	HZ-AEC	ERJ-170LR	17000118	
□	HZ-AED	ERJ-170LR	17000119	
□	HZ-AEE	ERJ-170LR	17000121	
□	HZ-AEF	ERJ-170LR	17000123	
□	HZ-AEG	ERJ-170LR	17000124	
□	HZ-AEH	ERJ-170LR	17000135	
□	HZ-AEI	ERJ-170LR	17000142	
□	HZ-AEJ	ERJ-170LR	17000145	
□	HZ-AEK	ERJ-170LR	17000149	
□	HZ-AEL	ERJ-170LR	17000152	
□	HZ-AEM	ERJ-170LR	17000155	
□	HZ-AEN	ERJ-170LR	17000158	
□	HZ-AEO	ERJ-170LR	17000161	

□	HZ-APA	MD-90-30	53491/2191	
□	HZ-APB	MD-90-30	53492/2205	
□	HZ-APC	MD-90-30	53493/2209	
□	HZ-APD	MD-90-30	53494/2213	
□	HZ-APE	MD-90-30	53495/2215	
□	HZ-APF	MD-90-30	53496/2216	
□	HZ-APG	MD-90-30	53497/2219	
□	HZ-APH	MD-90-30	53498/2221	
□	HZ-API	MD-90-30	53499/2223	
□	HZ-APJ	MD-90-30	53500/2225	
□	HZ-APK	MD-90-30	53501/2226	
□	HZ-APL	MD-90-30	53502/2227	
□	HZ-APM	MD-90-30	53503/2229	
□	HZ-APN	MD-90-30	53504/2230	
□	HZ-APO	MD-90-30	53505/2231	
□	HZ-APP	MD-90-30	53506/2232	
□	HZ-APQ	MD-90-30	53507/2235	
□	HZ-APR	MD-90-30	53508/2237	
□	HZ-APS	MD-90-30	53509/2250	
□	HZ-APT	MD-90-30	53510/2251	
□	HZ-APU	MD-90-30	53511/2255	
□	HZ-APV	MD-90-30	53512/2256	
□	HZ-APX	MD-90-30	53514/2260	
□	HZ-APY	MD-90-30	53515/2262	
□	HZ-APZ	MD-90-30	53516/2263	
□	HZ-AP3	MD-90-30	53518/2289	
□	HZ-AP4	MD-90-30	53519/2290	
□	HZ-AP7	MD-90-30	53517/2288	
□	HZ-ANA	MD-11F	48773/609	
□	HZ-ANB	MD-11F	48775/616	
□	HZ-ANC	MD-11F	48776/617	
□	HZ-AND	MD-11F	48777/618	
□	HZ-AGG	B737-268	20883/366	
□	TC-OAH	A300B4-605R	584	>OHY
□	TC-ETF	A321-231	1438	<KKK
□	TC-ETG	B757-256	26254/905	<KKK
□	TC-OGS	B757-256	29307/924	<KKK
□	TC-OGT	B757-256	29308/935	<KKK

SILVERWING

| □ | HZ-AJW | A319-112 | 1494 |

SNAS AVIATION RSE

□	HZ-SNA	B727-264F	20896/1051	
□	HZ-SNB	B727-223F	21084/1199	
□	HZ-SNC	B727-230F	20905/1091	<BCS
□	HZ-SND	B727-223F	20994/1190	<BCS
□	HZ-SNF	B727-230F	22643/1762	

I - ITALY

AIR DOLOMITI EN / DLA

□	I-ADLL	ATR 42-500	518	
□	I-ADLQ	ATR 42-500	606	[MGL]♦
□	I-ADCA	ATR 72-212A	658	
□	I-ADCB	ATR 72-212A	660	
□	I-ADCC	ATR 72-212A	662	
□	I-ADCD	ATR 72-212A	664	♦
□	I-ADCE	ATR 72-212A	668	♦
□	I-ADLJ	ATR 72-212A	686	
□	I-ADLK	ATR 72-212A	706	
□	I-ADLN	ATR 72-212A	557	
□	I-ADLO	ATR 72-212A	585	
□	I-ADLS	ATR 72-212A	634	
□	I-ADLT	ATR 72-212A	638	
□	I-ADLW	ATR 72-212A	707	
□	I-ADJK	ERJ-195LR	19000245	
□	I-ADJL	ERJ-195LR	19000256	
□	I-ADJM	ERJ-195LR	19000258	

Reg	Type	Serial	
I-ADJN	ERJ-195LR	19000270	
I-ADJO	ERJ-195LR	19000280	

AIR ITALY   I9 / AEY

Reg	Type	Serial	
EI-IGR	B737-36N/W	28561/2896	♦
EI-IGS	B737-36N/W	28562/2908	♦
I-AIGL	B737-33A	23636/1438	
I-AIGM	B737-33A	24299/1598	
I-AIGN	B737-84P/W	35074/2217	
I-AIGP	B737-76N/W	37233/2578	
I-AIGG	B767-304ER	28041/614	
I-AIGH	B767-23BER	23973/208	
I-AIGI	B767-23BER	23974/214	
I-AIGJ	B767-304ER	28039/610	

AIR VALLEE   DO / RVL

Reg	Type	Serial	
I-AIRJ	Do 328 Jet	3186	
I-AIRX	Do 328 Jet	3142	

ALITALIA   AZ / AZA

Reg	Type	Serial	
EI-IMC	A319-112	2057	♦
EI-IME	A319-112	1740	♦
EI-IMF	A319-112	2083	♦
EI-IMG	A319-112	2086	♦
EI-IMH	A319-112	2101	♦
EI-IMI	A319-112	1745	♦
EI-IMJ	A319-112	1779	♦
EI-IML	A319-112	2127	♦
EI-IMO	A319-112	1770	♦
I-BIMA	A319-112	1722	
I-BIMB	A319-112	2033	
I-BIMD	A319-112	2074	
EI-DSA	A320-216	2869	
EI-DSB	A320-216	2932	
EI-DSC	A320-216	2995	
EI-DSD	A320-216	3076	
EI-DSE	A320-216	3079	
EI-DSF	A320-216	3080	
EI-DSG	A320-216	3115	
EI-DSH	A320-216	3178	
EI-DSI	A320-216	3213	
EI-DSJ	A320-216	3295	
EI-DSK	A320-216	3328	
EI-DSL	A320-216	3343	
EI-DSM	A320-216	3362	
EI-DSN	A320-216	3412	
EI-DSO	A320-216	3464	
EI-DSP	A320-216	3482	
EI-DSR	A320-216	3502	
EI-DSS	A320-216	3515	
EI-DST	A320-216	3532	
EI-DSU	A320-216	3563	
EI-DSV	A320-216	3598	
EI-DSW	A320-216	3609	
EI-DSX	A320-216	3643	
EI-DSY	A320-216	3666	
EI-DSZ	A320-216	3695	
EI-DTA	A320-216	3732	
EI-DTB	A320-216	3815	
EI-DTC	A320-216	3831	
EI-DTD	A320-216	3846	
EI-DTE	A320-216	3885	
EI-DTF	A320-216	3906	
EI-DTG	A320-216	3921	
EI-DTH	A320-216	3956	
EI-DTI	A320-216	3976	
EI-DTJ	A320-216	3978	
EI-DTK	A320-216	4075	
EI-DTL	A320-216	4108	
EI-DTM	A320-216	4119	
EI-DTN	A320-216	4143	
EI-DTO	A320-216	4152	
EI-EIA	A320-216	4195	♦
EI-EIB	A320-216	4249	♦
EI-EIC	A320-216	4520	♦
EI-EID	A320-216	4523	♦
EI-EIE	A320-216	4536	♦
EI-	A320-216		o/o♦
EI-	A320-216		o/o♦
EI-	A320-216		o/o♦
EI-	A320-216		o/o♦
EI-	A320-216		o/o♦
EI-	A320-216		o/o♦
EI-	A320-216		o/o♦
EI-	A320-216		o/o♦
EI-	A320-216		o/o♦
EI-	A320-216		o/o♦
EI-	A320-216		o/o♦
EI-	A320-216		o/o♦
EI-	A320-216		o/o♦
EI-	A320-216		o/o♦
EI-	A320-216		o/o♦
EI-	A320-216		o/o♦
EI-	A320-216		o/o♦
EI-	A320-216		o/o♦
EI-	A320-216		o/o♦
EI-	A320-216		o/o♦
EI-IKB	A320-214	1226	♦
EI-IKL	A320-214	1489	♦
EI-IKU	A320-214	1217	♦
I-BIKA	A320-214	0951	
I-BIKC	A320-214	1448	
I-BIKD	A320-214	1457	
I-BIKE	A320-214	0999	
I-BIKF	A320-214	1473	
I-BIKG	A320-214	1480	
I-BIKI	A320-214	1138	
I-BIKO	A320-214	1168	
I-WEBA	A320-214	3138	
I-WEBB	A320-214	3161	
EI-IXC	A321-112	0526	♦
EI-IXG	A321-112	0516	♦
EI-IXH	A321-112	0940	♦
EI-IXI	A321-112	0494	♦
EI-IXJ	A321-112	0959	♦
EI-IXV	A321-112	0819	♦
EI-IXZ	A321-112	0848	♦
I-BIXA	A321-112	0477	
I-BIXB	A321-112	0524	
I-BIXD	A321-112	0532	
I-BIXE	A321-112	0488	
I-BIXF	A321-112	0515	
I-BIXK	A321-112	1220	
I-BIXL	A321-112	0513	
I-BIXM	A321-112	0514	
I-BIXN	A321-112	0576	
I-BIXO	A321-112	0495	
I-BIXP	A321-112	0583	
I-BIXQ	A321-112	0586	
I-BIXR	A321-112	0593	
I-BIXS	A321-112	0599	
I-BIXT	A321-112	0765	
I-BIXU	A321-112	0434	
EI-DIP	A330-202	339	
EI-DIR	A330-202	272	
EI-EJG	A330-202	1123	♦
EI-EJH	A330-202	1135	♦
EI-	A330-202		o/o♦
EI-	A330-202		o/o♦
EI-	A330-202		o/o♦
EI-	A330-202		o/o♦
EI-	A330-202		o/o♦
EI-	A330-202		o/o♦
D-AGMR	B737-430	27007/2367	

☐	EI-COI	B737-430	27002/2323	
☐	EI-CWE	B737-42C	24232/2060	
☐	EI-CWF	B737-42C	24814/2270	
☐	EI-CWW	B737-4Y0	24906/2009	
☐	EI-CWX	B737-4Y0	24912/2064	
☐	EI-DMR	B737-436	25851/2387	
☐	EI-DOH	B737-31S	29056/2928	
☐	EI-DOS	B737-49R	28881/2833	
☐	EI-DOV	B737-48E	27632/2857	
☐	F-GKTA	B737-3M8	24413/1884	
☐	EI-CRD	B767-31BER	26259/534	
☐	EI-CRF	B767-31BER	25170/542	
☐	EI-CRM	B767-343ER	30009/746	
☐	EI-DBP	B767-35HER	26389/459	
☐	EI-DDW	B767-3S1ER	26608/559	
☐	I-DEIG	B767-33AER	27918/603	
☐	EI-DBK	B777-243ER	32783/455	
☐	EI-DBL	B777-243ER	32781/459	
☐	EI-DBM	B777-243ER	32782/463	
☐	EI-DDH	B777-243ER	32784/477	
☐	I-DISA	B777-243ER	32855/413	
☐	I-DISB	B777-243ER	32859/426	
☐	I-DISD	B777-243ER	32860/439	
☐	I-DISE	B777-243ER	32856/421	
☐	I-DISO	B777-243ER	32857/424	
☐	I-DISU	B777-243ER	32858/425	
☐	I-DACQ	MD-82	49974/1774	[FCO]
☐	I-DACR	MD-82	49975/1775	
☐	I-DACS	MD-82	53053/1806	
☐	I-DACT	MD-82	53054/1856	
☐	I-DACU	MD-82	53055/1857	[NAP]
☐	I-DACV	MD-82	53056/1880	
☐	I-DACW	MD-82	53057/1894	[FCO]
☐	I-DACX	MD-82	53060/1944	[FCO]
☐	I-DACY	MD-82	53059/1942	[FCO]
☐	I-DACZ	MD-82	53058/1927	
☐	I-DAND	MD-82	53061/1957	
☐	I-DANF	MD-82	53062/1960	
☐	I-DANG	MD-82	53176/1972	
☐	I-DANH	MD-82	53177/1973	
☐	I-DANL	MD-82	53178/1994	[FCO]
☐	I-DANM	MD-82	53179/1997	[FCO]
☐	I-DANP	MD-82	53180/2002	[FCO]
☐	I-DANQ	MD-82	53181/2005	
☐	I-DANR	MD-82	53203/2007	[FCO]
☐	I-DANU	MD-82	53204/2009	
☐	I-DANV	MD-82	53205/2028	[FCO]
☐	I-DANW	MD-82	53206/2034	
☐	I-DATA	MD-82	53216/2048	[FCO]
☐	I-DATC	MD-82	53222/2080	
☐	I-DATD	MD-82	53223/2081	[FCO]
☐	I-DATE	MD-82	53217/2053	
☐	I-DATG	MD-82	53225/2086	
☐	I-DATH	MD-82	53226/2087	[FCO]
☐	I-DATI	MD-82	53218/2060	
☐	I-DATJ	MD-82	53227/2103	[FCO]
☐	I-DATM	MD-82	53230/2106	
☐	I-DATO	MD-82	53219/2062	[FCO]
☐	I-DATQ	MD-82	53233/2110	
☐	I-DATR	MD-82	53234/2111	[FCO]
☐	I-DATS	MD-82	53235/2113	[FCO]
☐	I-DAVB	MD-82	49216/1262	
☐	I-DAVJ	MD-82	49431/1377	
☐	I-DAVR	MD-82	49550/1584	[FCO]
☐	I-DAVT	MD-82	49552/1597	

ALITALIA EXPRESS   XM / SMX

☐	EI-DOT	CRJ-900ER	15066
☐	EI-DOU	CRJ-900ER	15068
☐	EI-DRI	CRJ-900ER	15076
☐	EI-DRJ	CRJ-900ER	15077
☐	EI-DRK	CRJ-900ER	15075

☐	EI-DUK	CRJ-900ER	15104
☐	EI-DVP	CRJ-900ER	15116
☐	EI-DVR	CRJ-900ER	15118
☐	EI-DVS	CRJ-900ER	15119
☐	EI-DVT	CRJ-900ER	15123
☐	EI-DFG	ERJ-170LR	17000008
☐	EI-DFH	ERJ-170LR	17000009
☐	EI-DFI	ERJ-170LR	17000010
☐	EI-DFJ	ERJ-170LR	17000011
☐	EI-DFK	ERJ-170LR	17000032
☐	EI-DFL	ERJ-170LR	17000036

BLU EXPRESS.COM   BV / BPA

☐	EI-CUA	B737-4K5	24901/1854	<BPA
☐	EI-CUD	B737-4Q8	26298/2564	<BPA
☐	EI-CUN	B737-4K5	27074/2281	<BPA
☐	EI-DVY	B737-31S	29059/2967	<BPA
☐	EI-DXB	B737-31S	29060/2979	<BPA
☐	EI-EEW	B737-375	23808/1434	
☐	EI-ERD	B737-36N	28563/2921	♦
☐	I-LLAG	B767-330ER	25137/377	

BLUE PANORAMA AIRLINES   BV / BPA

☐	EI-CUA	B737-4K5	24901/1854	
☐	EI-CUD	B737-4Q8	26298/2564	
☐	EI-CUN	B737-4K5	27074/2281	
☐	EI-DVY	B737-31S	29059/2967	
☐	EI-DXB	B737-31S	29060/2979	
☐	EI-DXC	B737-4Q8	26300/2604	♦
☐	EI-DKL	B757-231	28482/770	
☐	EI-DNA	B757-231	28483/777	
☐	EI-CXO	B767-3G5ER	28111/612	
☐	EI-CZH	B767-3G5ER	29435/720	
☐	EI-EED	B767-31AER	27619/595	

CARGOITALIA   2G / CRG

☐	EI-EMS	MD-11BCF	48766/600	♦
☐	EI-UPE	MD-11C	48427/471	♦
☐	EI-UPI	MD-11C	48428/474	
☐	I-CGIA	DC-10-30F	47843/335	[FNI]

CARGOLUX ITALIA   C8 / ICV

☐	LX-KCV	B747-4R7F	25868/1125

EAGLE AIRLINES   E3 / EGS

☐	I-GIOA	Fokker 100	11315	♦
☐	I-GIOB	Fokker 100	11364	o/o ♦
☐	I-GIOI	Fokker 100	11307	♦

ITALI AIRLINES   9X / ACL

☐	I-ACLG	Do 328 Jet	3133
☐	I-ACLH	Do 328 Jet	3152
☐	I-BSTI	SA.227AC Metro III	AC-470
☐	I-BSTS	SA.227AC Metro III	AC-603
☐	I-DAVA	MD-82	49215/1253
☐	I-DAWW	MD-82	49212/1233
☐	I-DAWZ	MD-82	49214/1245

ITALIATOUR AIRLINES

☐	I-CLBA	Avro 146-RJ85	E2300	[BSL]

LUFTHANSA ITALIA

☐	D-AILI	A319-114	0651
☐	D-AKNF	A319-112	0646
☐	D-AKNG	A319-112	0654

☐ D-AKNH	A319-112	0794	
☐ D-AKNI	A319-112	1016	
☐ D-AKNJ	A319-112	1172	

MERIDIANA FLY — IG / EEZ

☐ EI-DEZ	A319-112	1283	
☐ EI-DFA	A319-112	1305	
☐ EI-DFP	A319-112	1048	
☐ I-EEZQ	A319-112	0548	♦
☐ EI-EZO	A320-232	1723	♦
☐ EI-EZR	A320-214	1198	♦
☐ I-EEZE	A320-214	1937	
☐ I-EEZF	A320-214	1983	
☐ I-EEZG	A320-214	2001	
☐ I-EEZH	A320-214	0737	
☐ I-EEZI	A320-214	0749	
☐ I-EEZK	A320-214	1125	
☐ I-EEZN	A320-232	1715	
☐ I-EEZP	A320-233	2102	
☐ EI-EZL	A330-223	802	
☐ I-EEZJ	A330-223	665	
☐ I-EEZM	A330-223	822	
☐ EI-CIW	MD-83	49785/1628	
☐ EI-CKM	MD-83	49792/1655	
☐ EI-CNR	MD-83	53199/1968	
☐ EI-CRE	MD-83	49854/1601	
☐ EI-CRH	MD-83	49935/1773	
☐ EI-CRW	MD-83	49951/1915	
☐ I-SMEB	MD-82	53064/1908	
☐ I-SMEC	MD-83	49808/1836	
☐ I-SMEL	MD-82	49247/1151	
☐ I-SMEM	MD-82	49248/1152	
☐ I-SMEN	MD-83	53013/1738	
☐ I-SMEP	MD-82	49740/1618	
☐ I-SMER	MD-82	49901/1766	
☐ I-SMES	MD-82	49902/1948	
☐ I-SMET	MD-82	49531/1362	
☐ I-SMEV	MD-82	49669/1493	
☐ I-SMEZ	MD-82	49903/1949	

MINILINER — MNL

☐ I-MLGT	F.27 Friendship 500	10379	
☐ I-MLHT	F.27 Friendship 500	10382	
☐ I-MLQT	F.27 Friendship 400	10295	
☐ I-MLRT	F.27 Friendship 500	10377	
☐ I-MLTT	F.27 Friendship 500	10378	
☐ I-MLUT	F.27 Friendship 500	10369	
☐ I-MLVT	F.27 Friendship 500	10373	
☐ I-MLXT	F.27 Friendship 500	10374	
☐ I-MLCT	Fokker 50	20191	
☐ I-MLDT	Fokker 50	20197	
☐ PH-LMA	Fokker 50	20118	>APF
☐ PH-LMB	Fokker 50	20119	>APF

MISTRALAIR — MSA

☐ EI-DUS	B737-3M8(QC)	24021/1630	
☐ EI-DVA	B737-36E(QC)	25159/2068	
☐ EI-DVC	B737-33A(QC)	25426/2172	
☐ EI-ELY	B737-4S3	25595/2233	♦
☐ EI-ELZ	B737-4Q8	26308/2665	♦
☐ EI-SLA	ATR 42-300F	149	< ABR
☐ EI-SLC	ATR 42-300F	082	< ABR

NEOS — NO / NOS

☐ I-NDMJ	B767-306ER/W	27958/589	♦
☐ I-NDOF	B767-306ER	27610/605	
☐ I-NEOS	B737-86N/W	32733/1078	

☐ I-NEOT	B737-86N/W	33004/1144	
☐ I-NEOU	B737-86N/W	29887/1263	
☐ I-NEOW	B737-86N/W	32685/2186	
☐ I-NEOX	B737-86N/W	33677/1486	
☐ I-NEOZ	B737-86N/W	34257/2024	♦

SKYBRIDGE AUROPS

☐ I-SKYB	EMB.120RT	120087	

SOREM

☐ I-CFST	CL-215	1072	1
☐ I-SRMA	CL-215	1004	A1
☐ I-SRMC	CL-215	1076	S2
☐ I-SRMD	CL-215	1097	S3
☐ I-SRME	CL-215	1049	S4
☐ I-DPCC	CL-415	2066	27
☐ I-DPCD	CL-415	2003	7
☐ I-DPCE	CL-415	2004	8
☐ I-DPCF	CL-415	2059	23
☐ I-DPCG	CL-415	2060	24
☐ I-DPCH	CL-415	2062	25
☐ I-DPCI	CL-415	2058	26
☐ I-DPCN	CL-415	2070	28
☐ I-DPCO	CL-415	2009	10
☐ I-DPCP	CL-415	2020	11
☐ I-DPCQ	CL-415	2021	12
☐ I-DPCR	CL-415	2074	♦
☐ I-DPCS	CL-415	2073	♦
☐ I-DPCT	CL-415	2029	18
☐ I-DPCU	CL-415	2030	14
☐ I-DPCV	CL-415	2035	15
☐ I-DPCW	CL-415	2036	6
☐ I-DPCY	CL-415	2047	20
☐ I-DPCZ	CL-415	2048	21

VOLIAMO

☐ HA-LEW	B737-2K2C	20836/354	

WINDJET — IV / JET

☐ EI-DVD	A319-113	0647	
☐ EI-DVU	A319-113	0660	
☐ EI-ECX	A319-132	2698	
☐ EI-ECY	A319-132	2723	
☐ EI-CUM	A320-232	0542	
☐ EI-DFO	A320-211	0371	
☐ EI-DNP	A320-212	0421	
☐ EI-DOE	A320-211	0215	
☐ EI-DOP	A320-232	0816	
☐ EI-ELG	A320-232	0877	
☐ F-GJVC	A320-211	0204	
☐ I-LINH	A320-231	0163	

JA - JAPAN

AIR CENTRAL — NV / CRF

☐ JA841A	DHC-8-402Q	4080	
☐ JA853A	DHC-8-402Q	4135	
☐ JA854A	DHC-8-402Q	4151	

AIR DO — HD / ADO

☐ JA300K	B737-54K	27434/2872	<ANA
☐ JA8404	B737-54K	27381/2708	<ANA
☐ JA8504	B737-54K	27432/2783	
☐ JA8595	B737-54K	28461/2850	
☐ JA01HD	B767-33AER	28159/689	
☐ JA98AD	B767-33AER	27476/687	
☐ JA8258	B767-381	23758/179	

AIR NEXT — 7A / NXA

☐	JA302K	B737-54K	28990/3002	<ANA
☐	JA304K	B737-54K	28992/3030	<ANA
☐	JA306K	B737-54K	29794/3109	<ANA
☐	JA307K	B737-54K	29795/3116	<ANA
☐	JA351K	B737-5Y0	25189/2240	<ANA
☐	JA352K	B737-5Y0	26097/2534	<ANA
☐	JA353K	B737-5Y0	26104/2552	<ANA
☐	JA354K	B737-5Y0	26105/2553	<ANA
☐	JA359K	B737-5L9	28128/2817	<ANA

ALL NIPPON — EL / ANK

☐	JA01AN	B737-781/W	33916/1781	<ANA
☐	JA02AN	B737-781/W	33872/1850	<ANA
☐	JA03AN	B737-781/W	33873/1871	<ANA
☐	JA04AN	B737-781/W	33874/1890	<ANA
☐	JA05AN	B737-781/W	33875/1971	<ANA
☐	JA06AN	B737-781/W	33876/1992	<ANA
☐	JA07AN	B737-781/W	33900/2071	<ANA
☐	JA08AN	B737-781/W	33877/2086	<ANA
☐	JA09AN	B737-781/W	33878/2145	<ANA
☐	JA10AN	B737-781ER/W	33879/2157	<ANA
☐	JA11AN	B737-781/W	33882/2268	<ANA
☐	JA12AN	B737-781/W	33881/2301	<ANA
☐	JA13AN	B737-781ER/W	33880/2232	<ANA
☐	JA14AN	B737-781/W	33883/2370	<ANA
☐	JA15AN	B737-781/W	33888/2394	<ANA
☐	JA16AN	B737-781/W	33889/2488	<ANA
☐	JA17AN	B737-781/W	33884/2513	<ANA
☐	JA18AN	B737-781/W	33885/2582	<ANA
☐	JA51AN	B737-881/W	33886/2607	<ANA
☐	JA52AN	B737-881/W	33887/2643	<ANA
☐	JA53AN	B737-881/W	33891/2739	<ANA
☐	JA54AN	B737-881/W	33890/2833	<ANA
☐	JA55AN	B737-881/W	33892/2889	<ANA
☐	JA56AN	B737-881/W	33893/2926	<ANA
☐	JA57AN	B737-881/W	33894/2975	<ANA
☐	JA58AN	B737-881/W	33895/3029	<ANA
☐	JA59AN	B737-881/W	33896/3073	<ANA
☐	JA60AN	B737-881/W	33897/3126	<ANA
☐	JA61AN	B737-881/W	33906/3379	<ANA♦
☐	JA62AN	B737-881/W	33899/3414	<ANA♦
☐	JA63AN	B737-881/W	33901/3449	<ANA♦
☐	JA64AN	B737-881/W	33902/3478	<ANA♦
☐	JA65AN	B737-881/W	33903/3502	<ANA♦
☐	JA301K	B737-54K	27435/2875	<ANA
☐	JA303K	B737-54K	28991/3017	<ANA
☐	JA305K	B737-54K	28993/3075	<ANA
☐	JA355K	B737-5L9	28129/2823	<ANA
☐	JA356K	B737-5L9	28083/2784	<ANA
☐	JA357K	B737-5L9	28131/2828	<ANA
☐	JA358K	B737-5L9	28130/2825	<ANA
☐	JA392K	B737-46M	28550/2847	>ADO
☐	JA8195	B737-54K	27433/2815	<ANA
☐	JA8196	B737-54K	27966/2824	<ANA
☐	JA8404	B737-54K	27381/2708	>ADO
☐	JA8500	B737-54K	27431/2751	<ANA
☐	JA8596	B737-54K	28462/2853	<ANA
☐	JA801K	DHC-8Q-314	565	
☐	JA802K	DHC-8Q-314	577	
☐	JA803K	DHC-8Q-314	583	
☐	JA804K	DHC-8Q-314	591	
☐	JA805K	DHC-8Q-314	592	

ALL NIPPON NETWORK — EH / ANA

☐	JA801K	DHC-8Q-314	565	<ANK
☐	JA802K	DHC-8Q-314	577	<ANK
☐	JA803K	DHC-8Q-314	583	<ANK
☐	JA804K	DHC-8Q-314	591	<ANK
☐	JA805K	DHC-8Q-314	592	<ANK

☐	JA841A	DHC-8-402Q	4080	<ANA
☐	JA842A	DHC-8-402Q	4082	<ANA
☐	JA843A	DHC-8-402Q	4084	<ANA
☐	JA844A	DHC-8-402Q	4091	<ANA
☐	JA845A	DHC-8-402Q	4096	<ANA
☐	JA846A	DHC-8-402Q	4097	<ANA
☐	JA847A	DHC-8-402Q	4099	<ANA
☐	JA848A	DHC-8-402Q	4102	<ANA
☐	JA849A	DHC-8-402Q	4106	<ANA
☐	JA850A	DHC-8-402Q	4108	<ANA
☐	JA851A	DHC-8-402Q	4109	<ANA
☐	JA852A	DHC-8-402Q	4131	<ANA
☐	JA853A	DHC-8-402Q	4135	<ANA
☐	JA854A	DHC-8-402Q	4151	<ANA
☐	JA855A	DHC-8-402Q	4292	<ANA
☐	JA856A	DHC-8-402Q	4335	<ANA♦
☐	JA	DHC-8-402Q		o/o♦
☐	JA	DHC-8-402Q		o/o♦
☐	JA	DHC-8-402Q		o/o♦

AMAKUSA AIRLINES — AHX

☐	JA81AM	DHC-8Q-103	537

ANA - ALL NIPPON AIRWAYS — NH / ANA

☐	JA203A	A320-214	2061	
☐	JA204A	A320-214	2998	
☐	JA205A	A320-214	3099	
☐	JA206A	A320-214	3147	
☐	JA207A	A320-214	3148	
☐	JA208A	A320-214	3189	
☐	JA8300	A320-211	0549	
☐	JA8304	A320-211	0531	
☐	JA8313	A320-211	0534	
☐	JA8382	A320-211	0139	
☐	JA8384	A320-211	0151	
☐	JA8385	A320-211	0167	
☐	JA8386	A320-211	0170	
☐	JA8387	A320-211	0196	
☐	JA8388	A320-211	0212	
☐	JA8389	A320-211	0219	
☐	JA8390	A320-211	0245	
☐	JA8391	A320-211	0300	
☐	JA8392	A320-211	0328	
☐	JA8393	A320-211	0365	
☐	JA8394	A320-211	0383	
☐	JA8395	A320-211	0413	
☐	JA8396	A320-211	0482	
☐	JA8400	A320-211	0554	
☐	JA8609	A320-211	0501	
☐	JA8654	A320-211	0507	
☐	JA8946	A320-211	0669	
☐	JA8947	A320-211	0685	
☐	JA8997	A320-211	0658	
☐	JA	A320-214		o/o
☐	JA	A320-214		o/o
☐	JA	A320-214		o/o
☐	JA300K	B737-54K	27434/2872	>ADO
☐	JA301K	B737-54K	27435/2875	>ANK
☐	JA302K	B737-54K	28990/3002	>ANX
☐	JA303K	B737-54K	28991/3017	>ANK
☐	JA304K	B737-54K	28992/3030	>NXA
☐	JA305K	B737-54K	28993/3075	>ANK
☐	JA306K	B737-54K	29794/3109	>NXA
☐	JA307K	B737-54K	29795/3116	>NXA
☐	JA351K	B737-5Y0	25189/2240	>NXA
☐	JA352K	B737-5Y0	26097/2534	>NXA
☐	JA353K	B737-5Y0	26104/2552	>NXA
☐	JA354K	B737-5Y0	26105/2553	>NXA
☐	JA355K	B737-5L9	28129/2823	>ANK
☐	JA356K	B737-5L9	28083/2784	>ANK
☐	JA357K	B737-5L9	28131/2828	>ANK
☐	JA358K	B737-5L9	28130/2825	>ANK
☐	JA359K	B737-5L9	28128/2817	>NXA

	Reg	Type	c/n	Notes
☐	JA392K	B737-46M	28550/2847	>SNJ
☐	JA8195	B737-54K	27433/2815	>ANK
☐	JA8196	B737-54K	27966/2824	>ANK
☐	JA8404	B737-54K	27381/2708	>ANK
☐	JA8419	B737-54K	27430/2723	
☐	JA8500	B737-54K	27431/2751	>ANK
☐	JA8596	B737-54K	28462/2853	>ANK
☐	JA01AN	B737-781/W	33916/1781	>ANK
☐	JA02AN	B737-781/W	33872/1850	>ANK
☐	JA03AN	B737-781/W	33873/1871	>ANK
☐	JA04AN	B737-781/W	33874/1890	>ANK
☐	JA05AN	B737-781/W	33875/1971	>ANK
☐	JA06AN	B737-781/W	33876/1992	>ANK
☐	JA07AN	B737-781/W	33900/2071	>ANK
☐	JA08AN	B737-781/W	33877/2086	>ANK
☐	JA09AN	B737-781/W	33878/2145	>ANK
☐	JA10AN	B737-781ER/W	33879/2157	>ANK
☐	JA11AN	B737-781/W	33882/2268	>ANK
☐	JA12AN	B737-781/W	33881/2301	>ANK
☐	JA13AN	B737-781ER/W	33880/2232	>ANK
☐	JA14AN	B737-781/W	33883/2370	>ANK
☐	JA15AN	B737-781/W	33888/2394	>ANK
☐	JA16AN	B737-781/W	33889/2488	>ANK
☐	JA17AN	B737-781/W	33884/2513	>ANK
☐	JA18AN	B737-781/W	33885/2582	>ANK
☐	JA	B737-781/W		o/o♦
☐	JA	B737-781/W		o/o♦
☐	JA	B737-781/W		o/o♦
☐	JA	B737-781/W		o/o♦
☐	JA	B737-781/W		o/o♦
☐	JA51AN	B737-881/W	33886/2607	>ANK
☐	JA52AN	B737-881/W	33887/2643	>ANK
☐	JA53AN	B737-881/W	33891/2739	>ANK
☐	JA54AN	B737-881/W	33890/2833	>ANK
☐	JA55AN	B737-881/W	33892/2889	>ANK
☐	JA56AN	B737-881/W	33893/2926	>ANK
☐	JA57AN	B737-881/W	33894/2975	>ANK
☐	JA58AN	B737-881/W	33895/3029	>ANK
☐	JA59AN	B737-881/W	33896/3073	>ANK
☐	JA60AN	B737-881/W	33897/3126	>ANK
☐	JA61AN	B737-881/W	33906/3379	>ANK♦
☐	JA62AN	B737-881/W	33899/3414	>ANK♦
☐	JA63AN	B737-881/W	33901/3449	>ANK♦
☐	JA64AN	B737-881/W	33902/3478	>ANK♦
☐	JA65AN	B737-881/W	33903/3502	>ANK♦
☐	JA66AN	B737-881/W		o/o♦
☐	JA67AN	B737-881/W		o/o♦
☐	JA8099	B747-481D	25292/891	
☐	JA8956	B747-481D	25640/920	
☐	JA8957	B747-481D	25642/927	
☐	JA8958	B747-481	25641/928	
☐	JA8959	B747-481D	25646/952	
☐	JA8960	B747-481D	25643/972	
☐	JA8961	B747-481D	25644/975	
☐	JA8963	B747-481D	25647/991	
☐	JA8964	B747-481D	27163/996	
☐	JA8965	B747-481D	27436/1060	
☐	JA8966	B747-481D	27442/1066	
☐	JA601A	B767-381	27943/669	
☐	JA601F	B767-381F	33404/885	>AJV
☐	JA602A	B767-381	27944/684	
☐	JA602F	B767-381F	33509/937	>AJV
☐	JA603A	B767-381ER	32972/877	
☐	JA604A	B767-381ER	32973/881	
☐	JA604F	B767-381F	35709/947	>AJV
☐	JA605A	B767-381ER	32974/882	
☐	JA606A	B767-381ER	32975/883	
☐	JA607A	B767-381ER	32976/884	
☐	JA608A	B767-381ER	32977/886	
☐	JA609A	B767-381ER	32978/888	
☐	JA610A	B767-381ER	32979/895	
☐	JA611A	B767-381ER	32980/914	
☐	JA612A	B767-381ER	33506/920	
☐	JA613A	B767-381ER	33507/924	
☐	JA614A	B767-381ER	33508/931	
☐	JA615A	B767-381ER	35877/951	
☐	JA616A	B767-381ER	35876/953	
☐	JA617A	B767-381ER	37719/971	
☐	JA618A	B767-381ER	37720/976	
☐	JA619A	B767-381ER	40564/993	♦
☐	JA620A	B767-381ER	40565/996	♦
☐	JA621A	B767-381ER	40566/998	♦
☐	JA622A	B767-381ER	40567/1000	o/o♦
☐	JA623A	B767-381ER	40894/1001	o/o♦
☐	JA	B767-381ER		o/o♦
☐	JA	B767-381ER		o/o♦
☐	JA8256	B767-381	23756/176	
☐	JA8257	B767-381	23757/177	
☐	JA8258	B767-381	23758/179	>ADO
☐	JA8259	B767-381	23759/185	
☐	JA8271	B767-381	24002/199	
☐	JA8272	B767-381	24003/212	
☐	JA8273	B767-381	24004/218	
☐	JA8274	B767-381	24005/222	
☐	JA8275	B767-381	24006/223	
☐	JA8285	B767-381	24350/245	
☐	JA8286	B767-381ERBCF	24400/269	
☐	JA8287	B767-381	24351/271	
☐	JA8288	B767-381	24415/276	
☐	JA8289	B767-381	24416/280	
☐	JA8290	B767-381	24417/290	
☐	JA8291	B767-381	24755/295	
☐	JA8322	B767-381	25618/458	
☐	JA8323	B767-381ERBCF	25654/463	
☐	JA8324	B767-381	25655/465	
☐	JA8342	B767-381	27445/573	
☐	JA8356	B767-381ERBCF	25136/379	
☐	JA8357	B767-381	25293/401	
☐	JA8358	B767-381ER	25616/432	
☐	JA8359	B767-381	25617/439	
☐	JA8360	B767-381	25055/352	
☐	JA8362	B767-381ERBCF	24632/285	
☐	JA8363	B767-381	24756/300	
☐	JA8368	B767-381	24880/336	
☐	JA8567	B767-381	25656/510	
☐	JA8568	B767-381	25657/515	
☐	JA8569	B767-381	27050/516	
☐	JA8578	B767-381	25658/519	
☐	JA8579	B767-381	25659/520	
☐	JA8664	B767-381ER	27339/556	
☐	JA8669	B767-381	27444/567	
☐	JA8670	B767-381	25660/539	
☐	JA8674	B767-381	25661/543	
☐	JA8677	B767-381	25662/551	
☐	JA8970	B767-381ER	25619/645	
☐	JA8971	B767-381ER	27942/651	
☐	N742AX	B767-232 (SCD)	22217/27	<ABX
☐	N744AX	B767-232 (SCD)	22221/53	<ABX
☐	JA701A	B777-281	27938/77	
☐	JA702A	B777-281	27033/75	
☐	JA703A	B777-281	27034/81	
☐	JA704A	B777-281	27035/131	
☐	JA705A	B777-281	29029/137	
☐	JA706A	B777-281	27036/141	
☐	JA707A	B777-281ER	27037/247	
☐	JA708A	B777-281ER	28277/278	
☐	JA709A	B777-281ER	28278/286	
☐	JA710A	B777-281ER	28279/302	
☐	JA711A	B777-281	33406/482	
☐	JA712A	B777-281	33407/495	
☐	JA713A	B777-281	32647/509	
☐	JA714A	B777-281	28276/523	
☐	JA715A	B777-281ER	32646/563	
☐	JA716A	B777-281ER	33414/574	
☐	JA717A	B777-281ER	33415/580	
☐	JA731A	B777-381ER	28281/488	

	Reg	Type	c/n	
☐	JA732A	B777-381ER	27038/511	
☐	JA733A	B777-381ER	32648/529	
☐	JA734A	B777-381ER	32649/557	
☐	JA735A	B777-381ER	34892/571	
☐	JA736A	B777-381ER	34893/589	
☐	JA751A	B777-381	28272/142	
☐	JA752A	B777-381	28274/160	
☐	JA753A	B777-381	28273/132	
☐	JA754A	B777-381	27939/172	
☐	JA755A	B777-381	28275/104	
☐	JA756A	B777-381	27039/440	
☐	JA757A	B777-381	27040/442	
☐	JA777A	B777-381ER	32650/593	
☐	JA778A	B777-381ER	32651/606	
☐	JA779A	B777-381ER	34894/631	
☐	JA780A	B777-381ER	34895/639	
☐	JA781A	B777-381ER	27041/667	
☐	JA782A	B777-381ER	33416/691	
☐	JA783A	B777-381ER	27940/737	
☐	JA784A	B777-381ER	37950/833	
☐	JA785A	B777-381ER	37951/855	♦
☐	JA786A	B777-381ER	37948/866	♦
☐	JA787A	B777-381ER	37949/870	♦
☐	JA788A	B777-381ER	40686/873	♦
☐	JA789A	B777-381ER	40687/878	♦
☐	JA8197	B777-281	27027/16	
☐	JA8198	B777-281	27028/21	
☐	JA8199	B777-281	27029/29	
☐	JA8967	B777-281	27030/37	
☐	JA8968	B777-281	27031/38	
☐	JA8969	B777-281	27032/50	
☐	JA801A	B787-881	34485/7	o/o♦
☐	JA802A	B787-881	34486/9	o/o♦
☐	JA803A	B787-881	34488/8	o/o♦
☐	JA804A	B787-881	34497/11	o/o♦
☐	JA805A	B787-881	34508/12	o/o♦
☐	JA806A	B787-881	34490/13	o/o♦
☐	JA807A	B787-881	34510/22	o/o♦
☐	JA808A	B787-881	34514/24	o/o♦
☐	JA809A	B787-881	34498/14	o/o♦
☐	JA810A	B787-881	34491/15	o/o♦
☐	JA811A	B787-881		o/o♦
☐	JA812A	B787-881		o/o♦
☐	JA813A	B787-881		o/o♦
☐	JA814A	B787-881		o/o♦
☐	JA815A	B787-881		o/o♦

FUJI DREAM AIRLINES — JH / FDA

	Reg	Type	c/n	
☐	JA01FJ	ERJ-170STD	17000271	
☐	JA02FJ	ERJ-170STD	17000289	
☐	JA03FJ	ERJ-175STD	17000304	
☐	JA04FJ	ERJ-170SU	17000129	♦
☐	JA05FJ	ERJ-175STD	17000316	♦

HOKKAIDO AIR SYSTEM — NTH

	Reg	Type	c/n
☐	JA01HC	SAAB SF.340B	340B-432
☐	JA02HC	SAAB SF.340B	340B-440
☐	JA03HC	SAAB SF.340B	340B-458

IBEX AIRLINES — FW / IBX

	Reg	Type	c/n	
☐	JA01RJ	CRJ-100ER	7052	
☐	JA02RJ	CRJ-100ER	7033	
☐	JA03RJ	CRJ-200ER	7624	
☐	JA04RJ	CRJ-200ER	7798	
☐	JA05RJ	CRJ-702NG	10279	
☐	JA06RJ	CRJ-702NG	10303	♦

J-AIR — JL / JAL

	Reg	Type	c/n
☐	JA201J	CRJ-200ER	7452
☐	JA202J	CRJ-200ER	7484
☐	JA203J	CRJ-200ER	7626
☐	JA204J	CRJ-200ER	7643
☐	JA205J	CRJ-200ER	7767
☐	JA206J	CRJ-200ER	7834
☐	JA207J	CRJ-200ER	8050
☐	JA208J	CRJ-200ER	8059
☐	JA209J	CRJ-200ER	8062
☐	JA211J	ERJ-170STD	17000251
☐	JA212J	ERJ-170STD	17000268
☐	JA213J	ERJ-170STD	17000285
☐	JA214J	ERJ-170STD	17000295
☐	JA215J	ERJ-170STD	17000297
☐	JA216J	ERJ-170STD	17000299

	Reg	Type	c/n	
☐	JA217J	ERJ-170STD	17000308	♦
☐	JA218J	ERJ-170STD	17000314	♦
☐	JA219J	ERJ-170STD	17000315	♦
☐	JA	ERJ-170STD		o/o♦

JAL EXPRESS — JC / JEX

	Reg	Type	c/n	
☐	JA307J	B737-846/W	35336/2450	<JAL
☐	JA308J	B737-846/W	35337/2479	<JAL
☐	JA309J	B737-846/W	35338/2522	<JAL
☐	JA311J	B737-846/W	35340/2571	<JAL
☐	JA313J	B737-846/W	35342/2633	<JAL
☐	JA314J	B737-846/W	35343/2701	<JAL
☐	JA316J	B737-846/W	35345/2762	<JAL
☐	JA319J	B737-846/W	35348/2867	<JAL
☐	JA322J	B737-846/W	35351/3002	<JAL
☐	JA323J	B737-846/W	35352/3057	<JAL
☐	JA324J	B737-846/W	35353/3105	<JAL
☐	JA325J	B737-846/W	35354/3117	<JAL
☐	JA326J	B737-846/W	35355/3159	<JAL
☐	JA327J	B737-846/W	35356/3201	<JAL♦
☐	JA328J	B737-846/W	35357/3279	<JAL♦
☐	JA329J	B737-846/W	35358/3315	<JAL♦
☐	JA330J	B737-846/W	35359/3341	<JAL♦
☐	JA331J	B737-846/W	40346/3366	<JAL♦
☐	JA332J	B737-846/W	40347/3385	<JAL♦
☐	JA333J	B737-846/W	40348/3465	<JAL♦
☐	JA334J	B737-846/W	40349/3489	<JAL♦
☐	JA335J	B737-846/W	40350/3525	<JAL♦
☐	JA336J	B737-846/W	40351/3543	<JAL♦
☐	JA8991	B737-446	27916/2718	
☐	JA8992	B737-446	27917/2729	
☐	JA8993	B737-446	28087/2812	<JAL
☐	JA8994	B737-446	28097/2907	<JAL
☐	JA8995	B737-446	28831/2911	<JAL
☐	JA8996	B737-446	28832/2953	<JAL
☐	JA8998	B737-446	28994/3044	<JAL
☐	JA8999	B737-446	29864/3111	<JAL
☐	JA8262	MD-81	49463/1488	<JAL
☐	JA8374	MD-81	53043/1982	<JAL
☐	JA8556	MD-81	53301/2082	<JAL

JAPAN AIR COMMUTER — 3X / JAC

	Reg	Type	c/n
☐	JA841C	DHC-8-402Q	4072
☐	JA842C	DHC-8-402Q	4073
☐	JA843C	DHC-8-402Q	4076
☐	JA844C	DHC-8-402Q	4092
☐	JA845C	DHC-8-402Q	4101
☐	JA846C	DHC-8-402Q	4107
☐	JA847C	DHC-8-402Q	4111
☐	JA848C	DHC-8-402Q	4121
☐	JA849C	DHC-8-402Q	4133
☐	JA850C	DHC-8-402Q	4158
☐	JA851C	DHC-8-402Q	4177
☐	JA001C	SAAB SF.340B	340B-419
☐	JA002C	SAAB SF.340B	340B-459
☐	JA8594	SAAB SF.340B	340B-399
☐	JA8642	SAAB SF.340B	340B-365
☐	JA8649	SAAB SF.340B	340B-368

☐	JA8703	SAAB SF.340B	340B-355
☐	JA8704	SAAB SF.340B	340B-361
☐	JA8886	SAAB SF.340B	340B-281
☐	JA8887	SAAB SF.340B	340B-308
☐	JA8888	SAAB SF.340B	340B-331
☐	JA8900	SAAB SF.340B	340B-378

JAPAN AIRLINES JL / JAL

☐	JA011D	A300B4-622R	783	
☐	JA012D	A300B4-622R	797	
☐	JA014D	A300B4-622R	836	
☐	JA015D	A300B4-622R	837	
☐	JA016D	A300B4-622R	838	
☐	JA8375	A300B4-622R	602	
☐	JA8376	A300B4-622R	617	
☐	JA8377	A300B4-622R	621	
☐	JA8527	A300B4-622R	724	
☐	JA8529	A300B4-622R	729	
☐	JA8561	A300B4-622R	670	
☐	JA8562	A300B4-622R	679	
☐	JA8563	A300B4-622R	683	
☐	JA8564	A300B4-622R	703	
☐	JA8566	A300B4-622R	730	
☐	JA8573	A300B4-622R	737	
☐	JA8657	A300B4-622R	753	
☐	JA8659	A300B4-622R	770	
☐	JA8993	B737-446	28087/2812	>JEX
☐	JA8994	B737-446	28097/2907	>JEX
☐	JA8995	B737-446	28831/2911	>JEX
☐	JA8996	B737-446	28832/2953	>JEX
☐	JA8998	B737-446	28994/3044	>JEX
☐	JA8999	B737-446	29864/3111	>JEX
☐	JA301J	B737-846/W	35330/2095	
☐	JA302J	B737-846/W	35331/2162	
☐	JA303J	B737-846/W	35332/2225	
☐	JA304J	B737-846/W	35333/2253	
☐	JA305J	B737-846/W	35334/2289	
☐	JA306J	B737-846/W	35335/2395	
☐	JA307J	B737-846/W	35336/2450	>JEX
☐	JA308J	B737-846/W	35337/2479	>JEX
☐	JA309J	B737-846/W	35338/2522	>JEX
☐	JA310J	B737-846/W	35339/2510	
☐	JA311J	B737-846/W	35340/2571	>JEX
☐	JA312J	B737-846/W	35341/2584	
☐	JA313J	B737-846/W	35342/2633	>JEX
☐	JA314J	B737-846/W	35343/2701	>JEX
☐	JA315J	B737-846/W	35344/2731	
☐	JA316J	B737-846/W	35345/2762	>JEX
☐	JA317J	B737-846/W	35346/2824	
☐	JA318J	B737-846/W	35347/2830	
☐	JA319J	B737-846/W	35348/2867	>JEX
☐	JA320J	B737-846/W	35349/2953	
☐	JA321J	B737-846/W	35350/2977	
☐	JA322J	B737-846/W	35351/3002	>JEX
☐	JA323J	B737-846/W	35352/3057	>JEX
☐	JA324J	B737-846/W	35353/3105	>JEX
☐	JA325J	B737-846/W	35354/3117	>JEX
☐	JA326J	B737-846/W	35355/3159	>JEX
☐	JA327J	B737-846/W	35356/3201	>JEX♦
☐	JA328J	B737-846/W	35357/3279	>JEX♦
☐	JA329J	B737-846/W	35358/3315	>JEX♦
☐	JA330J	B737-846/W	35359/3341	>JEX♦
☐	JA331J	B737-846/W	40346/3366	>JEX♦
☐	JA332J	B737-846/W	40347/3385	>JEX♦
☐	JA333J	B737-846/W	40348/3465	>JEX♦
☐	JA334J	B737-846/W	40349/3489	>JEX♦
☐	JA335J	B737-846/W	40350/3525	>JEX♦
☐	JA336J	B737-846/W	40351/3543	>JEX♦
☐	JA8074	B747-446	24426/768	
☐	JA8075	B747-446	24427/780	[VCV]♦
☐	JA8076	B747-446	24777/797	
☐	JA8077	B747-446	24784/798	
☐	JA8078	B747-446	24870/821	

☐	JA8080	B747-446	24886/825	
☐	JA8081	B747-446	25064/851	
☐	JA8084	B747-446D	25214/879	
☐	JA8086	B747-446	25308/885	
☐	JA8087	B747-446	26346/897	
☐	JA8088	B747-446	26341/902	
☐	JA8089	B747-446	26342/905	
☐	JA8090	B747-446D	26347/907	
☐	JA8902	B747-446BCF	26344/929	[VCV]♦
☐	JA8904	B747-446D	26348/941	
☐	JA8907	B747-446D	26351/963	
☐	JA8916	B747-446	26362/1202	
☐	JA8917	B747-446	29899/1208	
☐	JA8918	B747-446	27650/1234	
☐	JA8920	B747-446	27648/1253	
☐	JA8921	B747-446	27645/1262	
☐	JA8922	B747-446	27646/1280	[VCV]♦
☐	JA601J	B767-346ER	32886/875	
☐	JA602J	B767-346ER	32887/879	
☐	JA603J	B767-346ER	32888/880	
☐	JA604J	B767-346ER	33493/905	
☐	JA605J	B767-346ER	33494/911	
☐	JA606J	B767-346ER	33495/915	
☐	JA607J	B767-346ER	33496/917	
☐	JA608J	B767-346ER	33497/919	
☐	JA609J	B767-346ER	33845/921	
☐	JA610J	B767-346ER	33846/925	
☐	JA611J	B767-346ER	33847/927	
☐	JA612J	B767-346ER	33848/929	
☐	JA613J	B767-346ER	33849/935	
☐	JA614J	B767-346ER	33851/938	
☐	JA615J	B767-346ER	33850/942	
☐	JA616J	B767-346ER	35813/954	
☐	JA617J	B767-346ER	35814/957	
☐	JA618J	B767-346ER	35815/964	
☐	JA619J	B767-346ER	37550/969	
☐	JA620J	B767-346ER	37547/974	
☐	JA621J	B767-346ER	37548/975	
☐	JA622J	B767-346ER	37549/977	
☐	JA623J	B767-346ER	36131/978	
☐	JA651J	B767-346ER	40363/994	♦
☐	JA652J	B767-346ER	40364/995	♦
☐	JA653J	B767-346ER	40365/997	♦
☐	JA654J	B767-346ER	40366/999	♦
☐	JA	B767-346ER		o/o♦
☐	JA	B767-346ER		o/o♦
☐	JA	B767-346ER		o/o♦
☐	JA	B767-346ER		o/o♦
☐	JA8231	B767-246	23212/117	
☐	JA8233	B767-246	23214/122	[VCV]♦
☐	JA8264	B767-346	23965/186	
☐	JA8265	B767-346	23961/192	
☐	JA8266	B767-346	23966/191	
☐	JA8267	B767-346	23962/193	
☐	JA8268	B767-346	23963/224	
☐	JA8269	B767-346	23964/225	
☐	JA8299	B767-346	24498/277	
☐	JA8364	B767-346	24782/327	
☐	JA8365	B767-346	24783/329	
☐	JA8397	B767-346	27311/547	
☐	JA8398	B767-346	27312/548	
☐	JA8399	B767-346	27313/554	
☐	JA8975	B767-346	27658/581	
☐	JA8976	B767-346	27659/667	
☐	JA8980	B767-346	28837/673	
☐	JA8986	B767-346	28838/680	
☐	JA8987	B767-346	28553/688	
☐	JA8988	B767-346	29863/772	
☐	JA007D	B777-289	27639/134	
☐	JA008D	B777-289	27640/146	
☐	JA009D	B777-289	27641/159	
☐	JA010D	B777-289	27642/213	
☐	JA701J	B777-246ER	32889/410	
☐	JA702J	B777-246ER	32890/417	

	Reg	Type	Serial	Note
☐	JA703J	B777-246ER	32891/427	
☐	JA704J	B777-246ER	32892/435	
☐	JA705J	B777-246ER	32893/446	
☐	JA706J	B777-246ER	33394/464	
☐	JA707J	B777-246ER	32894/475	
☐	JA708J	B777-246ER	32895/483	
☐	JA709J	B777-246ER	32896/489	
☐	JA710J	B777-246ER	33395/525	
☐	JA711J	B777-246ER	33396/533	
☐	JA712J	B777-246ER	37879/ .	o/o
☐	JA713J	B777-246ER	37880/ .	o/o
☐	JA714J	B777-246ER	37881/ .	o/o
☐	JA715J	B777-246ER	37882/ .	o/o
☐	JA716J	B777-246ER	37883/ .	o/o
☐	JA731J	B777-346ER	32431/429	
☐	JA732J	B777-346ER	32430/423	
☐	JA733J	B777-346ER	32432/521	
☐	JA734J	B777-346ER	32433/527	
☐	JA735J	B777-346ER	32434/577	
☐	JA736J	B777-346ER	32435/583	
☐	JA737J	B777-346ER	36126/668	
☐	JA738J	B777-346ER	32436/724	
☐	JA739J	B777-346ER	32437/736	
☐	JA740J	B777-346ER	36127/744	
☐	JA741J	B777-346ER	36128/812	
☐	JA742J	B777-346ER	36129/816	
☐	JA743J	B777-346ER	36130/821	
☐	JA751J	B777-346	27654/458	
☐	JA752J	B777-346	27655/460	
☐	JA771J	B777-246	27656/437	
☐	JA772J	B777-246	27657/507	
☐	JA773J	B777-246	27653/635	
☐	JA8941	B777-346	28393/152	
☐	JA8942	B777-346	28394/158	
☐	JA8943	B777-346	28395/196	
☐	JA8944	B777-346	28396/212	
☐	JA8945	B777-346	28397/238	
☐	JA8977	B777-289	27636/45	
☐	JA8978	B777-289	27637/79	
☐	JA8979	B777-289	27638/107	
☐	JA8981	B777-246	27364/23	
☐	JA8982	B777-246	27365/26	
☐	JA8983	B777-246	27366/39	
☐	JA8984	B777-246	27651/68	
☐	JA8985	B777-246	27652/72	
☐	JA	B777-		o/o
☐	JA821A	B787-846	34831/20	o/o♦
☐	JA	B787-846	34833/21	o/o♦
☐	JA	B787-846	34832/23	o/o♦
☐	JA	B787-846	34834/27	o/o♦
☐	JA	B787-846		o/o♦
☐	JA	B787-846		o/o♦
☐	JA	B787-846		o/o♦
☐	JA	B787-846		o/o♦
☐	JA8262	MD-81	49463/1488	>JEX
☐	JA8374	MD-81	53043/1982	>JEX
☐	JA8497	MD-81	49281/1200	
☐	JA8554	MD-81	53299/2075	
☐	JA8556	MD-81	53301/2082	>JEX
☐	JA8557	MD-81	53302/2085	
☐	JA001D	MD-90-30	53555/2207	
☐	JA002D	MD-90-30	53556/2210	
☐	JA003D	MD-90-30	53557/2211	
☐	JA004D	MD-90-30	53558/2212	
☐	JA005D	MD-90-30	53559/2236	
☐	JA006D	MD-90-30	53560/2245	
☐	JA8004	MD-90-30	53359/2164	
☐	JA8020	MD-90-30	53360/2190	
☐	JA8029	MD-90-30	53361/2202	
☐	JA8062	MD-90-30	53352/2098	
☐	JA8063	MD-90-30	53353/2120	
☐	JA8064	MD-90-30	53354/2125	
☐	JA8065	MD-90-30	53355/2131	
☐	JA8066	MD-90-30	53356/2157	
☐	JA8069	MD-90-30	53357/2164	
☐	JA8070	MD-90-30	53358/2179	

JAPAN TRANSOCEAN AIR — NU / JTA

	Reg	Type	Serial
☐	JA8523	B737-4Q3	26603/2618
☐	JA8524	B737-4Q3	26604/2684
☐	JA8525	B737-4Q3	26605/2752
☐	JA8526	B737-4Q3	26606/2898
☐	JA8597	B737-4Q3	27660/3043
☐	JA8930	B737-4K5	27102/2394
☐	JA8931	B737-429	25247/2106
☐	JA8932	B737-429	25248/2120
☐	JA8933	B737-429	25226/2104
☐	JA8934	B737-4K5	27830/2670
☐	JA8938	B737-4Q3	29485/3085
☐	JA8939	B737-4Q3	29486/3088
☐	JA8940	B737-4Q3	29487/3122

JP EXPRESS — 9N / AJV

	Reg	Type	Serial	Note
☐	JA601F	B767-381F	33404/885	<ANA
☐	JA602F	B767-381F	33509/937	<ANA
☐	JA604F	B767-381F	35709/947	<ANA

NIPPON CARGO AIRLINES — KZ / NCA

	Reg	Type	Serial	Note
☐	JA01KZ	B747-481F	34016/1360	
☐	JA02KZ	B747-481F	34017/1363	
☐	JA03KZ	B747-4KZF	34018/1378	
☐	JA04KZ	B747-4KZF	34283/1384	
☐	JA05KZ	B747-4KZF	36132/1394	
☐	JA06KZ	B747-4KZF	36133/1397	
☐	JA07KZ	B747-4KZF	36134/1405	
☐	JA08KZ	B747-4KZF	36135/1408	
☐	JA11KZ	B747-8KZF	36136/1421	o/o
☐	JA12KZ	B747-8KZF	36137/1422	o/o
☐	JA13KZ	B747-8KZF	36138/1431	o/o

ORIENTAL AIR BRIDGE — NGK

	Reg	Type	Serial
☐	JA801B	DHC-8Q-201	566
☐	JA802B	DHC-8Q-201	579

RYUKYU AIR COMMUTER — RAC

	Reg	Type	Serial
☐	JA8935	DHC-8Q-103B	593
☐	JA8936	DHC-8Q-314	635
☐	JA8972	DHC-8Q-103	472
☐	JA8973	DHC-8Q-103	501
☐	JA8974	DHC-8Q-103B	540

SKYMARK AIRLINES — BC / SKY

	Reg	Type	Serial	Note
☐	JA73NA	B737-8HX/W	36849/3372	♦
☐	JA73NB	B737-8HX/W	36848/3394	♦
☐	JA73NC	B737-8FZ/W	31743/3450	♦
☐	JA73ND	B737-8FZ/W	33440/3474	♦
☐	JA73NE	B737-82Y/W	40713/3501	♦
☐	JA	B737-8		o/o♦
☐	JA	B737-8		o/o♦
☐	JA737H	B737-86N	34247/1830	
☐	JA737K	B737-86N	34249/1857	
☐	JA737L	B737-86N	32694/1960	
☐	JA737M	B737-86N	32683/2136	
☐	JA737N	B737-8HX	36845/2339	
☐	JA737P	B737-8HX	29681/2493	
☐	JA737Q	B737-86N/W	35228/2630	
☐	JA737R	B737-86N/W	35630/2666	
☐	JA737T	B737-8Q8/W	35290/2818	
☐	JA737U	B737-8FZ/W	29680/2888	
☐	JA737X	B737-8AL/W	36692/3088	
☐	JA737Y	B737-8FZ/W	29663/3113	
☐	JA737Z	B737-82Y/W	40712/3308	♦

SKYNET ASIA AIRWAYS — 6J / SNJ

☐	JA391K	B737-4Y0	24545/1805
☐	JA392K	B737-46M	28550/2847	<ANA
☐	JA737A	B737-46Q	29000/3033
☐	JA737B	B737-46Q	29001/3040
☐	JA737E	B737-4Y0	26069/2352
☐	JA737F	B737-43Q	28492/2837
☐	JA737G	B737-43Q	28491/2832
☐	JA737V	B737-4M0	29201/3018
☐	JA737W	B737-4M0	29202/3025

STARFLYER — 7G / SFJ

☐	JA01MC	A320-214	2620
☐	JA02MC	A320-214	2658
☐	JA03MC	A320-214	2695
☐	JA04MC	A320-214	3025
☐	JA05MC	A320-214	4555	♦

JU - MONGOLIA

AERO MONGOLIA — MNG

☐	JU-8251	Fokker 50	20251
☐	JU-8257	Fokker 50	20257	♦
☐	JU-8258	Fokker 50	20258
☐	JU-8428	Fokker 100	11428
☐	JU-8452	Fokker 100	11352

EZNIS AIRWAYS — EZA

☐	JU-9901	SAAB SF.340B	340B-259
☐	JU-9903	SAAB SF.340B	340B-297
☐	JU-9905	SAAB SF.340B	340B-359

MIAT - MONGOLIAN AIRLINES — OM / MGL

☐	EI-CSG	B737-8AS/W	29922/571
☐	EI-CXV	B737-8CX/W	32364/1166
☐	JU-1004	An-24RV	17306807	[ULN]
☐	JU-1006	An-24RV	47309807	[ULN]
☐	JU-1009	An-24RV	57310104	[ULN]
☐	JU-1010	A310-304	526
☐	JU-1014	An-26B-100	14101

JY - JORDAN

BARQ AVIATION

☐	N162AT	L1011-500 Tristar	193B-1220	[VCV]
☐	N164AT	L1011-500 Tristar	193B-1238	[FJR]
☐	N194AT	L1011-100 Tristar	193B-1230	[FJR]

JORDAN AVIATION — R5 / JAV

☐	JY-JAH	A310-304	481
☐	JY-JAV	A310-222	357	Opf UN
☐	JY-JAC	A320-211	0029
☐	JY-JAE	B727-2N4	21846/1549
☐	JY-JAB	B737-33A	23630/1312
☐	JY-JAD	B737-322	24662/1862
☐	JY-JAN	B737-322	23956/1564
☐	JY-JAO	B737-322	24672/1915
☐	JY-JAP	B737-46B	24124/1679
☐	JY-JAQ	B737-46J	27826/2694	♦
☐	JY-JAX	B737-322	23955/1550
☐	JY-JAY	B737-3S3	29244/3059	♦
☐	JY-JAG	B767-204ER	24757/299
☐	JY-JAI	B767-204ER	24736/296
☐	JY-JAL	B767-204ER	24239/243

JORDAN INTERNATIONAL CARGO — J4 / JCI

☐	JY-JIA	Il-76TD	23437093

ROYAL FALCON

☐	JY-JRE	A319-112	1124	♦
☐	JY-RFF	B737-4K5	27831/2677
☐	JY-JRD	B767-3P6ER	26237/544
☐	JY-JRF	B767-233	22526/92	>IRQ

ROYAL JORDANIAN — RJ / RJA

☐	JY-AGM	A310-304	491
☐	JY-AGN	A310-304	531
☐	JY-AGQ	A310-304F	445
☐	JY-AGR	A310-304F	490
☐	JY-AYL	A319-132	3428
☐	JY-AYM	A319-132	3685
☐	JY-AYN	A319-132	3803
☐	JY-AYP	A319-132	3832
☐	F-OHGV	A320-232	2649
☐	F-OHGX	A320-231	2953
☐	JY-AYD	A320-232	2598
☐	JY-AYF	A320-232	2692
☐	JY-AYI	A320-212	0569	>RWA
☐	JY-AYG	A321-231	2730
☐	JY-AYH	A321-231	2793
☐	JY-AYJ	A321-231	3458
☐	JY-AYK	A321-231	3522
☐	JY-AY	A321-231		o/o
☐	JY-AIE	A330-223	970	♦
☐	JY-AIF	A330-223	979	♦
☐	JY-AIA	A340-212	038
☐	JY-AIB	A340-212	043
☐	JY-AIC	A340-212	014
☐	JY-AID	A340-212	022
☐	JY-EMA	ERJ-195AR	19000107
☐	JY-EMB	ERJ-195AR	19000131
☐	JY-EMC	ERJ-175LR	17000223
☐	JY-EMD	ERJ-175LR	17000232
☐	JY-EME	ERJ-195AR	19000050
☐	JY-EMF	ERJ-195AR	19000067
☐	JY-EMG	ERJ-195AR	19000088
☐	JY-EMH	ERJ-175LR	17000316

PETRA AIRLINES

☐	JY-PTA	A320-212	0459	♦

ROYAL WINGS AIRLINES — RY / RYW

☐	JY-AYI	A320-212	0569	<RJA

SKYGATE INTERNATIONAL — SGD

☐	(EX-058)	L1011-250 Tristar	193C-1228	[VCV]
☐	JY-SGI	L1011-250 Tristar	193C-1234	[AMM]

SOLITAIRE AIR

☐	JY-SOA	B737-4Q8	25109/2561	♦

STARJET — MBM

☐	A6-BSM	L-1011-500 Tristar	193G-1222	[CDG]
☐	EX-088	L-1011-500 Tristar	193G-1179

TRANSWORLD AVIATION

☐ JY-TWB	An-26	
☐ JY-TWC	B737-2T4C	23065/989

J2 - DJIBOUTI

DAALLO AIRLINES — D3 / DAO

☐ (J2-KCV)	B747-212B	21938/436	[OPF]
☐ J2-SHE	An-24RV	67310505	
☐ J2-SHF	B747SP-09	21300/304	[SHJ]
☐ UP-I1802	Il-18E	185008603	<MGK

SILVER AIR — SVJ

☐ J2-KCC	B737-268	20576/297	[ADD]
☐ J2-KCE	B737-268	21360/485	
☐ J2-SRH	B737-268	21280/471	[ADD]
☐ J2-SRS	B737-268	21361/488	

TEEBAH AIRLINES — TBN

☐ 9L-LEL	B727-247	21483/1350	>IAW

LN - NORWAY

CLASSIC NORWAY AIR

☐ LN-SVZ	BAeJetstream 31	641

HELITRANS — HTA

☐ LN-FAN	BAeJetstream 32	864	>BCI
☐ LN-FAQ	BAeJetstream 32EP	953	
☐ LN-HTB	BAeJetstream 32EP	795	
☐ LN-HTC	ATR 42-300(QC)	122	♦

LUFTTRANSPORT — L5 / LTR

☐ LN-LYR	Do228-202K	8166
☐ LN-MOL	Do228-202K	8156

NORWEGIAN — DY / NAX

☐ LN-KHA	B737-31S/W	29100/2984
☐ LN-KHB	B737-31S/W	29264/3070
☐ LN-KHC	B737-31S/W	29265/3073
☐ LN-KKA	B737-33A	25033/2025
☐ LN-KKB	B737-33A	27457/2756
☐ LN-KKC	B737-3Y5	25615/2478
☐ LN-KKD	B737-33V	29339/3119
☐ LN-KKE	B737-33A	27285/2608
☐ LN-KKF	B737-3K2	24326/1683 [OSL]
☐ LN-KKG	B737-3K2	24327/1712
☐ LN-KKH	B737-3K2	24328/1856
☐ LN-KKI	B737-3K2	24329/1858
☐ LN-KKJ	B737-36N	28564/2936
☐ LN-KKL	B737-36N	28671/2955
☐ LN-KKM	B737-3Y0	24676/1829
☐ LN-KKN	B737-3Y0	24910/2030
☐ LN-KKO	B737-3Y0	24909/2021
☐ LN-KKP	B737-3M8	25040/2017
☐ LN-KKQ	B737-36Q	28658/2865
☐ LN-KKR	B737-3Y0	24256/1629
☐ LN-KKS	B737-33A	24094/1729
☐ LN-KKT	B737-3L9	27336/2587
☐ LN-KKU	B737-3L9	27337/2594
☐ LN-KKV	B737-3Y5	25613/2446
☐ LN-KKW	B737-3K9	24213/1794
☐ LN-KKX	B737-33S/W	29072/3012
☐ LN-KKY	B737-3S3	29245/3061
☐ LN-KKZ	B737-33A	27458/2959

☐ LN-DYA	B737-8JP/W	39162/2994	
☐ LN-DYB	B737-8JP/W	39163/3054	
☐ LN-DYC	B737-8JP/W	39164/3196	♦
☐ LN-DYD	B737-8JP/W	39002/3231	♦
☐ LN-DYE	B737-8JP/W	39003/3401	♦
☐ LN-DYF	B737-8JP/W	39004/3482	♦
☐ LN-DYG	B737-8JP/W	39165/3507	♦
☐ LN-DYH	B737-8JP/W	40865/3410	♦
☐ LN-DYI	B737-8JP/W	40866/3432	♦
☐ LN-DYJ	B737-8JP/W	39045/3530	♦
☐ LN-DYK	B737-8JP/W	39046/3557	o/o♦
☐ LN-DYL	B737-8JP/W	40867/3565	o/o♦
☐ LN-DYM	B737-8JP/W	39005/3572	o/o♦
☐ LN-	B737-8JP/W		o/o♦
☐ LN-	B737-8JP/W		o/o♦
☐ LN-	B737-8JP/W		o/o♦
☐ LN-	B737-8JP/W		o/o♦
☐ LN-	B737-8JP/W		o/o♦
☐ LN-	B737-8JP/W		o/o♦
☐ LN-	B737-8JP/W		o/o♦
☐ LN-	B737-8JP/W		o/o♦
☐ LN-NOB	B737-8FZ/W	34954/2483	
☐ LN-NOC	B737-81Q/W	30785/1007	
☐ LN-NOD	B737-8Q8/W	35280/2629	
☐ LN-NOE	B737-8Q8/W	35283/2742	
☐ LN-NOF	B737-86N/W	36809/2647	
☐ LN-NOG	B737-86N/W	35647/2927	
☐ LN-NOH	B737-86N/W	36814/3015	
☐ LN-NOI	B737-86N/W	36920/3131	
☐ LN-NOJ	B737-86N/W	37884/3223	♦
☐ LN-NOL	B737-8Q8/W	37159/2868	
☐ LN-NOM	B737-86N/W	28642/813	
☐ LN-NON	B737-86N/W	28620/542	
☐ LN-NOO	B737-86Q/W	30289/1399	
☐ LN-NOP	B737-86N/W	32655/1662	
☐ LN-NOR	B737-81D/W	39412/3553	o/o♦
☐ LN-NOQ	B737-86N/W	32658/1695	
☐ LN-NOS	B737-8BK/W	33018/1488	
☐ LN-NOT	B737-8JP/W	37816/3194	♦
☐ LN-NOU	B737-8FZ/W	29674/3140	
☐ LN-NOV	B737-8FZ/W	31713/3215	♦
☐ LN-NOW	B737-8FZ/W	37817/3364	♦

WIDEROE'S FLYVESELSKAP — WF / WIF

☐ LN-ILS	DHC-8-103	396	
☐ LN-WDE	DHC-8-402Q	4183	
☐ LN-WDF	DHC-8-402Q	4244	
☐ LN-WDG	DHC-8-402Q	4266	
☐ LN-WDH	DHC-8-402Q	4273	
☐ LN-WDI	DHC-8-402Q	4286	
☐ LN-WDJ	DHC-8-402Q	4290	
☐ LN-WDK	DHC-8-402Q	4337	♦
☐ LN-WFC	DHC-8-311A	236	
☐ LN-WFD	DHC-8-311	407	
☐ LN-WFH	DHC-8-311A	238	
☐ LN-WFO	DHC-8Q-311	493	
☐ LN-WFP	DHC-8Q-311	495	
☐ LN-WFS	DHC-8Q-311	535	
☐ LN-WFT	DHC-8Q-311	532	
☐ LN-WIA	DHC-8-103B	359	
☐ LN-WIB	DHC-8-103B	360	
☐ LN-WIC	DHC-8-103B	367	
☐ LN-WID	DHC-8-103B	369	
☐ LN-WIE	DHC-8-103B	371	
☐ LN-WIF	DHC-8-103B	372	
☐ LN-WIG	DHC-8-103B	382	
☐ LN-WIH	DHC-8-103B	383	
☐ LN-WII	DHC-8-103B	384	
☐ LN-WIJ	DHC-8-103B	386	
☐ LN-WIL	DHC-8-103B	398	
☐ LN-WIM	DHC-8-103B	403	
☐ LN-WIN	DHC-8-103B	409	
☐ LN-WIO	DHC-8-103B	417	
☐ LN-WIP	DHC-8-103A	239	
☐ LN-WIR	DHC-8-103A	273	

☐	LN-WIT	DHC-8-103	310
☐	LN-WIU	DHC-8-103	378

LV - ARGENTINA

AEROCHACO

☐	LV-BSC	MD-87	49727/1621
☐	LV-BZH	MD-87	49780/1674

AEROLINEAS ARGENTINAS · AR / ARG

☐	LV-BIT	A340-313	093	
☐	LV-BMT	A340-312	048	
☐	LV-CEK	A340-343	094	♦
☐	LV-ZPJ	A340-211	074	
☐	LV-ZPO	A340-211	063	
☐	LV-ZPX	A340-211	080	
☐	LV-ZRA	A340-211	085	[EZE]
☐	LV-AYE	B737-5H6	26456/2527	
☐	LV-AYI	B737-528	25234/2411	
☐	LV-AZU	B737-528	25235/2428	
☐	LV-BAR	B737-528	26450/2503	
☐	LV-BAT	B737-5H6	27356/2654	
☐	LV-BAX	B737-5H6	26448/2484	
☐	LV-BBN	B737-5H6	26454/2511	
☐	LV-BBW	B737-5Y0	24897/2003	
☐	LV-BDD	B737-5Y0	24899/2093	
☐	LV-BDV	B737-5Y0	24900/2095	
☐	LV-BEO	B737-5Y0	25176/2155	
☐	LV-BIH	B737-53A	24786/1898	
☐	LV-BIM	B737-53A	25425/2177	
☐	LV-BIX	B737-53A	24788/1921	
☐	LV-BNM	B737-5K5	24926/1966	
☐	LV-BNS	B737-5K5	24776/1848	
☐	LV-BOT	B737-505	24652/1917	
☐	LV-BYY	B737-7BD/W	33938/2863	
☐	LV-BZA	B737-76N/W	32674/1952	
☐	LV-BZO	B737-76N/W	32676/1974	
☐	LV-CAD	B737-76N/W	32680/2089	
☐	LV-CAM	B737-73V/W	30243/919	
☐	LV-CAP	B737-76N/W	32695/1919	
☐	LV-CBF	B737-76N/W	32696/1922	
☐	LV-CBG	B737-73V/W	30235/672	
☐	LV-CBS	B737-73V/W	30236/715	
☐	LV-CBT	B737-76N/W	34756/2208	
☐	LV-CCR	B737-73V/W	30237/730	
☐	LV-GOO	B737-7BD	35962/2932	
☐	LV-WSY	B737-281	20562/293	>DLU
☐	LV-WTX	B737-281	20561/292	
☐	LV-ZRO	B737-236	23164/1060	[EZE]
☐	LV-ZSW	B737-236	23170/1086	
☐	LV-ZTT	B737-236	21806/699	[EZE]
☐	LV-ZTY	B737-236	23159/1047	
☐	LV-ZXC	B737-236	23160/1053	
☐	LV-ZXP	B737-228	23003/939	[EZE]
☐	LV-ZXU	B737-236	23226/1105	
☐	LV-ZYG	B737-236	21795/645	[EZE]
☐	LV-ZYI	B737-228	23010/959	
☐	LV-ZYN	B737-236	21794/643	
☐	LV-ZZD	B737-228	23011/971	
☐	LV-ZZI	B737-236	23166/1067	
☐	LV-ALJ	B747-475	25422/912	
☐	LV-AXF	B747-475	24895/837	
☐	LV-BBU	B747-475	24883/823	
☐	LV-MLP	B747-287B	21726/403	
☐	LV-MLR	B747-287B	21727/404	[EZE]
☐	LV-OEP	B747-287B	22297/487	
☐	LV-OPA	B747-287B	22593/552	[EZE]
☐	LV-VBX	MD-88	53047/2016	
☐	LV-VBZ	MD-88	53049/2031	
☐	LV-VCB	MD-88	53351/2043	[AEP]
☐	LV-VGB	MD-88	53446/2046	[AEP]

AERO VIP · AOG

☐	LV-BYW	CRJ-900	15209

ANDES LINEAS AEREAS · ANS

☐	LV-CFD	CRJ-900ER	15064	♦
☐	LV-BHF	MD-82	49508/1449	
☐	LV-BTH	MD-83	49952/1934	
☐	LV-BZR	MD-87	49706/1614	
☐	LV-CDD	MD-83	49579/1465	♦

AUSTRAL LINEAS AEREAS · AU / AUT

☐	LV-ZTE	B737-228	23349/1135	[AEP]
☐	LV-ZTX	B737-228	23504/1267	[EZE]
☐	LV-ZXB	B737-228	23009/958	
☐	LV-ZXH	B737-228	23503/1256	[AEP]
☐	LV-ZXV	B737-228	23793/1426	[EZE]
☐	LV-CET	ERJ-190AR	19000383	♦
☐	LV-CEU	ERJ-190AR	19000389	♦
☐	LV-CEV	ERJ-190AR	19000390	♦
☐	LV-CHO	ERJ-190AR	19000395	♦
☐	LV-CHQ	ERJ-190AR	19000397	♦
☐	LV-CHR	ERJ-190AR	19000400	♦
☐	LV-CHS	ERJ-190AR	19000402	♦
☐	LV-CID	ERJ-190AR	19000409	♦
☐	LV-CIE	ERJ-190AR	19000414	♦
☐	LV-	ERJ-190AR		o/o♦
☐	LV-	ERJ-190AR		o/o♦
☐	LV-	ERJ-190AR		o/o♦
☐	LV-	ERJ-190AR		o/o♦
☐	LV-ARF	MD-83	49252/1169	
☐	LV-AYD	MD-83	53015/1818	
☐	LV-BAY	MD-83	49284/1209	
☐	LV-BDE	MD-83	49943/1887	[AEP]
☐	LV-BDO	MD-83	49941/1793	
☐	LV-BEG	MD-83	49630/1591	[AEP]
☐	LV-BGV	MD-83	49904/1680	[AEP]
☐	LV-BGZ	MD-82	49906/1786	
☐	LV-BHH	MD-82	49741/1630	
☐	LV-BHN	MD-83	53190/2148	
☐	LV-VAG	MD-83	53117/1951	
☐	LV-WFN	MD-81	48025/952	[AEP]
☐	LV-WGM	MD-83	49784/1627	
☐	LV-WGN	MD-83	49934/1764	
☐	LV-BOA	MD-88	53174/1854	
☐	LV-BOH	MD-88	53175/1868	
☐	LV-BOR	MD-88	49929/1741	[AEP]
☐	LV-BTI	MD-88	49927/1716	
☐	LV-BTW	MD-88	49926/1715	
☐	LV-BXA	MD-88	49928/1732	

LADE - LINEAS AEREAS DEL ESTADO · LDE

☐	T-31	SAAB SF.340B	340B-270
☐	T-32	SAAB SF.340B	340B-226
☐	T-33	SAAB SF.340B	340B-288
☐	T-34	SAAB SF.340B	340B-217
☐	T-44	F.27 Friendship 600	10454
☐	T-45	F.27 Friendship 600	10368
☐	TC-71	F.27 Friendship 400M	10403
☐	TC-74	F.27 Friendship 400M	10408
☐	TC-75	F.27 Friendship 500	10621
☐	TC-79	F.27 Friendship 400M	10575
☐	TC-52	F.28 Fellowship 1000C	11074
☐	TC-53	F.28 Fellowship 1000C	11020
☐	TC-55	F.28 Fellowship 1000C	11024
☐	TC-91	B707-387B	21070/897

LAN ARGENTINA — 4M / DSM

	Reg	Type	c/n	Notes
☐	LV-BET	A320-233	1854	<LAN
☐	LV-BFO	A320-233	1877	<LAN
☐	LV-BFY	A320-233	1858	<LAN
☐	LV-BGI	A320-233	1903	<LAN
☐	LV-BHU	A320-233	1512	<LAN
☐	LV-BOI	A320-233	1491	<LAN
☐	LV-BRA	A320-233	1304	<LAN
☐	LV-BRY	A320-233	1351	<LAN
☐	LV-BSJ	A320-233	1332	<LAN
☐	LV-BTA	A320-233	1548	<LAN
☐	LV-CDQ	B767-316ER/W	35229/949	<LAN♦

SOL LINEAS AEREAS — 8R / OLS

	Reg	Type	c/n
☐	LV-BEW	SAAB SF.340A	340A-150
☐	LV-BEX	SAAB SF.340A	340A-014
☐	LV-BMD	SAAB SF.340A	340A-123
☐	LV-BTP	SAAB SF.340A	340A-131

LX - LUXEMBOURG

CARGOLUX — CV / CLX

	Reg	Type	c/n	Notes
☐	LX-ACV	B747-4B5BCF	24200/748	✗5/>. ♦
☐	LX-LCV	B747-4R7F	29053/1139	
☐	LX-NCV	B747-4R7F	29730/1203	
☐	LX-OCV	B747-4R7F	29731/1222	
☐	LX-PCV	B747-4R7F	29732/1231	
☐	LX-RCV	B747-4R7F	30400/1235	
☐	LX-SCV	B747-4R7F	29733/1281	
☐	LX-TCV	B747-4R7F	30401/1311	19/3
☐	LX-UCV	B747-4R7F	33827/1345	✗5/>.
☐	LX-VCA	B747-8R7F	35808/1420	o/o♦
☐	LX-VCB	B747-8R7F	35806/1423	o/o♦
☐	LX-VCC	B747-8R7F	35807/1424	o/o♦
☐	LX-VCD	B747-8R7F	35809/	o/o♦
☐	LX-VCV	B747-4R7F	34235/1366	
☐	LX-WCV	B747-4R7F	35804/1390	
☐	LX-YCV	B747-4R7F	35805/1407	
☐	LX-ZCV	B747-481BDSF	24801/805	♦
☐	N741WA	B747-4H6 (BDSF)	25702/999	<WOA♦

LUXAIR — LG / LGL

	Reg	Type	c/n	Notes
☐	LX-LGQ	B737-7C9/W	33802/1442	
☐	LX-LGR	B737-7C9/W	33803/1468	
☐	LX-LGS	B737-7C9/W	33956/1634	
☐	LX-LGT	B737-8K5/W	28228/484	
☐	LX-LGA	DHC-8-402Q	4159	
☐	LX-LGC	DHC-8-402Q	4162	
☐	LX-LGD	DHC-8-402Q	4171	
☐	LX-LGE	DHC-8-402Q	4284	
☐	LX-LGF	DHC-8-402Q	4349	♦
☐	LX-LGI	ERJ-145LU	145369	
☐	LX-LGJ	ERJ-145LU	145395	
☐	LX-LGK	ERJ-135LR	14500886	
☐	LX-LGL	ERJ-135LR	14500893	
☐	LX-LGW	ERJ-145LU	145135	
☐	LX-LGX	ERJ-145LU	145147	
☐	LX-LGY	ERJ-145LU	145242	
☐	LX-LGZ	ERJ-145LU	145258	

WEST AIR EUROPE — WLX

	Reg	Type	c/n	Notes
☐	LX-WAL	BAeATPF	2059	<SWN
☐	LX-WAO	BAeATP (LFD)	2043	<SWN
☐	LX-WAP	BAeATPF	2057	<SWN
☐	LX-WAS	BAeATP	2058	<SWN
☐	LX-WAT	BAeATP (LFD)	2011	<SWN
☐	LX-WAV	BAeATP (LFD)	2041	<SWN
☐	LX-WAW	BAeATP (LFD)	2021	
☐	LX-WAB	ATR 72-201F	227	

LY - LITHUANIA

APATAS — LYT

	Reg	Type	c/n
☐	LY-AVA	LET L-410UVP-E3	882036
☐	LY-AVP	LET L-410UVP	851514
☐	LY-AVT	LET L-410UVP-E3	882033

AURELA — LSK

	Reg	Type	c/n
☐	LY-SKA	B737-35B	23972/1537
☐	LY-SKW	B737-382	25162/2241

AVIAVILSA — LVR

	Reg	Type	c/n	Notes
☐	LY-APK	An-26B	27312201	<GZP
☐	LY-APN	An-26B	27312010	
☐	LY-ETM	ATR 42-300F	67	

DANU ORO TRANSPORTAS — DNU

	Reg	Type	c/n	Notes
☐	LY-ARI	ATR 42-300	012A	
☐	LY-DAT	ATR 42-500	445	♦
☐	LY-LWH	ATR 42-300	148	
☐	LY-OOV	ATR 42-300F	5	
☐	LY-RUM	ATR 42-300	10	<DTR
☐	LY-RUN	SAAB SF.340A	340A-086	<DTR
☐	LY-RUS	SAAB SF.340A	340A-074	

NORDIC SOLUTIONS AIR SVCS — N9 / NVD

	Reg	Type	c/n
☐	LY-NSA	SAAB SF.340AF	340A-055
☐	LY-NSB	SAAB SF.340AF	340A-045
☐	LY-NSC	SAAB SF.340AF	340A-037

SMALL PLANET AIRLINES — LLC

	Reg	Type	c/n	Notes
☐	LY-AWD	B737-522	26739/2494	
☐	LY-AWE	B737-522	26684/2388	
☐	LY-AWH	B737-3Y0	23924/1542	
☐	LY-BSD	B737-2T4	22701/886	
☐	LY-FLC	B737-31S	29055/2923	
☐	LY-FLD	B737-322	24664/1877	
☐	LY-FLE	B737-3L9	27061/2347	♦
☐	LY-FLH	B737-382	25161/2226	♦
☐	LY-FLA	B757-29J/W	27203/588	
☐	LY-FLG	B757-204	27237/602	
☐	LY-SBC	SAAB 2000	2000-025	

STAR1 AIRLINES — HCW

	Reg	Type	c/n
☐	LY-STG	B737-73S	29083/392

LZ - BULGARIA

AIR MAX — RMX

	Reg	Type	c/n
☐	LZ-RMK	LET L-410UVP	851406

AIR SCORPIO — SCU

	Reg	Type	c/n
☐	LZ-CCB	Cessna 402B	402B0581
☐	LZ-MNR	An-26	87307504
☐	LZ-MNT	An-26	2209
☐	LZ-RMC	LET L-410UVP-E12	882207

AIRGO AIRLINES OF SOFIA

	Reg	Type	c/n	Notes
☐	LZ-BPS	BAeATP (LFD)	2005	♦

BH AIR — BGH

☐	LZ-BHB	A320-212	0294	
☐	LZ-BHC	A320-212	0349	
☐	LZ-BHD	A320-212	0221	
☐	LZ-BHE	A320-211	0305	
☐	TC-OAN	A321-231	1421	<OHY

BULGARIA AIR — FB / LZB

☐	LZ-FBE	A320-214	3780	
☐	LZ-FBF	A319-111	3028	
☐	LZ-BOQ	B737-522	26687/2402	
☐	LZ-BOU	B737-3L9	23717/1365	
☐	LZ-BOV	B737-330	23833/1439	
☐	LZ-BOW	B737-330	23834/1454	

BULGARIAN AIR CHARTER — BUC

☐	LZ-LDC	MD-82	49217/1268	
☐	LZ-LDE	MD-82	53221/2079	♦
☐	LZ-LDF	MD-82	49219/1310	
☐	LZ-LDG	MD-83	53149/1817	
☐	LZ-LDH	MD-83	53150/1831	
☐	LZ-LDK	MD-82	49432/1378	
☐	LZ-LDL	MD-82	53229/2105	♦
☐	LZ-LDM	MD-82	53228/2104	♦
☐	LZ-LDP	MD-82	49973/1762	♦
☐	LZ-LDR	MD-82	49277/1181	
☐	LZ-LDW	MD-82	49795/1639	♦
☐	LZ-LDY	MD-82	49213/1243	
☐	LZ-LDZ	MD-83	49930/1720	

CARGO AIR — VEA

☐	LZ-CGO	B737-301F	23237/1222	
☐	LZ-CGP	B737-35BF	23970/1467	♦

HELI AIR — HLR

☐	LZ-CBG	An-12A	2340804	[SOF]
☐	LZ-CCE	LET L-410UVP-E	871816	
☐	LZ-CCF	LET L-410UVP-E	861722	Opf UN
☐	LZ-CCG	LET L-410UVP-E	902503	
☐	LZ-CCP	LET L-410UVP-E20	912540	
☐	LZ-CCR	LET L-410UVP-E10	892301	
☐	LZ-CCS	LET L-410UVP-E	902425	Opf UN
☐	LZ-CCT	LET L-410UVP-E10	912528	Opf UN
☐	LZ-LSB	LET L-410UVP-E2	861802	Opf UN

HEMUS AIR — DU / HMS

☐	LZ-HBA	BAe146 Srs.200	E2072	
☐	LZ-HBB	BAe146 Srs.200	E2073	
☐	LZ-HBC	BAe146 Srs.200	E2093	
☐	LZ-HBD	BAe146 Srs.300	E3141	>TBM
☐	LZ-HBE	BAe146 Srs.300	E3131	
☐	LZ-HBF	BAe146 Srs.300	E3159	
☐	LZ-HBG	BAe146 Srs.300	E3146	
☐	LZ-HBZ	BAe146 Srs.200	E2103	>TBM
☐	LZ-TIM	Avro 146-RJ70	E1258	Opf Govt
☐	LZ-FBA	A319-112	3564	
☐	LZ-FBB	A319-112	3309	
☐	LZ-FBC	A320-214	2540	
☐	LZ-FBD	A320-214	2596	o/o
☐	LZ-ATR	ATR 42-300	151	>LBY
☐	LZ-ATS	ATR 42-300	130	

VIA - AIR VIA — VIM

☐	LZ-MDA	A320-232	2732	
☐	LZ-MDB	A320-232	3125	
☐	LZ-MDC	A320-232	4270	♦
☐	LZ-MDD	A320-232	4305	♦
☐	LZ-MDM	A320-232	2804	
☐	LZ-	A320-232		o/o♦
☐	LZ-	A320-232		o/o♦

WIZZ AIR BULGARIA AIRLINES — 8Z / WVL

☐	LZ-WZA	A320-232	2571	<WZZ
☐	LZ-WZB	A320-232	3562	<WZZ
☐	LZ-WZC	A320-232	4308	<WZZ♦

N - UNITED STATES OF AMERICA

ABX AIR — GB / ABX

☐	N312AA	B767-233SF	22315/94	
☐	N702AX	B767-231ER	22566/29	
☐	N707AX	B767-231ER	22570/63	
☐	N708AX	B767-231ER	22571/64	
☐	N709AX	B767-231ER	22572/65	
☐	N713AX	B767-205ER	23058/101	
☐	N739AX	B767-232 (SCD)	22216/26	
☐	N740AX	B767-232 (SCD)	22213/6	
☐	N741AX	B767-232 (SCD)	22215/17 for conv	
☐	N742AX	B767-232 (SCD)	22217/27	>ANA
☐	N743AX	B767-232 (SCD)	22218/31	
☐	N744AX	B767-232 (SCD)	22221/53	>ANA
☐	N745AX	B767-232 (SCD)	22222/56	
☐	N747AX	B767-232 (SCD)	22224/56	
☐	N749AX	B767-232	22226/78 for conv	
☐	N750AX	B767-232 (SCD)	22227/83	
☐	N752AX	B767-281	23434/171	
☐	N767AX	B767-281	22785/51	
☐	N768AX	B767-281	22786/54	
☐	N769AX	B767-281F	22787/58	
☐	N773AX	B767-281	22788/61	
☐	N774AX	B767-281	22789/67	
☐	N775AX	B767-281	22790/69	
☐	N783AX	B767-281	23016/80	
☐	N784AX	B767-281	23017/82	
☐	N785AX	B767-281	23018/84	
☐	N786AX	B767-281	23019/85	
☐	N787AX	B767-281F	23020/96	
☐	N788AX	B767-281	23021/103	
☐	N790AX	B767-281	23140/106	
☐	N791AX	B767-281	23141/108	
☐	N792AX	B767-281 (SCD)	23142/110	
☐	N793AX	B767-281	23143/114	
☐	N794AX	B767-281	23144/115	
☐	N795AX	B767-281F	23145/116	
☐	N796AX	B767-281	23146/121	
☐	N797AX	B767-281	23147/123	
☐	N798AX	B767-281 (SCD)	23431/143	

AERO FLITE

☐	N262NR	CL-215	1081	262
☐	N263NR	CL-215	1082	263
☐	N264V	CL-215	1090	264
☐	N266NR	CL-215	1102	266
☐	N267V	CL-215	1103	267

AERO UNION

☐	N900AU	P-3A Orion	185-5104	0
☐	N920AU	P-3A Orion	185-5039	20
☐	N921AU	P-3A Orion	185-5098	21
☐	N922AU	P-3A Orion	185-5100	22
☐	N923AU	P-3A Orion	185-5085	23
☐	N925AU	P-3A Orion	185-5074	25
☐	N927AU	P-3A Orion	185-5082	27

AIR CARGO CARRIERS — 2Q / SNC

☐	N58DD	Short SD.3-30	SH3008

	Registration	Type	Serial
☐	N167RC	Short SD.3-30	SH3038
☐	N330AC	Short SD.3-30	SH3007
☐	N334AC	Short SD.3-30	SH3029
☐	N336MV	Short SD.3-30	SH3018
☐	N390GA	Short SD.3-30	SH3077
☐	N936MA	Short SD.3-30	SH3036
☐	N2629P	Short SD.3-30	SH3079
☐	N124CA	Short SD.3-60	SH3652
☐	N136LR	Short SD.3-60	SH3752
☐	N151CA	Short SD.3-60	SH3653
☐	N360AB	Short SD.3-60	SH3756
☐	N360RW	Short SD.3-60	SH3613
☐	N360SA	Short SD.3-60	SH3601
☐	N367AC	Short SD.3-60	SH3626
☐	N368AC	Short SD.3-60	SH3651
☐	N376AC	Short SD.3-60	SH3736
☐	N601CA	Short SD.3-60	SH3623
☐	N617FB	Short SD.3-60	SH3617
☐	N688AN	Short SD.3-60	SH3633
☐	N701A	Short SD.3-60	SH3627
☐	N742CC	Short SD.3-60	SH3742
☐	N764JR	Short SD.3-60	SH3764
☐	N972AA	Short SD.3-60	SH3754
☐	N973AA	Short SD.3-60	SH3749
☐	N3732X	Short SD.3-60	SH3732
☐	N4498Y	Short SD.3-60	SH3625

AIR MIDWEST — ZV / AMW

	Registration	Type	Serial	
☐	N138YV	Beech 1900D	UE-138	<ASH
☐	N142ZV	Beech 1900D	UE-142	<ASH
☐	N159YV	Beech 1900D	UE-159	<ASH
☐	N10675	Beech 1900D	UE-229	<ASH

AIR SUNSHINE — YI / RSI

	Registration	Type	Serial	
☐	N123HY	EMB.110P1	110321	
☐	N744BA	SAAB SF.340A	340A-105	
☐	N792BA	SAAB SF.340A	340A-092	[FLL]♦
☐	N793BA	SAAB SF.340A	340A-093	[FLL]♦

AIR TAHOMA — 5C / HMA

	Registration	Type	Serial	
☐	N581P	Convair 580	29	
☐	N582P	Convair 580	475	[LCK]
☐	N584E	Convair 580	24	
☐	N585P	Convair 580	163	
☐	N588X	Convair 580	52	
☐	N590X	Convair 580	130	[LCK]
☐	N150PA	Convair 240-27	278	
☐	N156PA	Convair 240-27	324	[LCK]
☐	N99380	Convair 240-27 (T-29B)	249	

AIRNOW — RLR

	Registration	Type	Serial
☐	N24AN	EMB.110P1	110318
☐	N31AN	EMB.110P1	110372
☐	N36AN	EMB.110P1	110451
☐	N42AN	EMB.110P1	110456
☐	N51BA	EMB.110P1	110404
☐	N62CZ	EMB.110P1	110388
☐	N64CZ	EMB.110P1	110399
☐	N83BA	EMB.110P1	110351
☐	N97BA	EMB.110P1	110322
☐	N101TN	EMB.110P1	110271
☐	N621KC	EMB.110P1	110335
☐	N710NH	EMB.110P1	110250
☐	N830AC	EMB.110P1	110205

AIRSERV INTERNATIONAL

	Registration	Type	Serial
☐	N899AS	DHC-6 Twin Otter 300	347

AIRTRAN AIRWAYS — FL / TRS

	Registration	Type	FL / TRS	
☐	N603AT	B717-22A	55127/5074	771
☐	N717JL	B717-2BD	55042/5115	740
☐	N891AT	B717-2BD	55043/5131	741
☐	N892AT	B717-2BD	55044/5134	742
☐	N893AT	B717-2BD	55045/5136	743
☐	N894AT	B717-2BD	55046/5137	744
☐	N895AT	B717-2BD	55047/5139	745
☐	N896AT	B717-2BD	55048/5141	746
☐	N899AT	B717-2BD	55049/5143	747
☐	N906AT	B717-231	55087/5060	795
☐	N910AT	B717-231	55086/5056	794
☐	N915AT	B717-231	55085/5055	793
☐	N919AT	B717-231	55084/5052	792
☐	N920AT	B717-231	55083/5049	791
☐	N921AT	B717-231	55082/5046	790
☐	N922AT	B717-2BD	55050/5144	748
☐	N923AT	B717-2BD	55051/5148	749
☐	N924AT	B717-231	55080/5043	789
☐	N925AT	B717-231	55079/5042	788
☐	N926AT	B717-231	55078/5039	787
☐	N927AT	B717-231	55077/5038	786
☐	N928AT	B717-231	55076/5035	785
☐	N929AT	B717-231	55075/5032	784
☐	N930AT	B717-231	55072/5025	782
☐	N932AT	B717-231	55073/5028	783
☐	N933AT	B717-231	55071/5024	781
☐	N934AT	B717-231	55070/5022	780
☐	N935AT	B717-231	55069/5019	779
☐	N936AT	B717-231	55058/5017	778
☐	N937AT	B717-231	55091/5075	799
☐	N938AT	B717-2BD	55098/5155	751
☐	N939AT	B717-2BD	55099/5156	752
☐	N940AT	B717-2BD	55004/5005	702
☐	N942AT	B717-2BD	55005/5006	703
☐	N943AT	B717-2BD	55006/5007	704
☐	N944AT	B717-2BD	55007/5008	705
☐	N945AT	B717-2BD	55008/5009	706
☐	N946AT	B717-2BD	55009/5010	707
☐	N947AT	B717-2BD	55010/5011	708
☐	N948AT	B717-2BD	55011/5012	709
☐	N949AT	B717-2BD	55003/5004	701
☐	N950AT	B717-2BD	55012/5018	710
☐	N951AT	B717-2BD	55013/5021	711
☐	N952AT	B717-2BD	55014/5027	712
☐	N953AT	B717-2BD	55015/5033	713
☐	N954AT	B717-2BD	55016/5036	714
☐	N955AT	B717-2BD	55017/5040	715
☐	N956AT	B717-2BD	55018/5044	716
☐	N957AT	B717-2BD	55019/5047	717
☐	N958AT	B717-2BD	55020/5051	718
☐	N959AT	B717-2BD	55021/5057	719
☐	N960AT	B717-2BD	55022/5058	720
☐	N961AT	B717-2BD	55023/5062	721
☐	N963AT	B717-2BD	55024/5066	722
☐	N964AT	B717-2BD	55025/5071	723
☐	N965AT	B717-2BD	55026/5076	724
☐	N966AT	B717-2BD	55027/5081	725
☐	N967AT	B717-2BD	55028/5082	726
☐	N968AT	B717-2BD	55029/5091	727
☐	N969AT	B717-2BD	55030/5094	728
☐	N970AT	B717-2BD	55031/5096	729
☐	N971AT	B717-2BD	55032/5097	730
☐	N972AT	B717-2BD	55033/5099	731
☐	N974AT	B717-2BD	55034/5101	732
☐	N975AT	B717-2BD	55035/5102	733
☐	N977AT	B717-2BD	55036/5106	734
☐	N978AT	B717-2BD	55037/5108	735
☐	N979AT	B717-2BD	55038/5109	736
☐	N980AT	B717-2BD	55039/5111	737
☐	N981AT	B717-2BD	55040/5113	738
☐	N982AT	B717-2BD	55041/5114	739
☐	N983AT	B717-2BD	55052/5150	750
☐	N985AT	B717-231	55090/5068	798

N986AT	B717-231	55089/5067	797
N987AT	B717-231	55088/5063	796
N988AT	B717-23S	55068/5065	760
N989AT	B717-23S	55152/5085	761
N990AT	B717-23S	55134/5088	762
N991AT	B717-23S	55135/5090	763
N992AT	B717-2BD	55136/5100	764
N993AT	B717-2BD	55137/5103	765
N994AT	B717-2BD	55138/5104	766
N995AT	B717-2BD	55139/5105	767
N996AT	B717-2BD	55140/5107	768
N997AT	B717-2BD	55141/5110	769
N998AT	B717-2BD	55142/5112	770
N126AT	B737-76N/W	32679/1514	300
N149AT	B737-76N/W	32681/1526	301
N166AT	B737-7BD/W	33917/1550	302
N167AT	B737-7BD/W	33918/1572	304
N168AT	B737-76N/W	32653/1566	303
N169AT	B737-76N/W	32744/1584	305
N173AT	B737-76N/W	32661/1593	306
N174AT	B737-76N/W	32667/1623	307
N175AT	B737-76N/W	32652/1627	308
N176AT	B737-76N/W	32654/1641	309
N184AT	B737-76N/W	32656/1671	310
N240AT	B737-76N/W	32657/1687	311
N261AT	B737-76N/W	32660/1710	312
N267AT	B737-7BD/W	33919/1730	313
N272AT	B737-7BD/W	33921/1778	315
N273AT	B737-76N/W	32662/1788	316
N276AT	B737-76N/W	32664/1804	317
N278AT	B737-76N/W	32665/1827	318
N279AT	B737-76N/W	32666/1833	319
N281AT	B737-7BD/W	33922/1845	320
N283AT	B737-7BD/W	34479/1874	321
N284AT	B737-76N/W	32668/1876	322
N285AT	B737-76N/W	32670/1898	323
N287AT	B737-76N/W	32671/1925	325
N288AT	B737-7BD/W	33924/1940	326
N289AT	B737-76N/W	32673/1943	327
N290AT	B737-7BD/W	33925/1967	328
N291AT	B737-76N/W	32675/1970	329
N292AT	B737-7BD/W	33926/1997	330
N295AT	B737-76N/W	32677/2002	331
N296AT	B737-7BD/W	34861/2041	332
N299AT	B737-76N/W	32678/2055	333
N300AT	B737-7BD/W	33923/2083	334
N307AT	B737-7BD/W	34862/2094	335
N308AT	B737-7BD/W	35109/2126	336
N309AT	B737-7BD/W	33929/2129	337
N311AT	B737-7BD/W	33930/2143	338
N312AT	B737-7BD/W	35110/2147	339
N313AT	B737-7BD/W	33927/2169	340
N315AT	B737-7BD/W	35788/2178	341
N316AT	B737-7BD/W	33928/2190	342
N318AT	B737-7BD/W	33931/2214	344
N326AT	B737-7BD/W	33933/2278	345
N328AT	B737-7BD/W	33934/2296	346
N329AT	B737-7BD/W	36091/2304	347
N330AT	B737-7BD/W	36399/2312	348
N336AT	B737-7BD/W	36716/2505	350
N337AT	B737-7BD/W	36717/2526	351
N338AT	B737-7BD/W	33943/2552	352
N344AT	B737-7BD/W	36718/2568	353
N353AT	B737-7BD/W	36724/2813	
N354AT	B737-7BD/W	36725/2815	
N	B737-7BD/W		o/o♦
N	B737-7BD/W		o/o♦
N	B737-7BD/W		o/o♦
N	B737-7BD/W		o/o♦
N480AC	B737-7BD/W	34480/1900	♦

ALASKA AIRLINES AS / ASA

N703AS	B737-490	28893/3039	
N705AS	B737-490	29318/3042	
N706AS	B737-490	28894/3050	
N708AS	B737-490	28895/3098	
N709AS	B737-490(SF)	28896/3099	
N713AS	B737-490	30161/3110	
N754AS	B737-4Q8	25095/2265	
N755AS	B737-4Q8	25096/2278	
N756AS	B737-4Q8	25097/2299	
N760AS	B737-4Q8	25098/2320	
N762AS	B737-4Q8F	25099/2334	
N763AS	B737-4Q8F	25100/2346	
N764AS	B737-4Q8F	25101/2348	
N765AS	B737-4Q8F	25102/2350	
N767AS	B737-490	27081/2354	
N768AS	B737-490F	27082/2356	
N769AS	B737-4Q8	25103/2452	
N771AS	B737-4Q8	25104/2476	
N772AS	B737-4Q8	25105/2505	
N773AS	B737-4Q8	25106/2518	[VCV]♦
N778AS	B737-4Q8	25110/2586	
N779AS	B737-4Q8	25111/2605	
N786AS	B737-4S3	24795/1870	
N788AS	B737-490	28885/2891	
N791AS	B737-490	28886/2902	
N792AS	B737-490	28887/2903	
N793AS	B737-490	28888/2990	
N794AS	B737-490	28889/3000	
N795AS	B737-490	28890/3006	
N796AS	B737-490	28891/3027	
N797AS	B737-490	28892/3036	
N799AS	B737-490	29270/3038	
N607AS	B737-790/W	29751/313	
N609AS	B737-790/W	29752/350	
N611AS	B737-790/W	29753/385	
N612AS	B737-790/W	30162/406	
N613AS	B737-790/W	30163/430	
N614AS	B737-790/W	30343/439	
N615AS	B737-790/W	30344/472	
N617AS	B737-790/W	30542/532	
N618AS	B737-790/W	30543/536	
N619AS	B737-790/W	30164/597	
N622AS	B737-790/W	30165/661	
N623AS	B737-790/W	30166/700	
N624AS	B737-790/W	30778/724	
N625AS	B737-790/W	30792/754	
N626AS	B737-790/W	30793/763	
N627AS	B737-790/W	30794/796	
N644AS	B737-790/W	30795/1277	
N506AS	B737-890/W	35690/2627	
N508AS	B737-890/W	35691/2662	
N512AS	B737-890/W	39043/2711	
N513AS	B737-890/W	35192/2721	
N514AS	B737-890/W	35193/2727	
N516AS	B737-890/W	39044/2751	
N517AS	B737-890/W	35197/2770	
N518AS	B737-890/W	35693/2785	
N519AS	B737-890/W	36482/2800	
N520AS	B737-890/W	36481/2812	
N523AS	B737-890/W	35194/2816	
N524AS	B737-890/W	35195/2850	
N525AS	B737-890/W	35692/2859	
N526AS	B737-890/W	35196/2862	
N527AS	B737-890/W	35694/2913	
N528AS	B737-890/W	35695/2930	
N529AS	B737-890/W	35198/3229	♦
N530AS	B737-890/W	36578/3257	♦
N531AS	B737-890/W	35199/3287	♦
N532AS	B737-890/W	36346/3317	♦
N533AS	B737-890/W	35201/3511	♦
N534AS	B737-890/W	35202/3523	♦
N535AS	B737-890/W	35200/3558	o/o♦
N	B737-890/W		o/o♦
N546AS	B737-890/W	30022/1640	
N548AS	B737-890/W	30020/1738	
N549AS	B737-8FH/W	30824/1664	

☐ N551AS	B737-890/W	34593/1860	
☐ N552AS	B737-890/W	34595/1882	
☐ N553AS	B737-890/W	34594/1906	
☐ N556AS	B737-890/W	35175/1980	
☐ N557AS	B737-890/W	35176/2010	
☐ N558AS	B737-890/W	35177/2031	
☐ N559AS	B737-890/W	35178/2026	
☐ N560AS	B737-890/W	35179/2072	
☐ N562AS	B737-890/W	35091/2084	
☐ N563AS	B737-890/W	35180/2090	
☐ N564AS	B737-890/W	35103/2099	
☐ N565AS	B737-890/W	35181/2134	
☐ N566AS	B737-890/W	35182/2164	
☐ N568AS	B737-890/W	35183/2166	
☐ N569AS	B737-890/W	35184/2192	
☐ N570AS	B737-890/W	35185/2212	
☐ N577AS	B737-890/W	35186/2221	
☐ N579AS	B737-890/W	35187/2226	
☐ N581AS	B737-890/W	35188/2259	
☐ N583AS	B737-890/W	35681/2333	
☐ N584AS	B737-890/W	35682/2365	
☐ N585AS	B737-890/W	35683/2385	
☐ N586AS	B737-890/W	35189/2393	
☐ N587AS	B737-890/W	35684/2422	
☐ N588AS	B737-890/W	35685/2454	
☐ N589AS	B737-890/W	35686/2458	
☐ N590AS	B737-890/W	35687/2478	
☐ N592AS	B737-890/W	35190/2511	
☐ N593AS	B737-890/W	35107/2545	
☐ N594AS	B737-890/W	35191/2560	
☐ N596AS	B737-890/W	35688/2587	
☐ N597AS	B737-890/W	35689/2601	
☐ N302AS	B737-990/W	30017/596	
☐ N303AS	B737-990/W	30016/683	
☐ N305AS	B737-990/W	30013/774	
☐ N306AS	B737-990/W	30014/802	
☐ N307AS	B737-990/W	30015/838	
☐ N309AS	B737-990/W	30857/902	
☐ N315AS	B737-990/W	30019/1218	
☐ N317AS	B737-990/W	30856/1296	
☐ N318AS	B737-990/W	30018/1326	
☐ N319AS	B737-990/W	33679/1344	
☐ N320AS	B737-990/W	33680/1380	
☐ N323AS	B737-990/W	30021/1454	

ALASKA CENTRAL EXPRESS — KO / AER

☐ N111AX	Beech 1900C-1	UC-81	
☐ N113AX	Beech 1900C-1	UC-41	
☐ N114AX	Beech 1900C-1	UC-36	
☐ N115AX	Beech 1900C-1	UC-2	
☐ N117AX	Beech 1900C-1	UC-17	♦

ALLEGIANT AIR — G4 / AAY

☐ N901NV	B757-204	26963/450	♦
☐ N902NV	B757-204	26964/452	♦
☐ N903NV	B757-204	26966/520	o/o♦
☐ N399NV	MD-87	49413/1681	[MHV]
☐ N401NV	MD-88	49761/1623	
☐ N402NV	MD-88	49763/1626	
☐ N403NV	MD-88	49764/1632	
☐ N404NV	MD-88	49765/1645	
☐ N405NV	MD-83	49623/1499	
☐ N406NV	MD-82	49900/1765	
☐ N407NV	MD-82	53244/1901	
☐ N408NV	MD-82	53246/1918	
☐ N409NV	MD-83	49574/1413	
☐ N410NV	MD-83	49965/2044	
☐ N411NV	MD-82	53245/1978	
☐ N412NV	MD-88	49759/1606	
☐ N414NV	MD-88	49766/1657	
☐ N415NV	MD-82	49909/1625	♦
☐ N416NV	MD-82	49555/1402	♦

☐ N418NV	MD-82	49615/1543	♦
☐ N419NV	MD-82	53366/1999	♦
☐ N422NV	MD-82	49381/1231	♦
☐ N423NV	MD-82	53008/1895	[IGM]♦
☐ N428NV	MD-82	49420/1254	[IGM]♦
☐ N429NV	MD-82	49385/1244	♦
☐ N515PT	MD-87	49612/1827	[IGM]♦
☐ N860GA	MD-83	49786/1631	
☐ N861GA	MD-83	49557/1436	
☐ N862GA	MD-83	49556/1415	
☐ N863GA	MD-83	49911/1653	
☐ N864GA	MD-83	49912/1659	
☐ N865GA	MD-83	49998/1800	
☐ N866GA	MD-83	49910/1638	
☐ N868GA	MD-83	49554/1379	
☐ N869GA	MD-83	53294/1917	
☐ N871GA	MD-83	53296/1937	
☐ N872GA	MD-83	53295/1922	
☐ N873GA	MD-83	49658/1461	
☐ N874GA	MD-83	49643/1423	
☐ N875GA	MD-83	53468/2130	
☐ N876GA	MD-83	53469/2116	
☐ N877GA	MD-83	53467/2102	
☐ N878GA	MD-83	53487/2132	
☐ N879GA	MD-83	53486/2130	
☐ N880GA	MD-83	49625/1503	
☐ N881GA	MD-83	49708/1561	
☐ N883GA	MD-83	49710/1547	
☐ N884GA	MD-83	49401/1357	
☐ N886GA	MD-82	49931/1754	
☐ N887GA	MD-82	49932/1756	
☐ N891GA	MD-83	49423/1283	
☐ N892GA	MD-83	49826/1578	
☐ N893GA	MD-83	53051/1718	
☐ N894GA	MD-82	49660/1445	
☐ N895GA	MD-82	49667/1466	
☐ N945MA	MD-87	49725/1552	
☐ N948MA	MD-87	49778/1646	
☐ N949MA	MD-87	49779/1670	
☐ N952MA	MD-87	49673/1508	

ALOHA AIR CARGO

☐ N826AL	Boeing 737-2B2C	23051/1002	
☐ N840AL	Boeing 737-2X6C	23124/1046	
☐ N841AL	Boeing 737-2X6C	23123/1042	
☐ N842AL	Boeing 737-290QC	23126/1032	
☐ N843KH	SAAB SF.340A	340A-046	♦

ALPINE AIR EXPRESS — 5A / AIP

☐ N125BA	Beech 1900C	UB-6	
☐ N127BA	Beech 1900C	UB-7	
☐ N153GA	Beech 1900C	UB-34	
☐ N154GA	Beech 1900C	UB-25	
☐ N155CJ	Beech 1900D	UE-55	
☐ N172GA	Beech 1900C	UB-11	
☐ N190GA	Beech 1900C	UB-1	
☐ N192GA	Beech 1900C	UB-17	
☐ N194GA	Beech 1900C	UB-8	
☐ N197GA	Beech 1900C	UB-16	
☐ N198GA	Beech 1900C	UB-5	

AMERICAN AIRLINES — AA / AAL

☐ N800NN	B737-823/W	29564/2964	3DY
☐ N801NN	B737-823/W	29565/2972	3EA
☐ N802NN	B737-823/W	31073/2982	3EB
☐ N803NN	B737-823/W	29566/2995	3EC
☐ N804NN	B737-823/W	29567/3004	3ED
☐ N805NN	B737-823/W	31075/3013	3EE
☐ N806NN	B737-823/W	29561/3028	3EF
☐ N807NN	B737-823/W	31077/3035	3EG
☐ N808NN	B737-823/W	33206/3042	3EH
☐ N809NN	B737-823/W	33519/3050	3EJ

	Reg	Type	C/n	Code
☐	N810NN	B737-823/W	33207/3056	3EK
☐	N811NN	B737-823/W	31079/3063	3EL
☐	N812NN	B737-823/W	33520/3070	3EM
☐	N813NN	B737-823/W	30918/3077	3EN
☐	N814NN	B737-823/W	29562/3085	3EP
☐	N815NN	B737-823/W	33208/3094	3ER
☐	N816NN	B737-823/W	31081/3102	3ES
☐	N817NN	B737-823/W	29558/3017	3ET
☐	N818NN	B737-823/W	30910/3112	3EU
☐	N819NN	B737-823/W	31083/3118	3EV
☐	N820NN	B737-823/W	29559/3125	3EW
☐	N821NN	B737-823/W	30912/3137	3EX
☐	N822NN	B737-823/W	31085/3149	3EY
☐	N823NN	B737-823/W	29560/3156	3FA
☐	N824NN	B737-823/W	30916/3170	3FB◆
☐	N825NN	B737-823/W	31087/3178	3FC◆
☐	N826NN	B737-823/W	31089/3185	3FD◆
☐	N827NN	B737-823/W	33209/3193	3FE◆
☐	N829NN	B737-823/W	33210/3200	3FF◆
☐	N830NN	B737-823/W	31091/3209	3FG◆
☐	N831NN	B737-823/W	33211/3217	3FH◆
☐	N832NN	B737-823/W	33521/3228	3FJ◆
☐	N833NN	B737-823/W	31093/3236	3FK◆
☐	N834NN	B737-823/W	29576/3244	3FL◆
☐	N835NN	B737-823/W	29577/3252	3FM◆
☐	N836NN	B737-823/W	31095/3260	3FN◆
☐	N837NN	B737-823/W	30908/3268	3FP◆
☐	N838NN	B737-823/W	31097/3276	3FR◆
☐	N839NN	B737-823/W	29557/3282	3FS◆
☐	N840NN	B737-823/W	33518/3291	3FT◆
☐	N841NN	B737-823/W	30914/3298	3FU◆
☐	N842NN	B737-823/W	31099/3307	3FV◆
☐	N843NN	B737-823/W	30906/3328	3FW◆
☐	N844NN	B737-823/W	33212/3334	3FX◆
☐	N845NN	B737-823/W	40579/3340	3FY◆
☐	N846NN	B737-823/W	31101/3347	3GA◆
☐	N847NN	B737-823/W	29575/3361	3GB◆
☐	N848NN	B737-823/W	31103/3367	3GC◆
☐	N849NN	B737-823/W	33213/3373	3GD◆
☐	N850NN	B737-823/W	40580/3380	3GE◆
☐	N851NN	B737-823/W	29556/3390	3GF◆
☐	N852NN	B737-823/W	40581/3396	3GG◆
☐	N853NN	B737-823/W	31105/3404	3GH◆
☐	N854NN	B737-823/W	33214/3412	3GJ◆
☐	N855NN	B737-823/W	40852/3422	3GK◆
☐	N856NN	B737-823/W	31107/3427	3GL◆
☐	N857NN	B737-823/W	30907/3434	3GM◆
☐	N858NN	B737-823/W	30904/3440	3GN◆
☐	N859NN	B737-823/W	29555/3456	3GP◆
☐	N860NN	B737-823/W	40583/3462	3GR◆
☐	N861NN	B737-823/W	31109/3468	3GS◆
☐	N862NN	B737-823/W	30905/3475	3GT◆
☐	N863NN	B737-823/W	30903/3481	3GU◆
☐	N864NN	B737-823/W	31111/3487	3GV◆
☐	N865NN	B737-823/W	29554/3493	3GW◆
☐	N866NN	B737-823/W	40584/3499	3GX◆
☐		B737-823/W		o/o◆
☐		B737-823/W		o/o◆
☐		B737-823/W		o/o◆
☐		B737-823/W		o/o◆
☐		B737-823/W		o/o◆
☐		B737-823/W		o/o◆
☐		B737-823/W		o/o◆
☐		B737-823/W		o/o◆
☐		B737-823/W		o/o◆
☐		B737-823/W		o/o◆
☐		B737-823/W		o/o◆
☐		B737-823/W		o/o◆
☐		B737-823/W		o/o◆
☐		B737-823/W		o/o◆
☐		B737-823/W		o/o◆
☐	N901AN	B737-823/W	29503/184	3AA
☐	N902AN	B737-823/W	29504/190	3AB
☐	N903AN	B737-823/W	29505/196	3AC
☐	N904AN	B737-823/W	29506/207	3AD
☐	N905AN	B737-823/W	29507/231	3AE
☐	N906AN	B737-823/W	29508/240	3AF
☐	N907AN	B737-823/W	29509/254	3AG
☐	N908AN	B737-823/W	29510/263	3AH
☐	N909AN	B737-823/W	29511/267	3AJ
☐	N910AN	B737-823/W	29512/271	3AK
☐	N912AN	B737-823/W	29513/289	3AL
☐	N913AN	B737-823/W	29514/293	3AM
☐	N914AN	B737-823/W	29515/316	3AN
☐	N915AN	B737-823/W	29516/322	3AP
☐	N916AN	B737-823/W	29517/332	3AR
☐	N917AN	B737-823/W	29518/344	3AS
☐	N918AN	B737-823/W	29519/353	3AT
☐	N919AN	B737-823/W	29520/363	3AU
☐	N920AN	B737-823/W	29521/378	3AV
☐	N921AN	B737-823/W	29522/383	3AW
☐	N922AN	B737-823/W	29523/398	3AX
☐	N923AN	B737-823/W	29524/405	3AY
☐	N924AN	B737-823/W	29525/434	3BA
☐	N925AN	B737-823/W	29526/440	3BB
☐	N926AN	B737-823/W	29527/453	3BC
☐	N927AN	B737-823/W	30077/462	3BD
☐	N928AN	B737-823/W	29528/473	3BE
☐	N929AN	B737-823/W	30078/488	3BF
☐	N930AN	B737-823/W	29529/503	3BG
☐	N931AN	B737-823/W	30079/509	3BH
☐	N932AN	B737-823/W	29530/527	3BJ
☐	N933AN	B737-823/W	30080/531	3BK
☐	N934AN	B737-823/W	29531/553	3BL
☐	N935AN	B737-823/W	30081/559	3BM
☐	N936AN	B737-823/W	29532/575	3BN
☐	N937AN	B737-823/W	30082/579	3BP
☐	N938AN	B737-823/W	29533/608	3BR
☐	N939AN	B737-823/W	30083/612	3BS
☐	N940AN	B737-823/W	30598/616	3BT
☐	N941AN	B737-823/W	29534/624	3BU
☐	N942AN	B737-823/W	30084/629	3BV
☐	N943AN	B737-823/W	30599/635	3BW
☐	N944AN	B737-823/W	29535/645	3BX
☐	N945AN	B737-823/W	30085/649	3BY
☐	N946AN	B737-823/W	30600/655	3CA
☐	N947AN	B737-823/W	29536/671	3CB
☐	N948AN	B737-823/W	30086/679	3CC
☐	N949AN	B737-823/W	29537/699	3CD
☐	N950AN	B737-823/W	30087/704	3CE
☐	N951AA	B737-823/W	29538/720	3CF
☐	N952AA	B737-823/W	30088/726	3CG
☐	N953AN	B737-823/W	29539/741	3CH
☐	N954AN	B737-823/W	30089/745	3CJ
☐	N955AN	B737-823/W	29540/762	3CK
☐	N956AN	B737-823/W	30090/764	3CL
☐	N957AN	B737-823/W	29541/788	3CM
☐	N958AN	B737-823/W	30091/797	3CN
☐	N959AN	B737-823/W	30828/801	3CP
☐	N960AN	B737-823/W	29542/818	3CR
☐	N961AN	B737-823/W	30092/822	3CS
☐	N962AN	B737-823/W	30858/825	3CT
☐	N963AN	B737-823/W	29543/834	3CU
☐	N964AN	B737-823/W	30093/837	3CV
☐	N965AN	B737-823/W	29544/860	3CW
☐	N966AN	B737-823/W	30094/863	3CX
☐	N967AN	B737-823/W	29545/883	3CY
☐	N968AN	B737-823/W	30095/886	3DA
☐	N969AN	B737-823/W	29546/910	3DB
☐	N970AN	B737-823/W	30096/915	3DC
☐	N971AN	B737-823/W	29547/937	3DD
☐	N972AN	B737-823/W	30097/941	3DE
☐	N973AN	B737-823/W	29548/971	3DF
☐	N974AN	B737-823/W	30098/977	3DG
☐	N975AN	B737-823/W	29549/992	3DH
☐	N976AN	B737-823/W	30099/1001	3DJ
☐	N978AN	B737-823/W	30100/1022	3DL
☐	N979AN	B737-823/W	29568/2838	3DM
☐	N980AN	B737-823/W	33203/2846	3DN

☐ N981AN	B737-823/W	29569/2870	3DP
☐ N982AN	B737-823/W	31067/2876	3DR
☐ N983AN	B737-823/W	29570/2899	3DS
☐ N987AN	B737-823/W	31067/2907	3DT
☐ N989AN	B737-823/W	33205/2915	3DU
☐ N990AN	B737-823/W	29563/2935	3DV
☐ N991AN	B737-823/W	30920/2945	3DW
☐ N992AN	B737-823/W	31067/2954	3DX
☐ N172AJ	B757-223/W	32400/1012	5FT
☐ N173AN	B757-223/W	32399/1005	5FS
☐ N174AA	B757-223/W	31308/998	5FR
☐ N175AN	B757-223/W	32394/992	5FK
☐ N176AA	B757-223/W	32395/994	5FL
☐ N177AN	B757-223/W	32396/996	5FM
☐ N178AA	B757-223/W	32398/1002	5FN
☐ N179AA	B757-223/W	32397/1000	5FP
☐ N181AN	B757-223/W	29591/852	5EN
☐ N182AN	B757-223/W	29592/853	5EP
☐ N183AN	B757-223ER/W	29593/862	5ER
☐ N184AN	B757-223ER/W	29594/866	5ES
☐ N185AN	B757-223/W	32379/962	5ET
☐ N186AN	B757-223/W	32380/964	5EU
☐ N187AN	B757-223/W	32381/965	5EV
☐ N188AN	B757-223/W	32382/969	5EW
☐ N189AN	B757-223/W	32383/970	5EX
☐ N190AA	B757-223/W	32384/973	5EY
☐ N191AN	B757-223/W	32385/977	5FA
☐ N192AN	B757-223/W	32386/979	5FB
☐ N193AN	B757-223/W	32387/981	5FC
☐ N194AN	B757-223/W	32388/983	5FD
☐ N195AN	B757-223/W	32389/984	5FE
☐ N196AA	B757-223/W	32390/986	5FF
☐ N197AN	B757-223/W	32391/988	5FG
☐ N198AA	B757-223/W	32392/989	5FH
☐ N199AN	B757-223/W	32393/991	5FJ
☐ N601AN	B757-223/W	27052/661	5DU
☐ N602AN	B757-223/W	27053/664	5DV
☐ N603AA	B757-223/W	27054/670	5DW
☐ N604AA	B757-223/W	27055/677	5DX
☐ N605AA	B757-223/W	27056/680	5DY
☐ N606AA	B757-223/W	27057/707	5EA
☐ N607AM	B757-223/W	27058/712	5EB
☐ N608AA	B757-223ER/W	27446/720	5EC
☐ N609AA	B757-223ER/W	27447/722	5ED
☐ N610AA	B757-223/W	24486/234	610
☐ N611AM	B757-223/W	24487/236	611
☐ N612AA	B757-223/W	24488/240	612
☐ N613AA	B757-223/W	24489/242	613
☐ N614AA	B757-223/W	24490/243	614
☐ N615AM	B757-223/W	24491/245	615
☐ N616AA	B757-223/W	24524/248	616
☐ N617AM	B757-223/W	24525/253	617
☐ N618AA	B757-223/W	24526/260	618
☐ N619AA	B757-223/W	24577/269	619
☐ N620AA	B757-223/W	24578/276	620
☐ N621AM	B757-223/W	24579/283	621
☐ N622AA	B757-223/W	24580/289	622
☐ N623AA	B757-223/W	24581/296	623
☐ N624AA	B757-223/W	24582/297	624
☐ N625AA	B757-223/W	24583/303	625
☐ N626AA	B757-223/W	24584/304	626
☐ N627AA	B757-223/W	24585/308	627
☐ N628AA	B757-223/W	24586/309	628
☐ N629AA	B757-223/W	24587/315	629
☐ N630AA	B757-223/W	24588/316	630
☐ N631AA	B757-223/W	24589/317	631
☐ N632AA	B757-223/W	24590/324	632
☐ N633AA	B757-223/W	24591/324	633
☐ N634AA	B757-223/W	24592/327	634
☐ N635AA	B757-223/W	24593/328	635
☐ N636AM	B757-223/W	24594/336	636
☐ N637AM	B757-223/W	24595/337	637
☐ N638AA	B757-223/W	24596/344	638
☐ N639AA	B757-223/W	24597/345	639
☐ N640A	B757-223/W	24598/350	640
☐ N641AA	B757-223/W	24599/351	641
☐ N642AA	B757-223/W	24600/357	642
☐ N643AA	B757-223/W	24601/360	643
☐ N645AA	B757-223/W	24603/370	5BR
☐ N646AA	B757-223/W	24604/375	5BS
☐ N647AM	B757-223/W	24605/378	5BT
☐ N648AA	B757-223/W	24606/379	5BU
☐ N649AA	B757-223/W	24607/383	5BV
☐ N650AA	B757-223/W	24608/384	5BW
☐ N652AA	B757-223/W	24610/391	5BY
☐ N653A	B757-223/W	24611/397	5CA
☐ N654A	B757-223/W	24612/398	5CB
☐ N655AA	B757-223/W	24613/402	5CC
☐ N656AA	B757-223/W	24614/404	5CD
☐ N657AM	B757-223/W	24615/409	5CE
☐ N658AA	B757-223/W	24616/410	5CF
☐ N659AA	B757-223/W	24617/417	5CG
☐ N660AM	B757-223/W	25294/418	5CH
☐ N661AA	B757-223/W	25295/423	5CJ
☐ N662AA	B757-223/W	25296/425	5CK
☐ N663AM	B757-223/W	25297/432	5CL
☐ N664AA	B757-223/W	25298/433	5CM
☐ N665AA	B757-223/W	25299/436	5CN
☐ N666A	B757-223/W	25300/451	5CP
☐ N668AA	B757-223/W	25333/460	5CS
☐ N669AA	B757-223/W	25334/463	5CT
☐ N670AA	B757-223/W	25335/468	5CU
☐ N671AA	B757-223/W	25336/473	5CV
☐ N672AA	B757-223/W	25337/474	5CW
☐ N673AN	B757-223/W	29423/812	5EE
☐ N674AN	B757-223/W	29424/816	5EF
☐ N675AN	B757-223/W	29425/817	5EG
☐ N676AN	B757-223/W	29426/827	5EH
☐ N677AN	B757-223/W	29427/828	5EJ
☐ N678AN	B757-223/W	29428/837	5EK
☐ N679AN	B757-223/W	29589/842	5EL
☐ N680AN	B757-223/W	29590/847	5EM
☐ N681AA	B757-223/W	25338/483	5CX
☐ N682AA	B757-223/W	25339/484	5CY
☐ N683A	B757-223/W	25340/491	5DA
☐ N684AA	B757-223/W	25341/504	5DB
☐ N685AA	B757-223/W	25342/507	5DC
☐ N686AA	B757-223/W	25343/509	5DD
☐ N687AA	B757-223ER/W	25695/536	5DE
☐ N688AA	B757-223ER/W	25730/548	5DF
☐ N689AA	B757-223ER/W	25731/562	5DG
☐ N690AA	B757-223ER/W	25696/566	5DH
☐ N691AA	B757-223ER/W	25697/568	5DJ
☐ N602AA	B757-223/W	26972/578	5DK
☐ N693AA	B757-223/W	26973/580	5DL
☐ N694AN	B757-223/W	26974/582	5DM
☐ N695AN	B757-223/W	26975/621	5DN
☐ N696AN	B757-223/W	26976/627	5DP
☐ N697AN	B757-223/W	26977/633	5DR
☐ N698AN	B757-223/W	26980/635	5DS
☐ N699AN	B757-223/W	27051/660	5DT
☐ N7667A	B757-223/W	25301/459	5CR
☐ N319AA	B767-223ER	22320/128	319
☐ N320AA	B767-223ER	22321/130	320
☐ N321AA	B767-223ER	22322/139	321
☐ N322AA	B767-223ER	22323/140	322
☐ N323AA	B767-223ER	22324/146	323
☐ N324AA	B767-223ER	22325/147	324
☐ N325AA	B767-223ER	22326/157	325
☐ N327AA	B767-223ER	22327/159	327
☐ N328AA	B767-223ER	22328/160	328
☐ N329AA	B767-223ER	22329/164	329
☐ N332AA	B767-223ER	22331/168	332
☐ N335AA	B767-223ER	22333/194	335
☐ N336AA	B767-223ER	22334/195	336
☐ N338AA	B767-223ER	22335/196	338
☐ N339AA	B767-223ER	22336/198	339
☐ N342AN	B767-323ER	33081/896	342
☐ N343AN	B767-323ER	33082/899	343
☐ N344AN	B767-323ER	33083/900	344

	Reg	Type	c/n	Fleet
☐	N345AN	B767-323ER/W	33084/906	345
☐	N346AN	B767-323ER	33085/907	346
☐	N347AN	B767-323ER	33086/908	347
☐	N348AN	B767-323ER	33087/910	348
☐	N349AN	B767-323ER	33088/913	349
☐	N350AN	B767-323ER	33089/916	350
☐	N351AA	B767-323ER	24032/202	351
☐	N352AA	B767-323ER	24033/205	352
☐	N353AA	B767-323ER	24034/206	353
☐	N354AA	B767-323ER	24035/211	354
☐	N355AA	B767-323ER	24036/221	355
☐	N357AA	B767-323ER	24038/227	357
☐	N358AA	B767-323ER	24039/228	358
☐	N359AA	B767-323ER	24040/230	359
☐	N360AA	B767-323ER	24041/232	360
☐	N361AA	B767-323ER	24042/235	361
☐	N362AA	B767-323ER	24043/237	362
☐	N363AA	B767-323ER	24044/238	363
☐	N366AA	B767-323ER	25193/388	366
☐	N368AA	B767-323ER	25195/404	368
☐	N369AA	B767-323ER	25196/422	369
☐	N370AA	B767-323ER	25197/425	370
☐	N371AA	B767-323ER	25198/431	371
☐	N372AA	B767-323ER	25199/433	372
☐	N373AA	B767-323ER/W	25200/435	373
☐	N374AA	B767-323ER	25201/437	374
☐	N376AN	B767-323ER	25445/447	376
☐	N377AN	B767-323ER/W	25446/453	377
☐	N378AN	B767-323ER	25447/469	378
☐	N379AA	B767-323ER	25448/481	379
☐	N380AN	B767-323ER/W	25449/489	380
☐	N381AN	B767-323ER/W	25450/495	381
☐	N382AN	B767-323ER/W	25451/498	382
☐	N383AN	B767-323ER	26995/500	383
☐	N384AA	B767-323ER	26996/512	384
☐	N385AM	B767-323ER/W	27059/536	385
☐	N386AA	B767-323ER	27060/540	386
☐	N387AM	B767-323ER/W	27184/541	387
☐	N388AA	B767-323ER	27448/563	388
☐	N389AA	B767-323ER/W	27449/564	389
☐	N390AA	B767-323ER	27450/565	390
☐	N391AA	B767-323ER	27451/566	391
☐	N392AN	B767-323ER	29429/700	392
☐	N393AN	B767-323ER	29430/701	393
☐	N394AN	B767-323ER	29431/703	394
☐	N395AN	B767-323ER	29432/709	395
☐	N396AN	B767-323ER	29603/739	396
☐	N397AN	B767-323ER	29604/744	397
☐	N398AN	B767-323ER	29605/748	398
☐	N399AN	B767-323ER/W	29606/752	399
☐	N7375A	B767-323ER	25202/441	375
☐	N39356	B767-323ER	24037/226	356
☐	N39364	B767-323ER/W	24045/240	364
☐	N39365	B767-323ER	24046/241	365
☐	N39367	B767-323ER	25194/394	367
☐	N750AN	B777-223ER	30259/332	7BJ
☐	N751AN	B777-223ER	30798/333	7BK
☐	N752AN	B777-223ER	30260/339	7BL
☐	N753AN	B777-223ER	30261/341	7BM
☐	N754AN	B777-223ER	30262/345	7BN
☐	N755AN	B777-223ER	30263/354	7BP
☐	N756AM	B777-223ER	30264/358	7BR
☐	N757AN	B777-223ER	32636/363	7BS
☐	N758AN	B777-223ER	32637/371	7BT
☐	N759AN	B777-223ER	32638/376	7BU
☐	N760AN	B777-223ER	31477/379	7BV
☐	N761AJ	B777-223ER	31478/393	7BW
☐	N762AN	B777-223ER	31479/399	7BX
☐	N765AN	B777-223ER	32879/433	7BY
☐	N766AN	B777-223ER	32880/445	7CA
☐	N767AJ	B777-223ER	33539/555	7CB
☐	N768AA	B777-223ER	33540/566	7CC
☐	N770AN	B777-223ER	29578/185	7AA
☐	N771AN	B777-223ER	29579/190	7AB
☐	N772AN	B777-223ER	29580/198	7AC
☐	N773AN	B777-223ER	29583/199	7AD
☐	N774AN	B777-223ER	29581/208	7AE
☐	N775AN	B777-223ER	29584/209	7AF
☐	N776AN	B777-223ER	29582/215	7AG
☐	N777AN	B777-223ER	29585/218	7AH
☐	N778AN	B777-223ER	29587/223	7AJ
☐	N779AN	B777-223ER	29955/225	7AK
☐	N780AN	B777-223ER	29956/241	7AL
☐	N781AN	B777-223ER	29586/266	7AM
☐	N782AN	B777-223ER	30003/270	7AN
☐	N783AN	B777-223ER	30004/271	7AP
☐	N784AN	B777-223ER	29588/272	7AR
☐	N785AN	B777-223ER	30005/274	7AS
☐	N786AN	B777-223ER	30250/276	7AT
☐	N787AL	B777-223ER	30010/277	7AU
☐	N788AN	B777-223ER	30011/283	7AV
☐	N789AN	B777-223ER	30252/285	7AW
☐	N790AN	B777-223ER	30251/287	7AX
☐	N791AN	B777-223ER	30254/289	7AY
☐	N792AN	B777-223ER	30253/292	7BA
☐	N793AN	B777-223ER	30255/299	7BB
☐	N794AN	B777-223ER	30256/313	7BC
☐	N795AN	B777-223ER	30257/315	7BD
☐	N796AN	B777-223ER	30796/316	7BE
☐	N797AN	B777-223ER	30012/321	7BF
☐	N798AN	B777-223ER	30797/324	7BG
☐	N799AN	B777-223ER	30258/328	7BH
☐	N110HM	MD-83	49787/1636	4WU
☐	N208AA	MD-82	49159/1107	208
☐	N218AA	MD-82	49168/1100	[ROW]
☐	N219AA	MD-82	49171/1112	[ROW]
☐	N223AA	MD-82	49173/1114	[ROW]
☐	N227AA	MD-82	49177/1121	227
☐	N232AA	MD-82	49179/1123	[ROW]
☐	N233AA	MD-82	49180/1124	[ROW]
☐	N245AA	MD-82	49257/1160	245
☐	N249AA	MD-82	49269/1164	249
☐	N251AA	MD-82	49270/1165	251
☐	N253AA	MD-82	49286/1175	253
☐	N255AA	MD-82	49287/1176	255
☐	N258AA	MD-82	49288/1187	258
☐	N259AA	MD-82	49289/1193	269
☐	N262AA	MD-82	49290/1195	262
☐	N266AA	MD-82	49291/1210	266
☐	N271AA	MD-82	49293/1212	271
☐	N274AA	MD-82	49271/1166	274
☐	N278AA	MD-82	49294/1213	278
☐	N279AA	MD-82	49295/1214	[ROW]
☐	N283AA	MD-82	49296/1215	[ROW]
☐	N287AA	MD-82	49299/1218	[ROW]
☐	N290AA	MD-82	49302/1221	290
☐	N291AA	MD-82	49303/1222	291
☐	N292AA	MD-82	49304/1223	292
☐	N293AA	MD-82	49305/1226	293
☐	N298AA	MD-82	49310/1247	298
☐	N403A	MD-82	49314/1256	403
☐	N408AA	MD-82	49319/1266	[ROW]
☐	N410AA	MD-82	49321/1273	[ROW]
☐	N411AA	MD-82	49322/1280	[ROW]
☐	N412AA	MD-82	49323/1281	412
☐	N413AA	MD-82	49324/1289	[ROW]
☐	N415AA	MD-82	49326/1295	[ROW]
☐	N416AA	MD-82	49327/1296	[ROW]
☐	N417AA	MD-82	49328/1301	[ROW]
☐	N418AA	MD-82	49329/1302	[ROW]
☐	N419AA	MD-82	49331/1306	[ROW]
☐	N420AA	MD-82	49332/1307	420
☐	N422AA	MD-82	49334/1312	422
☐	N423AA	MD-82	49335/1320	423
☐	N424AA	MD-82	49336/1321	424
☐	N426AA	MD-82	49338/1327	426
☐	N427AA	MD-82	49339/1328	[ROW]
☐	N429AA	MD-82	49341/1336	[ROW]
☐	N430AA	MD-82	49342/1337	[ROW]
☐	N431AA	MD-82	49343/1339	431

☐	N432AA	MD-82	49350/1376	432
☐	N433AA	MD-83	49451/1388	433
☐	N434AA	MD-83	49452/1389	434
☐	N435AA	MD-83	49453/1390	435
☐	N436AA	MD-83	49454/1391	436
☐	N437AA	MD-83	49455/1392	437
☐	N438AA	MD-83	49456/1393	438
☐	N439AA	MD-83	49457/1398	439
☐	N440AA	MD-82	49459/1407	440
☐	N441AA	MD-82	49460/1408	441
☐	N442AA	MD-82	49468/1409	442
☐	N446AA	MD-82	49472/1426	446
☐	N447AA	MD-82	49473/1427	447
☐	N448AA	MD-82	49474/1431	448
☐	N449AA	MD-82	49475/1432	449
☐	N450AA	MD-82	49476/1439	450
☐	N451AA	MD-82	49477/1441	451
☐	N452AA	MD-82	49553/1450	452
☐	N453AA	MD-82	49558/1451	453
☐	N454AA	MD-82	49559/1460	454
☐	N455AA	MD-82	49560/1462	455
☐	N456AA	MD-82	49561/1474	456
☐	N457AA	MD-82	49562/1475	457
☐	N458AA	MD-82	49563/1485	458
☐	N459AA	MD-82	49564/1486	459
☐	N460AA	MD-82	49565/1496	460
☐	N461AA	MD-82	49566/1497	461
☐	N462AA	MD-82	49592/1505	462
☐	N463AA	MD-82	49593/1506	463
☐	N464AA	MD-82	49594/1507	464
☐	N465A	MD-82	49595/1509	465
☐	N466AA	MD-82	49596/1510	466
☐	N467AA	MD-82	49597/1511	467
☐	N468AA	MD-82	49598/1513	468
☐	N469AA	MD-82	49599/1515	469
☐	N470AA	MD-82	49600/1516	470
☐	N471AA	MD-82	49601/1518	471
☐	N472AA	MD-82	49647/1520	472
☐	N473AA	MD-82	49648/1521	473
☐	N474	MD-82	49649/1526	474
☐	N475AA	MD-82	49650/1527	475
☐	N476AA	MD-82	49651/1528	476
☐	N477AA	MD-82	49652/1529	477
☐	N478AA	MD-82	49653/1534	478
☐	N479AA	MD-82	49654/1535	479
☐	N480AA	MD-82	49655/1536	480
☐	N481AA	MD-82	49656/1545	481
☐	N482AA	MD-82	49675/1546	482
☐	N483A	MD-82	49676/1550	483
☐	N484AA	MD-82	49677/1551	484
☐	N485AA	MD-82	49678/1555	485
☐	N486AA	MD-82	49679/1557	486
☐	N487AA	MD-82	49680/1558	487
☐	N488AA	MD-82	49681/1560	488
☐	N489AA	MD-82	49682/1562	489
☐	N490AA	MD-82	49683/1563	490
☐	N491AA	MD-82	49684/1564	491
☐	N492AA	MD-82	49730/1565	492
☐	N493AA	MD-82	49731/1566	493
☐	N494AA	MD-82	49732/1567	494
☐	N495AA	MD-82	49733/1607	495
☐	N496AA	MD-82	49734/1619	496
☐	N497AA	MD-82	49735/1635	497
☐	N498AA	MD-82	49736/1640	498
☐	N499AA	MD-82	49737/1641	499
☐	N501AA	MD-82	49738/1648	501
☐	N505AA	MD-82	49799/1652	505
☐	N510AM	MD-82	49804/1669	510
☐	N513AA	MD-82	49890/1686	513
☐	N516AM	MD-82	49893/1696	516
☐	N552AA	MD-82	53034/1826	552
☐	N553AA	MD-82	53083/1828	553
☐	N554AA	MD-82	53084/1830	554
☐	N555AN	MD-82	53085/1839	555
☐	N556AA	MD-82	53086/1840	556

☐	N557AN	MD-82	53087/1841	557
☐	N558AA	MD-82	53088/1852	558
☐	N559AA	MD-82	53089/1853	559
☐	N560AA	MD-82	53090/1858	560
☐	N561AA	MD-82	53091/1863	561
☐	N562AA	MD-83	49344/1370	562
☐	N563AA	MD-83	49345/1371	563
☐	N564AA	MD-83	49346/1372	564
☐	N565AA	MD-83	49347/1373	565
☐	N566AA	MD-83	49348/1374	566
☐	N567AM	MD-83	53293/2021	567
☐	N568AA	MD-83	49349/1375	568
☐	N569AA	MD-83	49351/1385	569
☐	N570AA	MD-83	49352/1386	570
☐	N571AA	MD-83	49353/1387	571
☐	N572AA	MD-83	49458/1406	572
☐	N573AA	MD-82	53092/1864	573
☐	N574AA	MD-82	53151/1866	574
☐	N575AM	MD-82	53152/1875	575
☐	N576AA	MD-82	53153/1876	576
☐	N577AA	MD-82	53154/1878	577
☐	N578AA	MD-82	53155/1883	578
☐	N579AA	MD-82	53156/1884	579
☐	N580AA	MD-82	53157/1885	580
☐	N581AA	MD-82	53158/1891	581
☐	N582AA	MD-82	53159/1892	582
☐	N583AA	MD-82	53160/1893	583
☐	N584AA	MD-82	53247/1902	584
☐	N585AA	MD-82	53248/1903	585
☐	N586AA	MD-82	53249/1904	586
☐	N587AA	MD-82	53250/1907	587
☐	N588AA	MD-83	53251/1909	588
☐	N589AA	MD-83	53252/1910	589
☐	N590AA	MD-83	53253/1919	590
☐	N591AA	MD-83	53254/1920	591
☐	N592AA	MD-83	53255/1932	592
☐	N593AA	MD-83	53256/1933	593
☐	N594AA	MD-83	53284/1966	594
☐	N595AA	MD-83	53285/1989	595
☐	N596AA	MD-83	53286/2000	596
☐	N597AA	MD-83	53287/2006	597
☐	N598AA	MD-83	53288/2011	598
☐	N599AA	MD-83	53289/2012	599
☐	N919TW	MD-82	49368/1198	[ROW]
☐	N923TW	MD-82	49379/1205	[ROW]
☐	N931TW	MD-82	49527/1382	4WA
☐	N940AS	MD-83	49825/1577	[ROW]
☐	N941AS	MD-83	49925/1616	[ROW]
☐	N948TW	MD-83	49575/1414	4WS
☐	N951TW	MD-83	53470/2135	4XA
☐	N953U	MD-82	49267/1239	[ROW]
☐	N954U	MD-82	49426/1399	4UB
☐	N955U	MD-82	49427/1401	4UC
☐	N961TW	MD-83	53611/2264	4XT
☐	N962TW	MD-83	53612/2265	4XU
☐	N963TW	MD-83	53613/2266	4XV
☐	N964TW	MD-83	53614/2267	4XW
☐	N965TW	MD-83	53615/2268	4XX
☐	N966TW	MD-83	53616/2269	4XY
☐	N967TW	MD-83	53617/2270	4YA
☐	N968TW	MD-83	53618/2271	4YB
☐	N969TW	MD-83	53619/2272	4YC
☐	N970TW	MD-83	53620/2273	[TUL]
☐	N971TW	MD-83	53621/2274	[TUL]
☐	N972TW	MD-83	53622/2275	4YF
☐	N973TW	MD-83	53623/2276	4YG
☐	N974TW	MD-83	53624/2277	4YH
☐	N975TW	MD-83	53625/2278	4YJ
☐	N976TW	MD-83	53626/2279	4YK
☐	N978TW	MD-83	53628/2281	4YM
☐	N979TW	MD-83	53629/2282	4YN
☐	N980TW	MD-83	53630/2283	4YP
☐	N982TW	MD-83	53632/2285	4YR
☐	N983TW	MD-83	53633/2286	4YS
☐	N984TW	MD-83	53634/2287	4YT

	Reg	Type	c/n	Fleet
☐	N3507A	MD-82	49801/1661	507
☐	N3515	MD-82	49892/1695	515
☐	N7506	MD-82	49800/1660	506
☐	N7508	MD-82	49802/1662	508
☐	N7509	MD-82	49803/1663	509
☐	N7512A	MD-82	49806/1673	512
☐	N7514A	MD-82	49891/1694	514
☐	N7517A	MD-82	49894/1697	517
☐	N7518A	MD-82	49895/1698	518
☐	N7519A	MD-82	49896/1707	519
☐	N7520A	MD-82	49897/1708	520
☐	N7521A	MD-82	49898/1709	521
☐	N7522A	MD-82	49899/1722	522
☐	N7525A	MD-82	49917/1735	525
☐	N7526A	MD-82	49918/1743	526
☐	N7527A	MD-82	49919/1744	527
☐	N7528A	MD-82	49920/1750	528
☐	N7530	MD-82	49922/1753	530
☐	N7531A	MD-82	49923/1758	531
☐	N7532A	MD-82	49924/1759	532
☐	N7533A	MD-82	49987/1760	533
☐	N7534A	MD-82	49988/1768	534
☐	N7535A	MD-82	49989/1769	535
☐	N7536A	MD-82	49990/1770	536
☐	N7537A	MD-82	49991/1780	537
☐	N7538A	MD-82	49992/1781	538
☐	N7539A	MD-82	49993/1782	539
☐	N7540A	MD-82	49994/1790	540
☐	N7541A	MD-82	49995/1791	541
☐	N7542A	MD-82	49996/1792	542
☐	N7543A	MD-82	53025/1802	543
☐	N7544A	MD-82	53026/1804	544
☐	N7546A	MD-82	53028/1813	546
☐	N7547A	MD-82	53029/1814	547
☐	N7548A	MD-82	53030/1816	548
☐	N7549A	MD-82	53031/1819	549
☐	N7550	MD-82	53032/1820	550
☐	N9302B	MD-83	49528/1383	4WB
☐	N9304C	MD-83	49530/1397	4WD
☐	N9307R	MD-83	49663/1437	[ROW]
☐	N9401W	MD-83	53137/1872	4WJ
☐	N9402W	MD-83	53138/1886	4WK
☐	N9403W	MD-83	53139/1899	4WL
☐	N9404V	MD-83	53140/1923	4WM
☐	N9405T	MD-83	53141/1935	4WN
☐	N9406W	MD-83	53126/2026	4WP
☐	N9407R	MD-83	49400/1356	4WR
☐	N9409F	MD-83	53121/1971	4WT
☐	N9412W	MD-83	53187/2118	4WU
☐	N9413T	MD-83	53188/2119	4WW
☐	N9414W	MD-83	53189/2121	4WX
☐	N9420D	MD-83	49824/1554	4WY
☐	N9615W	MD-83	53562/2192	4XB
☐	N9616G	MD-83	53563/2196	4XC
☐	N9617R	MD-83	53564/2199	4XD
☐	N9618A	MD-83	53565/2201	4XE
☐	N9619V	MD-83	53566/2206	4XF
☐	N9620D	MD-83	53591/2208	4XG
☐	N9621A	MD-83	53592/2234	4XH
☐	N9622A	MD-83	53593/2239	4XJ
☐	N9624T	MD-83	53594/2241	4XK
☐	N9625W	MD-83	53595/2244	4XL
☐	N9626F	MD-83	53596//2247	4XM
☐	N9627R	MD-83	53597/2249	4XN
☐	N9628W	MD-83	53598/2252	4XP
☐	N9629H	MD-83	53599/2254	4XR
☐	N9630A	MD-83	53561/2174	4XS
☐	N9677W	MD-83	53627/2280	4YL
☐	N9681B	MD-83	53631/2284	4XT
☐	N14551	MD-82	53033/1822	551
☐	N16545	MD-82	53027/1805	545
☐	N33414	MD-82	49325/1290	414
☐	N33502	MD-82	49739/1649	502
☐	N44503	MD-82	49797/1650	503
☐	N59523	MD-82	49915/1723	523

	Reg	Type	c/n	Fleet
☐	N70401	MD-82	49312/1249	401
☐	N70425	MD-82	49337/1325	425
☐	N70504	MD-82	49798/1651	504
☐	N70524	MD-82	49916/1729	524
☐	N70529	MD-82	49921/1752	529
☐	N73444	MD-82	49470/1417	444
☐	N76200	MD-83	53290/2013	200
☐	N76201	MD-83	53291/2019	201
☐	N76202	MD-83	53292/2020	202
☐	N77421	MD-82	49333/1311	421
☐	N90511	MD-82	49805/1672	511

AMERICAN CONNECTION — AX / LOF

	Reg	Type	c/n
☐	N295SK	ERJ-140LR	145513
☐	N297SK	ERJ-140LR	145522
☐	N299SK	ERJ-140LR	145532
☐	N371SK	ERJ-140LR	145535
☐	N372SK	ERJ-140LR	145538
☐	N373SK	ERJ-140LR	145543
☐	N374SK	ERJ-140LR	145544
☐	N375SK	ERJ-140LR	145569
☐	N376SK	ERJ-140LR	145578
☐	N377SK	ERJ-140LR	145579
☐	N378SK	ERJ-140LR	145593
☐	N379SK	ERJ-140LR	145606
☐	N380SK	ERJ-140LR	145613
☐	N381SK	ERJ-140LR	145619
☐	N382SK	ERJ-140LR	145624
☐	N811HK	ERJ-145ER	145256

AMERICAN EAGLE — MQ / EGF

	Reg	Type	c/n
☐	N4AE	ATR 72-212	244
☐	N260AE	ATR 72-201	263
☐	N270AT	ATR 72-212	270
☐	N288AM	ATR 72-212	288
☐	N308AE	ATR 72-212	309
☐	N322AC	ATR 72-212	320
☐	N342AT	ATR 72-212	345
☐	N348AE	ATR 72-212	349
☐	N355AT	ATR 72-212	355
☐	N369AT	ATR 72-212	369
☐	N377AT	ATR 72-212	377
☐	N399AT	ATR 72-212	399
☐	N407AT	ATR 72-212	407
☐	N408AT	ATR 72-212	408
☐	N410AT	ATR 72-212	410
☐	N414WF	ATR 72-212	414
☐	N417AT	ATR 72-212	417
☐	N420AT	ATR 72-212	420
☐	N425MJ	ATR 72-212	425
☐	N426AT	ATR 72-212	426
☐	N429AT	ATR 72-212	429
☐	N431AT	ATR 72-212	431
☐	N434AT	ATR 72-212	434
☐	N440AM	ATR 72-212	440
☐	N447AM	ATR 72-212	447
☐	N448AM	ATR 72-212	448
☐	N451AT	ATR 72-212	451
☐	N494AE	ATR 72-212A	494
☐	N498AT	ATR 72-212A	498
☐	N499AT	ATR 72-212A	499
☐	N529AM	ATR 72-212A	529
☐	N533AT	ATR 72-212A	533
☐	N536AT	ATR 72-212A	536
☐	N538AT	ATR 72-212A	538
☐	N540AM	ATR 72-212A	540
☐	N541AT	ATR 72-212	521
☐	N545AT	ATR 72-212A	545
☐	N548AT	ATR 72-212A	548
☐	N550LL	ATR 72-212A	550
☐	N500AE	CRJ-701ER	10025
☐	N501BG	CRJ-701ER	10017

	Reg	Type	Serial	Note
☐	N502AE	CRJ-701ER	10018	
☐	N503AE	CRJ-701ER	10021	
☐	N504AE	CRJ-701ER	10044	
☐	N505AE	CRJ-701ER	10053	
☐	N506AE	CRJ-701ER	10056	
☐	N507AE	CRJ-701ER	10059	
☐	N508AE	CRJ-701ER	10072	
☐	N509AE	CRJ-701ER	10078	
☐	N510AE	CRJ-701ER	10105	
☐	N511AE	CRJ-701ER	10107	
☐	N512AE	CRJ-701ER	10110	
☐	N513AE	CRJ-701ER	10114	
☐	N514AE	CRJ-701ER	10119	
☐	N515AE	CRJ-701ER	10121	
☐	N516AE	CRJ-701ER	10123	
☐	N517AE	CRJ-701ER	10124	
☐	N518AE	CRJ-701ER	10126	
☐	N519AE	CRJ-701ER	10131	
☐	N520DC	CRJ-701ER	10140	
☐	N521AE	CRJ-701ER	10142	
☐	N522AE	CRJ-701ER	10147	
☐	N523AE	CRJ-701ER	10152	
☐	N524AE	CRJ-701ER	10154	
☐	N525AE	CRJ-702ER NG	10302	♦
☐	N526EA	CRJ-702ER NG	10304	♦
☐	N527EA	CRJ-702ER NG	10305	♦
☐	N528EG	CRJ-702ER NG	10306	♦
☐	N529EA	CRJ-702ER NG	10307	♦
☐	N530EA	CRJ-702ER NG	10308	♦
☐	N531EG	CRJ-702ER NG	10309	♦
☐	N532EA	CRJ-702ER NG	10310	♦
☐	N533AE	CRJ-702ER NG	10311	♦
☐	N534AE	CRJ-702ER NG	10312	♦
☐	N535EA	CRJ-702ER NG	10313	♦
☐	N536EA	CRJ-702ER NG	10315	♦
☐	N537EA	CRJ-702ER NG	10316	♦
☐	N538EG	CRJ-702ER NG	10317	♦
☐	N539EA	CRJ-702ER NG	10318	♦
☐	N540EG	CRJ-702ER NG	10319	♦
☐	N541EA	CRJ-702ER NG	10320	♦
☐	N	CRJ-702ER NG		o/o ♦
☐	N	CRJ-702ER NG		o/o ♦
☐	N	CRJ-702ER NG		o/o ♦
☐	N	CRJ-702ER NG		o/o ♦
☐	N	CRJ-702ER NG		o/o ♦
☐	N700LE	ERJ-135LR	145156	
☐	N701MH	ERJ-135LR	145162	
☐	N702AE	ERJ-135LR	145164	[IGM]
☐	N703MR	ERJ-135LR	145173	[IGM]
☐	N704PG	ERJ-135LR	145174	[IGM]
☐	N705AE	ERJ-135LR	145184	[IGM]
☐	N706RG	ERJ-135LR	145194	[IGM]
☐	N707EB	ERJ-135LR	145195	[CHI]
☐	N708AE	ERJ-135LR	145205	
☐	N709GB	ERJ-135LR	145211	[IGM]
☐	N710TB	ERJ-135LR	145224	[IGM]
☐	N711PH	ERJ-135LR	145235	
☐	N712AE	ERJ-135LR	145247	
☐	N713AE	ERJ-135LR	145249	
☐	N715AE	ERJ-135LR	145262	[IGM]
☐	N716AE	ERJ-135LR	145264	
☐	N717AE	ERJ-135LR	145272	
☐	N718AE	ERJ-135LR	145275	[IGM]
☐	N719AE	ERJ-135LR	145276	
☐	N720AE	ERJ-135LR	145279	
☐	N721HS	ERJ-135LR	145283	
☐	N722AE	ERJ-135LR	145287	
☐	N723AE	ERJ-135LR	145288	
☐	N724AE	ERJ-135LR	145301	
☐	N725AE	ERJ-135LR	145312	
☐	N726AE	ERJ-135LR	145314	[IGM]
☐	N727AE	ERJ-135LR	145326	[IGM]
☐	N728AE	ERJ-135LR	145328	
☐	N729AE	ERJ-135LR	145343	[IGM]
☐	N730KW	ERJ-135LR	145346	
☐	N731BE	ERJ-135LR	145356	[IGM]
☐	N732DH	ERJ-135LR	145358	[ABI]
☐	N733KR	ERJ-135LR	145368	
☐	N734EK	ERJ-135LR	145371	
☐	N735TS	ERJ-135LR	145386	
☐	N736DT	ERJ-135LR	145388	
☐	N737MW	ERJ-135LR	145396	
☐	N738NR	ERJ-135LR	145401	
☐	N739AE	ERJ-135LR	145402	
☐	N800AE	ERJ-140LR	145425	
☐	N801AE	ERJ-140LR	145469	
☐	N802AE	ERJ-140LR	145471	
☐	N803AE	ERJ-140LR	145483	
☐	N804AE	ERJ-140LR	145487	
☐	N805AE	ERJ-140LR	145489	
☐	N806AE	ERJ-140LR	145503	
☐	N807AE	ERJ-140LR	145506	
☐	N808AE	ERJ-140LR	145519	
☐	N809AE	ERJ-140LR	145521	
☐	N810AE	ERJ-140LR	145525	
☐	N811AE	ERJ-140LR	145529	
☐	N812AE	ERJ-140LR	145531	
☐	N813AE	ERJ-140LR	145539	
☐	N814AE	ERJ-140LR	145541	
☐	N815AE	ERJ-140LR	145545	
☐	N816AE	ERJ-140LR	145552	
☐	N817AE	ERJ-140LR	145554	
☐	N818AE	ERJ-140LR	145561	
☐	N819AE	ERJ-140LR	145566	
☐	N820AE	ERJ-140LR	145576	
☐	N821AE	ERJ-140LR	145577	
☐	N822AE	ERJ-140LR	145581	
☐	N823AE	ERJ-140LR	145582	
☐	N824AE	ERJ-140LR	145584	
☐	N825AE	ERJ-140LR	145589	
☐	N826AE	ERJ-140LR	145592	
☐	N827AE	ERJ-140LR	145602	
☐	N828AE	ERJ-140LR	145604	
☐	N829AE	ERJ-140LR	145609	
☐	N830AE	ERJ-140LR	145615	
☐	N831AE	ERJ-140LR	145616	
☐	N832AE	ERJ-140LR	145627	
☐	N833AE	ERJ-140LR	145629	
☐	N834AE	ERJ-140LR	145631	
☐	N835AE	ERJ-140LR	145634	
☐	N836AE	ERJ-140LR	145635	
☐	N837AE	ERJ-140LR	145647	
☐	N838AE	ERJ-140LR	145651	
☐	N839AE	ERJ-140LR	145653	
☐	N840AE	ERJ-140LR	145656	
☐	N841AE	ERJ-140LR	145667	
☐	N842AE	ERJ-140LR	145673	
☐	N843AE	ERJ-140LR	145680	
☐	N844AE	ERJ-140LR	145682	
☐	N845AE	ERJ-140LR	145685	
☐	N846AE	ERJ-140LR	145692	
☐	N847AE	ERJ-140LR	145707	
☐	N848AE	ERJ-140LR	145710	
☐	N849AE	ERJ-140LR	145716	
☐	N850AE	ERJ-140LR	145722	
☐	N851AE	ERJ-140LR	145734	
☐	N852AE	ERJ-140LR	145736	
☐	N853AE	ERJ-140LR	145742	
☐	N854AE	ERJ-140LR	145743	
☐	N855AE	ERJ-140LR	145747	
☐	N856AE	ERJ-140LR	145748	
☐	N857AE	ERJ-140LR	145752	
☐	N858AE	ERJ-140LR	145754	
☐	N600BP	ERJ-145LR	145044	
☐	N601DW	ERJ-145LR	145046	
☐	N602AE	ERJ-145LR	145048	[IGM]
☐	N603KC	ERJ-145LR	145055	
☐	N604AE	ERJ-145LR	145058	
☐	N605KS	ERJ-145LR	145059	

☐	N606AE	ERJ-145LR	145062
☐	N607AE	ERJ-145LR	145062
☐	N608LM	ERJ-145LR	145068
☐	N609DP	ERJ-145LR	145069
☐	N610AE	ERJ-145LR	145073
☐	N611AE	ERJ-145LR	145074
☐	N612AE	ERJ-145LR	145079
☐	N613AE	ERJ-145LR	145081
☐	N614AE	ERJ-145LR	145086
☐	N615AE	ERJ-145LR	145087
☐	N616AE	ERJ-145LR	145092
☐	N617AE	ERJ-145LR	145093
☐	N618AE	ERJ-145LR	145097
☐	N619AE	ERJ-145LR	145101
☐	N620AE	ERJ-145LR	145102
☐	N621AE	ERJ-145LR	145105
☐	N622AE	ERJ-145LR	145108
☐	N623AE	ERJ-145LR	145109
☐	N624AE	ERJ-145LR	145111
☐	N625AE	ERJ-145LR	145115
☐	N626AE	ERJ-145LR	145117
☐	N627AE	ERJ-145LR	145121
☐	N628AE	ERJ-145LR	145124
☐	N629AE	ERJ-145LR	145130
☐	N630AE	ERJ-145LR	145132
☐	N631AE	ERJ-145LR	145139
☐	N632AE	ERJ-145LR	145143
☐	N633AE	ERJ-145LR	145148
☐	N634AE	ERJ-145LR	145150
☐	N635AE	ERJ-145LR	145158
☐	N636AE	ERJ-145LR	145160
☐	N637AE	ERJ-145LR	145170
☐	N638AE	ERJ-145LR	145172
☐	N639AE	ERJ-145LR	145182
☐	N640AE	ERJ-145LR	145183
☐	N641AE	ERJ-145LR	145191
☐	N642AE	ERJ-145LR	145193
☐	N643AE	ERJ-145LR	145200
☐	N644AE	ERJ-145LR	145204
☐	N645AE	ERJ-145LR	145212
☐	N646AE	ERJ-145LR	145213
☐	N647AE	ERJ-145LR	145222
☐	N648AE	ERJ-145LR	145225
☐	N649PP	ERJ-145LR	145234
☐	N650AE	ERJ-145LR	145417
☐	N651AE	ERJ-145LR	145422
☐	N652RS	ERJ-145LR	145432
☐	N653AE	ERJ-145LR	145433
☐	N654AE	ERJ-145LR	145437
☐	N655AE	ERJ-145LR	145452
☐	N656AE	ERJ-145LR	145740
☐	N657AE	ERJ-145LR	145744
☐	N658AE	ERJ-145LR	145760
☐	N659AE	ERJ-145LR	145762
☐	N660CL	ERJ-145LR	145764
☐	N661JA	ERJ-145LR	145766
☐	N662EH	ERJ-145LR	145777
☐	N663AR	ERJ-145LR	145778
☐	N664MS	ERJ-145LR	145779
☐	N665BC	ERJ-145LR	145783
☐	N667GB	ERJ-145LR	145784
☐	N668HH	ERJ-145LR	145785
☐	N669MB	ERJ-145LR	145788
☐	N670AE	ERJ-145LR	145790
☐	N671AE	ERJ-145LR	145793
☐	N672AE	ERJ-145LR	145794
☐	N673AE	ERJ-145LR	145797
☐	N674RJ	ERJ-145LR	14500801
☐	N675AE	ERJ-145LR	14500806
☐	N676AE	ERJ-145LR	14500807
☐	N677AE	ERJ-145LR	14500810
☐	N678AE	ERJ-145LR	14500813
☐	N679AE	ERJ-145LR	14500814
☐	N680AE	ERJ-145LR	14500820
☐	N681AE	ERJ-145LR	14500824

☐	N682AE	ERJ-145LR	14500826
☐	N683AE	ERJ-145LR	14500833
☐	N684JW	ERJ-145LR	14500835
☐	N685AE	ERJ-145LR	14500836
☐	N686AE	ERJ-145LR	14500843
☐	N687JS	ERJ-145LR	14500846
☐	N688AE	ERJ-145LR	14500849
☐	N689EC	ERJ-145LR	14500853
☐	N690AE	ERJ-145LR	14500858
☐	N691AE	ERJ-145LR	14500860
☐	N692AE	ERJ-145LR	14500866
☐	N693AE	ERJ-145LR	14500868
☐	N694AE	ERJ-145LR	14500869
☐	N695AE	ERJ-145LR	14500870
☐	N696AE	ERJ-145LR	14500874
☐	N697AB	ERJ-145LR	14500875
☐	N698CB	ERJ-145LR	14500877
☐	N699AE	ERJ-145LR	14500883
☐	N900AE	ERJ-145LR	14500885
☐	N902BC	ERJ-145LR	14500887
☐	N905JH	ERJ-145LR	14500892
☐	N906AE	ERJ-145LR	14500894
☐	N907AE	ERJ-145LR	14500895
☐	N908AE	ERJ-145LR	14500897
☐	N909AE	ERJ-145LR	14500899
☐	N918AE	ERJ-145LR	14500902
☐	N922AE	ERJ-145LR	14500906
☐	N923AE	ERJ-145LR	14500907
☐	N925AE	ERJ-145LR	14500908
☐	N928AE	ERJ-145LR	14500911
☐	N931AE	ERJ-145LR	14500912
☐	N932AE	ERJ-145LR	14500915
☐	N933JN	ERJ-145LR	14500918
☐	N935AE	ERJ-145LR	14500920
☐	N939AE	ERJ-145LR	14500923
☐	N941LT	ERJ-145LR	14500926
☐	N942LL	ERJ-145LR	14500930

AMERIFLIGHT   AMF

☐	N19RZ	Beech 1900C-1	UC-75
☐	N21RZ	Beech 1900C-1	UC-106
☐	N26RZ	Beech 1900C-1	UC-134
☐	N34RZ	Beech 1900C-1	UC-151
☐	N49UC	Beech 1900C-1	UC-49
☐	N111YV	Beech 1900C-1	UC-111
☐	N112YV	Beech 1900C-1	UC-112
☐	N330AF	Beech 1900C	UB-38
☐	N331AF	Beech 1900C	UB-44
☐	N1568G	Beech 1900C-1	UC-58
☐	N2049K	Beech 1900C-1	UC-164
☐	N3052K	Beech 1900C	UB-70
☐	N3071A	Beech 1900C	UB-46
☐	N3229A	Beech 1900C	UB-51
☐	N7203C	Beech 1900C	UB-28
☐	N31701	Beech 1900C	UB-2
☐	N31702	Beech 1900C	UB-3
☐	N31703	Beech 1900C	UB-10
☐	N31704	Beech 1900C	UB-12
☐	N31705	Beech 1900C	UB-60
☐	N179CA	EMB.120ER	120179
☐	N189CA	EMB.120ER	120189
☐	N201YW	EMB.120RT	120201
☐	N246AS	EMB.120ER	120100
☐	N247CA	EMB.120ER	120225
☐	N257AS	EMB.120ER	120126
☐	N258AS	EMB.120ER	120131
☐	N152AF	SA.227AC Metro III	AC-520
☐	N155AF	SA.227AC Metro III	AC-455
☐	N191AF	SA.227AC Metro III	AC-491
☐	N240DH	SA.227AT Expediter	AT-602B
☐	N241DH	SA.227AT Expediter	AT-607B
☐	N242DH	SA.227AT Expediter	AT-608B
☐	N243DH	SA.227AT Expediter	AT-609B

☐	N244DH	SA.227AT Expediter	AT-618B
☐	N245DH	SA.227AT Expediter	AT-624B
☐	N246DH	SA.227AT Expediter	AT-625B
☐	N247DH	SA.227AT Expediter	AT-626B
☐	N248DH	SA.227AT Expediter	AT-630B
☐	N249DH	SA.227AT Expediter	AT-631B
☐	N360AE	SA.227AC Metro III	AC-675
☐	N362AE	SA.227AC Metro III	AC-677B
☐	N377PH	SA.227AC Metro III	AC-574
☐	N421MA	SA.227AC Metro III	AC-634
☐	N422MA	SA.227AC Metro III	AC-635
☐	N423MA	SA.227AC Metro III	AC-636
☐	N424MA	SA.227AC Metro III	AC-639
☐	N426MA	SA.227AC Metro III	AC-645
☐	N428MA	SA.227AC Metro III	AC-646
☐	N443AF	SA.227AC Metro III	AC-443
☐	N473AF	SA.227AC Metro III	AC-473
☐	N475AF	SA.227AC Metro III	AC-475
☐	N476AF	SA.227AC Metro III	AC-476
☐	N488AF	SA.227AC Metro III	AC-488
☐	N529AF	SA.227AC Metro III	AC-752
☐	N544UP	SA.227AT Expediter	AT-544
☐	N548UP	SA.227AT Expediter	AT-548
☐	N556UP	SA.227AT Expediter	AT-556
☐	N560UP	SA.227AT Expediter	AT-560
☐	N561UP	SA.227AT Expediter	AT-561
☐	N566UP	SA.227AT Expediter	AT-566
☐	N569UP	SA.227AT Expediter	AT-569
☐	N573G	SA.227AT Merlin IVC	AT-446B
☐	N578AF	SA.227AC Metro III	AC-578
☐	N671AV	SA.227AC Metro III	AC-671
☐	N672AV	SA.227AC Metro III	AC-672
☐	N673AV	SA.227AC Metro III	AC-673
☐	N698AF	SA.227AC Metro III	AC-698
☐	N801AF	SA.227AC Metro III	AC-701
☐	N807M	SA.227AT Merlin IVC	AT-454B
☐	N838AF	SA.227AC Metro III	AC-738

AMERIJET INTERNATIONAL · M6 / AJT

☐	N199AJ	B727-2F9F/W	21426/1285	
☐	N395AJ	B727-233F/W	21100/1148	
☐	N495AJ	B727-233F/W	20937/1103	
☐	N598AJ	B727-212F/W	21947/1506	
☐	N794AJ	B727-227F/W	21243/1197	
☐	N804AJ	B727-2D3F/W	21021/1082	[GYR]
☐	N905AJ	B727-231F/W	21989/1590	
☐	N909PG	R727-2K5F	21852/1553	
☐	N994AJ	B727-233F/W	20942/1130	

AMERISTAR JET CHARTER · AJI

☐	N732TW	B737-2H4	22731/864	[ELP]
☐	N733TW	B737-2H4	22732/877	
☐	N783TW	DC-9-15F	47010/97	
☐	N784TW	DC-9-15F	47014/141	
☐	N785TW	DC-9-15F	47015/156	

ARCTIC CIRCLE AIR SERVICE · 5F / CIR

| ☐ | N168LM | Short SD.3-30 | SH3104 |
| ☐ | N261AG | Short SD.3-30 | SH3117 |

ARCTIC TRANSPORTATION SVCS · 7S / RCT

☐	N424CA	CASA 212-200	CC20-7-242
☐	N437RA	CASA 212-200	CC21-2-166
☐	N439RA	CASA 212-200	CC50-9-287
☐	N440RA	CASA 212-200	CC20-6-174
☐	N1906	Short SC.7 Skyvan 3A	SH1906

ASIA PACIFIC AIRLINES · MGE

☐	N319NE	B727-212F/W	21349/1289
☐	N705AA	B727-223F/W	22462/1751
☐	N86425	B727-212F/W	21459/1329

ASTAR AIR CARGO · ER / DHL

☐	N362DH	A300B4-103F	084	[IGM]
☐	N363DH	A300B4-103F	085	[IGM]
☐	N364DH	A300B4-203F	141	[IGM]
☐	N365DH	A300B4-203F	149	[IGM]
☐	N366DH	A300B4-203F	249	[IGM]
☐	N367DH	A300B4-203F	265	[IGM]
☐	N741DH	B727-2Q9F	21931/1531	[IGM]
☐	N742DH	B727-225F	21290/1238	[IGM]
☐	N745DH	B727-224F	20665/1149	[IGM]
☐	N747DH	B727-224F	22253/1702	[IGM]
☐	N748DH	B727-225F	22440/1692	[IGM]
☐	N749DH	B727-223F	22013/1659	[IGM]
☐	N751DH	B727-264	22982/1802	[IGM]
☐	N752DH	B727-223F	22466/1763	[IGM]
☐	N753DH	B727-223F	22468/1766	[IGM]
☐	N754DH	B727-223F	22008/1646	[IGM]
☐	N760AT	B727-2B7F	21954/1525	[IGM]
☐	N770AT	B727-2B7F	21953/1516	[IGM]
☐	N780DH	B727-223F	22006/1636	[IGM]
☐	N782DH	B727-227F	21998/1577	[IGM]
☐	N783DH	B727-227F	21999/1581	[IGM]
☐	N784DH	B727-227F	22001/1585	[IGM]
☐	N785AT	B727-214F	21691/1480	[IGM]
☐	N786AT	B727-214F	21692/1482	[IGM]
☐	N788AT	B727-214F	21958/1533	[IGM]
☐	N793DH	B727-247F	21393/1307	[IGM]
☐	N801DH	DC-8-73AF	46033/431	
☐	N802DH	DC-8-73AF	46076/451	
☐	N804DH	DC-8-73AF	46124/511	
☐	N805DH	DC-8-73AF	46125/515	
☐	N806DH	DC-8-73CF	46002/394	
☐	N807DH	DC-8-73CF	45990/375	
☐	N873SJ	DC-8-73F	46091/519	

ATI - AIR TRANSPORT INTL · 8C / ATN

☐	N761CX	B767-223 (SCD)	22318/111	
☐	N762CX	B767-232 (SCD)	22225/77	♦
☐	N763CX	B767-232 (SCD)	22223/74	♦
☐	N41CX	DC-8-62CF	46129/523	
☐	N71CX	DC-8-62F	45961/361	
☐	N602AL	DC-8-73F	45991/380	
☐	N603AL	DC-8-73F	46003/401	
☐	N604BX	DC-8-73CF	46046/444	
☐	N605AL	DC-8-73F	46106/490	
☐	N606AL	DC-8-73F	46044/432	
☐	N721CX	DC-8-72CF	46013/427	
☐	N722CX	DC-8-72CF	46130/542	
☐	N728PL	DC-8-62F	45918/353	
☐	N799AL	DC-8-62F	45922/335	
☐	N820BX	DC-8-71F	46065/460	
☐	N821BX	DC-8-71F	45811/262	
☐	N822BX	DC-8-71F	45813/284	
☐	N823BX	DC-8-71F	46064/459	
☐	N825BX	DC-8-71F	45978/381	[MHV]♦
☐	N826BX	DC-8-71F	45998/399	[ROW]
☐	N828BX	DC-8-71F	45993/392	
☐	N829BX	DC-8-71F	45994/387	[MHV]
☐	N830BX	DC-8-71F	45973/358	

ATLANTIC AIR CARGO

| ☐ | N437GB | DC-3 | 19999 | Freighter |
| ☐ | N705GB | DC-3 | 13854 | Freighter |

ATLAS AIR · 5Y / GTI

☐	N355MC	B747-341(SF)	23395/629	>PAC
☐	N408MC	B747-47UF	29261/1192	>UAE
☐	N409MC	B747-47UF	30558/1242	
☐	N412MC	B747-47UF	30559/1244	

☐ N415MC	B747-47UF	32837/1304	>UAE
☐ N416MC	B747-47UF	32838/1307	>PAC
☐ N418MC	B747-47UF	32840/1319	
☐ N419MC	B747-48EF	28367/1096	
☐ N429MC	B747-481BCF	24833/812	
☐ N492MC	B747-47UF	29253/1169	
☐ N493MC	B747-47UF	29254/1179	
☐ N496MC	B747-47UF	29257/1217	
☐ N497MC	B747-47UF	29258/1220	>UAE
☐ N498MC	B747-47UF	29259/1227	
☐ N499MC	B747-47UF	29260/1240	
☐ N508MC	B747-230M	21644/256	
☐ N512MC	B747-230M	21220/294	[ROW]
☐ N516MC	B747-243M	22507/497	[ROW]
☐ N517MC	B747-243B(SF)	23300/613	
☐ N522MC	B747-2D7B(SF)	21783/417	
☐ N523MC	B747-2D7B(SF)	21782/402	
☐ N524MC	B747-2D7B(SF)	21784/424	
☐ N526MC	B747-2D7B(SF)	22337/479	
☐ N528MC	B747-2D7B(SF)	22472/597	[ROW]
☐ N537MC	B747-271C	22403/524	[ROW]
☐ N540MC	B747-243M	22508/499	

BALTIA AIRLINES — BTL

☐ N705BL	B747-282B	21035/256	♦
☐ N706BL	B747-251B	21705/374	o/o♦

BASLER AIRLINES — BFC

☐ N300BF	Basler BT-67	15299/26744

BERING AIR — 8E / BRG

☐ N15GA	Beech 1900D	UE-37
☐ N148SK	Beech 1900D	UE-148
☐ N349TA	CASA 212-200	CC60-9-349

BERRY AVIATION — BYA

☐ N335PH	Do328-100	3013
☐ N339PH	Do328-100	3015
☐ N473PS	Do328-100	3010
☐ N900LH	Do328-100	3014
☐ N165BA	SA.226TC Metro II	TC-215
☐ N226BA	SA.226TC Metro II	TC-321
☐ N323BA	SA.226TC Metro II	TC-280
☐ N373PH	SA.227AC Metro III	AC-538
☐ N589BA	SA.227AC Metro III	AC-589
☐ N590BA	SA.227AC Metro III	AC-590
☐ N680AX	SA.227AC Metro III	AC-680
☐ N691AX	SA.227AC Metro III	AC-691
☐ N697AX	SA.227AC Metro III	AC-697
☐ N729C	SA.227AC Metro III	AC-571
☐ N789C	SA.227AC Metro III	AC-540
☐ N26959	SA.227AC Metro III	AC-662B
☐ N27442	SA.227AC Metro III	AC-750B

BIGHORN AIRWAYS

☐ N107BH	CASA C.212-200	CC20-4-165
☐ N112BH	CASA C.212-200	CC50-11-292
☐ N117BH	CASA C.212-200	CC23-1-171
☐ N257MC	Do228-202	8102
☐ N263MC	Do228-202	8141
☐ N266MC	Do228-202	8150

BIMINI ISLAND AIR — BMY

☐ N325SV	SAAB SF.340A	340A-072
☐ N460BA	SAAB SF.340A	340A-033

BOSTON-MAINE AIRWAYS — E9 / CXS

☐ N342PA	B727-222	21893/1503

☐ N348PA	B727-222	21921/1639	[BQK]
☐ N525PA	BAeJetstream 31	666	
☐ N529PA	BAeJetstream 31	771	
☐ N530PA	BAeJetstream 31	732	
☐ N531PA	BAeJetstream 31	748	
☐ N538PA	BAeJetstream 31	751	
☐ N539PA	BAeJetstream 31	741	

BROOKS AVIATION

☐ N99FS	DC-3	12425

BROOKS FUEL

☐ N708Z	C-54G	36067	
☐ N3054U	DC-4	10547	162
☐ N51802	C-54G	35930	
☐ N96358	C-54E	27284	

BUSINESS AVIATION COURIER — DKT

☐ N366AE	SA.227AC Metro III	AC-681B
☐ N371PH	SA.227AC Metro III	AC-576
☐ N387PH	SA.227AC Metro III	AC-531
☐ N685BA	SA.227AC Metro III	AC-685
☐ N3108B	SA.227AC Metro III	AC-509
☐ N3116N	SA.227AC Metro III	AC-596

BUTLER AIRCRAFT

☐ N401US	DC-7	45145/767	62
☐ N531BA	L182-1A Hercules (C-130A)	3139	67
☐ N838D	DC-7	45347/936	60
☐ N6353C	DC-7	45486/964	66

C & M AIRWAYS — RWG

☐ N640CM	Convair 640	104	[ELP]
☐ N3420	Convair 640	64	[ELP]
☐ N563PC	DC-9-15RC	47055/194	

CAPE AIR — 9K / CAP

☐ N14834	ATR 42-320	193	
☐ N42836	ATR 42-320	200	836

CAPITAL CARGO INTL AL — PT / CCI

☐ N286SC	B727-2A1F	21601/1694	
☐ N287SC	B727-2A1F	21345/1673	
☐ N308AS	B727-227F	22002/1627	
☐ N357KP	B727-230F	20675/924	
☐ N708AA	B727-223F	22465/1761	
☐ N713AA	B727-223F	22469/1769	
☐ N715AA	B727-223F	22470/1771	
☐ N755DH	B727-225F	21857/1539	
☐ N801EA	B727-225F	22432/1658	
☐ N808EA	B727-225F	22439/1689	
☐ N815EA	B727-225F	22552/1773	
☐ N898AA	B727-223F	22014/1663	
☐ N899AA	B727-223F	22015/1666	
☐ N89427	B727-227F	21365/1273	
☐ N605DL	B757-232F	22812/46	
☐ N620DL	B757-232F	22910/111	
☐ N315AA	B767-223F	22317/109	

CARIBBEAN SUN AIRLINES — WAL

☐ N802WA	MD-83	53052/1731

CENTURION II AIR CARGO — WE / CWC

☐ N279AX	DC-10-30F	47816/316	[SFB]
☐ N612GC	DC-10-30F	47840/337	
☐ N984AR	MD-11BCF	48429/500	

☐	N988AR	MD-11F	48434/476	◆

CHAMPLAIN AIR

☐	N59NA	DC-3	9043
☐	N700CA	DC-3	12438

COLGAN AIR   9L / CJC

☐	N202SR	SAAB SF.340B	340B-202
☐	N210CJ	SAAB SF.340B	340B-210
☐	N251CJ	SAAB SF.340B	340B-251

CORPORATE AIR   CPT

☐	N210AS	EMB.120FC	120006	
☐	N223AS	EMB.120FC	120021	[OPF]
☐	N319BH	Beech 1900C	UB-36	
☐	N330SB	Short SD.3-30	SH3013	
☐	N331SB	Short SD.3-30	SH3015	
☐	N7254R	Beech 1900C	UB-22	

CUSTOM AIR TRANSPORT   5R / CTT

☐	N511PE	B727-232F	20634/917	
☐	N902PG	B727-281F	20725/958	[ROW]
☐	N7635U	B727-222F	19908/653	
☐	N7644U	B727-222F	20038/716	[ROW]
☐	N7645U	B727-222F	20039/720	
☐	N24343	B727-231F	21630/1458	

DELTA AIR LINES   DL / DAL

☐	N301NB	A319-114	1058	3101
☐	N302NB	A319-114	1062	3102
☐	N314NB	A319-114	1191	3114
☐	N315NB	A319-114	1230	3115
☐	N316NB	A319-114	1249	3116
☐	N317NB	A319-114	1324	3117
☐	N318NB	A319-114	1325	3118
☐	N319NB	A319-114	1346	3119
☐	N320NB	A319-114	1392	3120
☐	N321NB	A319-114	1414	3121
☐	N322NB	A319-114	1434	3122
☐	N323NB	A319-114	1453	3123
☐	N324NB	A319-114	1456	3124
☐	N325NB	A319-114	1483	3125
☐	N326NB	A319 114	1498	3126
☐	N327NB	A319-114	1501	3127
☐	N328NB	A319-114	1520	3128
☐	N329NB	A319-114	1543	3129
☐	N330NB	A319-114	1549	3130
☐	N331NB	A319-114	1567	3131
☐	N332NB	A319-114	1570	3132
☐	N333NB	A319-114	1582	3133
☐	N334NB	A319-114	1659	3134
☐	N335NB	A319-114	1662	3135
☐	N336NB	A319-114	1683	3136
☐	N337NB	A319-114	1685	3137
☐	N338NB	A319-114	1693	3138
☐	N339NB	A319-114	1709	3139
☐	N340NB	A319-114	1714	3140
☐	N341NB	A319-114	1738	3141
☐	N342NB	A319-114	1746	3142
☐	N343NB	A319-114	1752	3143
☐	N344NB	A319-114	1766	3144
☐	N345NB	A319-114	1774	3145
☐	N346NB	A319-114	1796	3146
☐	N347NB	A319-114	1800	3147
☐	N348NB	A319-114	1810	3148
☐	N349NB	A319-114	1815	3149
☐	N351NB	A319-114	1820	3151
☐	N352NB	A319-114	1824	3152
☐	N353NB	A319-114	1828	3153
☐	N354NB	A319-114	1833	3154
☐	N355NB	A319-114	1839	3155
☐	N357NB	A319-114	1875	3157
☐	N358NB	A319-114	1897	3158
☐	N359NB	A319-114	1923	3159
☐	N360NB	A319-114	1959	3160
☐	N361NB	A319-114	1976	3161
☐	N362NB	A319-114	1982	3162
☐	N363NB	A319-114	1990	3163
☐	N364NB	A319-114	2002	3164
☐	N365NB	A319-114	2013	3165
☐	N366NB	A319-114	2026	3166
☐	N368NB	A319-114	2039	3168
☐	N369NB	A319-114	2047	3169
☐	N370NB	A319-114	2087	3170
☐	N371NB	A319-114	2095	3171
☐	N309US	A320-211	0118	3209
☐	N310NW	A320-211	0121	3210
☐	N311US	A320-211	0125	3211
☐	N312US	A320-211	0152	3212
☐	N313US	A320-211	0153	3213
☐	N314US	A320-211	0160	3214
☐	N315US	A320-211	0171	3215
☐	N316US	A320-211	0192	3216
☐	N317US	A320-211	0197	3217
☐	N318US	A320-211	0206	3218
☐	N319US	A320-211	0208	3219
☐	N320US	A320-211	0213	3220
☐	N321US	A320-211	0262	3221
☐	N322US	A320-211	0263	3222
☐	N323US	A320-211	0272	3223
☐	N324US	A320-211	0273	3224
☐	N325US	A320-211	0281	3225
☐	N326US	A320-211	0282	3226
☐	N327NW	A320-211	0297	3227
☐	N328NW	A320-211	0298	3228
☐	N329NW	A320-211	0306	3229
☐	N330NW	A320-211	0307	3230
☐	N331NW	A320-211	0318	3231
☐	N332NW	A320-211	0319	3232
☐	N333NW	A320-211	0329	3233
☐	N334NW	A320-212	0339	3234
☐	N335NW	A320-212	0340	3235
☐	N336NW	A320-212	0355	3236
☐	N337NW	A320-212	0358	3237
☐	N338NW	A320-212	0360	3238
☐	N339NW	A320-212	0367	3239
☐	N340NW	A320-212	0372	3240
☐	N341NW	A320-212	0380	3241
☐	N342NW	A320-212	0381	3242
☐	N343NW	A320-212	0387	3243
☐	N344NW	A320-212	0388	3244
☐	N345NW	A320-212	0399	3245
☐	N347NW	A320-212	0408	3247
☐	N348NW	A320-212	0410	3248
☐	N349NW	A320-212	0417	3249
☐	N350NA	A320-212	0418	3250
☐	N351NW	A320-212	0766	3251
☐	N352NW	A320-212	0778	3252
☐	N353NW	A320-212	0786	3253
☐	N354NW	A320-212	0801	3254
☐	N355NW	A320-212	0807	3255
☐	N356NW	A320-212	0818	3256
☐	N357NW	A320-212	0830	3257
☐	N358NW	A320-212	0832	3258
☐	N359NW	A320-212	0846	3259
☐	N360NW	A320-212	0903	3260
☐	N361NW	A320-212	0907	3261
☐	N362NW	A320-212	0911	3262
☐	N363NW	A320-212	0923	3263
☐	N364NW	A320-212	0962	3264
☐	N365NW	A320-212	0964	3265
☐	N366NW	A320-212	0981	3266
☐	N367NW	A320-212	0988	3267
☐	N368NW	A320-212	0996	3268
☐	N369NW	A320-212	1011	3269
☐	N370NW	A320-212	1037	3270

□	N371NW	A320-212	1535	3271
□	N372NW	A320-212	1633	3272
□	N373NW	A320-212	1641	3273
□	N374NW	A320-212	1646	3274
□	N375NC	A320-212	1789	3275
□	N376NW	A320-212	1812	3276
□	N377NW	A320-212	2082	3277
□	N378NW	A320-212	2092	3278
□	N801NW	A330-323E	0524	3301
□	N802NW	A330-323E	0533	3302
□	N803NW	A330-323E	0542	3303
□	N804NW	A330-323E	0549	3304
□	N805NW	A330-323E	0552	3305
□	N806NW	A330-323E	0578	3306
□	N807NW	A330-323E	0588	3307
□	N808NW	A330-323E	0591	3308
□	N809NW	A330-323E	0663	3309
□	N810NW	A330-323E	0674	3310
□	N811NW	A330-323E	0690	3311
□	N812NW	A330-323E	0784	3312
□	N813NW	A330-323E	0799	3313
□	N814NW	A330-323E	0806	3314
□	N815NW	A330-323E	0817	3315
□	N816NW	A330-323E	0827	3316
□	N817NW	A330-323E	0843	3317
□	N818NW	A330-323E	0857	3318
□	N819NW	A330-323E	0858	3319
□	N820NW	A330-323E	0859	3320
□	N821NW	A330-323E	0865	3321
□	N851NW	A330-223	609	3351
□	N852NW	A330-223	614	3352
□	N853NW	A330-223	618	3353
□	N854NW	A330-223	620	3354
□	N855NW	A330-223	621	3355
□	N856NW	A330-223	631	3356
□	N857NW	A330-223	633	3357
□	N858NW	A330-223	718	3358
□	N859NW	A330-223	722	3359
□	N860NW	A330-223	778	3360
□	N861NW	A330-223	796	3361
□	N301DQ	B737-732/W	29687/2667	3601
□	N302DQ	B737-732/W	29648/2683	3602
□	N303DQ	B737-732/W	29688/2720	3603
□	N304DQ	B737-732/W	29683/2724	3604
□	N305DQ	B737-732/W	29645/2743	3605
□	N306DQ	B737-732/W	29633/2758	3606
□	N307DQ	B737-732/W	29679/2767	3607
□	N308DE	B737-732/W	29656/3022	3608
□	N309DE	B737-732/W	29634/3031	3609
□	N310DE	B737-732/W	29665/3058	3610
□	N371DA	B737-832/W	29619/115	3701
□	N372DA	B737-832/W	29620/118	3702
□	N373DA	B737-832/W	29621/123	3703
□	N374DA	B737-832/W	29622/128	3704
□	N375DA	B737-832	29623/145	3705
□	N376DA	B737-832/W	29624/176	3706
□	N377DA	B737-832/W	29625/264	3707
□	N378DA	B737-832/W	30265/340	3708
□	N379DA	B737-832/W	30349/351	3709
□	N380DA	B737-832/W	30266/361	3710
□	N381DN	B737-832/W	30350/365	3711
□	N382DA	B737-832/W	30345/389	3712
□	N383DN	B737-832/W	30346/393	3713
□	N384DA	B737-832/W	30347/412	3714
□	N385DN	B737-832/W	30348/418	3715
□	N386DA	B737-832/W	30373/446	3716
□	N387DA	B737-832/W	30374/457	3717
□	N388DA	B737-832	30375/469	3718
□	N389DA	B737-832/W	30376/513	3719
□	N390DA	B737-832/W	30536/518	3720
□	N391DA	B737-832/W	30560/535	3721
□	N392DA	B737-832/W	30561/564	3722
□	N393DA	B737-832/W	30377/584	3723
□	N394DA	B737-832/W	30562/589	3724
□	N395DN	B737-832/W	30773/604	3725
□	N396DA	B737-832/W	30378/632	3726♦
□	N397DA	B737-832/W	30537/638	3727
□	N398DA	B737-832/W	30774/641	3728
□	N399DA	B737-832/W	30379/657	3729
□	N3730B	B737-832	30538/662	3730
□	N3731T		30775/665	3731
□	N3732J	B737-832/W	30380/674	3732
□	N3733Z	B737-832/W	30539/685	3733
□	N3734B	B737-832/W	30776/689	3734
□	N3735D	B737-832/W	30381/694	3735
□	N3736C	B737-832/W	30540/709	3736
□	N3737C	B737-832/W	30799/712	3737
□	N3738B	B737-832/W	30382/723	3738
□	N3739P	B737-832/W	30541/729	3739
□	N3740C	B737-832/W	30800/732	3740
□	N3741S	B737-832/W	30487/750	3741
□	N3742C	B737-832/W	30835/755	3742
□	N3743H	B737-832/W	30836/770	3743
□	N3744F	B737-832/W	30837/805	3744
□	N3745B	B737-832/W	32373/831	3745
□	N3746H	B737-832/W	30488/842	3746
□	N3747D	B737-832/W	32374/846	3747
□	N3748Y	B737-832/W	30489/865	3748
□	N3749D	B737-832/W	30490/867	3749
□	N3750D	B737-832/w	32375/870	3750
□	N3751B	B737-832/W	30491/892	3751
□	N3752	B737-832/W	30492/894	3752
□	N3753	B737-832/W	32626/899	3753
□	N3754A	B737-832/W	29626/907	3754
□	N3755D	B737-832/W	29627/914	3755
□	N3756	B737-832/W	30493/917	3756
□	N3757D	B737-832/W	30813/921	3757
□	N3758Y	B737-832/W	30814/923	3758
□	N3759	B737-832/W	30815/949	3759
□	N3760C	B737-832/W	30816/952	3760
□	N3761R	B737-832/W	29628/964	3761
□	N3762Y	B737-832/W	30817/968	3762
□	N3763D	B737-832/W	29629/1003	3763
□	N3764D	B737-832/W	30818/1006	3764
□	N3765	B737-832/W	30819/1008	3765
□	N3766	B737-832/W	30820/1029	3766
□	N3767	B737-832/W	30821/1031	3767
□	N3768	B737-832/W	29630/1053	3768
□	N3769L	B737-832/W	30822/1057	3769
□	N3771K	B737-832/W	29632/1103	3771
□	N3772H	B737-832/W	30823/3274	3772♦
□	N3773D	B737-832/W	30825/3338	3773♦
□	N37700	B737-832/W	29631/1074	3770
□	N661US	B747-451	23719/696	6301
□	N662US	B747-451	23720/708	6302
□	N663US	B747-451	23818/715	6303
□	N664US	B747-451	23819/721	6304
□	N665US	B747-451	23820/726	6305
□	N666US	B747-451	23821/742	6306
□	N667US	B747-451	24222/799	6307
□	N668US	B747-451	24223/800	6308
□	N669US	B747-451	24224/803	6309
□	N670US	B747-451	24225/804	6310
□	N671US	B747-451	26477/1206	6311
□	N672US	B747-451	30267/1223	6312
□	N673US	B747-451	30268/1226	6313
□	N674US	B747-451	30269/1232	6314
□	N675NW	B747-451	33001/1297	6315
□	N676NW	B747-451	33002/1303	6316
□	N501US	B757-251	23190/53	5501
□	N502US	B757-251	23191/55	5502
□	N503US	B757-251	23192/59	5503
□	N507US	B757-251	23196/68	5507
□	N508US	B757-251	23197/69	[MZJ]
□	N513US	B757-251	23201/83	[MZJ]
□	N514US	B757-251	23202/86	5514

	Registration	Type	C/n	Fleet No.
☐	N516US	B757-251	23204/104	5516
☐	N517US	B757-251	23205/105	5517
☐	N518US	B757-251	23206/107	5518
☐	N519US	B757-251	23207/108	5519
☐	N520US	B757-251	23208/109	5520
☐	N521US	B757-251	23209/110	5521
☐	N522US	B757-251	23616/119	[MZJ]
☐	N523US	B757-251	23617/121	5523
☐	N525US	B757-251	23619/124	[MZJ]
☐	N526US	B757-251	23620/131	5526
☐	N528US	B757-251	23843/137	5528
☐	N529US	B757-251	23844/140	5529
☐	N530US	B757-251	23845/188	5530
☐	N531US	B757-251	23846/190	5531
☐	N532US	B757-251	24263/192	[MZJ]
☐	N533US	B757-251	24264/194	5533
☐	N534US	B757-251	24265/196	5534
☐	N535US	B757-251/W	26482/693	5635
☐	N536US	B757-251/W	26483/695	5636
☐	N537US	B757-251/W	26484/697	5637
☐	N538US	B757-251/W	26485/699	5638
☐	N539US	B757-251/W	26486/700	5639
☐	N540US	B757-251/W	26487/701	5640
☐	N541US	B757-251	26488/703	5641
☐	N542US	B757-251	26489/705	5642
☐	N543US	B757-251	26490/709	5643
☐	N544US	B757-251/W	26491/710	5644
☐	N545US	B757-251/W	26492/711	5645
☐	N546US	B757-251/W	26493/713	5646
☐	N547US	B757-251/W	26494/714	5647
☐	N548US	B757-251/W	26495/715	5648
☐	N549US	B757-251/W	26496/716	5649
☐	N550NW	B757-251	26497/968	5550
☐	N551NW	B757-251	26498/971	5551
☐	N552NW	B757-251/W	26499/975	5552
☐	N553NW	B757-251/W	26500/982	5553
☐	N554NW	B757-251/W	26501/987	5554
☐	N555NW	B757-251/W	33391/1011	5555
☐	N556NW	B757-251/W	33392/1013	5556
☐	N557NW	B757-251/W	33393/1016	5557
☐	N602DL	B757-232	22809/39	602
☐	N603DL	B757-232	22810/41	603
☐	N604DL	B757-232	22811/43	604
☐	N608DA	B757-232	22815/64	608
☐	N609DL	B757-232	22816/65	609
☐	N610DL	B757-232	22817/66	610
☐	N612DL	B757-232	22819/73	612
☐	N613DL	B757-232	22820/84	613
☐	N614DL	B757-232	22821/85	614
☐	N615DL	B757-232	22822/87	615
☐	N616DL	B757-232	22823/91	[SAT]
☐	N617DL	B757-232	22907/92	[MZJ]
☐	N618DL	B757-232	22908/95	[MZJ]
☐	N619DL	B757-232	22909/101	619
☐	N620DL	B757-232	22910/111	620
☐	N621DL	B757-232	22911/112	621
☐	N622DL	B757-232	22912/113	[MZJ]
☐	N623DL	B757-232	22913/118	623
☐	N624DL	B757-232	22914/120	624
☐	N625DL	B757-232	22915/126	625
☐	N626DL	B757-232	22916/128	626
☐	N627DL	B757-232	22917/129	627
☐	N628DL	B757-232	22918/133	628
☐	N629DL	B757-232	22919/134	629
☐	N630DL	B757-232	22920/135	630
☐	N631DL	B757-232	23612/138	631
☐	N632DL	B757-232	23613/154	632
☐	N633DL	B757-232	23614/157	633
☐	N634DL	B757-232	23615/158	634
☐	N635DL	B757-232	23762/159	635
☐	N636DL	B757-232	23763/164	636
☐	N637DL	B757-232	23760/171	637
☐	N638DL	B757-232/W	23761/177	638
☐	N639DL	B757-232	23993/198	639
☐	N640DL	B757-232/W	23994/201	640
☐	N641DL	B757-232/W	23995/202	641
☐	N642DL	B757-232	23996/205	642
☐	N643DL	B757-232	23997/206	643
☐	N644DL	B757-232	23998/207	644
☐	N645DL	B757-232	24216/216	645
☐	N646DL	B757-232	24217/217	[VCV]
☐	N647DL	B757-232	24218/222	647
☐	N648DL	B757-232/W	24372/223	648
☐	N649DL	B757-232/W	24389/229	649
☐	N650DL	B757-232/W	24390/230	650
☐	N651DL	B757-232	24391/238	651
☐	N652DL	B757-232	24392/239	652
☐	N653DL	B757-232	24393/261	653
☐	N654DL	B757-232	24394/264	654
☐	N655DL	B757-232	24395/265	655
☐	N656DL	B757-232	24396/266	656
☐	N657DL	B757-232	24419/286	657
☐	N658DL	B757-232	24420/287	[MZJ]
☐	N659DL	B757-232	24421/293	[MZJ]
☐	N660DL	B757-232	24422/294	660
☐	N661DN	B757-232	24972/335	[MZJ]
☐	N662DN	B757-232	24991/342	662
☐	N663DN	B757-232/W	24992/343	663
☐	N664DN	B757-232	25012/347	664
☐	N665DN	B757-232/W	25013/349	665
☐	N666DN	B757-232/W	25034/354	666
☐	N667DN	B757-232	25035/355	667
☐	N668DN	B757-232	25141/376	668
☐	N669DN	B757-232	25142/377	669
☐	N670DN	B757-232	25331/415	670
☐	N671DN	B757-232	25332/416	671
☐	N672DL	B757-232	25977/429	672
☐	N673DL	B757-232	25978/430	673
☐	N674DL	B757-232	25979/439	674
☐	N675DL	B757-232	25980/448	675
☐	N676DL	B757-232	25981/455	676
☐	N677DL	B757-232	25982/456	677
☐	N678DL	B757-232	25983/465	678
☐	N679DA	B757-232	26955/500	679
☐	N680DA	B757-232	26956/502	680
☐	N681DA	B757-232	26957/516	681
☐	N682DA	B757-232	26958/518	682
☐	N683DA	B757-232	27103/533	683
☐	N684DA	B757-232	27104/535	684
☐	N685DA	B757-232	27588/667	685
☐	N686DA	B757-232	27589/689	686
☐	N687DL	B757-232	27586/800	687
☐	N688DL	B757-232	27587/803	688
☐	N689DL	B757-232	27172/807	689
☐	N690DL	B757-232	27585/808	690
☐	N692DL	B757-232/W	29724/820	692
☐	N693DL	B757-232	29725/826	693
☐	N694DL	B757-232	29726/831	694
☐	N695DL	B757-232	29727/838	695
☐	N696DL	B757-232	29728/845	696
☐	N697DL	B757-232	30318/880	697
☐	N698DL	B757-232	29911/885	698
☐	N699DL	B757-232	29970/887	699
☐	N702TW	B757-2Q8/W	28162/732	6801
☐	N703TW	B757-2Q8ER/W	27620/736	6802
☐	N704X	B757-2Q8/W	28163/741	6803
☐	N705TW	B757-231/W	28479/742	6811
☐	N706TW	B757-2Q8/W	28165/743	6804
☐	N707TW	B757-2Q8ER/W	27625/744	6805
☐	N709TW	B757-2Q8/W	28168/754	6806
☐	N710TW	B757-2Q8/W	28169/757	6807
☐	N711ZX	B757-231/W	28481/758	6814
☐	N712TW	B757-2Q8ER/W	27624/760	6808
☐	N713TW	B757-2Q8/W	28173/764	6809
☐	N717TW	B757-231/W	28485/854	6812
☐	N718TW	B757-231/W	28486/869	6815
☐	N721TW	B757-231/W	29954/874	6810
☐	N722TW	B757-231/W	29385/893	6816
☐	N723TW	B757-231/W	29378/907	6817
☐	N727TW	B757-231/W	30340/901	6813

Reg	Type	Serial/Line	Code
N750AT	B757-212ER	23126/45	6902
N751AT	B757-212ER	23125/44	6901
N752AT	B757-212ER	23128/48	6904
N757AT	B757-212ER	23127/47	6903
N900PC	B757-26D	28446/740	691
N6700	B757-232	30337/890	6700
N6701	B757-232	30187/892	6701
N6702	B757-232	30188/898	6702
N6703D	B757-232	30234/908	6703
N6704Z	B757-232	30396/914	6704
N6705Y	B757-232	30397/917	6705
N6706Q	B757-232	30422/921	6706
N6707A	B757-232	30395/927	6707
N6708D	B757-232	30480/934	6708
N6709	B757-232	30481/937	6709
N6710E	B757-232	30482/939	6710
N6711M	B757-232	30483/941	6711
N6712B	B757-232	30484/942	6712
N6713Y	B757-232	30777/944	6713
N6714Q	B757-232	30485/949	6714
N6715C	B757-232	30486/953	6715
N6716C	B757-232	30838/955	6716
N67171	B757-232	30839/959	6717
N581NW	B757-351	32982/1001	5801
N582NW	B757-351	32981/1014	5802
N583NW	B757-351	32983/1019	5803
N584NW	B757-351	32984/1020	5804
N585NW	B757-351	32985/1021	5805
N586NW	B757-351	32987/1022	5806
N587NW	B757-351	32986/1023	5807
N588NW	B757-351	32988/1024	5808
N589NW	B757-351	32989/1025	5809
N590NW	B757-351	32990/1027	5810
N591NW	B757-351	32991/1030	5811
N592NW	B757-351	32992/1033	5812
N593NW	B757-351	32993/1034	5813
N594NW	B757-351	32994/1035	5814
N595NW	B757-351	32995/1036	5815
N596NW	B757-351	32996/1037	5816
N121DE	B767-332	23435/162	[VCV]
N124DE	B767-332	23438/189	[VCV]
N125DL	B767-332	24075/200	125
N126DL	B767-332	24076/201	126
N127DL	B767-332	24077/203	127
N128DL	B767-332	24078/207	128
N129DL	B767-332	24079/209	129
N130DL	B767-332	24080/216	130
N131DN	B767-332	24852/320	[MZJ]
N132DN	B767-332	24981/345	[VCV]
N133DN	B767-332	24982/348	[VCV]
N134DL	B767-332	25123/353	[VCV]
N135DL	B767-332	25145/356	[VCV]
N136DL	B767-332	25146/374	136
N137DL	B767-332	25306/392	137
N138DL	B767-332	25409/410	138
N139DL	B767-332	25984/427	139
N140LL	B767-332	25988/499	1401
N143DA	B767-332	25991/721	1403
N144DA	B767-332	27584/751	1404
N152DL	B767-3P6ER	24984/339	1502
N153DL	B767-3P6ER	24985/340	1503
N154DL	B767-3P6ER	25241/389	1504
N155DL	B767-3P6ER	25269/390	[VCV]♦
N156DL	B767-3P6ER	25354/406	1506
N169DZ	B767-332ER	29689/706	1601
N171DN	B767-332ER	24759/304	171
N171DZ	B767-332ER	29690/717	1701
N172DN	B767-332ER	24775/312	[VCV]
N172DZ	B767-332ER	29691/719	1702
N173DN	B767-332ER	24800/313	[VCV]
N173DZ	B767-332ER	29692/723	1703
N174DN	B767-332ER/W	24802/317	174
N174DZ	B767-332ER	29693/725	1704
N175DN	B767-332ER	24803/318	175
N175DZ	B767-332ER	29696/740	1705
N176DN	B767-332ER	25061/341	176
N176DZ	B767-332ER	29697/745	1706
N177DN	B767-332ER/W	25122/346	177
N177DZ	B767-332ER	29698/750	1707
N178DN	B767-332ER	25143/349	178
N178DZ	B767-332ER	30596/795	1708
N179DN	B767-332ER/W	25144/350	179
N180DN	B767-332ER	25985/428	180
N181DN	B767-332ER	25986/446	181
N182DN	B767-332ER	25987/461	182
N183DN	B767-332ER	27110/492	183
N184DN	B767-332ER	27111/496	184
N185DN	B767-332ER/W	27961/576	185
N186DN	B767-332ER/W	27962/585	186♦
N187DN	B767-332ER/W	27582/617	187
N188DN	B767-332ER	27583/631	188
N189DN	B767-332ER	25990/646	189
N190DN	B767-332ER	28447/653	190
N191DN	B767-332ER/W	28448/654	191
N192DN	B767-332ER/W	28449/664	192
N193DN	B767-332ER	28450/671	193
N194DN	B767-332ER/W	28451/675	[MZJ]
N195DN	B767-332ER	28452/676	195
N196DN	B767-332ER	28453/679	196
N197DN	B767-332ER	28454/683	197
N198DN	B767-332ER	28455/685	198
N199DN	B767-332ER	28456/690	199
N394DL	B767-324ER	27394/572	1521
N1200K	B767-332ER	28457/696	1200
N1201P	B767-332ER	28458/697	1201
N1402A	B767-332	25989/506	1402
N1501P	B767-3P6ER	24983/334	1501
N1602	B767-332ER	29694/735	1602
N1603	B767-332ER	29695/736	1603
N1604R	B767-332ER	30180/749	1604
N1605	B767-332ER	30198/753	1605
N1607B	B767-332ER/W	30388/787	1607
N1608	B767-332ER/W	30573/788	1608
N1609	B767-332ER/W	30574/789	1609
N1610D	B767-332ER/W	30594/790	1610
N1611B	B767-332ER	30595/794	1611
N1612T	B767-332ER/W	30575/838	1612
N1613B	B767-332ER/W	32776/847	1613
N16065	B767-322ER	30199/755	1606
N825MH	B767-432ER	29703/758	1801
N826MH	B767-432ER	29713/769	1802
N827MH	B767-432ER	29705/773	1803
N828MH	B767-432ER	29699/791	1804
N829MH	B767-432ER	29700/801	1805
N830MH	B767-432ER	29701/803	1806
N831MH	B767-432ER	29702/804	1807
N832MH	B767-432ER	29704/807	1808
N833MH	B767-432ER	29706/810	1809
N834MH	B767-432ER	29707/813	1810
N835MH	B767-432ER	29708/814	1811
N836MH	B767-432ER	29709/818	1812
N837MH	B767-432ER	29710/820	1813
N838MH	B767-432ER	29711/821	1814
N839MH	B767-432ER	29712/824	1815
N840MH	B767-432ER	29718/830	1816
N841MH	B767-432ER	29714/855	1817
N842MH	B767-432ER	29715/856	1818
N843MH	B767-432ER	29716/865	1819
N844MH	B767-432ER	29717/871	1820
N845MH	B767-432ER	29719/874	1821
N701DN	B777-232LR	29740/697	7101
N702DN	B777-232LR	29741/704	7102
N703DN	B777-232LR	32222/767	7103
N704DK	B777-232LR	29739/772	7104
N705DN	B777-232LR	29742/773	7105
N706DN	B777-232LR	30440/776	7106
N707DN	B777-232LR	39091/782	7107
N708DN	B777-232LR	39254/789	7108

	Registration	Type	Serial	Fleet
☐	N709DN	B777-232LR	40559/854	7109◆
☐	N710DN	B777-232LR	40560/857	7110◆
☐	N860DA	B777-232ER	29951/202	7001
☐	N861DA	B777-232ER	29952/207	7002
☐	N862DA	B777-232ER	29734/235	7003
☐	N863DA	B777-232ER	29735/245	7004
☐	N864DA	B777-232ER	29736/249	7005
☐	N865DA	B777-232ER	29737/257	7006
☐	N866DA	B777-232ER	29738/261	7007
☐	N867DA	B777-232ER	29743/387	7008
☐	N90S	DC-9-31	47244/498	[MZJ]
☐	N401EA	DC-9-51	47682/788	9885
☐	N600TR	DC-9-51	47783/899	9886
☐	N623NW	DC-9-32	47591/706	[MZJ]
☐	N670MC	DC-9-51	47659/807	9882
☐	N671MC	DC-9-51	47660/810	9883
☐	N675MC	DC-9-51	47651/780	[MZJ]
☐	N676MC	DC-9-51	47652/798	9881
☐	N677MC	DC-9-51	47756/873	9884
☐	N750NW	DC-9-41	47114/218	[MZJ]
☐	N751NW	DC-9-41	47115/261	9751
☐	N752NW	DC-9-41	47116/308	9752
☐	N753NW	DC-9-41	47117/319	[MZJ]
☐	N754NW	DC-9-41	47178/323	[MZJ]
☐	N755NW	DC-9-41	47179/335	9755
☐	N756NW	DC-9-41	47180/354	[MZJ]
☐	N758NW	DC-9-41	47286/359	[MZJ]
☐	N760NC	DC-9-51	47708/813	9851
☐	N760NW	DC-9-41	47288/369	9760
☐	N761NC	DC-9-51	47709/814	9852
☐	N762NC	DC-9-51	47710/818	9853
☐	N762NW	DC-9-41	47395/555	9762
☐	N763NW	DC-9-41	47396/557	9763
☐	N764NC	DC-9-51	47717/833	9855
☐	N765NC	DC-9-51	47718/834	9856
☐	N766NC	DC-9-51	47739/852	9857
☐	N767NC	DC-9-51	47724/853	9858
☐	N768NC	DC-9-51	47729/854	9859
☐	N769NC	DC-9-51	47757/877	9860
☐	N770NC	DC-9-51	47758/880	9861
☐	N771NC	DC-9-51	47769/881	9862
☐	N772NC	DC-9-51	47774/884	9863
☐	N773NC	DC-9-51	47775/888	9864
☐	N774NC	DC-9-51	47776/889	9865
☐	N775NC	DC-9-51	47785/904	9866
☐	N776NC	DC-9-51	47786/905	9867
☐	N777NC	DC-9-51	47787/912	0868
☐	N778NC	DC-9-51	48100/927	9869
☐	N779NC	DC-9-51	48101/931	9870
☐	N780NC	DC-9-51	48102/932	9871
☐	N781NC	DC-9-51	48121/935	9872
☐	N782NC	DC-9-51	48107/936	9873
☐	N783NC	DC-9-51	48108/937	9874
☐	N784NC	DC-9-51	48109/939	9875
☐	N785NC	DC-9-51	48110/945	9876
☐	N786NC	DC-9-51	48148/984	9877
☐	N787NC	DC-9-51	48149/990	9878
☐	N914RW	DC-9-31	47362/492	[MZJ]
☐	N915RW	DC-9-31	47139/169	[MZJ]
☐	N921RW	DC-9-31	47164/259	[MZJ]
☐	N923RW	DC-9-31	47183/272	[MZJ]
☐	N940N	DC-9-32	47572/708	[MZJ]
☐	N943N	DC-9-32	47647/773	[MZJ]
☐	N964N	DC-9-31	47416/512	[MZJ]
☐	N965N	DC-9-31	47417/518	[MZJ]
☐	N984US	DC-9-32	47383/538	[MZJ]
☐	N987US	DC-9-32	47458/646	[MZJ]
☐	N994Z	DC-9-32	47097/193	[MZJ]
☐	N1309T	DC-9-31	47316/439	[MZJ]
☐	N1334U	DC-9-31	47280/597	[MZJ]
☐	N3324L	DC-9-32	47103/205	[MZJ]
☐	N8920E	DC-9-31	45835/95	[MZJ]
☐	N8921E	DC-9-31	45836/96	[MZJ]
☐	N8929E	DC-9-31	45866/138	[MZJ]
☐	N8932E	DC-9-31	47141/227	[MZJ]
☐	N8938E	DC-9-31	47161/249	[MZJ]
☐	N8944E	DC-9-31	47167/266	[MZJ]
☐	N8960E	DC-9-31	45869/331	[MZJ]
☐	N8986E	DC-9-31	47402/482	[MZJ]
☐	N9332	DC-9-31	47264/329	[MZJ]
☐	N9341	DC-9-31	47390/490	[MZJ]
☐	N9343	DC-9-31	47439/501	[MZJ]
☐	N9344	DC-9-31	47440/502	[MZJ]
☐	N9346	DC-9-32	47376/517	[MZJ]
☐	N9347	DC-9-32	45827/135	[MZJ]
☐	N900DE	MD-88	53372/1970	9000
☐	N901DE	MD-88	53378/1980	9001
☐	N902DE	MD-88	53379/1983	9002
☐	N903DE	MD-88	53380/1986	9003
☐	N904DE	MD-88	53409/1990	9004
☐	N904DL	MD-88	49535/1347	904
☐	N905DE	MD-88	53410/1992	9005
☐	N905DL	MD-88	49536/1348	905
☐	N906DE	MD-88	53415/2027	9006
☐	N906DL	MD-88	49537/1355	906
☐	N907DE	MD-88	53416/2029	9007
☐	N907DL	MD-88	49538/1365	907
☐	N908DE	MD-88	53417/2032	9008
☐	N908DL	MD-88	49539/1366	908
☐	N909DE	MD-88	53418/2033	9009
☐	N909DL	MD-88	49540/1395	909
☐	N910DE	MD-88	53419/2036	9010
☐	N910DL	MD-88	49541/1416	910
☐	N911DE	MD-88	49967/2037	9011
☐	N911DL	MD-88	49542/1433	911
☐	N912DE	MD-88	49997/2038	9012
☐	N912DL	MD-88	49543/1434	912
☐	N913DE	MD-88	49956/2039	9013
☐	N913DL	MD-88	49544/1443	913
☐	N914DE	MD-88	49957/2049	9014
☐	N914DL	MD-88	49545/1444	914
☐	N915DE	MD-88	53420/2050	9015
☐	N915DL	MD-88	49546/1447	915
☐	N916DE	MD-88	53421/2051	9016
☐	N916DL	MD-88	49591/1448	916
☐	N917DE	MD-88	49958/2054	9017
☐	N917DL	MD-88	49573/1469	917
☐	N918DE	MD-88	49959/2055	9018
☐	N918DL	MD-88	49583/1470	[VCV]
☐	N919DE	MD-88	53422/2058	9019
☐	N919DL	MD-88	49584/1471	919
☐	N920DE	MD-88	53423/2059	9020
☐	N920DL	MD-88	49644/1473	920
☐	N921DL	MD-88	49645/1480	921
☐	N922DL	MD-88	49646/1481	922
☐	N923DL	MD-88	49705/1491	923
☐	N924DL	MD-88	49711/1492	[VCV]
☐	N925DL	MD-88	49712/1500	925
☐	N926DL	MD-88	49713/1523	926
☐	N927DA	MD-88	49714/1524	927
☐	N928DL	MD-88	49715/1530	928
☐	N929DL	MD-88	49716/1531	929
☐	N930DL	MD-88	49717/1532	930
☐	N931DL	MD-88	49718/1533	931
☐	N932DL	MD-88	49719/1570	932
☐	N933DL	MD-88	49720/1571	933
☐	N934DL	MD-88	49721/1574	934
☐	N935DL	MD-88	49722/1575	935
☐	N936DL	MD-88	49723/1576	936
☐	N937DL	MD-88	49810/1588	937
☐	N938DL	MD-88	49811/1590	938
☐	N939DL	MD-88	49812/1593	939
☐	N940DL	MD-88	49813/1599	940
☐	N941DL	MD-88	49814/1602	941
☐	N942DL	MD-88	49815/1605	942
☐	N943DL	MD-88	49816/1608	943
☐	N944DL	MD-88	49817/1612	944
☐	N945DL	MD-88	49818/1613	945
☐	N946DL	MD-88	49819/1629	946

☐ N947DL	MD-88	49878/1664	947
☐ N948DL	MD-88	49879/1666	948
☐ N949DL	MD-88	49880/1676	949
☐ N950DL	MD-88	49881/1677	950
☐ N951DL	MD-88	49882/1679	951
☐ N952DL	MD-88	49883/1683	952
☐ N953DL	MD-88	49884/1685	953
☐ N954DL	MD-88	49885/1689	954
☐ N955DL	MD-88	49886/1691	955
☐ N956DL	MD-88	49887/1699	956
☐ N957DL	MD-88	49976/1700	957
☐ N958DL	MD-88	49977/1701	958
☐ N959DL	MD-88	49978/1710	959
☐ N960DL	MD-88	49979/1711	960
☐ N961DL	MD-88	49980/1712	961
☐ N962DL	MD-88	49981/1725	962
☐ N963DL	MD-88	49982/1726	963
☐ N964DL	MD-88	49983/1747	964
☐ N965DL	MD-88	49984/1748	965
☐ N966DL	MD-88	53115/1795	966
☐ N967DL	MD-88	53116/1796	967
☐ N968DL	MD-88	53161/1808	968
☐ N969DL	MD-88	53172/1810	969
☐ N970DL	MD-88	53173/1811	970
☐ N971DL	MD-88	53214/1823	971
☐ N972DL	MD-88	53215/1824	972
☐ N973DL	MD-88	53241/1832	973
☐ N974DL	MD-88	53242/1833	974
☐ N975DL	MD-88	53243/1834	975
☐ N976DL	MD-88	53257/1845	976
☐ N977DL	MD-88	53258/1848	977
☐ N978DL	MD-88	53259/1849	978
☐ N979DL	MD-88	53266/1859	979
☐ N980DL	MD-88	53267/1860	980
☐ N981DL	MD-88	53268/1861	981
☐ N982DL	MD-88	53273/1870	982
☐ N983DL	MD-88	53274/1873	983
☐ N984DL	MD-88	53311/1912	984
☐ N985DL	MD-88	53312/1914	985
☐ N986DL	MD-88	53313/1924	986
☐ N987DL	MD-88	53338/1926	987
☐ N988DL	MD-88	53339/1928	988
☐ N989DL	MD-88	53341/1936	989
☐ N990DL	MD-88	53342/1939	990
☐ N991DL	MD-88	53343/1941	991
☐ N992DL	MD-88	53344/1943	992
☐ N993DL	MD-88	53345/1950	993
☐ N994DL	MD-88	53346/1952	994
☐ N995DL	MD-88	53362/1955	995
☐ N996DL	MD-88	53363/1958	996
☐ N997DL	MD-88	53364/1961	997
☐ N998DL	MD-88	53370/1963	998
☐ N999DN	MD-88	53371/1965	999
☐ N901DA	MD-90-30	53381/2100	9201
☐ N902DA	MD-90-30	53382/2094	9202
☐ N903DA	MD-90-30	53383/2095	9203
☐ N904DA	MD-90-30	53384/2096	9204
☐ N905DA	MD-90-30	53385/2097	9205
☐ N906DA	MD-90-30	53386/2099	9206
☐ N907DA	MD-90-30	53387/2115	9207
☐ N908DA	MD-90-30	53388/2117	9208
☐ N909DA	MD-90-30	53389/2122	9209
☐ N910DN	MD-90-30	53390/2123	9210
☐ N911DA	MD-90-30	53391/2126	9211
☐ N912DN	MD-90-30	53392/2136	9212
☐ N913DN	MD-90-30	53393/2154	9213
☐ N914DN	MD-90-30	53394/2156	9214
☐ N915DN	MD-90-30	53395/2159	9215
☐ N916DN	MD-90-30	53396/2161	9216
☐ N917DN	MD-90-30	53552/2163	
☐ N918DH	MD-90-30	53576/2195	
☐ N919DN	MD-90-30	53553/2165	
☐ N920DN	MD-90-30	53582/2198	[GSO]♦
☐ N921DN	MD-90-30	53583/2200	[MIA]♦
☐ N922DX	MD-90-30	53584/2203	[MHV]♦

☐ N923DN	MD-90-30	53585/2224	[MIA]♦
☐ N924DN	MD-90-30	53586/2233	[VCV]♦
☐ N925DN	MD-90-30	53587/2240	[MIA]♦
☐ N926DH	MD-90-30	53588/2248	[ATL]♦
☐ N927DN	MD-90-30	53589/2259	[MZJ]♦
☐ N928DN	MD-90-30	53589/2259	[MZJ]♦
☐ N929DN	MD-90-30	53459/2141	[MZJ]♦
☐ N930DN	MD-90-30	53458/2140	[VCV]♦
☐ N953DN	MD-90-30	53523/2143	[MZJ]♦
☐ N956DN	MD-90-30	53526/2170	[MZJ]♦

DELTA CONNECTION — DL / DAL

☐ N403CA	CRJ-200ER	7428	[VCV]
☐ N405SW	CRJ-200ER	7029	7029
☐ N406SW	CRJ-200ER	7030	7030
☐ N408CA	CRJ-200ER	7440	7440
☐ N408SW	CRJ-200ER	7055	7055
☐ N409CA	CRJ-200ER	7441	7441
☐ N409SW	CRJ-200ER	7056	7056
☐ N410SW	CRJ-200ER	7066	7066
☐ N411SW	CRJ-200ER	7067	7067
☐ N412SW	CRJ-200ER	7101	7101
☐ N416SW	CRJ-200ER	7089	7089
☐ N417SW	CRJ-200ER	7400	7400
☐ N418SW	CRJ-200ER	7446	7446
☐ N420CA	CRJ-200ER	7451	7451
☐ N423SW	CRJ-200ER	7456	7456
☐ N426SW	CRJ-200ER	7468	7468
☐ N427CA	CRJ-200ER	7460	7460
☐ N427SW	CRJ-200ER	7497	7497
☐ N429SW	CRJ-200ER	7518	7518
☐ N430CA	CRJ-200ER	7461	7461
☐ N430SW	CRJ-200ER	7523	7523
☐ N431SW	CRJ-200ER	7536	7536
☐ N432SW	CRJ-200ER	7548	7548
☐ N433SW	CRJ-200ER	7550	7550
☐ N435CA	CRJ-200ER	7473	7473
☐ N435SW	CRJ-200ER	7555	7555
☐ N436CA	CRJ-200ER	7482	7482
☐ N437SW	CRJ-200ER	7564	7564
☐ N438SW	CRJ-200ER	7574	7574
☐ N439SW	CRJ-200ER	7578	7578
☐ N440SW	CRJ-200ER	7589	7589
☐ N441SW	CRJ-200ER	7602	7602
☐ N442CA	CRJ-200ER	7483	7483
☐ N442SW	CRJ-200ER	7609	7609
☐ N443CA	CRJ-200ER	7539	7539
☐ N443SW	CRJ-200ER	7638	7638
☐ N445SW	CRJ-200ER	7651	7651
☐ N446CA	CRJ-200ER	7546	7546
☐ N446SW	CRJ-200ER	7666	7666
☐ N447CA	CRJ-200ER	7552	7552
☐ N447SW	CRJ-200ER	7677	7677
☐ N448SW	CRJ-200ER	7678	7678
☐ N449SW	CRJ-200ER	7699	7699
☐ N451CA	CRJ-200ER	7562	7562
☐ N452SW	CRJ-200ER	7716	7716
☐ N453SW	CRJ-200ER	7743	7743
☐ N454SW	CRJ-200ER	7749	7749
☐ N455CA	CRJ-200ER	7592	7592
☐ N455SW	CRJ-200ER	7760	7760
☐ N457SW	CRJ-200ER	7773	7773
☐ N459SW	CRJ-200ER	7782	7782
☐ N460SW	CRJ-200ER	7803	7803
☐ N461SW	CRJ-200ER	7811	7811
☐ N463SW	CRJ-200ER	7820	7820
☐ N464SW	CRJ-200ER	7827	7827
☐ N465SW	CRJ-200ER	7845	7845
☐ N466SW	CRJ-200ER	7856	7856
☐ N477CA	CRJ-200ER	7670	7670
☐ N487CA	CRJ-200ER	7729	7729
☐ N492SW	CRJ-100ER	7168	7168
☐ N528CA	CRJ-200ER	7841	7841
☐ N587SW	CRJ-100ER	7062	7062

	Reg	Type				Reg	Type		
☐	N588SW	CRJ-100ER	7069	7069	☐	N837AS	CRJ-200ER	7271	837
☐	N589SW	CRJ-100ER	7072	7072	☐	N838AS	CRJ-200ER	7276	838
☐	N590SW	CRJ-100ER	7077	7077	☐	N839AS	CRJ-200ER	7284	839
☐	N591SW	CRJ-100ER	7079	7079	☐	N839AY	CRJ-200LR	8039	8039
☐	N594SW	CRJ-100ER	7285	7285	☐	N840AS	CRJ-200ER	7290	840
☐	N595SW	CRJ-100ER	7292	7292	☐	N840AY	CRJ-200LR	8040	8040
☐	N597SW	CRJ-100ER	7293	7293	☐	N841AS	CRJ-200ER	7300	841
☐	N601XJ	CRJ-200LR	8044		☐	N841AY	CRJ-200LR	8041	8041
☐	N602XJ	CRJ-200LR	8045		☐	N842AS	CRJ-200ER	7304	842
☐	N629BR	CRJ-200ER	7251	7251	☐	N843AS	CRJ-200ER	7310	843
☐	N659BR	CRJ-200ER	7509	7509	☐	N844AS	CRJ-200ER	7317	844
☐	N675BR	CRJ-200ER	7635	7635	☐	N845AS	CRJ-200ER	7324	845
☐	N680BR	CRJ-200ER	7679		☐	N846AS	CRJ-200ER	7328	846
☐	N681BR	CRJ-200ER	7680		☐	N847AS	CRJ-200ER	7335	847
☐	N682BR	CRJ-200ER	7691		☐	N848AS	CRJ-200ER	7339	848
☐	N683BR	CRJ-200ER	7692		☐	N849AS	CRJ-200ER	7347	849
☐	N684BR	CRJ-200ER	7708		☐	N850AS	CRJ-200ER	7355	850
☐	N685BR	CRJ-200ER	7712	7712	☐	N851AS	CRJ-200ER	7360	851
☐	N686BR	CRJ-200ER	7715		☐	N852AS	CRJ-200ER	7369	852
☐	N710CA	CRJ-100ER	7241	7241	☐	N853AS	CRJ-200ER	7374	853
☐	N712CA	CRJ-100ER	7244	7244	☐	N854AS	CRJ-200ER	7382	854
☐	N713CA	CRJ-100ER	7245	7245	☐	N855AS	CRJ-200ER	7395	855
☐	N716CA	CRJ-100ER	7250	7250	☐	N856AS	CRJ-200ER	7404	856
☐	N720SW	CRJ-200ER	7297	7297	☐	N857AS	CRJ-200ER	7411	857
☐	N721CA	CRJ-100ER	7259	7259	☐	N858AS	CRJ-200ER	7417	858
☐	N739CA	CRJ-100ER	7273	7273	☐	N859AS	CRJ-200ER	7421	859
☐	N779CA	CRJ-100ER	7306	7306	☐	N860AS	CRJ-200ER	7433	860
☐	N781CA	CRJ-100ER	7312	7312	☐	N861AS	CRJ-200ER	7445	861
☐	N783CA	CRJ-100ER	7315	7315	☐	N862AS	CRJ-200ER	7476	7476
☐	N784CA	CRJ-100ER	7319	7319	☐	N863AS	CRJ-200ER	7487	7487
☐	N785CA	CRJ-100ER	7326	7326	☐	N864AS	CRJ-200ER	7502	864
☐	N786CA	CRJ-100ER	7333	7333	☐	N865AS	CRJ-200ER	7507	865
☐	N797CA	CRJ-100ER	7344	7344	☐	N866AS	CRJ-200ER	7517	7517
☐	N800AY	CRJ-200LR	8000	8000	☐	N867AS	CRJ-200ER	7463	867
☐	N801AY	CRJ-200LR	8001	8001	☐	N868AS	CRJ-200ER	7474	868
☐	N804CA	CRJ-100ER	7352	7352	☐	N868CA	CRJ-200ER	7427	7427
☐	N805AY	CRJ-200LR	8005	8005	☐	N869AS	CRJ-200ER	7479	869
☐	N807CA	CRJ-100ER	7364	7364	☐	N870AS	CRJ-200ER	7530	870
☐	N809CA	CRJ-100ER	7366	7366	☐	N871AS	CRJ-200ER	7537	871
☐	N810CA	CRJ-200ER	7370	7370	☐	N872AS	CRJ-200ER	7542	872
☐	N811CA	CRJ-200ER	7380	7380	☐	N873AS	CRJ-200ER	7549	873
☐	N812AY	CRJ-200LR	8012	8012	☐	N874AS	CRJ-200ER	7551	874
☐	N812CA	CRJ-200ER	7381	7381	☐	N875AS	CRJ-200ER	7559	875
☐	N813AY	CRJ-200LR	8013	8013	☐	N876AS	CRJ-200ER	7576	876
☐	N814CA	CRJ-200ER	7387	7387	☐	N877AS	CRJ-200ER	7579	877
☐	N815CA	CRJ-200ER	7397	7397	☐	N878AS	CRJ-200ER	7590	878
☐	N818CA	CRJ-200ER	7408	7408	☐	N879AS	CRJ-200ER	7600	879
☐	N819AY	CRJ-200LR	8019	8019	☐	N880AS	CRJ-200ER	7606	880
☐	N819CA	CRJ-200ER	7415	7415	☐	N881AS	CRJ-200ER	7496	881
☐	N820AS	CRJ-200ER	7188	820	☐	N882AS	CRJ-200ER	7503	882
☐	N820AY	CRJ-200LR	8020	8020	☐	N883AS	CRJ-200ER	7504	883
☐	N821AS	CRJ-200ER	7194	821	☐	N884AS	CRJ-200ER	7513	884
☐	N821AY	CRJ-200LR	8021	8021	☐	N885AS	CRJ-200ER	7521	885
☐	N823AS	CRJ-200ER	7196	823	☐	N886AS	CRJ-200ER	7531	886
☐	N823AY	CRJ-200LR	8023	8023	☐	N889AS	CRJ-200ER	7538	889
☐	N824AS	CRJ-200ER	7203	824	☐	N900EV	CRJ-200ER	7608	900
☐	N824AY	CRJ-200LR	8024	8024	☐	N901EV	CRJ-200ER	7616	901
☐	N825AS	CRJ-200ER	7207	825	☐	N902EV	CRJ-200ER	7620	902
☐	N825AY	CRJ-200LR	8025	8025	☐	N903EV	CRJ-200ER	7621	903
☐	N826AS	CRJ-200ER	7210	826	☐	N904EV	CRJ-200ER	7628	904
☐	N826AY	CRJ-200LR	8026	8026	☐	N905EV	CRJ-200ER	7632	905
☐	N827AS	CRJ-200ER	7212	827	☐	N906EV	CRJ-200ER	7642	906
☐	N827AY	CRJ-200LR	8027	8027	☐	N907EV	CRJ-200ER	7648	907
☐	N828AS	CRJ-200ER	7213	828	☐	N908EV	CRJ-200ER	7654	908
☐	N829AS	CRJ-200ER	7232	829	☐	N909EV	CRJ-200ER	7658	909
☐	N829AY	CRJ-200LR	8029	8029	☐	N910EV	CRJ-200ER	7727	7727
☐	N830AY	CRJ-200LR	8030	8030	☐	N912EV	CRJ-200ER	7728	7728
☐	N831AY	CRJ-200LR	8031	8031	☐	N913EV	CRJ-200ER	7731	7731
☐	N832AY	CRJ-200LR	8032	8032	☐	N914CA	CRJ-100ER	7012	7012
☐	N833AS	CRJ-200ER	7246	833	☐	N914EV	CRJ-200ER	7752	914
☐	N833AY	CRJ-200LR	8033	8033	☐	N915CA	CRJ-100ER	7013	7013
☐	N834AY	CRJ-200LR	8034	8034	☐	N915EV	CRJ-200ER	7754	7754
☐	N835AS	CRJ-200ER	7258	835	☐	N916CA	CRJ-100ER	7014	7014
☐	N835AY	CRJ-200LR	8035	8035	☐	N916EV	CRJ-200ER	7757	916
☐	N836AY	CRJ-200LR	8036	8036	☐	N917CA	CRJ-100ER	7017	7017

☐	N917EV	CRJ-200ER	7769	917
☐	N918CA	CRJ-100ER	7018	7018
☐	N919EV	CRJ-200ER	7780	919
☐	N920EV	CRJ-200ER	7810	920
☐	N921EV	CRJ-200ER	7819	921
☐	N922EV	CRJ-200ER	7822	922
☐	N923EV	CRJ-200ER	7826	923
☐	N924CA	CRJ-100ER	7026	7026
☐	N924EV	CRJ-200ER	7830	924
☐	N925EV	CRJ-200ER	7831	925
☐	N926EV	CRJ-200ER	7843	926
☐	N927CA	CRJ-100ER	7031	7031
☐	N927EV	CRJ-200ER	7844	927
☐	N928EV	CRJ-200ER	8006	928
☐	N929CA	CRJ-100ER	7035	7035
☐	N929EV	CRJ-200ER	8007	929
☐	N930EV	CRJ-200ER	8014	930
☐	N931CA	CRJ-100ER	7037	7037
☐	N931EV	CRJ-200ER	8015	931
☐	N932CA	CRJ-100ER	7038	7038
☐	N932EV	CRJ-200ER	8016	932
☐	N933CA	CRJ-100ER	7040	7040
☐	N933EV	CRJ-200ER	8022	933
☐	N934CA	CRJ-100ER	7042	7042
☐	N934EV	CRJ-200ER	8028	934
☐	N935EV	CRJ-200ER	8037	935
☐	N936CA	CRJ-100ER	7043	7043
☐	N936EV	CRJ-200ER	8038	936
☐	N937CA	CRJ-100ER	7044	7044
☐	N937EV	CRJ-200ER	8042	937
☐	N938CA	CRJ-100ER	7046	7046
☐	N940CA	CRJ-100ER	7048	7048
☐	N941CA	CRJ-100ER	7050	7050
☐	N954CA	CRJ-100ER	7100	7100
☐	N956CA	CRJ-100ER	7105	7105
☐	N957CA	CRJ-100ER	7109	7109
☐	N958CA	CRJ-100ER	7111	7111
☐	N959CA	CRJ-100ER	7116	7116
☐	N960CA	CRJ-100ER	7117	7117
☐	N962CA	CRJ-100ER	7123	7123
☐	N963CA	CRJ-100ER	7127	7127
☐	N964CA	CRJ-100ER	7129	7129
☐	N965CA	CRJ-100ER	7131	7131
☐	N966CA	CRJ-100ER	7132	7132
☐	N967CA	CRJ-100ER	7134	7134
☐	N969CA	CRJ-100ER	7141	7141
☐	N970EV	CRJ-200ER	7527	970
☐	N971CA	CRJ-100ER	7145	7145
☐	N971EV	CRJ-200ER	7528	971
☐	N972EV	CRJ-200ER	7534	972
☐	N973CA	CRJ-100ER	7146	7146
☐	N973EV	CRJ-200ER	7575	973
☐	N974EV	CRJ-200ER	7594	974
☐	N975EV	CRJ-200ER	7599	975
☐	N976EV	CRJ-200ER	7601	976
☐	N977EV	CRJ-200ER	7720	977
☐	N978EV	CRJ-200ER	7723	978
☐	N979EV	CRJ-200ER	7737	979
☐	N980EV	CRJ-200ER	7759	980
☐	N981EV	CRJ-200ER	7768	981
☐	N989CA	CRJ-100ER	7215	7215
☐	N8390A	CRJ-200LR	7390	8390
☐	N8409N	CRJ-200LR	7409	8409
☐	N8412F	CRJ-200LR	7412	8412
☐	N8416B	CRJ-200LR	7416	8416
☐	N8423C	CRJ-200LR	7423	8423
☐	N8432A	CRJ-200LR	7432	8432
☐	N8444F	CRJ-200LR	7444	8444
☐	N8458A	CRJ-200LR	7458	8458
☐	N8475B	CRJ-200LR	7475	8475
☐	N8477R	CRJ-200LR	7477	8477
☐	N8488D	CRJ-200LR	7488	8488
☐	N8492C	CRJ-200LR	7492	8492
☐	N8495B	CRJ-200LR	7495	8495
☐	N8501F	CRJ-200LR	7501	8501
☐	N8505Q	CRJ-200LR	7505	8505
☐	N8506C	CRJ-200LR	7506	8506
☐	N8515F	CRJ-200LR	7515	8515
☐	N8516C	CRJ-200LR	7516	8516
☐	N8524A	CRJ-200LR	7524	8524
☐	N8525B	CRJ-200LR	7525	8525
☐	N8532G	CRJ-200LR	7532	8532
☐	N8533D	CRJ-200LR	7533	8533
☐	N8541D	CRJ-200LR	7541	8541
☐	N8543F	CRJ-200LR	7543	8543
☐	N8554A	CRJ-200LR	7554	8554
☐	N8560F	CRJ-200LR	7560	8560
☐	N8577D	CRJ-200LR	7577	8577
☐	N8580A	CRJ-200LR	7580	8580
☐	N8587E	CRJ-200LR	7587	8587
☐	N8588D	CRJ-200LR	7588	8588
☐	N8598B	CRJ-200LR	7598	8598
☐	N8604C	CRJ-200LR	7604	8604
☐	N8611A	CRJ-200LR	7611	8611
☐	N8623A	CRJ-200LR	7623	8623
☐	N8631E	CRJ-200LR	7631	8631
☐	N8646A	CRJ-200LR	7646	8646
☐	N8659B	CRJ-200LR	7659	8659
☐	N8665A	CRJ-200LR	7665	8665
☐	N8672A	CRJ-200LR	7672	8672
☐	N8673D	CRJ-200LR	7673	8673
☐	N8674A	CRJ-200LR	7674	8674
☐	N8683B	CRJ-200LR	7683	8683
☐	N8688C	CRJ-200LR	7688	6888
☐	N8694A	CRJ-200LR	7694	8694
☐	N8696C	CRJ-200LR	7696	8696
☐	N8698A	CRJ-200LR	7698	8698
☐	N8709A	CRJ-200LR	7709	8709
☐	N8710A	CRJ-200LR	7710	8710
☐	N8718E	CRJ-200LR	7718	8718
☐	N8721B	CRJ-200LR	7721	8721
☐	N8733G	CRJ-200LR	7733	8733
☐	N8736A	CRJ-200LR	7736	8736
☐	N8745B	CRJ-200LR	7745	8745
☐	N8747B	CRJ-200LR	7747	8747
☐	N8751D	CRJ-200LR	7751	8751
☐	N8758D	CRJ-200LR	7758	8758
☐	N8771A	CRJ-200LR	7771	8771
☐	N8775A	CRJ-200LR	7775	8775
☐	N8783E	CRJ-200LR	7783	8783
☐	N8790A	CRJ-200LR	7790	8790
☐	N8794B	CRJ-200LR	7794	8794
☐	N8797A	CRJ-200LR	7797	8797
☐	N8800G	CRJ-200LR	7800	8800
☐	N8808H	CRJ-200LR	7808	8808
☐	N8828D	CRJ-200LR	7828	8828
☐	N8836A	CRJ-200LR	7836	8836
☐	N8837B	CRJ-200LR	7837	8837
☐	N8839E	CRJ-200LR	7839	8839
☐	N8847A	CRJ-200LR	7847	8847
☐	N8855A	CRJ-200LR	7855	8855
☐	N8869B	CRJ-200LR	7869	8869
☐	N8877A	CRJ-200LR	7877	8877
☐	N8883E	CRJ-200LR	7883	8883
☐	N8884E	CRJ-200LR	7884	8884
☐	N8886A	CRJ-200LR	7886	8886
☐	N8888D	CRJ-200LR	7888	8888
☐	N8891A	CRJ-200LR	7891	8891
☐	N8894A	CRJ-200LR	7894	8894
☐	N8896A	CRJ-200LR	7896	8896
☐	N8903A	CRJ-200LR	7903	8903
☐	N8907A	CRJ-200LR	7907	8907
☐	N8908D	CRJ-200LR	7908	8908
☐	N8913A	CRJ-200LR	7913	8913
☐	N8914A	CRJ-200LR	7914	8914
☐	N8918B	CRJ-200LR	7918	8918
☐	N8921B	CRJ-200LR	7921	8921
☐	N8923A	CRJ-200LR	7923	8923
☐	N8924B	CRJ-200LR	7924	8924
☐	N8928A	CRJ-200LR	7928	8928

	Reg	Type		
☐	N8930E	CRJ-200LR	7930	8930
☐	N8932C	CRJ-200LR	7932	8932
☐	N8933B	CRJ-200LR	7933	8933
☐	N8936A	CRJ-200LR	7936	8936
☐	N8938A	CRJ-200LR	7938	8938
☐	N8940E	CRJ-200LR	7940	8940
☐	N8942A	CRJ-200LR	7942	8942
☐	N8943A	CRJ-200LR	7943	8943
☐	N8944B	CRJ-200LR	7944	8944
☐	N8946A	CRJ-200LR	7946	8946
☐	N8948B	CRJ-200LR	7948	8948
☐	N8960A	CRJ-200LR	7960	8960
☐	N8964E	CRJ-200LR	7964	8964
☐	N8965E	CRJ-200LR	7965	8965
☐	N8968E	CRJ-200LR	7968	8968
☐	N8969A	CRJ-200LR	7969	8969
☐	N8970D	CRJ-200LR	7970	8970
☐	N8971A	CRJ-200LR	7971	8971
☐	N8972E	CRJ-200LR	7972	8972
☐	N8974C	CRJ-200LR	7974	8974
☐	N8976E	CRJ-200LR	7976	8976
☐	N8977A	CRJ-200LR	7977	8977
☐	N8980A	CRJ-200LR	7980	8980
☐	N8982A	CRJ-200LR	7982	8982
☐	N8986B	CRJ-200LR	7986	8986
☐	N317CA	CRJ-701ER	10055	10055
☐	N331CA	CRJ-701ER	10061	10061
☐	N340CA	CRJ-701ER	10062	10062
☐	N354CA	CRJ-701ER	10064	10064
☐	N355CA	CRJ-701ER	10067	10067
☐	N367CA	CRJ-701ER	10069	10069
☐	N368CA	CRJ-701ER	10075	10075
☐	N369CA	CRJ-701ER	10079	10079
☐	N371CA	CRJ-701ER	10082	10082
☐	N374CA	CRJ-701ER	10090	10090
☐	N376CA	CRJ-701ER	10092	10092
☐	N378CA	CRJ-701ER	10097	10097
☐	N379CA	CRJ-701ER	10102	10102
☐	N390CA	CRJ-701ER	10106	10106
☐	N391CA	CRJ-701ER	10108	10108
☐	N398CA	CRJ-701ER	10112	10112
☐	N603SK	CRJ-702ER	10248	10248
☐	N604SK	CRJ-702ER	10249	10239
☐	N606SK	CRJ-702ER	10250	10250
☐	N607SK	CRJ-702ER	10251	10251
☐	N608SK	CRJ-702ER	10252	10252
☐	N609SK	CRJ-701ER	10020	10020
☐	N611SK	CRJ-701ER	10035	10035
☐	N613SK	CRJ-701ER	10038	10038
☐	N614SK	CRJ-701ER	10051	10051
☐	N625CA	CRJ-701ER	10113	10113
☐	N641CA	CRJ-701ER	10122	10122
☐	N642CA	CRJ-701ER	10125	10125
☐	N653CA	CRJ-701ER	10129	10129
☐	N655CA	CRJ-701ER	10134	10134
☐	N656CA	CRJ-701ER	10143	10143
☐	N658CA	CRJ-701ER	10148	10148
☐	N659CA	CRJ-701ER	10153	10153
☐	N668CA	CRJ-701ER	10162	10162
☐	N669CA	CRJ-701ER	10176	10176
☐	N690CA	CRJ-701ER	10182	10182
☐	N707EV	CRJ-701ER	10057	
☐	N708EV	CRJ-701ER	10060	
☐	N709EV	CRJ-701ER	10068	
☐	N710EV	CRJ-701ER	10071	
☐	N712EV	CRJ-701ER	10074	
☐	N713EV	CRJ-701ER	10081	
☐	N716EV	CRJ-701ER	10084	
☐	N717EV	CRJ-701ER	10088	
☐	N718EV	CRJ-701ER	10095	
☐	N719EV	CRJ-701ER	10099	
☐	N720EV	CRJ-701ER	10115	
☐	N722EV	CRJ-701ER	10127	
☐	N723EV	CRJ-701ER	10132	
☐	N724EV	CRJ-701ER	10138	

	Reg	Type	
☐	N730EV	CRJ-701ER	10141
☐	N738EV	CRJ-701ER	10146
☐	N740EV	CRJ-701ER	10151
☐	N741EV	CRJ-701ER	10155
☐	N744EV	CRJ-701ER	10157
☐	N748EV	CRJ-701ER	10158
☐	N750EV	CRJ-701ER	10161
☐	N751EV	CRJ-701ER	10163
☐	N752EV	CRJ-701ER	10166
☐	N753EV	CRJ-701ER	10169
☐	N754EV	CRJ-701ER	10173
☐	N755EV	CRJ-701ER	10185
☐	N758EV	CRJ-701ER	10210
☐	N759EV	CRJ-701ER	10211
☐	N760EV	CRJ-701ER	10212
☐	N761ND	CRJ-701ER	10213
☐	N131EV	CRJ-900ER	15217
☐	N132EV	CRJ-900ER	15219
☐	N133EV	CRJ-900ER	15222
☐	N134EV	CRJ-900ER	15223
☐	N135EV	CRJ-900ER	15225
☐	N136EV	CRJ-900ER	15226
☐	N137EV	CRJ-900ER	15227
☐	N138EV	CRJ-900ER	15235
☐	N146PQ	CRJ-900ER	15146
☐	N147PQ	CRJ-900ER	15147
☐	N153PQ	CRJ-900ER	15153
☐	N161PQ	CRJ-900ER	15161
☐	N162PQ	CRJ-900ER	15162
☐	N166PQ	CRJ-900ER	15166
☐	N170PQ	CRJ-900ER	15170
☐	N176PQ	CRJ-900ER	15176
☐	N181PQ	CRJ-900ER	15181
☐	N186PQ	CRJ-900ER	15186
☐	N187PQ	CRJ-900ER	15187
☐	N195PQ	CRJ-900ER	15195
☐	N197PQ	CRJ-900ER	15197
☐	N200PQ	CRJ-900ER	15200
☐	N228PQ	CRJ-900ER	15228
☐	N232PQ	CRJ-900ER	15232
☐	N538CA	CRJ-900ER	15157
☐	N548CA	CRJ-900ER	15159
☐	N549CA	CRJ-900ER	15164
☐	N554CA	CRJ-900ER	15168
☐	N582CA	CRJ-900ER	15171
☐	N600LR	CRJ-900ER	15142
☐	N601LR	CRJ-900ER	15145
☐	N602LR	CRJ-900FR	15151
☐	N604LR	CRJ-900ER	15152
☐	N605LR	CRJ-900ER	15160
☐	N606LR	CRJ-900ER	15173
☐	N607LR	CRJ-900ER	15178
☐	N676CA	CRJ-900ER	15127
☐	N678CA	CRJ-900ER	15125
☐	N679CA	CRJ-900ER	15132
☐	N689CA	CRJ-900ER	15133
☐	N691CA	CRJ-900ER	15136
☐	N692CA	CRJ-900ER	15092
☐	N693CA	CRJ-900ER	15096
☐	N695CA	CRJ-900ER	15097
☐	N800SK	CRJ-900ER	15060
☐	N802SK	CRJ-900ER	15061
☐	N803SK	CRJ-900ER	15062
☐	N804SK	CRJ-900ER	15067
☐	N805SK	CRJ-900ER	15069
☐	N806SK	CRJ-900ER	15070
☐	N807SK	CRJ-900ER	15082
☐	N809SK	CRJ-900ER	15086
☐	N810SK	CRJ-900ER	15093
☐	N812SK	CRJ-900ER	15098
☐	N813SK	CRJ-900ER	15099
☐	N814SK	CRJ-900ER	15100
☐	N815SK	CRJ-900ER	15101
☐	N816SK	CRJ-900ER	15105
☐	N817SK	CRJ-900ER	15107

	Registration	Type	Serial	Fleet
☐	N820SK	CRJ-900ER	15108	
☐	N821SK	CRJ-900ER	15109	
☐	N822SK	CRJ-900ER	15203	
☐	N823SK	CRJ-900ER	15205	
☐	N824SK	CRJ-900ER	15208	
☐	N825SK	CRJ-900ER	15212	
☐	N901XJ	CRJ-900	15130	
☐	N902XJ	CRJ-900	15131	
☐	N903XJ	CRJ-900	15134	
☐	N904XJ	CRJ-900	15135	
☐	N905XJ	CRJ-900	15137	
☐	N906XJ	CRJ-900	15138	
☐	N907XJ	CRJ-900	15139	
☐	N908XJ	CRJ-900	15140	
☐	N909XJ	CRJ-900	15141	
☐	N910XJ	CRJ-900	15143	
☐	N912XJ	CRJ-900	15144	
☐	N913XJ	CRJ-900	15148	
☐	N914XJ	CRJ-900	15149	
☐	N915XJ	CRJ-900	15150	
☐	N916XJ	CRJ-900	15154	
☐	N917XJ	CRJ-900	15155	
☐	N918XJ	CRJ-900	15156	
☐	N919XJ	CRJ-900	15163	
☐	N920XJ	CRJ-900	15167	
☐	N921XJ	CRJ-900	15172	
☐	N922XJ	CRJ-900	15174	
☐	N923XJ	CRJ-900	15177	
☐	N924XJ	CRJ-900	15179	
☐	N925XJ	CRJ-900	15183	
☐	N926XJ	CRJ-900	15184	
☐	N927XJ	CRJ-900	15188	
☐	N928XJ	CRJ-900	15190	
☐	N929XJ	CRJ-900	15191	
☐	N930XJ	CRJ-900	15192	
☐	N931XJ	CRJ-900	15193	
☐	N932XJ	CRJ-900	15194	
☐	N933XJ	CRJ-900	15196	
☐	N934XJ	CRJ-900	15198	
☐	N935XJ	CRJ-900	15199	
☐	N936XJ	CRJ-900	15201	
☐	N937XJ	CRJ-900	15210	
☐	N272SK	ERJ-145LR	145306	8272
☐	N273SK	ERJ-145LR	145331	8273
☐	N274SK	ERJ-145LR	145344	8274
☐	N561RP	ERJ-145LR	145447	8561
☐	N562RP	ERJ-145LR	145451	8562
☐	N563RP	ERJ-145LR	145509	8563
☐	N564RP	ERJ-145LR	145524	8564
☐	N565RP	ERJ-145LR	145679	8565
☐	N566RP	ERJ-145LR	145691	8566
☐	N567RP	ERJ-145LR	145698	8567
☐	N568RP	ERJ-145LR	145800	8568
☐	N569RP	ERJ-145LR	14500816	8569
☐	N570RP	ERJ-145LR	14500821	8570
☐	N571RP	ERJ-145LR	14500827	8571
☐	N572RP	ERJ-145LR	14500828	8572
☐	N573RP	ERJ-145LR	14500837	8573
☐	N574RP	ERJ-145LR	14500845	8574
☐	N575RP	ERJ-145LR	14500847	8575
☐	N576RP	ERJ-145LR	14500856	8576
☐	N577RP	ERJ-145LR	14500862	8577
☐	N578RP	ERJ-145LR	14500865	8578
☐	N579RP	ERJ-145LR	14500871	8579
☐	N825MJ	ERJ-145LR	145179	
☐	N826MJ	ERJ-145LR	145214	
☐	N827MJ	ERJ-145LR	145217	
☐	N828MJ	ERJ-145LR	145218	
☐	N829MJ	ERJ-145LR	145228	
☐	N830MJ	ERJ-145LR	145259	
☐	N831MJ	ERJ-145LR	145273	
☐	N832MJ	ERJ-145LR	145310	
☐	N833MJ	ERJ-145LR	145327	
☐	N836MJ	ERJ-145LR	145359	
☐	N837MJ	ERJ-145LR	145367	
☐	N838MJ	ERJ-145LR	145384	
☐	N841MJ	ERJ-145LR	145448	
☐	N842MJ	ERJ-145LR	145457	
☐	N844MJ	ERJ-145LR	145481	
☐	N845MJ	ERJ-145LR	145502	
☐	N847MJ	ERJ-145LR	145517	
☐	N848MJ	ERJ-145LR	145530	
☐	N849MJ	ERJ-145LR	145534	
☐	N850MJ	ERJ-145LR	145568	
☐	N851MJ	ERJ-145LR	145572	
☐	N852MJ	ERJ-145LR	145567	
☐	N853MJ	ERJ-145LR	145464	
☐	N854MJ	ERJ-145LR	145490	
☐	N855MJ	ERJ-145LR	145614	
☐	N856MJ	ERJ-145LR	145626	
☐	N857MJ	ERJ-145LR	145765	
☐	N860MJ	ERJ-145LR	145773	
☐	N12569	ERJ-145LR	145630	
☐	N10575	ERJ-145LR	145640	
☐	N14570	ERJ-145LR	145632	
☐	N22909	ERJ-145LR	145459	
☐	N11137	ERJ-145XR	145721	
☐	N11165	ERJ-145XR	14500819	
☐	N11176	ERJ-145XR	14500881	
☐	N11181	ERJ-145XR	14500904	
☐	N11184	ERJ-145XR	14500917	
☐	N11193	ERJ-145XR	14500938	
☐	N12167	ERJ-145XR	14500834	
☐	N14168	ERJ-145XR	14500840	
☐	N14171	ERJ-145XR	14500859	
☐	N14173	ERJ-145XR	14500872	
☐	N14179	ERJ-145XR	14500896	
☐	N16170	ERJ-145XR	14500850	
☐	N16183	ERJ-145XR	14500914	
☐	N33182	ERJ-145XR	14500909	
☐	N201JQ	ERJ-175LR	17000235	
☐	N202JQ	ERJ-175LR	17000240	
☐	N203JQ	ERJ-175LR	17000242	
☐	N204JQ	ERJ-175LR	17000243	
☐	N206JQ	ERJ-175LR	17000249	
☐	N207JQ	ERJ-175LR	17000254	
☐	N208JQ	ERJ-175LR	17000257	
☐	N209JQ	ERJ-175LR	17000258	
☐	N210JQ	ERJ-175LR	17000260	
☐	N211JQ	ERJ-175LR	17000261	
☐	N212JQ	ERJ-175LR	17000264	
☐	N213JQ	ERJ-175LR	17000265	
☐	N214JQ	ERJ-175LR	17000267	
☐	N215JQ	ERJ-175LR	17000270	
☐	N216JQ	ERJ-175LR	17000273	
☐	N602CZ	ERJ-175LR	17000171	
☐	N603CZ	ERJ-175LR	17000176	
☐	N604CZ	ERJ-175LR	17000181	
☐	N605CZ	ERJ-175LR	17000186	
☐	N606CZ	ERJ-175LR	17000188	
☐	N607CZ	ERJ-175LR	17000192	
☐	N608CZ	ERJ-175LR	17000195	
☐	N609CZ	ERJ-175LR	17000197	
☐	N610CZ	ERJ-175LR	17000198	
☐	N612CZ	ERJ-175LR	17000201	
☐	N613CZ	ERJ-175AR	17000203	
☐	N614CZ	ERJ-175AR	17000205	
☐	N615CZ	ERJ-175LR	17000207	
☐	N616CZ	ERJ-175LR	17000209	
☐	N617CZ	ERJ-175LR	17000210	
☐	N619CZ	ERJ-175LR	17000213	
☐	N620CZ	ERJ-175LR	17000214	
☐	N621CZ	ERJ-175LR	17000218	
☐	N622CZ	ERJ-175LR	17000219	
☐	N623CZ	ERJ-175LR	17000221	
☐	N624CZ	ERJ-175LR	17000222	
☐	N625CZ	ERJ-175AR	17000225	
☐	N626CZ	ERJ-175AR	17000226	
☐	N627CZ	ERJ-175AR	17000229	

	Reg	Type	Serial	
☐	N628CZ	ERJ-175AR	17000233	
☐	N629CZ	ERJ-175AR	17000236	
☐	N630CZ	ERJ-175AR	17000238	
☐	N631CZ	ERJ-175AR	17000239	
☐	N632CZ	ERJ-175AR	17000244	
☐	N633CZ	ERJ-175AR	17000245	
☐	N634CZ	ERJ-175AR	17000246	
☐	N635CZ	ERJ-175AR	17000252	
☐	N636CZ	ERJ-175AR	17000253	
☐	N637CZ	ERJ-175AR	17000256	
☐	N638CZ	ERJ-175AR	17000259	
☐	N639CZ	ERJ-175AR	17000262	
☐	N855RW	ERJ-170SE	17000077	
☐	N859RW	ERJ-170SE	17000082	
☐	N860RW	ERJ-170SE	17000084	
☐	N862RW	ERJ-170SE	17000098	
☐	N867RW	ERJ-170SU	17000130	
☐	N868RW	ERJ-170SU	17000131	
☐	N869RW	ERJ-170SE	17000133	
☐	N870RW	ERJ-170SE	17000138	
☐	N958WH	ERJ-175LR	17000248	8205
☐	N365PX	SAAB SF.340B	340B-265	
☐	N408XJ	SAAB SF.340B	340B-408	
☐	N410XJ	SAAB SF.340B	340B-410	
☐	N411XJ	SAAB SF.340B	340B-411	
☐	N412XJ	SAAB SF.340B	340B-412	
☐	N413XJ	SAAB SF.340B	340B-413	
☐	N415XJ	SAAB SF.340B	340B-415	
☐	N416XJ	SAAB SF.340B	340B-416	
☐	N417XJ	SAAB SF.340B	340B-417	
☐	N418XJ	SAAB SF.340B	340B-418	
☐	N420XJ	SAAB SF.340B	340B-420	
☐	N421XJ	SAAB SF.340B	340B-421	
☐	N422XJ	SAAB SF.340B	340B-422	
☐	N423XJ	SAAB SF.340B	340B-423	
☐	N424XJ	SAAB SF.340B	340B-424	
☐	N426XJ	SAAB SF.340B	340B-426	
☐	N427XJ	SAAB SF.340B	340B-427	
☐	N428XJ	SAAB SF.340B	340B-428	
☐	N429XJ	SAAB SF.340B	340B-429	
☐	N430XJ	SAAB SF.340B	340B-430	
☐	N433XJ	SAAB SF.340B	340B-433	
☐	N434XJ	SAAB SF.340B	340B-434	
☐	N435XJ	SAAB SF.340B	340B-435	
☐	N436XJ	SAAB SF.340B	340B-436	
☐	N437XJ	SAAB SF.340B	340B-437	
☐	N438XJ	SAAB SF.340B	340B-438	
☐	N439XJ	SAAB SF.340B	340B-439	
☐	N441XJ	SAAB SF.340B	340B-441	
☐	N442XJ	SAAB SF.340B	340B-442	
☐	N443XJ	SAAB SF.340B	340B-443	
☐	N444XJ	SAAB SF.340B	340B-444	
☐	N445XJ	SAAB SF.340B	340B-445	
☐	N446XJ	SAAB SF.340B	340B-446	
☐	N447XJ	SAAB SF.340B	340B-447	
☐	N448XJ	SAAB SF.340B	340B-448	
☐	N449XJ	SAAB SF.340B	340B-449	
☐	N450XJ	SAAB SF.340B	340B-450	
☐	N451XJ	SAAB SF.340B	340B-451	
☐	N452XJ	SAAB SF.340B	340B-452	
☐	N453XJ	SAAB SF.340B	340B-453	
☐	N454XJ	SAAB SF.340B	340B-454	
☐	N456XJ	SAAB SF.340B	340B-456	
☐	N457XJ	SAAB SF.340B	340B-457	

DYNAMIC AIRWAYS

☐	N880DA	MD-88	49760/1620	♦

EG & G

☐	N273RH	B737-66N	29890/1276	
☐	N288DP	B737-66N	29892/1305	
☐	N319BD	B737-66N	28649/887	
☐	N365SR	B737-66N	29891/1294	

☐	N859WP	B737-66N	28652/938	
☐	N869HH	B737-66N	28650/932	

ERA AVIATION — 7H / ERH

☐	N881EA	DHC-8-106	233	
☐	N882EA	DHC-8-103	98	
☐	N883EA	DHC-8-106	260	
☐	N971EA	Beech 1900D	UE-387	
☐	N972EA	Beech 1900D	UE-389	
☐	N973EA	Beech 1900D	UE-391	

EVERGREEN HELICOPTERS — 7E

☐	N191EV	Beech 1900D	UE-114	
☐	N348CA	CASA C.212-200	CC20-7-175	
☐	N352CA	CASA C.212-200	CC40-1-190	
☐	N422CA	CASA C.212-200	CC40-5-238	
☐	N423CA	CASA C.212-200	S1-1-240	

EVERGREEN INTERNATIONAL AL — EZ / EIA

☐	N470EV	B747-273C	20653/237	947
☐	N471EV	B747-273C	20651/209	
☐	N478EV	B747SR-46 (SCD)	21033/254	[MZJ]
☐	N479EV	B747-132 (SCD)	19898/94	
☐	N480EV	B747-121 (SCD)	20348/106	[MZJ]
☐	N482EV	B747-212B (SCD)	20713/219	
☐	N485EV	B747-212B (SCD)	20712/218	
☐	N486EV	B747-212B (SCD)	20888/240	
☐	N487EV	B747-230B (SCD)	23286/614	
☐	N488EV	B747-230B (SCD)	23287/617	
☐	N489EV	B747-230B(SF)	23393/633	
☐	N490EV	B747-230F	24138/706	
■	N491EV	B747-412F	26561/1042	*13/2* ♦ *23/3.*
☐	N249BA	B747-409LCF	24309/766	
☐	N718BA	B747-4H6LCF	27042/932	
☐	N747BC	B747-4J6LCF	25879/904	
☐	N780BA	B747-409LCF	24310/778	
☐	N915F	DC-9-15RC	47061/207	[MZJ]
☐	N916F	DC-9-15RC	47044/265	[MZJ]
☐	N933F	DC-9-33RC	47191/280	[MZJ]
☐	N941F	DC-9-33F	47193/311	[MZJ]

EVERTS AIR CARGO — 3K / VTS

☐	N151	DC-6B	45496/992	
☐	N251CE	C-118A	44612/532	
☐	N351CE	C-118A	44599/505	
☐	N400UA	DC-6A	44258/467	
☐	N555SQ	DC-6B	45137/830	
☐	N1036F	C-118A	43581/295	[FAI]
☐	N1377K	C-118A	44596/499	[FAI]
☐	N6586C	DC-6BF	45222/849	
☐	N9056R	DC-6A/B	45498/1005	
☐	N99330	C-118A	43576/275	[FAI]
☐	N932AX	DC-9-33RC	47465/584	♦
☐	N1105G	EMB.120FC	120105	
☐	N1110J	EMB.120FC	120110	
☐	N7848B	Curtiss C-46R	273	Dumbo
☐	N12703	EMB.120FC	120084	[FAI]
☐	N54514	Curtiss C-46D	33285	

EVERTS AIR FUEL

☐	N100CE	C-118A	44662/629	♦
☐	N444CE	DC-6B	45478/962	
☐	N451CE	C-118B	43712/358	
☐	N747CE	C-118A	44661/628	
☐	N1822M	Curtiss C-46F Commando	22521	
☐	N1837M	Curtiss C-46F Commando	22388	
☐	N6174C	DC-6A	44075/451	
☐	N7780B	DC-6A	45372/875	

EXPRESSJET AIRLINES — CO / BTA

	Reg	Type	MSN
☐	N11189	ERJ-145XR	14500931
☐	N11192	ERJ-145XR	14500936
☐	N11199	ERJ-145XR	14500953
☐	N12163	ERJ-145XR	14500811
☐	N12175	ERJ-145XR	14500878
☐	N12201	ERJ-145XR	14500959
☐	N14162	ERJ-145XR	14500808
☐	N14174	ERJ-145XR	14500876
☐	N14188	ERJ-145XR	14500929
☐	N14198	ERJ-145XR	14500951
☐	N16178	ERJ-145XR	14500889
☐	N11544	ERJ-145LR	145557
☐	N11551	ERJ-145LR	145411
☐	N14907	ERJ-145LR	145468
☐	N18557	ERJ-145LR	145596
☐	N19554	ERJ-145LR	145587

FEDEX EXPRESS — FX / FDX

	Reg	Type	MSN	
☐	N650FE	A300F4-605R	726	
☐	N651FE	A300F4-605R	728	
☐	N652FE	A300F4-605R	735	
☐	N653FE	A300F4-605R	736	
☐	N654FE	A300F4-605R	738	
☐	N655FE	A300F4-605R	742	
☐	N656FE	A300F4-605R	745	
☐	N657FE	A300F4-605R	748	
☐	N658FE	A300F4-605R	752	
☐	N659FE	A300F4-605R	757	
☐	N660FE	A300F4-605R	759	
☐	N661FE	A300F4-605R	760	
☐	N662FE	A300F4-605R	761	
☐	N663FE	A300F4-605R	766	
☐	N664FE	A300F4-605R	768	
☐	N665FE	A300F4-605R	769	
☐	N667FE	A300F4-605R	771	
☐	N668FE	A300F4-605R	772	
☐	N669FE	A300F4-605R	774	
☐	N670FE	A300F4-605R	777	
☐	N671FE	A300F4-605R	778	
☐	N672FE	A300F4-605R	779	
☐	N673FE	A300F4-605R	780	
☐	N674FE	A300F4-605R	781	
☐	N675FE	A300F4-605R	789	
☐	N676FE	A300F4-605R	790	
☐	N677FE	A300F4-605R	791	
☐	N678FE	A300F4-605R	792	
☐	N679FE	A300F4-605R	793	
☐	N680FE	A300F4-605R	794	
☐	N681FE	A300F4-605R	799	
☐	N682FE	A300F4-605R	800	
☐	N683FE	A300F4-605R	801	
☐	N684FE	A300F4-605R	802	
☐	N685FE	A300F4-605R	803	
☐	N686FE	A300F4-605R	804	
☐	N687FE	A300F4-605R	873	
☐	N688FE	A300F4-605R	874	
☐	N689FE	A300F4-605R	875	
☐	N690FE	A300F4-605R	876	
☐	N691FE	A300F4-605R	877	
☐	N692FE	A300F4-605R	878	
☐	N716FD	A300B4-622F	358	
☐	N717FD	A300B4-622F	361	
☐	N718FD	A300B4-622F	365	
☐	N719FD	A300B4-622F	388	
☐	N720FD	A300B4-622F	417	
☐	N721FD	A300B4-622RF	477	
☐	N722FD	A300B4-622RF	479	
☐	N723FD	A300B4-622RF	543	
☐	N724FD	A300B4-622RF	530	
☐	N725FD	A300B4-622RF	572	
☐	N726FD	A300B4-622RF	575	
☐	N727FD	A300B4-622RF	579	
☐	N728FD	A300B4-622RF	581	
☐	N729FD	A300B4-622RF	657	
☐	N730FD	A300B4-622RF	659	
☐	N731FD	A300B4-605RF	709	
☐	N732FD	A300B4-605RF	713	
☐	N733FD	A300B4-605RF	715	
☐	N740FD	A300B4-622RF	559	
☐	N741FD	A300B4-622RF	611	
☐	N742FD	A300B4-622RF	613	
☐	N743FD	A300B4-622RF	630	
☐	N744FD	A300B4-622RF	664	
☐	N745FD	A300B4-622RF	668	
☐	N746FD	A300B4-622RF	688	
☐	N748FD	A300B4-622RF	633	
☐	N749FD	A300B4-622RF	536	
☐	N750FD	A300B4-622RF	555	
☐	N751FD	A300B4-622RF	625	
☐	N401FE	A310-203F	191	[VCV]
☐	N402FE	A310-203F	201	
☐	N403FE	A310-203F	230	
☐	N404FE	A310-203F	233	
☐	N405FE	A310-203F	237	
☐	N407FE	A310-203F	254	[VCV]
☐	N408FE	A310-203F	257	[VCV]
☐	N409FE	A310-203F	273	[VCV]
☐	N410FE	A310-203F	356	♦
☐	N411FE	A310-203F	359	[VCV]
☐	N412FE	A310-203F	360	[VCV]
☐	N414FE	A310-203F	400	[VCV]
☐	N416FE	A310-222F	288	[VCV]
☐	N417FE	A310-222F	333	
☐	N418FE	A310-222F	343	
☐	N419FE	A310-222F	345	[VCV]
☐	N421FE	A310-203F	342	
☐	N423FE	A310-203F	281	
☐	N425FE	A310-203F	264	
☐	N426FE	A310-203F	245	
☐	N427FE	A310-203F	362	
☐	N428FE	A310-203F	248	
☐	N429FE	A310-203F	364	
☐	N430FE	A310-203F	394	
☐	N431FE	A310-203F	316	
☐	N435FE	A310-203F	369	
☐	N436FE	A310-203F	454	
☐	N443FE	A310-203F	283	
☐	N445FE	A310-203F	297	
☐	N446FE	A310-222F	224	[VCV]♦
☐	N447FE	A310-222F	251	
☐	N448FE	A310-222F	260	
☐	N450FE	A310-222F	162	
☐	N451FE	A310-222F	303	
☐	N453FE	A310-222F	267	
☐	N454FE	A310-222F	278	
☐	N455FE	A310-222F	331	
☐	N456FE	A310-222F	318	
☐	N801FD	A310-324F	539	
☐	N802FD	A310-324F	542	
☐	N803FD	A310-324F	378	
☐	N804FD	A310-324F	549	
☐	N805FD	A310-324F	456	
☐	N806FD	A310-324F	458	
☐	N807FD	A310-324F	492	
☐	N808FD	A310-324F	439	
☐	N809FD	A310-324F	449	
☐	N810FD	A310-324F	452	
☐	N811FD	A310-324F	457	
☐	N812FD	A310-324F	467	
☐	N813FD	A310-324F	500	
☐	N814FD	A310-324F	534	
☐	N815FD	A310-324F	638	
☐	N816FD	A310-304F	593	
☐	N817FD	A310-304F	552	
☐	N68096	A310-324	589	[VCV]

	Reg	Type	c/n	Notes
☐	N900FX	ATR 42-320F	170	
☐	N901FX	ATR 42-320F	172	
☐	N902FX	ATR 42-320F	175	
☐	N903FX	ATR 42-320F	179	
☐	N906FX	ATR 42-320F	280	
☐	N907FX	ATR 42-320F	286	
☐	N908FX	ATR 42-300F	023	
☐	N909FX	ATR 42-300F	275	
☐	N910FX	ATR 42-300F	277	
☐	N911FX	ATR 42-300F	045	
☐	N912FX	ATR 42-300F	047	
☐	N913FX	ATR 42-320F	250	
☐	N914FX	ATR 42-300F	293	
☐	N915FX	ATR 42-300F	269	
☐	N916FX	ATR 42-300F	314	
☐	N917FX	ATR 42-320F	354	
☐	N918FX	ATR 42-300F	262	
☐	N919FX	ATR 42-320F	266	
☐	N920FX	ATR 42-320F	325	
☐	N921FX	ATR 42-300F	319	
☐	EI-FXG	ATR 72-202F	224	
☐	EI-FXH	ATR 72-202F	229	
☐	EI-FXI	ATR 72-202F	294	
☐	EI-FXJ	ATR 72-202F	292	
☐	EI-FXK	ATR 72-202F	256	
☐	N800FX	ATR 72-212	336	♦
☐	N801FX	ATR 72-212	338	♦
☐	N802FX	ATR 72-212	344	♦
☐	N803FX	ATR 72-212	362	♦
☐	N804FX	ATR 72-212	370	♦
☐	N805FX	ATR 72-212	372	♦
☐	N806FX	ATR 72-212	375	♦
☐	N807FX	ATR 72-212	383	♦
☐	N809FX	ATR 72-202F	217	
☐	N810FX	ATR 72-202F	220	
☐	N811FX	ATR 72-202F	283	
☐	N812FX	ATR 72-212F	404	
☐	N816FX	ATR 72-212F	347	
☐	N819FX	ATR 72-212F	359	
☐	N820FX	ATR 72-212F	248	
☐	N821FX	ATR 72-212F	253	
☐	N203FE	B727-2S2F	22925/1819	
☐	N204FE	B727-2S2F	22926/1820	
☐	N207FE	B727-2S2F	22929/1823	
☐	N211FE	B727-2S2F	22933/1827	
☐	N213FE	B727-2S2F	22935/1829	
☐	N215FE	B727-2S2F	22936/1830	
☐	N216FE	B727-2S2F	22937/1831	
☐	N217FE	B727-2S2F	22938/1832	
☐	N218FE	B727-233F	21101/1150	[VCV]♦
☐	N220FE	B727-233F	20934/1074	
☐	N221FE	B727-233F	20932/1069	
☐	N222FE	B727-233F	20933/1071	[VCV]
☐	N223FE	B727-233F	20935/1076	
☐	N233FE	B727-247F	21327/1249	♦
☐	N235FE	B727-247F	21329/1254	♦
☐	N236FE	B727-247F	21330/1260	♦
☐	N237FE	B727-247F	21331/1266	
☐	N240FE	B727-277F	20978/1083	
☐	N241FE	B727-277F	20979/1098	
☐	N243FE	B727-277F	21480/1352	[VCV]
☐	N244FE	B727-277F	21647/1436	
☐	N245FE	B727-277F	22016/1566	
☐	N254FE	B727-233F	20936/1078	[VCV]♦
☐	N257FE	B727-233F	20939/1112	
☐	N258FE	B727-233F	20940/1120	
☐	N262FE	B727-233F	21624/1468	
☐	N263FE	B727-233F	21625/1470	
☐	N264FE	B727-233F	21626/1472	
☐	N265FE	B727-233F	21671/1523	
☐	N266FE	B727-233F	21672/1538	
☐	N267FE	B727-233F	21673/1541	
☐	N268FE	B727-233F	21674/1543	
☐	N269FE	B727-233F	21675/1555	
☐	N271FE	B727-233F	22036/1596	[VCV]♦
☐	N273FE	B727-233F	22038/1612	
☐	N274FE	B727-233F	22039/1614	
☐	N275FE	B727-233F	22040/1626	
☐	N276FE	B727-233F	22041/1628	
☐	N277FE	B727-233F	22042/1630	
☐	N278FE	B727-233F	22345/1699	
☐	N279FE	B727-233F	22346/1704	
☐	N280FE	B727-223F	22347/1708	
☐	N281FE	B727-233F	22348/1714	
☐	N282FE	B727-233F	22349/1722	
☐	N283FE	B727-233F	22350/1745	
☐	N284FE	B727-233F	22621/1791	
☐	N285FE	B727-233F	22622/1792	
☐	N286FE	B727-233F	22623/1803	
☐	N287FE	B727-2D4F	21849/1527	
☐	N288FE	B727-2D4F	21850/1536	
☐	N462FE	B727-225F	22550/1739	
☐	N463FE	B727-225F	22551/1744	
☐	N464FE	B727-225F	21288/1234	
☐	N465FE	B727-225F	21289/1235	
☐	N466FE	B727-225F	21292/1240	
☐	N467FE	B727-225F	21449/1306	
☐	N468FE	B727-225F	21452/1312	
☐	N469FE	B727-225F	21581/1437	
☐	N479FE	B727-227F	21461/1337	
☐	N480FE	B727-227F	21462/1342	[VCV]
☐	N481FE	B727-227F	21463/1353	
☐	N482FE	B727-227F	21464/1355	
☐	N483FE	B727-227F	21465/1363	
☐	N484FE	B727-227F	21466/1372	
☐	N485FE	B727-227F	21488/1388	
☐	N486FE	B727-227F	21489/1390	
☐	N487FE	B727-227F	21490/1396	
☐	N488FE	B727-227F	21491/1402	
☐	N489FE	B727-227F	21492/1440	
☐	N490FE	B727-227F	21493/1442	
☐	N491FE	B727-227F	21529/1444	
☐	N492FE	B727-227F	21530/1446	
☐	N493FE	B727-227F	21531/1450	
☐	N494FE	B727-227F	21532/1453	
☐	N495FE	B727-227F	21669/1484	
☐	N498FE	B727-232F	20867/1068	
☐	N499FE	B727-232F	21018/1095	
☐	N226CL	B757-225	22612/114	[VCV]
☐	N240MQ	B757-2Y0	25240/388	[VCV]
☐	N901FD	B757-2B7F	27122/525	
☐	N903FD	B757-2B7SF	27124/540	
☐	N905FD	B757-2B7	27145/546	[VCV]
☐	N906FD	B757-2B7SF	27148/564	
☐	N910FD	B757-236SF	25054/362	
☐	N912FD	B757-28ASF	24260/204	
☐	N913FD	B757-28ASF	24017/162	
☐	N914FD	B757-28A	24367/208	[VCV]
☐	N915FD	B757-236SF	24120/174	
☐	N916FD	B757-27BSF	24137/178	
☐	N917FD	B757-23A	24291/215	
☐	N918FD	B757-23AER	24290/212	
☐	N919FD	B757-23ASF	24636/259	
☐	N920FD	B757-23AER	24289/209	
☐	N921FD	B757-23AF	24924/333	[VCV]
☐	N922FD	B757-23A	24293/220	[VCV]
☐	N923FD	B757-204F	26266/514	
☐	N924FD	B757-204	26267/538	[VCV]
☐	N925FD	B757-204	27238/604	[VCV]
☐	N928FD	B757-28A	24369/226	[VCV]♦
☐	N933FD	B757-21BSF	24330/200	
☐	N934FD	B757-21B	24331/203	
☐	N935FD	B757-2T7ER	22780/15	[VCV]
☐	N936FD	B757-2T7ER	23293/56	[VCV]
☐	N937FD	B757-2T7	23895/132	[VCV]♦
☐	N939FD	B757-23A	24528/250	♦
☐	N941FD	B757-225	22691/155	[VCV]
☐	N946FD	B757-236	24398/224	[VCV]♦
☐	N947FD	B757-236ER	24882/323	[VCV]♦

Reg	Type	Serial	Notes
☐ N948FD	B757-236ER	25059/363	[VCV]♦
☐ N949FD	B757-236ER	25060/364	[VCV]♦
☐ N950FD	B757-236	25806/601	[VCV]♦
☐ N954FD	B757-236	29113/784	o/o♦
☐ N955FD	B757-236	29114/793	o/o♦
☐ N957FD	B757-21B	24774/288	[VCV]♦
☐ N960FD	B757-236	25593/466	[VCV]♦
☐ N993FD	B757-2Q8	24965/438	[VCV]
☐ N994FD	B757-23A	25490/510	[VCV]
☐ N850FD	B777-FS2	37721/813	
☐ N851FD	B777-FS2	37722/834	♦
☐ N852FD	B777-FS2	37723/848	♦
☐ N853FD	B777-FS2	37724/829	
☐ N854FD	B777-FS2	37725/890	♦
☐ N855FD	B777-FS2	37726/892	♦
☐ N856FD	B777-FS2	37727/884	♦
☐ N857FD	B777-FS2	37728/886	♦
☐ N880FD	B777-F28	32967/718	♦
☐ N882FD	B777-F28	32969/827	♦
☐ N883FD	B777-FHT	39285/897	♦
☐ N884FD	B777-FHT	37137/917	o/o♦
☐ N	B777-FS2		o/o♦
☐ N	B777-FS2		o/o♦
☐ N	B777-FS2		o/o♦
☐ C-FEXB	C208B Caravan	208B0539	
☐ C-FEXF	C208B Caravan	208B0508	
☐ C-FEXV	C208B Caravan	208B0482	
☐ C-FEXY	C208B Caravan	208B0226	
☐ N700FX	C208B Caravan	208B0419	
☐ N701FX	C208B Caravan	208B0420	
☐ N702FX	C208B Caravan	208B0422	
☐ N703FX	C208B Caravan	208B0423	
☐ N705FX	C208B Caravan	208B0425	
☐ N706FX	C208B Caravan	208B0426	
☐ N707FX	C208B Caravan	208B0427	
☐ N709FX	C208B Caravan	208B0430	
☐ N710FX	C208B Caravan	208B0431	
☐ N711FX	C208B Caravan	208B0433	
☐ N712FX	C208B Caravan	208B0435	
☐ N713FX	C208B Caravan	208B0438	
☐ N715FX	C208B Caravan	208B0440	
☐ N716FX	C208B Caravan	208B0442	
☐ N717FX	C208B Caravan	208B0445	
☐ N718FX	C208B Caravan	208B0448	
☐ N719FX	C208B Caravan	208B0450	
☐ N720FX	C208B Caravan	208B0452	
☐ N721FX	C208B Caravan	208B0453	
☐ N722FX	C208B Caravan	208B0454	
☐ N723FX	C208B Caravan	208B0456	
☐ N724FX	C208B Caravan	208B0458	
☐ N725FX	C208B Caravan	208B0460	
☐ N726FX	C208B Caravan	208B0465	
☐ N727FX	C208B Caravan	208B0468	
☐ N728FX	C208B Caravan	208B0471	
☐ N729FX	C208B Caravan	208B0474	
☐ N730FX	C208B Caravan	208B0477	
☐ N731FX	C208B Caravan	208B0480	
☐ N740FX	C208B Caravan	208B0484	
☐ N741FX	C208B Caravan	208B0486	
☐ N742FX	C208B Caravan	208B0489	
☐ N744FX	C208B Caravan	208B0492	
☐ N745FX	C208B Caravan	208B0495	
☐ N746FX	C208B Caravan	208B0498	
☐ N747FE	C208B Caravan	208B0238	
☐ N747FX	C208B Caravan	208B0501	
☐ N748FE	C208B Caravan	208B0241	
☐ N748FX	C208B Caravan	208B0503	
☐ N749FE	C208B Caravan	208B0242	
☐ N750FX	C208B Caravan	208B0511	
☐ N751FE	C208B Caravan	208B0245	
☐ N751FX	C208B Caravan	208B0514	
☐ N752FE	C208B Caravan	208B0247	
☐ N752FX	C208B Caravan	208B0517	
☐ N753FX	C208B Caravan	208B0520	
☐ N754FX	C208B Caravan	208B0526	
☐ N755FE	C208B Caravan	208B0250	
☐ N755FX	C208B Caravan	208B0529	
☐ N756FE	C208B Caravan	208B0251	
☐ N756FX	C208B Caravan	208B0532	
☐ N757FX	C208B Caravan	208B0535	
☐ N760FE	C208B Caravan	208B0252	
☐ N761FE	C208B Caravan	208B0254	
☐ N762FE	C208B Caravan	208B0255	
☐ N763FE	C208B Caravan	208B0256	
☐ N764FE	C208B Caravan	208B0258	
☐ N765FE	C208B Caravan	208B0259	
☐ N766FE	C208B Caravan	208B0260	
☐ N767FE	C208B Caravan	208B0262	
☐ N768FE	C208B Caravan	208B0263	
☐ N769FE	C208B Caravan	208B0264	
☐ N770FE	C208B Caravan	208B0265	
☐ N771FE	C208B Caravan	208B0267	
☐ N772FE	C208B Caravan	208B0268	
☐ N773FE	C208B Caravan	208B0269	
☐ N774FE	C208B Caravan	208B0271	
☐ N775FE	C208B Caravan	208B0272	
☐ N776FE	C208B Caravan	208B0273	
☐ N778FE	C208B Caravan	208B0275	
☐ N779FE	C208B Caravan	208B0276	
☐ N780FE	C208B Caravan	208B0277	
☐ N781FE	C208B Caravan	208B0278	
☐ N782FE	C208B Caravan	208B0280	
☐ N783FE	C208B Caravan	208B0281	
☐ N784FE	C208B Caravan	208B0282	
☐ N785FE	C208B Caravan	208B0283	
☐ N786FE	C208B Caravan	208B0284	
☐ N787FE	C208B Caravan	208B0285	
☐ N788FE	C208B Caravan	208B0286	
☐ N789FE	C208B Caravan	208B0287	
☐ N790FE	C208B Caravan	208B0288	
☐ N792FE	C208B Caravan	208B0290	
☐ N793FE	C208B Caravan	208B0291	
☐ N794FE	C208B Caravan	208B0292	
☐ N795FE	C208B Caravan	208B0293	
☐ N796FE	C208B Caravan	2C8B0212	
☐ N797FE	C208B Caravan	208B0042	
☐ N798FE	C208B Caravan	208B0174	
☐ N799FE	C208B Caravan	20800065	
☐ N800FE	C208A Caravan	20800007	
☐ N801FE	C208A Caravan	20800009	
☐ N804FE	C208B Caravan	208B0039	
☐ N807FE	C208B Caravan	208B0041	
☐ N812FE	C208A Caravan	20800040	
☐ N819FE	C208A Caravan	20800056	
☐ N820FE	C208B Caravan	208B0111	
☐ N827FE	C208A Caravan	20800072	
☐ N828FE	C208B Caravan	208B0122	
☐ N830FE	C208A Caravan	20800075	
☐ N831FE	C208B Caravan	208B0225	
☐ N832FE	C208A Caravan	20800081	
☐ N833FE	C208A Caravan	20800084	
☐ N835FE	C208A Caravan	20800016	
☐ N841FE	C208B Caravan	208B0144	
☐ N842FE	C208B Caravan	208B0146	
☐ N843FE	C208B Caravan	208B0147	
☐ N844FE	C208B Caravan	208B0149	
☐ N845FE	C208B Caravan	208B0152	
☐ N846FE	C208B Caravan	208B0154	
☐ N847FE	C208B Caravan	208B0156	
☐ N848FE	C208B Caravan	208B0158	
☐ N849FE	C208B Caravan	208B0162	
☐ N850FE	C208B Caravan	208B0164	
☐ N851FE	C208B Caravan	208B0166	
☐ N852FE	C208B Caravan	208B0168	
☐ N853FE	C208B Caravan	208B0170	
☐ N855FE	C208B Caravan	208B0203	
☐ N856FE	C208B Caravan	208B0176	
☐ N857FE	C208B Caravan	208B0177	
☐ N858FE	C208B Caravan	208B0178	

☐ N859FE	C208B Caravan	208B0181		☐ N940FE	C208B Caravan	208B0040	
☐ N860FE	C208B Caravan	208B0182		☐ N943FE	C208B Caravan	208B0043	
☐ N861FE	C208B Caravan	208B0183		☐ N946FE	C208B Caravan	208B0048	
☐ N862FE	C208B Caravan	208B0184		☐ N947FE	C208B Caravan	208B0050	
☐ N863FE	C208B Caravan	208B0186		☐ N950FE	C208B Caravan	208B0056	
☐ N864FE	C208B Caravan	208B0187		☐ N952FE	C208B Caravan	208B0060	
☐ N865FE	C208B Caravan	208B0188		☐ N953FE	C208B Caravan	208B0062	
☐ N866FE	C208B Caravan	208B0189		☐ N954FE	C208B Caravan	208B0064	
☐ N867FE	C208B Caravan	208B0191		☐ N955FE	C208B Caravan	208B0066	
☐ N869FE	C208B Caravan	208B0195		☐ N956FE	C208B Caravan	208B0068	
☐ N870FE	C208B Caravan	208B0196		☐ N957FE	C208B Caravan	208B0070	
☐ N871FE	C208B Caravan	208B0198		☐ N958FE	C208B Caravan	208B0071	
☐ N872FE	C208B Caravan	208B0200		☐ N959FE	C208B Caravan	208B0073	
☐ N873FE	C208B Caravan	208B0202		☐ N960FE	C208B Caravan	208B0075	
☐ N874FE	C208B Caravan	208B0205		☐ N961FE	C208B Caravan	208B0077	
☐ N875FE	C208B Caravan	208B0206		☐ N962FE	C208B Caravan	208B0078	
☐ N876FE	C208B Caravan	208B0207		☐ N963FE	C208B Caravan	208B0080	
☐ N877FE	C208B Caravan	208B0232		☐ N964FE	C208B Caravan	208B0083	
☐ N878FE	C208B Caravan	208B0211		☐ N965FE	C208B Caravan	208B0084	
☐ N879FE	C208B Caravan	208B0213		☐ N966FE	C208B Caravan	208B0086	
☐ N880FE	C208B Caravan	208B0215		☐ N967FE	C208B Caravan	208B0088	
☐ N881FE	C208B Caravan	208B0204		☐ N968FE	C208B Caravan	208B0090	
☐ N882FE	C208B Caravan	208B0208		☐ N969FE	C208B Caravan	208B0092	
☐ N883FE	C208B Caravan	208B0210		☐ N970FE	C208B Caravan	208B0093	
☐ N884FE	C208B Caravan	208B0233		☐ N971FE	C208B Caravan	208B0094	
☐ N885FE	C208B Caravan	208B0185		☐ N972FE	C208B Caravan	208B0096	
☐ N886FE	C208B Caravan	208B0190		☐ N973FE	C208B Caravan	208B0098	
☐ N887FE	C208B Caravan	208B0216		☐ N975FE	C208B Caravan	208B0101	
☐ N888FE	C208B Caravan	208B0217		☐ N976FE	C208B Caravan	208B0103	
☐ N889FE	C208B Caravan	208B0218		☐ N977FE	C208B Caravan	208B0104	
☐ N890FE	C208B Caravan	208B0219		☐ N979FE	C208B Caravan	208B0106	
☐ N891FE	C208B Caravan	208B0221		☐ N980FE	C208B Caravan	208B0108	
☐ N892FE	C208B Caravan	208B0222		☐ N981FE	C208B Caravan	208B0110	
☐ N894FE	C208B Caravan	208B0224		☐ N983FE	C208B Caravan	208B0113	
☐ N895FE	C208B Caravan	208B0015		☐ N984FE	C208B Caravan	208B0115	
☐ N897FE	C208B Caravan	208B0227		☐ N985FE	C208B Caravan	208B0117	
☐ N898FE	C208B Caravan	208B0228		☐ N986FE	C208B Caravan	208B0194	
☐ N899FE	C208B Caravan	208B0235		☐ N987FE	C208B Caravan	208B0201	
☐ N900FE	C208B Caravan	208B0054		☐ N989FE	C208B Caravan	208B0124	
☐ N901FE	C208B Caravan	208B0001		☐ N990FE	C208B Caravan	208B0125	
☐ N902FE	C208B Caravan	208B0002		☐ N991FE	C208B Caravan	208B0127	
☐ N903FE	C208B Caravan	208B0003		☐ N992FE	C208B Caravan	208B0128	
☐ N904FE	C208B Caravan	208B0004		☐ N993FE	C208B Caravan	208B0130	
☐ N905FE	C208B Caravan	208B0005		☐ N994FE	C208B Caravan	208B0132	
☐ N906FE	C208B Caravan	208B0006		☐ N995FE	C208B Caravan	208B0133	
☐ N907FE	C208D Caravan	208B0007		☐ N996FE	C208B Caravan	208B0135	
☐ N908FE	C208B Caravan	208B0008		☐ N997FE	C208B Caravan	208B0197	
☐ N909FE	C208B Caravan	208B0009		☐ N998FF	C208B Caravan	208B0139	
☐ N910FE	C208B Caravan	208B0010		☐ N999FE	C208B Caravan	208B0231	
☐ N911FE	C208B Caravan	208B0011					
☐ N912FE	C208B Caravan	208B0012		☐ N301FE	MD-10-30CF	46800/96	
☐ N914FE	C208B Caravan	208B0014		☐ N302FE	MD-10-30CF	46801/103	
☐ N916FE	C208B Caravan	208B0016		☐ N303FE	MD-10-30CF	46802/110	
☐ N917FE	C208B Caravan	208B0017		☐ N304FE	MD-10-30CF	46992/257	
☐ N918FE	C208B Caravan	208B0018		☐ N306FE	MD-10-30F	48287/409	
☐ N919FE	C208B Caravan	208B0019		☐ N307FE	MD-10-30F	48291/412	
☐ N920FE	C208B Caravan	208B0020		☐ N308FE	MD-10-30F	48297/416	
☐ N921FE	C208B Caravan	208B0021		☐ N311FE	MD-10-30CF	46871/219	
☐ N922FE	C208B Caravan	208B0022		☐ N312FE	MD-10-30CF	48300/433	
☐ N923FE	C208B Caravan	208B0023		☐ N313FE	MD-10-30F	48311/440	
☐ N924FE	C208B Caravan	208B0024		☐ N314FE	MD-10-30F	48312/442	
☐ N925FE	C208B Caravan	208B0025		☐ N315FE	MD-10-30F	48313/443	[VCE]
☐ N926FE	C208B Caravan	208B0026		☐ N316FE	MD-10-30F	48314/444	
☐ N927FE	C208B Caravan	208B0027		☐ N317FE	MD-10-30CF	46835/277	
☐ N928FE	C208B Caravan	208B0028		☐ N318FE	MD-10-30CF	46837/282	
☐ N929FE	C208B Caravan	208B0029		☐ N319FE	MD-10-30CF	47820/317	
☐ N930FE	C208B Caravan	208B0030		☐ N320FE	MD-10-30F	47835/326	[VCV]
☐ N931FE	C208B Caravan	208B0031		☐ N321FE	MD-10-30F	47836/330	
☐ N933FE	C208B Caravan	208B0033		☐ N357FE	MD-10-10F	46939/203	
☐ N934FE	C208B Caravan	208B0034		☐ N358FE	MD-10-10F	46633/297	
☐ N935FE	C208B Caravan	208B0035		☐ N359FE	MD-10-10F	46635/307	
☐ N936FE	C208B Caravan	208B0036		☐ N360FE	MD-10-10F	46636/309	
☐ N937FE	C208B Caravan	208B0037		☐ N361FE	MD-10-10F	48260/344	
☐ N938FE	C208B Caravan	208B0038		☐ N362FE	MD-10-10F	48261/347	
☐ N939FE	C208B Caravan	208B0180		☐ N363FE	MD-10-10F	48263/353	
				☐ N365FE	MD-10-10F	46601/6	♦

☐	N366FE	MD-10-10F	46602/8	
☐	N367FE	MD-10-10F	46605/15	
☐	N368FE	MD-10-10F	46606/17	
☐	N369FE	MD-10-10F	46607/25	
☐	N370FE	MD-10-10F	46608/26	♦
☐	N371FE	MD-10-10F	46609/27	
☐	N372FE	MD-10-10F	46610/32	
☐	N373FE	MD-10-10F	46611/35	
☐	N374FE	MD-10-10F	46612/39	[VCV]
☐	N375FE	MD-10-10F	46613/42	
☐	N377FE	MD-10-10F	47965/59	[VCV]
☐	N381FE	MD-10-10F	46615/76	♦
☐	N383FE	MD-10-10F	46616/86	
☐	N384FE	MD-10-10F	46617/89	
☐	N385FE	MD-10-10F	46619/119	
☐	N386FE	MD-10-10F	46620/138	
☐	N387FE	MD-10-10F	46621/140	
☐	N388FE	MD-10-10F	46622/144	
☐	N389FE	MD-10-10F	46623/154	
☐	N390FE	MD-10-10F	46624/155	
☐	N392FE	MD-10-10F	46626/198	
☐	N394FE	MD-10-10F	46628/207	
☐	N395FE	MD-10-10F	46629/208	
☐	N396FE	MD-10-10F	46630/209	
☐	N397FE	MD-10-10F	46631/210	
☐	N398FE	MD-10-10F	46634/298	
☐	N399FE	MD-10-10F	48262/351	
☐	N550FE	MD-10-10F	46521/55	
☐	N554FE	MD-10-10F	46708/62	
☐	N556FE	MD-10-10F	46710/70	
☐	N559FE	MD-10-10F	46930/112	
☐	N560FE	MD-10-10F	46938/153	
☐	N562FE	MD-10-10F	46947/247	
☐	N563FE	MD-10-10F	46948/249	
☐	N564FE	MD-10-10F	46984/250	
☐	N566FE	MD-10-10F	46989/271	
☐	N567FE	MD-10-10F	46994/273	[VCV]♦
☐	N569FE	MD-10-10F	47828/319	
☐	N570FE	MD-10-10F	47829/321	
☐	N571FE	MD-10-10F	47830/323	
☐	N10060	MD-10-10F	46970/269	
☐	N40061	MD-10-10F	46973/272	
☐	N68049	MD-10-10CF	47803/139	
☐	N68050	MD-10-10CF	47804/142	
☐	N68051	MD-10-10CF	47805/145	
☐	N68052	MD-10-10CF	47806/148	
☐	N68053	MD-10-10CF	47807/173	
☐	N68054	MD-10-10CF	47808/177	
☐	N68057	MD-10-10CF	48264/379	
☐	N68059	MD-10-10F	46907/78	

☐	N521FE	MD-11F	48478/514
☐	N522FE	MD-11F	48476/510
☐	N523FE	MD-11F	48479/536
☐	N524FE	MD-11F	48480/538
☐	N525FE	MD-11F	48565/542
☐	N526FE	MD-11F	48600/560
☐	N527FE	MD-11F	48601/562
☐	N528FE	MD-11F	48623/605
☐	N529FE	MD-11F	48624/622
☐	N572FE	MD-11BBCF	48755/613
☐	N573FE	MD-11ER	48769/603
☐	N574FE	MD-11F	48499/486
☐	N575FE	MD-11F	48500/493
☐	N576FE	MD-11F	48501/513
☐	N577FE	MD-11F	48469/519
☐	N578FE	MD-11F	48458/449
☐	N579FE	MD-11F	48470/546
☐	N580FE	MD-11F	48471/558
☐	N582FE	MD-11F	48420/451
☐	N583FE	MD-11F	48421/452
☐	N584FE	MD-11F	48436/483
☐	N585FE	MD-11F	48481/482
☐	N586FE	MD-11F	48487/469
☐	N587FE	MD-11F	48489/492
☐	N588FE	MD-11F	48490/499

☐	N589FE	MD-11F	48491/503	
☐	N590FE	MD-11F	48505/462	
☐	N591FE	MD-11F	48527/504	
☐	N592FE	MD-11F	48550/526	
☐	N593FE	MD-11F	48551/527	
☐	N594FE	MD-11F	48552/530	
☐	N595FE	MD-11F	48553/531	
☐	N596FE	MD-11F	48554/535	
☐	N597FE	MD-11F	48596/537	
☐	N598FE	MD-11F	48597/540	
☐	N599FE	MD-11F	48598/550	
☐	N601FE	MD-11F	48401/447	
☐	N602FE	MD-11F	48402/448	
☐	N603FE	MD-11F	48459/470	
☐	N604FE	MD-11F	48460/497	
☐	N605FE	MD-11F	48514/515	
☐	N606FE	MD-11F	48602/549	
☐	N607FE	MD-11F	48547/517	
☐	N608FE	MD-11F	48548/521	
☐	N609FE	MD-11F	48549/545	
☐	N610FE	MD-11F	48603/551	
☐	N612FE	MD-11F	48605/555	
☐	N613FE	MD-11F	48749/598	
☐	N614FE	MD-11F	48528/507	
☐	N615FE	MD-11F	48767/602	
☐	N616FE	MD-11F	48747/594	
☐	N617FE	MD-11F	48748/595	
☐	N618FE	MD-11F	48754/604	
☐	N619FE	MD-11F	48770/607	
☐	N620FE	MD-11F	48791/635	
☐	N621FE	MD-11F	48792/636	
☐	N623FE	MD-11F	48794/638	
☐	N624FE	MD-11F	48443/458	
☐	N625FE	MD-11BCF	48753/608	♦
☐	N628FE	MD-11F	48447/464	
☐	N631FE	MD-11F	48454/477	

FLIGHT INTERNATIONAL AVIATION   FNT

☐	N175SW	SA.227AC Metro III	AC-621B
☐	N766C	SA.227AC Metro III	AC-559
☐	N781C	SA.227AC Metro III	AC-535
☐	N782C	SA.227AC Metro III	AC-525
☐	N26974	SA.227AC Metro III	AC-664

FLORIDA AIR CARGO

☐	N15MA	DC-3	19286

FLORIDA AIR TRANSPORT

☐	N70BF	C-118B	43720/373
☐	N381AA	DC-7BF	44921/666
☐	N406WA	C-54G	35944

FLORIDA WEST INTERNATIONAL AL   FWL

☐	N316LA	B767-316F	30842/860	
☐	N422LA	B767-346F	35818/960	♦
☐	N526LA	B767-346F	35817/959	♦

FOUR STAR AIR CARGO   HK / FSC

☐	N131FS	DC-3	16172/32920
☐	N132FS	DC-3	14333/25778
☐	N133FS	DC-3	15757/27202
☐	N135FS	DC-3	20063
☐	N138FS	DC-3	9967

FREEDOM AIR   FP / FRE

☐	N74NF	Short SD.3-60	SH3721
☐	N330FA	Short SD.3-30	SH3112
☐	N2843F	Short SD.3-60	SH3739

FRONTIER AIRLINES — F9 / FFT

	Reg	Type	c/n	
☐	N801FR	A318-111	1939	
☐	N802FR	A318-111	1991	
☐	N803FR	A318-111	2017	
☐	N804FR	A318-111	2051	
☐	N805FR	A318-111	1660	
☐	N806FR	A318-111	2218	
☐	N807FR	A318-111	2276	
☐	N902FR	A319-111	1515	
☐	N904FR	A319-111	1579	
☐	N905FR	A319-111	1583	
☐	N906FR	A319-111	1684	
☐	N908FR	A319-111	1759	
☐	N910FR	A319-112	1781	
☐	N912FR	A319-111	1803	
☐	N914FR	A319-111	1841	
☐	N918FR	A319-111	1943	
☐	N919FR	A319-111	1980	
☐	N920FR	A319-111	1997	
☐	N921FR	A319-111	2010	
☐	N922FR	A319-111	2012	
☐	N923FR	A319-111	2019	
☐	N924FR	A319-111	2030	
☐	N925FR	A319-111	2103	
☐	N926FR	A319-111	2198	
☐	N927FR	A319-111	2209	
☐	N928FR	A319-111	2236	
☐	N929FR	A319-111	2240	
☐	N930FR	A319-111	2241	
☐	N931FR	A319-111	2253	
☐	N932FR	A319-111	2258	
☐	N933FR	A319-111	2260	
☐	N934FR	A319-111	2287	
☐	N935FR	A319-111	2318	
☐	N936FR	A319-111	2392	
☐	N937FR	A319-111	2400	
☐	N938FR	A319-111	2406	
☐	N939FR	A319-111	2448	
☐	N940FR	A319-111	2465	
☐	N941FR	A319-112	2483	
☐	N942FR	A319-111	2497	
☐	N943FR	A319-112	2518	
☐	N945FR	A319-112	2751	
☐	N947FR	A319-111	2806	
☐	N948FR	A319-112	2836	
☐	N949FR	A319-112	2857	
☐	N951FR	A319-112	4127	♦
☐	N952FR	A319-112	4204	♦
☐	N953FR	A319-112	4254	♦
☐	N201FR	A320-214	3389	
☐	N202FR	A320-214	3431	
☐	N203FR	A320-214	1806	
☐	N204FR	A320-214	2325	
☐	N205FR	A320-214	4253	♦
☐	N206FR	A320-214	4272	♦
☐	N207FR	A320-214	4307	♦
☐	N208FR	A320-214	4562	♦
☐		A320-214		o/o♦
☐		A320-214		o/o♦
☐		A320-214		o/o♦
☐		A320-214		o/o♦
☐		A320-214		o/o♦
☐		A320-214		o/o♦
☐		A320-214		o/o♦
☐		A320-214		o/o♦
☐	N502LX	DHC-8-402Q	4168	
☐	N506LX	DHC-8-402Q	4176	
☐	N510LX	DHC-8-402Q	4186	
☐	N511LX	DHC-8-402Q	4265	

FRONTIER FLYING SERVICE — 2F / FTA

	Reg	Type	c/n
☐	N575A	Beech 1900C-1	UC-83
☐	N575F	Beech 1900C-1	UC-99
☐	N575G	Beech 1900C-1	UC-155
☐	N575P	Beech 1900C-1	UC-95
☐	N575Q	Beech 1900C-1	UC-160
☐	N575X	Beech 1900C-1	UC-149
☐	N575Z	Beech 1900C-1	UC-136
☐	N1553C	Beech 1900C-1	UC-24

GB AIRLINK — GBX

	Reg	Type	c/n
☐	N80GB	Short SC.7 Skyvan 3	SH1888

GO!

	Reg	Type	c/n
☐	N591ML	CRJ-200LR	7388
☐	N27318	CRJ-200LR	7318
☐	N37342	CRJ-200LR	7342
☐	N77302	CRJ-200LR	7302

GRAND CANYON AIRLINES — CVU

	Reg	Type	c/n
☐	N72GC	DHC-6 Twin Otter 300	264
☐	N74GC	DHC-6 Twin Otter 300	559
☐	N171GC	DHC-6 Twin Otter 300	406
☐	N173GC	DHC-6 Twin Otter 300	295
☐	N177GC	DHC-6 Twin Otter 300	263
☐	N178GC	DHC-6 Twin Otter 300	697

GREAT LAKES AIRLINES — ZK / GLA

	Reg	Type	c/n
☐	N92SK	Beech 1900D	UE-92
☐	N100UX	Beech 1900D	UE-100
☐	N122UX	Beech 1900D	UE-122
☐	N153GL	Beech 1900D	UE-153
☐	N154GL	Beech 1900D	UE-154
☐	N169GL	Beech 1900D	UE-169
☐	N170GL	Beech 1900D	UE-170
☐	N173YV	Beech 1900D	UE-173
☐	N182YV	Beech 1900D	UE-182
☐	N184UX	Beech 1900D	UE-184
☐	N192GL	Beech 1900D	UE-192
☐	N195GL	Beech 1900D	UE-195
☐	N201GL	Beech 1900D	UE-201
☐	N202UX	Beech 1900D	UE-202
☐	N208GL	Beech 1900D	UE-208
☐	N210GL	Beech 1900D	UE-210
☐	N211GL	Beech 1900D	UE-211
☐	N218YV	Beech 1900D	UE-218
☐	N219GL	Beech 1900D	UE-219
☐	N220GL	Beech 1900D	UE-220
☐	N231YV	Beech 1900D	UE-231
☐	N237YV	Beech 1900D	UE-237
☐	N240GL	Beech 1900D	UE-240
☐	N245GL	Beech 1900D	UE-245
☐	N247GL	Beech 1900D	UE-247
☐	N251GL	Beech 1900D	UE-251
☐	N253GL	Beech 1900D	UE-253
☐	N254GL	Beech 1900D	UE-254
☐	N255GL	Beech 1900D	UE-255
☐	N257GL	Beech 1900D	UE-257
☐	N261GL	Beech 1900D	UE-261
☐	N71GL	EMB.120ER	120071
☐	N96ZK	EMB.120ER	120096
☐	N108UX	EMB.120ER	120108
☐	N293UX	EMB.120ER	120293
☐	N297UX	EMB.120ER	120297
☐	N299UX	EMB.120ER	120299

GULF AND CARIBBEAN AIR — TSU

	Reg	Type	c/n	
☐	N131FL	Convair 580	155	13
☐	N141FL	Convair 580	111	14

☐ N151FL	Convair 580		51	15
☐ N171FL	Convair 580		318	17
☐ N181FL	Convair 580		387	18
☐ N191FL	Convair 580		326	19
☐ N361FL	Convair 5800		343	
☐ N371FL	Convair 5800		309	
☐ N381FL	Convair 5800		276	
☐ N391FL	Convair 5800		278	
☐ N991FL	Convair 580		508	
☐ N7813B	Convair 340-70		265	
☐ N221FL	B727-22C	19805/543	709	
☐ N251FL	B727-277F/W	20551/1054	♦	
☐ N281FL	B727-225F/W	20153/779	711	
☐ N471FL	AMD Falcon 20		163	
☐ N481FL	AMD Falcon 20C-5		27	
☐ N511FL	AMD Falcon 20C-5		122	
☐ N521FL	AMD Falcon 20C-5		68	
☐ N531FL	AMD Falcon 20		113	
☐ N541FL	AMD Falcon 20		48	

GULFSTREAM INTERNATIONAL   3M / GFT

☐ N45AR	Beech 1900D	UE-12	
☐ N46AR	Beech 1900D	UE-27	
☐ N266AS	EMB.120ER	120188	201

HAGELAND AVIATION SERVICES   H6 / HAG

☐ N404GV	Beech 1900C-1	UC-154
☐ N15503	Beech 1900C-1	UC-72

HAWAIIAN AIRLINES   HA / HAL

☐ N380HA	A330-243	1104	♦
☐ N381HA	A330-243	1114	♦
☐ N382HA	A330-243	1171	♦
☐ N	A330-243	o/o	♦
☐ N	A330-243	o/o	♦
☐ N475HA	B717-22A	55121/5050	
☐ N476HA	B717-22A	55118/5053	
☐ N477HA	B717-22A	55122/5061	
☐ N478HA	B717-22A	55123/5064	
☐ N479HA	B717-22A	55124/5069	
☐ N480HA	B717-22A	55125/5070	
☐ N481HA	B717-22A	55126/5073	
☐ N483HA	B717-22A	55128/5079	
☐ N484HA	B717-22A	55129/5080	
☐ N485HA	B717-22A	55130/5089	
☐ N486HA	B717-22A	55131/5092	
☐ N487HA	B717-22A	55132/5098	
☐ N488HA	B717-23S	55001/5002	
☐ N489HA	B717-23S	55002/5003	
☐ N490HA	B717-23S	55151/5041	
☐ N580HA	B767-33AER/W	28140/850	
☐ N581HA	B767-33AER/W	28141/853	
☐ N582HA	B767-33AER/W	28139/857	
☐ N583HA	B767-33AER	25531/423	
☐ N584HA	B767-3G5ER	24258/255	
☐ N585HA	B767-3G5ER	24257/251	
☐ N586HA	B767-3G5ER	24259/268	
☐ N587HA	B767-33AER/W	33421/887	
☐ N588HA	B767-3CBER/W	33466/890	♦
☐ N589HA	B767-33AER/W	33422/892	♦
☐ N590HA	B767-3CBER/W	33467/894	
☐ N591HA	B767-33AER	33423/897	
☐ N592HA	B767-3CBER/W	33468/898	
☐ N593HA	B767-33AER	33424/901	
☐ N594HA	B767-332	23275/136	
☐ N596HA	B767-332	23276/151	
☐ N597HA	B767-332	23277/152	
☐ N598HA	B767-332	23278/153	

HORIZON AIR   QX / QXE

☐ N600QX	CRJ-701	10005	600
☐ N601QX	CRJ-701	10009	601
☐ N603QX	CRJ-701	10011	603
☐ N604QX	CRJ-701	10019	604
☐ N605QX	CRJ-701	10022	605
☐ N606QX	CRJ-701	10023	606
☐ N608QX	CRJ-701	10026	608
☐ N609QX	CRJ-701	10031	609
☐ N611QX	CRJ-701	10041	611
☐ N612QX	CRJ-701	10042	612
☐ N613QX	CRJ-701	10045	613
☐ N614QX	CRJ-701	10049	614
☐ N615QX	CRJ-701	10065	615
☐ N616QX	CRJ-701	10128	616
☐ N617QX	CRJ-701	10130	617
☐ N618QX	CRJ-701	10205	618
☐ N619QX	CRJ-701	10246	619
☐ N353PH	DHC-8Q-202	496	
☐ N354PH	DHC-8Q-202	498	
☐ N358PH	DHC-8Q-202	506	
☐ N359PH	DHC-8Q-202	514	>UCA
☐ N360PH	DHC-8Q-202	515	>UCA
☐ N361PH	DHC-8Q-202	516	>UCA
☐ N362PH	DHC-8Q-202	518	>UCA
☐ N363PH	DHC-8Q-202	520	>UCA
☐ N364PH	DHC-8Q-202	524	>UCA
☐ N365PH	DHC-8Q-202	526	>UCA
☐ N366PH	DHC-8Q-202	510	>UCA
☐ N367PH	DHC-8Q-202	511	>UCA
☐ N368PH	DHC-8Q-202	512	>UCA
☐ N369PH	DHC-8Q-202	513	
☐ N374PH	DHC-8Q-202	528	
☐ N375PH	DHC-8Q-202	529	>UCA
☐ N379PH	DHC-8Q-202	530	>UCA
☐ N400QX	DHC-8-402Q	4030	
☐ N401QX	DHC-8-402Q	4031	
☐ N402QX	DHC-8-402Q	4032	
☐ N403QX	DHC-8-402Q	4037	
☐ N404QX	DHC-8-402Q	4046	
☐ N405QX	DHC-8-402Q	4047	
☐ N406QX	DHC-8-402Q	4048	
☐ N407QX	DHC-8-402Q	4049	
☐ N408QX	DHC-8-402Q	4050	
☐ N409QX	DHC-8-402Q	4051	
☐ N410QX	DHC-8-402Q	4053	
☐ N411QX	DHC-8-402Q	4055	
☐ N412QX	DHC-8-402Q	4059	
☐ N413QX	DHC-8-402Q	4060	
☐ N414QX	DHC-8-402Q	4061	
☐ N415QX	DHC-8-402Q	4081	
☐ N416QX	DHC-8-402Q	4083	
☐ N417QX	DHC-8-402Q	4086	
☐ N418QX	DHC-8-402Q	4143	
☐ N419QX	DHC-8-402Q	4145	
☐ N420QX	DHC-8-402Q	4147	
☐ N421QX	DHC-8-402Q	4149	
☐ N422QX	DHC-8-402Q	4150	
☐ N423QX	DHC-8-402Q	4153	
☐ N424QX	DHC-8-402Q	4006	
☐ N425QX	DHC-8-402Q	4039	
☐ N426QX	DHC-8-402Q	4154	
☐ N427QX	DHC-8-402Q	4156	
☐ N428QX	DHC-8-402Q	4160	
☐ N429QX	DHC-8-402Q	4161	
☐ N430QX	DHC-8-402Q	4163	
☐ N431QX	DHC-8-402Q	4164	
☐ N432QX	DHC-8-402Q	4166	
☐ N433QX	DHC-8-402Q	4210	
☐ N434MK	DHC-8-402Q	4227	
☐ N435QX	DHC-8-402Q	4232	
☐ N436QX	DHC-8-402Q	4236	
☐ N437QX	DHC-8-402Q	4240	

☐	N438QX	DHC-8-402Q	4243	
☐	N439QX	DHC-8-402Q	4246	
☐	N440QX	DHC-8-402Q	4347	♦
☐	N441QX	DHC-8-402Q	4348	♦
☐	N	DHC-8-402Q	4352	o/o♦
☐	N	DHC-8-402Q		o/o♦
☐	N	DHC-8-402Q		o/o♦
☐	N	DHC-8-402Q		o/o♦
☐	N	DHC-8-402Q		o/o♦
☐	N	DHC-8-402Q		o/o♦

IBC AIRWAYS — II / CSQ

☐	N431BC	SAAB SF.340B	340B-260
☐	N481BC	SAAB SF.340B	340B-274
☐	N541BC	SAAB SF.340A	340A-029
☐	N611BC	SAAB SF.340A	340A-060
☐	N631BC	SAAB SF.340A	340A-061
☐	N641BC	SAAB SF.340A	340A-069
☐	N651BC	SAAB SF.340A	340A-076
☐	N661BC	SAAB SF.340A	340A-125
☐	N671BC	SAAB SF.340A	340A-084
☐	N691BC	SAAB SF.340A	340A-041
☐	N831BC	SA.227AC Metro III	AC-654B
☐	N841BC	SA.227TC Metro II	TC-282
☐	N851BC	SA.227AT Merlin IVC	AT-495B
☐	N861BC	SA.227AC Metro III	AC-487B
☐	N871BC	SA.227AC Metro III	AC-659B
☐	N891BC	SA.227AC Metro III	AC-709B

INTERNATIONAL AIR RESPONSE

☐	N117TG	C-130A-1A Hercules	3018	31
☐	N118TG	C-130A-1A Hercules	3219	32
☐	N119TG	C-130A Hercules	3227	[CHD]
☐	N121TG	C-130A Hercules	3119	
☐	N125TG	C-130A Hercules	3138	[CHD]
☐	N126TG	C-130A-1A Hercules	3142	[CHD]♦
☐	N133HP	C-130A-1A Hercules	3189	
☐	N797AL	DC-8-63F	46163/556	[VCV]
☐	N995CF	DC-8-62F	46024/428	[VCV]
☐	N4887C	DC-7B	45351/903	33

ISLAND AIR — WP/MKU

☐	N805WP	DHC-8-103	353	
☐	N806WP	DHC-8-103	357	
☐	N808WP	DHC-8-103	026	[HNL]♦
☐	N809WP	DHC-8-103	032	
☐	N829EX	DHC-8-103	146	
☐	N979HA	DHC-8-103	373	

JETBLUE AIRWAYS — B6 / JBU

☐	N503JB	A320-232	1123	
☐	N504JB	A320-232	1156	
☐	N505JB	A320-232	1173	
☐	N506JB	A320-232	1235	
☐	N509JB	A320-232	1270	
☐	N510JB	A320-232	1280	
☐	N516JB	A320-232	1302	
☐	N517JB	A320-232	1327	
☐	N519JB	A320-232	1398	
☐	N520JB	A320-232	1446	
☐	N521JB	A320-232	1452	
☐	N523JB	A320-232	1506	
☐	N524JB	A320-232	1528	
☐	N527JL	A320-232	1557	♦
☐	N529JB	A320-232	1610	
☐	N534JB	A320-232	1705	
☐	N535JB	A320-232	1739	
☐	N536JB	A320-232	1784	
☐	N537JL	A320-232	1785	♦
☐	N547JB	A320-232	1849	

☐	N552JB	A320-232	1861
☐	N554JB	A320-232	1898
☐	N556JB	A320-232	1904
☐	N558JB	A320-232	1915
☐	N559JB	A320-232	1917
☐	N561JB	A320-232	1927
☐	N562JB	A320-232	1948
☐	N563JB	A320-232	2006
☐	N564JB	A320-232	2020
☐	N565JB	A320-232	2031
☐	N566JB	A320-232	2042
☐	N568JB	A320-232	2063
☐	N569JB	A320-232	2075
☐	N570JB	A320-232	2099
☐	N571JB	A320-232	2125
☐	N579JB	A320-232	2132
☐	N580JB	A320-232	2136
☐	N583JB	A320-232	2150
☐	N584JB	A320-232	2149
☐	N585JB	A320-232	2159
☐	N586JB	A320-232	2160
☐	N587JB	A320-232	2177
☐	N588JB	A320-232	2201
☐	N589JB	A320-232	2215
☐	N590JB	A320-232	2231
☐	N591JB	A320-232	2246
☐	N592JB	A320-232	2259
☐	N593JB	A320-232	2280
☐	N594JB	A320-232	2284
☐	N595JB	A320-232	2286
☐	N597JB	A320-232	2307
☐	N598JB	A320-232	2314
☐	N599JB	A320-232	2336
☐	N603JB	A320-232	2352
☐	N605JB	A320-232	2368
☐	N606JB	A320-232	2384
☐	N607JB	A320-232	2386
☐	N608JB	A320-232	2415
☐	N612JB	A320-232	2447
☐	N613JB	A320-232	2449
☐	N615JB	A320-232	2461
☐	N618JB	A320-232	2489
☐	N621JB	A320-232	2491
☐	N623JB	A320-232	2504
☐	N624JB	A320-232	2520
☐	N625JB	A320-232	2535
☐	N627JB	A320-232	2577
☐	N629JB	A320-232	2580
☐	N630JB	A320-232	2640
☐	N632JB	A320-232	2647
☐	N633JB	A320-232	2671
☐	N634JB	A320-232	2710
☐	N635JB	A320-232	2725
☐	N636JB	A320-232	2755
☐	N637JB	A320-232	2781
☐	N638JB	A320-232	2802
☐	N639JB	A320-232	2814
☐	N640JB	A320-232	2832
☐	N641JB	A320-232	2848
☐	N643JB	A320-232	2871
☐	N644JB	A320-232	2880
☐	N645JB	A320-232	2900
☐	N646JB	A320-232	2945
☐	N648JB	A320-232	2970
☐	N649JB	A320-232	2977
☐	N651JB	A320-232	2992
☐	N652JB	A320-232	3029
☐	N653JB	A320-232	3039
☐	N655JB	A320-232	3072
☐	N656JB	A320-232	3091
☐	N657JB	A320-232	3119
☐	N658JB	A320-232	3150
☐	N659JB	A320-232	3190
☐	N661JB	A320-232	3228
☐	N662JB	A320-232	3263

☐	N663JB	A320-232	3287
☐	N665JB	A320-232	3348
☐	N703JB	A320-232	3381
☐	N705JB	A320-232	3416
☐	N706JB	A320-232	3451
☐	N708JB	A320-232	3479
☐	N709JB	A320-232	3488
☐	N712JB	A320-232	3517
☐	N715JB	A320-232	3554
☐	N729JB	A320-232	3572
☐	N746JB	A320-232	3622
☐	N760JB	A320-232	3659
☐	N763JB	A320-232	3707
☐	N766JB	A320-232	3724
☐	N768JB	A320-232	3760
☐	N775JB	A320-232	3800
☐	N779JB	A320-232	3811
☐		A320-232	o/o♦
☐		A320-232	o/o♦
☐		A320-232	o/o♦
☐		A320-232	o/o♦
☐	N178JB	ERJ-190AR	19000004
☐	N179JB	ERJ-190AR	19000006
☐	N183JB	ERJ-190AR	19000007
☐	N184JB	ERJ-190AR	19000008
☐	N187JB	ERJ-190AR	19000009
☐	N190JB	ERJ-190AR	19000011
☐	N192JB	ERJ-190AR	19000014
☐	N193JB	ERJ-190AR	19000017
☐	N197JB	ERJ-190AR	19000020
☐	N198JB	ERJ-190AR	19000021
☐	N203JB	ERJ-190AR	19000023
☐	N206JB	ERJ-190AR	19000025
☐	N216JB	ERJ-190AR	19000026
☐	N228JB	ERJ-190AR	19000030
☐	N229JB	ERJ-190AR	19000032
☐	N231JB	ERJ-190AR	19000033
☐	N236JB	ERJ-190AR	19000035
☐	N238JB	ERJ-190AR	19000039
☐	N239JB	ERJ-190AR	19000040
☐	N247JB	ERJ-190AR	19000042
☐	N249JB	ERJ-190AR	19000045
☐	N258JB	ERJ-190AR	19000047
☐	N265JB	ERJ-190AR	19000049
☐	N266JB	ERJ-190AR	19000054
☐	N267JB	ERJ-190AR	19000065
☐	N273JB	ERJ-190AR	19000073
☐	N274JB	ERJ-190AR	19000082
☐	N279JB	ERJ-190AR	19000090
☐	N281JB	ERJ-190AR	19000103
☐	N283JB	ERJ-190AR	19000125
☐	N284JB	ERJ-190AR	19000144
☐	N289JB	ERJ-190AR	19000002
☐	N292JB	ERJ-190AR	19000179
☐	N294JB	ERJ-190AR	19000185
☐	N296JB	ERJ-190AR	19000219
☐	N298JB	ERJ-190AR	19000249
☐	N304JB	ERJ-190AR	19000257
☐	N306JB	ERJ-190AR	19000272
☐	N307JB	ERJ-190AR	19000286
☐	N309JB	ERJ-190AR	19000289
☐	N316JB	ERJ-190AR	19000292
☐	N317JB	ERJ-190AR	19000363 ♦
☐	N318JB	ERJ-190AR	19000364 ♦
☐	N323JB	ERJ-190AR	19000384 ♦
☐	N324JB	ERJ-190AR	19000388 ♦
☐	N	ERJ-190AR	o/o♦
☐	N	ERJ-190AR	o/o♦
☐	N	ERJ-190AR	o/o♦
☐	N	ERJ-190AR	o/o♦
☐	N	ERJ-190AR	o/o♦

JIM HANKINS AIR SERVICE — HKN

☐	N3BA	DC-3	12172

☐	N366MQ	Short SD.3-60	SH3639
☐	N8061A	DC-3	6085

KALITTA AIR — K4 / CKS

☐	N356NA	B747-446BCF	26356/1026	♦
☐	N616US	B747-251F	21120/258	[OSC]♦
☐	N619US	B747-251F	21321/308	[OSC]♦
☐	N629US	B747-251F	22388/444	[OSC]♦
☐	N630US	B747-2J9F	21668/400	[OSC]♦
☐	N631NW	B747-251B(SF)	23111/594	[OSC]♦
☐	N646NW	B747-222B(SF)	23737/675	[OSC]♦
☐	N700CK	B747-246B(SF)	22990/579	
☐	N701CK	B747-259B (SCD)	21730/372	
☐	N703CK	B747-212B(SF)	21939/449	
☐	N704CK	B747-246F	23391/654	
☐	N705CK	B747-246B (SCD)	21034/243	
☐	N706CK	B747-249F	21827/406	
☐	N707CK	B747-246F	21681/382	
☐	N708CK	B747-212B(SF)	21937/419	
☐	N709CK	B747-132 (SCD)	20247/159	
☐	N710CK	B747-2B4M	21097/262	
☐	N712CK	B747-122 (SCD)	19754/60	
☐	N713CK	B747-2B4M	21099/264	
☐	N715CK	B747-209B(SF)	22447/556	
☐	N716CK	B747-122 (SCD)	19753/52	
☐	N717CK	B747-123 (SCD)	20325/125	
☐	N740CK	B747-4H6FCF	24405/745	
☐	N741CK	B747-4H6FCF	24315/738	
☐	N742CK	B747-446BCF	24424/760	
☐	N743CK	B747-446BCF	26350/961	♦
☐	N744CK	B747-446BCF	26353/980	♦
☐	N745CK	B747-446BCF	26361/1188	♦
☐	N746CK	B747-246F	22989/571	
☐	N748CK	B747-221F	21744/392	
☐	N768CK	B747-346	23969/691	[OSC]
☐	N790CK	B747-251B(SF)	23112/595	♦
☐	N790CK	B747-251F	23888/682	♦
☐	N792CK	B747-212F	24177/710	♦
■	N793CK	B747-222B(SF)	23736/673	[OSC]♦ 3/3

KALITTA CHARTERS II — KFS

☐	N720CK	B727-2B6F	21298/1246	
☐	N722CK	B727-2H3F	20948/1084	
☐	N723CK	B727-2H3F	20545/877	
☐	N724CK	B727-225F	20383/831	
☐	N725CK	B727-224F	22252/1697	
☐	N726CK	B727-2M7	21951/1680	♦
☐	N915CK	DC-9-15RC	47086/219	

KEY LIME AIR — LYM

☐	N62Z	SA.226TC Metro II	TC-237
☐	N184SW	SA.227AC Metro III	AC-647
☐	N340AE	SA.227AC Metro III	AC-510
☐	N425MA	SA.227AC Metro III	AC-640
☐	N508FA	SA.227AC Metro III	AC-508
☐	N509SS	SA.226TC Metro II	TC-206
☐	N542FA	SA.227AC Metro III	AC-542
☐	N765FA	SA.227AC Metro III	AC-765
☐	N769KL	SA.227AC Metro III	AC-769B
☐	N770S	SA.226TC Metro II	TC-248
☐	N779BC	SA.227AC Metro III	BC-779B
☐	N787KL	SA.227BC Metro III	BC-787B
☐	N882DC	SA.227DC Metro 23	DC-882B
☐	N2691W	SA.227AC Metro III	AC-655B
☐	N2728G	SA.227AC Metro III	AC-731
☐	N81418	SA.226TC Metro II	TC-223

KITTY HAWK AIRCARGO — KR / KHA

☐	N90AX	B727-222F	20040/729	[ROW]
☐	N855AA	B727-223F	20996/1193	[ROW]
☐	N858AA	B727-223F	21085/1200	[ROW]

	N6808	B727-223F	19483/558	[ROW]
☐	N6808	B727-223F	19483/558	[ROW]
☐	N6809	B727-223F	19484/560	[ROW]
☐	N6827	B727-223F	20180/698	[ROW]
☐	N6831	B727-223F	20184/707	[ROW]
☐	N6833	B727-223F	20186/721	[ROW]
☐	N69740	B727-224F	20668/1154	[ROW]
☐	N77780	B727-232F	20635/918	

KOLOB CANYONS AIR SERVICES

☐	N481UE	BAeJetstream 32	895
☐	N894KA	BAeJetstream 32	894

LOGISTIC AIR

☐	N735LA	B737-268	20574/294	[RKT]
☐	N2409N	B737-242C	20496/268	[QUE]
☐	N24089	B737-242C	20455/254	[MZJ]
☐	N303TW	B747-257B	20116/112	[MZJ]
☐	N741LA	B747-246B	19824/122	[MZJ]
☐	5U-ACE	B747-230B	20527/179	[ROW]
☐	5U-ACF	B747-146B	23150/601	
☐	5U-ACG	B747-146B	22067/427	

LYNDEN AIR CARGO · L2 / LYC

☐	N401LC	L-382G-31C Hercules	4606
☐	N402LC	L-382G-35C Hercules	4698
☐	N403LC	L-382G-31C Hercules	4590
☐	N404LC	L-382G-38C Hercules	4763
☐	N405LC	L-382G-69C Hercules	5025
☐	N406LC	L-382G-35C Hercules	4676

LYNX AIR INTERNATIONAL · LXF

☐	N61NE	SA.227AC Metro III	AC-761B	
☐	N158SD	SAAB SF.340A	340A-158	[FLL]

M & N AVIATION

☐	N410MN	Beech 1900C	UC-167

M ARTINAIRE · MRA

☐	N354AE	SA.227AC Metro III	AC-633
☐	N370AE	SA.227AC Metro III	AC-506
☐	N592BA	SA.227AC Metro III	AC-592
☐	N26932	SA.227AC Metro III	AC-660

MAVERICK HELICOPTERS

☐	N567MA	Beech 1900D	UE-67
☐	N886MA	Beech 1900D	UE-86

MCNEELY CHARTER SERVICE · MDS

☐	N120SC	SA.226TC Merlin IVA	AT-067
☐	N2699Y	SA.227AC Metro III	AC-666

MESA AIRLINES · YV / ASH

☐	N138YV	Beech 1900D	UE-138	>AMW
☐	N139ZV	Beech 1900D	UE-139	>BSY
☐	N142ZV	Beech 1900D	UE-142	>AMW
☐	N143YV	Beech 1900D	UE-143	>AMW
☐	N144ZV	Beech 1900D	UE-144	>AMW
☐	N155ZV	Beech 1900D	UE-155	>AMW
☐	N159YV	Beech 1900D	UE-159	>AMW
☐	N161YV	Beech 1900D	UE-161	>AMW
☐	N162ZV	Beech 1900D	UE-162	>AMW
☐	N165YV	Beech 1900D	UE-165	>BSY
☐	N166YV	Beech 1900D	UE-166	>AMW
☐	N167YV	Beech 1900D	UE-167	>AMW
☐	N171ZV	Beech 1900D	UE-171	>BSY
☐	N174YV	Beech 1900D	UE-174	[ABQ]
☐	N176YV	Beech 1900D	UE-176	>AMW
☐	N237YV	Beech 1900D	UE-237	>BSY
☐	N242YV	Beech 1900D	UE-242	>AMW
☐	N244YV	Beech 1900D	UE-244	>AMW
☐	N10675	Beech 1900D	UE-229	>AMW

MIAMI AIR INTERNATIONAL · LL / BSK

☐	N732MA	B737-81Q/W	30618/830
☐	N733MA	B737-81Q/W	30619/856
☐	N734MA	B737-8Q8/W	30039/701
☐	N737KA	B737-7BX	30740/776
☐	N738MA	B737-8Q8/W	32799/1467
☐	N739MA	B737-8Q8/W	30670/1481
☐	N740EH	B737-8DC/W	34596/1875
☐	N742MA	B737-83N/W	30675/898
☐	N752MA	B737-48E	28198/2806
☐	N753MA	B737-48E	28053/2954

MIDWEST AIRLINES · YX / MEP

☐	N907ME	B717-2BL	55171/5121	[VCV]
☐	N922ME	B717-2BL	55184/5142	[VCV]
☐	N601ME	MD-88	49762/1624	[BYH]
☐	N804ME	MD-81	48030/962	
☐	N808ME	MD-82	48070/999	
☐	N809ME	MD-82	48071/1004	[BYH]
☐	N812ME	MD-81	48006/966	
☐	N813ME	MD-81	48007/971	[GSP]
☐	N814ME	MD-81	48010/992	[BYH]

MIDWEST CONNECT · AL / SYX

☐	N403SW	CRJ-200ER	7028
☐	N407SW	CRJ-200ER	7034
☐	N468CA	CRJ-200ER	7649
☐	N471CA	CRJ-200ER	7655
☐	N472CA	CRJ-200ER	7667
☐	N479CA	CRJ-200ER	7675
☐	N494CA	CRJ-200ER	7765
☐	N495CA	CRJ-200ER	7774
☐	N496CA	CRJ-200ER	7791
☐	N498CA	CRJ-200ER	7792
☐	N506CA	CRJ-200ER	7793
☐	N507CA	CRJ-200ER	7796
☐	N699BR	CRJ-200ER	7801
☐	N709BR	CRJ-200ER	7850
☐	N983CA	CRJ-100ER	7169
☐	N984CA	CRJ-100ER	7171
☐	N986CA	CRJ-100ER	7174
☐	N988CA	CRJ-100ER	7204
☐	N836RP	ERJ-135LR	145713

MOUNTAIN AIR CARGO · MTN

☐	N2679U	Short SD.3-30	SH3071
☐	N26288	Short SD.3-30	SH3074

NATIONAL AIRLINES · 5M / MUA

☐	N919CA	B747-428BCF	25302/884	♦
☐	TF-NAC	B747-428MBCF	25238/872	♦
☐	N259CA	B757-2Y0ER	26152/478	♦
☐	N963CA	B757-2Y0ER	26154/486	♦
☐	N290MA	BAeJetstream 32EP	800	
☐	N339TE	BAeJetstream 32	935	
☐	N343TE	BAeJetstream 32	955	
☐	N695MA	BAeJetstream 31	695	
☐	N743PE	BAeJetstream 31	755	
☐	N155CA	DC-8-73CF	46073/485	
☐	N865F	DC-8-63F	46088/464	
☐	N872SJ	DC-8-71F	46040/449	
☐	N921R	DC-8-63F	46145/548	

NORD AVIATION

☐ N321L	C-117D	43345
☐ N620NA	DC-6A	44677/527
☐ N57626	DC-3	4564

NORTH AMERICAN AIRLINES   NA / NAO

☐ N750NA	B757-28A	26277/658
☐ N752NA	B757-28A	28174/865
☐ N754NA	B757-28A	29381/958
☐ N755NA	B757-28A	30043/925
☐ N756NA	B757-28A	32448/967
☐ N760NA	B767-39HER	26257/488
☐ N764NA	B767-328ER	27135/493
☐ N765NA	B767-306ER	28098/607
☐ N767NA	B767-324ER	27569/601
☐ N768NA	B767-36NER	29898/754

NORTH STAR AIR CARGO   SBX

☐ N50NS	Short SC.7 Skyvan	SH1856
☐ N51NS	Short SC.7 Skyvan	SH1843
☐ N101WA	Short SC.7 Skyvan	SH1859
☐ N731E	Short SC.7 Skyvan	SH1853

NORTH STAR AVIATION

☐ N153KM	BAeJetstream 4101	41053
☐ N308UE	BAeJetstream 4101	41023
☐ N679AS	BAeJetstream 4101	41056
☐ N680AS	BAeJetstream 4101	41030

NORTHERN AIR CARGO   NC / NAC

☐ N779TA	DC-6A	45529/1035	
☐ N2907F	C-118A	44636/574	
☐ N310DL	B737-232	23082/1006	♦
☐ N320DL	B737-232F	23092/1023	
☐ N321DL	B737-232F	23093/1024	
☐ N322DL	B737-232F	23094/1026	

OMNI AIR INTERNATIONAL   OY / OAE

☐ N558AX	B757-23N	27971/690	
☐ N639AX	B757-28A	24368/213	
☐ N342AX	B767-328ER	27136/497	
☐ N351AX	B767-33AER	27908/578	
☐ N378AX	B767-33AER	28147/622	
☐ N396AX	B767-319ER	26264/555	♦
☐ N108AX	DC-10-30	47927/190	
☐ N270AX	DC-10-30	48318/446	
☐ N522AX	DC-10-30ER	48315/436	
☐ N531AX	DC-10-30ERF	48316/437	
☐ N540AX	DC-10-30	46595/299	[VCV]
☐ N603AX	DC-10-30	48267/434	
☐ N612AX	DC-10-30ER	48290/435	
☐ N621AX	DC-10-30ER	48319/438	
☐ N630AX	DC-10-30	46596/301	[VCV]
☐ N720AX	DC-10-30	48252/342	
☐ N810AX	DC-10-30ER	48265/345	
☐ N59083	DC-10-30	47926/170	[VCV]

PACE AIRLINES   Y5 / PCE

☐ N373PA	B737-3Y0	23749/1389
☐ N583CC	B737-291	21069/415
☐ N737DX	B737-408	24804/1851
☐ N801DM	B757-256/W	26240/561

PARAMOUNT JET

☐ N406BN	B727-291F	19991/521

PENAIR   KS / PEN

☐ N640PA	SA.227AC Metro III	AC-759B
☐ N892DC	SA.227DC Metro 23	DC-892B
☐ N109XJ	SAAB SF.340A	340A-109
☐ N665PA	SAAB SF.340B	340B-181
☐ N675PA	SAAB SF.340B	340B-206
☐ N676PA	SAAB SF.340B	340B-316
☐ N677PA	SAAB SF.340B	340B-328
☐ N679PA	SAAB SF.340B	340B-345
☐ N685PA	SAAB SF.340B	340B-212

PLATINUM AIRLINES

☐ N727PL	B727-232	20643/951

PLAYERS AIR   PYZ

☐ N650CT	EMB.120RT	120198
☐ N651CT	EMB.120RT	120197
☐ N653CT	EMB.120ER	120243

POLAR AIR CARGO   PO / PAC

☐ N355MC	B747-341(SF)	23395/629	<GTI
☐ N416MC	B747-47UF	32838/1307	<GTI
☐ N450PA	B747-46NF	30808/1257	
☐ N451PA	B747-46NF	30809/1259	
☐ N452PA	B747-46NF	30810/1260	
☐ N453PA	B747-46NF	30811/1283	
☐ N454PA	B747-46NF	30812/1310	

PRESIDENTAL AIRWAYS

☐ N961BW	CASA C.212-200	CC40-8-248	
☐ N962BW	CASA C.212-200	CC44-1-290	
☐ N963BW	CASA C.212-200	CC60-3-320	
☐ N966BW	CASA C.212-200	CC50-10-289	
☐ N967BW	CASA C.212-200	CD51-2-304	
☐ N969BW	CASA C.212-200	CC50-1-262	
☐ N2357G	CASA C.212-200	CD51-2-309	
☐ N4399T	CASA C.212-300	DF-1-393	
☐ N6369C	CASA C.212-200	MS03-08-379	
☐ N150RN	DHC-8-103	086	
☐ N511AV	DHC-8-102	051	♦
☐ N955BW	SA.227DC Metro 23	DC-821B	
☐ N956BW	SA.227DC Metro 23	DC-864B	
☐ N982BW	CASA CN-235-10	10	
☐ N990AV	DHC-8-102	99	♦

REPUBLIC AIRLINES

☐ N810MD	ERJ-170SU	17000026
☐ N813MA	ERJ-170SU	17000031
☐ N815MD	ERJ-170SU	17000034
☐ N818MD	ERJ-170SU	17000039
☐ N821MD	ERJ-170SU	17000042
☐ N823MD	ERJ-170SU	17000044
☐ N824MD	ERJ-170SU	17000045
☐ N826MD	ERJ-170SU	17000046
☐ N871RW	ERJ-170SU	17000140
☐ N872RW	ERJ-170SU	17000143
☐ N873RW	ERJ-170SU	17000144
☐ N874RW	ERJ-170SU	17000148
☐ N161HL	ERJ-190AR	19000154
☐ N162HL	ERJ-190AR	19000231
☐ N163HQ	ERJ-190AR	19000255
☐ N164HQ	ERJ-190AR	19000275
☐ N165HQ	ERJ-190AR	19000291
☐ N166HQ	ERJ-190AR	19000166
☐ N167HQ	ERJ-190AR	19000173
☐ N168HQ	ERJ-190AR	19000183
☐ N169HQ	ERJ-190AR	19000188

☐	N170HQ	ERJ-190AR	19000191	
☐	N171HQ	ERJ-190AR	19000197	
☐	N172HQ	ERJ-190AR	19000198	
☐	N173HQ	ERJ-190AR	19000206	
☐	N174HQ	ERJ-190AR	19000211	
☐	N175HQ	ERJ-190AR	19000216	
☐	N	ERJ-190AR		o/o♦
☐	N	ERJ-190AR		o/o♦
☐	N	ERJ-190AR		o/o♦
☐	N	ERJ-190AR		o/o♦
☐	N	ERJ-190AR		o/o♦
☐	N	ERJ-190AR		o/o♦

RHOADES INTERNATIONAL — RDS

☐	N376AS	AMI Turbo DC-3-65TP15602/27047	
☐	N587CA	Convair 640	463

ROBLEX AVIATION — ROX

☐	N151PR	Short SD.3-60	SH3725
☐	N165DD	Short SD.3-60	SH3740
☐	N377AR	Short SD.3-60	SH3755
☐	N411ER	Short SD.3-60	SH3726
☐	N875RR	Short SD.3-60	SH3741
☐	N948RR	Short SD.3-60	SH3751

ROSS AVIATION — NRG

☐	N148DE	DHC-6 Twin Otter 300	493
☐	N162DE	DHC-6 Twin Otter 300	429
☐	N166DE	DC-9-15RC	47152/170
☐	N229DE	DC-9-15RC	45826/79

ROYAL AIR FREIGHT — RAX

☐	N34A	EMB.110P1	110350
☐	N49RA	EMB.110P1	110424
☐	N64DA	EMB.110P1	110385
☐	N72RA	EMB.110P1	110377
☐	N73RA	EMB.110P1	110413

RYAN INTERNATIONAL AIRLINES — RD / RYN

☐	N151GX	B757-2G5	24451/227	[VCV]
☐	N526NA	B757-236	24794/278	
☐	N120DL	B767-332	23279/154	
☐	N123DN	B767-332	23437/188	
☐	N125RD	B767-383ER	24849/330	
☐	N637TW	B767-33AER	25403/409	
☐	N763BK	B767-3Z9ER	23765/165	
☐	N764RD	B767-3Y0ER	26204/464	
☐	N932RD	MD-83	49233/1203	
☐	N964AS	MD-83	53078/1996	
☐	N969NS	MD-83	53063/1851	
☐	N976AS	MD-83	53452/2109	

SCENIC AIRLINES — YR / SCE

☐	N140SA	DHC-6 Twin Otter 300	267
☐	N142SA	DHC-6 Twin Otter 300	241
☐	N146SA	DHC-6 Twin Otter 300	514
☐	N148SA	DHC-6 Twin Otter 300	409
☐	N226SA	DHC-6 Twin Otter 300	585
☐	N227SA	DHC-6 Twin Otter 300	517
☐	N228SA	DHC-6 Twin Otter 300	253
☐	N241SA	DHC-6 Twin Otter 300	556
☐	N297SA	DHC-6 Twin Otter 300	297
☐	N359AR	DHC-6 Twin Otter 300	359
☐	N692AR	DHC-6 Twin Otter 300	692

SEABORNE AIRLINES — BB

☐	N224SA	DHC-6 Twin Otter 300	247
☐	N288SA	DHC-6 Twin Otter 300	389

☐	N562CP	DHC-6 Twin Otter 300	562
☐	N573SA	DHC-6 Twin Otter 300	573
☐	N888PV	DHC-6 Twin Otter 300	620

SIERRA PACIFIC AIRLINES — SI / SPA

☐	N703S	B737-2T4	22529/750
☐	N712S	B737-2Y5	23038/949

SIERRA WEST AIRLINES — PKW

☐	N63NE	SA.227AC Metro III	AC-763B
☐	N681TR	SA.227AC Metro III	AC-682
☐	N8897Y	SA.226AT Merlin IVC	AT-492

SKY KING — F3 / SGB

☐	N147AW	B737-297	22630/860	
☐	N249TR	B737-2K5	22598/792	
☐	N251TR	B737-228	23792/1397	♦
☐	N252TR	B737-228	23001/936	
☐	N464AT	B737-2L9	21278/479	
☐	N465AT	B737-2L9	21528/517	
☐	N916SK	B737-4Q8	24706/1996	
☐	N977UA	B737-2L9	21508/518	

SKYLEASE AIR CARGO — WI / TDX

☐	N501TR	A300B4-203F	053	>MST♦
☐	N504TA	A300B4-203F	216	
☐	N952AR	MD-11F	48497/512	♦
☐	N985AR	MD-11C	48430/508	
☐	N986AR	MD-11C	48426/468	

SKYWAY ENTERPRISES — SKZ

☐	N366MQ	Short SD.3-60	SH3639
☐	N367MQ	Short SD.3-60	SH3640
☐	N377MQ	Short SD.3-60	SH3699
☐	N378MQ	Short SD.3-60	SH3700
☐	N380MQ	Short SD.3-60	SH3702
☐	N381MQ	Short SD.3-60	SH3703
☐	N383MQ	Short SD.3-60	SH3706
☐	N384MQ	Short SD.3-60	SH3711
☐	N385MQ	Short SD.3-60	SH3707
☐	N387MQ	Short SD.3-60	SH3710
☐	N112PS	DC-9-15F	47013/129
☐	N118SW	Short SD.3-30	SH3100

SKYWEST AIRLINES — OO / SKW

☐	N947SW	CRJ-200ER	7786	7786
☐	N216SW	EMB.120ER	120285	
☐	N217SW	EMB.120ER	120286	
☐	N224SW	EMB.120ER	120294	
☐	N271YV	EMB.120ER	120271	
☐	N296SW	EMB.120ER	120325	
☐	N299SW	EMB.120ER	120329	
☐	N301YV	EMB.120ER	120301	
☐	N576SW	EMB.120ER	120345	

SNOW AVIATION

☐	N130SA	C-130A Hercules	3035
☐	N307SA	C-130E Hercules	3688

SOUTH PACIFIC EXPRESS

☐	N711MP	Short SD.3-60	SH3698

SOUTHERN AIR — 9S / SOO

☐	N704SA	B747-2B5F	24195/718
☐	N708SA	B747-2B5F	24196/720

☐	N723SA	B747-246F	23641/684	[MHV]
☐	N740SA	B747-230B(SF)	21380/320	[MHV]
☐	N746SA	B747-206M (EUD)	21111/276	[MHV]♦
☐	N748SA	B747-206M (EUD)	21110/271	[MHV]
☐	N749SA	B747-3B5F	24194/713	
☐	N751SA	B747-228F	22678/535	[CGK]
☐	N752SA	B747-228F	21255/295	
☐	N753SA	B747-228F	21787/398	
☐	N754SA	B747-228F	21576/334	
☐	N758SA	B747-281F	23138/604	
☐	N760SA	B747-230M	21221/299	
☐	N761SA	B747-2F6SF	21832/421	
☐	N765SA	B747-2F6B (SCD)	21833/423	
☐	N783SA	B747-281F	23919/689	
☐	N789SA	B747-341(SF)	23394/627	
☐	N795SA	B747-243M	22506/492	
☐	N798SA	B747-246B(SF)	23389/635	[VCV]
☐	N815SA	B747-2L5B(SF)	22107/469	[MHV]
☐	N818SA	B747-346	23068/589	[VCV]
☐	N774SA	B777-FZB	37986/844	Lt THA
☐	N775SA	B777-FZB	37987/852	Lt THA o/o

SOUTHWEST AIRLINES — WN / SWA

☐	N300SW	B737-3H4	22940/1037	
☐	N302SW	B737-3H4	22942/1052	
☐	N303SW	B737-3H4	22943/1101	
☐	N304SW	B737-3H4	22944/1138	
☐	N305SW	B737-3H4	22945/1139	[MHV]♦
☐	N306SW	B737-3H4	22946/1148	[MHV]♦
☐	N307SW	B737-3H4	22947/1156	[GYR]♦
☐	N308SA	B737-3Y0	23498/1233	
☐	N310SW	B737-3H4	22949/1161	
☐	N311SW	B737-3H4	23333/1183	
☐	N312SW	B737-3H4	23334/1185	
☐	N313SW	B737-3H4	23335/1201	
☐	N314SW	B737-3H4	23336/1229	
☐	N315SW	B737-3H4	23337/1231	
☐	N316SW	B737-3H4	23338/1232	
☐	N317WN	B737-3Q8	24068/1506	
☐	N318SW	B737-3H4	23339/1255	
☐	N323SW	B737-3H4	23344/1378	
☐	N325SW	B737-3H4	23689/1398	
☐	N326SW	B737-3H4	23690/1400	
☐	N327SW	B737-3H4	23691/1407	
☐	N328SW	B737-3H4	23692/1521	
☐	N329SW	B737-3H4	23693/1525	
☐	N330SW	B737-3H4	23694/1529	
☐	N331SW	B737-3H4	23695/1536	
☐	N332SW	B737-3H4	23696/1545	
☐	N333SW	B737-3H4	23697/1547	
☐	N334SW	B737-3H4	23938/1549	
☐	N335SW	B737-3H4	23939/1553	
☐	N336SW	B737-3H4	23940/1557	
☐	N337SW	B737-3H4	23959/1567	
☐	N338SW	B737-3H4	23960/1571	
☐	N339SW	B737-3H4	24090/1591	
☐	N340LV	B737-3K2	23738/1360	
☐	N341SW	B737-3H4	24091/1593	
☐	N342SW	B737-3H4	24133/1682	
☐	N343SW	B737-3H4	24151/1686	
☐	N344SW	B737-3H4	24152/1688	
☐	N345SA	B737-3K2	23786/1386	
☐	N346SW	B737-3H4	24153/1690	
☐	N347SW	B737-3H4	24374/1708	
☐	N348SW	B737-3H4	24375/1710	
☐	N349SW	B737-3H4	24408/1734	
☐	N350SW	B737-3H4	24409/1748	
☐	N351SW	B737-3H4	24572/1790	
☐	N352SW	B737-3H4/W	24888/1942	
☐	N353SW	B737-3H4	24889/1947	
☐	N354SW	B737-3H4	25219/2092	
☐	N355SW	B737-3H4/W	25250/2103	
☐	N356SW	B737-3H4	25251/2105	
☐	N357SW	B737-3H4	26594/2294	

☐	N358SW	B737-3H4	26595/2295	
☐	N359SW	B737-3H4/W	26596/2297	
☐	N360SW	B737-3H4/W	26571/2307	
☐	N361SW	B737-3H4/W	26572/2309	
☐	N362SW	B737-3H4/W	26573/2322	
☐	N363SW	B737-3H4/W	26574/2429	
☐	N364SW	B737-3H4/W	26575/2430	
☐	N365SW	B737-3H4/W	26576/2433	
☐	N366SW	B737-3H4/W	26577/2469	
☐	N367SW	B737-3H4/W	26578/2470	
☐	N368SW	B737-3H4/W	26579/2473	
☐	N369SW	B737-3H4/W	26580/2477	
☐	N370SW	B737-3H4/W	26597/2497	
☐	N371SW	B737-3H4/W	26598/2500	
☐	N372SW	B737-3H4/W	26599/2504	
☐	N373SW	B737-3H4/W	26581/2509	
☐	N374SW	B737-3H4/W	26582/2515	
☐	N375SW	B737-3H4/W	26583/2520	
☐	N376SW	B737-3H4/W	26584/2570	
☐	N378SW	B737-3H4/W	26585/2579	
☐	N379SW	B737-3H4/W	26586/2580	
☐	N380SW	B737-3H4/W	26587/2610	
☐	N382SW	B737-3H4/W	26588/2611	
☐	N383SW	B737-3H4/W	26589/2612	
☐	N384SW	B737-3H4	26590/2613	
☐	N385SW	B737-3H4/W	26600/2617	
☐	N386SW	B737-3H4/W	26601/2626	
☐	N387SW	B737-3H4/W	26602/2627	
☐	N388SW	B737-3H4	26591/2628	
☐	N389SW	B737-3H4	26592/2629	
☐	N390SW	B737-3H4/W	26593/2642	
☐	N391SW	B737-3H4/W	27378/2643	
☐	N392SW	B737-3H4/W	27379/2644	
☐	N394SW	B737-3H4/W	27380/2645	
☐	N395SW	B737-3H4/W	27689/2667	
☐	N396SW	B737-3H4/W	27690/2668	
☐	N397SW	B737-3H4/W	27691/2695	
☐	N398SW	B737-3H4/W	27692/2696	
☐	N399WN	B737-3H4/W	27693/2697	
☐	N600WN	B737-3H4	27694/2699	
☐	N601WN	B737-3H4/W	27695/2702	
☐	N602SW	B737-3H4/W	27953/2713	
☐	N603SW	B737-3H4/W	27954/2714	
☐	N604SW	B737-3H4/W	27955/2715	
☐	N605SW	B737-3H4	27956/2716	
☐	N606SW	B737-3H4/W	27926/2740	
☐	N607SW	B737-3H4/W	27927/2741	
☐	N608SW	B737-3H4/W	27928/2742	
☐	N609SW	B737-3H4/W	27929/2744	
☐	N610WN	B737-3H4/W	27696/2745	
☐	N611SW	B737-3H4/W	27697/2750	♦
☐	N612SW	B737-3H4	27930/2753	
☐	N613SW	B737-3H4	27931/2754	
☐	N614SW	B737-3H4/W	28033/2755	
☐	N615SW	B737-3H4/W	27698/2757	
☐	N616SW	B737-3H4/W	27699/2758	
☐	N617SW	B737-3H4/W	27700/2759	
☐	N618WN	B737-3H4	28034/2761	
☐	N619SW	B737-3H4/W	28035/2762	
☐	N620SW	B737-3H4/W	28036/2766	
☐	N621SW	B737-3H4	28037/2767	
☐	N622SW	B737-3H4/W	27932/2779	
☐	N623SW	B737-3H4/W	27933/2780	
☐	N624SW	B737-3H4/W	27934/2781	
☐	N625SW	B737-3H4/W	27701/2787	
☐	N626SW	B737-3H4/W	27702/2789	
☐	N627SW	B737-3H4/W	27935/2790	
☐	N628SW	B737-3H4/W	27703/2795	
☐	N629SW	B737-3H4/W	27704/2796	
☐	N630WN	B737-3H4/W	27705/2797	
☐	N631SW	B737-3H4/W	27706/2798	
☐	N632SW	B737-3H4/W	27707/2799	
☐	N633SW	B737-3H4/W	27936/2807	
☐	N634SW	B737-3H4/W	27937/2808	
☐	N635SW	B737-3H4/W	27708/2813	

	Registration	Type	Serial/Line	Notes
☐	N636WN	B737-3H4/W	27709/2814	
☐	N637SW	B737-3H4/W	27710/2819	
☐	N638SW	B737-3H4/W	27711/2820	
☐	N639SW	B737-3H4/W	27712/2821	
☐	N640SW	B737-3H4/W	27713/2840	
☐	N641SW	B737-3H4/W	27714/2841	
☐	N642WN	B737-3H4/W	27715/2842	
☐	N643SW	B737-3H4/W	27716/2843	
☐	N644SW	B737-3H4/W	28329/2869	
☐	N645SW	B737-3H4/W	28330/2870	
☐	N646SW	B737-3H4/W	28331/2871	
☐	N647SW	B737-3H4/W	27717/2892	
☐	N648SW	B737-3H4/W	27718/2893	
☐	N649SW	B737-3H4/W	27719/2894	
☐	N650SW	B737-3H4/W	27720/2901	
☐	N651SW	B737-3H4/W	27721/2915	♦
☐	N652SW	B737-3H4/W	27722/2916	
☐	N653SW	B737-3H4/W	28398/2917	
☐	N654SW	B737-3H4/W	28399/2918	
☐	N655WN	B737-3H4/W	28400/2931	
☐	N656SW	B737-3H4/W	28401/2932	
☐	N657SW	B737-3L9	23331/1111	
☐	N658SW	B737-3L9	23332/1118	
☐	N659SW	B737-301	23229/1112	
☐	N660SW	B737-301	23230/1115	
☐	N661SW	B737-317	23173/1098	
☐	N662SW	B737-3Q8	23255/1125	
☐	N663SW	B737-3Q8	23256/1128	
☐	N664WN	B737-3Y0	23495/1206	
☐	N665WN	B737-3Y0	23497/1227	
☐	N669SW	B737-3A4	23752/1484	
☐	N670SW	B737-3G7	23784/1533	
☐	N671SW	B737-3G7	23785/1535	
☐	N676SW	B737-3A4	23288/1100	[MHV]♦
☐	N679AA	B737-3A4	23291/1211	[MHV]♦
☐	N682SW	B737-3Y0	23496/1217	
☐	N683SW	B737-3G7	24008/1576	
☐	N684WN	B737-3T0	23941/1520	
☐	N685SW	B737-3Q8	23401/1209	
☐	N686SW	B737-317	23175/1110	
☐	N687SW	B737-3Q8	23388/1187	
☐	N688SW	B737-3Q8	23254/1107	
☐	N689SW	B737-3Q8	23387/1163	
☐	N690SW	B737-3G7	23783/1531	
☐	N691WN	B737-3G7	23781/1494	
☐	N692SW	B737-3T5	23062/1083	
☐	N693SW	B737-317	23174/1104	
☐	N694SW	B737-3T5	23061/1080	
☐	N697SW	B737-3T0	23838/1505	
☐	N698SW	B737-317	23176/1213	
☐	N699SW	B737-3Y0	23826/1372	
☐	N501SW	B737-5H4	24178/1718	
☐	N502SW	B737-5H4	24179/1744	
☐	N503SW	B737-5H4	24180/1766	
☐	N504SW	B737-5H4	24181/1804	
☐	N505SW	B737-5H4	24182/1826	
☐	N506SW	B737-5H4	24183/1852	
☐	N507SW	B737-5H4	24184/1864	
☐	N508SW	B737-5H4	24185/1932	
☐	N509SW	B737-5H4	24186/1934	
☐	N510SW	B737-5H4	24187/1940	
☐	N511SW	B737-5H4	24188/2029	
☐	N512SW	B737-5H4	24189/2056	
☐	N513SW	B737-5H4	24190/2058	
☐	N514SW	B737-5H4	25153/2078	
☐	N515SW	B737-5H4	25154/2080	
☐	N519SW	B737-5H4	25318/2121	
☐	N520SW	B737-5H4	25319/2134	
☐	N521SW	B737-5H4	25320/2136	
☐	N522SW	B737-5H4	26564/2202	
☐	N523SW	B737-5H4	26565/2204	
☐	N524SW	B737-5H4	26566/2224	
☐	N525SW	B737-5H4	26567/2283	
☐	N526SW	B737-5H4	26568/2285	
☐	N527SW	B737-5H4	26569/2287	
☐	N528SW	B737-5H4	26570/2292	
☐	N200WN	B737-7H4/W	32482/1638	
☐	N201LV	B737-7H4/W	29854/1650	
☐	N202WN	B737-7H4/W	33999/1653	
☐	N203WN	B737-7H4/W	32483/1656	
☐	N204WN	B737-7H4/W	29855/1663	
☐	N205WN	B737-7H4/W	34010/1668	
☐	N206WN	B737-7H4/W	34011/1675	
☐	N207WN	B737-7H4/W	34012/1678	
☐	N208WN	B737-7H4/W	29856/1679	
☐	N209WN	B737-7H4/W	32484/1683	
☐	N210WN	B737-7H4/W	34162/1690	
☐	N211WN	B737-7H4/W	34163/1699	
☐	N212WN	B737-7H4/W	32485/1708	
☐	N213WN	B737-7H4/W	34217/1717	
☐	N214WN	B737-7H4/W	32486/1721	
☐	N215WN	B737-7H4/W	32487/1723	
☐	N216WR	B737-7H4/W	32488/1735	
☐	N217JC	B737-7H4/W	34232/1737	
☐	N218WN	B737-7H4/W	32489/1741	
☐	N219WN	B737-7H4/W	32490/1744	
☐	N220WN	B737-7H4/W	32491/1756	
☐	N221WN	B737-7H4/W	34259/1776	
☐	N222WN	B737-7H4/W	34290/1780	
☐	N223WN	B737-7H4/W	32492/1799	
☐	N224WN	B737-7H4/W	32493/1801	
☐	N225WN	B737-7H4/W	34333/1820	
☐	N226WN	B737-7H4/W	32494/1822	
☐	N227WN	B737-7H4/W	34450/1831	
☐	N228WN	B737-7H4/W	32496/1835	
☐	N229WN	B737-7H4/W	32498/1858	
☐	N230WN	B737-7H4/W	34592/1868	
☐	N231WN	B737-7H4/W	32499/1881	
☐	N232WN	B737-7H4/W	32500/1888	
☐	N233LV	B737-7H4/W	32501/1893	
☐	N234WN	B737-7H4/W	32502/1905	
☐	N235WN	B737-7H4/W	34630/1916	
☐	N236WN	B737-7H4/W	34631/1928	
☐	N237WN	B737-7H4/W	34632/1930	
☐	N238WN	B737-7H4/W	34713/1950	
☐	N239WN	B737-7H4/W	34714/1954	
☐	N240WN	B737-7H4/W	32503/1959	
☐	N241WN	B737-7H4/W	32504/1965	
☐	N242WN	B737-7H4/W	32505/1969	
☐	N243WN	B737-7H4/W	34863/1973	
☐	N244WN	B737-7H4/W	34864/1977	
☐	N245WN	B737-7H4/W	32506/1982	
☐	N246LV	B737-7H4/W	32507/1984	
☐	N247WN	B737-7H4/W	32508/1989	
☐	N248WN	B737-7H4/W	32509/2000	
☐	N249WN	B737-7H4/W	34951/2005	
☐	N250WN	B737-7H4/W	34972/2019	
☐	N251WN	B737-7H4/W	32510/2025	
☐	N252WN	B737-7H4/W	34973/2027	
☐	N253WN	B737-7H4/W	32511/2038	
☐	N254WN	B737-7H4/W	32512/2040	
☐	N255WN	B737-7H4/W	32513/2049	
☐	N256WN	B737-7H4/W	32514/2059	
☐	N257WN	B737-7H4/W	32515/2062	
☐	N258WN	B737-7H4/W	32516/2076	
☐	N259WN	B737-7H4/W	35554/2092	
☐	N260WN	B737-7H4/W	32518/2114	
☐	N261WN	B737-7H4/W	32517/2133	
☐	N262WN	B737-7H4/W	32519/2139	
☐	N263WN	B737-7H4/W	32520/2153	
☐	N264LV	B737-7H4/W	32521/2161	
☐	N265WN	B737-7H4/W	32522/2174	
☐	N266WN	B737-7H4/W	32523/2182	
☐	N267WN	B737-7H4/W	32525/2193	
☐	N268WN	B737-7H4/W	32524/2199	
☐	N269WN	B737-7H4/W	32526/2204	
☐	N270WN	B737-705/W	29089/83	
☐	N271LV	B737-705/W	29090/109	
☐	N272WN	B737-7H4/W	32527/2224	
☐	N273WN	B737-7H4/W	32528/2238	

☐	N274WN	B737-7H4/W	32529/2244	
☐	N275WN	B737-7H4/W	36153/2256	
☐	N276WN	B737-7H4/W	32530/2262	
☐	N277WN	B737-7H4/W	32531/2274	
☐	N278WN	B737-7H4/W	36441/2281	
☐	N279WN	B737-7H4/W	32532/2284	
☐	N280WN	B737-7H4/W	32533/2294	
☐	N281WN	B737-7H4/W	36528/2307	
☐	N282WN	B737-7H4/W	32534/2318	
☐	N283WN	B737-7H4/W	36610/2322	
☐	N284WN	B737-7H4/W	32535/2328	
☐	N285WN	B737-7H4/W	32536/2337	
☐	N286WN	B737-7H4/W	32471/1535	
☐	N287WN	B737-7H4/W	32537/2344	
☐	N288WN	B737-7H4/W	36611/2350	
☐	N289CT	B737-7H4/W	36633/2354	
☐	N290WN	B737-7H4/W	36632/2363	
☐	N291WN	B737-7H4/W	32539/2378	
☐	N292WN	B737-7H4/W	32538/2383	
☐	N293WN	B737-7H4/W	36612/2387	
☐	N294WN	B737-7H4/W	32540/2390	
☐	N295WN	B737-7H4/W	32541/2409	
☐	N296WN	B737-7H4/W	36613/2413	
☐	N297WN	B737-7H4/W	32542/2417	
☐	N298WN	B737-7H4/W	32543/2438	
☐	N299WN	B737-7H4/W	36614/2442	
☐	N400WN	B737-7H4/W	27891/806	
☐	N401WN	B737-7H4/W	29813/810	
☐	N402WN	B737-7H4/W	29814/811	
☐	N403WN	B737-7H4/W	29815/821	
☐	N404WN	B737-7H4/W	27892/880	
☐	N405WN	B737-7H4/W	27893/881	
☐	N406WN	B737-7H4/W	27894/885	
☐	N407WN	B737-7H4/W	29817/903	
☐	N408WN	B737-7H4/W	27895/934	
☐	N409WN	B737-7H4/W	27896/945	
☐	N410WN	B737-7H4/W	27897/946	
☐	N411WN	B737-7H4/W	29821/950	
☐	N412WN	B737-7H4/W	29818/956	
☐	N413WN	B737-7H4/W	29819/960	
☐	N414WN	B737-7H4/W	29820/967	
☐	N415WN	B737-7H4/W	29836/980	
☐	N416WN	B737-7H4/W	32453/990	
☐	N417WN	B737-7H4/W	29822/993	
☐	N418WN	B737-7H4/W	29823/1000	
☐	N419WN	B737-7H4/W	29824/1017	
☐	N420WN	B737-7H4/W	29825/1039	
☐	N421LV	B737-7H4/W	32452/1040	
☐	N422WN	B737-7H4/W	29826/1093	
☐	N423WN	B737-7H4/W	29827/1101	
☐	N424WN	B737-7H4/W	29828/1105	
☐	N425LV	B737-7H4/W	29829/1109	
☐	N426WN	B737-7H4/W	29830/1114	
☐	N427WN	B737-7H4/W	29831/1119	
☐	N428WN	B737-7H4/W	29844/1243	
☐	N429WN	B737-7H4/W	33658/1256	
☐	N430WN	B737-7H4/W	33659/1257	
☐	N431WN	B737-7H4/W	29845/1259	
☐	N432WN	B737-7H4/W	33715/1297	
☐	N433LV	B737-7H4/W	33716/1301	
☐	N434WN	B737-7H4/W	32454/1313	
☐	N435WN	B737-7H4/W	32455/1328	
☐	N436WN	B737-7H4/W	32456/1342	
☐	N437WN	B737-7H4/W	29832/1349	
☐	N438WN	B737-7H4/W	29833/1353	
☐	N439WN	B737-7H4/W	29834/1356	
☐	N440LV	B737-7H4/W	29835/1358	
☐	N441WN	B737-7H4/W	29837/1360	
☐	N442WN	B737-7H4/W	32459/1365	
☐	N443WN	B737-7H4/W	29838/1369	
☐	N444WN	B737-7H4/W	29839/1374	
☐	N445WN	B737-7H4/W	29841/1388	
☐	N446WN	B737-7H4/W	29842/1401	
☐	N447WN	B737-7H4/W	33720/1405	
☐	N448WN	B737-7H4/W	33721/1409	
☐	N449WN	B737-7H4/W	32469/1427	
☐	N450WN	B737-7H4/W	32470/1429	
☐	N451WN	B737-7H4/W	32495/1458	
☐	N452WN	B737-7H4/W	29846/1461	
☐	N453WN	B737-7H4/W	29847/1476	
☐	N454WN	B737-7H4/W	29851/1477	
☐	N455WN	B737-7H4/W	32462/1480	
☐	N456WN	B737-7H4/W	32463/1484	
☐	N457WN	B737-7H4/W	33856/1485	
☐	N458WN	B737-7H4/W	33857/1490	
☐	N459WN	B737-7H4/W	32497/1492	
☐	N460WN	B737-7H4/W	32464/1499	
☐	N461WN	B737-7H4/W	32465/1510	
☐	N462WN	B737-7H4/W	32466/1513	
☐	N463WN	B737-7H4/W	32467/1515	
☐	N464WN	B737-7H4/W	32468/1517	
☐	N465WN	B737-7H4/W	33829/1519	
☐	N466WN	B737-7H4/W	30677/1520	
☐	N467WN	B737-7H4/W	33830/1521	
☐	N468WN	B737-7H4/W	33858/1523	
☐	N469WN	B737-7H4/W	33859/1525	
☐	N470WN	B737-7H4/W	33860/1528	
☐	N472WN	B737-7H4/W	33831/1537	
☐	N473WN	B737-7H4/W	33832/1541	
☐	N474WN	B737-7H4/W	33861/1543	
☐	N475WN	B737-7H4/W	32474/1545	
☐	N476WN	B737-7H4/W	32475/1549	
☐	N477WN	B737-7H4/W	33988/1552	
☐	N478WN	B737-7H4/W	33989/1555	
☐	N479WN	B737-7H4/W	33990/1558	
☐	N480WN	B737-7H4/W	33998/1561	
☐	N481WN	B737-7H4/W	29853/1564	
☐	N482WN	B737-7H4/W	29852/1568	
☐	N483WN	B737-7H4/W	32472/1570	
☐	N484WN	B737-7H4/W	33841/1575	
☐	N485WN	B737-7H4/W	32473/1577	
☐	N486WN	B737-7H4/W	33852/1579	
☐	N487WN	B737-7H4/W	33854/1583	
☐	N488WN	B737-7H4/W	33853/1587	
☐	N489WN	B737-7H4/W	33855/1589	
☐	N490WN	B737-7H4/W	32476/1591	
☐	N491WN	B737-7H4/W	33867/1598	
☐	N492WN	B737-7H4/W	33866/1605	
☐	N493WN	B737-7H4/W	32477/1616	
☐	N494WN	B737-7H4/W	33868/1621	
☐	N495WN	B737-7H4/W	33869/1625	
☐	N496WN	B737-7H4/W	32478/1626	
☐	N497WN	B737-7H4/W	32479/1628	
☐	N498WN	B737-7H4/W	32480/1633	
☐	N499WN	B737-7H4/W	32481/1636	
☐	N550WN	B737-76Q/W	30279/1010	
☐	N551WN	B737-76Q/W	30280/1025	
☐	N554WN	B737-7BX/W	30746/1085	♦
☐	N555LV	B737-7H4/W		o/o♦
☐	N556WN	B737-7H4/W		o/o♦
☐	N700GS	B737-7H4/W	27835/4	
☐	N701GS	B737-7H4/W	27836/6	
☐	N703SW	B737-7H4/W	27837/12	
☐	N704SW	B737-7H4/W	27838/15	
☐	N705SW	B737-7H4/W	27839/20	
☐	N706SW	B737-7H4/W	27840/24	
☐	N707SA	B737-7H4/W	27841/1	
☐	N708SW	B737-7H4/W	27842/2	
☐	N709SW	B737-7H4/W	27843/3	
☐	N710SW	B737-7H4/W	27844/34	
☐	N711HK	B737-7H4/W	27845/38	
☐	N712SW	B737-7H4/W	27846/53	
☐	N713SW	B737-7H4/W	27847/54	
☐	N714CB	B737-7H4/W	27848/61	
☐	N715SW	B737-7H4/W	27849/62	
☐	N716SW	B737-7H4/W	27850/64	
☐	N717SA	B737-7H4/W	27851/70	
☐	N718SW	B737-7H4/W	27852/71	
☐	N719SW	B737-7H4/W	27853/82	
☐	N720WN	B737-7H4/W	27854/121	

	Reg	Type	c/n	
☐	N723SW	B737-7H4/W	27855/199	
☐	N724SW	B737-7H4/W	27856/201	
☐	N725SW	B737-7H4/W	27857/208	
☐	N726SW	B737-7H4/W	27858/213	
☐	N727SW	B737-7H4/W	27859/274	
☐	N728SW	B737-7H4/W	27860/276	
☐	N729SW	B737-7H4/W	27861/278	
☐	N730SW	B737-7H4/W	27862/284	
☐	N731SA	B737-7H4/W	27863/318	
☐	N732SW	B737-7H4/W	27864/319	
☐	N733SA	B737-7H4/W	27865/320	
☐	N734SA	B737-7H4/W	27866/324	
☐	N735SA	B737-7H4/W	27867/354	
☐	N736SA	B737-7H4/W	27868/357	
☐	N737JW	B737-7H4/W	27869/358	
☐	N738CB	B737-7H4/W	27870/360	
☐	N739GB	B737-7H4/W	29275/144	
☐	N740SW	B737-7H4/W	29276/155	
☐	N741SA	B737-7H4/W	29277/157	
☐	N742SW	B737-7H4/W	29278/172	
☐	N743SW	B737-7H4/W	29279/175	
☐	N744SW	B737-7H4/W	29490/232	
☐	N745SW	B737-7H4/W	29491/237	
☐	N746SW	B737-7H4/W	29798/299	
☐	N747SA	B737-7H4/W	29799/306	
☐	N748SW	B737-7H4/W	29800/331	
☐	N749SW	B737-7H4/W	29801/343	
☐	N750SA	B737-7H4/W	29802/366	
☐	N751SW	B737-7H4/W	29803/373	
☐	N752SW	B737-7H4/W	29804/387	
☐	N753SW	B737-7H4/W	29848/400	
☐	N754SW	B737-7H4/W	29849/416	
☐	N755SA	B737-7H4/W	27871/419	
☐	N756SA	B737-7H4/W	27872/422	
☐	N757LV	B737-7H4/W	29850/425	
☐	N758SW	B737-7H4/W	27873/437	
☐	N759GS	B737-7H4/W	30544/448	
☐	N760SW	B737-7H4/W	27874/468	
☐	N761RR	B737-7H4/W	27875/495	
☐	N762SW	B737-7H4/W	27876/512	
☐	N763SW	B737-7H4/W	27877/520	
☐	N764SW	B737-7H4/W	27878/521	
☐	N765SW	B737-7H4/W	29805/525	
☐	N766SW	B737-7H4/W	29806/537	
☐	N767SW	B737-7H4/W	29807/541	
☐	N768SW	B737-7H4/W	30587/580	
☐	N769SW	B737-7H4/W	30588/592	
☐	N770SA	B737-7H4/W	30589/595	
☐	N771SA	B737-7H4/W	27879/599	
☐	N772SW	B737-7H4/W	27880/601	
☐	N773SA	B737-7H4/W	27881/603	
☐	N774SW	B737-7H4/W	27882/609	
☐	N775SW	B737-7H4/W	30590/617	
☐	N776WN	B737-7H4/W	30591/620	
☐	N777QC	B737-7H4/W	30592/621	
☐	N778SW	B737-7H4/W	27883/626	
☐	N779SW	B737-7H4/W	27884/628	
☐	N780SW	B737-7H4/W	27885/643	
☐	N781WN	B737-7H4/W	30601/646	
☐	N782SA	B737-7H4/W	29808/670	
☐	N783SW	B737-7H4/W	29809/675	
☐	N784SW	B737-7H4/W	29810/677	
☐	N785SW	B737-7H4/W	30602/693	
☐	N786SW	B737-7H4/W	29811/698	
☐	N787SA	B737-7H4/W	29812/705	
☐	N788SA	B737-7H4/W	30603/707	
☐	N789SW	B737-7H4/W	29816/718	
☐	N790SW	B737-7H4/W	30604/721	
☐	N791SW	B737-7H4/W	27886/736	
☐	N792SW	B737-7H4/W	27887/737	
☐	N793SA	B737-7H4/W	27888/744	
☐	N794SW	B737-7H4/W	30605/748	
☐	N795SW	B737-7H4/W	30606/780	
☐	N796SW	B737-7H4/W	27889/784	
☐	N797MX	B737-7H4/W	27890/803	
☐	N798SW	B737-7AD/W	28436/41	
☐	N799SW	B737-7Q8/W	28209/14	
☐	N900WN	B737-7H4/W	32544/2460	
☐	N901WN	B737-7H4/W	32545/2462	
☐	N902WN	B737-7H4/W	36615/2469	
☐	N903WN	B737-7H4/W	32457/2473	
☐	N904WN	B737-7H4/W	36616/2480	
☐	N905WN	B737-7H4/W	36617/2491	
☐	N906WN	B737-7H4/W	36887/2494	
☐	N907WN	B737-7H4/W	36619/2500	
☐	N908WN	B737-7H4/W	36620/2509	
☐	N909WN	B737-7H4/W	32458/2517	
☐	N910WN	B737-7H4/W	36618/2521	
☐	N912WN	B737-7H4/W	36621/2532	
☐	N913WN	B737-7H4/W	29840/2536	
☐	N914WN	B737-7H4/W	36622/2540	
☐	N915WN	B737-7H4/W	36888/2546	
☐	N916WN	B737-7H4/W	36623/2558	
☐	N917WN	B737-7H4/W	36624/2562	
☐	N918WN	B737-7H4/W	29843/2572	
☐	N919WN	B737-7H4/W	36625/2591	
☐	N920WN	B737-7H4/W	32460/2597	
☐	N921WN	B737-7H4/W	36626/2600	
☐	N922WN	B737-7H4/W	32461/2620	
☐	N923WN	B737-7H4/W	36627/2634	
☐	N924WN	B737-7H4/W	36628/2640	
☐	N925WN	B737-7H4/W	36630/2656	
☐	N926WN	B737-7H4/W	36629/2663	
☐	N927WN	B737-7H4/W	36889/2679	
☐	N928WN	B737-7H4/W	36890/2687	
☐	N929WN	B737-7H4/W	36631/2689	
☐	N930WN	B737-7H4/W	36636/2784	
☐	N931WN	B737-7H4/W	36637/2799	
☐	N932WN	B737-7H4/W	36639/2837	
☐	N933WN	B737-7H4/W	36640/2847	
☐	N934WN	B737-7H4/W	36642/2878	
☐	N935WN	B737-7H4/W	36641/2894	
☐	N936WN	B737-7H4/W	36643/2909	
☐	N937WN	B737-7H4/W	36644/2925	
☐	N938WN	B737-7H4/W	36645/2929	
☐	N939WN	B737-7H4/W	36646/2933	
☐	N940WN	B737-7H4/W	36900/2943	
☐	N941WN	B737-7H4/W	36647/2961	
☐	N942WN	B737-7H4/W	36648/2985	
☐	N943WN	B737-7H4/W	36913/3195	♦
☐	N944WN	B737-7H4/W	36659/3220	♦
☐	N945WN	B737-7H4/W	36660/3226	♦
☐	N946WN	B737-7H4/W	36918/3251	♦
☐	N947WN	B737-7H4/W	36924/3290	♦
☐	N948WN	B737-7H4/W	36662/3296	♦
☐	N949WN	B737-7H4/W	36663/3358	♦
☐	N950WN	B737-7H4/W	36664/3365	♦
☐	N951WN	B737-7H4/W	36665/3388	♦
☐	N952WN	B737-7H4/W	36667/3477	♦
☐	N953WN	B737-7H4/W	36668/3510	♦
☐	N954WN	B737-7H4/W	36669/3547	o/o♦
☐	N955WN	B737-7H4/W		o/o♦
☐	N956WN	B737-7H4/W		o/o♦
☐	N957WN	B737-7H4/W		o/o♦
☐	N958WN	B737-7H4/W		o/o♦
☐	N959WN	B737-7H4/W		o/o♦
☐	N960WN	B737-7H4/W		o/o♦
☐	N961WN	B737-7Q8/W		o/o♦
☐	N962WN	B737-7H4/W		o/o♦
☐	N963WN	B737-7H4/W		o/o♦
☐	N964WN	B737-7H4/W		o/o♦
☐	N965WN	B737-7H4/W		o/o♦
☐	N966WN	B737-7H4/W		o/o♦
☐	N967WN	B737-7H4/W		

SPIRIT AIRLINES — NKS

	Reg	Type	c/n
☐	N502NK	A319-132	2433
☐	N503NK	A319-132	2470
☐	N504NK	A319-132	2473
☐	N505NK	A319-132	2485

☐	N506NK	A319-132	2490	
☐	N507NK	A319-132	2560	
☐	N508NK	A319-132	2567	
☐	N509NK	A319-132	2603	
☐	N510NK	A319-132	2622	
☐	N512NK	A319-132	2673	
☐	N514NK	A319-132	2679	
☐	N516NK	A319-132	2704	
☐	N517NK	A319-132	2711	
☐	N522NK	A319-132	2893	
☐	N523NK	A319-132	2898	
☐	N524NK	A319-132	2929	
☐	N525NK	A319-132	2942	
☐	N526NK	A319-132	2963	
☐	N527NK	A319-132	2978	
☐	N528NK	A319-132	2983	
☐	N529NK	A319-132	3007	
☐	N530NK	A319-132	3017	
☐	N531NK	A319-132	3026	
☐	N532NK	A319-132	3165	
☐	N533NK	A319-132	3393	
☐	N534NK	A319-132	3395	
☐		A319-132		o/o♦
☐	N601NK	A320-232	4206	♦
☐	N602NK	A320-232	4264	♦
☐	N603NK	A320-232	4321	♦
☐	N604NK	A320-232	4431	♦
☐	N605NK	A320-232	4548	♦
☐	N606NK	A320-232	4592	o/o♦
☐	N607NK	A320-232	4595	o/o♦
☐	N587NK	A321-231	2476	
☐	N588NK	A321-231	2590	

SPRINGFIELD AIR CHARTER

☐	N935MA	SAAB SF.340A	340A-073

SUBURBAN AIR FREIGHT   SUB

☐	N124GP	Beech 1900C	UB-23	
☐	N253SF	Beech 1900C-1	UC-53	♦
☐	N719GL	Beech 1900C	UB-19	

SUN COUNTY AIRLINES   SY / SCX

☐	N710SY	B737-73V	30241/1034	
☐	N711SY	B737-73V	30245/1058	
☐	N712SY	B737-7Q8	28219/183	♦
☐	N801SY	B737-8Q8/W	30332/777	
☐	N804SY	B737-8Q8/W	30689/908	
☐	N805SY	B737-8Q8/W	30032/985	
☐	N806SY	B737-8Q8/W	28215/75	
☐	N809SY	B737-8Q8/W	30683/1669	
☐	N813SY	B737-8Q8	28237/769	

TBM

☐	N466TM	C-130A-1A Hercules	3173	64
☐	N473TM	C-130A-1A Hercules	3081	63

TEPPER AVIATION

☐	N2679C	L-382G-69C Hercules	4796
☐	N2731G	L-382G-30C Hercules	4582
☐	N3796B	L-382G-39C Hercules	5027

TOLAIR SERVICES   TI / TOL

☐	N87T	DC-3	6148
☐	N147JR	Convair 240-57 (T-29C)	403
☐	N783T	DC-3	4219

TRANSAIR   P6 / MUI

☐	N221LM	Short SD.3-60	SH3722

☐	N351TA	Short SD.3-60	SH3759
☐	N729PC	Short SD.3-60	SH3729
☐	N808KR	Short SD.3-60	SH3734
☐	N808TR	Short SD.3-60	SH3718
☐	N827BE	Short SD.3-60	SH3746
☐	N4476F	Short SD.3-60	SH3731

TRANSNORTHERN AVIATION   TNV

☐	N27TN	C-117D	43332	♦
☐	N30TN	C-117D	43159	
☐	N3114G	SA.227AC Metro III	AC-583	

TRICOASTAL AIR   GAE

☐	N168GA	SA.226TC Metro	TC-207

UFLY AIRWAYS   6F / FAO

☐	N836NK	MD-83	53045/1777
☐	N836RA	MD-83	53046/1784

UNITED AIR LINES   UA / UAL

☐	N801UA	A319-131	0686	4001
☐	N802UA	A319-131	0690	4002
☐	N803UA	A319-131	0748	4003
☐	N804UA	A319-131	0759	4004
☐	N805UA	A319-131	0783	4005
☐	N806UA	A319-131	0788	4006
☐	N807UA	A319-131	0798	4007
☐	N808UA	A319-131	0804	4008
☐	N809UA	A319-131	0825	4009
☐	N810UA	A319-131	0843	4010
☐	N811UA	A319-131	0847	4011
☐	N812UA	A319-131	0850	4012
☐	N813UA	A319-131	0858	4013
☐	N814UA	A319-131	0862	4014
☐	N815UA	A319-131	0867	4015
☐	N816UA	A319-131	0871	4016
☐	N817UA	A319-131	0873	4017
☐	N818UA	A319-131	0882	4018
☐	N819UA	A319-131	0893	4019
☐	N820UA	A319-131	0898	4020
☐	N821UA	A319-131	0944	4021
☐	N822UA	A319-131	0948	4022
☐	N823UA	A319-131	0952	4023
☐	N824UA	A319-131	0965	4024
☐	N825UA	A319-131	0980	4025
☐	N826UA	A319-131	0989	4026
☐	N827UA	A319-131	1022	4027
☐	N828UA	A319-131	1031	4028
☐	N829UA	A319-131	1211	4029
☐	N830UA	A319-131	1243	4030
☐	N831UA	A319-131	1291	4031
☐	N832UA	A319-131	1321	4032
☐	N833UA	A319-131	1401	4033
☐	N834UA	A319-131	1420	4034
☐	N835UA	A319-131	1426	4035
☐	N836UA	A319-131	1460	4036
☐	N837UA	A319-131	1474	4037
☐	N838UA	A319-131	1477	4038
☐	N839UA	A319-131	1507	4039
☐	N840UA	A319-131	1522	4040
☐	N841UA	A319-131	1545	4041
☐	N842UA	A319-131	1569	4042
☐	N843UA	A319-131	1573	4043
☐	N844UA	A319-131	1581	4044
☐	N845UA	A319-131	1585	4045
☐	N846UA	A319-131	1600	4046
☐	N847UA	A319-131	1627	4047
☐	N848UA	A319-131	1647	4048
☐	N849UA	A319-131	1649	4049
☐	N850UA	A319-131	1653	4050
☐	N851UA	A319-131	1664	4051
☐	N852UA	A319-131	1671	4052

☐	N853UA	A319-131	1688	4053
☐	N854UA	A319-131	1731	4054
☐	N855UA	A319-131	1737	4055
☐	N401UA	A320-232	0435	4501
☐	N402UA	A320-232	0439	4502
☐	N403UA	A320-232	0442	4703
☐	N404UA	A320-232	0450	4704
☐	N405UA	A320-232	0452	4705
☐	N406UA	A320-232	0454	4506
☐	N407UA	A320-232	0456	4507
☐	N408UA	A320-232	0457	4508
☐	N409UA	A320-232	0462	4709
☐	N410UA	A320-232	0463	4910
☐	N411UA	A320-232	0464	4711
☐	N412UA	A320-232	0465	4712
☐	N413UA	A320-232	0470	4713
☐	N414UA	A320-232	0472	4814
☐	N415UA	A320-232	0475	4615
☐	N416UA	A320-232	0479	4616
☐	N417UA	A320-232	0483	4617
☐	N418UA	A320-232	0485	4618
☐	N419UA	A320-232	0487	4619
☐	N420UA	A320-232	0489	4620
☐	N421UA	A320-232	0500	4621
☐	N422UA	A320-232	0503	4622
☐	N423UA	A320-232	0504	4623
☐	N424UA	A320-232	0506	4624
☐	N425UA	A320-232	0508	4625
☐	N426UA	A320-232	0510	4626
☐	N427UA	A320-232	0512	4627
☐	N428UA	A320-232	0523	4628
☐	N429UA	A320-232	0539	4629
☐	N430UA	A320-232	0568	4630
☐	N431UA	A320-232	0571	4631
☐	N432UA	A320-232	0587	4632
☐	N433UA	A320-232	0589	4633
☐	N434UA	A320-232	0592	4634
☐	N435UA	A320-232	0613	4635
☐	N436UA	A320-232	0638	4636
☐	N437UA	A320-232	0655	4637
☐	N438UA	A320-232	0678	4838
☐	N439UA	A320-232	0683	4839
☐	N440UA	A320-232	0702	4840
☐	N441UA	A320-232	0751	4841
☐	N442UA	A320-232	0780	4842
☐	N443UA	A320-232	0820	4643
☐	N444UA	A320-232	0824	4844
☐	N445UA	A320-232	0826	4845
☐	N446UA	A320-232	0834	4846
☐	N447UA	A320-232	0836	4847
☐	N448UA	A320-232	0842	4848
☐	N449UA	A320-232	0851	4849
☐	N451UA	A320-232	0865	4851
☐	N452UA	A320-232	0955	4852
☐	N453UA	A320-232	1001	4853
☐	N454UA	A320-232	1104	4654
☐	N455UA	A320-232	1105	4655
☐	N456UA	A320-232	1128	4656
☐	N457UA	A320-232	1146	4857
☐	N458UA	A320-232	1163	4858
☐	N459UA	A320-232	1192	4859
☐	N460UA	A320-232	1248	4860
☐	N461UA	A320-232	1266	4661
☐	N462UA	A320-232	1272	4962
☐	N463UA	A320-232	1282	4663
☐	N464UA	A320-232	1290	4664
☐	N465UA	A320-232	1341	4865
☐	N466UA	A320-232	1343	4666
☐	N467UA	A320-232	1359	4867
☐	N468UA	A320-232	1363	4668
☐	N469UA	A320-232	1409	4869
☐	N470UA	A320-232	1427	4870
☐	N471UA	A320-232	1432	4871
☐	N472UA	A320-232	1435	4872
☐	N473UA	A320-232	1469	4873

☐	N474UA	A320-232	1475	4874
☐	N475UA	A320-232	1495	4875
☐	N476UA	A320-232	1508	4876
☐	N477UA	A320-232	1514	4877
☐	N478UA	A320-232	1533	4878
☐	N479UA	A320-232	1538	4879
☐	N480UA	A320-232	1555	4880
☐	N481UA	A320-232	1559	4881
☐	N482UA	A320-232	1584	4882
☐	N483UA	A320-232	1586	4883
☐	N484UA	A320-232	1609	4884
☐	N485UA	A320-232	1617	4885
☐	N486UA	A320-232	1620	4886
☐	N487UA	A320-232	1669	4887
☐	N488UA	A320-232	1680	4888
☐	N489UA	A320-232	1702	4889
☐	N490UA	A320-232	1728	4890
☐	N491UA	A320-232	1741	4891
☐	N492UA	A320-232	1755	4892
☐	N493UA	A320-232	1821	4893
☐	N494UA	A320-232	1840	4894
☐	N495UA	A320-232	1842	4895
☐	N496UA	A320-232	1845	4896
☐	N497UA	A320-232	1847	4897
☐	N498UA	A320-232	1865	4898
☐	N14604	B737-524/W	27317/2576	604♦
☐	N58606	B737-524/W	27319/2590	[GYR]
☐	N27610	B737-524/W	27323/2616	610♦
☐	N11612	B737-524/W	27325/2630	[GYR]
☐	N14613	B737-524/W	27326/2633	[GYR]
☐	N17614	B737-524/W	27327/2634	614♦
☐	N16617	B737-524/W	27330/2648	617
☐	N17619	B737-524/W	27332/2659	0619
☐	N17620	B737-524/W	27333/2660	620
☐	N19621	B737-524/W	27334/2661	0621
☐	N18622	B737-524/W	27526/2669	0622
☐	N19623	B737-524/W	27527/2672	623
☐	N13624	B737-524/W	27528/2675	624
☐	N46625	B737-524/W	27529/2683	625
☐	N32626	B737-524/W	27530/2686	626
☐	N17627	B737-524/W	27531/2700	627
☐	N14628	B737-524/W	27532/2712	628
☐	N14629	B737-524/W	27533/2725	629
☐	N59630	B737-524/W	27534/2726	630
☐	N62631	B737-524/W	27535/2728	631
☐	N16632	B737-524/W	27900/2736	632
☐	N24633	B737-524/W	27901/2743	0633
☐	N19638	B737-524/W	28899/2912	638
☐	N14639	B737-524/W	28900/2913	639
☐	N17640	B737-524/W	28901/2924	640
☐	N11641	B737-524/W	28902/2926	641
☐	N16642	B737-524/W	28903/2927	0642
☐	N17644	B737-524/W	28905/2934	0644
☐	N14645	B737-524/W	28906/2935	645
☐	N16646	B737-524/W	28907/2956	0646
☐	N16647	B737-524/W	28908/2958	647
☐	N16648	B737-524/W	28909/2960	0648
☐	N16649	B737-524/W	28910/2972	649
☐	N16650	B737-524/W	28911/2973	0650
☐	N11651	B737-524/W	28912/2980	0651
☐	N14652	B737-524/W	28913/2985	0652
☐	N14653	B737-524/W	28914/2986	653
☐	N14655	B737-524/W	28916/2994	[GYR]
☐	N16701	B737-724/W	28762/29	701
☐	N24702	B737-724/W	28763/32	702
☐	N16703	B737-724/W	28764/37	703
☐	N14704	B737-724/W	28765/43	704
☐	N25705	B737-724/W	28766/46	705
☐	N24706	B737-724/W	28767/47	706
☐	N23707	B737-724/W	28768/48	707
☐	N23708	B737-724/W	28769/52	708
☐	N16709	B737-724/W	28779/93	709
☐	N15710	B737-724/W	28780/94	710
☐	N54711	B737-724/W	28782/97	711

	Registration	Type	C/n	Fleet No.
☐	N15712	B737-724/W	28783/105	712
☐	N16713	B737-724/W	28784/107	713
☐	N33714	B737-724/W	28785/119	714
☐	N24715	B737-724/W	28786/125	715
☐	N13716	B737-724/W	28787/156	716
☐	N29717	B737-724/W	28936/182	717
☐	N13718	B737-724/W	28937/185	718
☐	N17719	B737-724/W	28938/195	719
☐	N13720	B737-724/W	28939/214	720
☐	N23721	B737-724/W	28940/219	721
☐	N27722	B737-724/W	28789/247	722
☐	N21723	B737-724/W	28790/253	723
☐	N27724	B737-724/W	28791/283	724
☐	N39726	B737-724/W	28796/315	726
☐	N38727	B737-724/W	28797/317	727
☐	N39728	B737-724/W	28944/321	728
☐	N24729	B737-724/W	28945/325	729
☐	N17730	B737-724/W	28798/338	730
☐	N14731	B737-724/W	28799/346	731
☐	N16732	B737-724/W	28948/352	732
☐	N27733	B737-724/W	28800/364	733
☐	N27734	B737-724/W	28949/371	734
☐	N14735	B737-724/W	28950/376	735
☐	N24736	B737-724/W	28803/380	736
☐	N13750	B737-724/W	28941/286	750
☐	N25201	B737-824/W	28958/443	201
☐	N24202	B737-824/W	30429/581	202
☐	N33203	B737-824/W	30613/591	203
☐	N35204	B737-824/W	30576/606	204
☐	N27205	B737-824/W	30577/615	205
☐	N11206	B737-824/W	30578/618	206
☐	N36207	B737-824/W	30579/627	207
☐	N26208	B737-824/W	30580/644	208
☐	N33209	B737-824/W	30581/647	209
☐	N26210	B737-824/W	28770/56	210
☐	N24211	B737-824/W	28771/58	211
☐	N24212	B737-824/W	28772/63	0212
☐	N27213	B737-824/W	28773/65	213
☐	N14214	B737-824/W	28774/74	214
☐	N26215	B737-824/W	28775/76	215
☐	N12216	B737-824/W	28776/79	216
☐	N16217	B737-824/W	28777/81	217
☐	N12218	B737-824/W	28778/84	218
☐	N14219	B737-824/W	28781/88	0219
☐	N18220	B737-824/W	28929/134	220
☐	N12221	B737-824/W	28930/153	221
☐	N34222	B737-824/W	28931/159	0222
☐	N18223	B737-824/W	28932/162	0223
☐	N24224	B737-824/W	28933/165	224
☐	N12225	B737-824/W	28934/168	225
☐	N26226	B737-824/W	28935/171	226
☐	N13227	B737-824/W	28788/262	227
☐	N14228	B737-824/W	28792/281	228
☐	N17229	B737-824/W	28793/287	229
☐	N14230	B737-824/W	28794/296	230
☐	N14231	B737-824/W	28795/300	231
☐	N26232	B737-824/W	28942/304	232
☐	N17233	B737-824/W	28943/328	233
☐	N16234	B737-824/W	28946/334	234
☐	N14235	B737-824/W	28947/342	235
☐	N35236	B737-824/W	28801/367	236
☐	N14237	B737-824/W	28802/374	237
☐	N12238	B737-824/W	28804/386	238
☐	N27239	B737-824/W	28951/391	239
☐	N14240	B737-824/W	28952/394	240
☐	N54241	B737-824/W	28953/395	241
☐	N14242	B737-824/W	28805/402	242
☐	N18243	B737-824/W	28806/403	243
☐	N17244	B737-824/W	28954/409	244
☐	N17245	B737-824/W	28955/411	245
☐	N27246	B737-824/W	28956/413	246
☐	N36247	B737-824/W	28807/431	247
☐	N13248	B737-824/W	28808/435	248
☐	N14249	B737-824/W	28809/438	249
☐	N14250	B737-824/W	28957/441	250
☐	N73251	B737-824/W	30582/650	251
☐	N37252	B737-824/W	30583/656	252
☐	N37253	B737-824/W	30584/660	253
☐	N76254	B737-824/W	30779/667	254
☐	N37255	B737-824/W	30610/686	255
☐	N73256	B737-824/W	30611/692	256
☐	N38257	B737-824/W	30612/706	257
☐	N77258	B737-824/W	30802/708	258
☐	N73259	B737-824/W	30803/854	259
☐	N35260	B737-824/W	30855/862	260
☐	N77261	B737-824/W	31582/897	261
☐	N33262	B737-824/W	32402/901	262
☐	N37263	B737-824/W	31583/906	263
☐	N33264	B737-824/W	31584/916	264
☐	N76265	B737-824/W	31585/928	265
☐	N33266	B737-824/W	32403/930	266
☐	N37267	B737-824/W	31586/939	267
☐	N38268	B737-824/W	31587/957	268
☐	N76269	B737-824/W	31588/966	269
☐	N73270	B737-824/W	31632/970	270
☐	N35271	B737-824/W	31589/982	271
☐	N36272	B737-824/W	31590/987	272
☐	N37273	B737-824/W	31591/1012	273
☐	N37274	B737-824/W	31592/1062	274
☐	N73275	B737-824/W	31593/1077	275
☐	N73276	B737-824/W	31594/1079	0276
☐	N37277	B737-824/W	31595/1099	277
☐	N73278	B737-824/W	31596/1390	278
☐	N79279	B737-824/W	31597/1411	0279
☐	N36280	B737-824/W	31598/1423	280
☐	N37281	B737-824/W	31599/1425	0281
☐	N34282	B737-824/W	31634/1440	282
☐	N73283	B737-824/W	31606/1456	0283
☐	N33284	B737-824/W	31635/1475	284
☐	N78285	B737-824/W	33452/1540	0285
☐	N33286	B737-824/W	31600/1506	286
☐	N37287	B737-824/W	31636/1509	287
☐	N76288	B737-824/W	33451/1516	288
☐	N33289	B737-824/W	31607/1542	0289
☐	N37290	B737-824/W	31601/1567	290
☐	N73291	B737-824/W	33454/1611	291
☐	N33292	B737-824/W	33455/1622	292
☐	N37293	B737-824/W	33453/1743	293
☐	N33294	B737-824/W	34000/1762	294
☐	N77295	B737-824/W	34001/1779	295
☐	N77296	B737-824/W	34002/1787	296
☐	N39297	B737-824/W	34003/1791	297
☐	N37298	B737-824/W	34004/1813	298
☐	N73299	B737-824/W	34005/1821	299
☐	N78501	B737-824/W	31602/1994	501
☐	N76502	B737-824/W	31603/2017	502
☐	N76503	B737-824/W	33461/2023	503
☐	N76504	B737-824/W	31604/2035	504
☐	N76505	B737-824/W	32834/2048	505
☐	N78506	B737-824/W	32832/2065	506
☐	N87507	B737-824/W	31637/2487	0507
☐	N76508	B737-824/W	31639/2514	0508
☐	N76509	B737-824/W	31638/2523	0509
☐	N77510	B737-824/W	32828/2579	0510
☐	N78511	B737-824/W	33459/2598	0511
☐	N87512	B737-824/W	33458/2601	512
☐	N87513	B737-824/W	31621/2655	0513
☐	N76514	B737-824/W	31626/2680	0514
☐	N76515	B737-824/W	31623/2713	515
☐	N76516	B737-824/W	37096/2718	0516
☐	N76517	B737-824/W	31628/2723	0517
☐	N77518	B737-824/W	31605/2740	0518
☐	N76519	B737-824/W	30132/3138	0519♦
☐	N77520	B737-824/W	31658/3158	0520♦
☐	N79521	B737-824/W	31662/3169	0521♦
☐	N76522	B737-824/W	31660/3175	0522♦
☐	N76523	B737-824/W	37101/3216	0523♦
☐	N78524	B737-824/W	31642/3241	0524♦
☐	N77525	B737-824/W	31659/3253	0525♦
☐	N76526	B737-824/W	38700/3289	0526♦

	Reg	Type	C/n	Fleet
☐	N87527	B737-824/W	38701/3305	0527♦
☐	N76528	B737-824/W	31663/3464	0528♦
☐	N76529	B737-824/W	31652/3490	0529♦
☐	N77530	B737-824/W	39998/3521	o/o♦
☐	N87531	B737-824/W	39999/3549	o/o♦
☐	N	B737-824/W		o/o♦
☐	N	B737-824/W		o/o♦
☐	N30401	B737-924/W	30118/820	401
☐	N79402	B737-924/W	30119/857	402
☐	N38403	B737-924/W	30120/884	403
☐	N32404	B737-924/W	30121/893	404
☐	N72405	B737-924/W	30122/911	405
☐	N73406	B737-924/W	30123/943	406
☐	N35407	B737-924/W	30124/951	407
☐	N37408	B737-924/W	30125/962	408
☐	N37409	B737-924/W	30126/1004	409
☐	N75410	B737-924/W	30127/1021	410
☐	N71411	B737-924/W	30128/1052	411
☐	N31412	B737-924/W	30129/1112	412
☐	N37413	B737-924ER/W	31664/2474	0413
☐	N47414	B737-924ER/W	32827/2490	0414
☐	N39415	B737-924ER/W	32826/2516	0415
☐	N39416	B737-924ER/W	37093/2528	416
☐	N38417	B737-924ER/W	31665/2541	417
☐	N39418	B737-924ER/W	33456/2547	418
☐	N37419	B737-924ER/W	31666/2553	419
☐	N37420	B737-924ER/W	33457/2565	420
☐	N27421	B737-924ER/W	37094/2577	421
☐	N37422	B737-924ER/W	31620/2614	422
☐	N39423	B737-924ER/W	32829/2645	423
☐	N38424	B737-924ER/W	37095/2651	424
☐	N75425	B737-924ER/W	33460/2657	425
☐	N75426	B737-924ER/W	31622/2676	426
☐	N37427	B737-924ER/W	37097/2707	427
☐	N75428	B737-924ER/W	31633/2737	428
☐	N75429	B737-924ER/W	30130/2750	429
☐	N77430	B737-924ER/W	37098/2774	430
☐	N77431	B737-924ER/W	32833/2787	431
☐	N75432	B737-924ER/W	32835/2817	432
☐	N75433	B737-924ER/W	33527/2842	0433
☐	N37434	B737-924ER/W	33528/2891	434
☐	N75435	B737-924ER/W	33529/2916	435
☐	N75436	B737-924ER/W	33531/2947	436
☐	N37437	B737-924ER/W	33532/2959	437
☐	N78438	B737-924ER/W	33533/2971	438
☐	N5/439	B737-924ER/W	33534/2990	439
☐	N45440	B737-924ER/W	33535/2996	440
☐	N53441	B737-924ER/W	30131/3014	441
☐	N53442	B737-924ER/W	33536/3027	0442
☐	N38443	B737-924ER/W	31655/3393	0443♦
☐	N36444	B737-924ER/W	301643/3417	0444♦
☐	N104UA	B747-422	26902/1141	8104
☐	N105UA	B747-451	26473/985	8105
☐	N107UA	B747-422	26900/1168	8107
☐	N116UA	B747-422	26908/1193	8116
☐	N117UA	B747-422	28810/1197	8117
☐	N118UA	B747-422	28811/1201	8118
☐	N119UA	B747-422	28812/1207	8119
☐	N120UA	B747-422	29166/1209	8120
☐	N121UA	B747-422	29167/1211	8121
☐	N122UA	B747-422	29168/1218	8122
☐	N127UA	B747-422	28813/1221	8127
☐	N128UA	B747-422	30023/1245	8128
☐	N171UA	B747-422	24322/733	8171
☐	N173UA	B747-422	24380/759	8173
☐	N174UA	B747-422	24381/762	8174
☐	N175UA	B747-422	24382/806	8175
☐	N177UA	B747-422	24384/819	8177
☐	N178UA	B747-422	24385/820	8178
☐	N179UA	B747-422	25158/866	8179
☐	N180UA	B747-422	25224/867	8180
☐	N181UA	B747-422	25278/881	8181
☐	N182UA	B747-422	25279/882	8182
☐	N187UA	B747-422	26876/939	8187
☐	N193UA	B747-422	26890/1085	[VCV]
☐	N194UA	B747-422	26892/1088	[VCV]
☐	N195UA	B747-422	26899/1113	[VCV]
☐	N196UA	B747-422	28715/1120	[VCV]
☐	N197UA	B747-422	26901/1121	8197
☐	N198UA	B747-422	28716/1124	[VCV]
☐	N199UA	B747-422	28717/1126	8199
☐	N501UA	B757-222	24622/241	5401
☐	N502UA	B757-222/W	24623/246	5702
☐	N503UA	B757-222	24624/247	5403
☐	N504UA	B757-222	24625/251	5404
☐	N505UA	B757-222	24626/254	5705
☐	N506UA	B757-222	24627/263	5406
☐	N507UA	B757-222	24743/270	5407
☐	N508UA	B757-222	24744/277	5708
☐	N509UA	B757-222	24763/284	5409
☐	N510UA	B757-222/W	24780/290	5710
☐	N511UA	B757-222	24799/291	5411
☐	N512UA	B757-222/W	24809/298	5712
☐	N513UA	B757-222	24810/299	5413
☐	N514UA	B757-222	24839/305	5414
☐	N515UA	B757-222	24840/306	5415
☐	N516UA	B757-222	24860/307	5416
☐	N517UA	B757-222/W	24861/310	5717
☐	N518UA	B757-222/W	24871/311	5718
☐	N519UA	B757-222	24872/312	5419
☐	N520UA	B757-222	24890/313	5420
☐	N521UA	B757-222	24891/319	5421
☐	N522UA	B757-222	24931/320	5422
☐	N523UA	B757-222	24932/329	5423
☐	N524UA	B757-222	24977/331	5424
☐	N525UA	B757-222/W	24978/338	5725
☐	N526UA	B757-222	24994/339	5426
☐	N527UA	B757-222	24995/341	5427
☐	N528UA	B757-222	25018/346	5428
☐	N529UA	B757-222	25019/352	5429
☐	N530UA	B757-222	25043/353	5430
☐	N532UA	B757-222/W	25072/366	5732
☐	N533UA	B757-222	25073/367	5433
☐	N534UA	B757-222	25129/372	5434
☐	N535UA	B757-222	25130/373	5435
☐	N536UA	B757-222	25156/380	5436
☐	N537UA	B757-222	25157/381	5437
☐	N538UA	B757-222	25222/385	5438
☐	N539UA	B757-222	25223/386	5439
☐	N540UA	B757-222	25252/393	5440
☐	N541UA	B757-222	25253/394	5441
☐	N542UA	B757-222	25276/396	5442
☐	N543UA	B757-222ER/W	25698/401	5543
☐	N544UA	B757-222ER/W	25322/405	5544
☐	N545UA	B757-222ER/W	25323/406	5545
☐	N546UA	B757-222ER/W	25367/413	5546
☐	N547UA	B757-222ER	25368/414	5547
☐	N548UA	B757-222ER	25396/420	5548
☐	N549UA	B757-222ER/W	25397/421	5549
☐	N550UA	B757-222ER	25398/426	5550
☐	N551UA	B757-222ER	25399/427	5551
☐	N552UA	B757-222ER	26641/431	5552
☐	N553UA	B757-222	25277/434	5453
☐	N554UA	B757-222/W	26644/435	5754
☐	N555UA	B757-222/W	26647/442	5755
☐	N556UA	B757-222	26650/447	5456
☐	N557UA	B757-222	26653/454	5757
☐	N558UA	B757-222	26654/462	5458
☐	N559UA	B757-222	26657/467	5459
☐	N560UA	B757-222	26660/469	5760
☐	N561UA	B757-222	26661/479	5461
☐	N562UA	B757-222	26664/487	5462
☐	N563UA	B757-222	26665/488	5463
☐	N564UA	B757-222	26666/490	5464
☐	N565UA	B757-222	26669/492	5465
☐	N566UA	B757-222	26670/494	5466
☐	N567UA	B757-222	26673/497	5467
☐	N568UA	B757-222	26674/498	5468
☐	N569UA	B757-222	26677/499	5469

	Registration	Type	c/n	Fleet
☐	N570UA	B757-222	26678/501	5470
☐	N571UA	B757-222	26681/506	5471
☐	N572UA	B757-222	26682/508	5472
☐	N573UA	B757-222	26685/512	5473
☐	N574UA	B757-222	26686/513	5474
☐	N575UA	B757-222	26689/515	5475
☐	N576UA	B757-222	26690/524	5676
☐	N577UA	B757-222	26693/527	5677
☐	N578UA	B757-222	26694/531	5678
☐	N579UA	B757-222	26697/539	5679
☐	N580UA	B757-222	26698/542	5680
☐	N581UA	B757-222	26701/543	5681
☐	N582UA	B757-222	26702/550	5682
☐	N583UA	B757-222	26705/556	5683
☐	N584UA	B757-222	26706/559	5684
☐	N585UA	B757-222	26709/563	5685
☐	N586UA	B757-222	26710/567	5686
☐	N587UA	B757-222	26713/570	5687
☐	N588UA	B757-222	26717/571	5688
☐	N589UA	B757-222ER	28707/773	5589
☐	N590UA	B757-222ER/W	28708/785	5590
☐	N592UA	B757-222	28143/719	5492
☐	N593UA	B757-222	28144/724	5493
☐	N594UA	B757-222	28145/727	5494
☐	N595UA	B757-222ER	28748/789	5595
☐	N596UA	B757-222ER/W	28749/794	5596
☐	N597UA	B757-222ER	28750/841	5597
☐	N598UA	B757-222ER	28751/844	5598
☐	N58101	B757-224/W	27291/614	0101
☐	N14102	B757-224/W	27292/619	0102
☐	N33103	B757-224/W	27293/623	0103
☐	N17104	B757-224/W	27294/629	104
☐	N17105	B757-224/W	27295/632	0105
☐	N14106	B757-224/W	27296/637	0106
☐	N14107	B757-224/W	27297/641	107
☐	N21108	B757-224/W	27298/645	0108
☐	N12109	B757-224/W	27299/648	0109
☐	N13110	B757-224/W	27300/650	110
☐	N57111	B757-224/W	27301/652	0111
☐	N18112	B757-224/W	27302/653	0112
☐	N13113	B757-224/W	27555/668	0113
☐	N12114	B757-224/W	27556/682	0114
☐	N14115	B757-224/W	27557/686	0115
☐	N12116	B757-224/W	27558/702	0116
☐	N19117	B757-224/W	27559/706	0117
☐	N14118	B757-224/W	27560/748	0118
☐	N18119	B757-224/W	27561/753	0119
☐	N14120	B757-224/W	27562/761	0120
☐	N14121	B757-224/W	27563/766	121
☐	N17122	B757-224/W	27564/768	0122
☐	N26123	B757-224/W	28966/781	123
☐	N29124	B757-224/W	27565/786	0124
☐	N12125	B757-224/W	28967/788	0125
☐	N17126	B757-224/W	27566/790	126
☐	N48127	B757-224/W	28968/791	0127
☐	N17128	B757-224/W	27567/795	128
☐	N29129	B757-224/W	28969/796	129
☐	N19130	B757-224/W	28970/799	0130
☐	N34131	B757-224/W	28971/806	131
☐	N33132	B757-224/W	29281/809	132
☐	N17133	B757-224/W	29282/840	133
☐	N67134	B757-224/W	29283/848	134
☐	N41135	B757-224/W	29284/851	0135
☐	N19136	B757-224/W	29285/856	0136
☐	N34137	B757-224/W	30229/899	0137
☐	N13138	B757-224/W	30351/903	0138
☐	N17139	B757-224/W	30352/911	0139
☐	N41140	B757-224/W	30353/913	0140
☐	N19141	B757-224/W	30354/933	0141
☐	N75851	B757-324/W	32810/990	0851
☐	N57852	B757-324/W	32811/995	852
☐	N75853	B757-324/W	32812/997	853
☐	N75854	B757-324/W	32813/999	854
☐	N57855	B757-324/W	32814/1038	855♦
☐	N74856	B757-324/W	32815/1039	0856♦
☐	N57857	B757-324/W	32816/1040	0857
☐	N75858	B757-324/W	32817/1042	0858
☐	N56859	B757-324/W	32818/1043	859
☐	N73860	B757-33N/W	32584/972	860
☐	N75861	B757-33N/W	32585/976	861
☐	N57862	B757-33N/W	32586/978	862
☐	N57863	B757-33N/W	32587/980	863♦
☐	N57864	B757-33N/W	32588/985	864
☐	N77865	B757-33N/W	32589/1003	865
☐	N78866	B757-33N/W	32591/1007	866♦
☐	N77867	B757-33N/W	32592/1008	867
☐	N57868	B757-33N/W	32590/1017	868♦
☐	N57869	B757-33N/W	32593/1018	869♦
☐	N57870	B757-33N/W	33525/1031	0870♦
☐	N77871	B757-33N/W	33526/1032	871
☐	N641UA	B767-322ER	25091/360	6341
☐	N642UA	B767-322ER	25092/367	6342
☐	N643UA	B767-322ER	25093/368	6343
☐	N644UA	B767-322ER	25094/369	6344
☐	N646UA	B767-322ER	25283/420	6346
☐	N647UA	B767-322ER	25284/424	6347
☐	N648UA	B767-322ER	25285/443	[MZJ]
☐	N649UA	B767-322ER	25286/444	6349
☐	N651UA	B767-322ER	25389/452	6351
☐	N652UA	B767-322ER	25390/457	6352
☐	N653UA	B767-322ER	25391/460	6353
☐	N654UA	B767-322ER	25392/462	6354
☐	N655UA	B767-322ER	25393/468	6355
☐	N656UA	B767-322ER	25394/472	6356
☐	N657UA	B767-322ER	27112/479	6357
☐	N658UA	B767-322ER	27113/480	6358
☐	N659UA	B767-322ER	27114/485	6359
☐	N660UA	B767-322ER	27115/494	6360
☐	N661UA	B767-322ER	27158/507	6361
☐	N662UA	B767-322ER	27159/513	6362
☐	N663UA	B767-322ER	27160/514	6363
☐	N664UA	B767-322ER	29236/707	6764
☐	N665UA	B767-322ER	29237/711	6765
☐	N666UA	B767-322ER	29238/715	6766
☐	N667UA	B767-322ER	29239/717	6767
☐	N668UA	B767-322ER	30024/742	6768
☐	N669UA	B767-322ER	30025/757	6769
☐	N670UA	B767-322ER	29240/763	6770
☐	N671UA	B767-322ER	30026/766	6771
☐	N672UA	B767-322ER	30027/773	6772
☐	N673UA	B767-322ER	29241/779	6773
☐	N674UA	B767-322ER	29242/782	6774
☐	N675UA	B767-322ER	29243/800	6775
☐	N676UA	B767-322ER	30028/834	6776
☐	N677UA	B767-322ER	30029/852	6777
☐	N76151	B767-224ER	30430/811	151
☐	N73152	B767-224ER	30431/815	152
☐	N76153	B767-224ER	30432/819	153
☐	N69154	B767-224ER	30433/823	154
☐	N68155	B767-224ER	30434/825	155
☐	N76156	B767-224ER	30435/827	156
☐	N67157	B767-224ER	30436/833	157
☐	N67158	B767-224ER	30437/839	158
☐	N68159	B767-224ER	30438/845	159
☐	N68160	B767-224ER	30439/851	160
☐	N66051	B767-424ER	29446/799	051
☐	N67052	B767-424ER	29447/805	052
☐	N59053	B767-424ER	29448/809	053
☐	N76054	B767-424ER	29449/816	054
☐	N76055	B767-424ER	29450/826	0055
☐	N66056	B767-424ER	29451/842	056
☐	N66057	B767-424ER	29452/859	057
☐	N67058	B767-424ER	29453/862	058
■	N69059	B767-424ER	29454/864	0059
☐	N78060	B767-424ER	29455/866	060
☐	N68061	B767-424ER	29456/868	061
☐	N76062	B767-424ER	29457/869	062
☐	N69063	B767-424ER	29458/872	063

	Reg	Type	c/n	Fleet
☐	N76064	B767-424ER	29459/873	064
☐	N76065	B767-424ER	29460/876	065
☐	N77066	B767-424ER	29461/878	066
☐	N204UA	B777-222ER	28713/191	2904
☐	N206UA	B777-222ER	30212/216	2906
☐	N209UA	B777-222ER	30215/259	2609
☐	N210UA	B777-222ER	30216/264	2510
☐	N211UA	B777-222	30217/282	2511
☐	N212UA	B777-222	30218/293	2512
☐	N213UA	B777-222	30219/295	2513
☐	N214UA	B777-222	30220/296	2514
☐	N215UA	B777-222	30221/297	2515
☐	N216UA	B777-222ER	30549/291	2616
☐	N217UA	B777-222ER	30550/294	2617
☐	N218UA	B777-222ER	30222/317	2618
☐	N219UA	B777-222ER	30551/318	2619
☐	N220UA	B777-222ER	30223/340	2620
☐	N221UA	B777-222ER	30552/347	2621
☐	N222UA	B777-222ER	30553/352	2622
☐	N223UA	B777-222ER	30224/357	2623
☐	N224UA	B777-222ER	30225/375	2624
☐	N225UA	B777-222ER	30554/377	2625
☐	N226UA	B777-222ER	30226/380	2626
☐	N227UA	B777-222ER	30555/381	2627
☐	N228UA	B777-222ER	30556/384	2628
☐	N229UA	B777-222ER	30557/388	2629
☐	N768UA	B777-222	26919/11	2368
☐	N769UA	B777-222	26921/12	2369
■	N771UA	B777-222	26932/3	2371
☐	N772UA	B777-222	26930/5	2372
☐	N773UA	B777-222	26929/4	2373
☐	N774UA	B777-222	26936/2	2374
☐	N775UA	B777-222	26947/22	2375
☐	N776UA	B777-222	26937/27	2376
☐	N777UA	B777-222	26916/7	2377
■	N778UA	B777-222	26940/34	2378
☐	N779UA	B777-222	26941/35	2379
☐	N780UA	B777-222	26944/36	2380
☐	N781UA	B777-222	26945/40	2381
☐	N782UA	B777-222ER	26948/57	2982
☐	N783UA	B777-222ER	26950/60	2983
☐	N784UA	B777-222ER	26951/69	2984
☐	N785UA	B777-222ER	26954/73	2985
☐	N786UA	B777-222ER	26938/52	2986
☐	N787UA	B777-222ER	26939/43	2987
☐	N788UA	B777-222ER	26942/82	2988
☐	N791UA	B777-222ER	26933/93	2991
☐	N792UA	B777-222ER	26934/96	2992
☐	N793UA	B777-222ER	26946/97	2993
■	N794UA	B777-222ER	26953/105	2994
☐	N795UA	B777-222ER	26927/108	2995
☐	N796UA	B777-222ER	26931/112	2996
☐	N797UA	B777-222ER	26924/116	2997
☐	N798UA	B777-222ER	26928/123	2998
☐	N799UA	B777-222ER	26926/139	2999
☐	N78001	B777-224ER	27577/161	0001
☐	N78002	B777-224ER	27578/165	002
☐	N78003	B777-224ER	27579/167	003
☐	N78004	B777-224ER	27580/169	004
☐	N78005	B777-224ER	27581/177	005
☐	N77006	B777-224ER	29476/183	006
☐	N74007	B777-224ER	29477/197	0007
☐	N78008	B777-224ER	29478/200	0008
☐	N78009	B777-224ER	29479/211	0009
☐	N76010	B777-224ER	29480/220	010
☐	N79011	B777-224ER	29859/227	0011
☐	N77012	B777-224ER	29860/234	0012
☐	N78013	B777-224ER	29861/243	013
☐	N77014	B777-224ER	29862/253	014
☐	N27015	B777-224ER	28678/273	015
☐	N57016	B777-224ER	28679/279	016
☐	N78017	B777-224ER	31679/391	017
☐	N37018	B777-224ER	31680/397	018
☐	N77019	B777-224ER	35547/617	019
☐	N69020	B777-224ER	31687/625	0020

	Reg	Type	c/n	Fleet
☐	N76021	B777-224ER	39776/858	021♦
☐	N77022	B777-224ER	39777/868	022♦
☐	N	B787-8		o/o♦
☐	N	B787-8		o/o♦
☐	N	B787-8		o/o♦
☐	N	B787-8		o/o♦
☐	N	B787-8		o/o♦
☐	N	B787-8		o/o♦

UNITED EXPRESS   UA

	Reg	Type	c/n	Fleet
☐	N81533	Beech 1900D	UE-137	
☐	N81535	Beech 1900D	UE-147	
☐	N81536	Beech 1900D	UE-152	
☐	N38537	Beech 1900D	UE-158	
☐	N81538	Beech 1900D	UE-199	
☐	N82539	Beech 1900D	UE-168	
☐	N16540	Beech 1900D	UE-172	
☐	N17541	Beech 1900D	UE-203	
☐	N47542	Beech 1900D	UE-198	
☐	N49543	Beech 1900D	UE-181	
☐	N53545	Beech 1900D	UE-185	
☐	N81546	Beech 1900D	UE-187	
☐	N69547	Beech 1900D	UE-189	
☐	N69549	Beech 1900D	UE-194	
☐	N87550	Beech 1900D	UE-205	
☐	N87551	Beech 1900D	UE-206	
☐	N87552	Beech 1900D	UE-216	
☐	N87554	Beech 1900D	UE-227	
☐	N87555	Beech 1900D	UE-234	
☐	N81556	Beech 1900D	UE-239	
☐	N87557	Beech 1900D	UE-246	
☐	N154SF	CRJ-200LR	7154	154
☐	N473CA	CRJ-200ER	7668	472
☐	N571ML	CRJ-200LR	7209	
☐	N592ML	CRJ-200LR	7410	
☐	N645BR	CRJ-200ER	7383	462
☐	N647BR	CRJ-200ER	7399	463
☐	N648BR	CRJ-200ER	7406	
☐	N650BR	CRJ-200ER	7418	457
☐	N650ML	CRJ-200LR	7137	
☐	N652BR	CRJ-200ER	7429	458
☐	N653BR	CRJ-200ER	7438	460
☐	N667BR	CRJ-200ER	7535	461
☐	N702BR	CRJ-200ER	7462	459
☐	N715SF	CRJ-200LR	7115	
☐	N830AS	CRJ-200ER	7236	♦
☐	N832AS	CRJ-200ER	7243	♦
☐	N834AS	CRJ-200ER	7254	♦
☐	N836AS	CRJ-200ER	7263	♦
☐	N903SW	CRJ-200ER	7425	7425
☐	N905SW	CRJ-200ER	7437	7437
☐	N906SW	CRJ-200ER	7510	7510
☐	N907SW	CRJ-200ER	7511	7511
☐	N908SW	CRJ-200ER	7540	7540
☐	N909SW	CRJ-200ER	7558	7558
☐	N910SW	CRJ-200ER	7566	7566
☐	N912SW	CRJ-200ER	7595	7595
☐	N913SW	CRJ-200ER	7597	7597
☐	N915SW	CRJ-200ER	7615	7615
☐	N916SW	CRJ-200ER	7634	7634
☐	N917SW	CRJ-200ER	7641	7641
☐	N918SW	CRJ-200ER	7645	7645
☐	N919SW	CRJ-200ER	7657	7657
☐	N920SW	CRJ-200ER	7660	7660
☐	N923SW	CRJ-200ER	7664	7664
☐	N924SW	CRJ-200ER	7681	7681
☐	N925SW	CRJ-200ER	7682	7682
☐	N926SW	CRJ-200ER	7687	7687
☐	N927SW	CRJ-200ER	7693	7693
☐	N928SW	CRJ-200ER	7701	7701
☐	N929SW	CRJ-200ER	7703	7703
☐	N930SW	CRJ-200ER	7713	7713
☐	N932SW	CRJ-200ER	7714	7714

	Reg	Type		
☐	N934SW	CRJ-200ER	7722	7722
☐	N935SW	CRJ-200ER	7725	7725
☐	N936SW	CRJ-200ER	7726	7726
☐	N937SW	CRJ-200ER	7735	7735
☐	N938SW	CRJ-200ER	7741	7741
☐	N939SW	CRJ-200ER	7742	7742
☐	N941SW	CRJ-200ER	7750	7750
☐	N943SW	CRJ-200ER	7762	7762
☐	N944SW	CRJ-200ER	7764	7764
☐	N945SW	CRJ-200ER	7770	7770
☐	N946SW	CRJ-200ER	7776	7776
☐	N948SW	CRJ-200ER	7789	7789
☐	N951SW	CRJ-200ER	7795	7795
☐	N952SW	CRJ-200ER	7805	7805
☐	N953SW	CRJ-200ER	7813	7813
☐	N954SW	CRJ-200ER	7815	7815
☐	N955SW	CRJ-200ER	7817	7817
☐	N956SW	CRJ-200ER	7825	7825
☐	N957SW	CRJ-200ER	7829	7829
☐	N958SW	CRJ-200ER	7833	7833
☐	N959SW	CRJ-200ER	7840	7840
☐	N960SW	CRJ-200ER	7853	7853
☐	N961SW	CRJ-200ER	7857	7857
☐	N962SW	CRJ-200ER	7859	7859
☐	N963SW	CRJ-200ER	7865	7865
☐	N964SW	CRJ-200ER	7868	7867
☐	N965SW	CRJ-200ER	7871	7871
☐	N967SW	CRJ-200ER	7872	7872
☐	N969SW	CRJ-200ER	7876	7876
☐	N970SW	CRJ-200ER	7881	7881
☐	N971SW	CRJ-200ER	7947	7947
☐	N973SW	CRJ-200ER	7949	7949
☐	N975SW	CRJ-200ER	7951	7951
☐	N976SW	CRJ-200ER	7952	7952
☐	N978SW	CRJ-200ER	7953	7953
☐	N979SW	CRJ-200ER	7954	7954
☐	N980SW	CRJ-200ER	7955	7955
☐	N982SW	CRJ-200ER	7956	7956
☐	N983SW	CRJ-200ER	7961	7961
☐	N986SW	CRJ-200ER	7967	7967
☐	N17156	CRJ-200LR	7156	
☐	N17175	CRJ-200LR	7175	
☐	N27172	CRJ-200LR	7172	
☐	N27185	CRJ-200LR	7185	
☐	N37208	CRJ-200LR	7208	
☐	N37228	CRJ-200LR	7228	
☐	N47202	CRJ-200LR	7202	
☐	N75994	CRJ-200LR	7367	
☐	N75995	CRJ-200LR	7361	
☐	N77181	CRJ-200LR	7181	
☐	N77195	CRJ-200LR	7195	
☐	N151GJ	CRJ-702ER	10216	
☐	N152GJ	CRJ-702ER	10218	
☐	N153GJ	CRJ-702ER	10219	
☐	N154GJ	CRJ-702ER	10224	
☐	N155GJ	CRJ-702ER	10225	
☐	N156GJ	CRJ-702ER	10227	
☐	N157GJ	CRJ-702ER	10230	
☐	N158GJ	CRJ-702ER	10237	
☐	N159GJ	CRJ-702ER	10238	
☐	N160GJ	CRJ-702ER	10239	
☐	N161GJ	CRJ-702ER	10253	
☐	N162GJ	CRJ-702ER	10254	
☐	N163GJ	CRJ-702ER	10255	
☐	N164GJ	CRJ-702ER	10256	
☐	N165GJ	CRJ-702ER	10257	
☐	N166GJ	CRJ-702ER	10266	
☐	N167GJ	CRJ-702ER	10269	
☐	N168GJ	CRJ-702ER	10272	
☐	N169GJ	CRJ-702ER	10273	
☐	N170GJ	CRJ-702ER	10280	
☐	N171GJ	CRJ-702ER	10282	
☐	N172GJ	CRJ-702ER	10283	
☐	N173GJ	CRJ-702ER	10287	
☐	N174GJ	CRJ-702ER	10296	
☐	N175GJ	CRJ-702ER	10297	
☐	N501MJ	CRJ-701ER	10047	
☐	N502MJ	CRJ-701ER	10050	
☐	N503MJ	CRJ-701ER	10058	
☐	N504MJ	CRJ-701ER	10066	
☐	N505MJ	CRJ-701ER	10070	
☐	N506MJ	CRJ-701ER	10073	
☐	N507MJ	CRJ-701ER	10077	
☐	N508MJ	CRJ-701ER	10087	
☐	N509MJ	CRJ-701ER	10094	
☐	N510MJ	CRJ-701ER	10101	
☐	N511MJ	CRJ-701ER	10104	
☐	N512MJ	CRJ-701ER	10109	
☐	N513MJ	CRJ-701ER	10111	
☐	N514MJ	CRJ-701ER	10116	
☐	N515MJ	CRJ-701ER	10117	
☐	N516LR	CRJ-701ER	10258	
☐	N518LR	CRJ-701ER	10259	
☐	N519LR	CRJ-701ER	10260	
☐	N521LR	CRJ-701ER	10261	
☐	N522LR	CRJ-701ER	10262	
☐	N701SK	CRJ-701ER	10133	10133
☐	N702SK	CRJ-701ER	10136	10136
☐	N703SK	CRJ-701ER	10139	10139
☐	N705SK	CRJ-701ER	10145	10145
☐	N706SK	CRJ-701ER	10149	10149
☐	N707SK	CRJ-701ER	10003	10003
☐	N708SK	CRJ-701ER	10156	10156
☐	N709SK	CRJ-701ER	10159	10159
☐	N710SK	CRJ-701ER	10170	10170
☐	N712SK	CRJ-701ER	10172	10172
☐	N713SK	CRJ-701ER	10174	10174
☐	N715SK	CRJ-701ER	10179	10179
☐	N716SK	CRJ-701ER	10180	10180
☐	N718SK	CRJ-701ER	10184	10184
☐	N719SK	CRJ-701ER	10188	10188
☐	N724SK	CRJ-701ER	10189	10189
☐	N726SK	CRJ-701ER	10190	10190
☐	N727SK	CRJ-701ER	10191	10191
☐	N728SK	CRJ-701ER	10192	10192
☐	N730SK	CRJ-701ER	10193	10193
☐	N732SK	CRJ-701ER	10194	10194
☐	N738SK	CRJ-701ER	10195	10195
☐	N740SK	CRJ-701ER	10196	10196
☐	N742SK	CRJ-701ER	10197	10197
☐	N743SK	CRJ-701ER	10199	10199
☐	N744SK	CRJ-701ER	10200	10200
☐	N745SK	CRJ-701ER	10201	10201
☐	N746SK	CRJ-701ER	10202	10202
☐	N748SK	CRJ-701ER	10203	10203
☐	N750SK	CRJ-701ER	10207	10207
☐	N751SK	CRJ-701ER	10208	10208
☐	N752SK	CRJ-701ER	10209	10209
☐	N753SK	CRJ-701ER	10214	10214
☐	N754SK	CRJ-701ER	10215	10215
☐	N755SK	CRJ-701ER	10220	10220
☐	N756SK	CRJ-701ER	10221	10221
☐	N758SK	CRJ-701ER	10222	10222
☐	N760SK	CRJ-701ER	10223	10223
☐	N762SK	CRJ-702ER	10226	10226
☐	N763SK	CRJ-702ER	10228	10228
☐	N764SK	CRJ-702ER	10229	10229
☐	N765SK	CRJ-702ER	10231	10231
☐	N766SK	CRJ-702ER	10232	10232
☐	N767SK	CRJ-702ER	10233	10233
☐	N768SK	CRJ-702ER	10234	10234
☐	N770SK	CRJ-702ER	10243	10243
☐	N771SK	CRJ-702ER	10244	10244
☐	N772SK	CRJ-702ER	10235	10235
☐	N773SK	CRJ-702ER	10236	10236
☐	N774SK	CRJ-702ER	10240	10240
☐	N776SK	CRJ-702ER	10241	10241
☐	N778SK	CRJ-702ER	10242	10242
☐	N779SK	CRJ-702ER	10276	10276
☐	N780SK	CRJ-702ER	10277	10277

Reg	Type			
N782SK	CRJ-702ER	10278	10278	
N783SK	CRJ-702ER	10281	10281	
N784SK	CRJ-702ER	10284	10284	
N785SK	CRJ-702ER	10285	10285	
N786SK	CRJ-702ER	10286	10286	
N787SK	CRJ-702ER	10288	10288	
N788SK	CRJ-702ER	10290	10290	
N789SK	CRJ-702ER	10291	10291	
N790SK	CRJ-702ER	10292	10292	
N791SK	CRJ-702ER	10293	10293	
N792SK	CRJ-702ER	10294	10294	
N793SK	CRJ-702ER	10295	10295	
N794SK	CRJ-702ER	10298	10298	
N795SK	CRJ-702ER	10299	10299	
N796SK	CRJ-702ER	10300	10300	
N797SK	CRJ-702ER	10301	10301	
N	CRJ-702ER		o/o♦	
N	CRJ-702ER		o/o♦	
N	CRJ-702ER		o/o♦	
N	CRJ-702ER		o/o♦	
N	CRJ-702ER		o/o♦	
N351PH	DHC-8Q-202	490	763	
N358PH	DHC-8Q-202	506	775	
N359PH	DHC-8Q-202	514	764	
N360PH	DHC-8Q-202	515	762	
N361PH	DHC-8Q-202	516	767	
N362PH	DHC-8Q-202	518	766	
N363PH	DHC-8Q-202	520	760	
N364PH	DHC-8Q-202	524	765	
N365PH	DHC-8Q-202	526	773	
N366PH	DHC-8Q-202	510	769	
N367PH	DHC-8Q-202	511	774	
N368PH	DHC-8Q-202	512	768	
N369PH	DHC-8Q-202	513	770	
N374PH	DHC-8Q-202	528	771	
N375PH	DHC-8Q-202	529	761	
N379PH	DHC-8Q-202	530	771	
N436YV	DHC-8Q-202	436		
N444YV	DHC-8Q-202	444		
N445YV	DHC-8Q-202	445		
N446YV	DHC-8Q-202	446		
N454YV	DHC-8Q-202	454		
N455YV	DHC-8Q-202	455		
N456YV	DHC-8Q-202	456		
N34NG	DHC-8-402Q	4340	♦	
N187WQ	DHC-8 402Q	4187	777	
N188WQ	DHC-8-402Q	4188	778	
N190WQ	DHC-8-402Q	4190	779	
N191WQ	DHC-8-402Q	4191	780	
N195WQ	DHC-8-402Q	4195	781	
N196WQ	DHC-8-402Q	4196	782	
N199WQ	DHC-8-402Q	4199	783	
N202WQ	DHC-8-402Q	4202	785	
N203WQ	DHC-8-402Q	4203	786	
N204WQ	DHC-8-402Q	4204	787	
N208WQ	DHC-8-402Q	4208	788	
N209WQ	DHC-8-402Q	4209	789	
N213WQ	DHC-8-402Q	4213	790	
N214WQ	DHC-8-402Q	4214	791	
N323NG	DHC-8-402Q	4323	♦	
N328NG	DHC-8-402Q	4328	♦	
N332NG	DHC-8-402Q	4332	♦	
N333NG	DHC-8-402Q	4333	♦	
N336NG	DHC-8-402Q	4336	♦	
N338NG	DHC-8-402Q	4388	♦	
N339NG	DHC-8-402Q	4339	♦	
N341NG	DHC-8-402Q	4341	♦	
N342NG	DHC-8-402Q	4342	♦	
N346NG	DHC-8-402Q	4346	♦	
N351NG	DHC-8-402Q	4351	o/o♦	
N354NG	DHC-8-402Q	4354	o/o♦	
N	DHC-8-402Q		o/o♦	
N	DHC-8-402Q		o/o♦	
N	DHC-8-402Q		o/o♦	
N	DHC-8-402Q		o/o♦	
N221SW	EMB.120ER	120290		
N223SW	EMB.120ER	120291		
N226SW	EMB.120ER	120296		
N229SW	EMB.120ER	120305		
N233SW	EMB.120ER	120307		
N234SW	EMB.120ER	120308		
N235SW	EMB.120ER	120310		
N236SW	EMB.120ER	120312		
N237SW	EMB.120ER	120314		
N251YV	EMB.120ER	120251		
N270YV	EMB.120ER	120270		
N284YV	EMB.120ER	120284		
N288SW	EMB.120ER	120316		
N290SW	EMB.120ER	120317		
N291SW	EMB.120ER	120318		
N292SW	EMB.120ER	120319		
N292UX	EMB.120ER	120292		
N294SW	EMB.120ER	120321		
N295SW	EMB.120ER	120322		
N295UX	EMB.120ER	120295		
N297SW	EMB.120ER	120327		
N298SW	EMB.120ER	120328		
N308SW	EMB.120ER	120326		
N393SW	EMB.120ER	120330		
N560SW	EMB.120ER	120334		
N561SW	EMB.120ER	120335		
N562SW	EMB.120ER	120336		
N564SW	EMB.120ER	120339		
N565SW	EMB.120ER	120340		
N566SW	EMB.120ER	120341		
N567SW	EMB.120ER	120342		
N568SW	EMB.120ER	120343		
N569SW	EMB.120ER	120344		
N578SW	EMB.120ER	120346		
N579SW	EMB.120ER	120347		
N580SW	EMB.120ER	120348		
N581SW	EMB.120ER	120349		
N582SW	EMB.120ER	120350		
N583SW	EMB.120ER	120351		
N584SW	EMB.120ER	120352		
N585SW	EMB.120ER	120353		
N586SW	EMB.120ER	120354		
N16501	ERJ-135ER	145145	[IGM]	
N16502	ERJ-135ER	145166	[IGM]	
N19503	ERJ-135ER	145176	[IGM]	
N25504	ERJ-135ER	145186	[CLE]	
N14505	ERJ-135ER	145192	[IGM]	
N27506	ERJ-135ER	145206	[IGM]	
N17507	ERJ-135ER	145215	[IGM]	
N14508	ERJ-135ER	145220	[IGM]	
N15509	ERJ-135ER	145238	[IGM]	
N16510	ERJ-135ER	145251	[IGM]	
N16511	ERJ-135ER	145267	[IGM]	
N27512	ERJ-135ER	145274	[IGM]	
N17513	ERJ-135LR	145292	[IGM]	
N14514	ERJ-135LR	145303	[IGM]	
N29515	ERJ-135LR	145309	[IGM]	
N14516	ERJ-135LR	145323	[IGM]	
N24517	ERJ-135LR	145332	[IGM]	
N28518	ERJ-135LR	145334	[IGM]	
N12519	ERJ-135LR	145366	[IGM]	
N16520	ERJ-135LR	145372	[IGM]	
N17521	ERJ-135LR	145378	[IGM]	
N14522	ERJ-135LR	145383	[IGM]	
N27523	ERJ-135LR	145389	[IGM]	
N17524	ERJ-135LR	145399	[IGM]	
N16525	ERJ-135LR	145403	[IGM]	
N11526	ERJ-135LR	145410		
N15527	ERJ-135LR	145413		
N12528	ERJ-135LR	145504		
N28529	ERJ-135LR	145512		
N12530	ERJ-135LR	145533		

	Reg	Type	Number	Code
☐	N265SK	ERJ-145LR	145226	
☐	N266SK	ERJ-145LR	145241	436
☐	N267SK	ERJ-145LR	145268	437
☐	N268SK	ERJ-145LR	145270	
☐	N269SK	ERJ-145LR	145293	
☐	N270SK	ERJ-145LR	145304	
☐	N271SK	ERJ-145LR	145305	
☐	N275SK	ERJ-145LR	145345	439
☐	N276SK	ERJ-145LR	145348	
☐	N277SK	ERJ-145LR	145355	440
☐	N278SK	ERJ-145LR	145370	
☐	N279SK	ERJ-145LR	145379	
☐	N281SK	ERJ-145LR	145391	
☐	N283SK	ERJ-145LR	145424	442
☐	N284SK	ERJ-145LR	145427	
☐	N285SK	ERJ-145LR	145435	444
☐	N286SK	ERJ-145LR	145443	
☐	N287SK	ERJ-145LR	145460	
☐	N288SK	ERJ-145LR	145461	
☐	N289SK	ERJ-145LR	145463	
☐	N290SK	ERJ-145LR	145474	
☐	N292SK	ERJ-145LR	145488	
☐	N294SK	ERJ-145LR	145497	
☐	N296SK	ERJ-145LR	145514	
☐	N806HK	ERJ-145ER	145112	
☐	N807HK	ERJ-145ER	145119	
☐	N810HK	ERJ-145LR	145231	
☐	N832HK	ERJ-145LR	145771	
☐	N833HK	ERJ-145LR	145240	
☐	N835HK	ERJ-145LR	145670	
☐	N836HK	ERJ-145LR	145695	
☐	N838HK	ERJ-145LR	145321	
☐	N839HK	ERJ-145LR	14500829	
☐	N840HK	ERJ-145LR	145341	
☐	N841HK	ERJ-145LR	145382	
☐	N842HK	ERJ-145LR	14500830	
☐	N843HK	ERJ-145LR	14500822	
☐	N844HK	ERJ-145LR	14500838	
☐	N845HK	ERJ-145LR	14500842	
☐	N846HK	ERJ-145LR	14500855	
☐	N847HK	ERJ-145LR	14500857	
☐	N851HK	ERJ-145LR	145340	
☐	N852HK	ERJ-145LR	145353	
☐	N858MJ	ERJ-145LR	145767	
☐	N859MJ	ERJ-145LR	145769	
☐	N11535	ERJ-145LR	145518	535
☐	N11536	ERJ-145LR	145520	536
☐	N21537	ERJ-145LR	145523	537
☐	N13538	ERJ-145LR	145527	538
☐	N11539	ERJ-145LR	145536	539
☐	N12540	ERJ-145LR	145537	540
☐	N16541	ERJ-145LR	145542	541
☐	N14542	ERJ-145LR	145547	542
☐	N14543	ERJ-145LR	145553	543
☐	N26545	ERJ-145LR	145558	545
☐	N16546	ERJ-145LR	145562	546
☐	N11547	ERJ-145LR	145563	547
☐	N11548	ERJ-145LR	145565	548
☐	N26549	ERJ-145LR	145571	549
☐	N13550	ERJ-145LR	145575	550
☐	N12552	ERJ-145LR	145583	552
☐	N13553	ERJ-145LR	145585	553
☐	N15555	ERJ-145LR	145594	555
☐	N18556	ERJ-145LR	145595	556
☐	N14558	ERJ-145LR	145598	558
☐	N16559	ERJ-145LR	145603	559
☐	N17560	ERJ-145LR	145605	560
☐	N16561	ERJ-145LR	145610	561
☐	N14562	ERJ-145LR	145611	562
☐	N12563	ERJ-145LR	145612	563
☐	N12564	ERJ-145LR	145618	564
☐	N11565	ERJ-145LR	145621	565
☐	N13566	ERJ-145LR	145622	566
☐	N12567	ERJ-145LR	145623	567
☐	N14568	ERJ-145LR	145628	568
☐	N16571	ERJ-145LR	145633	571
☐	N15572	ERJ-145LR	145636	572
☐	N14573	ERJ-145LR	145638	573
☐	N15574	ERJ-145LR	145639	574
☐	N12900	ERJ-145LR	145511	900
☐	N48901	ERJ-145LR	145501	901
☐	N14902	ERJ-145LR	145496	902
☐	N13903	ERJ-145LR	145479	903
☐	N14904	ERJ-145LR	145477	904
☐	N14905	ERJ-145LR	145476	905
☐	N29906	ERJ-145LR	145472	906
☐	N13908	ERJ-145LR	145465	908
☐	N15910	ERJ-145LR	145455	910
☐	N16911	ERJ-145LR	145446	911
☐	N15912	ERJ-145LR	145439	912
☐	N13913	ERJ-145LR	145438	913
☐	N13914	ERJ-145LR	145430	914
☐	N36915	ERJ-145LR	145421	915
☐	N14916	ERJ-145LR	145415	916
☐	N29917	ERJ-145LR	145414	917
☐	N16918	ERJ-145LR	145397	918
☐	N16919	ERJ-145LR	145393	919
☐	N14920	ERJ-145LR	145380	920
☐	N12921	ERJ-145LR	145354	921
☐	N12922	ERJ-145LR	145338	922
☐	N14923	ERJ-145LR	145318	923
☐	N12924	ERJ-145LR	145311	924
☐	N14925	ERJ-145EP	145004	925
☐	N15926	ERJ-145EP	145005	926
☐	N16927	ERJ-145EP	145006	927
☐	N17928	ERJ-145EP	145007	928
☐	N13929	ERJ-145EP	145009	929
☐	N14930	ERJ-145EP	145011	930
☐	N15932	ERJ-145EP	145015	932
☐	N14933	ERJ-145EP	145018	933
☐	N12934	ERJ-145EP	145019	934
☐	N13935	ERJ-145EP	145022	935
☐	N13936	ERJ-145EP	145025	936
☐	N14937	ERJ-145EP	145026	937
☐	N14938	ERJ-145EP	145029	938
☐	N14939	ERJ-145EP	145030	939
☐	N14940	ERJ-145EP	145033	940
☐	N15941	ERJ-145EP	145035	941
☐	N14942	ERJ-145EP	145037	942
☐	N14943	ERJ-145EP	145040	943
☐	N16944	ERJ-145EP	145045	944
☐	N14945	ERJ-145EP	145049	945
☐	N12946	ERJ-145EP	145052	946
☐	N14947	ERJ-145EP	145054	947
☐	N15948	ERJ-145EP	145056	948
☐	N13949	ERJ-145LR	145057	949
☐	N14950	ERJ-145LR	145061	950
☐	N16951	ERJ-145LR	145063	951
☐	N14952	ERJ-145LR	145067	952
☐	N14953	ERJ-145LR	145071	953
☐	N16954	ERJ-145LR	145072	954
☐	N13955	ERJ-145LR	145075	955
☐	N13956	ERJ-145LR	145078	956
☐	N12957	ERJ-145LR	145080	957
☐	N13958	ERJ-145LR	145085	958
☐	N14959	ERJ-145LR	145091	959
☐	N14960	ERJ-145LR	145100	960
☐	N16961	ERJ-145LR	145103	961
☐	N27962	ERJ-145LR	145110	962
☐	N16963	ERJ-145LR	145116	963
☐	N13964	ERJ-145LR	145123	964
☐	N13965	ERJ-145LR	145125	965
☐	N19966	ERJ-145LR	145131	966
☐	N12967	ERJ-145LR	145133	967
☐	N13968	ERJ-145LR	145138	968
☐	N13969	ERJ-145LR	145141	969
☐	N13970	ERJ-145LR	145146	970
☐	N22971	ERJ-145LR	145149	971
☐	N14972	ERJ-145LR	145151	972
☐	N15973	ERJ-145LR	145159	973

	Reg	Type	Serial	No.
☐	N14974	ERJ-145LR	145161	974
☐	N13975	ERJ-145LR	145163	975
☐	N16976	ERJ-145LR	145171	976
☐	N14977	ERJ-145LR	145175	977
☐	N13978	ERJ-145LR	145180	978
☐	N13979	ERJ-145LR	145181	979
☐	N15980	ERJ-145LR	145202	980
☐	N16981	ERJ-145LR	145208	981
☐	N18982	ERJ-145LR	145223	982
☐	N15983	ERJ-145LR	145239	983
☐	N17984	ERJ-145LR	145246	984
☐	N15985	ERJ-145LR	145248	985
☐	N15986	ERJ-145LR	145254	986
☐	N16987	ERJ-145LR	145261	987
☐	N13988	ERJ-145LR	145265	988
☐	N13989	ERJ-145LR	145271	989
☐	N13990	ERJ-145LR	145277	990
☐	N14991	ERJ-145LR	145278	991
☐	N13992	ERJ-145LR	145284	992
☐	N14993	ERJ-145LR	145289	993
☐	N13994	ERJ-145LR	145291	994
☐	N13995	ERJ-145LR	145295	995
☐	N12996	ERJ-145LR	145296	996
☐	N13997	ERJ-145LR	145298	997
☐	N14998	ERJ-145LR	145302	998
☐	N16999	ERJ-145LR	145307	999
☐	N18101	ERJ-145XR	145590	101
☐	N18102	ERJ-145XR	145643	102
☐	N24103	ERJ-145XR	145645	103
☐	N41104	ERJ-145XR	145646	104
☐	N14105	ERJ-145XR	145649	105
☐	N11106	ERJ-145XR	145650	106
☐	N11107	ERJ-145XR	145654	107
☐	N17108	ERJ-145XR	145655	108
☐	N11109	ERJ-145XR	145657	109
☐	N34110	ERJ-145XR	145658	110
☐	N34111	ERJ-145XR	145659	111
☐	N16112	ERJ-145XR	145660	112
☐	N11113	ERJ-145XR	145662	113
☐	N18114	ERJ-145XR	145664	114
☐	N17115	ERJ-145XR	145666	115
☐	N14116	ERJ-145XR	145672	116
☐	N14117	ERJ-145XR	145674	117
☐	N13118	ERJ-145XR	145675	118
☐	N11119	ERJ-145XR	145677	119
☐	N18120	ERJ-145XR	145681	120
☐	N11121	ERJ-145XR	145683	121
☐	N12122	ERJ-145XR	145684	122
☐	N13123	ERJ-145XR	145688	123
☐	N13124	ERJ-145XR	145689	124
☐	N14125	ERJ-145XR	145690	125
☐	N12126	ERJ-145XR	145693	126
☐	N11127	ERJ-145XR	145697	127
☐	N24128	ERJ-145XR	145700	128
☐	N21129	ERJ-145XR	145703	129
☐	N21130	ERJ-145XR	145704	130
☐	N31131	ERJ-145XR	145705	131
☐	N13132	ERJ-145XR	145708	132
☐	N13133	ERJ-145XR	145712	133
☐	N25134	ERJ-145XR	145714	134
☐	N12135	ERJ-145XR	145718	135
☐	N12136	ERJ-145XR	145719	136
☐	N17138	ERJ-145XR	145727	138
☐	N23139	ERJ-145XR	145731	139
☐	N11140	ERJ-145XR	145732	140
☐	N26141	ERJ-145XR	145733	141
☐	N12142	ERJ-145XR	145735	142
☐	N14143	ERJ-145XR	145739	143
☐	N21144	ERJ-145XR	145741	144
☐	N12145	ERJ-145XR	145745	145
☐	N17146	ERJ-145XR	145746	146
☐	N16147	ERJ-145XR	145749	147
☐	N14148	ERJ-145XR	145751	148
☐	N16149	ERJ-145XR	145753	149
☐	N11150	ERJ-145XR	145756	150
☐	N16151	ERJ-145XR	145758	151
☐	N27152	ERJ-145XR	145759	152
☐	N14153	ERJ-145XR	145761	153
☐	N21154	ERJ-145XR	145772	154
☐	N11155	ERJ-145XR	145782	155
☐	N10156	ERJ-145XR	145786	156
☐	N12157	ERJ-145XR	145787	157
☐	N14158	ERJ-145XR	145791	158
☐	N17159	ERJ-145XR	145792	159
☐	N12160	ERJ-145XR	145799	160
☐	N13161	ERJ-145XR	14500805	161
☐	N11164	ERJ-145XR	14500817	164
☐	N12166	ERJ-145XR	14500831	166
☐	N17169	ERJ-145XR	14500844	169
☐	N12172	ERJ-145XR	14500864	172
☐	N14177	ERJ-145XR	14500888	177
☐	N14180	ERJ-145XR	14500900	180
☐	N17185	ERJ-145XR	14500922	185
☐	N14186	ERJ-145XR	14500924	186
☐	N11187	ERJ-145XR	14500927	187
☐	N27190	ERJ-145XR	14500934	190
☐	N11191	ERJ-145XR	14500935	191
☐	N11194	ERJ-145XR	14500940	
☐	N12195	ERJ-145XR	14500943	195
☐	N17196	ERJ-145XR	14500945	196
☐	N21197	ERJ-145XR	14500947	197
☐	N27200	ERJ-145XR	14500956	200
☐	N13202	ERJ-145XR	14500962	202
☐	N14203	ERJ-145XR	14500964	203
☐	N14204	ERJ-145XR	14500968	204
☐	N631RW	ERJ-170SE	17000007	
☐	N632RW	ERJ-170SE	17000050	
☐	N633RW	ERJ-170SE	17000054	
☐	N634RW	ERJ-170SE	17000055	
☐	N635RW	ERJ-170SE	17000056	
☐	N636RW	ERJ-170SE	17000052	
☐	N637RW	ERJ-170SE	17000051	
☐	N638RW	ERJ-170SE	17000053	
☐	N639RW	ERJ-170SE	17000057	
☐	N640RW	ERJ-170SE	17000058	
☐	N641RW	ERJ-170SE	17000062	
☐	N642RW	ERJ-170SE	17000063	
☐	N643RW	ERJ-170SE	17000060	
☐	N644RW	ERJ-170SE	17000061	
☐	N645RW	ERJ-170SE	17000064	
☐	N646RW	ERJ-170SE	17000066	
☐	N647RW	ERJ-170SE	17000067	
☐	N648RW	ERJ-170SE	17000068	
☐	N649RW	ERJ-170SE	17000070	
☐	N650RW	ERJ-170SE	17000071	
☐	N651RW	ERJ-170SE	17000072	
☐	N652RW	ERJ-170SE	17000075	
☐	N653RW	ERJ-170SE	17000076	
☐	N654RW	ERJ-170SE	17000104	
☐	N655RW	ERJ-170SE	17000105	
☐	N656RW	ERJ-170SE	17000113	
☐	N657RW	ERJ-170SE	17000115	
☐	N856RW	ERJ-170SE	17000078	
☐	N858RW	ERJ-170SE	17000079	
☐	N858RW	ERJ-170SE	17000080	
☐	N861RW	ERJ-170SE	17000094	
☐	N863RW	ERJ-170SE	17000100	
☐	N864RW	ERJ-170SE	17000117	
☐	N865RW	ERJ-170SE	17000122	
☐	N184CJ	SAAB SF.340B	340B-184	
☐	N191MJ	SAAB SF.340B	340B-191	
☐	N193CJ	SAAB SF.340B	340B-193	
☐	N194CJ	SAAB SF.340B	340B-194	
☐	N196CJ	SAAB SF.340B	340B-196	
☐	N198CJ	SAAB SF.340B	340B-198	
☐	N204CJ	SAAB SF.340B	340B-204	
☐	N220MJ	SAAB SF.340B	340B-220	
☐	N237MJ	SAAB SF.340B	340B-237	
☐	N239CJ	SAAB SF.340B	340B-239	

☐	N242CJ	SAAB SF.340B	340B-242
☐	N277MJ	SAAB SF.340B	340B-277
☐	N309CE	SAAB SF.340B	340B-201
☐	N311CE	SAAB SF.340B	340B-214
☐	N314CE	SAAB SF.340B	340B-335
☐	N334CJ	SAAB SF.340B	340B-334
☐	N343CJ	SAAB SF.340B	340B-343
☐	N352CJ	SAAB SF.340B	340B-352
☐	N356CJ	SAAB SF.340B	340B-356

UNIVERSAL AIRLINES   PNA

☐	N170UA	DC-6A	45518/998
☐	N500UA	DC-6A	44597/501
☐	N600UA	DC-6BF	44894/651

UPS AIRLINES   5X / UPS

☐	N120UP	A300F4-622R	805
☐	N121UP	A300F4-622R	806
☐	N122UP	A300F4-622R	807
☐	N124UP	A300F4-622R	808
☐	N125UP	A300F4-622R	809
☐	N126UP	A300F4-622R	810
☐	N127UP	A300F4-622R	811
☐	N128UP	A300F4-622R	812
☐	N129UP	A300F4-622R	813
☐	N130UP	A300F4-622R	814
☐	N131UP	A300F4-622R	815
☐	N133UP	A300F4-622R	816
☐	N134UP	A300F4-622R	817
☐	N135UP	A300F4-622R	818
☐	N136UP	A300F4-622R	819
☐	N137UP	A300F4-622R	820
☐	N138UP	A300F4-622R	821
☐	N139UP	A300F4-622R	822
☐	N140UP	A300F4-622R	823
☐	N141UP	A300F4-622R	824
☐	N142UP	A300F4-622R	825
☐	N143UP	A300F4-622R	826
☐	N144UP	A300F4-622R	827
☐	N145UP	A300F4-622R	828
☐	N146UP	A300F4-622R	829
☐	N147UP	A300F4-622R	830
☐	N148UP	A300F4-622R	831
☐	N149UP	A300F4-622R	832
☐	N150UP	A300F4-622R	833
☐	N151UP	A300F4-622R	834
☐	N152UP	A300F4-622R	835
☐	N153UP	A300F4-622R	839
☐	N154UP	A300F4-622R	840
☐	N155UP	A300F4-622R	841
☐	N156UP	A300F4-622R	845
☐	N157UP	A300F4-622R	846
☐	N158UP	A300F4-622R	847
☐	N159UP	A300F4-622R	848
☐	N160UP	A300F4-622R	849
☐	N161UP	A300F4-622R	850
☐	N162UP	A300F4-622R	851
☐	N163UP	A300F4-622R	852
☐	N164UP	A300F4-622R	853
☐	N165UP	A300F4-622R	854
☐	N166UP	A300F4-622R	861
☐	N167UP	A300F4-622R	862
☐	N168UP	A300F4-622R	863
☐	N169UP	A300F4-622R	864
☐	N170UP	A300F4-622R	865
☐	N171UP	A300F4-622R	866
☐	N172UP	A300F4-622R	867
☐	N173UP	A300F4-622R	868
☐	N174UP	A300F4-622R	869
☐	N676UP	B747-123(SF)	20101/57 [ROW]
☐	N677UP	B747-123(SF)	20391/143 [ROW]
☐	N681UP	B747-121(SF)	19661/70 [ROW]
☐	N682UP	B747-121(SF)	20349/110 [ROW]

☐	N683UP	B747-121(SF)	20353/131
☐	N570UP	B747-44AF	35667/1388
☐	N572UP	B747-44AF	35669/1396
☐	N573UP	B747-44AF	35662/1401
☐	N574UP	B747-44AF	35663/1403
☐	N575UP	B747-44AF	35664/1406
☐	N576UP	B747-44AF	35665/1410
☐	N577UP	B747-44AF	35666/1412
☐	N578UP	B747-45EM	27154/994
☐	N579UP	B747-45EM	26062/1016
☐	N580UP	B747-428F	25632/968
☐	N581UP	B747-4R7F	25866/1002
☐	N583UP	B747-4R7F	25867/1008
☐	N401UP	B757-24APF	23723/139
☐	N402UP	B757-24APF	23724/141
☐	N403UP	B757-24APF	23725/143
☐	N404UP	B757-24APF	23726/147
☐	N405UP	B757-24APF	23727/149
☐	N406UP	B757-24APF	23728/176
☐	N407UP	B757-24APF	23729/181
☐	N408UP	B757-24APF	23730/184
☐	N409UP	B757-24APF	23731/186
☐	N410UP	B757-24APF	23732/189
☐	N411UP	B757-24APF	23851/191
☐	N412UP	B757-24APF	23852/193
☐	N413UP	B757-24APF	23853/195
☐	N414UP	B757-24APF	23854/197
☐	N415UP	B757-24APF	23855/199
☐	N416UP	B757-24APF	23903/318
☐	N417UP	B757-24APF	23904/322
☐	N418UP	B757-24APF	23905/326
☐	N419UP	B757-24APF	23906/330
☐	N420UP	B757-24APF	23907/334
☐	N421UP	B757-24APF	25281/395
☐	N422UP	B757-24APF	25324/399
☐	N423UP	B757-24APF	25325/403
☐	N424UP	B757-24APF	25369/407
☐	N425UP	B757-24APF	25370/411
☐	N426UP	B757-24APF	25457/477
☐	N427UP	B757-24APF	25458/481
☐	N428UP	B757-24APF	25459/485
☐	N429UP	B757-24APF	25460/489
☐	N430UP	B757-24APF	25461/493
☐	N431UP	B757-24APF	25462/569
☐	N432UP	B757-24APF	25463/573
☐	N433UP	B757-24APF	25464/577
☐	N434UP	B757-24APF	25465/579
☐	N435UP	B757-24APF	25466/581
☐	N436UP	B757-24APF	25467/625
☐	N437UP	B757-24APF	25468/628
☐	N438UP	B757-24APF	25469/631
☐	N439UP	B757-24APF	25470/634
☐	N440UP	B757-24APF	25471/636
☐	N441UP	B757-24APF	27386/638
☐	N442UP	B757-24APF	27387/640
☐	N443UP	B757-24APF	27388/642
☐	N444UP	B757-24APF	27389/644
☐	N445UP	B757-24APF	27390/646
☐	N446UP	B757-24APF	27735/649
☐	N447UP	B757-24APF	27736/651
☐	N448UP	B757-24APF	27737/654
☐	N449UP	B757-24APF	27738/656
☐	N450UP	B757-24APF	25472/659
☐	N451UP	B757-24APF	27739/675
☐	N452UP	B757-24APF	25473/679
☐	N453UP	B757-24APF	25474/683
☐	N454UP	B757-24APF	25475/687
☐	N455UP	B757-24APF	25476/691
☐	N456UP	B757-24APF	25477/728
☐	N457UP	B757-24APF	25478/729
☐	N458UP	B757-24APF	25479/730
☐	N459UP	B757-24APF	25480/733
☐	N460UP	B757-24APF	25481/734
☐	N461UP	B757-24APF	28265/755

♦

	Reg	Type	Serial	Notes
☐	N462UP	B757-24APF	28266/759	
☐	N463UP	B757-24APF	28267/763	
☐	N464UP	B757-24APF	28268/765	
☐	N465UP	B757-24APF	28269/767	
☐	N466UP	B757-24APF	25482/769	
☐	N467UP	B757-24APF	25483/771	
☐	N468UP	B757-24APF	25484/774	
☐	N469UP	B757-24APF	25485/776	
☐	N470UP	B757-24APF	25486/778	
☐	N471UP	B757-24APF	28842/813	
☐	N472UP	B757-24APF	28843/815	
☐	N473UP	B757-24APF	28846/823	
☐	N474UP	B757-24APF	28844/879	
☐	N475UP	B757-24APF	28845/882	
☐	N301UP	B767-34AF	27239/580	
☐	N302UP	B767-34AF	27240/590	
☐	N303UP	B767-34AF	27241/594	
☐	N304UP	B767-34AF	27242/598	
☐	N305UP	B767-34AF	27243/600	
☐	N306UP	B767-34AF	27759/622	
☐	N307UP	B767-34AF	27760/624	
☐	N308UP	B767-34AF	27761/626	
☐	N309UP	B767-34AF	27740/628	
☐	N310UP	B767-34AF	27762/630	
☐	N311UP	B767-34AF	27741/632	
☐	N312UP	B767-34AF	27763/634	
☐	N313UP	B767-34AF	27764/636	
☐	N314UP	B767-34AF	27742/638	
☐	N315UP	B767-34AF	27743/640	
☐	N316UP	B767-34AF	27744/660	
☐	N317UP	B767-34AF	27745/666	
☐	N318UP	B767-34AF	27746/670	
☐	N319UP	B767-34AF	27758/672	
☐	N320UP	B767-34AF	27747/674	
☐	N322UP	B767-34AF	27748/678	
☐	N323UP	B767-34AF	27749/682	
☐	N324UP	B767-34AF	27750/724	
☐	N325UP	B767-34AF	27751/726	
☐	N326UP	B767-34AF	27752/728	
☐	N327UP	B767-34AF	27753/730	
☐	N328UP	B767-34AF	27754/732	
☐	N329UP	B767-34AF	27755/756	
☐	N330UP	B767-34AF	27756/760	
☐	N331UP	B767-34AF	27757/764	
☐	N332UP	B767-34AF	32843/854	
☐	N334UP	B767-34AF	32844/858	
☐	N335UP	B767-34AF	37856/979	
☐	N336UP	B767-34AF	37857/983	
☐	N337UP	B767-34AF	37858/986	
☐	N338UP	B767-34AF	37944/988	♦
☐	N339UP	B767-34AF	37859/989	♦
☐	N340UP	B767-34AF	37860/991	♦
☐	N341UP	B767-34AF	37861/992	♦
☐		B767-34AF		o/o♦
☐		B767-34AF		o/o♦
☐		B767-34AF		o/o♦
☐		B767-34AF		o/o♦
☐		B767-34AF		o/o♦
☐		B767-34AF		o/o♦
☐		B767-34AF		o/o♦
☐		B767-34AF		o/o♦
☐		B767-34AF		o/o♦
☐		B767-34AF		o/o♦
☐		B767-34AF		o/o♦
☐		B767-34AF		o/o♦
☐		B767-34AF		o/o♦
☐	N700UP	DC-8-71CF	45900/316	[ROW]
☐	N702UP	DC-8-71CF	45902/294	
☐	N715UP	DC-8-71F	45915/295	[ROW]
☐	N718UP	DC-8-71F	46018/420	[ROW]
☐	N729UP	DC-8-71F	46029/425	[ROW]
☐	N752UP	DC-8-71CF	45952/338	[ROW]
☐	N811UP	DC-8-73CF	46089/501	[ROW]

	Reg	Type	Serial	Notes
☐	N812UP	DC-8-73CF	46112/520	[ROW]
☐	N814UP	DC-8-73CF	46090/504	[ROW]
☐	N819UP	DC-8-73F	46019/411	
☐	N840UP	DC-8-73CF	46140/528	
☐	N851UP	DC-8-73CF	46051/440	[ROW]
☐	N852UP	DC-8-73CF	46052/442	
☐	N866UP	DC-8-73CF	45966/393	[ROW]
☐	N867UP	DC-8-73CF	45967/385	[ROW]
☐	N868UP	DC-8-73CF	45968/389	[ROW]
☐	N874UP	DC-8-73PF	46074/468	[ROW]
☐	N880UP	DC-8-73F	46080/466	
☐	N894UP	DC-8-73CF	46094/482	[ROW]
☐	N250UP	MD-11F	48745/596	
☐	N251UP	MD-11F	48744/592	
☐	N252UP	MD-11F	48768/601	
☐	N253UP	MD-11F	48439/554	
☐	N254UP	MD-11F	48406/547	
☐	N255UP	MD-11F	48404/523	
☐	N256UP	MD-11F	48405/524	
☐	N257UP	MD-11F	48451/505	
☐	N258UP	MD-11F	48416/466	
☐	N259UP	MD-11F	48417/467	
☐	N260UP	MD-11F	48418/501	
☐	N270UP	MD-11F	48576/574	
☐	N271UP	MD-11F	48572/556	
☐	N272UP	MD-11F	48571/552	
☐	N273UP	MD-11F	48574/566	
☐	N274UP	MD-11F	48575/568	
☐	N275UP	MD-11F	48774/610	
☐	N276UP	MD-11F	48579/599	
☐	N277UP	MD-11F	48578/588	
☐	N278UP	MD-11F	48577/583	
☐	N279UP	MD-11F	48573/559	
☐	N280UP	MD-11F	48634/614	
☐	N281UP	MD-11F	48538/533	
☐	N282UP	MD-11F	48452/472	
☐	N283UP	MD-11F	48484/484	
☐	N284UP	MD-11F	48541/621	
☐	N285UP	MD-11F	48457/498	
☐	N286UP	MD-11F	48453/473	
☐	N287UP	MD-11	48539/571	
☐	N288UP	MD-11F	48540/611	
☐	N289UP	MD-11	48455/487	
☐	N290UP	MD-11F	48456/494	
☐	N291UP	MD-11F	48477/511	
☐	N292UP	MD-11F	48566/543	
☐	N293UP	MD-11F	48473/481	
☐	N294UP	MD-11F	48472/480	
☐	N295UP	MD-11F	48475/489	
☐	N296UP	MD-11F	48474/485	

US AIRWAYS — US / USA

	Reg	Type	Serial
☐	N700UW	A319-112	0885
☐	N701UW	A319-112	0890
☐	N702UW	A319-112	0896
☐	N703UW	A319-112	0904
☐	N704US	A319-112	0922
☐	N705UW	A319-112	0929
☐	N708UW	A319-112	0972
☐	N709UW	A319-112	0997
☐	N710UW	A319-112	1019
☐	N711UW	A319-112	1033
☐	N712US	A319-112	1038
☐	N713UW	A319-112	1040
☐	N714US	A319-112	1046
☐	N715UW	A319-112	1051
☐	N716UW	A319-112	1055
☐	N717UW	A319-112	1069
☐	N721UW	A319-112	1095
☐	N722US	A319-112	1097
☐	N723UW	A319-112	1109
☐	N724UW	A319-112	1122
☐	N725UW	A319-112	1135
☐	N730US	A319-112	1182

	Reg	Type	c/n	
☐	N732US	A319-112	1203	
☐	N733UW	A319-112	1205	
☐	N737UW	A319-112	1245	
☐	N738US	A319-112	1254	
☐	N740UW	A319-112	1265	
☐	N741UW	A319-112	1269	
☐	N742PS	A319-112	1275	
☐	N744P	A319-112	1287	
☐	N745VJ	A319-112	1289	
☐	N746UW	A319-112	1297	
☐	N747UW	A319-112	1301	
☐	N748UW	A319-112	1311	
☐	N749US	A319-112	1313	
☐	N750UW	A319-112	1315	
☐	N751UW	A319-112	1317	
☐	N752US	A319-112	1319	
☐	N753US	A319-112	1326	
☐	N754UW	A319-112	1328	
☐	N755US	A319-112	1331	
☐	N756US	A319-112	1340	
☐	N757UW	A319-112	1342	
☐	N758US	A319-112	1348	
☐	N760US	A319-112	1354	
☐	N762US	A319-112	1358	
☐	N763US	A319-112	1360	
☐	N764US	A319-112	1369	
☐	N765US	A319-112	1371	
☐	N766US	A319-112	1378	
☐	N767UW	A319-112	1382	
☐	N768US	A319-112	1389	
☐	N769US	A319-112	1391	
☐	N770UW	A319-112	1393	
☐	N801AW	A319-132	0889	
☐	N802AW	A319-132	0924	
☐	N803AW	A319-132	0931	
☐	N804AW	A319-132	1043	
☐	N805AW	A319-132	1049	
☐	N806AW	A319-132	1056	
☐	N807AW	A319-132	1064	
☐	N808AW	A319-132	1088	
☐	N809AW	A319-132	1111	
☐	N810AW	A319-132	1116	
☐	N812AW	A319-132	1178	
☐	N813AW	A319-132	1223	
☐	N814AW	A319-132	1281	
☐	N815AW	A319-132	1323	
☐	N816AW	A319-132	1350	
☐	N817AW	A319-132	1373	
☐	N818AW	A319-132	1375	
☐	N819AW	A319-132	1395	
☐	N820AW	A319-132	1397	
☐	N821AW	A319-132	1406	
☐	N822AW	A319-132	1410	
☐	N823AW	A319-132	1463	
☐	N824AW	A319-132	1490	
☐	N825AW	A319-132	1527	
☐	N826AW	A319-132	1534	
☐	N827AW	A319-132	1547	
☐	N828AW	A319-132	1552	
☐	N829AW	A319-132	1563	
☐	N830AW	A319-132	1565	
☐	N831AW	A319-132	1576	
☐	N832AW	A319-132	1643	
☐	N833AW	A319-132	1844	
☐	N834AW	A319-132	2302	
☐	N835AW	A319-132	2458	
☐	N836AW	A319-132	2570	
☐	N837AW	A319-132	2595	
☐	N838AW	A319-132	2615	
☐	N839AW	A319-132	2669	
☐	N840AW	A319-132	2690	
☐	N102UW	A320-214	0844	
☐	N103US	A320-214	0861	
☐	N104UW	A320-214	0863	
☐	N105UW	A320-214	0868	
☐	N107US	A320-214	1052	
☐	N108UW	A320-214	1061	
☐	N109UW	A320-214	1065	
☐	N110UW	A320-214	1112	
☐	N111US	A320-214	1114	
☐	N112US	A320-214	1134	
☐	N113UW	A320-214	1141	
☐	N114UW	A320-214	1148	
☐	N117UW	A320-214	1224	
☐	N118US	A320-214	1264	
☐	N119US	A320-214	1268	
☐	N121UW	A320-214	1294	
☐	N122US	A320-214	1298	
☐	N123UW	A320-214	1310	
☐	N124US	A320-214	1314	
☐	N125UW	A320-214	4086	
☐	N126UW	A320-214	4149	
☐	N127UW	A320-214	4202	♦
☐	N128UW	A320-214	4242	♦
☐	N601AW	A320-232	1935	
☐	N602AW	A320-232	0565	
☐	N604AW	A320-232	1196	
☐	N620AW	A320-231	0052	
☐	N621AW	A320-231	0053	
☐	N622AW	A320-231	0054	
☐	N624AW	A320-231	0055	
☐	N625AW	A320-231	0064	
☐	N626AW	A320-231	0065	
☐	N627AW	A320-231	0066	
☐	N628AW	A320-231	0067	
☐	N629AW	A320-231	0076	
☐	N631AW	A320-231	0077	
☐	N632AW	A320-231	0081	
☐	N633AW	A320-231	0082	
☐	N634AW	A320-231	0091	
☐	N637AW	A320-231	0099	
☐	N640AW	A320-232	0448	
☐	N642AW	A320-232	0584	
☐	N644AW	A320-231	0317	
☐	N647AW	A320-232	0762	
☐	N648AW	A320-232	0770	
☐	N649AW	A320-232	0803	
☐	N650AW	A320-232	0856	
☐	N651AW	A320-232	0866	
☐	N652AW	A320-232	0953	
☐	N653AW	A320-232	1003	
☐	N654AW	A320-232	1050	
☐	N655AW	A320-232	1075	
☐	N656AW	A320-232	1079	
☐	N657AW	A320-232	1083	
☐	N658AW	A320-232	1110	
☐	N659AW	A320-232	1166	
☐	N660AW	A320-232	1234	
☐	N661AW	A320-232	1284	
☐	N662AW	A320-232	1274	
☐	N663AW	A320-232	1419	
☐	N664AW	A320-232	1621	
☐	N665AW	A320-232	1644	
☐	N667AW	A320-232	1710	
☐	N668AW	A320-232	1764	
☐	N669AW	A320-232	1792	
☐	N672AW	A320-232	2193	
☐	N673AW	A320-232	2312	
☐	N675AW	A320-232	2405	
☐	N676AW	A320-232	2422	
☐	N677AW	A320-232	2430	
☐	N678AW	A320-232	2482	
☐	N679AW	A320-232	2613	
☐	N680AW	A320-232	2630	
☐		A320-232		o/o♦
☐		A320-232		o/o♦
☐		A320-232		o/o♦
☐		A320-232		o/o♦
☐		A320-232		o/o♦
☐		A320-232		o/o♦

☐	N161UW	A321-211	1403
☐	N162UW	A321-211	1412
☐	N163US	A321-211	1417
☐	N165US	A321-211	1431
☐	N167US	A321-211	1442
☐	N169UW	A321-211	1455
☐	N170US	A321-211	1462
☐	N171US	A321-211	1465
☐	N172US	A321-211	1472
☐	N173US	A321-211	1481
☐	N174US	A321-211	1492
☐	N176UW	A321-211	1499
☐	N177US	A321-211	1517
☐	N178US	A321-211	1519
☐	N179UW	A321-211	1521
☐	N180US	A321-211	1525
☐	N181UW	A321-211	1531
☐	N182UW	A321-211	1536
☐	N183UW	A321-211	1539
☐	N184US	A321-211	1651
☐	N185UW	A321-211	1666
☐	N186US	A321-211	1701
☐	N187US	A321-211	1704
☐	N188US	A321-211	1724
☐	N189UW	A321-211	1425
☐	N190UW	A321-211	1436
☐	N191UW	A321-211	1447
☐	N192UW	A321-211	1496
☐	N193UW	A321-211	3584
☐	N194UW	A321-211	3629
☐	N195UW	A321-211	3633
☐	N196UW	A321-211	3879
☐	N197UW	A321-211	3928
☐	N507AY	A321-231	3712
☐	N508AY	A321-231	3740
☐	N509AY	A321-231	3796
☐	N510UW	A321-231	3858
☐	N519UW	A321-231	3881
☐	N520UW	A321-231	3924
☐	N521UW	A321-231	3944
☐	N523UW	A321-231	3960
☐	N524UW	A321-231	3977
☐	N534UW	A321-231	3989
☐	N535UW	A321-231	3993
☐	N536UW	A321-231	4025
☐	N537UW	A321-231	4041
☐	N538UW	A321-231	4050
☐	N539UW	A321-231	4082
☐	N540UW	A321-231	4107
☐	N541UW	A321-231	4123
☐	N542UW	A321-231	4134
☐		A321-231	o/o♦
☐		A321-231	o/o♦
☐		A321-231	o/o♦
☐		A321-231	o/o♦
☐		A321-231	o/o♦
☐	N270AY	A330-323X	315
☐	N271AY	A330-323X	323
☐	N272AY	A330-323X	333
☐	N273AY	A330-323X	337
☐	N274AY	A330-323X	342
☐	N275AY	A330-323X	370
☐	N276AY	A330-323X	375
☐	N277AY	A330-323X	380
☐	N278AY	A330-323X	388
☐	N279AY	A330-243	1011
☐	N280AY	A330-243	1022
☐	N281AY	A330-243	1041
☐	N282AY	A330-243	1069
☐	N283AY	A330-243	1076
☐	N284AY	A330-243	1095
☐	N285AY	A330-243	1100 ♦
☐	N154AW	B737-3G7	23776/1417

☐	N155AW	B737-3G7	23777/1419	
☐	N156AW	B737-3G7	23778/1455	
☐	N157AW	B737-3G7	23779/1457	
☐	N158AW	B737-3G7	23780/1459	
☐	N302AW	B737-3G7	24009/1578	
☐	N303AW	B737-3G7	24010/1606	
☐	N305AW	B737-3G7	24012/1612	
☐	N313AW	B737-3S3	23712/1336	
☐	N314AW	B737-3S3	23733/1345	
☐	N315AW	B737-3S3	23734/1359	
☐	N316AW	B737-3S3	23713/1341	
☐	N332AW	B737-3B7	23384/1427	
☐	N334AW	B737-3Y0	23748/1381	
☐	N504AU	B737-3B7	23379/1362	
☐	N505AU	B737-3B7	23380/1366	
☐	N506AU	B737-3B7	23381/1394	
☐	N516AU	B737-3B7	23702/1475	
☐	N529AU	B737-3B7	24411/1713	
☐	N530AU	B737-3B7	24412/1735	
☐	N531AU	B737-3B7	24478/1743	
☐	N532AU	B737-3B7	24479/1745	
☐	N533AU	B737-3B7	24515/1767	
☐	N574US	B737-301	23739/1469	
☐	N588US	B737-301	23933/1559	[GYR]
☐	N404US	B737-401	23886/1487	
☐	N405US	B737-401	23885/1512	
☐	N406US	B737-401	23876/1528	
☐	N409US	B737-401	23879/1573	
☐	N417US	B737-401	23984/1674	
☐	N418US	B737-401	23985/1676	
☐	N419US	B737-401	23986/1684	
☐	N420US	B737-401	23987/1698	
☐	N421US	B737-401	23988/1714	
☐	N422US	B737-401	23989/1716	
☐	N423US	B737-401	23990/1732	
☐	N424US	B737-401	23991/1746	
☐	N425US	B737-401	23992/1764	
☐	N426US	B737-4B7	24548/1789	
☐	N427US	B737-4B7	24549/1791	
☐	N430US	B737-4B7	24552/1797	
☐	N432US	B737-4B7	24554/1817	
☐	N433US	B737-4B7	24555/1819	
☐	N434US	B737-4B7	24556/1821	
☐	N435US	B737-4B7	24557/1835	
☐	N438US	B737-4B7	24560/1849	
☐	N439US	B737-4B7	24781/1874	
☐	N440US	B737-4B7	24811/1890	
☐	N441US	B737-4B7	24812/1892	
☐	N442US	B737-4B7	24841/1906	
☐	N443US	B737-4B7	24842/1908	
☐	N444US	B737-4B7	24862/1910	
☐	N445US	B737-4B7	24863/1914	
☐	N449US	B737-4B7	24893/1946	
☐	N450UW	B737-4B7	24933/1954	
☐	N451UW	B737-4B7	24934/1956	
☐	N452UW	B737-4B7	24979/1980	
☐	N453UW	B737-4B7	24980/1982	
☐	N454UW	B737-4B7	24996/1986	
☐	N455UW	B737-4B7	24997/1990	
☐	N456UW	B737-4B7	25020/1992	
☐	N457UW	B737-4B7	25021/1995	
☐	N458UW	B737-4B7	25022/2010	
☐	N459UW	B737-4B7	25023/2020	
☐	N460UW	B737-4B7	25024/2026	
☐	N200UU	B757-2B7/W	27809/673	
☐	N201UU	B757-2B7/W	27810/678	
☐	N202UW	B757-2B7/W	27811/681	
☐	N203UW	B757-23N/W	30548/930	
☐	N204UW	B757-23N/W	30886/945	
☐	N205UW	B757-23N/W	30887/946	
☐	N206UW	B757-2B7/W	27808/666	
☐	N901AW	B757-2S7	23321/76	
☐	N902AW	B757-2S7	23322/79	
☐	N903AW	B757-2S7	23323/80	

☐	N904AW	B757-2S7	23566/96
☐	N905AW	B757-2S7	23567/97
☐	N906AW	B757-2S7	23568/99
☐	N908AW	B757-2G7/W	24233/244
☐	N909AW	B757-2G7/W	24522/252
☐	N910AW	B757-2G7/W	24523/256
☐	N923UW	B757-225	22203/26 [VCV]
☐	N925UW	B757-225	22205/28
☐	N935UW	B757-2B7/W	27201/605
☐	N936UW	B757-2B7	27244/607
☐	N937UW	B757-2B7/W	27245/630
☐	N938UW	B757-2B7/W	27246/643
☐	N939UW	B757-2B7/W	27303/647
☐	N940UW	B757-2B7/W	27805/655
☐	N941UW	B757-2B7/W	27806/657
■	N942UW	B757-2B7/W	27807/662 3/3
☐	N245AY	B767-201ER	23897/173
☐	N246AY	B767-201ER	23898/175
☐	N248AY	B767-201ER	23900/190
☐	N249AU	B767-201ER	23901/197
☐	N250AY	B767-201ER	23902/217
☐	N251AY	B767-2B7ER	24764/306
☐	N252AU	B767-2B7ER	24765/308
☐	N253AY	B767-2B7ER	24894/338
☐	N255AY	B767-2B7ER	25257/383
☐	N256AY	B767-2B7ER	26847/486

US AIRWAYS EXPRESS   USX

☐	N124CJ	Beech 1900D	UE-24	LVA
☐	N171CJ	Beech 1900D	UE-71	LVU
☐	N172MJ	Beech 1900D	UE-72	LVI
☐	N191CJ	Beech 1900D	UE-19	LVW
☐	N221CJ	Beech 1900D	UE-221	LVG
☐	N202PS	CRJ-200ER	7858	202
☐	N206PS	CRJ-200ER	7860	206
☐	N207PS	CRJ-200ER	7873	207
☐	N209PS	CRJ-200ER	7874	209
☐	N213PS	CRJ-200ER	7879	213
☐	N215PS	CRJ-200ER	7880	215
☐	N216PS	CRJ-200ER	7882	216
☐	N218PS	CRJ-200ER	7885	218
☐	N220PS	CRJ-200ER	7887	220
☐	N221PS	CRJ-200ER	7889	221
☐	N223JS	CRJ-200ER	7892	223
☐	N226JS	CRJ-200ER	7895	226
☐	N228PS	CRJ-200ER	7897	228
☐	N229PS	CRJ-200ER	7898	229
☐	N230PS	CRJ-200ER	7904	230
☐	N237PS	CRJ-200ER	7906	237
☐	N241PS	CRJ-200ER	7909	241
☐	N242JS	CRJ-200ER	7911	242
☐	N244PS	CRJ-200ER	7912	244
☐	N245PS	CRJ-200ER	7919	245
☐	N246PS	CRJ-200ER	7920	246
☐	N247JS	CRJ-200ER	7922	247
☐	N248PS	CRJ-200ER	7925	248
☐	N249PS	CRJ-200ER	7926	249
☐	N250PS	CRJ-200ER	7929	250
☐	N251PS	CRJ-200ER	7931	251
☐	N253PS	CRJ-200ER	7934	253
☐	N254PS	CRJ-200ER	7935	254
☐	N256PS	CRJ-200ER	7937	256
☐	N257PS	CRJ-200ER	7939	257
☐	N258PS	CRJ-200ER	7941	258
☐	N259PS	CRJ-200ER	7945	259
☐	N260JS	CRJ-200ER	7957	260
☐	N261PS	CRJ-200ER	7959	261
☐	N262PS	CRJ-200ER	7962	262
☐	N401AW	CRJ-200LR	7280	401
☐	N403AW	CRJ-200LR	7288	403
☐	N404AW	CRJ-200LR	7294	404
☐	N405AW	CRJ-200LR	7362	405
☐	N406AW	CRJ-200LR	7402	406

☐	N407AW	CRJ-200LR	7424	407
☐	N408AW	CRJ-200LR	7568	408
☐	N409AW	CRJ-200LR	7447	409
☐	N410AW	CRJ-200LR	7490	410
☐	N411ZW	CRJ-200LR	7569	411
☐	N412AW	CRJ-200LR	7582	412
☐	N413AW	CRJ-200LR	7585	413
☐	N414ZW	CRJ-200LR	7586	414
☐	N415AW	CRJ-200LR	7593	415
☐	N416AW	CRJ-200LR	7603	416
☐	N417AW	CRJ-200LR	7610	417
☐	N418AW	CRJ-200LR	7618	418
☐	N419AW	CRJ-200LR	7633	419
☐	N420AW	CRJ-200LR	7640	420
☐	N421ZW	CRJ-200LR	7346	421
☐	N422AW	CRJ-200LR	7341	422
☐	N423AW	CRJ-200LR	7636	423
☐	N424AW	CRJ-200LR	7656	424
☐	N425AW	CRJ-200LR	7663	425
☐	N426AW	CRJ-200LR	7669	426
☐	N427ZW	CRJ-200LR	7685	427
☐	N428AW	CRJ-200LR	7695	428
☐	N429AW	CRJ-200LR	7711	429
☐	N430AW	CRJ-200LR	7719	430
☐	N431AW	CRJ-200LR	7256	431
☐	N432AW	CRJ-200LR	7257	432
☐	N433AW	CRJ-200LR	7289	433
☐	N434AW	CRJ-200LR	7322	434
☐	N435AW	CRJ-200LR	7724	435
☐	N436AW	CRJ-200LR	7734	436
☐	N437AW	CRJ-200LR	7744	437
☐	N438AW	CRJ-200LR	7748	438
☐	N439AW	CRJ-200LR	7753	439
☐	N440AW	CRJ-200LR	7766	440
☐	N441ZW	CRJ-200LR	7777	441
☐	N442AW	CRJ-200LR	7778	442
☐	N443AW	CRJ-200LR	7781	443
☐	N444ZW	CRJ-200LR	7788	444
☐	N445AW	CRJ-200LR	7804	445
☐	N446AW	CRJ-200LR	7806	446
☐	N447AW	CRJ-200LR	7812	447
☐	N448AW	CRJ-200LR	7814	448
☐	N449AW	CRJ-200LR	7818	449
☐	N450AW	CRJ-200LR	7823	450
☐	N451AW	CRJ-200LR	7832	451
☐	N452AW	CRJ-200LR	7835	452
☐	N453AW	CRJ-200LR	7838	453
☐	N454AW	CRJ-200LR	7842	454
☐	N455AW	CRJ-200LR	7848	455
☐	N456ZW	CRJ-200LR	7849	456
☐	N457AW	CRJ-200LR	7854	457
☐	N458AW	CRJ-200LR	7861	458
☐	N459AW	CRJ-200LR	7863	459
☐	N460AW	CRJ-200LR	7867	460
☐	N461AW	CRJ-200LR	7870	461
☐	N462AW	CRJ-200LR	7875	462
☐	N463AW	CRJ-200LR	7878	463
☐	N464AW	CRJ-200LR	7890	464
☐	N465AW	CRJ-200LR	7893	465
☐	N466AW	CRJ-200LR	7899	466
☐	N467AW	CRJ-200LR	7900	467
☐	N468AW	CRJ-200LR	7916	468
☐	N469AW	CRJ-200LR	7917	469
☐	N470ZW	CRJ-200LR	7927	470
☐	N570ML	CRJ-200LR	7206	YJX
☐	N651ML	CRJ-200LR	7139	YCD
☐	N7264V	CRJ-200LR	7264	
☐	N7291Z	CRJ-200LR	7291	
☐	N7305V	CRJ-200LR	7305	
☐	N17231	CRJ-200LR	7231	
☐	N17275	CRJ-200LR	7275	
☐	N17337	CRJ-200LR	7337	
☐	N17358	CRJ-200LR	7358	
☐	N27173	CRJ-200LR	7173	
☐	N27314	CRJ-200LR	7314	

	Reg	Type	c/n	Code
☐	N37178	CRJ-200LR	7178	
☐	N75984	CRJ-200LR	7489	YJW
☐	N77260	CRJ-200LR	7260	
☐	N77286	CRJ-200LR	7286	
☐	N97325	CRJ-200LR	7325	
☐	N702PS	CRJ-701ER	10135	702
☐	N703PS	CRJ-701ER	10137	703
☐	N705PS	CRJ-701ER	10144	705
☐	N706PS	CRJ-701ER	10150	706
☐	N708PS	CRJ-701ER	10160	708
☐	N709PS	CRJ-701ER	10165	709
☐	N710PS	CRJ-701ER	10167	710
☐	N712PS	CRJ-701ER	10168	712
☐	N716PS	CRJ-701ER	10171	716
☐	N718PS	CRJ-701ER	10175	718
☐	N719PS	CRJ-701ER	10177	719
☐	N720PS	CRJ-701ER	10178	720
☐	N723PS	CRJ-701ER	10181	723
☐	N725PS	CRJ-701ER	10186	725
☐	N726PS	CRJ-701ER		o/o
☐	N728PS	CRJ-701ER		o/o
☐	N729PS	CRJ-701ER		o/o
☐	N730PS	CRJ-701ER		o/o
☐	N736PS	CRJ-701ER		o/o
☐	N740PS	CRJ-701ER		o/o
☐	N741PS	CRJ-701ER		o/o
☐	N743PS	CRJ-701ER		o/o
☐	N744PS	CRJ-701ER		o/o
☐	N745PS	CRJ-701ER		o/o
☐	N746PS	CRJ-701ER		o/o
☐	N748PS	CRJ-701ER		o/o
☐	N749PS	CRJ-701ER		o/o
☐	N750PS	CRJ-701ER		o/o
☐	N751PS	CRJ-701ER		o/o
☐	N752PS	CRJ-701ER		o/o
☐	N753PS	CRJ-701ER		o/o
☐	N754PS	CRJ-701ER		o/o
☐	N755PS	CRJ-701ER		o/o
☐	N756PS	CRJ-701ER		o/o
☐	N	CRJ-701ER		o/o
☐	N	CRJ-701ER		o/o
☐	N	CRJ-701ER		o/o
☐	N	CRJ-701ER		o/o
☐	N	CRJ-701ER		o/o
☐	N	CRJ-701ER		o/o
☐	N	CRJ-701ER		o/o
☐	N	CRJ-701ER		o/o
☐	N	CRJ-701ER		o/o
☐	N	CRJ-701ER		o/o
☐	N	CRJ-701ER		o/o
☐	N902FJ	CRJ-900ER	15002	
☐	N903FJ	CRJ-900ER	15003	
☐	N904FJ	CRJ-900ER	15004	
☐	N905J	CRJ-900ER	15005	
☐	N906FJ	CRJ-900ER	15006	
☐	N907FJ	CRJ-900ER	15007	
☐	N908FJ	CRJ-900ER	15008	
☐	N909FJ	CRJ-900ER	15009	
☐	N910FJ	CRJ-900ER	15010	
☐	N911FJ	CRJ-900ER	15011	
☐	N912FJ	CRJ-900ER	15012	
☐	N913FJ	CRJ-900ER	15013	
☐	N914FJ	CRJ-900ER	15014	
☐	N915FJ	CRJ-900ER	15015	
☐	N916FJ	CRJ-900ER	15016	
☐	N917FJ	CRJ-900ER	15017	
☐	N918FJ	CRJ-900ER	15018	
☐	N919FJ	CRJ-900ER	15019	
☐	N920FJ	CRJ-900ER	15020	
☐	N921FJ	CRJ-900ER	15021	
☐	N922FJ	CRJ-900ER	15022	
☐	N923FJ	CRJ-900ER	15023	
☐	N924FJ	CRJ-900ER	15024	
☐	N925FJ	CRJ-900ER	15025	

	Reg	Type	c/n	Code
☐	N926LR	CRJ-900ER	15026	
☐	N927LR	CRJ-900ER	15027	
☐	N928LR	CRJ-900ER	15028	
☐	N929LR	CRJ-900ER	15029	
☐	N930LR	CRJ-900ER	15030	
☐	N931LR	CRJ-900ER	15031	
☐	N932LR	CRJ-900ER	15032	
☐	N933LR	CRJ-900ER	15033	
☐	N934FJ	CRJ-900ER	15034	
☐	N935LR	CRJ-900ER	15035	
☐	N938LR	CRJ-900ER	15038	
☐	N939LR	CRJ-900ER	15039	
☐	N942LR	CRJ-900ER	15042	
☐	N956LR	CRJ-900ER	15056	
☐	N326EN	DHC-8-311	234	HDF
☐	N327EN	DHC-8-311A	261	HDD
☐	N328EN	DHC-8-311A	281	HDC
☐	N329EN	DHC-8-311	290	HDG
☐	N330EN	DHC-8-311A	274	HDI
☐	N331EN	DHC-8-311A	279	HDJ
☐	N333EN	DHC-8-311	221	HDK
☐	N335EN	DHC-8-311	375	HDN
☐	N336EN	DHC-8-311A	336	HAD
☐	N337EN	DHC-8-311A	284	HDH
☐	N343EN	DHC-8-311A	340	HDE
☐	N437YV	DHC-8-202	437	
☐	N449YV	DHC-8Q-202	449	
☐	N804EX	DHC-8-102A	227	ESA
☐	N805EX	DHC-8-102A	228	ESB
☐	N806EX	DHC-8-102A	263	ESC
☐	N807EX	DHC-8-102A	292	ESD
☐	N808EX	DHC-8-102A	299	ESE
☐	N809EX	DHC-8-102A	302	ESF
☐	N810EX	DHC-8-102A	308	ESG
☐	N812EX	DHC-8-102A	312	ESH
☐	N814EX	DHC-8-102A	318	ESI
☐	N815EX	DHC-8-102A	321	ESJ
☐	N816EX	DHC-8-102A	329	ESK
☐	N837EX	DHC-8-102A	217	ERH
☐	N838EX	DHC-8-102A	220	ERK
☐	N906HA	DHC-8-102	009	HAS
☐	N907HA	DHC-8-102	011	HSB
☐	N908HA	DHC-8-102	015	HSC
☐	N911HA	DHC-8-102	034	HSF
☐	N912HA	DHC-8-102	040	HSG
☐	N914HA	DHC-8-102	053	HSH
☐	N930HA	DHC-8 102	126	HSW
☐	N931HA	DHC-8-102	132	HSZ
☐	N933HA	DHC-8-102	134	HBA
☐	N934HA	DHC-8-102	139	HBB
☐	N935HA	DHC-8-102	142	HBC
☐	N936HA	DHC-8-102	145	HRA
☐	N937HA	DHC-8-102	148	HRB
☐	N938HA	DHC-8-102	152	HRC
☐	N940HA	DHC-8-102	156	HRE
☐	N941HA	DHC-8-102	161	HRF
☐	N942HA	DHC-8-102	163	HRG
☐	N943HA	DHC-8-102	167	HRH
☐	N987HA	DHC-8-201	425	
☐	N988HA	DHC-8-201	426	
☐	N989HA	DHC-8-201	427	
☐	N991HA	DHC-8-201	431	
☐	N257JQ	ERJ-145LR	14500812	JBJ
☐	N258JQ	ERJ-145LR	145768	JBI
☐	N259JQ	ERJ-145LR	145763	JBH
☐	N280SK	ERJ-145LR	145381	JRM
☐	N291SK	ERJ-145LR	145486	JRX
☐	N293SK	ERJ-145LR	145500	JRY
☐	N298SK	ERJ-145LR	145508	JRZ
☐	N370SK	ERJ-145LR	145515	JBA
☐	N801HK	ERJ-145ER	145053	TRK
☐	N802HK	ERJ-145ER	145066	TRL
☐	N803HK	ERJ-145ER	145077	TRM
☐	N804HK	ERJ-145ER	145082	TRA

☐ N805HK	ERJ-145ER	145096	TRB
☐ N808HK	ERJ-145ER	145157	TRD
☐ N809HK	ERJ-145ER	145187	TRE
☐ N812HK	ERJ-145ER	145373	TRG
☐ N839MJ	ERJ-145LR	145416	YRO
☐ N840MJ	ERJ-145LR	145429	YRP
☐ N843MJ	ERJ-145LR	145478	YRT
☐ N846MJ	ERJ-145LR	145507	YRW
☐ N977RP	ERJ-145MP	145185	JBH
☐ N978RP	ERJ-145LR	145169	JBX
☐ N801MA	ERJ-170SU	17000012	801
☐ N802MD	ERJ-170SU	17000013	802
☐ N803MD	ERJ-170SU	17000015	803
☐ N805MD	ERJ-170SU	17000018	805
☐ N806MD	ERJ-170SU	17000019	806
☐ N807MD	ERJ-170SU	17000020	807
☐ N808MD	ERJ-170SU	17000021	808
☐ N809MD	ERJ-170SU	17000022	809
☐ N811MD	ERJ-170SU	17000028	811
☐ N812MD	ERJ-170SU	17000030	812
☐ N814MD	ERJ-170SU	17000033	814
☐ N816MA	ERJ-170SU	17000037	816
☐ N817MD	ERJ-170SU	17000038	817
☐ N819MD	ERJ-170SU	17000040	819
☐ N820MD	ERJ-170SU	17000041	820
☐ N822MD	ERJ-170SU	17000043	822
☐ N827MD	ERJ-170SU	17000047	827
☐ N828MD	ERJ-170SU	17000048	828
☐ N829MD	ERJ-170SU	17000049	829
☐ N101HQ	ERJ-175LR	17000156	
☐ N102HQ	ERJ-175LR	17000157	
☐ N103HQ	ERJ-175LR	17000159	
☐ N104HQ	ERJ-175LR	17000160	
☐ N105HQ	ERJ-175LR	17000163	
☐ N106HQ	ERJ-175LR	17000164	
☐ N107HQ	ERJ-175LR	17000165	
☐ N108HQ	ERJ-175LR	17000166	
☐ N109HQ	ERJ-175LR	17000168	
☐ N110HQ	ERJ-175LR	17000172	
☐ N111HQ	ERJ-175LR	17000173	
☐ N112HQ	ERJ-175LR	17000174	
☐ N113HQ	ERJ-175LR	17000177	
☐ N114HQ	ERJ-175LR	17000179	
☐ N115HQ	ERJ-175LR	17000182	
☐ N116HQ	ERJ-175LR	17000183	
☐ N117HQ	ERJ-175LR	17000184	
☐ N118HQ	ERJ-175LR	17000189	
☐ N119HQ	ERJ-175LR	17000190	
☐ N120HQ	ERJ-175LR	17000193	
☐ N121HQ	ERJ-175LR	17000194	
☐ N122HQ	ERJ-175LR	17000196	
☐ N123HQ	ERJ-175LR	17000199	
☐ N124HQ	ERJ-175LR	17000200	
☐ N125HQ	ERJ-175LR	17000202	
☐ N126HQ	ERJ-175LR	17000204	
☐ N127HQ	ERJ-175LR	17000206	
☐ N128HQ	ERJ-175LR	17000208	
☐ N129HQ	ERJ-175LR	17000211	
☐ N130HQ	ERJ-175LR	17000212	
☐ N131HQ	ERJ-175LR	17000215	
☐ N132HQ	ERJ-175LR	17000216	
☐ N133HQ	ERJ-175LR	17000217	
☐ N134HQ	ERJ-175LR	17000220	
☐ N135HQ	ERJ-175LR	17000224	
☐ N136HQ	ERJ-170LR	17000228	
☐ N137HQ	ERJ-170LR	17000231	
☐ N138HQ	ERJ-170LR	17000234	
☐ N944UW	ERJ-190AR	19000058	
☐ N945UW	ERJ-190AR	19000062	
☐ N946UW	ERJ-190AR	19000072	
☐ N947UW	ERJ-190AR	19000078	
☐ N948UW	ERJ-190AR	19000081	
☐ N949UW	ERJ-190AR	19000102	

☐ N950UW	ERJ-190AR	19000106	
☐ N951UW	ERJ-190AR	19000112	
☐ N952UW	ERJ-190AR	19000119	
☐ N953UW	ERJ-190AR	19000133	
☐ N954UW	ERJ-190AR	19000139	
☐ N955UW	ERJ-190AR	19000152	
☐ N956UW	ERJ-190AR	19000156	
☐ N957UW	ERJ-190AR	19000161	
☐ N958UW	ERJ-190AR	19000164	
☐ N9CJ	SAAB SF.340B	340B-224	LVE
☐ N203CJ	SAAB SF.340B	340B-203	LNI
☐ N233CJ	SAAB SF.340B	340B-233	LVF
☐ N249CJ	SAAB SF.340B	340B-249	
☐ N252CJ	SAAB SF.340B	340B-252	LVJ
☐ N321CJ	SAAB SF.340B	340B-321	LVH
☐ N338CJ	SAAB SF.340B	340B-338	LNG
☐ N339CJ	SAAB SF.340B	340B-339	LNA
☐ N341CJ	SAAB SF.340B	340B-341	LND
☐ N344CJ	SAAB SF.340B	340B-344	LNF
☐ N346CJ	SAAB SF.340B	340B-346	LNB
☐ N347CJ	SAAB SF.340B	340B-347	LNH
☐ N350CJ	SAAB SF.340B	340B-350	LNE
☐ N362PX	SAAB SF.340B	340B-258	

US FOREST SERVICE

☐ N115Z	Basler Turbo-67 (DC-3TP)	16819/33567	
☐ N141Z	DHC-6 Twin Otter 300	803	
☐ N142Z	Basler Turbo-67 (DC-3TP)	20494	
☐ N143Z	DHC-6 Twin Otter 300	437	
☐ N173Z	Short SD.3-30	SH3116	
☐ N175Z	Short SD.3-30	SH3115	
☐ N178Z	Short SD.3-30	SH3119	
☐ N179Z	Short SD.3-30	SH3109	

USA 3000 AIRLINES — U5 / GWY

☐ N260AV	A320-214	1564	
☐ N261AV	A320-214	1615	
☐ N262AV	A320-214	1725	
☐ N263AV	A320-214	1860	
☐ N264AV	A320-214	1867	

USA JET AIRLINES — JUS

☐ N192US	DC-9-15RC	47156/228	
☐ N194US	DC-9-15RC	47016/173	[YIP]
☐ N195US	DC-9-15RC	47017/186	
☐ N205US	DC-9-32CF	47690/843	
☐ N208US	DC-9-32F	47220/296	[YIP]
☐ N215US	DC-9-32	47480/607	
☐ N231US	DC-9-32	48114/919	
☐ N327US	DC-9-33F	47414/536	
☐ N949NS	MD-83	53022/1909	♦

VIRGIN AMERICA — VX / VRD

☐ N521VA	A319-112	2773	
☐ N522VA	A319-112	2811	
☐ N523VA	A319-112	3181	
☐ N524VA	A319-112	3204	
☐ N525VA	A319-112	3324	
☐ N526VA	A319-112	3347	
☐ N527VA	A319-112	3417	
☐ N528VA	A319-112	3445	
☐ N529VA	A319-112	3684	
☐ N530VA	A319-112	3686	
☐ N621VA	A320-214	2616	
☐ N622VA	A320-214	2674	
☐ N623VA	A320-214	2740	
☐ N624VA	A320-214	2778	
☐ N625VA	A320-214	2800	
☐ N626VA	A320-214	2830	
☐ N627VA	A320-214	2851	

☐	N628VA	A320-214	2993	
☐	N629VA	A320-214	3037	
☐	N630VA	A320-214	3101	
☐	N631VA	A320-214	3135	
☐	N632VA	A320-214	3155	
☐	N633VA	A320-214	3230	
☐	N634VA	A320-214	3359	
☐	N635VA	A320-214	3398	
☐	N636VA	A320-214	3460	
☐	N637VA	A320-214	3465	
☐	N638VA	A320-214	3503	
☐	N639VA	A320-214	3016	♦
☐	N640VA	A320-214	3349	♦
☐	N641VA	A320-214	3656	♦
☐	N642VA	A320-214	3670	♦
☐	N835VA	A320-214	4448	♦
☐	N836VA	A320-214	4480	♦
☐	N837VA	A320-214	4558	♦
☐	N838VA	A320-214	4559	♦
☐	N839VA	A320-214	4610	o/o♦
☐	N840VA	A320-214	4616	o/o♦
☐		A320-214		o/o♦
☐		A320-214		o/o♦

VISION AIRLINES

☐	N920AE	BAeJetstream 32EP	920
☐	N732VA	B737-3T0	23366/1174
☐	N742VA	B737-448	24773/1850
☐	N743VA	B737-4B6	25262/2088
☐	N781VA	B737-8Q8/W	28214/78
☐	N766VA	B767-2Q8ER	24448/740
☐	N767VA	B767-222ER	21870/13
☐	N768VA	B767-222ER	21869/11
☐	N769VA	B767-222ER	21866/7
☐	N801VA	DHC-8Q-202	494 ♦
☐	N402VA	Do228-202K	8085
☐	N403VA	Do228-202K	8171
☐	N404VA	Do228-203F	8120
☐	N405VA	Do228-203F	8144
☐	N409VA	Do228-201	8097
☐	N38VP	Do 328 Jet	3174
☐	N328DA	Do 328 Jet	3171
☐	N329MX	Do328-100	3049
☐	N330MX	Do328-100	3067
☐	N331MX	Do328-100	3074
☐	N431JS	Do328-110	3028 o/o
☐	N905HB	Do 328 Jet	3178
☐	N906HB	Do 328 Jet	3179

WESTERN AIR EXPRESS — WAE

☐	N158WA	SA.226TC Metro II	TC-411
☐	N159WA	SA.226TC Metro II	TC-334
☐	N160WA	SA.226TC Metro IIA	TC-399
☐	N162WA	SA.226TC Metro IIA	TC-418

WIGGINS AIRWAYS — WIG

☐	N656WA	DHC-6 Twin Otter 100	47

WORLD AIRWAYS — WO / WOA

☐	N136WA	DC-10-30	47844/336	[MZJ]
☐	N137WA	DC-10-30	48282/355	
☐	N138WA	DC-10-30	47845/356	[CEW]
☐	N223NW	DC-10-30	46580/183	[MZJ]
☐	N224NW	DC-10-30	46581/184	[MZJ]
☐	N702TZ	DC-10-30	46912/188	[MZJ]
☐	N705TZ	DC-10-30	46915/199	
☐	N269WA	MD-11	48450/479	♦
☐	N270WA	MD-11	48449/455	

☐	N271WA	MD-11	48518/525	271
☐	N272WA	MD-11	48437/506	272
☐	N273WA	MD-11	48519/539	273
☐	N274WA	MD-11F	48633/563	274
☐	N275WA	MD-11CF	48631/579	275
☐	N276WA	MD-11CF	48632/582	276
☐	N277WA	MD-11ER	48743/590	277
☐	N278WA	MD-11ER	48746/597	278
☐	N279WA	MD-11F	48756/623	279
☐	N380WA	MD-11F	48407/456	380
☐	N381WA	MD-11F	48523/516	381
☐	N382WA	MD-11F	48411/453	
☐	N383WA	MD-11F	48412/454	
☐	N384WA	MD-11F	48435/478	
☐	N740WA	B747-4H6 (BDSF)	25700/974	
☐	N741WA	B747-4H6 (BDSF)	25702/999	>CLX♦
☐	N742WA	B747-412BCF	27071/1072	♦
☐	N743WA	B747-412SF	26562/1074	♦

XTRA AIRWAYS — XP / CXP

☐	N42XA	B737-429	25729/2217	
☐	N43XA	B737-4S3	24796/1887	
☐	N188AQ	B737-322	24670/1909	♦
☐	N279AD	B737-4Q8	26279/2221	

OB - PERU

AERO TRANSPORTE — AMP

☐	OB-1778-P	An-26B-100	14205
☐	OB-1869-T	An-32B	3305

AEROCONDOR — Q6 / CDP

☐	OB-1793-P	B737-2H6	20583/303	
☐	OB-1627	F.27 Friendship 100	10116	
☐	OB-1650-P	An-24RV	37308802	
☐	OB-1693-P	F.27 Friendship 200	10181	[LIM]
☐	OB-1770-P	Fokker 50	20280	
☐	OB-1828	An-26	87307409	
☐	OB-1829-P	Fokker 50	20260	

AMAZON SKY

☐	OB-1859-P	An-26B-100	6209

CIELOS AIRLINES — A2 / CIU

☐	N609GC	DC-10-30F	46932/158
☐	N614GC	DC-10-30F	46931/137
☐	OB-1749	DC-10-30CF	46891/127
☐	OB-1812-P	DC-10-30CF	46975/248

LAN PERU — LP / LPE

☐	CC-COU	A319-132	2089	<LAN
☐	CC-COX	A319-132	2096	<LAN
☐	CC-COY	A319-132	2295	<LAN
☐	CC-COZ	A319-132	2304	<LAN
☐	CC-CPE	A319-132	2321	<LAN
☐	CC-CPF	A319-132	2572	<LAN
☐	CC-CPI	A319-132	2585	<LAN
☐	CC-CPM	A319-132	2864	<LAN
☐	CC-CPO	A319-132	2872	<LAN
☐	CC-CPQ	A319-132	2886	<LAN
☐	CC-CPX	A319-132	2887	<LAN
☐	CC-CQK	A319-132	2892	<LAN
☐	CC-CQL	A319-132	2894	<LAN
☐	CC-CQM	A320-233	3280	<LAN

PERUVIAN AIRLINES — PVN

☐	OB-1954-P	B737-247	23188/1071	♦

☐ OB-1955	B737-2T7	22761/850	♦
☐ OB-1956	B737-2T7	22762/856	♦
☐ OB-	B737-217	21716/560	
☐ OB-	B737-33A	23627/1302	♦

STAR PERU · 2I / SRU

☐ OB-1794-P	B737-2Y5	23039/954
☐ OB-1800-P	B737-291	21641/537
☐ OB-1823-P	B737-2T2	22793/892
☐ OB-1839-P	B737-204	22640/867
☐ OB-1841-P	B737-204	22058/629
☐ OB-1851-P	B737-230	22133/772
☐ OB-1717	An-24RV	27308010
☐ OB-1734-P	An-24RV	17307006
☐ OB-1769	An-24RV	57310110
☐ OB-1772-P	An-26B-100	10704
☐ OB-1877-P	BAe146 Srs.100	E1199
☐ OB-1879-P	BAe146 Srs.100	E1095
☐ OB-1885-P	BAe146 Srs.200	E2087
☐ OB-1914-P	BAe146 Srs.300	E3181
☐ OB-1923-P	BAe146 Srs.300	E3185
☐ OB-1930-P	BAe146 Srs.200	E2201 ♦
☐ OB-1943-P	BAe146 Srs.200	E2133 ♦
☐ OB-1948-P	BAe146 Srs.200	E2156 ♦

TACA PERU · T0 / TPU

☐ N471TA	A319-132	1066	<TAI
☐ N472TA	A319-132	1113	<TAI

TRANSPORTES AEREOS CIELOS ANDINOS

☐ OB-1651	An-24RV	27308303
☐ OB-1859-P	An-26	
☐ OB-1876-T	An-26B-100	17311506
☐ OB-1887-P	An-26-100	87306606
☐ OB-1893-P	An-26-100	8401

OD - LEBANON

CIRRUS MIDDLE EAST

☐ OD-NOR	B737-247	22754/870

FLYING CARPET AIR TRANSPORT SVS · FCR

☐ OD-AMB	B737-2H4	23109/1016

MIDDLE EAST AIRLINES · ME / MEA

☐ F-OMRN	A320-232	4339	♦
☐ F-OMRO	A320-232	4296	♦
☐ OD-MRR	A320-232	3837	
☐ OD-MRS	A320-232	3804	
☐ OD-MRT	A320-232	3736	
☐	A320-232		o/o♦
☐ F-ORME	A321-231	1878	
☐ F-ORMF	A321-231	1953	
☐ F-ORMG	A321-231	1956	
☐ F-ORMH	A321-231	1967	
☐ F-ORMI	A321-231	1977	
☐ F-ORMJ	A321-231	2055	
☐ F-ORMA	A330-243	926	
☐ OD-MEA	A330-243	984	
☐ OD-MEB	A330-243	998	
☐ OD-MEC	A330-243	995	

TMA · TMA

☐ OD-TMA	A300F4-622RF	872	♦

WINGS OF LEBANON · WLB

☐ OD-HAJ	B737-3Q8	26313/2704
☐ OD-WOL	B737-232	23083/1008

OE - AUSTRIA

AIR ALPS AVIATION · A6 / LPV

☐ OE-LKA	Do328-110	3110
☐ OE-LKB	Do328-110	3036
☐ OE-LKC	Do328-110	3119
☐ OE-LKD	Do328-110	3072

AMERER AIR · AMK

☐ OE-ILW	F.27 Friendship 500	10681

AUSTRIAN AIRLINES · OS / AUA

☐ OE-LDA	A319-112	2131
☐ OE-LDB	A319-112	2174
☐ OE-LDC	A319-112	2262
☐ OE-LDD	A319-112	2416
☐ OE-LDE	A319-112	2494
☐ OE-LDF	A319-112	2547
☐ OE-LDG	A319-112	2652
☐ OE-LBN	A320-214	0768
☐ OE-LBO	A320-214	0776
☐ OE-LBP	A320-214	0797
☐ OE-LBQ	A320-214	1137
☐ OE-LBR	A320-214	1150
☐ OE-LBS	A320-214	1189
☐ OE-LBT	A320-214	1387
☐ OE-LBU	A320-214	1478
☐ OE-LBA	A321-111	0552
☐ OE-LBB	A321-111	0570
☐ OE-LBC	A321-111	0581
☐ OE-LBD	A321-211	0920
☐ OE-LBE	A321-211	0935
☐ OE-LBF	A321-211	1458
☐ OE-LNJ	B737-8Z9/W	28177/69
☐ OE-LNK	B737-8Z9/W	28178/222
☐ OE-LNL	B737-6Z9	30137/526
☐ OE-LNM	B737-6Z9	30138/546
☐ OE-LNN	B737-7Z9/W	30418/815
☐ OE-LNO	B737-7Z9/W	30419/874
☐ OE-LNP	B737-8Z9/W	30420/1100
☐ OE-LNQ	B737-8Z9/W	30421/1345
☐ OE-LNR	B737-8Z9/W	33833/1680
☐ OE-LNS	B737-8Z9/W	34262/1720
☐ OE-LNT	B737-8Z9/W	33834/1938
☐ OE-LAE	B767-3Z9ER/W	30383/812
☐ OE-LAT	B767-31AER	25273/393
☐ OE-LAW	B767-3Z9ER	26417/448
☐ OE-LAX	B767-3Z9ER/W	27095/467
☐ OE-LAY	B767-3Z9ER/W	29867/731
☐ OE-LAZ	B767-3Z9ER/W	30331/759
☐ OE-LPA	B777-2Z9ER	28698/87
☐ OE-LPB	B777-2Z9ER	28699/163
☐ OE-LPC	B777-2Z9ER	29313/386
☐ OE-LPD	B777-2Z9ER	35960/607

AUSTRIAN ARROWS

☐ OE-LCJ	CRJ-200LR	7142
☐ OE-LCN	CRJ-200LR	7365
☐ OE-LCR	CRJ-200LR	7910
☐ OE-LGA	DHC-8-402Q	4014
☐ OE-LGB	DHC-8-402Q	4015

☐	OE-LGC	DHC-8-402Q	4026
☐	OE-LGD	DHC-8-402Q	4027
☐	OE-LGE	DHC-8-402Q	4042
☐	OE-LGF	DHC-8-402Q	4068
☐	OE-LGG	DHC-8-402Q	4074
☐	OE-LGH	DHC-8-402Q	4075
☐	OE-LGI	DHC-8-402Q	4100
☐	OE-LGJ	DHC-8-402Q	4104
☐	OE-LGK	DHC-8-402Q	4280
☐	OE-LGL	DHC-8-402Q	4310 ♦
☐	OE-LGM	DHC-8-402Q	4319 ♦
☐	OE-LGN	DHC-8-402Q	4326 ♦
☐	OE-LTG	DHC-8Q-314	438
☐	OE-LTH	DHC-8Q-314	442
☐	OE-LTM	DHC-8Q-314	527
☐	OE-LTN	DHC-8Q-314	531 [LNZ]♦
☐	OE-LTO	DHC-8Q-314	553
☐	OE-LTP	DHC-8Q-314	554 [LNZ]♦
☐	OE-LFG	Fokker 70	11549
☐	OE-LFH	Fokker 70	11554
☐	OE-LFI	Fokker 70	11529
☐	OE-LFJ	Fokker 70	11532
☐	OE-LFK	Fokker 70	11555
☐	OE-LFL	Fokker 70	11573
☐	OE-LFP	Fokker 70	11560
☐	OE-LFQ	Fokker 70	11568
☐	OE-LFR	Fokker 70	11572
☐	OE-LVA	Fokker 100	11490
☐	OE-LVB	Fokker 100	11502
☐	OE-LVC	Fokker 100	11446
☐	OE-LVD	Fokker 100	11515
☐	OE-LVE	Fokker 100	11499
☐	OE-LVF	Fokker 100	11483
☐	OE-LVG	Fokker 100	11520
☐	OE-LVH	Fokker 100	11456
☐	OE-LVI	Fokker 100	11468
☐	OE-LVJ	Fokker 100	11359
☐	OE-LVK	Fokker 100	11397
☐	OE-LVL	Fokker 100	11404
☐	OE-LVM	Fokker 100	11361
☐	OE-LVN	Fokker 100	11367
☐	OE-LVO	Fokker 100	11460

GROSSMANN AIR TRANSPORT — HTG

☐	OE-HTG	Do328-300 (Envoy 3)	3162

INTERSKY — 3L / ISK

☐	OE-LIA	DHC-8Q-311	505
☐	OE-LIC	DHC-8Q-314	503
☐	OE-LIE	DHC-8Q-315	546
☐	OE-LSB	DHC-8Q-314	525

MAPJET — MPJ

☐	OE-LMP	A310-322	410 [BRU]
☐	OE-IKB	MD-83	49448/1313
☐	OE-LOG	MD-83	49359/1349
☐	OE-LRW	MD-83	49629/1583

NIKI — HG / NLY

☐	OE-LED	A319-112	3407
☐	OE-LEK	A319-112	3019
☐	OE-LEA	A320-214	2529
☐	OE-LEB	A320-214	4231 ♦
☐	OE-LEC	A320-214	4316 ♦
☐	OE-LEE	A320-214	2749
☐	OE-LEF	A320-214	4368 ♦
☐	OE-LEG	A320-214	4581 ♦
☐	OE-LEO	A320-214	2668
☐	OE-LEU	A320-214	2902

☐	OE-LEX	A320-214	2867
☐	OE-	A320-214	o/o♦
☐	OE-	A320-214	o/o♦
☐	OE-	A320-214	o/o♦
☐	OE-	A320-214	o/o♦
☐	OE-	A320-214	o/o♦
☐	OE-	A320-214	o/o♦
☐	OE-LES	A321-211	3504
☐	OE-LET	A321-211	3830
☐	OE-	A321-211	o/o♦
☐	OE-	A321-211	o/o♦
☐	OE-IHA	ERJ-190LR	19000285
☐	OE-IHB	ERJ-190LR	19000294
☐	OE-IHC	ERJ-190LR	19000349 ♦
☐	OE-IHD	ERJ-190LR	19000354 ♦
☐	OE-	ERJ-190LR	o/o♦
☐	OE-	ERJ-190LR	o/o♦

ROBIN HOOD AVIATION — RH / RHA

☐	OE-GIR	SAAB SF.340A	340A-134
☐	OE-GOD	SAAB SF.340A	340A-153

TYROLEAN JET SERVICE — TJS

☐	OE-HMS	Do 328 Jet	3121
☐	OE-HTJ	Do 328 Jet	3114

WELCOME AIR — 2W / WLC

☐	OE-GBB	Do328-110	3078
☐	OE-LIR	Do328-110	3115
☐	OE-LJR	Do 328 Jet	3213

OH - FINLAND

AIR ALAND

☐	LY-RIK	SAAB SF.340A	340A-112

AIR FINLAND — OF / FIF

☐	OH-AFI	B757-2K2	26330/717
☐	OH-AFJ	B757-28A	26269/612
☐	OH-AFK	B757-28A	25622/530

BLUE1 — K1 / BLF

☐	OH-SAJ	Avro 146-RJ85	E2388
☐	OH-SAK	Avro 146-RJ85	E2389
☐	OH-SAL	Avro 146-RJ85	E2392
☐	OH-SAO	Avro 146-RJ85	E2393
☐	OH-SAP	Avro 146-RJ85	E2394
☐	OH-BLG	B717-23S	55059/5023 ♦
☐	OH-BLH	B717-23S	55060/5026 ♦
☐	OH-BLI	B717-23S	55061/5029 ♦
☐	OH-BLJ	B717-23S	55065/5048 ♦
☐	OH-BLM	B717-23S	55056/5054 ♦
☐	OH-BLP	B717-23S	55064/5037 ♦

FINNAIR — AY / FIN

☐	OH-LVA	A319-112	1073
☐	OH-LVB	A319-112	1107
☐	OH-LVC	A319-112	1309
☐	OH-LVD	A319-112	1352
☐	OH-LVE	A319-112	1791
☐	OH-LVF	A319-112	1808
☐	OH-LVG	A319-112	1916
☐	OH-LVH	A319-112	1184
☐	OH-LVI	A319-112	1364
☐	OH-LVK	A319-112	2124
☐	OH-LVL	A319-112	2266

☐	OH-LXA	A320-214	1405	
☐	OH-LXB	A320-214	1470	
☐	OH-LXC	A320-214	1544	
☐	OH-LXD	A320-214	1588	
☐	OH-LXE	A320-214	1678	
☐	OH-LXF	A320-214	1712	
☐	OH-LXG	A320-214	1735	
☐	OH-LXH	A320-214	1913	
☐	OH-LXI	A320-214	1989	
☐	OH-LXK	A320-214	2065	
☐	OH-LXL	A320-214	2146	
☐	OH-LXM	A320-214	2154	
☐	OH-LZA	A321-211	0941	
☐	OH-LZB	A321-211	0961	
☐	OH-LZC	A321-211	1185	
☐	OH-LZD	A321-211	1241	
☐	OH-LZE	A321-211	1978	
☐	OH-LZF	A321-211	2208	
☐	OH-LTM	A330-302E	994	
☐	OH-LTN	A330-302E	1007	
☐	OH-LTO	A330-302E	1013	
☐	OH-LTP	A330-302E	1023	
☐	OH-LTR	A330-302E	1067	
☐	OH-LTS	A330-302E	1078	
☐	OH-LTT	A330-302E	1088	♦
☐	OH-LTU	A330-302E	1173	♦
☐	OH-LQA	A340-311	058	
☐	OH-LQB	A340-313E	835	
☐	OH-LQC	A340-313E	844	
☐	OH-LQD	A340-313E	921	
☐	OH-LQE	A340-313E	938	
☐	OH-LQF	A340-313X	168	<AFR♦
☐	OH-LQG	A340-313X	174	<AFR♦
☐	OH-LBO	B757-2Q8/W	28172/772	
☐	OH-LBR	B757-2Q8/W	28167/775	
☐	OH-LBS	B757-2Q8/W	27623/792	
☐	OH-LBT	B757-2Q8/W	28170/801	
☐	OH-LEE	ERJ-170LR	17000093	
☐	OH-LEF	ERJ-170LR	17000106	
☐	OH-LEG	ERJ-170LR	17000107	
☐	OH-LEH	ERJ-170LR	17000112	
☐	OH-LEI	ERJ-170LR	17000120	
☐	OH-LEK	ERJ-170LR	17000127	
☐	OH-LEL	ERJ-170LR	17000139	
☐	OH-LEO	ERJ-170LR	17000150	
☐	OH-LKE	ERJ-190LR	19000059	
☐	OH-LKF	ERJ-190LR	19000066	
☐	OH-LKG	ERJ-190LR	19000079	
☐	OH-LKH	ERJ-190LR	19000086	
☐	OH-LKI	ERJ-190LR	19000117	
☐	OH-LKK	ERJ-190LR	19000127	
☐	OH-LKL	ERJ-190LR	19000153	
☐	OH-LKM	ERJ-190LR	19000160	
☐	OH-LKN	ERJ-190LR	19000252	
☐	OH-LKO	ERJ-190LR	19000267	
☐	OH-	ERJ-190LR		o/o♦
☐	OH-	ERJ-190LR		o/o♦
☐	OH-LGC	MD-11F	48512/529	
☐	N513AY	MD-11	48513/564	[QPG]

FINNCOMM AIRLINES   FC / WBA

☐	OH-ATA	ATR 42-500	641	
☐	OH-ATB	ATR 42-500	643	
☐	OH-ATC	ATR 42-500	651	
☐	OH-ATD	ATR 42-500	655	
☐	OH-ATE	ATR 72-212A	741	
☐	OH-ATF	ATR 72-212A	744	
☐	OH-ATG	ATR 72-212A	757	
☐	OH-ATH	ATR 72-212A	769	

☐	OH-ATI	ATR 72-212A	783	
☐	OH-ATJ	ATR 72-212A	792	
☐	OH-ATK	ATR 72-212A	848	
☐	OH-ATL	ATR 72-212A	851	
☐	OH-	ATR 72-212A		♦
☐	OH-	ATR 72-212A		♦
☐	OH-	ATR 72-212A		♦
☐	OH-	ATR 72-212A		♦

OK - CZECH REPUBLIC

CENTRAL CONNECT AIRLINES   3B / CCG

☐	OK-CCC	SAAB SF.340B	340B-208
☐	OK-CCD	SAAB SF.340B	340A-161
☐	OK-CCE	SAAB SF.340A	340A-108
☐	OK-CCF	SAAB SF.340A	340A-101
☐	OK-CCG	SAAB SF.340A	340A-104
☐	OK-CCK	SAAB SF.340A	340A-078
☐	OK-CCL	SAAB SF.340A	340A-159
☐	OK-CCN	SAAB SF.340B	340B-230
☐	OK-CCO	SAAB SF.340B	340B-188

CSA CZECH AIRLINES   OK / CSA

☐	OK-MEK	A319-112	3043	
☐	OK-MEL	A319-112	3094	
☐	OK-NEM	A319-112	3406	
☐	OK-NEN	A319-112	3436	
☐	OK-NEO	A319-112	3452	
☐	OK-NEP	A319-112	3660	
☐	OK-OER	A319-112	3892	
☐	OK-PET	A319-112	4258	♦
☐	OK-	A319-112		o/o♦
☐	OK-	A319-112		o/o♦
☐	OK-	A319-112		o/o♦
☐	OK-	A319-112		o/o♦
☐	OK-GEA	A320-214	1439	
☐	OK-GEB	A320-214	1450	
☐	OK-LEE	A320-214	2719	
☐	OK-LEF	A320-214	2758	
☐	OK-LEG	A320-214	2789	
☐	OK-MEH	A320-214	3031	
☐	OK-MEI	A320-214	3060	
☐	OK-MEJ	A320-214	3097	
☐	OK-CEC	A321-211	0674	
☐	OK-CED	A321-211	0684	
☐	OK-JFJ	ATR 42-500	623	
☐	OK-JFK	ATR 42-500	625	
☐	OK-JFL	ATR 42-500	629	
☐	OK-KFM	ATR 42-500	635	
☐	OK-KFN	ATR 42-500	637	
☐	OK-KFO	ATR 42-500	633	
☐	OK-KFP	ATR 42-500	639	
☐	OK-VFI	ATR 42-320	173	
☐	OK-XFA	ATR 72-202	285	
☐	OK-XFB	ATR 72-202	297	
☐	OK-XFC	ATR 72-202	299	
☐	OK-XFD	ATR 72-202	303	
☐	OK-CGK	B737-55S	28471/2885	
☐	OK-DGL	B737-55S	28472/3004	
☐	OK-EGO	B737-55S	28475/3096	
☐	OK-WGX	B737-436	25349/2156	
☐	OK-WGY	B737-436	25839/2188	
☐	OK-XGA	B737-55S	26539/2300	
☐	OK-XGB	B737-55S	26540/2317	
☐	OK-XGC	B737-55S	26541/2319	
☐	OK-XGD	B737-55S	26542/2337	
☐	OK-XGE	B737-55S	26543/2339	

CZECH CHARTER AIRLINES

☐ OK-CCA	B737-31S	29058/2946	o/o♦

LR AIRLINES — LRB

☐ OK-LRA	LET L-410UVP-E	892216

SILVER AIR — SLD

☐ OK-SLD	LET L-410UVP-E9	22634
☐ OK-WDC	LET L-410UVP-E	912531
☐ OK-WDT	LET L-410UVP-E	912615

SKYDIVE & AIR SERVICE

☐ OK-ASA	LET L-410UVP-E	902439
☐ OK-SAS	LET L-410UVP	831040

SMARTWINGS — QS / TVS

☐ OK-SWU	B737-522	26703/2498
☐ OK-SWV	B737-522	26696/2440

TRAVEL SERVICE AIRLINES — QS / TVS

☐ OK-TVB	B737-8CX/W	32362/1125	
☐ OK-TVD	B737-86N	28595/285	
☐ OK-TVF	B737-8FH/W	29669/1692	
☐ OK-TVG	B737-8Q8/W	30719/2257	
☐ OK-TVH	B737-8Q8/W	35275/2604	>SMR♦
☐ OK-TVJ	B737-8Q8/W	29351/1471	
☐ OK-TVK	B737-86N/W	32740/1444	
☐ OK-TVL	B737-8FN/W	37076/3147	
☐ OK-TVM	B737-8FN/W	37077/3163	
☐ OK-TVN	B737-8BK/W	29643/2303	♦
☐ OK-TVO	B737-8CX/W	32360/1084	♦
☐ OK-TVP	B737-8K5/W	32907/1117	♦
☐ OK-	B737-8		o/o♦
☐ OK-	B737-8		o/o♦

VAN AIR EUROPE — 6Z / VAA

☐ OK-RDA	LET L-410UVP-E9	861813
☐ OK-TCA	LET L-410UVP-E	902431
☐ OK-UBA	LET L-410UVP-E19	892319

OM - SLOVAKIA

AIREXPLORE

☐ OM-AEX	B737-4Y0	25178/2199	♦

CENTRAL CHARTER AIRLINES SLOVAKIA

☐ OM-CCA	B737-36M	28333/2810	♦

DANUBE WINGS — V5

☐ OM-VRA	ATR 72-201	373
☐ OM-VRB	ATR 72-202	367
☐ OM-VRC	ATR 72-202	307

DUBNICA AIR

☐ OM-ODQ	LET L-410UVP	841320
☐ OM-PGA	LET L-410UVP-T	820909
☐ OM-SAB	LET L-410MA	750405

SLOVAK GOVERNMENT FLYING SVS — SSG

☐ OM-BYE	Yak-40	9440338
☐ OM-BYL	Yak-40	9940560
☐ OM-BYO	Tu-154M	89A803
☐ OM-BYR	Tu-154M	98A1012

TRAVEL SERVICE SLOVAKIA

☐ OM-TVA	B737-86N/W	32243/869	♦

OO - BELGIUM

AIR SERVICE LIEGE — LGG

☐ OO-PHB	Beech 1900D	UE-106

BRUSSELS AIRLINES — TV / DAT

☐ OO-SSC	A319-112	1086	♦
☐ OO-SSD	A319-112	1102	♦
☐ OO-SSG	A319-112	1160	
☐ OO-SSK	A319-112	1336	
☐ OO-SSM	A319-112	1388	
☐ OO-SSP	A319-113	0644	
☐ OO-SSR	A319-112	4275	♦
☐ OO-SNA	A320-214	1441	o/o♦
☐ OO-SFM	A330-301	030	
☐ OO-SFN	A330-301	037	
☐ OO-SFO	A330-301	045	
☐ OO-SFV	A330-322	095	♦
☐ OO-SFW	A330-322	082	
☐ OO-DJE	BAe146 Srs.200	E2164	[BRU]
☐ OO-DJJ	BAe146 Srs.200	E2196	[BRU]
☐ OO-DJK	Avro 146-RJ85	E2271	
☐ OO-DJL	Avro 146-RJ85	E2273	
☐ OO-DJN	Avro 146-RJ85	E2275	
☐ OO-DJO	Avro 146-RJ85	E2279	
☐ OO-DJP	Avro 146-RJ85	E2287	
☐ OO-DJQ	Avro 146-RJ85	E2289	
☐ OO-DJR	Avro 146-RJ85	E2290	
☐ OO-DJS	Avro 146-RJ85	E2292	
☐ OO-DJT	Avro 146-RJ85	E2294	
☐ OO-DJV	Avro 146-RJ85	E2295	
☐ OO-DJW	Avro 146-RJ85	E2296	
☐ OO-DJX	Avro 146-RJ85	E2297	
☐ OO-DJY	Avro 146-RJ85	E2302	
☐ OO-DJZ	Avro 146-RJ85	E2305	
☐ OO-DWA	Avro 146-RJ100	E3308	
☐ OO-DWB	Avro 146-RJ100	E3315	
☐ OO-DWC	Avro 146-RJ100	E3322	
☐ OO-DWD	Avro 146-RJ100	E3324	
☐ OO-DWE	Avro 146-RJ100	E3327	
☐ OO-DWF	Avro 146-RJ100	E3332	
☐ OO-DWG	Avro 146-RJ100	E3336	
☐ OO-DWH	Avro 146-RJ100	E3340	
☐ OO-DWI	Avro 146-RJ100	E3342	
☐ OO-DWJ	Avro 146-RJ100	E3355	
☐ OO-DWK	Avro 146-RJ100	E3360	
☐ OO-DWL	Avro 146-RJ100	E3361	
☐ OO-MJE	BAe146 Srs.200	E2192	[BRU]
☐ OO-LTM	B737-3M8	25070/2037	
☐ OO-VEG	B737-36N/W	28568/2987	
☐ OO-VEH	B737-36N/W	28571/3022	
☐ OO-VEK	B737-405	24270/1726	
☐ OO-VEN	B737-36N	28586/3090	
☐ OO-VEP	B737-43Q	28489/2827	
☐ OO-VES	B737-43Q	28493/2838	
☐ OO-VET	B737-4Q8	28202/3009	
☐ OO-VEX	B737-36N/W	28670/2948	

EUROPEAN AIR TRANSPORT — QY / BCS

☐ OO-DLW	A300B4-203F	199	[LEJ]
☐ OO-DLZ	A300B4-203F	219	[LEJ]

JETAIRFLY — TB / JAF

☐ OO-JAA	B737-8BK/W	29660/2355	♦
☐ OO-JAF	B737-8K5	35133/2313	

☐ OO-JAN	B737-76N/W	28609/417	
☐ OO-JAO	B737-7K5/W	35141/2603	♦
☐ OO-JAQ	B737-8K5/W	35148/2790	
☐ OO-JAR	B737-7K5/W	35150/2825	
☐ OO-JAS	B737-7K5/W	35144/2652	
☐ OO-JAT	B737-5K5	24927/1968	
☐ OO-JAX	B737-8K5/W	37238/3452	♦
☐ OO-JBG	B737-8K5/W	35142/2660	
☐ OO-TUA	B737-4K5	24127/1707	
☐ OO-VAC	B737-8BK/W	33014/1367	
☐ OO-JAP	B767-38EER	30840/829	
☐ OO-TUC	B767-341ER	24844/324	

THOMAS COOK AL BELGIUM — FQ / TCW

☐ OO-TCH	A320-214	1929	
☐ OO-TCI	A320-214	1975	
☐ OO-TCJ	A320-214	1787	
☐ OO-TCN	A320-232	0425	
☐ OO-TCO	A320-214	1306	
☐ OO-TCP	A320-214	0653	
☐ OO-TCR	A320-214	0453	♦

TNT AIRWAYS — 3V / TAY

☐ EC-HQT	A300B4-203F	124	[MHV]
☐ OO-TZB	A300B4-203F	261	
☐ TF-ELF	A300B4-622RF	529	<ABD♦
☐ OO-TAA	BAe146 Srs.300QT	E3151	
☐ OO-TAD	BAe146 Srs.300QT	E3166	
☐ OO-TAE	BAe146 Srs.300QT	E3182	
☐ OO-TAF	BAe146 Srs.300QT	E3186	
☐ OO-TAH	BAe146 Srs.300QT	E3168	
☐ OO-TAJ	BAe146 Srs.300QT	E3153	
☐ OO-TAK	BAe146 Srs.300QT	E3150	
☐ OO-TAQ	BAe146 Srs.200QT	E2078	♦
☐ OO-TAR	BAe146 Srs.200QT	E2067	
☐ OO-TAS	BAe146 Srs.300QT	E3154	
☐ OO-TAU	BAe146 Srs.200QT	E2100	
☐ OO-TAW	BAe146 Srs.200QT	E2089	
☐ OO-TAY	BAe146 Srs.200(QC)	E2211	
☐ OO-TAZ	BAe146 Srs.200(QC)	E2188	
☐ OO-TNA	B737-3T0(SF)	23569/1258	
☐ OO-TNB	B737-3T0(SF)	23578/1358	
☐ OO-TNC	B737-301(SF)	23513/1327	
☐ OO-TNE	B737-3Q8(SF)	23535/1301	
☐ OO-TNF	B737-3Q8(QC)	24131/1541	
☐ OO-TNG	B737-3Y0(QC)	24255/1625	
☐ OO-TNH	B737-301(SF)	23930/1539	
☐ OO-TNJ	B737-301(SF)	23260/1146	
☐ OO-TNK	B737-301(SF)	23258/1126	
☐ OO-TNL	B737-34S(SF)	29109/3001	♦
☐ OO-THA	B747-4HAERF	35232/1381	
☐ OO-THB	B747-4HAERF	35234/1386	
☐ OO-THC	B747-4HAERF	35235/1389Opf UAE	
☐ OO-THD	B747-4HAERF	35236/1399Opf UAE	
☐ OO-TSA	B777-FHT	o/o♦	
☐ OO-	B777-FHT	o/o♦	
☐ OO-	B777-FHT	o/o♦	

VLM AIRLINES — VG / VLM

☐ OO-VLE	Fokker 50	20132
☐ OO-VLF	Fokker 50	20208
☐ OO-VLI	Fokker 50	20226
☐ OO-VLJ	Fokker 50	20105
☐ OO-VLL	Fokker 50	20144
☐ OO-VLM	Fokker 50	20135
☐ OO-VLN	Fokker 50	20145
☐ OO-VLO	Fokker 50	20127
☐ OO-VLP	Fokker 50	20209
☐ OO-VLQ	Fokker 50	20159

☐ OO-VLR	Fokker 50	20121
☐ OO-VLS	Fokker 50	20109
☐ OO-VLV	Fokker 50	20160
☐ OO-VLX	Fokker 50	20177
☐ OO-VLY	Fokker 50	20181
☐ OO-VLZ	Fokker 50	20264

OY - DENMARK

AIR GREENLAND — GL / GRL

☐ OY-GRN	A330-223	230	
☐ OY-GRL	B757-236	25620/449	
☐ OY-POF	DHC-6 Twin Otter 300	235	
☐ OY-CBT	DHC-7-103	10	
☐ OY-CBU	DHC-7-103	20	
☐ OY-CTC	DHC-7-102	101	
☐ OY-GRD	DHC-7-103	9	
☐ OY-GRE	DHC-7-103	106	
☐ OY-GRF	DHC-7-102	113	
☐ OY-GRG	DHC-8Q-202	504	♦
☐ OY-GRH	DHC-8Q-202	488	♦

ATLANTIC AIRWAYS — RC / FLI

☐ OY-RCC	Avro 146-RJ100	E3357
☐ OY-RCD	Avro 146-RJ85	E2235
☐ OY-RCE	Avro 146-RJ85	E2233

BALTIC AIR SERVICE

☐ OY-ASY	EMB.110P1	110308
☐ OY-BHT	EMB.110P2	110161

BENAIR AIR SERVICE — BDI

☐ OY-BJP	SA.227AC Metro III	AC-499
☐ OY-MUG	Short SD.3-60	SH3716
☐ OY-PBH	LET L-410UVP-E20	972736
☐ OY-PBI	LET L-410UVP-E20	871936
☐ OY-PBV	Short SD.3-60	SH3747
☐ OY-PBW	Short SD.3-60	SH3760

CIMBER AIR — QI / CIM

☐ OY-CIJ	ATR 42-500	497	
☐ OY-CIK	ATR 42-500	501	>OMA
☐ OY-CIL	ATR 42-500	514	
☐ OY-CIM	ATR 72-212A	468	♦
☐ OY-CIN	ATR 72-212A	568	
☐ OY-CIO	ATR 72-212A	595	>MAU
☐ OY-RTC	ATR 72-202	508	
☐ OY-RTD	ATR 72-211	509	
☐ OY-RTF	ATR 72-202	496	
☐ OY-RTH	ATR 42-500	549	<EWG
☐ OY-MBI	CRJ-200LR	7436	
☐ OY-MBT	CRJ-200LR	7617	
☐ OY-RJA	CRJ-200LR	7413	
☐ OY-RJB	CRJ-200LR	7419	
☐ OY-RJC	CRJ-200LR	7015	
☐ OY-RJD	CRJ-200LR	7007	
☐ OY-RJE	CRJ-200LR	7009	
☐ OY-RJF	CRJ-200LR	7019	
☐ OY-RJG	CRJ-200LR	7104	
☐ OY-RJH	CRJ-200LR	7090	
☐ OY-RJI	CRJ-200LR	7093	
☐ OY-RJJ	CRJ-200ER	7784	

CIMBER STERLING — CIM

☐ OY-MRE	B737-7L9/W	28008/203
☐ OY-MRF	B737-7L9/W	28009/221
☐ OY-MRG	B737-7L9/W	28010/396

☐	OY-MRH	B737-7L9/W	28013/682
☐	OY-MRS	B737-76N/W	32737/1130
☐	OY-MRU	B737-73S/W	29079/194

DANISH AIR TRANSPORT — DX / DTR

☐	LY-RUM	ATR 42-300	010
☐	OY-CIR	ATR 42-310	107
☐	OY-CIU	ATR 42-310	112
☐	OY-JRJ	ATR 42-320	036
☐	OY-JRY	ATR 42-300	063
☐	OY-RUB	ATR 72-202	301
☐	OY-RUD	ATR 72-201	162
☐	OY-JRU	MD-87	49403/1404
☐	OY-RUE	MD-83	49936/1778

JETTIME — JTG

☐	OY-JTA	B737-33A	23631/1337
☐	OY-JTB	B737-3Y0	24464/1753
☐	OY-JTC	B737-3L9/W	23718/1402
☐	OY-JTD	B737-3Y0/W	24678/1853
☐	OY-JTE	B737-3L9	27834/2692
☐	OY-JTF	B737-382QC	24364/1657 ♦

NORTH FLYING — M3 / NFA

☐	OY-NPB	SA.227AC Metro III	AC-420
☐	OY-NPD	SA.227DC Metro 23	DC-865B
☐	OY-NPE	SA.227DC Metro 23	DC-867B
☐	OY-NPF	SA.227DC Metro 23	DC-880B

PRIMERA AIR SCANDINAVIA — PF

☐	OY-PSA	B737-8Q8/W	30688/2280
☐	OY-PSB	B737-8Q8/W	30722/2261
☐	OY-PSC	B737-86N/W	33419/1251
☐	OY-PSD	B737-86N/W	28618/514
☐	OY-PSE	B737-8Q8/W	30664/743
☐	OY-PSF	B737-7Q8/W	28210/22

STAR AIR — S6 / SRR

☐	OY-SRF	B767-219ER(SF)	23327/134
☐	OY-SRG	B767-219ER(SF)	23328/149
☐	OY-SRH	B767-204ER(SF)	24457/256
☐	OY-SRI	B767-25E(SF)	27193/527
☐	OY-SRJ	B767-25E(SF)	27195/535
☐	OY-SRK	B767-204ER(SF)	23072/107
☐	OY-SRL	B767-232(SF)	22219/37
☐	OY-SRM	B767-25E(SF)	27192/524
☐	OY-SRN	B767-219ER(SF)	23326/124
☐	OY-SRO	B767-25E(SF)	27194/532
☐	OY-SRP	B767-232(SF)	22220/38

SUN-AIR OF SCANDINAVIA — EZ / SUS

☐	OY-NCA	Do 328-110	3047
☐	OY-NCC	Do 328-110	3083
☐	OY-NCD	Do 328-120	3104
☐	OY-NCG	Do 328-110	3055
☐	OY-NCK	Do 328-110	3061
☐	OY-NCL	Do 328 Jet	3192
☐	OY-NCM	Do 328 Jet	3190
☐	OY-NCN	Do 328 Jet	3193
☐	OY-NCO	Do 328 Jet	3210
☐	OY-NCP	Do 328 Jet	3132
☐	OY-NCS	Do 328-110	3070
☐	OY-SVB	BAeJetstream 31	985
☐	OY-SVF	BAeJetstream 31	686

THOMAS COOK SCANDINAVIA — DK / VKG

☐	OY-VKA	A321-211	1881	
☐	OY-VKB	A321-211	1921	
☐	OY-VKC	A321-211	1932	
☐	OY-VKD	A321-211	1960	<MYT
☐	OY-VKE	A321-211	1887	<MYT
☐	OY-VKM	A320-214	1889	
☐	OY-VKS	A320-214	1954	
☐	OY-VKT	A321-211	1972	
☐	OY-VKF	A330-243	309	
☐	OY-VKG	A330-343X	349	
☐	OY-VKH	A330-343X	356	
☐	OY-VKI	A330-343X	357	

TRANSAVIA DENMARK — PH / TDK

☐	OY-TDA	B737-8K2/W	30646/1122
☐	OY-TDB	B737-8K2/W	30650/1158

P - NORTH KOREA

AIR KORYO — JS / KOR

☐	P-527	An-24B	67302207
☐	P-532	An-24RV	47309707
☐	P-533	An-24RV	47309708
☐	P-534	An-24RV	47309802
☐	P-537	An-24B	67302408
☐	P-835	Il-18D	188011205
☐	P-836	Il-18V	185008204
☐	P-618	Il-62M	2546624Opf Govt
☐	P-881	Il-62M	3647853
☐	P-882	Il-62M	2850236Opf Govt
☐	P-885	Il-62M	3933913
☐	P-912	Il-76MD	1003403104
☐	P-913	Il-76MD	1003404126
☐	P-914	Il-76MD	1003404146
☐	P-813	Tu-134B-3	66215
☐	P-814	Tu-134B-3	66368
☐	P-551	Tu-154B	75A129
☐	P-552	Tu-154B	76A143
☐	P-553	Tu-154B	77A191
☐	P-561	Tu-154B-2	83A573
☐	P-632	Tu-204-300	64012
☐	P-633	Tu-204-100	64048 ♦

PH - NETHERLANDS

AMSTERDAM AIRLINES — WD / AAN

☐	PH-AAX	A320-231	0430
☐	PH-AAY	A320-232	0527

ARKEFLY / TUI NETHERLANDS — OR / TFL

☐	PH-TFA	B737-8FH/W	35100/2424
☐	PH-TFB	B737-8K5/W	35149/2820
☐	PH-TFC	B737-8K5/W	35146/2875
☐	PH-AHQ	B767-383ER	24477/337
☐	PH-AHX	B767-383ER	24847/315
☐	PH-AHY	B767-383ER	24848/325
■	PH-OYI	B767-304ER/W	29138/783 17/3 ♦

CHC AIRWAYS — AW / SCH

☐	5A-DLX	DHC-8-311A	254

KLM CITYHOPPER — WA / KLC

☐	PH-KVG	Fokker 50	20211 [NWI]♦
☐	PH-KVH	Fokker 50	20217 [NWI]♦
☐	PH-KVI	Fokker 50	20218 [NWI]♦
☐	PH-KVK	Fokker 50	20219 [NWI]♦
☐	PH-LXP	Fokker 50	20276
☐	PH-LXR	Fokker 50	20277
☐	PH-JCH	Fokker 70	11528

	Reg	Type	MSN/Line	Notes
☐	PH-JCT	Fokker 70	11537	
☐	PH-KBX	Fokker 70	11547	
☐	PH-KZA	Fokker 70	11567	
☐	PH-KZB	Fokker 70	11562	
☐	PH-KZC	Fokker 70	11566	
☐	PH-KZD	Fokker 70	11582	
☐	PH-KZE	Fokker 70	11576	
☐	PH-KZF	Fokker 70	11577	
☐	PH-KZG	Fokker 70	11578	
☐	PH-KZH	Fokker 70	11583	
☐	PH-KZI	Fokker 70	11579	
☐	PH-KZK	Fokker 70	11581	
☐	PH-KZL	Fokker 70	11536	
☐	PH-KZM	Fokker 70	11561	
☐	PH-KZN	Fokker 70	11553	
☐	PH-KZO	Fokker 70	11538	
☐	PH-KZP	Fokker 70	11539	
☐	PH-KZR	Fokker 70	11551	
☐	PH-KZS	Fokker 70	11540	
☐	PH-KZT	Fokker 70	11541	
☐	PH-KZU	Fokker 70	11543	
☐	PH-KZV	Fokker 70	11556	
☐	PH-KZW	Fokker 70	11558	
☐	PH-WXA	Fokker 70	11570	
☐	PH-WXC	Fokker 70	11574	
☐	PH-WXD	Fokker 70	11563	
☐	PH-KLD	Fokker 100	11269	[WOE]
☐	PH-OFC	Fokker 100	11263	[WOE]
☐	PH-OFE	Fokker 100	11260	
☐	PH-OFF	Fokker 100	11274	[WOE]
☐	PH-OFH	Fokker 100	11277	[WOE]
☐	PH-OFI	Fokker 100	11279	
☐	PH-OFL	Fokker 100	11444	♦
☐	PH-OFM	Fokker 100	11475	
☐	PH-OFN	Fokker 100	11477	
☐	PH-OFO	Fokker 100	11462	
☐	PH-OFP	Fokker 100	11472	
☐	PH-EZA	ERJ-190STD	19000224	
☐	PH-EZB	ERJ-190STD	19000235	
☐	PH-EZC	ERJ-190STD	19000250	
☐	PH-EZD	ERJ-190STD	19000279	
☐	PH-EZE	ERJ-190STD	19000288	
☐	PH-EZF	ERJ-190STD	19000304	
☐	PH-EZG	ERJ-190STD	19000315	
☐	PH-EZH	ERJ-190STD	19000319	
☐	PH-EZI	ERJ-190STD	19000322	
☐	PH-EZK	ERJ-190STD	19000326	
☐	PH-EZL	ERJ-190STD	19000334	♦
☐	PH-EZM	ERJ-190STD	19000338	♦
☐	PH-EZN	ERJ-190STD	19000342	♦
☐	PH-EZO	ERJ-190STD	19000347	♦
☐	PH-EZP	ERJ-190STD	19000348	♦
☐	PH-EZR	ERJ-190STD	19000375	♦
☐	PH-EZS	ERJ-190STD	19000380	♦

KLM ROYAL DUTCH AIRLINES   KL / KLM

	Reg	Type	MSN/Line	Notes
☐	PH-AOA	A330-203	682	
☐	PH-AOB	A330-203	686	
☐	PH-AOC	A330-203	703	
☐	PH-AOD	A330-203	738	
☐	PH-AOE	A330-203	770	
☐	PH-AOF	A330-203	801	
☐	PH-AOH	A330-203	811	
☐	PH-AOI	A330-203	819	
☐	PH-AOK	A330-203	834	
☐	PH-AOL	A330-203	900	
☐	PH-AOM	A330-203	1161	♦
☐	PH-BDO	B737-306	24262/1642	
☐	PH-BDP	B737-306	24404/1681	[NWI]♦
☐	PH-BDT	B737-406	24530/1772	
☐	PH-BDW	B737-406	24858/1903	
☐	PH-BPB	B737-4Y0	24344/1723	

	Reg	Type	MSN/Line	Notes
☐	PH-BPC	B737-4Y0	24468/1747	
☐	PH-BTA	B737-406	25412/2161	
☐	PH-BTB	B737-406	25423/2184	
☐	PH-BTD	B737-306	27420/2406	
☐	PH-BTE	B737-306	27421/2438	
☐	PH-BTF	B737-406	27232/2591	
☐	PH-BTG	B737-406	27233/2601	
☐	PH-BTH	B737-306	28719/2930	
☐	HB-JJA	B737-7AK/W	34303/1758	<PTI
☐	PH-BGD	B737-7K2/W	30366/2675	
☐	PH-BGE	B737-7K2/W	30371/2705	
☐	PH-BGF	B737-7K2/W	30365/2714	
☐	PH-BGG	B737-7K2/W	30367/2835	
☐	PH-BGH	B737-7K2/W	38053/3119	
☐	PH-BGI	B737-7K2/W	30364/3172	♦
☐	PH-BGK	B737-7K2/W	38054/3292	♦
☐	PH-BGL	B737-7K2/W	30369/3407	♦
☐	PH-BGM	B737-7K2/W	39255/3569	o/o♦
☐	PH-	B737-		o/o♦
☐	PH-	B737-		o/o♦
☐	PH-	B737-		o/o♦
☐	PH-	B737-		o/o♦
☐	PH-	B737-		o/o♦
☐	PH-	B737-		o/o♦
☐	PH-	B737-		o/o♦
☐	PH-	B737-		o/o♦
☐	PH-BCA	B737-8K2/W	37820/3480	♦
☐	PH-BGA	B737-8K2/W	37593/2569	
☐	PH-BGB	B737-8K2/W	37594/2594	
☐	PH-BGC	B737-8K2/W	30361/2619	
☐	PH-BXA	B737-8K2/W	29131/198	
☐	PH-BXB	B737-8K2/W	29132/261	
☐	PH-BXC	B737-8K2/W	29133/305	
☐	PH-BXD	B737-8K2/W	29134/355	
☐	PH-BXE	B737-8K2/W	29595/552	
☐	PH-BXF	B737-8K2/W	29596/583	
☐	PH-BXG	B737-8K2/W	30357/605	
☐	PH-BXH	B737-8K2/W	29597/630	
☐	PH-BXI	B737-8K2/W	30358/633	
☐	PH-BXK	B737-8K2/W	29598/639	
☐	PH-BXL	B737-8K2/W	30359/659	
☐	PH-BXM	B737-8K2/W	30355/714	
☐	PH-BXN	B737-8K2/W	30356/728	
☐	PH-BXU	B737-8BK/W	33028/1936	
☐	PH-BXV	B737-8K2/W	30370/2205	
☐	PH-BXW	B737-8K2/W	30360/2467	
☐	PH-BXY	B737-8K2/W	30372/2503	
☐	PH-BXZ	B737-8K2/W	30368/2533	
☐	PH-BXO	B737-9K2/W	29599/866	
☐	PH-BXP	B737-9K2/W	29600/924	
☐	PH-BXR	B737-9K2/W	29601/959	
☐	PH-BXS	B737-9K2/W	29602/981	
☐	PH-BXT	B737-9K2/W	32944/1498	
☐	PH-BFA	B747-406	23999/725	
☐	PH-BFB	B747-406	24000/732	
☐	PH-BFC	B747-406M	23982/735	
☐	PH-BFD	B747-406M	24001/737	
☐	PH-BFE	B747-406M	24201/763	
☐	PH-BFF	B747-406M	24202/770	
☐	PH-BFG	B747-406	24517/782	
☐	PH-BFH	B747-406M	24518/783	
☐	PH-BFI	B747-406M	25086/850	
☐	PH-BFK	B747-406	25087/854	
☐	PH-BFL	B747-406	25356/888	
☐	PH-BFM	B747-406M	26373/896	
☐	PH-BFN	B747-406	26372/969	
☐	PH-BFO	B747-406M	25413/938	
☐	PH-BFP	B747-406M	26374/992	
☐	PH-BFR	B747-406M	27202/1014	
☐	PH-BFS	B747-406	28195/1090	
☐	PH-BFT	B747-406	28459/1112	

	Reg	Type	Serial
☐	PH-BFU	B747-406	28196/1127
■	PH-BFV	B747-406	28460/1225 o/3.
☐	PH-BFW	B747-406	30454/1258
☐	PH-BFY	B747-406	30455/1302
☐	PH-CKA	B747-406ERF	33694/1326
☐	PH-CKB	B747-406ERF	33695/1328
☐	PH-CKC	B747-406ERF	33696/1341
☐	PH-CKD	B747-406ERF	35233/1382
■	PH-BQA	B777-206ER	33711/454
☐	PH-BQB	B777-206ER	33712/457
☐	PH-BQC	B777-206ER	29397/461
☐	PH-BQD	B777-206ER	33713/465
■	PH-BQE	B777-206ER	28691/468
■	PH-BQF	B777-206ER	29398/474
☐	PH-BQG	B777-206ER	32704/476
☐	PH-BQH	B777-206ER	32705/493
■	PH-BQI	B777-206ER	33714/497
☐	PH-BQK	B777-206ER	29399/499
☐	PH-BQL	B777-206ER	34711/552
☐	PH-BQM	B777-206ER	34712/559
☐	PH-BQN	B777-206ER	32720/561
■	PH-BQO	B777-206ER	35295/609
☐	PH-BQP	B777-206ER	32721/630
☐	PH-BVA	B777-306ER	35671/694
☐	PH-BVB	B777-306ER	36145/706
■	PH-BVC	B777-306ER	37582/787 3/3
☐	PH-BVD	B777-306ER	35979/807
■	PH-BVF	B777-306ER	39972/915 ♦
■	PH-BVE	B777-306ER	3/3 o/o♦
■	PH-KCA	MD-11	48555/557
☐	PH-KCB	MD-11	48556/561
■	PH-KCC	MD-11	48557/569
■	PH-KCD	MD-11	48558/573 3/3
■	PH-KCE	MD-11	48559/575 3/3
■	PH-KCF	MD-11	48560/578
■	PH-KCG	MD-11	48561/585
■	PH-KCH	MD-11	48562/591
☐	PH-KCI	MD-11	48563/593
☐	PH-KCK	MD-11	48564/612

MARTINAIR — MP / MPH
	Reg	Type	Serial
☐	PH-MPP	B747-412BCF	24061/717 [AMS]♦
☐	PH-MPR	B747-412BCF	24226/809
☐	PH-MPS	B747-412BCF	24066/791 [MZJ]
☐	PH-MCI	B767-31AER	25312/400
☐	PH-MCJ	B767-33AER	25535/491
☐	PH-MCL	B767-31AER	26469/415
☐	PH-MCM	B767-31AER	26470/416
■	PH-MCP	MD-11CF	48616/577
☐	PH-MCR	MD-11CF	48617/581
☐	PH-MCS	MD-11CF	48618/584
☐	PH-MCT	MD-11CF	48629/486
☐	PH-MCU	MD-11F	48757/606
☐	PH-MCW	MD-11CF	48788/632
☐	PH-MCY	MD-11F	48445/460

ORANGE AIRCRAFT LEASING — RNG
	Reg	Type	Serial
☐	PH-RAQ	ATR 42-300	139 [MST]
☐	PH-RNG	Beech 1900D	UE-70

TRANSAVIA AIRLINES — HV / TRA
	Reg	Type	Serial
☐	PH-XRA	B737-7K2/W	30784/873
☐	PH-XRB	B737-7K2/W	28256/1298
☐	PH-XRC	B737-7K2/W	29347/1318 ♦
☐	PH-XRD	B737-7K2/W	30659/1329
☐	PH-XRE	B737-7K2/W	30668/1482
☐	PH-XRV	B737-7K2/W	34170/1701
☐	PH-XRW	B737-7K2/W	33465/1316
☐	PH-XRX	B737-7K2/W	33464/1299
☐	PH-XRY	B737-7K2/W	33463/1292
☐	PH-XRZ	B737-7K2/W	33462/1278
☐	PH-HSA	B737-8K2/W	34171/2950
☐	PH-HSB	B737-8K2/W	34172/3242 ♦
☐	PH-HSC	B737-8K2/W	34173/3266 ♦
☐	PH-	B737-8K2/W	o/o♦
☐	PH-	B737-8K2/W	o/o♦
☐	PH-HSW	B737-8K2/W	37160/2880
☐	PH-HZD	B737-8K2/W	28376/252
☐	PH-HZE	B737-8K2/W	28377/277
☐	PH-HZF	B737-8K2/W	28378/291
☐	PH-HZG	B737-8K2/W	28379/498
☐	PH-HZI	B737-8K2/W	28380/524
☐	PH-HZJ	B737-8K2/W	30389/549
☐	PH-HZK	B737-8K2/W	30390/555
☐	PH-HZL	B737-8K2/W	30391/814
☐	PH-HZM	B737-8K2/W	30392/833
☐	PH-HZN	B737-8K2/W	32943/1478
☐	PH-HZO	B737-8K2/W	34169/2243
☐	PH-HZW	B737-8K2/W	29345/1132

PJ - NETHERLANDS ANTILLES

DUTCH ANTILLES AIRLINES
	Reg	Type	Serial
☐	PJ-DAA	Fokker 100	11310
☐	PJ-DAB	Fokker 100	11331

DUTCH ANTILLES EXPRESS — 9H / DNL
	Reg	Type	Serial
☐	PJ-SLH	ATR 42-320	90
☐	PJ-XLM	ATR 42-320	378
☐	PJ-XLN	ATR 42-500	513

INSELAIR INTERNATIONAL — 7I / INC
	Reg	Type	Serial
☐	PJ-MDA	MD-83	49449/1354
☐	PJ-MDB	MD-82	48021/1078 <SFR
☐	PJ-MDC	MD-82	49434/1446
☐	PJ-MDD	MD-82	49972/1757
☐	PJ-	MD-82	49194/1130 o/o

PK - INDONESIA

AIR MALEO
	Reg	Type	Serial
☐	PK-VKD	DAe146 Srs.100	F1104 [Clark]

AIR MARK INDONESIA AVIATION
	Reg	Type	Serial
☐	EW-262TK	An-32A	2103
☐	PK-AIY	F.27 Mk 050F (Fokker 50)	20227

AIRFAST INDONESIA — AFE
	Reg	Type	Serial
☐	PK-OCP	B737-27A	23794/1424
☐	PK-OCT	MD-82	49889/1761
☐	PK-OCU	MD-82	53017/1797
☐	PK-OSP	BAe146 Srs.100	E1124

AVIASTAR MANDIRI
	Reg	Type	Serial
☐	PK-BRE	BAe146 Srs.200	E2139
☐	PK-BRF	BAe146 Srs.200	E2210
☐	PK-BRW	Fokker 50	20307 ♦

BATAVIA AIR — 7P / BTV
	Reg	Type	Serial
☐	PK-YVA	A319-132	2648
☐	PK-YVC	A319-132	2660
☐	PK-	A319-132	o/o
☐	PK-YUC	A320-233	0460 ♦
☐	PK-YUE	A320-233	0461 ♦
☐	PK-YVD	A320-231	0449

☐ PK-YVE	A320-231	0441	
☐ PK-YVF	A320-233	1676	
☐ PK-YVG	A320-231	0168	
☐ PK-YVH	A320-232	0710	♦
☐ PK-YVI	A330-202	330	
☐ PK-YVJ	A330-202	205	
☐ PK-	A330-202	211	o/o
☐ PK-	ATR 72-212A		o/o
☐ PK-	ATR 72-212A		o/o
☐ PK-YTA	B737-266	21192/451	
☐ PK-YTC	B737-2M8	22090/664	
☐ PK-YTD	B737-2T4	22802/901	[CGK]
☐ PK-YTE	B737-405	25303/2137	
☐ PK-YTG	B737-2Q8	22453/748	[CGK]
☐ PK-YTH	B737-204	20806/338	[CGK]
☐ PK-YTI	B737-2L9	22407/698	[CGK]
☐ PK-YTJ	B737-204	21693/541	
☐ PK-YTK	B737-4Y0	24687/1865	
☐ PK-YTL	B737-2P5	23113/1010	[CGK]
☐ PK-YTM	B737-3B7	22957/1127	[CGK]
☐ PK-YTN	B737-217	22659/874	
☐ PK-YTP	B737-4Y0	24345/1731	
☐ PK-YTQ	B737-281	21767/585	[CGK]
☐ PK-YTR	B737-281	21766/583	
☐ PK-YTS	B737-2T4	22055/633	
☐ PK-YTU	B737-3Y9	25604/2405	
☐ PK-YTV	B737-2M8	21955/659	
☐ PK-YTW	B737-3B7	23318/1234	[CGK]
☐ PK-YTX	B737-3B7	22953/1022	
☐ PK-YTY	B737-3B7	22955/1043	[CGK]
☐ PK-YTZ	B737-4Y0	23869/1639	[CGK]
☐ PK-YVK	B737-301	23233/1200	
☐ PK-YVL	B737-322	24638/1784	
☐ PK-YVM	B737-322	24253/1650	
☐ PK-YVN	B737-48E	25766/2543	
☐ PK-YVO	B737-4Y0	23868/1616	
☐ PK-YVP	B737-4Y0	23979/1661	
☐ PK-YVQ	B737-4S3	25594/2223	
☐ PK-YVR	B737-4Y0	24494/1757	
☐ PK-YVS	B737-4H6	27352/2624	
☐ PK-YVT	B737-4H6	27191/2676	
☐ PK-YVU	B737-33A	24097/1741	
☐ PK-YVV	B737-3B7	23316/1212	
☐ PK-YVW	B737-3B7	23319/1250	
☐ PK-YVX	B737-33A	24093/1727	
☐ PK-YVY	B737-3B7	22952/1015	[CGK]
☐ PK-YVZ	B737-3B7	23317/1221	
☐ PK-YCM	F.28Fellowship 4000	11168	[CGK]

CARDIG AIR

☐ PK-BBA	B737-347SF	23597/1287	
☐ PK-BBB	B737-347SF	23598/1289	

CITILINK

☐ PK-GHV	B737-3Y0	24914/2054	[CGK]

DERAYA AIR TAXI   DRY

☐ PK-DGA	BAeATP (F)	2026	
☐ PK-DGI	BAeATP (F)	2027	
☐ PK-DSB	Short SD.3-30	SH3056	
☐ PK-DSH	Short SD.3-60	SH3757	
☐ PK-DSR	Short SD.3-30	SH3060	
☐ PK-DSS	Short SD.3-60	SH3743	
☐ PK-	Short SD.3-60	SH3757	

EASTINDO

☐ PK-RGE	Fokker 100	11445	

GADING SARI AVIATION SERVICES

☐ 9M-PMM	B737-205C	20458/278	<TSE

GARUDA INDONESIA   GA / GIA

☐ PK-GPA	A330-341	138	
☐ PK-GPC	A330-341	140	
☐ PK-GPD	A330-341	144	for IBE
☐ PK-GPE	A330-341	148	
☐ PK-GPF	A330-341	153	
☐ PK-GPG	A330-341	165	
☐ PK-GPH	A330-243	1020	
☐ PK-GPI	A330-243	1052	
☐ PK-GPJ	A330-243	988	
☐ PK-GPK	A330-243	1028	
☐ PK-GPL	A330-243	1184	♦
☐ PK-GCA	B737-3L9	24569/1775	
☐ PK-GCC	B737-3Q8	28200/2854	
☐ PK-GGA	B737-5U3	28726/2920	
☐ PK-GGC	B737-5U3	28727/2937	
☐ PK-GGD	B737-5U3	28728/2938	
☐ PK-GGE	B737-5U3	28729/2950	
☐ PK-GGF	B737-5U3	28730/2952	
☐ PK-GGG	B737-3U3	28731/2949	
☐ PK-GGN	B737-3U3	28735/3029	
☐ PK-GGO	B737-3U3	28736/3032	
☐ PK-GGP	B737-3U3	28737/3047	
☐ PK-GGQ	B737-3U3	28739/3064	
☐ PK-GGR	B737-3U3	28741/3079	
☐ PK-GGV	B737-3Q8	26293/2541	
☐ PK-GHW	B737-3M8	25039/2007	
☐ PK-GHX	B737-3L9	26440/2234	
☐ PK-GWK	B737-4U3	25713/2531	
☐ PK-GWL	B737-4U3	25714/2535	
☐ PK-GWM	B737-4U3	25715/2537	
☐ PK-GWN	B737-4U3	25716/2540	
☐ PK-GWO	B737-4U3	25717/2546	
☐ PK-GWP	B737-4U3	25718/2548	
☐ PK-GWQ	B737-4U3	25719/2549	
☐ PK-GWT	B737-4K5	26316/2711	
☐ PK-GWU	B737-4Q8	24708/2076	
☐ PK-GZA	B737-497	25663/2382	
☐ PK-GZH	B737-4M0	29203/3049	
☐ PK-GZK	B737-4M0	29206/3058	
☐ PK-GZL	B737-4M0	29207/3078	
☐ PK-GZM	B737-4M0	29208/3081	
☐ PK-GZN	B737-4M0	29209/3087	
☐ PK-GZO	B737-4M0	29210/3091	
☐ PK-GZP	B737-46Q	28661/2910	
☐ PK-GZQ	B737-4S3	25134/2083	
☐ PK-GEE	B737-8CX/W	32361/1098	
☐ PK-GEF	B737-8CX/W	32363/1139	
☐ PK-GEG	B737-83N/W	30033/1149	
☐ PK-GEH	B737-83N/W	30643/1106	
☐ PK-GEI	B737-86N/W	29883/1083	
☐ PK-GEJ	B737-86N/W	33003/1121	
☐ PK-GEK	B737-85F/W	30568/793	
☐ PK-GEL	B737-8AS/W	29927/727	
☐ PK-GEM	B737-8AS/W	29928/735	
☐ PK-GEN	B737-8AS/W	29929/753	
☐ PK-GEO	B737-8AS/W	29930/757	
☐ PK-GEP	B737-8AS/W	29931/1020	
☐ PK-GEQ	B737-86N/W	32659/1709	
☐ PK-GER	B737-86J/W	30876/759	
☐ PK-GFA	B737-86N/W	36549/3331	♦
☐ PK-GFC	B737-86N/W	39390/3348	♦
☐ PK-GFD	B737-8U3/W	40807/3337	♦
☐ PK-GFE	B737-86N/W	36804/3374	♦
☐ PK-GFF	B737-8U3/W	36436/3370	♦
☐ PK-GFG	B737-8U3/W	37819/3402	♦
☐ PK-GFH	B737-8U3/W	36850/3389	♦
☐ PK-GFI	B737-86N/W	36805/3438	♦
☐ PK-GFI	B737-86N/W	37885/3445	♦

☐ PK-GFK	B737-86N/W	37887/3463	♦
☐ PK-GFL	B737-86N/W	36808/3505	♦
☐ PK-GFM	B737-8U3/W	39920/3518	♦
☐ PK-	B737-8		o/o♦
☐ PK-	B737-8		o/o♦
☐ PK-	B737-8		o/o♦
☐ PK-	B737-8		o/o♦
☐ PK-	B737-8		o/o♦
☐ PK-	B737-8		o/o♦
☐ PK-	B737-8		o/o♦
☐ PK-	B737-8		o/o♦
☐ PK-	B737-8		o/o♦
☐ PK-	B737-8		o/o♦
☐ PK-	B737-8		o/o♦
☐ PK-	B737-8		o/o♦
☐ PK-	B737-8		o/o♦
☐ PK-GMA	B737-8U3/W	30151/2942	
☐ PK-GMC	B737-8U3/W	30155/3081	
☐ PK-GMD	B737-8U3/W	30156/3100	
☐ PK-GME	B737-8U3/W	30157/3123	
☐ PK-GMF	B737-8U3/W	30140/3129	
☐ PK-GMG	B737-8U3/W	30141/3166	
☐ PK-GMH	B737-8U3/W	30142/3213	♦
☐ PK-GMI	B737-8U3/W	30143/3243	♦
☐ PK-GMJ	B737-8U3/W	30144/3249	♦
☐ PK-GMK	B737-8U3/W	30145/3171	♦
☐ PK-GML	B737-8U3/W	31763/3177	♦
☐ PK-GMM	B737-8U3/W	30147/3285	♦
☐ PK-GMN	B737-8U3/W	30146/3303	♦
☐ PK-GMO	B737-8U3/W	30147/3327	♦
☐ PK-GMP	B737-8U3/W	30148/3353	♦
☐ PK-GMQ	B737-8U3/W	30149/3405	♦
☐ PK-GMR	B737-8U3/W	30150/3429	♦
☐ PK-	B737-8		♦
☐ PK-	B737-8		♦
☐ PK-	B737-8		♦
☐ PK-GSG	B747-4U3	25704/1011	
☐ PK-GSH	B747-4U3	25705/1029	
☐ PK-GSI	B747-441	24956/917	
☐ PK-	B777-3U3ER		o/o
☐ PK-	B777-3U3ER		o/o
☐ PK-	B777-3U3ER		o/o
☐ PK-	B777-3U3ER		o/o

GATARI AIR SERVICE — GHS

☐ PK-HNS	ATR 42-500	601	
☐ PK-HNT	ATR 42-500	614	♦
☐ PK-HNH	F.28Fellowship 4000	11218	
☐ PK-HNJ	F.28Fellowship 3000RC	11134	[HLP]
☐ PK-HNN	F.28Fellowship 3000R	11119	[HLP]
☐ PK-HNP	F.28Fellowship 4000	11216	[HLP]

GT AIR

☐ PK-LTP	F.27 Friendship 500	10398
☐ PK-LTQ	F.27 Friendship 500	10389/10528

INDONESIA AIR TRANSPORT — IDA

☐ PK-THT	ATR 42-500	611	♦
☐ PK-TSY	ATR 42-300	118	
☐ PK-TSZ	ATR 42-300	59	
☐ PK-TRU	BAC One-Eleven 492GM	262	[AOR]
☐ PK-TST	BAC One-Eleven 423ET	118	[AOR]
☐ PK-TSJ	F.27 Friendship 500RFC	10525	
☐ PK-TSO	Fokker 50	20186	
☐ PK-TSP	Fokker 50	20316	

INDONESIA AIRASIA — QZ / AWQ

☐ PK-AXA	A320-216	3610
☐ PK-AXC	A320-216	3648
☐ PK-AXD	A320-216	3182
☐ PK-AXE	A320-216	3715
☐ PK-AXF	A320-216	3765
☐ PK-AXG	A320-216	3813
☐ PK-AXH	A320-216	3875
☐ PK-AXI	A320-216	3963
☐ PK-AXJ	A320-216	4035
☐ PK-AXK	A320-216	4147
☐ PK-AXL	A320-216	4346 ♦
☐ PK-AXM	A320-216	4462 ♦
☐ PK-AXN	A320-216	4477 ♦
☐ PK-AXO	A320-216	4486 ♦
☐ PK-AXP	A320-216	4571 ♦
☐ PK-AWO	B737-322	24659/1836
☐ PK-AWP	B737-3Y0	24905/2001
☐ PK-AWQ	B737-3B7	23376/1308 <AXM
☐ PK-AWT	B737-3B7	23345/1170 <AXM
☐ PK-AWU	B737-301	23257/1124
☐ PK-AWX	B737-3Y0	24547/1813

JATAYU AIR — VJ / JTY

☐ PK-JAC	B727-232	21587/1492	[CGK]
☐ PK-JAG	B727-232	21306/1270	
☐ PK-JGN	B727-223	21384/1328	[CGK]
☐ PK-JGP	B737-204	22364/696	[CGK]
☐ PK-JGS	B737-222	19949/197	[PCB]
☐ PK-JGW	B737-2N7	21226/458	[MES]
☐ PK-LIA	B737-2P5	21440/502	[CGK]

KALSTAR

☐ PK-KSE	ATR 42-320	415
☐ PK-KSI	ATR 42-320	348

KARTIKA AIRLINES — 3Y / KAE

☐ PK-KAD	B737-284	22338/691
☐ PK-KAO	B737-284	22339/692

LION AIRLINES — JT / LNI

☐ PK-LIF	B737-4Y0	24467/1733	
☐ PK-LIG	B737-4Y0	24513/1779	[CGK]
☐ PK-LIH	B737-4Y0	24520/1803	
☐ PK-LII	B737-46B	24123/1663	
☐ PK-LIQ	B737-4Y0	24911/2033	[PNK]♦
☐ PK-LIR	B737-4Y0	24692/1963	
☐ PK-LIS	B737-4Y0	24693/1972	
☐ PK-LIT	B737-4Y0	24512/1777	
☐ PK-LIU	B737-3G7	23218/1076	
☐ PK-LIV	B737-3G7	23219/1090	
☐ PK-LIW	B737-4Y0	24684/1841	
☐ PK-LFF	B737-9GPER/W	35679/2093	
☐ PK-LFG	B737-9GPER/W	35680/1981	
☐ PK-LFH	B737-9GPER/W	35710/2285	
☐ PK-LFI	B737-9GPER/W	35711/2319	
☐ PK-LFJ	B737-9GPER/W	35712/2349	
☐ PK-LFK	B737-9GPER/W	35713/2437	
☐ PK-LFL	B737-9GPER/W	35714/2461	
☐ PK-LFM	B737-9GPER/W	35715/2485	
☐ PK-LFO	B737-9GPER/W	35716/2504	
☐ PK-LFP	B737-9GPER/W	35717/2455	
☐ PK-LFQ	B737-9GPER/W	35718/2670	
☐ PK-LFR	B737-9GPER/W	35719/2694	
☐ PK-LFS	B737-9GPER/W	35720/2756	
☐ PK-LFT	B737-9GPER/W	35721/2793	
☐ PK-LFU	B737-9GPER/W	35722/2836	
☐ PK-LFV	B737-9GPER/W	35723/2848	
☐ PK-LFW	B737-9GPER/W	35724/2879	
☐ PK-LFY	B737-9GPER/W	35725/2897	
☐ PK-LFZ	B737-9GPER/W	35726/2904	
☐ PK-LGF	B737-96NER/W	35223/2559	
☐ PK-LGG	B737-96NER/W	35225/2590	

	Reg	Type	Serial	Notes
☐	PK-LGH	B737-96NER/W	35227/2621	
☐	PK-LGI	B737-96NER/W	36539/2596	
☐	PK-LGJ	B737-9GPER/W	35727/2934	
☐	PK-LGK	B737-9GPER/W	35728/2984	
☐	PK-LGL	B737-9GPER/W	35729/3008	
☐	PK-LGM	B737-9GPER/W	35730/3075	
☐	PK-LGO	B737-9GPER/W	35731/3093	
☐	PK-LGP	B737-9GPER/W	35732/3111	
☐	PK-LGQ	B737-9GPER/W	35733/3135	
☐	PK-LGR	B737-9GPER/W	35734/3153	
☐	PK-LGS	B737-9GPER/W	35735/3183	♦
☐	PK-LGT	B737-9GPER/W	35736/3207	♦
☐	PK-LGU	B737-9GPER/W	35737/3225	♦
☐	PK-LGV	B737-9GPER/W	37268/3297	♦
☐	PK-LGW	B737-9GPER/W	37269/3321	♦
☐	PK-LGY	B737-9GPER/W	37270/3333	♦
☐	PK-LGZ	B737-9GPER/W	37271/3345	♦
☐	PK-LHH	B737-9GPER/W	37275/3375	♦
☐	PK-LHI	B737-9GPER/W	32276/3381	♦
☐	PK-LHJ	B737-9GPER/W	37272/3411	♦
☐	PK-LHK	B737-9GPER/W	37273/3423	♦
☐	PK-LHL	B737-9GPER/W	37274/3441	♦
☐	PK-LHM	B737-9GPER/W	37277/3513	♦
☐	PK-LHO	B737-9GPER/W	37278/3555	o/o♦
☐	PK-LHP	B737-9GPER/W	37279/3573	o/o♦
☐	PK-LHQ	B737-9GPER/W	37380/3537	o/o♦
☐	PK-	B737-9GPER/W		o/o♦
☐	PK-	B737-9GPER/W		o/o♦
☐	PK-	B737-9GPER/W		o/o♦
☐	PK-	B737-9GPER/W		o/o♦
☐	PK-	B737-9GPER/W		o/o♦
☐	PK-	B737-9GPER/W		o/o♦
☐	PK-	B737-9GPER/W		o/o♦
☐	PK-	B737-9GPER/W		o/o♦
☐	PK-LHF	B747-412	24063/736	
☐	PK-LHG	B747-412	24065/761	
☐	PK-LMI	MD-82	49263/1163	
☐	PK-LMM	MD-82	48069/1032	[CGK]
☐	PK-LMO	MD-82	49373/1201	
☐	PK-LMR	MD-82	49116/1061	[CGK]
☐	PK-LMW	MD-82	49443/1291	
☐	PK-LMY	MD-82	49250/1186	
☐	PK-LIK	MD-90-30	53570/2181	
☐	PK-LIL	MD-90-30	53573/2182	
☐	PK-LIM	MD-90-30	53489/2129	
☐	PK-LIO	MD-90-30	53490/2133	
☐	PK-LIP	MD-90-30	53551/2144	

MANUNGGAL AIR

	Reg	Type	Serial	Notes
☐	PK-VTA	BAe146 Srs.100	E1015	
☐	PK-VTM	BAe146 Srs.100	E1009	
☐	PK-VTR	Transall C-160NG	233	[HLP]
☐	PK-VTS	Transall C-160P	207	[HLP]

MERPATI NUSANTARA AIRLINES — MZ / MNA

	Reg	Type	Serial	Notes
☐	PK-MFA	ATR 72-212	379	♦
☐	PK-	ATR 72-212	385	o/o♦
☐	PK-MZA	CAIC MA60	0407	
☐	PK-MZB	CAIC MA60	0406	
☐	PK-MZC	CAIC MA60	0409	
☐	PK-MZD	CAIC MA60	0410	o/o
☐	PK-MZE	CAIC MA60	0501	o/o
☐	PK-MZF	CAIC MA60	0502	o/o
☐	PK-MZG	CAIC MA60	0505	o/o
☐	PK-MZI	CAIC MA60	0506	o/o
☐	PK-MZJ	CAIC MA60	0601	o/o
☐	PK-MZK	CAIC MA60	0602	o/o
☐	PK-MZL	CAIC MA60	0603	o/o
☐	PK-MZM	CAIC MA60	0604	o/o
☐	PK-MBC	B737-230	22129/754	[SUB]
☐	PK-MBE	B737-230	22142/797	
☐	PK-MBH	B737-2S3	22279/650	
☐	PK-MBJ	B737-2U4	22576/761	
☐	PK-MBN	B737-377	24304/1622	
☐	PK-MBO	B737-377	24305/1641	
☐	PK-MBP	B737-33A	23632/1344	
☐	PK-MBQ	B737-217	22260/784	
☐	PK-MBS	B737-217	22342/810	[SUB]
☐	PK-MBU	B737-217	22259/771	[SUB]
☐	PK-MBX	B737-228	23005/943	[SUB]
☐	PK-MBY	B737-228	23004/941	[SUB]
☐	PK-MBZ	B737-228	23007/948	[SUB]
☐	PK-MDC	B737-2L9	21685	
☐	PK-MDD	B737-2S3	22278/646	
☐	PK-MDE	B737-322	24660/1838	
☐	PK-MDF	B737-3S1	24856/1911	
☐	PK-MDG	B737-3Q8	26296/2581	
☐	PK-MDH	B737-301	23932/1554	
☐	PK-MDJ	B737-301	23931/1552	
☐	PK-MDK	B737-3B7	23858/1509	
☐	PK-MDO	B737-4Q8	24069/1635	
☐	PK-MDQ	B737-3Q8	24300/1666	
☐	PK-MDZ	B737-4Q8	26280/2239	
☐	PK-MNC	CASA-Nurtanio CN-2355/N002		
☐	PK-MND	CASA-Nurtanio CN-2357/N003		[SUB]
☐	PK-MNE	CASA-Nurtanio CN-2359/N004		
☐	PK-MNF	CASA-Nurtanio CN-23510/N005		[SUB]
☐	PK-MNG	CASA-Nurtanio CN-23514/N006		
☐	PK-MNI	CASA-Nurtanio CN-23516/N007		
☐	PK-MNJ	CASA-Nurtanio CN-23519/N009		[SUB]
☐	PK-MNK	CASA-Nurtanio CN-23520/N010		
☐	PK-MNM	CASA-Nurtanio CN-23526/N012		
☐	PK-MNP	CASA-Nurtanio CN-23530/N015		
☐	PK-MFF	F.27 Friendship 500	10551	[SUB]
☐	PK-MFG	F.27 Friendship 500	10552	[SUB]
☐	PK-MFJ	F.27 Friendship 500	10598	[SUB]
☐	PK-MFK	F.27 Friendship 500	10607	[SUB]
☐	PK-MFQ	F.27 Friendship 500	10623	[SUB]
☐	PK-MFV	F.27 Friendship 500	10625	[SUB]
☐	PK-MFW	F.27 Friendship 500	10626	[SUB]
☐	PK-MFY	F.27 Friendship 500	10629	
☐	PK-MJA	Fokker 100	11453	[SUB]
☐	PK-MJC	Fokker 100	11463	
☐	PK-MJD	Fokker 100	11474	

NUSANTARA AIR CHARTER

	Reg	Type	Serial
☐	PK-JKC	BAe146 Srs.200	E2113
☐	PK-JKM	F.28Fellowship 4000	11116
☐	PK-JKW	BAe146 Srs.200	E2204

PELITA AIR — 6D / PAS

	Reg	Type	Serial	Notes
☐	PK-PKT	DHC-7-110	54	
☐	PK-PSV	DHC-7-103	105	
☐	PK-PSW	DHC-7-103	100	
☐	PK-PSX	DHC-7-103	94	
☐	PK-PSY	DHC-7-103	86	
☐	PK-PSZ	DHC-7-103	75	
☐	PK-PFZ	Fokker 100	11486	
☐	PK-PJJ	Avro 146-RJ85	E2239	
☐	PK-PJK	F.28 Fellowship 4000	11192	[PCB]
☐	PK-PJL	F.28 Fellowship 4000	11111	
☐	PK-PJM	F.28 Fellowship 4000	11178	[PCB]
☐	PK-PJN	Fokker 100	11288	
☐	PK-PJY	F.28 Fellowship 4000	11146	

PREMIAIR

	Reg	Type	Serial	Notes
☐	PK-RJI	Fokker 100	11328	VIP

RIAU AIRLINES — RIU

	Reg	Type	Serial
☐	PK-RAL	Fokker 50	20282
☐	PK-RAS	Fokker 50	20261

RPX AIRLINES — RH / RPH

☐ PK-RPH	B737-2K2C	20943/405
☐ PK-RPI	B737-2K2C	20944/408

SRIWIJAYA AIR — SJ / SJY

☐ PK-CJA	B737-284	22301/683	
☐ PK-CJC	B737-33A	24025/1556	
☐ PK-CJD	B737-204	22057/621	
☐ PK-CJE	B737-2T4	23446/1165	
☐ PK-CJF	B737-284	22343/695	
☐ PK-CJG	B737-2H6	23320/1120	
☐ PK-CJH	B737-2B7	22883/935	
☐ PK-CJI	B737-2B7	23135/1054	[CGK]
☐ PK-CJJ	B737-2B7	22880/927	
☐ PK-CJK	B737-236	22032/742	
☐ PK-CJL	B737-284	21301/474	
☐ PK-CJM	B737-2B7	22884/956	
☐ PK-CJN	B737-2B7	23134/1050	[CGK]
☐ PK-CJO	B737-284	22300/674	
☐ PK-CJP	B737-2B7	23132/1044	[CGK]
☐ PK-CJR	B737-284	21225/464	
☐ PK-CJS	B737-3L9	27925/2763	
☐ PK-CJT	B737-33A	24791/1984	
☐ PK-CJU	B737-4Q8	24234/1627	
☐ PK-CJV	B737-4Y0	24689/1883	
☐ PK-CJW	B737-4Y0	24690/1885	
☐ PK-CJY	B737-3Q8	24698/1846	♦
☐ PK-CKA	B737-4Q8	25169/2237	
☐ PK-CKC	B737-4Q8	26285/2416	
☐ PK-CKD	B737-4Y0	25180/2201	
☐ PK-	B737-3Q8	24987/2268	

TIMAX CARGO AIRLINES

☐ PK-YGZ	B727-31F	20112/700

TRANSWISATA AIR

☐ PK-TWA	F.28Fellowship 4000	11234
☐ PK-TWC	Fokker 50	20272
☐ PK-TWF	Fokker 50	20142
☐ PK-TWM	F.28Fellowship 4000	11183
☐ PK-TWN	Fokker 100	11335
☐ PK-TWR	Fokker 50	20317

TRAVIRA AIR

☐ PK-TUB	DHC-8Q-315	590	o/o♦
☐ PK-TVY	DHC-8-315	549	
☐ PK-TVZ	B737-5L9	28996/2998	

TRIGANA AIR SERVICE — TGN

☐ PK-YRE	ATR 42-300	027
☐ PK-YRH	ATR 42-300	097
☐ PK-YRI	ATR 72-202	326
☐ PK-YRK	ATR 42-300	106
☐ PK-YRN	ATR 42-300	102
☐ PK-YRR	ATR 42-310	214
☐ PK-YRV	ATR 42-300	190
☐ PK-YRX	ATR 72-202	342
☐ PK-YRY	ATR 72-202	201
☐ PK-YRG	F.27 Friendship 500	10397
☐ PK-YRT	B737-2K5	22599/814

TRI-MG INTRA ASIA AIRLINES — GY / TMG

☐ PK-YGR	B727-223F	20893/1189
☐ PK-YGZ	B727-31F	20112/700

WINGS AIR — IW / WON

☐ PK-WFF	ATR 72-212A	869
☐ PK-WFG	ATR 72-212A	882

☐ PK-WFH	ATR 72-212A	883	
☐ PK-WFI	ATR 72-212A	871	
☐ PK-WFJ	ATR 72-212A	898	♦
☐ PK-WFK	ATR 72-212A	905	♦
☐ PK-WFL	ATR 72-212A	915	♦
☐ PK-WFM	ATR 72-212A	922	♦
☐ PK-WFO	ATR 72-212A	936	♦
☐ PK-WFP	ATR 72-212A	937	♦
☐ PK-	ATR 72-212A		o/o♦
☐ PK-	ATR 72-212A		o/o♦
☐ PK-	ATR 72-212A		o/o♦
☐ PK-	ATR 72-212A		o/o♦
☐ PK-	ATR 72-212A		o/o♦
☐ PK-WIA	DHC-8-301	194	
☐ PK-WID	DHC-8-301	116	
☐ PK-WIE	DHC-8-301	108	
☐ PK-LMG	MD-82	49417/1278	[CGK]
☐ PK-LMP	MD-82	49117/1063	<LNI
☐ PK-LMS	MD-82	49114/1066	[CGK]
☐ PK-LMT	MD-82	49118/1065	<LNI
☐ PK-LMU	MD-82	49429/1242	[CGK]
☐ PK-WIF	MD-82	49481/1308	<LNI
☐ PK-WIG	MD-82	49489/1351	[CGK]
☐ PK-WIH	MD-82	49582/1411	<LNI
☐ PK-WIK	MD-82	49788/1637	<LNI
☐ PK-WIL	MD-82	48083/1043	<LNI
☐ PK-WIO	MD-82	49102/1076	[CGK]
☐ PK-WIP	MD-82	49190/1180	[CGK]

XPRESS AIR — XN / XAR

☐ PK-TXD	B737-284	22400/766
☐ PK-TXF	B737-284	21302/475
☐ PK-TXG	B737-5L9	25066/2038
☐ PK-YGN	LET L-410UVP-E	902434

PP / PR / PT - BRAZIL

ABSA CARGO — M3 / TUS

☐ PR-ABB	B767-316F/W	29881/778	<LAN♦
☐ PR-ABD	B767-316F/W	34245/934	<LAN
☐ PR-ACG	B767-316F/W	30780/806	<LAN♦

AIR BRASIL CARGO — BSL

☐ PR-AIB	B727-227F	21363/1258

ATA BRASIL — ABZ

☐ PR-GMA	B727-224F	20659/979	[GYN]
☐ PR-LSW	B737-248C	20219/208	
☐ PR-MGA	B737-204C	20282/245	

AVIANCA BRAZIL — ONE

☐ PR-AVB	A319-115	4222	♦
☐ PR-AVC	A319-115	4287	♦
☐ PR-AVD	A319-115	4336	♦
☐ PR-BRB	B737-3Q4	24210/1577	
☐ PR-BRD	B737-3M8	24376/1717	
☐ PR-OAD	Fokker 100	11370	
☐ PR-OAE	Fokker 100	11426	
☐ PR-OAF	Fokker 100	11415	
☐ PR-OAG	Fokker 100	11412	
☐ PR-OAI	Fokker 100	11417	
☐ PR-OAJ	Fokker 100	11418	
☐ PR-OAK	Fokker 100	11425	
☐ PR-OAL	Fokker 100	11435	
☐ PR-OAM	Fokker 100	11436	
☐ PR-OAQ	Fokker 100	11467	
☐ PR-OAR	Fokker 100	11481	

☐	PR-OAS	Fokker 100	11405	
☐	PR-OAT	Fokker 100	11411	
☐	PR-OAU	Fokker 100	11427	

AZUL AD / AZU

☐	PR-AZR	ATR 72-202QC	519	♦
☐	PR-AZS	ATR 72-202	502	♦
☐	PR-	ATR 72-		o/o♦
☐	PR-	ATR 72-		o/o♦
☐	PR-	ATR 72-		o/o♦
☐	PR-AYA	ERJ-195AR	19000237	
☐	PR-AYB	ERJ-195AR	19000239	
☐	PR-AYC	ERJ-195AR	19000240	
☐	PR-AYD	ERJ-195AR	19000247	
☐	PR-AYE	ERJ-195AR	19000260	
☐	PR-AYF	ERJ-195AR	19000353	♦
☐	PR-AYG	ERJ-195AR	19000356	♦
☐	PR-AYH	ERJ-195AR	19000361	♦
☐	PR-AYI	ERJ-195AR	19000366	♦
☐	PR-AYJ	ERJ-195AR	19000370	♦
☐	PR-AYK	ERJ-195AR	19000374	♦
☐	PR-AYL	ERJ-195AR	19000378	♦
☐	PR-AYM	ERJ-195AR	19000382	♦
☐	PR-AYN	ERJ-195AR	19000386	♦
☐	PR-AYO	ERJ-195AR	19000391	♦
☐	PR-AYP	ERJ-195AR	19000396	
☐	PR-AYQ	ERJ-195AR	19000407	o/o♦
☐	PR-	ERJ-195AR		o/o♦
☐	PR-	ERJ-195AR		o/o♦
☐	PR-	ERJ-195AR		o/o♦
☐	PR-	ERJ-195AR		o/o♦
☐	PR-	ERJ-195AR		o/o♦
☐	PR-	ERJ-195AR		o/o♦
☐	PR-	ERJ-195AR		o/o♦
☐	PR-	ERJ-195AR		o/o♦
☐	PR-AZA	ERJ-190AR	19000150	
☐	PR-AZB	ERJ-190AR	19000241	
☐	PR-AZC	ERJ-190AR	19000242	
☐	PR-AZD	ERJ-190AR	19000271	
☐	PR-AZE	ERJ-190AR	19000282	
☐	PR-AZF	ERJ-190AR	19000295	
☐	PR-AZG	ERJ-190AR	19000329	
☐	PR-AZH	ERJ-190AR	19000330	
☐	PR-AZI	ERJ-190AR	19000336	♦
☐	PR-AZL	ERJ-190AR	19000147	

BETA CARGO AIR BET

☐	PP-BEL	DC-8-73AF	46047/447	
☐	PP-BEM	DC-8-73F	46086/478	
☐	PP-BET	DC-8-73CF	46103/483	
☐	PP-BEX	DC-8-73F	46104/488	
☐	PP-BRR	B707-323C	20088/727	[GRU]

GOL TRANSPORTES AEREOS G3 / GLO

☐	PR-GEA	B737-7EH/W	37595/3026	
☐	PR-GIF	B737-73S	29076/98	
☐	PR-GIG	B737-73S	29077/104	
☐	PR-GIH	B737-76N/W	32743/1503	
☐	PR-GII	B737-7L9	28011/1203	
☐	PR-GIJ	B737-7L9	28012/1092	>SNB
☐	PR-GIK	B737-7Q8	28224/369	
☐	PR-GIL	B737-7Q8	30635/713	
☐	PR-GIM	B737-73V	30238/913	
☐	PR-GIN	B737-73V	30242/690	
☐	PR-GOA	B737-7L9	28005/11	
☐	PR-GOB	B737-75B	28099/13	
☐	PR-GOC	B737-75B	28101/17	
☐	PR-GOD	B737-75B	28105/66	
☐	PR-GOE	B737-75B	28106/68	
☐	PR-GOF	B737-76Q	30273/843	
☐	PR-GOG	B737-76Q	30275/900	

☐	PR-GOH	B737-76N	32440/954	
☐	PR-GOI	B737-76N	32574/983	
☐	PR-GOL	B737-7L9	28004/10	
☐	PR-GOM	B737-76N	28613/463	
☐	PR-GON	B737-76N	30051/436	
☐	PR-GOO	B737-76N	30135/1068	
☐	PR-GOQ	B737-76N	33417/1215	
☐	PR-GOR	B737-76N	33380/1231	
☐	PR-GOV	B737-76N	28580/135	
☐	PR-GOW	B737-76N	28584/170	
☐	PR-GOX	B737-7K9	28088/19	
☐	PR-GOY	B737-7K9	28089/25	
☐	PR-VBH	B737-73V	30239/944	
☐	PR-VBI	B737-73V	30246/1064	
☐	PR-VBO	B737-73V	30247/1066	
☐	PR-VBW	B737-7BX	30739/758	
☐	PR-VBY	B737-73A/W	28499/390	
☐	PR-VBZ	B737-73A/W	28500/414	
☐	PR-	B737-7EH/W		o/o♦
☐	PR-	B737-7EH/W		o/o♦
☐	PR-GGA	B737-8EH/W	35063/2476	
☐	PR-GGB	B737-8EH/W	35064/2498	
☐	PR-GGD	B737-8EH/W	34275/2588	
☐	PR-GGE	B737-8EH/W	35824/2665	
☐	PR-GGF	B737-8EH/W	35826/2749	
☐	PR-GGG	B737-8EH/W	36566/2809	
☐	PR-GGH	B737-8EH/W	36147/2864	
☐	PR-GGJ	B737-8EH/W	35825/2786	
☐	PR-GGK	B737-8EH/W	35065/2561	
☐	PR-GGL	B737-8EH/W	36148/2890	
☐	PR-GGM	B737-8EH/W	36149/2920	
☐	PR-GGN	B737-8EH/W	35827/2991	
☐	PR-GGO	B737-8EH/W	35828/3025	
☐	PR-GGP	B737-8EH/W	35829/3076	
☐	PR-GGQ	B737-8EH/W	37596/3103	
☐	PR-GGR	B737-8EH/W	36150/3106	
☐	PR-GGT	B737-8EH/W	35830/3115	
☐	PR-GGU	B737-8EH/W	37597/3133	
☐	PR-GGV	B737-8EH/W	37598/3136	
☐	PR-GGW	B737-8EH/W	35831/3165	
☐	PR-GGX	B737-8EH/W	36596/3180	♦
☐	PR-GGY	B737-8EH/W	37599/3191	♦
☐	PR-GGZ	B737-8EH/W	37600/3205	♦
☐	PR-GID	B737-76N/W	29904/347	
☐	PR-GIE	B737-8BK/W	33027/1918	
☐	PR-GIO	B737-85F/W	30477/976	
☐	PR-GIP	B737-85F/W	30571/936	
☐	PR-GIQ	B737-86N/W	28616/483	
☐	PR-GIR	B737-8Q8	28213/50	
☐	PR-GIT	B737-809	28403/117	
☐	PR-GIU	B737-809	29103/129	
☐	PR-GIV	B737-86N/W	28578/89	
☐	PR-GIW	B737-86N/W	28575/91	
☐	PR-GIX	B737-8Q8	30636/768	
☐	PR-GOJ	B737-8CX	32359/1041	[PTY]
☐	PR-GOP	B737-8BK	30621/1194	
☐	PR-GOT	B737-8BK	30625/1248	
☐	PR-GTA	B737-8EH/W	34474/1843	
☐	PR-GTB	B737-8EH/W	34475/2020	
☐	PR-GTC	B737-8EH/W	34277/2028	
☐	PR-GTE	B737-8EH/W	34278/2052	
☐	PR-GTF	B737-8EH/W	34279/2061	
☐	PR-GTG	B737-8EH/W	34654/2075	
☐	PR-GTH	B737-8EH/W	34655/2091	
☐	PR-GTI	B737-8EH/W	34280/2100	
☐	PR-GTJ	B737-8EH/W	34656/2110	
☐	PR-GTK	B737-8EH/W	34281/2116	
☐	PR-GTL	B737-8EH/W	34962/2215	
☐	PR-GTM	B737-8EH/W	34963/2240	
☐	PR-GTN	B737-8EH/W	34267/2311	
☐	PR-GTO	B737-8EH/W	34964/2332	
☐	PR-GTP	B737-8EH/W	34965/2341	
☐	PR-GTQ	B737-8EH/W	36146/2358	
☐	PR-GTR	B737-8EH/W	34966/2367	

☐ PR-GTT	B737-8EH/W	34268/2407	
☐ PR-GTU	B737-8EH/W	34269/2412	
☐ PR-GTV	B737-8EH/W	34270/2420	
☐ PR-GTY	B737-8EH/W	34273/2464	
☐ PR-GTZ	B737-8EH/W	34274/2468	
☐ PR-GUA	B737-8EH/W	37601/3301	♦
☐ PR-GUB	B737-8EH/W	35832/3309	♦
☐ PR-GUC	B737-8EH/W	35835/3430	♦
☐ PR-GUD	B737-8EH/W	35836/3466	♦
☐ PR-GUE	B737-8EH/W	35837/3473	♦
☐ PR-GUF	B737-8EH/W	35838/3508	♦
☐ PR-	B737-8EH/W	o/o♦	
☐ PR-	B737-8EH/W	o/o♦	
☐ PR-	B737-8EH/W	o/o♦	

MTA CARGO — MTA

☐ N501TR	A300B4-203F	053	<TDX♦
☐ PP-MTA	DC-10-30CF	47908/215	
☐ PR-MTC	DC-10-30F	46540/268	

PANTANAL — P8 / PTN

☐ PT-MFJ	ATR 42-320	343
☐ PT-MFM	ATR 42-300	376
☐ PT-MFT	ATR 42-320	306
☐ PT-MFU	ATR 42-310	070
☐ PT-MFV	ATR 42-300	043

PASSAREDO — PTB

☐ PR-PSF	ERJ-145EP	145016	
☐ PR-PSG	ERJ-145EP	145021	
☐ PR-PSH	ERJ-145LR	145597	
☐ PR-PSK	ERJ-145LU	145387	
☐ PR-PSL	ERJ-145LR	145269	♦
☐ PR-PSM	ERJ-145LR	145281	♦
☐ PR-PSN	ERJ-145MP	145407	♦
☐ PR-PSQ	ERJ-145MP	145244	♦
☐ PR-PSR	ERJ-145MP	145339	♦

PLATINUM LINHAS AEREAS — PLJ

☐ PR-PLH	B727-225	22434/1671

PUMA AIR LINHAS AEREAS — PLY

☐ PR-GLK	B737-322	24668/1905	♦

RICO LINHAS AEREAS — C7 / RLE

☐ PR-RLA	B737-241	21009/417	[MAO]
☐ (PR-RLB)	B737-241	21008/402	[MAO]
☐ (PR-RLC)	B737-241	21000/378	
☐	An-32	o/o♦	
☐	An-32	o/o♦	

RIO LINHAS AEREAS

☐ PR-IOA	B772-214F	21512/1343	♦
☐ PR-IOB	B727-264F	22983/1806	♦
☐ PR-IOC	B727-264F	22984/1813	♦
☐ PR-IOD	B727-264F	23014/1816	♦
☐ PR-IOF	B727-214F	21961/1479	♦
☐ PR-IOG	B727-214F	21962/1480	♦
☐ PR-RLJ	B727-214F	21513/1365	

SIDERAL AIR CARGO

☐ PR-SDL	B737-3S3F	24060/1519	♦

SKYMASTER AIRLINES — SKC

☐ PR-SKC	DC-8-63F	46143/547
☐ PR-SKI	DC-8-62F	46154/554
☐ PR-SKM	DC-8-63F	46137/527

☐ PT-MTE	B707-321C	20017/753	
☐ PT-MTR	B707-369C	20084/758	
☐ PT-WUS	B707-324C	19352/576	[GRU]

TAF LINHAS AEREAS — TSD

☐ PR-MTD	B727-227F	21248/1218
☐ PR-MTG	B737-217	22255/666
☐ PR-MTH	B737-232	23102/1045
☐ PR-MTJ	B727-2M7F	21952/1693
☐ PR-MTK	B727-222F	20037/701
☐ PR-MTL	B727-2J7F	20879/1033
☐ PT-MTC	B727-228F	20409/845
☐ PT-MTF	B737-241	21007/400

TAM LINHAS AEREAS — JJ / TAM

☐ PR-MAH	A319-132	1608	
☐ PR-MAI	A319-132	1703	
☐ PR-MAL	A319-132	1801	
☐ PR-MAM	A319-132	1826	
☐ PR-MAN	A319-132	1831	
☐ PR-MAO	A319-132	1837	
☐ PR-MAQ	A319-132	1855	
☐ PR-MBI	A319-132	1575	
☐ PR-MBN	A319-132	3032	
☐ PR-MBU	A319-132	3588	
☐ PR-MBV	A319-132	3595	
☐ PR-MBW	A319-132	3710	
☐ PR-MYB	A319-112	3727	
☐ PR-MYC	A319-112	3733	
☐ PT-MZA	A319-132	0976	
☐ PT-MZB	A319-132	1010	
☐ PT-MZC	A319-132	1092	
☐ PT-MZD	A319-132	1096	
☐ PT-MZE	A319-132	1103	
☐ PT-MZF	A319-132	1139	
☐ PT-TMA	A319-132	4000	
☐ PT-TMB	A319-132	4163	♦
☐ PT-TMC	A319-132	4171	♦
☐ PT-TMD	A319-132	4192	♦
☐ PT-TME	A319-132	4389	♦
☐ PT-TMF	A319-132	2467	♦
☐ PT-	A319-132	o/o♦	
☐ PT-	A319-132	o/o♦	
☐ PT-	A319-132	o/o♦	
☐ PR-MAA	A320-232	1595	
☐ PR-MAB	A320-232	1663	
☐ PR-MAC	A320-232	1672	
☐ PR-MAD	A320-232	1771	
☐ PR-MAE	A320-232	1804	
☐ PR-MAG	A320-232	1832	
☐ PR-MAJ	A320-232	1818	
☐ PR-MAK	A320-232	1825	
☐ PR-MAP	A320-232	1857	
☐ PR-MAR	A320-232	1888	
☐ PR-MAS	A320-232	2372	
☐ PR-MAV	A320-232	2393	
☐ PR-MAW	A320-232	2417	
☐ PR-MAX	A320-232	2602	
☐ PR-MAY	A320-232	2661	
☐ PR-MAZ	A320-232	2513	
☐ PR-MBA	A320-232	2734	
☐ PR-MBB	A320-232	2737	
☐ PR-MBC	A320-232	2783	
☐ PR-MBD	A320-232	2838	
☐ PR-MBE	A320-232	2859	
☐ PR-MBF	A320-232	2896	
☐ PR-MBG	A320-232	1459	
☐ PR-MBH	A320-232	2904	
☐ PR-MBJ	A320-232	2445	
☐ PR-MBL	A320-233	2044	
☐ PR-MBM	A320-233	1339	
☐ PR-MBO	A320-232	3156	
☐ PR-MBP	A320-232	1215	

☐	PR-MBQ	A320-232	1652	
☐	PR-MBR	A320-232	1802	
☐	PR-MBS	A320-232	1835	
☐	PR-MBX	A320-232	1591	
☐	PR-MBY	A320-232	1891	
☐	PR-MBZ	A320-232	1827	
☐	PR-MHA	A320-214	2924	
☐	PR-MHB	A320-214	1692	
☐	PR-MHC	A320-214	1717	
☐	PR-MHD	A320-214	1775	
☐	PR-MHE	A320-214	3111	
☐	PR-MHF	A320-214	3180	
☐	PR-MHG	A320-214	3002	
☐	PR-MHI	A320-214	3035	
☐	PR-MHJ	A320-214	3047	
☐	PR-MHK	A320-214	3058	
☐	PR-MHM	A320-214	3211	
☐	PR-MHN	A320-214	3240	
☐	PR-MHO	A320-214	3278	
☐	PR-MHP	A320-214	3266	
☐	PR-MHQ	A320-214	3284	
☐	PR-MHR	A320-214	3313	
☐	PR-MHS	A320-214	3325	
☐	PR-MHT	A320-214	1757	
☐	PR-MHU	A320-214	3391	
☐	PR-MHV	A320-214	3540	
☐	PR-MHW	A320-214	3630	
☐	PR-MHX	A320-214	3565	
☐	PR-MHY	A320-214	3594	
☐	PR-MHZ	A320-214	3658	
☐	PR-MYA	A320-214	3662	
☐	PR-MYD	A320-214	3750	
☐	PR-MYE	A320-214	3908	
☐	PR-MYF	A320-214	3972	
☐	PR-MYG	A320-214	4320	
☐	PR-MYH	A320-214	4441	♦
☐	PR-MYI	A320-214	4446	♦
☐	PR-MYJ	A320-214	4465	♦
☐	PR-MYK	A320-214	4544	♦
☐	PR-	A320-2		o/o♦
☐	PR-	A320-2		o/o♦
☐	PR-	A320-2		o/o♦
☐	PR-	A320-2		o/o♦
☐	PR-	A320-2		o/o♦
☐	PT-MZG	A320-232	1143	
☐	PT-MZH	A320-232	1158	
☐	PT-MZI	A320-232	1246	
☐	PT-MZJ	A320-232	1251	
☐	PT-MZK	A320-232	1368	
☐	PT-MZL	A320-232	1376	
☐	PT-MZN	A320-231	0440	
☐	PT-MZO	A320-231	0250	
☐	PT-MZQ	A320-231	0335	
☐	PT-MZR	A320-231	0334	
☐	PT-MZT	A320-232	1486	
☐	PT-MZU	A320-232	1518	
☐	PT-MZV	A320-232	0758	
☐	PT-MZW	A320-232	1580	
☐	PT-MZX	A320-232	1613	
☐	PT-MZY	A320-232	1628	
☐	PT-MZZ	A320-232	1593	
☐	PT-MXA	A321-231	3222	
☐	PT-MXB	A321-231	3229	
☐	PT-MXC	A321-231	3294	
☐	PT-MXD	A321-231	3761	
☐	PT-MXE	A321-231	3816	
☐	PT-MXF	A321-231	4352	♦
☐	PT-MXG	A321-231	4358	♦
☐	PT-MXH	A321-231	4570	♦
☐	PT-	A321-231		o/o♦
☐	PT-MVA	A330-223	232	
☐	PT-MVB	A330-223	238	
☐	PT-MVC	A330-223	247	
☐	PT-MVD	A330-223	259	

☐	PT-MVE	A330-223	361	
☐	PT-MVF	A330-223	466	
☐	PT-MVG	A330-203	472	
☐	PT-MVH	A330-203	477	
☐	PT-MVK	A330-203	486	
☐	PT-MVL	A330-203	700	
☐	PT-MVM	A330-223	869	
☐	PT-MVN	A330-223	876	
☐	PT-MVO	A330-223	949	
☐	PT-MVP	A330-223	961	
☐	PT-MVQ	A330-223	968	
☐	PT-MVR	A330-223	977	
☐	PT-MVS	A330-223	1112	♦
☐	PT-MVT	A330-223	1118	♦
☐	PT-	A330-223		o/o♦
☐	PT-	A330-223		o/o♦
☐	PT-MSL	A340-541	464	
☐	PT-MSN	A340-541	445	
☐	PT-MSQ	B767-33AER	27468/584	
☐	PT-MSR	B767-33AER	27377/561	
☐	PT-MSU	B767-33AER	27376/560	
☐	PT-MUA	B777-32WER	37664/727	
☐	PT-MUB	B777-32WER	37665/733	
☐	PT-MUC	B777-32WER	37666/740	
☐	PT-MUD	B777-32WER	37667/751	
☐	PT-MQC	Fokker 100	11371	
☐	PT-MRE	Fokker 100	11348	

TAVAJ LINHAS AEREAS — 4U / TVJ

☐	PT-LAG	F.27 Friendship 600	10197	
☐	PT-LAH	F.27 Friendship 600	10178	

TOTAL LINHAS AEREAS — TTL

☐	PR-TTB	B727-223	22007/1643	
☐	PR-TTO	B727-2M7F	21200/1206	
☐	PR-TTP	B727-2M7F	21502/1339	
☐	PR-TTW	B727-225F	22438/1685	♦
☐	PT-MTQ	B727-243F	22053/1620	
☐	PT-MTT	B727-243F	22167/1752	

TRIP LINHAS AEREAS — 8R

☐	PP-ATV	ATR 42-300	298	
☐	PP-PTC	ATR 42-300	035	
☐	PP-PTD	ATR 42-320	091	
☐	PP-PTE	ATR 42-300	014	>CRN
☐	PP-PTF	ATR 42-300	072	
☐	PP-PTG	ATR 42-320	128	
☐	PP-PTI	ATR 42-320	374	
☐	PP-PTJ	ATR 42-320	284	
☐	PP-PTV	ATR 42-500	503	
☐	PP-PTW	ATR 42-500	510	
☐	PR-TKB	ATR 42-500	610	♦
☐	PR-TKC	ATR 42-500	609	♦
☐	PR-TKD	ATR 42-500	604	♦
☐	PR-TKE	ATR 42-500	556	♦
☐	PR-TTE	ATR 42-300	400	
☐	PR-TTF	ATR 42-300	021	
☐	PR-TTG	ATR 42-320	020	
☐	PR-TTH	ATR 42-500	506	
☐	PR-TTK	ATR 42-500	504	
☐	PR-TTM	ATR 42-500	551	
☐	PT-MFE	ATR 42-300	295	
☐	PT-TTL	ATR 42-320	380	
☐	PP-PTH	ATR 72-202	365	
☐	PP-PTK	ATR 72-202	352	
☐	PP-PTL	ATR 72-212A	773	
☐	PP-PTM	ATR 72-212A	798	
☐	PP-PTN	ATR 72-212A	832	

☐	PP-PTO	ATR 72-212A	837	
☐	PP-PTP	ATR 72-212A	865	
☐	PP-PTQ	ATR 72-212A	874	
☐	PP-PTR	ATR 72-212A	785	♦
☐	PP-PTT	ATR 72-212A	846	♦
☐	PP-PTU	ATR 72-212A	891	♦
☐	PP-PTX	ATR 72-212A	666	♦
☐	PP-PTY	ATR 72-212A	911	♦
☐	PP-PTZ	ATR 72-212A	918	♦
☐	PR-TKA	ATR 72-212A	926	♦
☐	PR-TTI	ATR 72-212	454	
☐	PR-TTJ	ATR 72-212	463	
☐	PR-	ATR 72-212A	o/o♦	
☐	PR-	ATR 72-212A	o/o♦	
☐	PP-PJA	ERJ-175LR	17000272	
☐	PP-PJB	ERJ-175LR	17000277	
☐	PP-PJC	ERJ-175LR	17000287	
☐	PP-PJD	ERJ-175LR	17000017	
☐	PP-PJE	ERJ-175LR	17000291	♦
☐	PP-PJF	ERJ-175LR	17000309	♦
☐	PP-PJG	ERJ-175LR	17000137	♦
☐	PP-PJH	ERJ-175LR	17000147	♦
☐	PP-PJJ	ERJ-190LR	19000163	♦
☐	PP-PJK	ERJ-190LR	19000178	♦
☐	PP-PJL	ERJ-190LR	19000189	♦
☐	PP-	ERJ-190LR	o/o♦	
☐	PP-	ERJ-190LR	o/o♦	

VARIG — RG / VRN

☐	PP-VNT	B737-33A	23828/1446	
☐	PP-VNY	B737-3K9	24864/1918	
☐	PP-VQN	B737-33A	24098/1783	
☐	PP-VTA	B737-3K9	23797/1416	[ROW]
☐	PP-VTB	B737-3K9	23798/1429	
☐	PR-VBA	B737-8AS/W	29916/210	
☐	PR-VBB	B737-8AS/W	29917/298	
☐	PR-VBC	B737-8AS/W	29918/307	
☐	PR-VBD	B737-8AS/W	29919/341	
☐	PR-VBE	B737-8AS/W	29920/362	
☐	PR-VBF	B737-8EH/W	34276/2716	
☐	PR-VBG	B737-8EH/W	35066/2700	
☐	PR-VBJ	B737-86N/W	36434/2706	
☐	PR-VBK	B737-8EH/W	34271/2445	<GLO
☐	PR-VBL	B737-8EH/W	34272/2449	<GLO
☐	PR-VBM	B737-7EA	32406/859	
☐	PR-VBN	B737-76N	28577/124	
☐	PR-VBP	B737-7EA	32407/904	
☐	PR-VBU	B737-76N/W	29905/372	
☐	PR-VBV	B737-76N/W	30050/429	
☐	PR-VBX	B737-7BX	30738/716	
☐	PR-VAB	B767-33AER	27477/337	[VNF]
☐	PR-VAC	B767-27GER	27048/475	♦
☐	PR-VAF	B767-38EER	25132/417	
☐	PR-VAN	B767-328ER	27427/579	[GIG]

VARIG LOG — LC / VLO

☐	PP-VQV	B727-243F	22166/1725	
☐	PR-LGC	B727-2A1F	21342/1256	
☐	PR-LGH	B757-225 (PCF)	22211/74	
☐	PR-LGJ	B757-225 (PCF)	22210/42	

WEBJET LINHAS AEREAS — WEB

☐	PR-WJA	B737-322	24663/1875
☐	PR-WJB	B737-341	25050/2125
☐	PR-WJC	B737-341	25051/2127
☐	PR-WJD	B737-3Y0	23922/1538
☐	PR-WJE	B737-33A	25057/2046
☐	PR-WJF	B737-341	24936/1951
☐	PR-WJG	B737-322	24452/1728
☐	PR-WJH	B737-341	26856/2321

☐	PR-WJI	B737-341	26857/2326	
☐	PR-WJJ	B737-341	24935/1935	
☐	PR-WJK	B737-33A	23830/1462	
☐	PR-WJL	B737-36N	28590/3097	
☐	PR-WJM	B737-36Q	28660/2883	
☐	PR-WJN	B737-36Q	29327/3023	
☐	PR-WJO	B737-3Q8	26295/2557	
☐	PR-WJP	B737-3Q8	26309/2674	
☐	PR-WJQ	B737-3U3	28742/2992	
☐	PR-WJR	B737-36N	28566/2964	
☐	PR-WJS	B737-3Y0	24465/1755	
☐	PR-WJT	B737-3Y0	24908/2015	
☐	PR-WJU	B737-36N	28560/2888	♦
☐	PR-WJV	B737-36N	28567/2971	♦
☐	PR-WJW	B737-33A	27267/2600	♦
☐	PR-WJX	B737-33A	25033/2025	♦

WHITEJETS

☐	PR-WTA	A310-304	494	♦

PZ - SURINAME

SURINAM AIRWAYS — PY / SLM

☐	PZ-TCM	B747-306M	23508/657	
☐	PZ-TCN	B737-36N	28668/2890	
☐	PZ-TCO	B737-36N	28669/2897	
■	PZ-TCP	A340-311	049	07/1/08.4.14

P2 - PAUA NEW GUINEA

AIR NIUGINI — PX / ANG

☐	P2-ANA	B767-366ER	24541/275	<ICE
☐	P2-ANB	B757-256	29312/943	<ICE
☐	P2-ANK	DHC-8Q-202	461	
☐	P2-ANL	DHC-8-102	153	
☐	P2-ANM	DHC-8Q-314	523	
☐	P2-ANN	DHC-8-315	401	
☐	P2-ANO	DHC-8-311A	252	
☐	P2-ANP	DHC-8-102	177	
☐	P2-ANX	DHC-8Q-202	463	
☐	P2-ANZ	DHC-8Q-201	421	
☐	P2-PXT	DHC-8-402Q	4329	♦
☐	P2-PXU	DHC-8-402Q	4316	♦
☐	P2-ANC	Fokker 100	11471	
☐	P2-AND	Fokker 100	11473	
☐	P2-ANE	Fokker 100	11264	
☐	P2-ANF	Fokker 100	11351	
☐	P2-ANH	Fokker 100	11301	
☐	P2-ANQ	Fokker 100	11451	
☐	P2-ANI	F.28 Fellowship 4000	11223	[POM]
☐	P2-ANJ	F.28 Fellowship 4000	11219	[POM]
☐	P2-ANR	F.28 Fellowship 4000	11207	[KUL]
☐	P2-ANS	F.28 Fellowship 4000	11195	[POM]

AIRLINES OF PAPUA NEW GUINEA — CG / TOK

☐	P2-MCG	DHC-8-102	006
☐	P2-MCH	DHC-8-102	012
☐	P2-MCI	DHC-8-102	197
☐	P2-MCJ	DHC-8-102	125
☐	P2-MCL	DHC-8-102	027
☐	P2-MCP	DHC-8-102	033
☐	P2-MCQ	DHC-8-103A	243
☐	P2-MCT	DHC-8-102	135
☐	P2-MCU	DHC-8-102	208

ASIA PACIFIC AIRLINES

☐	P2-NAX	DHC-8-103	229	<NJS
☐	P2-NAZ	DHC-8-106	316	<NJS

RA - RUSSIA

ABAKAN-AVIA ABG

☐ RA-76457	Il-76T	093421621
☐ RA-76509	Il-76T	083413415
☐ RA-76780	Il-76T	013430901

AERO RENT NRO

☐ RA-21506	Yak-40KD	9840259
☐ RA-42434	Yak-42D	43050170517
☐ RA-65557	Tu-134A	66380
☐ RA-65790	Tu-134A-3	63100
☐ RA-87397	Yak-40	9410933
☐ RA-88306	Yak-40KD	9640651

AEROBRATSK BRP

☐ RA-88205	Yak-40	9630749
☐ RA-88215	Yak-40K	9630150

AEROFLOT PLUS PLS

☐ RA-65559	Tu-134A	7349909
☐ RA-65694	Tu-134B-3	63235
☐ RA-65790	Tu-134A-3	63100

AEROFLOT RUSSIAN AIRLINES SU / AFL

☐ VP-BDM	A319-111	2069	
☐ VP-BDN	A319-111	2072	
☐ VP-BDO	A319-111	2091	
☐ VP-BUK	A319-111	3281	
☐ VP-BUN	A319-111	3298	
☐ VP-BUO	A319-111	3336	
☐ VP-BWA	A319-111	2052	
☐ VP-BWG	A319-111	2093	
☐ VP-BWJ	A319-111	2179	
☐ VP-BWK	A319-111	2222	
☐ VP-BWL	A319-111	2243	
☐ VQ-BBA	A319-111	3794	
☐ VQ-BBD	A319-131	3838	
☐ VQ-BCO	A319-131	3942	
☐ VQ-BCP	A319-131	3998	
☐ VP-BDK	A320-214	2106	
☐ VP-BKC	A320-214	3545	
☐ VP-BKX	A320-214	3410	
☐ VP-BKY	A320-214	3511	
☐ VP-BME	A320-214	3699	
☐ VP-BMF	A320-214	3711	
☐ VP-BQP	A320-214	2875	
☐ VP-BQU	A320-214	3373	
☐ VP-BQV	A320-214	2920	
☐ VP-BQW	A320-214	2947	
☐ VP-BRX	A320-214	3063	
☐ VP-BRY	A320-214	3052	
☐ VP-BRZ	A320-214	3157	
☐ VP-BWD	A320-214	2116	
☐ VP-BWE	A320-214	2133	
☐ VP-BWF	A320-214	2144	
☐ VP-BWH	A320-214	2151	
☐ VP-BWI	A320-214	2163	
☐ VP-BWM	A320-214	2233	
☐ VP-BZO	A320-214	3574	
☐ VP-BZP	A320-214	3631	
☐ VP-BZQ	A320-214	3627	
☐ VP-BZR	A320-214	3640	
☐ VP-BZS	A320-214	3644	
☐ VQ-BAX	A320-214	3778	
☐ VQ-BAY	A320-214	3786	
☐ VQ-BAZ	A320-214	3789	
☐ VQ-BBB	A320-214	3823	
☐ VQ-BBC	A320-214	3835	
☐ VQ-BCM	A320-214	3923	
☐ VQ-BCN	A320-214	3954	
☐ VQ-BEH	A320-214	4133	
☐ VQ-BEJ	A320-214	4160	
☐ VQ-BHL	A320-214	4453	♦
☐ VQ-BHN	A320-214	4498	♦
☐ VQ-BIW	A320-214	4579	♦
☐ VQ-	A320-214		o/o♦
☐ VQ-	A320-214		o/o♦
☐ VQ-	A320-214		o/o♦
☐ VP-BQR	A321-211	2903	
☐ VP-BQS	A321-211	2912	
☐ VP-BQT	A321-211	2965	
☐ VP-BQX	A321-211	2957	
☐ VP-BRW	A321-211	3191	
☐ VP-BUM	A321-211	3267	
☐ VP-BUP	A321-211	3334	
☐ VP-BWN	A321-211	2330	
☐ VP-BWO	A321-211	2337	
☐ VP-BWP	A321-211	2342	
☐ VQ-BEA	A321-211	4058	
☐ VQ-BED	A321-211	4074	
☐ VQ-BEE	A321-211	4099	
☐ VQ-BEF	A321-211	4103	
☐ VQ-BEG	A321-211	4116	
☐ VQ-BEI	A321-211	4148	
☐ VQ-BHK	A321-211	4461	♦
☐ VQ-BHM	A321-211	4500	♦
☐ VQ-	A321-211		o/o♦
☐ VP-BLX	A330-243	963	
☐ VP-BLY	A330-243	973	
☐ VQ-BBE	A330-243	1014	
☐ VQ-BBF	A330-243	1045	
☐ VQ-BBG	A330-243	1047	
☐ VQ-BCQ	A330-343E	1058	
☐ VQ-BCU	A330-343E	1065	
☐ VQ-BCV	A330-343E	1072	
☐ VQ-BEK	A330-343E	1077	
☐ VQ-BEL	A330-343E	1103	♦
☐ VQ-	A330-343E		o/o♦
☐ VQ-	A330-343E		o/o♦
☐ VQ-	A330-343E		o/o♦
☐ VQ-	A330-343E		o/o♦
☐ VP-BAV	B767-36NER	30107/761	
☐ VP-BAX	B767-36NER	30109/767	
☐ VP-BAY	B767-36NER	30110/775	
☐ VP-BAZ	B767-36NER	30111/776	
☐ VP-BDI	B767-38AER	29618/792	
☐ VP-BWT	B767-38AER	29617/741	
☐ VP-BWU	B767-3T7ER	25076/366	
☐ VP-BWV	B767-3T7ER	25117/370	
☐ VP-BWW	B767-306ER	27959/609	
☐ VP-BWX	B767-306ER	27960/625	
☐ RA-96005	Il-96-300	74393201002	
☐ RA-96007	Il-96-300	74393201004	
☐ RA-96008	Il-96-300	74393201005	
☐ RA-96010	Il-96-300	74393201007	
☐ RA-96011	Il-96-300	74393201008	
☐ RA-96015	Il-96-300	74393201012	
☐ RA-	Il-96-300		o/o
☐ RA-	Il-96-300		o/o
☐ RA-	Il-96-300		o/o
☐ RA-	Il-96-300		o/o
☐ RA-	Il-96-300		o/o
☐ RA-	Il-96-300		o/o
☐ VP-BDP	MD-11F	48502/520	
☐ VP-BDQ	MD-11F	48504/548	
☐ VP-BDR	MD-11F	48503/528	
☐ RA-89001	Sukhoi Superjet 100	95008	o/o♦
☐ RA-89002	Sukhoi Superjet 100	95010	o/o♦
☐ RA-89003	Sukhoi Superjet 100	95011	o/o♦

□	RA-89004	Sukhoi Superjet 100	95012	o/o♦
□	RA-	Sukhoi Superjet 100		o/o♦
□	RA-	Sukhoi Superjet 100		o/o♦
□	RA-	Sukhoi Superjet 100		o/o♦
□	RA-	Sukhoi Superjet 100		o/o♦
□	RA-	Sukhoi Superjet 100		o/o♦
□	RA-85135	Tu-154M	92A922	
□	RA-85627	Tu-154M	87A756	
□	RA-85637	Tu-154M	87A767	
□	RA-85735	Tu-154M	92A917	
□	RA-85760	Tu-154M	92A942	
□	RA-85765	Tu-154M	90A832	

AEROKUZBASS　　　　　NKZ

| □ | RA-85747 | Tu-154M | 92A930 |
| □ | RA-85749 | Tu-154M | 92A931 |

AIR BASHKORTOSTAN　　　BBT

| □ | RA-73015 | B757-230 | 25901/464 | <MOV |

AIRBRIDGE CARGO　　　RU / ABW

□	VP-BIC	B747-329(SF)	24837/810	
□	VP-BIG	B747-46NERF	35420/1395	
□	VP-BII	B747-281F	24576/818	
□	VP-BIJ	B747-281F	25171/886	
□	VP-BIK	B747-46NERF	35421/1400	
□	VP-BIM	B747-4HAERF	35237/1402	
■	VQ-BFX	B747-428ERF	33096/1317	>4>.
□	VQ-BGY	B747-428ERF	33097/1361	♦
□	VQ-BHE	B747-4KZF	36784/1411	♦
□	VQ-BHZ	B747-8HVF	37580/1430	o/o♦
□	VQ-BIA	B747-4KZF	36785/1418	♦
□	VQ-BIM	B747-446F	33749/1352	♦
□	VQ-	B747-8HVF		o/o♦
□	RA-64051	Tu-204-120C	64051	o/o
□	RA-64052	Tu-204-120C	64052	o/o

AIRSTARS AIRWAYS　　　PL / ASE

□	RA-76476	Il-76TD	43451528
□	RA-76750	Il-76TD	83485561
□	RA-86523	Il-62M	2241647
□	RA-96002	Il-96-300	74393201001

AK BARS AERO　　　　BGM

□	VQ-BHF	CRJ-200LR	7802	♦
□	VQ-BHH	CRJ-200LR	7826	♦
□	VQ-BHI	CRJ-200LR	7809	♦
□	VQ-BHJ	CRJ-200LR	7821	♦
□	RA-87209	Yak-40K	9810657	
□	RA-87227	Yak-40K	9810559	
□	RA-87239	Yak-40	9530643	
□	RA-87247	Yak-40	9531543	
□	RA-87342	Yak-40	9511139	
□	RA-87447	Yak-40	9430436	
□	RA-87462	Yak-40	9430137	
□	RA-87505	Yak-40	9510740	
□	RA-87517	Yak-40	9521940	
□	RA-87588	Yak-40	9222022	
□	RA-87849	Yak-40	9331830	
□	RA-88165	Yak-40	9611946	
□	RA-88182	Yak-40	9620248	

ALANIA AIRLINE　　　2D / OST

| □ | RA-42435 | Yak-42D | 43060170617 |

ALROSA AVIA　　　　LRO

| □ | RA-65693 | Tu-134B-3 | 63221 |

| □ | RA-65907 | Tu-134A | 63996 |

ALROSA AVIATION　　　6R / DRU

□	RA-26552	An-26	3107	[YKS]
□	RA-26668	An-26B-100	8201	
□	RA-46488	An-24RV	27308106	
□	RA-46621	An-24RV	37308708	
□	RA-47272	An-24B	7306402	
□	RA-47694	An-24B	27307601	
□	RA-76357	Il-76TD	1023414467	
□	RA-76360	Il-76TD	1033414492	
□	RA-76373	Il-76TD	1033415507	
□	RA-76420	Il-76TD	1023413446	
□	RA-65101	Tu-134A-3	60260	<ORB
□	RA-65146	Tu-134B-3	61000	
□	RA-65715	Tu-134B-3	63536	
□	RA-85654	Tu-154M	89A796	
□	RA-85675	Tu-154M	90A835	
□	RA-85684	Tu-154M	90A851	
□	RA-85728	Tu-154M	92A910	
□	RA-85757	Tu-154M	92A939	
□	RA-85782	Tu-154M	93A966	

AMUR ARTEL STARATELEI AVIAKOMPANIA

| □ | RA-26001 | An-26 | 9705 |
| □ | RA-26048 | An-26B | 10901 |

AMURSKIE AVIALINII

| □ | RA-87395 | Yak-40 | 9410733 |
| □ | RA-87938 | Yak-40K | 9710153 |

ANGARA AIRLINES　　　AGU

□	RA-26511	An-26-100	6808
□	RA-26655	An-26-100	7802
□	RA-46625	An-24RV	37308804
□	RA-46662	An-24RV	47309410
□	RA-46697	An-24RV	47309908
□	RA-46712	An-24RV	57310408
□	RA-47818	An-24RV	17307107
□	RA-47848	An-24B	17307410

ARKHANGELSK AIRLINES

| □ | RA-46667 | An-24RV | 47309508 |

ASTAIR

| □ | RA-85031 | Tu-154M | 87A751 |

ATRANS - AVIATRANS CARGO A/L　V8 / VAS

□	RA-11868	An-12B	9346310
□	RA-12990	An-12B	347304
□	RA-26218	An-26B	5408
□	RA-93913	An-12B	4342609
□	RA-93916	An-26	9105

AVIACON ZITOTRANS　　ZR / AZS

□	RA-76352	Il-76TD	1023411378
□	RA-76386	Il-76TD	1033418600
□	RA-76807	Il-76TD	1013405176
□	RA-76842	Il-76TD	1033418616

AVIAENERGO　　　　7U / ERG

□	RA-65962	Tu-134A-3	3351901
□	RA-85809	Tu-154M	94A985
□	RA-86583	Il-62M	1356851

AVIAL AVIATION CO — NVI

☐	RA-11113	An-12TB	1347908
☐	RA-11115	An-12BP	1348003
☐	RA-11372	An-12BP	401912
☐	RA-11906	An-12BP	2340802
☐	RA-69314	An-12BP	5343004

AVIALESOOKHRANA VLADMIR AIR ENT

☐	RA-26002	An-26	7309706	
☐	RA-26005	An-26	9809	
☐	RA-26011	An-26B	9908	
☐	RA-26040	An-26B	10703	[IKT]
☐	RA-26532	An-26	7410	
☐	RA-46480	An-24RV	27308008	

AVIAST AIR — 6I / VVA

☐	RA-11756	An-12BP	4342208	>SHU
☐	RA-11962	An-12BP	5343007	
☐	RA-76843	Il-76TD	1013408269	
☐	RA-76849	Il-76TD	23440161	[BKA]

AVIANOVA — AO

☐	EI-EEI	A320-232	0661	
☐	EI-EEL	A320-232	0543	
☐	EI-ELD	A320-232	1918	
☐	EI-ELN	A320-232	1993	♦

AVIASTAR TU — 4B / TUP

☐	RA-64021	Tu-204-100C	64021
☐	RA-64024	Tu-204-100C	64024
☐	RA-64032	Tu-204-100C	64032

BARKOL AVIAKOMPANIA — VOG

☐	RA-87280	Yak-40	9322025
☐	RA-87372	Yak-40	9340332
☐	RA-87957	Yak-40K	9821857
☐	RA-88229	Yak-40	9641850

BURAL — BUN

☐	RA-46408	An-24B	77304003	
☐	RA-46506	An-24RV	37308402	>SIB
☐	RA-46614	An-24RV	37308701	

BUSINESS AERO

☐	RA-42344	Yak-42	27082950208

BYLINA — BYL

☐	RA-88263	Yak-40	9711852
☐	RA-88274	Yak-40	9721253

CENTER-SOUTH AIRLINES — CTS

☐	RA-87276	Yak-40	9311227
☐	RA-87655	Yak-40	9211820
☐	RA-87921	Yak-40	9731155
☐	RA-87966	Yak-40	9820958
☐	RA-88236	Yak-40	9640551

CENTRE-AVIA AIRLINES — J7 / CVC

☐	RA-42325	Yak-42D	44021480306
☐	RA-42341	Yak-42D	17062920907
☐	RA-42353	Yak-42D	47113961108
☐	RA-42385	Yak-42D	30162690612
☐	RA-42423	Yak-42	4216606
☐	RA-42542	Yak-42D	11140804
☐	RA-87507	Yak-40	9520940

CHUKOTAVIA

☐	RA-26099	An-26B-100	11905
☐	RA-26128	An-26B	12702
☐	RA-26590	An-26B	13910
☐	RA-46616	An-24RV	37308703
☐	RA-47159	An-24B	89901701

CONTINENTAL AIRWAYS — PC / PVV

☐	RA-85773	Tu-154M	93A955

DAGHESTAN AIRLINES — N2 / DAG

☐	RA-46654	An-24RV	47309209
☐	RA-65569	Tu-134B-3	63340
☐	RA-65570	Tu-134A-3	66550
☐	RA-85495	Tu-154B-2	81A495
☐	RA-85756	Tu-154M	92A938
☐	RA-85828	Tu-154M	97A1009
☐	RA-85840	Tu-154M	98A1011

DALAVIA — H8 / KHB

☐	RA-46474	An-24RV	27308002
☐	RA-46522	An-24RV	47310001
☐	RA-46529	An-24RV	57310008
☐	RA-46643	An-24RV	37309001
☐	RA-47354	An-24RV	67310603
☐	RA-47367	An-24RV	77310806
☐	RA-26000	An-26	7309604
☐	RA-26058	An-26B	11101
☐	RA-86131	Il-62M	4255244
☐	RA-86493	Il-62M	4140748
☐	RA-86525	Il-62M	4851612
☐	RA-86560	Il-62M	2153347
☐	RA-85114	Tu-154M	89A814
☐	RA-85477	Tu-154B-2	81A477
☐	RA-85734	Tu-154M	86A734
☐	RA-85752	Tu-154M	92A934
☐	RA-85797	Tu-154M	93A981
☐	RA-85802	Tu-154M	93A961
☐	RA-64502	Tu-214	42625002
☐	RA-64503	Tu-214	43103003
☐	RA-64507	Tu-214	42305007
☐	RA-64510	Tu-214	42305010
☐	RA-64512	Tu-214	42305012

DAURIA

☐	RA-26053	An-26B	17310909	
☐	RA-26543	An-26	5732709	[IKT]
☐	RA-47268	An-24B	7306306	
☐	RA-47838	An-24B	17307310	

DOMODEDOVO AIRLINES — E3 / DMO

☐	RA-86519	Il-62M	4140212	
☐	RA-76799	Il-76TD	1003403075	>ESL
☐	RA-96006	Il-96-300	74393201003	
☐	RA-96009	Il-96-300	74393201006	[DME]
☐	RA-96013	Il-96-300	74393202013	[DME]
☐	RA-85841	Tu-154M	90A858	

DONAVIA — D9 / DNV

☐	VP-BLF	B737-528	25232/2231
☐	VP-BLG	B737-528	25233/2251
☐	VP-BVU	B737-5Q8	25166/2129
☐	VP-BWY	B737-528	27305/2574
☐	VP-BWZ	B737-528	27304/2572
☐	VP-BYU	B737-5Q8	25167/2173

☐ VP-BYV	B737-5Q8	25160/2114	
☐ VQ-BAN	B737-4Q8	25113/2656	
☐ VQ-BAO	B737-4Q8	25114/2666	
☐ VQ-BCS	B737-43Q	28494/2839	
☐ RA-86124	Il-86	51483210092	[SVO]
☐ RA-86140	Il-86	51483211102	
☐ RA-86141	Il-86	51483211103	
☐ RA-85149	Tu-154M	89A797	
☐ RA-85626	Tu-154M	87A753	
☐ RA-85630	Tu-154M	87A759	
☐ RA-85640	Tu-154M	87A772	

ELBRUS AVIA — NLK

☐ RA-42346	Yak-42D	4520423708311
☐ RA-42371	Yak-42D	4520422914225
☐ RA-42422	Yak-42D	4520424304017

EVENKIA AVIA

☐ RA-26008	An-26B-100	9902
☐ RA-26118	An-26B-100	12207
☐ RA-69354	An-32	1606
☐ RA-87900	Yak-40K	9720254

FLIGHT INSPECTION & SYSTEMS — LTS

☐ RA-26571	An-26	67303909
☐ RA-26631	An-26ASLK	77305503
☐ RA-26673	An-26ASLK	97308408
☐ RA-46395	An-24ALK	7306209

GAZPROMAVIA — 4G / GZP

☐ RA-74005	An-74TK-100C	36547095892	
☐ RA-74008	An-74TK-100	36547095900	
☐ RA-74012	An-74D	36547098959	
☐ RA-74016	An-74TK-200	365470991034	
☐ RA-74032	An-74TK-100	36547098962	
☐ RA-74035	An-74TK-100	36547098963	
☐ RA-74036	An-74-200	36547098965	
☐ RA-74044	An-74-200	36547097936	
☐ RA-74056	An-74-200	36547098951	
☐ RA-74058	An-74-200	36547098956	
☐ RA-73000	B737-76N	28630/664	
☐ RA-73004	B737-76N	28635/734	
☐ RA-76370	Il-76TD	1033414458	>VDA
☐ RA-76402	Il-76TD	1023413430	>VDA
☐ RA-76445	Il-76TD	1023410330	>VDA
☐ RA-76446	Il-76TD	1023412418	>VDA
☐ RA-65045	Tu-134A-3	49500	
☐ RA-85625	Tu-154M	87A752	
☐ RA-85751	Tu-154M	92A933	[VKO]
☐ RA-85774	Tu-154M	93A956	
☐ RA-85778	Tu-154M	93A962	
☐ RA-21505	Yak-40K	9830159	
☐ RA-87511	Yak-40	9521340	
☐ RA-88186	Yak-40K	9620648	
☐ RA-88300	Yak-40K	9641451	
☐ RA-98113	Yak-40	9710253	
☐ RA-42425	Yak-42D	13030160316	
☐ RA-42436	Yak-42D	16050180518	
☐ RA-42437	Yak-42D	36060180618	
☐ RA-42438	Yak-42D	36090180918	
☐ RA-42439	Yak-42D	39040190419	
☐ RA-42442	Yak-42D	20020190219	
☐ RA-42451	Yak-42D	27080180818	
☐ RA-42452	Yak-42D	409016	

GEODYNAMICA CENTRE — CGS

☐ RA-30001	An-30	1402
☐ RA-30006	An-30	1407
☐ RA-30039	An-30	710

GLOBUS — GLP

☐ VP-BTA	B737-4Q8	25168/2210	
☐ VP-BTH	B737-42C	24231/1871	
☐ RA-85611	Tu-154M	85A715	
☐ RA-85612	Tu-154M	86A721	
☐ RA-85623	Tu-154M	87A749	[DME]

GROZNYY AVIA

☐ RA-42379	Yak-42D	10145430911
☐ RA-42418	Yak-42D	32191181015

IFLY

☐ EI-DUA	Boeing 757-256	26247/860
☐ EI-DUC	Boeing 757-256	26248/863
☐ EI-DUD	Boeing 757-256	26249/881

INTERAVIA AIRLINES — 8D / SUW

☐ RA-86533	Il-62M	1343123
☐ RA-86567	Il-62M	4256314
☐ RA-86575	Il-62M	1647928
☐ RA-86577	Il-62M	2748552
☐ RA-42339	Yak-42D	46062670707
☐ RA-42356	Yak-42D	28114000109
☐ RA-42359	Yak-42D	38114170409

IRAERO

☐ RA-46846	An-24RV	27307504
☐ RA-47321	An-24RV	67310507
☐ RA-47804	An-24RV	17306903
☐ RA-26051	An-26B	10906
☐ RA-26130	An-26B	12704
☐ RA-26131	An-26B	12707
☐ RA-26692	An-26	9409

IZHAVIA — IZA

☐ RA-46620	An-24RV	37308707
☐ RA-46637	An-24RV	37308903
☐ RA-47315	An-24RV	67310502
☐ RA-65056	Tu-134A-3	49860
☐ RA-42450	Yak-42	4520424601019
☐ RA-42524	Yak-42D	11030603

JET 2000

☐ RA-87216	Yak-40	9510440

JET AIR GROUP

☐ P4-AIR	MD-87ER	49412/1424
☐ RA-65723	Tu-134A-3M	66440
☐ RA-65930	Tu-134A-3M	66500

KAPO — KAO

☐ RA-26597	An-26B	13310
☐ RA-86126	Il-62MF	4154535
☐ RA-86576	Il-62MF	4546257
☐ RA-86579	Il-62MF	2951636
☐ RA-86945	Il-62M	3850145

KATEKAVIA — KTK

☐ RA-46491	An-24RV	27308204
☐ RA-46493	An-24RV	27308206
☐ RA-46497	An-24RV	27308210
☐ RA-46520	An-24RV	37308506
☐ RA-46604	An-24RV	37308601
☐ RA-46683	An-24RV	47309706
☐ RA-46689	An-24RV	47309806
☐ RA-46693	An-24RV	47309904
☐ RA-47351	An-24RV	67310510
☐ RA-47358	An-24RV	67310607
☐ RA-48102	An-24RT	1911804

KHABAROVSK AIRLINES

☐ RA-26174	An-26B-100	97308304
☐ RA-87651	Yak-40	9141220
☐ RA-88251	Yak-40K	9710552

KIROV AVIA ENTERPRISE — KTA

☐ RA-46660	An-24RV	47309307
☐ RA-47295	An-24RV	7306608
☐ RA-26086	An-26B	12302
☐ RA-26677	An-26B	8603

KMV MINERALNYE VODY AL — KV / MVD

☐ RA-85380	Tu-154B-2	79A380	
☐ RA-85457	Tu-154B-2	80A457	
☐ RA-85494	Tu-154B-2	81A494	
☐ RA-85715	Tu-154M	91A891	
☐ RA-85746	Tu-154M	92A929	
☐ RA-85790	Tu-154M	93A974	
☐ RA-85792	Tu-154M	93A976	
☐ RA-85826	Tu-154M	89A812	
☐ RA-64016	Tu-204-100	1450743464016	
☐ RA-64022	Tu-204-100	1450742064022	
☐ RA-	Tu-204-300		o/o
☐ RA-	Tu-204-300		o/o

KNAAPO — KNM

☐ RA-11125	An-12BP	3341006
☐ RA-11371	An-12BP	347406
☐ RA-11789	An-12BP	6343905

KOLAVIA — 7K / KGL

☐ TC-KLA	A320-232	2029
☐ TC-KLB	A320-232	2077
☐ RA-65045	Tu-134A-3	49500
☐ RA-65943	Tu-134A-3	63580
☐ RA-65944	Tu-134A-3	12096
☐ RA-85522	Tu-154B-2	82A522
☐ RA-85761	Tu-154M	93A944
☐ RA-85784	Tu-154M	93A968

KOSMOS AIRLINES — KSM

☐ RA-11025	An-12TB	6344103
☐ RA-65010	Tu-134A	46130
☐ RA-65097	Tu-134AK	60540
☐ RA-65719	Tu-134AK	63637
☐ RA-65726	Tu-134AK	63720
☐ RA-65727	Tu-134B-3	03564820
☐ RA-65805	Tu-134B-3	64775
☐ RA-65935	Tu-134A-3	66180

KOSTROMA AIR ENTERPRISE — KMW

☐ RA-26595	An-26	47313401
☐ RA-27210	An-26-100	5410

KUBAN AIRLINES — GW / KIL

☐ VQ-BHB	B737-3Q8	26310/2680	♦
☐ VQ-BHC	B737-3Q8	26311/2681	♦
☐ VQ-BHD	B737-3Q8	26312/2693	♦
☐ RA-42331	Yak-42	45051280906	
☐ RA-42336	Yak-42	26062200407	
☐ RA-42342	Yak-42	17063021007	
☐ RA-42350	Yak-42	47113720808	
☐ RA-42363	Yak-42D	48114380809	
☐ RA-42367	Yak-42D	19141330510	
☐ RA-42375	Yak-42D	49144100411	
☐ RA-42386	Yak-42D	40163100812	
☐ RA-42421	Yak-42D	4520422303017	
☐ RA-42541	Yak-42	11140704	

LIPETSKAVIA

☐ RA-87372	Yak-40	9340332

LUKIAVIATRANS — PKV

☐ RA-30042	An-30	0901
☐ RA-30053	An-30D	1008
☐ RA-30067	An-30	1208
☐ RA-46632	An-30	0201

MCHS ROSSII — SUM

☐ RF-31122	An-74P	36547136012	
☐ RF-31350	An-74P	36547097940	
☐ RF-32765	Be-200ChS	76820001301	
☐ RF-32766	Be-200ChS	76820001402	
☐ RF-32767	Be-200ChS	76820002501	
☐ RF-32768	Be-200ChS	76820002602	
☐ RF-	Be-200ChS		o/o
☐ RA-86570	Il-62M	1356344	
☐ RA-76362	Il-76TD	1033416533	
☐ RA-76363	Il-76TD	1033417540	
☐ RA-76429	Il-76TD	1043419639	
☐ RA-76840	Il-76TD	1033417553	
☐ RA-76841	Il-76TD	1033418601	
☐ RA-76845	Il-76TDP	1043420696	
☐ RA-87482	Yak-40	9441038	
☐ RA-42441	Yak-42D	14020180218	
☐ RA-42446	Yak-42D		

MORDOVIA AIR

☐ RA-26247	An-26B-100	4103
☐ RA-46505	An-24RV	37308309
☐ RA-46640	An-24RV	37308908

MOSKOVIA — 3R / GAI

☐ RA-11309	An-12BP	347510
☐ RA-11310	An-12BP	4342601
☐ RA-12162	An-12BP	3341509
☐ RA-30028	An-30	0501
☐ VQ-BDI	B737-73A	28497/216
☐ VQ-BER	B737-7L9/W	28006/26
☐ VQ-BFR	B737-883	30468/668
☐ VQ-BFU	B737-883	30467/634
☐ RA-65606	Tu-134A-3	46300
☐ RA-85615	Tu-154M	86A731
☐ RA-85736	Tu-154M	92A918
☐ RA-85743	Tu-154M	92A926

MOSKVA AIR COMPANY — 3G / AYZ

☐ RA-	An-148	o/o♦
☐ RA-	An-148	o/o♦

☐	RA-	An-148	o/o♦
☐	RA-	An-148	o/o♦
☐	RA-	An-148	o/o♦
☐	RA-	An-148	o/o♦
☐	RA-	An-148	o/o♦
☐	RA-	An-148	o/o♦
☐	RA-	An-148	o/o♦
☐	RA-	An-148	o/o♦
☐	RA-	An-148	o/o♦
☐	RA-	An-148	o/o♦
☐	VP-BBL	B737-347	23183/1108
☐	VP-BBM	B737-347	23442/1239
☐	VP-BMI	B737-81Q	29052/557
☐	VQ-BBR	B737-8AS/W	32778/1140 ♦
☐	VQ-BBS	B737-8AS/W	32779/1167 ♦
☐	VQ-BCH	B737-8AS/W	32780/1178 ♦
☐	VQ-BDU	B737-8AS/W	29936/1236
☐	VQ-BDV	B737-8AS/W	29937/1238
☐	VQ-BJY	B737-8K2/W	28248/1126 ♦
☐		B737-8	o/o♦
☐		B737-8	o/o♦
☐		B737-8	o/o♦
☐		B737-8	o/o♦
☐	RA-	EMB.120ER	120172
☐	RA-	EMB.120ER	120133
☐	RA-02851	EMB.120ER	120125
☐	RA-02852	EMB.120ER	120128
☐	RA-02854	EMB.120ER	120136
☐	RA-02856	EMB.120ER	120240
☐	EW-78779	Il-76TD	83489662 <TXC
☐	RA-76401	Il-76TD	1023412399 <UHS
☐	RA-76783	Il-76TD	93498974 <UHS
☐	RA-76817	Il-76TD	1023412387 <ESL
☐	RA-86109	Il-86	51483208077
☐	RA-86123	Il-86	51483210091
☐	RA-86125	Il-86	51483210093
☐	RA-86136	Il-86	51483210094
☐	RA-86138	Il-86	51483210096
☐	RA-85140	Tu-154M	85A716
☐	RA-85709	Tu-154M	91A884
☐	RA-85740	Tu-154M	91A895

NAPO AVIATRANS   NPO

☐	RA-12193	An-12BK	9346805
☐	RA-12194	An-12BK	347203
☐	RA-12195	An-12BK	347410

NORDAVIA REGIONAL AIRLINES   5N / AUL

☐	RA-46528	An-24RV	47310007
☐	RA-46651	An-24RV	47309202
☐	RA-26104	An-26BRL	27312002
☐	VP-BKP	B737-59D	25065/2028
☐	VP-BKT	B737-33R	28871/2900
☐	VP-BKU	B737-505	25789/2229
☐	VP-BKV	B737-505	27155/2449
☐	VP-BOH	B737-59D	25038/1969
☐	VP-BOI	B737-505	24650/1792
☐	VP-BQI	B737-5Y0	25186/2236
☐	VP-BQL	B737-5Y0	25185/2220
☐	VP-BRE	B737-53C	24827/2243
☐	VP-BRG	B737-53C	24826/2041
☐	VP-BRI	B737-5Y0	25289/2288 >AFL
☐	VP-BRK	B737-5Y0	25288/2286
☐	VP-BRN	B737-5Y0	25191/2260
☐	VP-BRP	B737-505	24651/1842
☐	VP-BXM	B737-59D	24695/1872
☐	VP-BXN	B737-53A	24754/1868

☐	RA-65034	Tu-134A-3	48565	
☐	RA-65043	Tu-134A-3	49400	
☐	RA-65052	Tu-134A-3	49825	
☐	RA-65083	Tu-134A-3	60090	>UTA
☐	RA-65096	Tu-134A-3	60257	
☐	RA-65108	Tu-134A-3	60332	>UTA
☐	RA-65116	Tu-134A-3	60420	
☐	RA-65564	Tu-134A-3	63165	

NORDSTAR

☐	VQ-BDN	B737-8K5/W	32905/1046	
☐	VQ-BDO	B737-8K5/W	32906/1087	
☐	VQ-BDP	Boeing 737-8Q8/W	28221/226	
☐	VQ-BDW	B737-8K5/W	27977/9	♦
☐	VQ-BDZ	B737-8K5/W	27978/40	♦

NORDWIND   N4 / NWS

☐	VQ-BAK	B757-2Q8	26332/688	
☐	VQ-BAL	B757-2Q8	27351/639	
☐	VQ-BBT	B757-2Q8	29443/821	
☐	VQ-BBU	B757-2Q8	29442/819	
☐	VQ-BHR	B757-2Q8/W	30046/1006	♦
☐	VQ-BJK	B757-2Q8	29380/836	
☐	VQ-BKE	B757-231/W	28484/825	♦
☐	VQ-BOG	B767-341ER	30342/774	♦
☐	VQ-BRA	B767-33AER	27310/545	♦

NOVOSIBIRSK AIR ENTERPRISE   NBE

☐	RA-46642	An-24RV	37308910
☐	RA-46659	An-24RV	47309306
☐	RA-46682	An-24RV	47309704
☐	RA-47306	An-24RV	57310306
☐	RA-30007	An-30D	1408

ORENAIR   R2 / ORB

☐	VP-BEW	B737-505	26297/2578	
☐	VP-BGP	B737-4Y0	24691/1904	
☐	VP-BGQ	B737-4Y0	24683/1901	
☐	VP-BGR	B737-505	25790/2245	
☐	VP-BPE	B737-5H6	26445/2327	
☐	VP-BPF	B737-5H6	26446/2358	
☐	VP-BPG	B737-8AS/W	29924/578	
☐	VP-BPI	B737-83N/W	28244/958	
☐	VP-BPY	B737-83N/W	28247/1091	
☐	VQ-BCJ	B737-8AS/W	29932/1030	
☐	VQ-BEM	B737-85R/W	29036/164	
☐	VQ-BEN	B737-85R/W	29037/177	
☐	VQ-BFY	B737-86N/W	29884/1094	♦
☐	VQ-BFZ	B737-86N/W	28644/839	♦
☐	VQ-BJC	B737-8K5/W	27992/523	♦
☐	RA-65049	Tu-134A-3	49755	
☐	RA-65054	Tu-134A	49840	
☐	RA-65090	Tu-134A	60185	>SVR
☐	RA-65101	Tu-134A-3	60260	>DRU
☐	RA-65110	Tu-134A-3	60343	
☐	RA-65117	Tu-134A-3	60450	
☐	RA-65136	Tu-134A-3	60885	>UTA
☐	RA-85602	Tu-154B-2	84A602	
☐	RA-85603	Tu-154B-2	84A603	
☐	RA-85604	Tu-154B-2	85A604	
☐	RA-85768	Tu-154M	94A949	

PERM AIRLINES   P9 / PGP

☐	RA-26520	An-26-100	87307101
☐	RA-26636	An-26-100	87306306
☐	RA-47756	An-24B	79901209
☐	RA-65064	Tu-134A-3	49886
☐	RA-65751	Tu-134A-3	61066
☐	RA-65775	Tu-134A-3	62530

PETROPAVLOVSK-KAMCHATSKY AIR ENT

☐ RA-26122	An-26B	12401
☐ RA-26251	An-26-100	9109
☐ RA-87385	Yak-40K	9411632
☐ RA-87947	Yak-40K	9621145
☐ RA-87949	Yak-40K	9621345
☐ RA-87988	Yak-40	9541244
☐ RA-88241	Yak-40K	9641351

POLAR AIRLINES

☐ RA-46333	An-24B	97305510
☐ RA-46374	An-24B	7306005
☐ RA-47161	An-24B	89901703
☐ RA-47260	An-24B	27307802
☐ RA-26030	An-26B	10501
☐ RA-26061	An-26B	11108
☐ RA-26538	An-26-100	47302102
☐ RA-26635	An-26	6305
☐ RA-26674	An-26	8506
☐ RA-26685	An-26	1307

POLET AVIAKOMPANIA   YQ / POT

☐ RA-46676	An-24RV	47309608	
☐ RA-46690	An-24RV	47309901	
☐ RA-48096	An-24RV	57310406	
☐ RA-30024	An-30	0502	
☐ RA-30048	An-30	0910	
☐ RA-82010	An-124-100	3616017	
☐ RA-82014	An-124-100	9773054732039	
☐ RA-82024	An-124	19530502033	[ULY]
☐ RA-82026	An-124	19530502127	[ULY]
☐ RA-82068	An-124-100	9773051359127	
☐ RA-82075	An-124-100	3459147	
☐ RA-82077	An-124-100	4459151	
☐ RA-82080	An-124-100	1462161	
☐ RA-	An-148		o/o♦
☐ RA-	An-148		o/o♦
☐ RA-	An-148		o/o♦
☐ RA-	An-148		o/o♦
☐ RA-	An-148		o/o♦
☐ RA-	An-148		o/o♦
☐ RA-	Il-76-90VD		o/o♦
☐ RA-	Il-76-90VD		o/o♦
☐ RA-	Il-76-90VD		o/o♦
☐ RA-96101	Il-96-400T	74393201001	
☐ RA-96102	Il-96-400T	73439201002	
☐ RA-96103	Il-96-400T	97693201003	♦
☐ RA-	Il-96-400T		o/o♦
☐ VQ-BGC	SAAB SF.340B	340B-232	♦
☐ VQ-BGD	SAAB SF.340B	340B-250	♦
☐ VQ-BGE	SAAB SF.340B	340B-273	♦
☐ VQ-BGF	SAAB SF.340B	340B-218	♦
☐ VP-BPL	SAAB 2000	2000-029	
☐ VP-BPM	SAAB 2000	2000-057	
☐ VP-BPN	SAAB 2000	2000-058	
☐ VP-BPQ	SAAB 2000	2000-060	
☐ VP-BPR	SAAB 2000	2000-061	
☐ RA-88304	Yak-40S2	9510439	

POLYARNYA AVIA

☐ RA-46834	An-24RV	17306801

PTROGRESS AVIAKOMPANIA

☐ RA-26180	An-26	9737810

☐ RA-26192	An-24RT	1911805

PSKOVAVIA   PSW

☐ RA-26107	An-26B	27312008
☐ RA-26120	An-26B	27312304
☐ RA-26134	An-26B	12805
☐ RA-26142	An-26B	37312904

RED WINGS   VAZ

☐ RA-64018	Tu-204-100	64018	
☐ RA-64019	Tu-204-100	64019	
☐ RA-64020	Tu-204-100	64020	
☐ RA-64043	Tu-204-100	64043	o/o
☐ RA-64046	Tu-204-100	64046	
☐ RA-64047	Tu-204-100	64047	
☐ RA-64049	Tu-204-100	64049	
☐ RA-64050	Tu-204-100	64050	
☐ RA-64051	Tu-204-100	64051	o/o
☐ RA-64053	Tu-204-100	64053	o/o

REGIONAL AIRLINES

☐ VQ-BBX	EMB.120ER	120205	
☐ VQ-BBY	EMB.120ER	120265	
☐ VQ-BCB	EMB.120ER	120231	
☐ VQ-BCL	EMB.120ER	120304	
☐ VQ-	EMB.120ER	120202	o/o
☐ VQ-	EMB.120ER	120236	o/o

ROSNEFT-BALTIKA   RNB

☐ RA-21500	Yak-40K	9741356
☐ RA-87244	Yak-40	9531243

ROSSIYA RUSSIAN AIRLINES   FV / SDM

☐ VP-BIQ	A319-111	1890	
☐ VP-BIT	A319-112	1761	
☐ VP-BIU	A319-114	0649	
☐ VQ-BAQ	A319-111	1560	
☐ VQ-BAR	A319-111	1488	
☐ VQ-BAS	A319-111	1863	
☐ VQ-BAT	A319-112	1876	
☐ VQ-BAU	A319-112	1851	
☐ VQ-BAV	A319-111	1743	
☐ EI-DXY	A320-212	0525	
☐ EI-DZR	A320-212	0427	
☐ VQ-BBM	A320-214	1578	
☐ VQ-BDQ	A320-214	1767	
☐ VQ-BDR	A320-214	1130	♦
☐ VQ-BDY	A320-214	1657	♦
☐ VQ-BEY	A320-214	0426	♦
☐ RA-61701	An-148-100B	2701504001	
☐ RA-61702	An-148-100B	2701504002	
☐ RA-61703	An-148-100B	2701504003	
☐ RA-61704	An-148-100B	2701504004	
☐ RA-61705	An-148-100B	2701504005	
☐ EI-CDD	B737-548	24989/1989	
☐ EI-CDE	B737-548	25115/2050	
☐ EI-CDF	B737-548	25737/2232	
☐ EI-CDG	B737-548	25738/2261	
☐ EI-CDH	B737-548	25739/2271	
☐ EI-DZH	B767-3Q8ER	29390/870	
☐ EI-EAR	B767-3Q8ER	27616/714	
☐ EI-ECB	B767-3Q8ER	27617/722	
☐ RA-86466	Il-62M	2749316	
☐ RA-86467	Il-62M	3749733	
☐ RA-86468	Il-62M	4749857	
☐ RA-86536	Il-62M	4445948	
☐ RA-86540	Il-62M	3546548	

□	RA-86559	Il-62M	2153258	
□	RA-86561	Il-62M	4154842	
□	RA-86710	Il-62M	2647646	
□	RA-86712	Il-62M	4648339	
□	RA-96012	Il-96-300	74393201009	
□	RA-96016	Il-96-300PU	74393202010	
□	RA-96018	Il-96-300PU	74393202018	
□	RA-65093	Tu-134A-3	60215	
□	RA-65109	Tu-134A-3	60339	[LED]
□	RA-65553	Tu-134A-3	66300	
□	RA-65555	Tu-134A-3	66350	
□	RA-65912	Tu-134A-3	63985	
□	RA-65921	Tu-134A-3	63997	
□	RA-85187	Tu-154M	91A919	
□	RA-85629	Tu-154M	87A758	
□	RA-85645	Tu-154M	88A782	
□	RA-85658	Tu-154M	89A808	
□	RA-85659	Tu-154M	89A809	
□	RA-85739	Tu-154M	92A925	
□	RA-85769	Tu-154M	93A951	
□	RA-85770	Tu-154M	93A952	
□	RA-85771	Tu-154M	93A953	
□	RA-85779	Tu-154M	93A963	
□	RA-85785	Tu-154M	93A969	
□	RA-85800	Tu-154M	94A984	
□	RA-85832	Tu-154M	92A908	
□	RA-85834	Tu-154M	98A1014	
□	RA-85835	Tu-154M	98A1015	
□	RA-85836	Tu-154M	98A1018	
□	RA-85843	Tu-154M	95A991	
□	RA-64504	Tu-214	41203004	
□	RA-64505	Tu-214	42204005	
□	RA-64506	Tu-214	44204006	
□	RA-64515	Tu-214	44204015	
□	RA-87203	Yak-40	9741456	
□	RA-87969	Yak-40	9831358	
□	RA-87971	Yak-40D	9831558	
□	RA-88200	Yak-40	9630149	

RUSAIR   CGI

□	RA-65124	Tu-134A	60560	
□	RA-65566	Tu-134A	63952	
□	RA-65771	Tu-134A-3	62445	♦
□	RA-65908	Tu-134A	63870	
□	RA-87311	Yak-40	9320629	
□	RA-87494	Yak-40	9541745	
□	RA-87502	Yak-40	9510140	
□	RA-42368	Yak-42D	29141660610	

RUS JET

□	RA-65737	Tu-134B-3	64195
□	RA-87418	Yak-40	9421034
□	RA-88240	Yak-40K	9641151
□	RA-42365	Yak-42D	4520424811447
□	RA-42411	Yak-42D	4520421219043

RUSLINE   RLU

□	VP-BAO	CRJ-100	7177
□	VQ-BBV	CRJ-200	7454
□	VQ-BBW	CRJ-200	7426
□	RA-65087	Tu-134A-3	60155
□	RA-65756	Tu-134A	62179
□	RA-65903	Tu-134A	63750
□	RA-65934	Tu-134A	66143
□	RA-65941	Tu-134A-3	60642
□	RA-87248	Yak-40K	9540144

□	RA-87380	Yak-40	9421225
□	RA-87828	Yak-40	9242024
□	RA-87981	Yak-40K	9540444
□	RA-88308	Yak-40	9230224

RUSSIAN SKY AIRLINES   P7 / ESL

□	RA-76799	Il-76TD	10034030375	<DMO
□	RA-76817	Il-76TD	1023412387	>AYZ

RYAZANAVIA TRANS   RYZ

□	RA-47359	An-24RV	67310608
□	RA-47362	An-24RV	67310706

S-AIR   RLS

□	RA-65550	Tu-134A-3	66200
□	RA-65692	Tu-134A-3	63215
□	RA-65721	Tu-134A-3M	66130
□	RA-65926	Tu-134A-3	66101
□	RA-65932	Tu-134A-3	66405
□	RA-42402	Yak-42D	21165830713
□	RA-42427	Yak-42D	23050160516

S7 AIRLINES   S7 / SBI

□	VP-BTJ	A310-304	520	
□	VP-BTL	A310-204	487	
□	VP-BTM	A310-204	486	
□	VP-BHF	A319-114	1819	
□	VP-BHG	A319-114	1870	
□	VP-BHI	A319-114	2028	
□	VP-BHJ	A319-114	2369	
□	VP-BHK	A319-114	2373	
□	VP-BHL	A319-114	2464	
□	VP-BHP	A319-114	2618	
□	VP-BHQ	A319-114	2641	
□	VP-BHV	A319-114	2474	
□	VP-BTN	A319-114	1126	
□	VP-BTO	A319-114	1129	
□	VP-BTP	A319-114	1131	
□	VP-BTQ	A319-114	1149	
□	VP-BTS	A319-114	1164	
□	VP-BTT	A319-114	1167	
□	VP-BTU	A319-114	1071	
□	VP-BTV	A319-114	1078	
□	VP-BTW	A319-114	1090	
□	VP-BTX	A319-114	1091	
□	VP-BCZ	A320-214	3446	
□	VP-BCP	A320-214	3473	
□	VP-BCS	A320-214	3490	
□	VP-BDT	A320-214	3494	
□	VQ-BCI	A320-214	2623	
□	VQ-BDE	A320-214	3866	
□	VQ-BDF	A320-214	3880	
□	VQ-BES	A320-214	4032	
□	VQ-BET	A320-214	4150	
□	VQ-	A320-214		o/o
□	VQ-	A320-214		o/o
□	VQ-	A320-214		o/o
□	VQ-	A320-214		o/o
□	VQ-	A320-214		o/o
□	VQ-	A320-214		o/o
□	VQ-	A320-214		o/o
□	VQ-	A320-214		o/o
□	VP-BAN	B737-4Y0	26071/2361	
□	VP-BND	B737-83N/W	28245/1054	
□	VP-BNG	B737-83N/W	30640/1035	
□	VP-BQD	B737-83N/W	28239/847	
□	VP-BQF	B737-83N/W	28243/984	
□	VP-BQG	B737-46J	27171/2465	
□	VQ-	B737-800		o/o

☐ VQ-	B737-800		o/o
☐ VQ-	B737-800		o/o
☐ VQ-	B737-800		o/o
☐ VQ-	B737-800		o/o
☐ VP-BVH	B767-33AER	28495/643	
☐ VQ-BBI	B767-328ER	27428/586	
☐ RA-85610	Tu-154M	84A705	[OVB]
☐ RA-85613	Tu-154M	86A722	
☐ RA-85618	Tu-154M	86A737	
☐ RA-85619	Tu-154M	86A738	
☐ RA-85620	Tu-154M	86A739	[OVB]
☐ RA-85622	Tu-154M	87A746	
☐ RA-85624	Tu-154M	87A750	
☐ RA-85628	Tu-154M	87A757	[OVB]
☐ RA-85632	Tu-154M	87A761	
☐ RA-85633	Tu-154M	87A762	
☐ RA-85635	Tu-154M	87A764	
☐ RA-85652	Tu-154M	88A794	[OVB]
☐ RA-85674	Tu-154M	90A834	
☐ RA-85687	Tu-154M	90A857	
☐ RA-85688	Tu-154M	90A859	
☐ RA-85690	Tu-154M	90A861	
☐ RA-85697	Tu-154M	91A870	[DME]
☐ RA-85699	Tu-154M	91A874	
☐ RA-85724	Tu-154M	92A906	
☐ RA-85827	Tu-154M	87A745	[OVB]
☐ RA-85829	Tu-154M	87A755	
☐ RA-85848	Tu-154M	89A804	

SAKHA AVIATION SCHOOL

☐ RA-74003	An-74	36547070690

SAMARA AIRLINES   E5 / BRZ

☐ RA-76475	Il-76TD	43451523	
☐ RA-76791	Il-76TD	93497936	
☐ RA-65105	Tu-134A	60308	
☐ RA-65122	Tu-134A-3	60518	
☐ RA-65753	Tu-134A-3	61099	
☐ RA-65758	Tu-134A-3	62230	
☐ RA-65792	Tu-134A-3	63121	
☐ RA-65797	Tu-134A-3	63173	
☐ RA-85057	Tu-154M	07A1001	
☐ RA-85332	Tu-154B-2	79A332	
☐ RA-85585	Tu-154B-2	83A585	
☐ RA-85601	Tu-154B-2	84A601	
☐ RA-85707	Tu-154M	91A882	
☐ RA-85716	Tu-154M	91A892	
☐ RA-85723	Tu-154M	92A905	
☐ RA-85731	Tu-154M	92A913	
☐ RA-85817	Tu-154M	95A1007	
☐ RA-85818	Tu-154M	85A719	
☐ RA-85821	Tu-154M	89A805	
☐ RA-85822	Tu-154M	89A806	
☐ RA-85823	Tu-154M	88A775	

SARATOV AIRLINES   6W / SOV

☐ RA-42316	Yak-42	22020300405	[RTW]
☐ RA-42326	Yak-42D	44021540406	
☐ RA-42328	Yak-42	15050580606	
☐ RA-42378	Yak-42D	10144940811	
☐ RA-42389	Yak-42D	40165420113	
☐ RA-42432	Yak-42D	44100161016	
☐ RA-42550	Yak-42D	11140205	
☐ RA-87844	Yak-40	9331330	

SAT AIRLINES   HZ / SHU

☐ RA-11364	An-12V	347601
☐ RA-12988	An-12B	347206
☐ RA-48984	An-12BP	402913

☐ RA-46530	An-24B	57310009
☐ RA-46618	An-24RV	37308705
☐ RA-46639	An-24RV	37308905
☐ RA-47198	An-24RV	27307702
☐ RA-47317	An-24RV	67310504
☐ RA-47366	An-24RV	77310804
☐ RA-26132	An-26B	37312708
☐ RA-26138	An-26B	12810
☐ RA-73003	B737-2J8	22859/890
☐ RA-73005	B737-232	23100/1038
☐ RA-73013	B737-5L9	28721/2856
☐ RA-67251	DHC-8-311	533
☐ RA-67257	DHC-8-201	457
☐ RA-67259	DHC-8-201	459
☐ RA-67261	DHC-8-102	460

SATURN AVIAKOMPANIA   RMO

☐ RA-88289	An-26B	11804
☐ RA-87225	Yak-40K	9841359
☐ RA-87936	Yak-40K	9740756

SEVERSTAL AIRCOMPANY   D2 / SSF

☐ RA-87224	Yak-40K	9841259
☐ RA-87954	Yak-40	9811357
☐ RA-88180	Yak-40	9622047
☐ RA-88188	Yak-40	9620848
☐ RA-88296	Yak-40	9421634

SHAR INK   UGP

☐ RA-74001	An-74TK-100	36547070655
☐ RA-74014	An-74-200	36547098968
☐ RA-74015	An-74-200	36547098969
☐ RA-74020	An-74TK-100	36547195014
☐ RA-74047	An-74-200	36547097941

SIBAVIATRANS   5M / SIB

☐ RA-46674	An-24RV	47309606
☐ RA-49278	An-24RV	47309808
☐ RA-49279	An-24RV	17306905
☐ RA-49287	An-24RV	27307607
☐ RA-48113	An-32	1709
☐ RA-65571	Tu-134AK	63955
☐ RA-65605	Tu-134A	09070
☐ RA-65615	Tu-134A-3	4352205
☐ RA-65881	Tu-134A-3	35220
☐ RA-65694	Tu-134B-3	63235
☐ RA-21503	Yak-40K	9820358

SIRIUS AERO   CIG

☐ RA-65079	Tu-134A-3	60054
☐ RA-65099	Tu-134A-3	63700
☐ RA-65604	Tu-134AK	62561
☐ RA-65722	Tu-134A-3M	66420
☐ RA-65928	Tu-134A-3M	66491
☐ RA-65978	Tu-134A-3	63357

SKOL AVIAKOMPANIA   CDV

☐ RA-46848	An-24RV	27307506
☐ RA-87240	Yak-40	9530743
☐ RA-87940	Yak-40	9540444

SKYEXPRESS   XW / SXR

☐ VP-BET	B737-53C	24825/1894

☐ VP-BFB	B737-5Y0	26067/2304	
☐ VP-BFJ	B737-53A	24859/1919	
☐ VP-BFK	B737-5L9	24928/1961	
☐ VP-BFM	B737-53A	24921/1962	
☐ VP-BFN	B737-53A	24922/1964	
☐ VP-BHA	B737-529	26538/2298	
☐ VP-BOT	B737-341	25048/2085	
☐ VP-BOU	B737-341	25049/2091	

SVERDLOVSK 2ND AIR ENTERPRISE   UKU

☐ RA-74004	An-74	36547094890
☐ RA-74006	An-74	36547095896
☐ RA-74048	An-74D	36547098943
☐ RA-87253	Yak-40	9321026
☐ RA-87503	Yak-40AT	9520240
☐ RA-87524	Yak-40	9520641
☐ RA-87974	Yak-40K	9621346
☐ RA-88159	Yak-40	9621346
☐ RA-88234	Yak-40	9640351

TATARSTAN AIR   U9 / TAK

☐ VQ-BAP	B737-322	24665/1889	
☐ VQ-BBN	B737-53A	24785/1882	
☐ VQ-BBO	B737-548	25165/2463	
☐ VQ-BDB	B737-4D7	28702/2978	
☐ VQ-BDC	B737-341	26852/2273	
☐ RA-86142	Il-86	51483210097	[DME]
☐ RA-86143	Il-86	51483210099	
☐ RA-86926	Il-86	51463210100	
☐ RA-65065	Tu-134A-3	49890	
☐ RA-65102	Tu-134A-3	60267	
☐ RA-65691	Tu-134A	63195	
☐ RA-65970	Tu-134A	3351910	
☐ RA-65973	Tu-134A	3352003	
☐ RA-85101	Tu-154M	88A783	
☐ RA-85109	Tu-154M	88A790	
☐ RA-85136	Tu-154M	88A791	
☐ RA-85798	Tu-154M	93A982	
☐ RA-85799	Tu-154M	94A983	
☐ RA-88287	Yak-40K	9940360	
☐ RA-42333	Yak-42	26061560107	
☐ RA-42335	Yak-42	26062040307	
☐ RA-42347	Yak-42	37113220508	
☐ RA-42357	Yak-42	28114080209	
☐ RA-42374	Yak-42D	39143400211	
☐ RA-42380	Yak-42D	20145491011	
☐ RA-42413	Yak-42D	22190660515	
☐ RA-42433	Yak-42D	13010170117	

TOMSKAVIA   TSK

☐ RA-26039	An-26B	10702
☐ RA-46679	An-24RV	47309701
☐ RA-47254	An-24RV	27307706
☐ RA-47355	An-24RV	67310604

TRANSAERO AIRLINES   UN / TSO

☐ EI-CXK	B737-4S3	25596/2255
☐ EI-CXN	B737-329	23772/1432
☐ EI-CXR	B737-329	24355/1709
☐ EI-CZK	B737-4Y0	24519/1781
☐ EI-DDK	B737-4S3	24165/1720
☐ EI-DDY	B737-4Y0	24904/1988
☐ EI-DNM	B737-4S3	24166/1722
☐ EI-DTU	B737-5Y0	25175/2150
☐ EI-DTV	B737-5Y0	25183/2218
☐ EI-DTW	B737-5Y0	25188/2238
☐ EI-DTX	B737-5Q8	28052/2965

☐ EI-EDZ	B737-8K5/W	27980/45	
☐ EI-EEA	B737-8K5/W	27989/59	
☐ VP-BPA	B737-5K5	25037/2022	
☐ VP-BPD	B737-5K5	25062/2044	
☐ VP-BVQ	B737-524/W	28915/2993	♦
☐ VP-BYI	B737-524	28921/3052	
☐ VP-BYJ	B737-524	28923/3060	
☐ VP-BYN	B737-524	28924/3063	♦
☐ VP-BYO	B737-524	28922/3055	♦
☐ VP-BYP	B737-524	28927/3074	♦
☐ VP-BYQ	B737-524	28919/3045	♦
☐ VP-BYT	B737-524	28928/3077	
☐ EI-XLB	B747-446	26359/1153	♦
☐ EI-XLC	B747-446	27100/1236	♦
☐ N914UN	B747-446	26360/1166	♦
☐ VP-BGU	B747-346	23482/640	
☐ VP-BGW	B747-346	24019/695	
☐ VP-BGX	B747-346	24156/716	
☐ VP-BGY	B747-346	23640/668	
☐ VP-BKJ	B747-444	26638/995	
☐ VP-BKL	B747-444	28468/1162	
☐ VP-BPX	B747-267B	22872/566	
☐ VP-BQC	B747-219B	22725/563	
☐ VP-BQE	B747-219B	22722/523	
☐ VP-BQH	B747-219B	22791/568	
☐ VP-BVR	B747-444	26637/943	
☐ VQ-BHW	B747-4F6	28959/1158	♦
☐ VQ-BHX	B747-4F6	28960/1167	♦
☐ EI-CXZ	B767-216ER	24973/347	
☐ EI-CZD	B767-216ER	23623/142	
☐ EI-DBF	B767-3Q8ER	24745/355	
☐ EI-DBG	B767-3Q8ER	24746/378	
☐ EI-DBU	B767-37EER	25077/385	
☐ EI-DBW	B767-201ER	23899/182	
☐ EI-DFS	B767-33AER	25346/403	
☐ EI-UNA	B767-3P6ER	26233/501	
☐ EI-UNB	B767-3P6ER	26234/538	
☐ EI-UNC	B767-319ER	29388/785	♦
☐ EI-UND	B767-3P6ER	26236/436	
☐ EI-UNF	B767-3P6ER	26238/440	
☐ EI-UNR	B777-212ER	28511/122	♦
☐ EI-UNT	B777-212ER	28999/150	♦
☐ EI-UNU	B777-212ER	28998/149	♦
☐ EI-UNV	B777-222ER	28714/205	♦
☐ EI-UNW	B777-222ER	30214/254	
☐ EI-UNX	B777-222ER	30213/232	
☐ EI-UNZ	B777-222	26925/13	<VTB
☐ RA-64509	Tu-214	47305009	
☐ RA-64516	Tu-214	42709016	
☐ RA-64517	Tu-214	42305017	
☐ RA-64518	Tu-214	42305018	
☐ RA-64549	Tu-214	42305013	

TRANSAVIA GARATIA

☐ RA-26024	An-26B-100	10306
☐ RA-26081	An-26B-100	11703
☐ RA-26682	An-26B-100	97308706
☐ RA-26687	An-26B-100	8902
☐ RA-87235	Yak-40	9530143
☐ RA-87336	Yak-40	9610539

TULPAR AIR   TUL

☐ RA-21504	Yak-40K	9831758
☐ RA-87496	Yak-40	9541945
☐ RA-87535	Yak-40	9521941
☐ RA-87977	Yak-40	9321128
☐ RA-88269	Yak-40	9720753
☐ RA-42330	Yak-42D	25051220806
☐ RA-42415	Yak-42D	22190890715
☐ RA-42440	Yak-42D	100181018

TUVA AIRLINES

☐ RA-87425	Yak-40	9420135
☐ RA-87925	Yak-40	9731655
☐ RA-88212	Yak-40	9631849

TYUMEN SPETSAVIA — TUM

☐ RA-26088	An-26	17311209
☐ RA-26102	An-26	17311909
☐ RA-26662	An-26	97308101

URAL AIRLINES — U6 / SVR

☐ VP-BFZ	A320-214	0735	
☐ VP-BPU	A320-211	0220	
☐ VP-BPV	A320-211	0203	
☐ VP-BQY	A320-211	0140	
☐ VP-BQZ	A320-211	0157	
☐ VQ-BAG	A320-214	1063	
☐ VQ-BCY	A320-214	1484	
☐ VQ-BCZ	A320-214	1777	
☐ VQ-BDJ	A320-214	2175	
☐ VQ-BDM	A320-214	2187	
☐ VQ-BFV	A320-214	1152	♦
☐ VQ-BFW	A320-214	2327	♦
☐ VQ-BCX	A321-211	1720	
☐ VQ-BDA	A321-211	1012	
☐ RA-46532	An-24RV	57310101	
☐ RA-47182	An-24B	99901907	
☐ RA-47187	An-24B	99902002	
☐ RA-86078	Il-86	51483205049	
☐ RA-86093	Il-86	51483207064	
☐ RA-86120	Il-86	51483209088	
☐ RA-65090	Tu-134A	60185	
☐ RA-85337	Tu-154B-2	79A337	
☐ RA-85374	Tu-154B-2	79A374	
☐ RA-85375	Tu-154B-2	79A375	
☐ RA-85508	Tu-154B-2	81A508	
☐ RA-85807	Tu-154M	94A988	
☐ RA-85814	Tu-154M	95A994	
☐ RA-85833	Tu-154M	01A1020	
☐ RA-85844	Tu-154M	03A992	

UTAIR AIRLINES — UT / UTA

☐ RA-46362	An-24B	7305903
☐ RA-46388	An-24B	7306201
☐ RA-46481	An-24RV	27308009
☐ RA-46509	An-24RV	37308405
☐ RA-46609	An-24RV	37308606
☐ RA-46619	An-24RV	37308706
☐ RA-46828	An-24B	17306705
☐ RA-47271	An-24RV	7306401
☐ RA-47273	An-24B	7306403
☐ RA-47289	An-24B	7306509
☐ RA-47357	An-24RV	67310606
☐ RA-47827	An-24B	17307208
☐ RA-47829	An-24B	17307210
☐ VP-BCA	ATR 42-300	051
☐ VP-BCB	ATR 42-300	054
☐ VP-BCD	ATR 42-300	042
☐ VP-BCF	ATR 42-300	068
☐ VP-BCG	ATR 42-300	057
☐ VP-BLI	ATR 42-300	233
☐ VP-BLJ	ATR 42-300	255
☐ VP-BLN	ATR 42-300	278
☐ VP-BLO	ATR 42-300	289
☐ VP-BLU	ATR 42-300	287
☐ VP-BPJ	ATR 42-300	165
☐ VP-BPK	ATR 42-300	166

☐ VP-BYW	ATR 72-201	174	
☐ VP-BYX	ATR 72-201	251	
☐ VP-BYZ	ATR 72-201	332	
☐ VP-BVL	B737-524	28926/3069	
☐ VP-BVN	B737-524	27540/2776	
☐ VP-BVZ	B737-524	28925/3066	
☐ VP-BXO	B737-524/W	27314/2566	
☐ VP-BXQ	B737-524/W	27315/2571	
☐ VP-BXR	B737-524/W	27316/2573	
☐ VP-BXU	B737-524/W	27318/2582	
☐ VP-BXV	B737-524/W	27322/2607	
☐ VP-BXY	B737-524/W	27328/2640	
☐ VP-BXZ	B737-524/W	27329/2641	
☐ VP-BYK	B737-524	28918/3026	
☐ VP-BYL	B737-524	28920/3048	
☐ VP-BYM	B737-524	28917/3019	
☐ VQ-BAC	B737-524/W	27321/2597	
☐ VQ-BAD	B737-524/W	27331/2652	
☐ VQ-BAE	B737-524/W	27320/2596	
☐ VQ-BIC	B737-45S	28478/3132	♦
☐ VQ-BID	B737-45S	28477/3131	♦
☐ VQ-BIE	B737-45S	28476/3103	♦
☐ VQ-BIF	B737-45S	28474/3028	♦
☐ VQ-BEY	B757-2Q8/W	29382/1010	♦
☐ VQ-BEZ	B757-2Q8/W	29377/857	♦
☐ VQ-BGJ	CRJ-200LR	7121	♦
☐ VQ-BGK	CRJ-200LR	7122	♦
☐ VQ-BGL	CRJ-200LR	7128	♦
☐ VQ-BGO	CRJ-200LR	7135	♦
☐ VQ-BGP	CRJ-200LR	7165	♦
☐ VQ-BGR	CRJ-200LR	7220	♦
☐ VQ-BGT	CRJ-200LR	7266	♦
☐ VQ-BGU	CRJ-200LR	7298	♦
☐ VQ-BGV	CRJ-200LR	7378	♦
☐ VQ-BGW	CRJ-200LR	7391	♦
☐ VQ-BGX	CRJ-200LR	7394	♦
☐ VQ-	CRJ-200LR	7114	o/o♦
☐ RA-65005	Tu-134A-3	44065	
☐ RA-65024	Tu-134A	48420	
☐ RA-65033	Tu-134A-3	48540	
☐ RA-65055	Tu-134A	49856	
☐ RA-65127	Tu-134A-3	60627	
☐ RA-65136	Tu-134A-3	60885	
☐ RA-65148	Tu-134A-3	61025	
☐ RA-65560	Tu-134A	60321	
☐ RA-65565	Tu-134A-1	63998	
☐ RA-65572	Tu-134AK-3	63960	
☐ RA-65607	Tu-134A	48560	
☐ RA-65608	Tu-134A	38040	
☐ RA-65609	Tu-134A-3	46155	
☐ RA-65611	Tu-134A-3	3351903	
☐ RA-65614	Tu-134A	4352207	
☐ RA-65620	Tu-134A-3	35180	
☐ RA-65621	Tu-134A-3	48320	
☐ RA-65622	Tu-134A-3	60495	
☐ RA-65716	Tu-134A-3	63595	
☐ RA-65728	Tu-134B-3	49858	
☐ RA-65755	Tu-134A-3	62165	
☐ RA-65777	Tu-134A-3	62552	
☐ RA-65780	Tu-134A-3	62622	
☐ RA-65793	Tu-134A-3	63128	
☐ RA-65901	Tu-134A-3	63731	
☐ RA-65902	Tu-134A-3	63742	
☐ RA-65916	Tu-134A-3	66152	
☐ RA-65977	Tu-134A	63245	
☐ RA-85013	Tu-154M	90A840	
☐ RA-85016	Tu-154M	90A844	
☐ RA-85018	Tu-154M	90A852	
☐ RA-85056	Tu-154M	90A845	
☐ RA-85069	Tu-154M	90A863	
☐ RA-85595	Tu-154B-2	84A595	

☐	RA-85681	Tu-154M	90A848
☐	RA-85727	Tu-154M	92A909
☐	RA-85733	Tu-154M	92A915
☐	RA-85755	Tu-154M	92A937
☐	RA-85777	Tu-154M	93A959
☐	RA-85788	Tu-154M	93A972
☐	RA-85789	Tu-154M	93A973
☐	RA-85796	Tu-154M	94A980
☐	RA-85805	Tu-154M	94A986
☐	RA-85806	Tu-154M	94A987
☐	RA-85808	Tu-154M	94A989
☐	RA-85813	Tu-154M	95A990
☐	RA-85820	Tu-154M	98A995
☐	RA-87907	Yak-40	9731254
☐	RA-87941	Yak-40	9540545
☐	RA-87997	Yak-40	9540145
☐	RA-88209	Yak-40K	9730353
☐	RA-88227	Yak-40	9641550

UTAIR EXPRESS — UR / KMV

☐	RA-13344	An-24RV	37308310
☐	RA-46468	An-24RV	27307906
☐	RA-46494	An-24RV	27308207
☐	RA-46603	An-24RV	37308510
☐	RA-46610	An-24RV	37308607
☐	RA-46640	An-24RV	37308908
☐	RA-46692	An-24RV	47309903
☐	RA-47820	An-24RV	17307201

UVAUGA — UHS

☐	RA-26025	An-26B	10308
☐	RA-26513	An-26	6810
☐	RA-26544	An-26	2710
☐	RA-76401	Il-76TD	1023412399	>AYZ
☐	RA-76783	Il-76TD	93498974	>AYZ
☐	RA-85470	Tu-154B-2	81A470
☐	RA-85609	Tu-154M	84A704
☐	RA-87299	Yak-40	9341528
☐	RA-87315	Yak-40	9331429
☐	RA-87580	Yak-40	9221222
☐	RA-42528	Yak-42D	11041003	[ULY]

VIM AIRLINES — NN / MOV

☐	RA-73007	B757-230	24749/295
☐	RA-73008	B757-230	25436/419
☐	RA-73009	B757-230	25437/422
☐	RA-73010	B757-230	25438/428
☐	RA-73011	B757-230	25439/437
☐	RA-73012	B757-230	25440/443
☐	RA-73014	B757-230	25441/446
☐	RA-73015	B757-230	25901/464	>BBT
☐	RA-73016	B757-230	26433/521
☐	RA-73017	B757-230	26434/532
☐	RA-73018	B757-230	26435/537
☐	RA-73019	B757-230	26436/588	[DME]
☐	RA-42340	Yak-42D	46062700807
☐	RA-42343	Yak-42	17082850108
☐	RA-42370	Yak-42D	29142030810
☐	RA-42408	Yak-42D	41166980914

VLADIVOSTOK AIR — XF / VLK

☐	VP-BEQ	A320-212	0422
☐	VP-BRB	A320-212	0528
☐	VP-BFX	A320-214	0714
☐	VP-BFY	A320-214	0730
☐	VQ-BCG	A320-214	1200

☐	VQ-BCW	A330-301	070
☐	VQ-BEQ	A330-301	086
☐	VQ-BEU	A330-301	055	o/o♦
☐	RA-85562	Tu-154B-2	82A562
☐	RA-85676	Tu-154M	90A836
☐	RA-85685	Tu-154M	90A853
☐	RA-85766	Tu-154M	92A923
☐	RA-85803	Tu-154M	89A822
☐	RA-85837	Tu-154M	91A876
☐	RA-85849	Tu-154M	89A815
☐	RA-64026	Tu-204-300	64026
☐	RA-64038	Tu-204-300	64038
☐	RA-64039	Tu-204-300	64039
☐	RA-64040	Tu-204-300	64040
☐	RA-64044	Tu-204-300	64044
☐	RA-64045	Tu-204-300	64045
☐	RA-87273	Yak-40	9310927
☐	RA-87958	Yak-40K	9821957
☐	RA-88172	Yak-40K	9611047
☐	RA-88216	Yak-40	9630250

VOLGA AVIA EXPRESS — WLG

☐	VP-BMN	CRJ-200ER	7179
☐	VP-BMR	CRJ-200ER	7192
☐	VQ-BFA	CRJ-200ER	7627
☐	VQ-BFB	CRJ-200ER	7637
☐	VQ-BFF	CRJ-200LR	7470
☐	VQ-BFI	CRJ-200ER	7671
☐	RA-76484	Il-76TD	63469081
☐	RA-65019	Tu-134A	48375
☐	RA-65086	Tu-134A-3	60130
☐	RA-88171	Yak-40	9620947
☐	RA-88228	Yak-40	9641750
☐	RA-42384	Yak-42D	30162300412
☐	RA-42406	Yak-42D	4520424116683
☐	RA-42549	Yak-42D	11040105

VOLGA-DNEPR AIRLINES — VI / VDA

☐	RA-82042	An-124-100	4055093
☐	RA-82043	An-124-100	4155101
☐	RA-82044	An-124-100	4155109
☐	RA-82045	An-124-100	2255113
☐	RA-82046	An-124-100	2255117
☐	RA-82047	An-124-100	3259121
☐	RA-82074	An-124-100	1459142
☐	RA-82078	An-124-100	4559153
☐	RA-82079	An-124-100	2062157
☐	RA-82081	An-124-100M	1462165
☐	EW-76734	Il-76TD	73476312
☐	EW-78843	Il-76TD	1003403082
☐	RA-76370	Il-76TD	1033414458	<GZP
☐	RA-76402	Il-76TD	1023413430	<GZP
☐	RA-76445	Il-76TD	1023410330	<GZP
☐	RA-76446	Il-76TD	1023412418	<GZP
☐	RA-76483	Il-76TD	63468042
☐	RA-76493	Il-76TD	43456700
☐	RA-76950	Il-76-90VD	2053420697
☐	RA-76951	Il-76-90VD	2073421704
☐	RA-87400	Yak-40	9421233
☐	RA-87484	Yak-40	9441238
☐	RA-88231	Yak-40K	9642050

VOLOGDA AIR ENTERPRISE — VGV

☐	RA-87284	Yak-40	9311927
☐	RA-87484	Yak-40	9441238
☐	RA-87665	Yak-40	9240925
☐	RA-87669	Yak-40	9021760

☐ RA-87842	Yak-40	9321030	
☐ RA-88247	Yak-40	9642051	

VYBORG AIRLINES — VBG

☐ RA-91014	Il-114	1023823024	
☐ RA-91015	Il-114	1033828025	

YAK SERVICE — AKY

☐ RA-87648	Yak-40	9140920	
☐ RA-87659	Yak-40	9240325	
☐ RA-88294	Yak-40	9331029	
☐ RA-88295	Yak-40	9331329	
☐ RA-42387	Yak-42	40164360912	
☐ RA-42412	Yak-42D	22190550415	

YAKUTIA AIRLINES — K7 / SYL

☐ RA-11354	An-12BP	401812	[YKS]
☐ RA-11767	An-12BP	401909	[YKS]
☐ RA-46496	An-24RV	27308209	
☐ RA-46510	An-24RV	37308406	
☐ RA-46665	An-24RV	47309506	
☐ RA-47352	An-24RV	67310601	
☐ RA-47353	An-24RV	67310602	
☐ RA-47360	An-24RV	67310704	
☐ RA-47819	An-24RV	17307108	
☐ RA-26105	An-26B-100	12003	
☐ RA-26660	An-26-100	97308008	
☐ RA-41250	An-140-100	05A001	
☐ RA-41251	An-140-100	07A012	
☐ RA-41252	An-140-100	09A014	
☐ RA-41253	An-140-100	36525305032	♦
☐ VQ-BEO	B737-76Q/W	30293/1496	
☐ VQ-BMP	B737-86N/W	28617/504	o/o♦
☐ VQ-BOY	B737-85F	28825/188	♦
☐ VP-BFG	B757-256/W	26244/616	
☐ VP-BFI	B757-27B	24838/302	
☐ VQ-BCF	B757-23N/W	27974/737	
☐ VQ-BCK	B757-256/W	26245/617	
☐ VQ-BMW	B757-23N/W	29330/843	♦
☐ RA-85007	Tu-154M	88A777	
☐ RA-85700	Tu-154M	91A875	
☐ RA-85791	Tu-154M	93A975	
☐ RA-85794	Tu-154M	93A978	
☐ RA-85812	Tu-154M	94A1005	

YAMAL AIRLINES — YL / LLM

☐ RA-46694	An-24RV	47309905	
☐ RA-46695	An-24RV	47309906	
☐ RA-26133	An-26B	37312709	
☐ RA-72918	An-72	36572040548	
☐ RA-74052	An-74-200	36547098944	
☐ VP-BRQ	B737-528	25230/2191	
☐ VP-BRS	B737-528	25231/2208	
☐ VP-BRU	B737-528	25206/2099	
☐ VP-BRV	B737-528	25227/2108	
☐ VQ-BAB	B737-56N	28565/2944	
☐ VQ-BII	B737-48E	25773/2905	♦
☐ RA-65132	Tu-134A-3	60639	
☐ RA-65143	Tu-134A	60967	
☐ RA-65552	Tu-134A-3	66270	
☐ RA-65554	Tu-134A-3	66320	
☐ RA-65906	Tu-134A	66175	
☐ RA-65914	Tu-134A-3	66109	

☐ RA-65915	Tu-134A-3	66120	
☐ RA-65919	Tu-134A-3	66168	
☐ RA-65983	Tu-134A-3	63350	
☐ RA-87222	Yak-40K	9832058	
☐ RA-87340	Yak-40	9510939	
☐ RA-87381	Yak-40	9411232	
☐ RA-87416	Yak-40	9420834	
☐ RA-88264	Yak-40K	9711952	

ZAPOLYARYE AVIAKOMPANIA — NSK

☐ RA-11363	An-12B	347505	
☐ RA-26620	An-26-100	5104	
☐ RA-85725	Tu-154M	92A907	

RDPL - LAOS

LAO AIR — LLL

☐ RDPL-34156	An-12BP	402001	

LAO AIRLINES — QV / LAO

☐ RDPL-34173	ATR 72-202	870	
☐ RDPL-34174	ATR 72-202	878	
☐ RDPL-34175	ATR 72-202	929	♦
☐ RDPL-34176	ATR 72-202	938	♦
☐ RDPL-34168	AVIC I Y-7 MA60	0402	
☐ RDPL-34169	AVIC I Y-7 MA60	0403	
☐ RDPL-34171	AVIC I Y-7 MA60	0507	
☐ RDPL-34172	AVIC I Y-7 MA60	0508	

LAO CAPRICORN AIR

☐ RDPL-34153	An-12TB	1347907	
☐ RDPL-34163	Il-76TD	053460832	♦

RP - PHILIPPINES

AIR LINK INTERNATIONAL AIRWAYS

☐ RP-C2252	NAMC YS-11A-500	2079	

AIRPHIL EXPRESS — 2P / GAP

☐ RP-C3227	A320-214	2183	
☐ RP-C3228	A320-214	2162	
☐ RP-C8388	A320-214	4415	♦
☐ RP-C8389	A320-214	4475	♦
☐ RP-C8390	A320-214	4504	♦
☐ RP-C8391	A320-214	4512	♦
☐ RP-C2025	B737-222	19077/103	
☐ RP-C3011	B737-2H4	21533/524	
☐ RP-C3012	B737-2H4	21448/509	
☐ RP-C3015	B737-2H4	21534/526	
☐ RP-C8001	B737-2B7	23116/999	[MNL]
☐ RP-C8002	B737-2B7	22886/974	[MNL]
☐ RP-C8003	B737-2B7	22888/979	[MNL]
☐ RP-C8007	B737-2B7	22878/921	
☐ RP-C8009	B737-201	22879/926	[MNL]
☐ RP-C8011	B737-247	23606/1379	
☐ RP-C8022	B737-247	23607/1387	[MNL]
☐ RP-C4007	B737-332	25996/2488	<PAL
☐ RP-C4011	B737-3Y0	24770/1941	<PAL
☐ RP-C3016	DHC-8Q-314	653	
☐ RP-C3017	DHC-8Q-314	657	
☐ RP-C3018	DHC-8Q-314	658	
☐ RP-C3030	DHC-8-402Q	4064	
☐ RP-C3031	DHC-8-402Q	4069	
☐ RP-C3032	DHC-8-402Q	4070	
☐ RP-C3033	DHC-8-402Q	4071	
☐ RP-C3036	DHC-8-402Q	4023	

CEBU PACIFIC AIR   5J / CEB

☐	RP-C3189	A319-111	2556
☐	RP-C3190	A319-111	2586
☐	RP-C3191	A319-111	2625
☐	RP-C3192	A319-111	2638
☐	RP-C3193	A319-111	2786
☐	RP-C3194	A319-111	2790
☐	RP-C3195	A319-111	2831
☐	RP-C3196	A319-111	2821
☐	RP-C3197	A319-111	2852
☐	RP-C3198	A319-111	2876
☐	RP-C3240	A320-214	2419
☐	RP-C3241	A320-214	2439
☐	RP-C3242	A320-214	2994
☐	RP-C3243	A320-214	3048
☐	RP-C3244	A320-214	3272
☐	RP-C3245	A320-214	3433
☐	RP-C3246	A320-214	3472
☐	RP-C3247	A320-214	3487
☐	RP-C3248	A320-214	3646
☐	RP-C3249	A320-214	3762
☐	RP-C3250	A320-214	3767
☐	RP-C3260	A320-214	4447 ♦
☐	RP-C3261	A320-214	4508 ♦
☐	RP-C3262	A320-214	4537 ♦
☐	RP-C3263	A320-214	4574 ♦
☐	RP-C	A320-214	o/o ♦
☐	RP-C	A320-214	o/o ♦
☐	RP-C	A320-214	o/o ♦
☐	RP-C	A320-214	o/o ♦
☐	RP-C7250	ATR 72-212A	779
☐	RP-C7251	ATR 72-212A	784
☐	RP-C7252	ATR 72-212A	820
☐	RP-C7253	ATR 72-212A	828
☐	RP-C7255	ATR 72-212A	842
☐	RP-C7256	ATR 72-212A	847
☐	RP-C7257	ATR 72-212A	857

INTERISLAND AIRLINES   ISN

☐	RP-C2639	An-26	77305509
☐	RP-C2695	Yak-40A	9522041
☐	RP-C2805	Yak-40	9342031

LIONAIR

☐	RP-C5525	BAe146 Srs.200	E2031 ♦

PACIFIC EAST ASIA CARGO AL   Q8 / PEC

☐	RP-C5353	B727-23F	19131/218
☐	RP-C5355	B727-223F	20185/710 <TMG

PACIFIC PEARL AIRWAYS

☐	RP-C8777	B737-232	23088/1018

PHILIPPINE AIRLINES   PR / PAL

☐	RP-C8600	A319-112	2878
☐	RP-C8601	A319-112	2925
☐	RP-C8602	A319-112	2954
☐	RP-C8603	A319-112	3108
☐	RP-C3221	A320-214	0706
☐	RP-C3223	A320-214	0745
☐	RP-C3231	A320-214	1210
☐	RP-C8604	A320-214	3087
☐	RP-C8605	A320-214	3107
☐	RP-C8606	A320-214	3187
☐	RP-C8607	A320-214	3205
☐	RP-C8609	A320-214	3273
☐	RP-C8610	A320-214	3310
☐	RP-C8611	A320-214	3455

☐	RP-C8612	A320-214	3553
☐	RP-C8613	A320-214	3579
☐	RP-C8614	A320-214	3652
☐	RP-C8615	A320-214	3731
☐	RP-C3330	A330-301	183
☐	RP-C3331	A330-301	184
☐	RP-C3332	A330-301	188
☐	RP-C3333	A330-301	191
☐	RP-C3335	A330-301	189
☐	RP-C3336	A330-301	198
☐	RP-C3337	A330-301	200
☐	RP-C3340	A330-301	203
☐	RP-C3430	A340-313X	173
☐	RP-C3431	A340-313X	176
☐	RP-C3432	A340-313X	187
☐	RP-C3434	A340-313X	196
☐	RP-C4007	B737-332	25996/2488 >GAP
☐	RP-C4011	B737-3Y0	24770/1941 >GAP
☐	RP-C7471	B747-4F6	27261/1005
☐	RP-C7472	B747-4F6	27262/1012
☐	RP-C7473	B747-4F6	27828/1039
☐	RP-C7475	B747-469M	27663/1068
☐	RP-C8168	B747-4F6	27827/1038
☐	RP-C7776	B777-36NER	37712/841
☐	RP-C7777	B777-36NER	37709/826

ROYAL STAR AVIATION

☐	RP-C8328	Do 328 Jet	3136

SOUTH EAST ASIAN AIRLINES   DG / SRQ

☐	RP-C2403	Do24ATT	5345
☐	RP-C2814	Do228-200	8019
☐	RP-C4328	Do328-120	3042
☐	RP-C5328	Do328-110	3046
☐	RP-C6328	Do328-110	3027
☐	RP-C7328	Do328-110	3069
☐	RP-C9328	Do328-110	3003

SPIRIT OF MANILA AIRLINES

☐	RP-C7701	B737-301	23234/1208
☐	RP-C7702	MD-83	49939/1787
☐	RP-C7703	MD-83	49946/1898

TRANSGLOBAL AIRWAYS

☐	RP-C8015	B737-2B1C	20536/289
☐	RP-C8018	MD-83	49985/1838

ZEST AIRWAYS   6K / EZD

☐	RP-C8890	A319-132	1074 ♦
☐	RP-C8897	A320-232	2141
☐	RP-C8988	A320-232	2147
☐	RP-C8989	A320-232	3621
☐	RP-C8991	A320-232	4533 ♦
☐	RP-C8992	A320-232	2137 ♦
☐	RP-C2895	DHC-7-102	35
☐	RP-C2915	DHC-7-102	92
☐	RP-C2955	DHC-7-102	90
☐	RP-C2978	DHC-7-102	79
☐	RP-C2988	DHC-7-102	78 [MNL]
☐	RP-C2996	DHC-7-102	18
☐	RP-C8892	AVIC I Y-7 MA60	0703
☐	RP-C8894	AVIC I Y-7 MA60	0710
☐	RP-C8895	AVIC I Y-7 MA60	0711
☐	RP-C8896	AVIC I Y-7 MA60	0712

☐ RP-C4000	ITPN CASA CN.235	N020	
☐ RP-C5000	ITPN CASA CN.235	N001	
☐ RP-C3338	NAMC YS-11A-227	2142	
☐ RP-C3339	NAMC YS-11A-222	2147	
☐ RP-C3588	NAMC YS-11A-213	2168	[MNL]
☐ RP-C3592	NAMC YS-11A-213	2108	

SE - SWEDEN

AIR SWEDEN · SXN

☐ SE-DMT	MD-81	48003/944	
☐ SE-RJM	A320-212	0289	♦
☐ SE-RJN	A320-231	0169	♦
☐ SE-RJP	MD-82	49209/1191	♦

AMAPOLA FLYG · APF

☐ PH-LMA	Fokker 50	20118	<MNL
☐ SE-KTC	Fokker 50	20124	
☐ SE-KTD	Fokker 50	20125	
☐ SE-LIP	Fokker 50	20147	
☐ SE-LJG	Fokker 50	20168	
☐ SE-LJH	Fokker 50	20171	
☐ SE-LJI	Fokker 50	20180	
☐ SE-LJV	Fokker 50	20103	
☐ SE-LJY	Fokker 50	20259	

AVITRANS NORDIC · 2Q / ETS

☐ SE-ISR	SAAB SF.340A	340A-017
☐ SE-ISY	SAAB SF.340A	340A-080
☐ SE-KCS	SAAB SF.340A/(QC)	340A-066
☐ SE-KCT	SAAB SF.340A/(QC)	340A-070
☐ SE-KXE	SAAB SF.340A	340A-111
☐ SE-KXI	SAAB SF.340B	340B-176
☐ SE-LJK	SAAB SF.340A	340A-089
☐ SE-LJL	SAAB SF.340A	340A-091
☐ SE-LJR	SAAB SF.340B	340B-168
☐ SE-LJS	SAAB SF.340B	340B-215
☐ SE-LJT	SAAB SF.340B	340B-221

CITY AIRLINE · CF / SDR

☐ SE-DZB	ERJ-145EP	145113	
☐ SE-RAA	ERJ-135ER	145210	
☐ SE-RAB	ERJ-135LR	145453	
☐ SE-RAC	ERJ-145LR	145098	
☐ SE-RAD	ERJ-145EU	145458	♦
☐ SE-RAE	ERJ-145EU	145482	♦
☐ SE-RIA	ERJ-145MP	145320	
☐ SE-DMK	MD-87	53337/1962	o/o♦

DIREKTFLYG · HS / HSV

☐ SE-LHB	BAeJetstream 32EP	844
☐ SE-LHC	BAeJetstream 32EP	846
☐ SE-LHE	BAeJetstream 32EP	854
☐ SE-LHF	BAeJetstream 32EP	855
☐ SE-LHG	BAeJetstream 32EP	857
☐ SE-LHH	BAeJetstream 32EP	848
☐ SE-LHI	BAeJetstream 32EP	841
☐ SE-LXD	BAeJetstream 32	977
☐ SE-LXE	BAeJetstream 32	970

GOLDEN AIR · DC / GAO

☐ OH-FAF	SAAB SF.340B	340B-167	<WBA
☐ SE-ISE	SAAB SF.340A	340A-156	
☐ SE-ISG	SAAB SF.340B	340B-162	
☐ SE-KTK	SAAB SF.340B	340B-276	
☐ SE-KXG	SAAB SF.340B	340A-164	
☐ SE-LMR	SAAB SF.340A	340A-141	>NTJ

☐ SE-KXK	SAAB 2000	2000-012	
☐ SE-LOM	SAAB 2000	2000-035	
☐ SE-LTU	SAAB 2000	2000-062	
☐ SE-LTV	SAAB 2000	2000-063	
☐ SE-LTX	SAAB 2000	2000-024	
☐ SE-LXH	SAAB 2000	2000-007	
☐ SE-MDA	ATR 72-212A	778	
☐ SE-MDB	ATR 72-212A	822	
☐ SE-MDC	ATR 72-212A	894	
☐ SE-MDH	ATR 72-212A	917	♦
☐ SE-MDI	ATR 72-212A	930	♦

INTERNATIONAL BUSINESS AIR · 6I / IBZ

☐ SE-LEF	SA.227AC Metro III	AC-451B	I
☐ SE-LIL	SA.227AC Metro III	AC-432B	
☐ SE-LKC	EMB.120ER	120046	

MALMO AVIATION · TF / SCW

☐ SE-DJN	Avro 146-RJ85	E2231	♦
☐ SE-DJO	Avro 146-RJ85	E2226	♦
☐ SE-DJP	Avro 146-RJ70	E1254	♦
☐ SE-DSO	Avro 146-RJ100	E3221	
☐ SE-DSP	Avro 146-RJ100	E3242	
☐ SE-DSR	Avro 146-RJ100	E3244	
☐ SE-DSS	Avro 146-RJ100	E3245	
☐ SE-DST	Avro 146-RJ100	E3247	
☐ SE-DSU	Avro 146-RJ100	E3248	
☐ SE-DSV	Avro 146-RJ100	E3250	
☐ SE-DSX	Avro 146-RJ100	E3255	
☐ SE-DSY	Avro 146-RJ100	E3263	

NEXTJET · 2N / NTJ

☐ SE-LLO	BAeATP	2023	
☐ SE-MAK	BAeATP	2040	<SWN
☐ SE-MAL	BAeATP	2045	
☐ SE-KXY	Beech 1900D	UE-236	
☐ SE-LCX	Beech 1900D	UE-275	
☐ SE-LEP	SAAB SF.340A	340A-127	
☐ SE-LJN	SAAB SF.340A	340A-114	
☐ SE-LMR	SAAB SF.340A	340A-141	<GAO

NOVAIR · 1I / NVR

☐ CS-TRA	A330-243	461	<OBS
☐ SE-RDN	A321-231	2211	
☐ SE-RDO	A321-231	2216	
☐ SE-RDP	A321-231	2410	

SCANDINAVIAN AIRLINES SYSTEM · SK / SAS

☐ OY-KBO	A319-132	2850	
☐ OY-KBP	A319-132	2888	
☐ OY-KBR	A319-131	3231	
☐ OY-KBT	A319-131	3292	
☐ LN-RKI	A321-232	1817	
☐ LN-RKK	A321-232	1848	
☐ OY-KBB	A321-232	1642	
☐ OY-KBE	A321-232	1798	
☐ OY-KBF	A321-232	1807	
☐ OY-KBH	A321-232	1675	
☐ OY-KBK	A321-232	1587	
☐ OY-KBL	A321-232	1619	
☐ LN-RKH	A330-343X	497	
☐ OY-KBN	A330-343X	496	
☐ SE-REE	A330-343X	515	
☐ SE-REF	A330-343X	568	
☐ LN-RKF	A340-313X	413	[LDE]♦
☐ LN-RKG	A340-313X	424	

☐	OY-KBA	A340-313X	435
☐	OY-KBC	A340-313X	467
☐	OY-KBD	A340-313X	470
☐	OY-KBI	A340-313X	430
☐	LN-BRE	B737-405	24643/1860
☐	LN-BRH	B737-505	24828/1925
☐	LN-BRI	B737-405	24644/1938
☐	LN-BRJ	B737-505	24273/2018
☐	LN-BRO	B737-505	24647/2143
☐	LN-BRQ	B737-405	25348/2148
☐	LN-BRV	B737-505	25791/2351
☐	LN-BRX	B737-505	25797/2434
☐	LN-BUC	B737-505	26304/2649
☐	LN-BUD	B737-505	25794/2803 [KRS]
☐	LN-BUE	B737-505	27627/2800
☐	LN-BUF	B737-405	25795/2867
☐	LN-BUG	B737-505	27631/2866
☐	LN-RCN	B737-883	28318/529
☐	LN-RCT	B737-683	30189/303
☐	LN-RCU	B737-683	30190/335
☐	LN-RCW	B737-683	28308/333
☐	LN-RCX	B737-883	30196/733
☐	LN-RCY	B737-883	28324/767
☐	LN-RCZ	B737-883	30197/798
☐	LN-RNN	B737-783	28315/464
☐	LN-RNO	B737-783	28316/476
☐	LN-RNU	B737-783/W	34548/3116
☐	LN-RNW	B737-783/W	34549/3210 ♦
☐	LN-RPA	B737-683	28290/100
☐	LN-RPB	B737-683	28294/137
☐	LN-RPE	B737-683	28306/329
☐	LN-RPF	B737-683	28307/330
☐	LN-RPG	B737-683	28310/255
☐	LN-RPH	B737-683	28605/375
☐	LN-RPJ	B737-783	30192/486
☐	LN-RPK	B737-783	28317/500
☐	LN-RPL	B737-883	30469/673
☐	LN-RPM	B737-883	30195/696
☐	LN-RPN	B737-883	30470/717
☐	LN-RPS	B737-683	28298/191
☐	LN-RPT	B737-683	28299/193
☐	LN-RPU	B737-683	28312/407
☐	LN-RPW	B737-683	28289/92
☐	LN-RPX	B737-683	28291/112
☐	LN-RPY	B737-683	28292/116
☐	LN-RPZ	B737-683	28293/120
☐	LN-RRA	B737-783/W	30471/2288
☐	LN-RRB	B737-783/W	32276/2331
☐	LN-RRC	B737-683	28300/209
☐	LN-RRD	B737-683	28301/227
☐	LN-RRE	B737-85P/W	35706/2586
☐	LN-RRF	B737-85P/W	35707/2610
☐	LN-RRG	B737-85P/W	35708/2653
☐	LN-RRH	B737-883/W	34546/2898
☐	LN-RRJ	B737-883/W	34547/2956
☐	LN-RRK	B737-883/W	32278/1169
☐	LN-RRL	B737-883/W	28328/1424
☐	LN-RRM	B737-783	28314/458
☐	LN-RRN	B737-783	30191/404
☐	LN-RRO	B737-683	28288/49
☐	LN-RRP	B737-683	28311/382
☐	LN-RRR	B737-683	28309/368
☐	LN-RRS	B737-883	28325/1014
☐	LN-RRT	B737-883	28326/1036
☐	LN-RRU	B737-883	28327/1070
☐	LN-RRW	B737-883	32277/1554
☐	LN-RRX	B737-683	28296/21
☐	LN-RRY	B737-683	28297/30
☐	LN-RRZ	B737-683	28295/149
☐	LN-TUA	B737-705	28211/33
☐	LN-TUD	B737-705	28217/142
☐	LN-TUF	B737-705	28222/245
☐	LN-TUH	B737-705	29093/471
☐	LN-TUI	B737-705	29094/507

☐	LN-TUJ	B737-705	29095/773
☐	LN-TUK	B737-705	29096/794
☐	LN-TUL	B737-705	29097/1072
☐	LN-TUM	B737-705	29098/1116
☐	OY-KKS	B737-683	28322/614
☐	SE-DNX	B737-683	28304/270
☐	SE-DOR	B737-683	28305/290
☐	SE-DTH	B737-683	28313/447
☐	LN-RNL	CRJ-900	15250
☐	OY-KFA	CRJ-900	15206
☐	OY-KFB	CRJ-900	15211
☐	OY-KFC	CRJ-900	15218
☐	OY-KFD	CRJ-900	15221
☐	OY-KFE	CRJ-900	15224
☐	OY-KFF	CRJ-900	15231
☐	OY-KFG	CRJ-900	15237
☐	OY-KFH	CRJ-900	15240
☐	OY-KFI	CRJ-900	15242
☐	OY-KFK	CRJ-900	15244
☐	OY-KFL	CRJ-900	15246
☐	LN-RDA	DHC-8-402Q	4013 [NYO]
☐	LN-RDI	DHC-8-402Q	4024 [CPH]
☐	LN-RDJ	DHC-8-402Q	4010 [CPH]
☐	LN-RDO	DHC-8-402Q	4036 [CPH]
☐	LN-RDP	DHC-8-402Q	4012 [NYO]
☐	LN-RDT	DHC-8-402Q	4038 [NYO]
☐	LN-RNC	Fokker 50	20176
☐	LN-RND	Fokker 50	20178
☐	LN-RNE	Fokker 50	20179
☐	LN-RNG	Fokker 50	20184 [NWI]♦
☐	LN-RLE	MD-82	49382/1232
☐	LN-RLF	MD-82	49383/1236
☐	LN-RMK	MD-87	49610/1705
☐	LN-RML	MD-82	53002/1835
☐	LN-RMM	MD-82	53005/1855
☐	LN-RMO	MD-82	53315/1947
☐	LN-RMR	MD-82	53365/1998
☐	LN-RMS	MD-82	53368/2003
☐	LN-RMT	MD-82	53001/1815
☐	LN-RMU	MD-87	53340/1967 [ARN]
☐	LN-RON	MD-82	53347/1979 [OSL]
☐	LN-ROP	MD-82	49384/1237
☐	LN-ROS	MD-82	49421/1263
☐	LN-ROT	MD-82	49422/1264
☐	LN-ROU	MD-82	49424/1284
☐	LN-ROW	MD-82	49438/1353 [LDE]
☐	LN-ROX	MD-82	49603/1442
☐	OY-KGT	MD-82	49380/1225
☐	OY-KHC	MD-82	49436/1303
☐	OY-KHE	MD-82	49604/1456
☐	OY-KHG	MD-82	49613/1519
☐	OY-KHM	MD-82	49914/1693
☐	OY-KHN	MD-82	53000/1812
☐	OY-KHP	MD-82	53007/1882
☐	OY-KHR	MD-82	53275/1896 [ARN]
☐	OY-KHU	MD-87	53336/1953 [MAD]♦
☐	SE-DIC	MD-87	49607/1512 [LDE]
☐	SE-DIK	MD-82	49728/1553
☐	SE-DIL	MD-82	49913/1665
☐	SE-DIN	MD-87	49999/1803
☐	SE-DIP	MD-87	53010/1921
☐	SE-DIR	MD-82	53004/1846
☐	SE-DIS	MD-82	53006/1869
☐	SE-DIU	MD-87	53011/1931
☐	SE-DMB	MD-82	53314/1946
☐	SE-DMI	MD-82	49437/1345

SKYWAYS EXPRESS   JZ / SKX

☐	SE-LEA	Fokker 50	20116
☐	SE-LEC	Fokker 50	20112

☐	SE-LED	Fokker 50	20111
☐	SE-LEH	Fokker 50	20108
☐	SE-LEL	Fokker 50	20110
☐	SE-LEU	Fokker 50	20115
☐	SE-LEZ	Fokker 50	20128
☐	SE-LIO	Fokker 50	20146
☐	SE-LIR	Fokker 50	20151
☐	SE-LIS	Fokker 50	20152
☐	SE-LIT	Fokker 50	20194

TOR AIR

☐	SE-RJA	B737-4Q8	26302/2620

TRANSWEDE — 5T / TWE

☐	SE-DJN	Avro 146-RJ85	E2231
☐	SE-DJO	Avro 146-RJ85	E2226
☐	SE-DJP	Avro 146-RJ70	E1254

TUIFLY NORDIC — 6B / BLX

☐	SE-DZK	B737-804/W	28231/538	
☐	SE-DZN	B737-804/W	32903/1127	
☐	SE-DZV	B737-804/W	32904/1302	
☐	SE-RFT	B737-8K5/W	38097/3548	♦
☐	SE-RFO	B757-28AER/W	25623/528	
☐	SE-RFP	B757-204/W	27219/596	
☐	SE-RFS	B767-304ER/W	28040/613	

WEST AIR EUROPE — PT / SWN

☐	SE-KXP	BAeATP (LFD)	2056	
☐	SE-LGU	BAeATP	2022	
☐	SE-LGV	BAeATP	2034	
☐	SE-LGX	BAeATP	2036	
☐	SE-LGY	BAeATP	2035	
☐	SE-LHX	BAeATP	2020	
☐	SE-LNX	BAeATP	2061	
☐	SE-LNY	BAeATP	2062	
☐	SE-LPU	BAeATP	2060	
☐	SE-LPX	BAeATP	2063	
☐	SE-MAF	BAeATP	2002	
☐	SE-MAH	BAeATP	2004	
☐	SE-MAI	BAeATP (LFD)	2010	
☐	SE-MAJ	BAeATP (LFD)	2038	
☐	SE-MAN	BAeATP (LFD)	2006	
☐	SE-MAP	BAeATP (LFD)	2037	
☐	SE-MAR	BAeATP	2053	
☐	SE-MAY	BAeATP	2044	
☐	SE-MEE	BAeATP	2019	♦
☐	SE-	BAeATP	2031	♦
☐	SE-DUX	CRJ-200F	7010	
☐	SE-DUY	CRJ-200F	7023	

SP - POLAND

AIR ITALY POLSKA — 4Q / AEI

☐	EI-EOJ	B737-8BK/W	33022/1672	♦
☐	EI-IGC	B757-230	24747/275	

ENTER AIR

☐	SP-ENA	B737-4Q8	26320/2563	♦
☐	SP-ENB	B737-4Q8	26299/2602	♦
☐	SP-ENC	B737-4Q8	25376/2689	♦
☐	SP-ENF	B737-4C9	25429/2215	♦
☐	SP-ENZ	B737-85F	28823/174	♦

EUROLOT — K2 / ELO

☐	SP-EDA	ATR 42-500	516
☐	SP-EDE	ATR 42-500	443

☐	SP-EDF	ATR 42-500	559
☐	SP-LFA	ATR 72-202	246
☐	SP-LFB	ATR 72-202	265
☐	SP-LFC	ATR 72-202	272
☐	SP-LFD	ATR 72-202	279
☐	SP-LFE	ATR 72-202	328
☐	SP-LFF	ATR 72-202	402
☐	SP-LFG	ATR 72-202	411
☐	SP-LFH	ATR 72-202	478

EXIN — EXN

☐	SP-FDP	An-26B	11903
☐	SP-FDR	An-26B	11305
☐	SP-FDS	An-26B	12205
☐	SP-FDT	An-26B	12102

JET AIR — O2 / JEA

☐	SP-KTR	ATR 42-300	92
☐	SP-KWD	BAeJetstream 3202	847
☐	SP-KWE	BAeJetstream 3201	842
☐	SP-KWF	BAeJetstream 3201	845
☐	SP-KWN	BAeJetstream 3201	856

LOT - POLISH AIRLINES — LO / LOT

☐	SP-LKC	B737-55D	27418/2397	
☐	SP-LKD	B737-55D	27419/2401	
☐	SP-LKE	B737-55D	27130/2448	
☐	SP-LKF	B737-55D	27368/2603	
☐	SP-LLA	B737-45D	27131/2458	
☐	SP-LLB	B737-45D	27156/2492	
☐	SP-LLC	B737-45D	27157/2502	
☐	SP-LLE	B737-45D	27914/2804	
☐	SP-LLF	B737-45D	28752/2874	
☐	SP-LLG	B737-45D	28753/2895	
☐	SP-LLK	B737-4Q8	25740/2461	
☐	SP-LLL	B737-4Q8	25164/2447	
☐	SP-LPA	B767-35DER	24865/322	
☐	SP-LPB	B767-35DER	27902/577	
☐	SP-LPC	B767-35DER	28656/659	
☐	SP-LPE	B767-341ER	24843/314	
☐	SP-LPF	B767-319ER	24876/413	>AEA
☐	SP-LPG	B767-306ER	26263/592	
☐	SP-	B787-8		o/o♦
☐	SP-	B787-8		o/o♦
☐	SP-	B787-8		o/o♦
☐	SP-LGE	ERJ-145MP	145285	
☐	SP-LGF	ERJ-145MP	145308	
☐	SP-LGG	ERJ-145MP	145319	
☐	SP-LGH	ERJ-145MP	145329	
☐	SP-LGO	ERJ-145MP	145560	
☐	SP-LDA	ERJ-170STD	17000023	
☐	SP-LDB	ERJ-170STD	17000024	
☐	SP-LDC	ERJ-170STD	17000025	
☐	SP-LDD	ERJ-170STD	17000027	
☐	SP-LDE	ERJ-170LR	17000029	
☐	SP-LDF	ERJ-170LR	17000035	
☐	SP-LDG	ERJ-170LR	17000065	
☐	SP-LDH	ERJ-170LR	17000069	
☐	SP-LDI	ERJ-170LR	17000073	
☐	SP-LDK	ERJ-170LR	17000074	
☐	SP-LIA	ERJ-175LR	17000125	
☐	SP-LIB	ERJ-175LR	17000132	
☐	SP-LIC	ERJ-175LR	17000134	
☐	SP-LID	ERJ-175LR	17000136	
☐	SP-LIE	ERJ-175LR	17000153	
☐	SP-LIF	ERJ-175LR	17000154	
☐	SP-LIG	ERJ-175LR	17000283	
☐	SP-LIH	ERJ-175LR	17000288	
☐	SP-LII	ERJ-175LR	17000290	

□ SP-LIK	ERJ-175LR	17000303	
□ SP-LIL	ERJ-175LR	17000306	♦
□ SP-LIM	ERJ-175LR	17000311	♦
□ SP-LIN	ERJ-175LR	17000313	♦
□ SP-LIO	ERJ-175LR	17000321	♦
□ SP-	ERJ-195LR		o/o♦
□ SP-	ERJ-195LR		o/o♦
□ SP-	ERJ-195LR		o/o♦

SKY TAXI — IGA

□ SP-MRB	SAAB SF.340A ((QC))340A-100	
□ SP-MRC	SAAB SF.340A	340A-143

SPRINT AIR — SXP

□ SP-KPE	SAAB SF.340A/(QC)340A-130	
□ SP-KPF	SAAB SF.340A/(QC)340A-135	
□ SP-KPG	SAAB SF.340A/(QC)340A-065	
□ SP-KPH	SAAB SF.340A/(QC)340A-015	
□ SP-KPK	SAAB SF.340AF	340A-026
□ SP-KPL	SAAB SF.340A	340A-038
□ SP-KPN	SAAB SF.340A	340A-118
□ SP-KPO	SAAB SF.340A/(QC)340A-010	
□ SP-KPR	SAAB SF.340A/(QC)340A-139	
□ SP-KPU	SAAB SF.340AF	340A-145
□ SP-KPV	SAAB SF.340A	340A-071

WHITE EAGLE GENERAL AVIATION — WEA

□ SP-KCA	ATR 42-300	085
□ SP-KTR	ATR 42-300	092

ST - SUDAN

ABABEEL AVIATION

□ EX-036	Il-76TD	93495863	<CKW
□ ST-ARL	An-26	2606	
□ ST-AWT	An-26		
□ ST-WTS	An-74-200	36547098960	

AIR TAXI & CARGO — WAM

□ ST-TKO	An-32B	3110	<PXA

AIR WEST CARGO — AWZ

□ ST-AWR	Il-76TD	0033447365	[FJR]
□ ST-EWC	Il-76TD	0023438129	
□ ST-EWD	Il-76TD	0063466989	
□ ST-EWX	Il-76TD	1013409282	
□ UN-A3101	A310-322	399	<SOZ

ALMAJARA AVIATION — MJA

□ ST-ATH	Il-76MD	63472158

AYR AVIATION

□ ST-SMZ	An-32	3205

AZZA AIR TRANSPORT — AZZ

□ ST-APS	Il-76TD	1023409316	
□ ST-ARV	An-12BP	8345310	
□ ST-ASA	An-12	402010	
□ ST-AZN	An-12	9346808	
□ ST-AZZ	Il-76TD	1023408265	
□ ST-DAS	An-12	7345209	
□ ST-JAC	An-26B-100	10203	
□ ST-JCC	B707-384C	18948/495	[KRT]♦

BADR AIRLINES — BDR

□ ST-BDE	Il-76TD	1013408252

□ ST-BDK	An-72-100	36572060642	
□ ST-BDN	Il-76TD	1023413443	
□ ST-BDR	An-74		
□ ST-BDT	An-74	36547097935	
□ ST-BDX	An-74-200	36547096924	
□ ST-SAL	An-26B	17311907	

BENTIU AIR TRANSPORT — BNT

□ ST-NDC	An-26	17310908
□ ST-SRA	An-26	17311807

EL MAGAL AVIATION — MGG

□ ST-APJ	An-12BP	2400701	
□ ST-EIB	An-32B	2903	
□ ST-ISG	WSK-PZL/An-28	1AJ005-01	
□ ST-MGD	Il-76TD	1013407230	
□ ST-NSP	An-32	2109	
□ S9-PSE	An-32	2803	<GLE

FEEDER AIRLINES — FDD

□ ST-NEW	Fokker 50	20138
□ ST-NEX	Fokker 50	20248

FORTY EIGHT AVIATION

□ ST-OHO	Il-62M	1052128	♦

IMAATONG SOUTH SUDAN AIRLINES

□ 5Y-BTD	F.27 Friendship 300M	10154	[WIL]

KATA TRANSPORTATION COMPANY

□ ST-AZM	An-12BK	346907
□ ST-HIS	An-26B	7310310

MARSLAND AVIATION — M7 / MSL

□ ST-ARJ	An-26	5602	
□ ST-ARP	An-24RV	37308809	
□ ST-MRL	Yak-42	4520424116690	
□ ST-MRS	Tu-134B-3	63333	[FJR]

MID AIRLINES — 7Y / NYL

□ ST-ARG	Fokker 50	20130
□ ST-ARH	Fokker 50	20131
□ ST-ARZ	Fokker 50	20134

NOVA AIRLINES

□ ST-NVA	Fokker 50	20227	[MST]
□ ST-NVB	CRJ-200ER	7807	
□ ST-NVC	CRJ-200ER	7686	

SACSO AIR LINES

□ ST-ARJ	An-26	77305602

SUDAN AIRWAYS — SD / SUD

□ ST-ASS	A300B4-622	252	
□ ST-AST	A310-322	437	
□ ST-ATA	A300B4-622R	775	
□ ST-ATB	A300B4-622R	666	
□ D6-CAS	A320-214	3040	<
□ ST-AFA	B707-3J8C	20897/885	
□ ST-ASD	Fokker 50	20201	
□ ST-ASF	Fokker 50	20155	
□ ST-ASI	Fokker 50	20247	
□ ST-ASJ	Fokker 50	20246	
□ ST-ASO	Fokker 50	20256	

SUDANESE STATES AVIATION

☐ ST-AQW	Boeing 707-320C	20517/854	[KRT]♦

SUN AIR   AWZ

☐ ST-SDA	B737-2T4	23274/1099	
☐ ST-SDB	B737-2T4	23273/1097	>MSL

TRANS ATTICO   ML / ETC

☐ ET-AKZ	DHC-8-202	469	<TNW
☐ ST-AQM	An-26	1404	
☐ ST-AQR	Il-76TD	0043453575	
☐ ST-AQU	An-32B	2009	
☐ ST-ASX	Il-76	73479392	

SU - EGYPT

AIR ARABIA EGYPT

☐ SU-AAA	A320-214	2764	♦
☐ SU-AAB	A320-214	3152	♦

AIR CAIRO   MSC

☐ SU-BPU	A320-214	2937
☐ SU-BPV	A320-214	2966
☐ SU-BPW	A320-214	3282
☐ SU-BPX	A320-214	3323

AIR MEMPHIS   MHS

☐ SU-BME	MD-83	49628/1582	
☐ SU-PBG	A320-233	1353	
☐ SU-PBH	A320-233	1300	
☐ SU-PBO	DC-9-31	48131/940	
☐ SU-YAH	Fokker 50	20123	♦
☐ SU-YAI	Fokker 50	20143	♦

ALEXANDRIA AIRLINES   KHH

☐ SU-KHM	B737-5C9	26438/2413

ALMASRIA UNIVERSAL AIRLINES   UJ / LMU

☐ SU-TCA	A320-232	0932
☐ SU-TCB	A320-232	0943

AMC AIRLINES   YJ / AMC

☐ SU-AYK	B737-266	21194/455	[CAI]
☐ SU-BPG	B737-86N/W	32669/1895	
☐ SU-BPZ	B737-86N/W	35213/2300	
☐ SU-BQA	B737-86N/W	35220/2406	
☐ SU-BOZ	MD-83	53192/2155	

CAIRO AVIATION   CCE

☐ SU-EAF	Tu-204-120	64027	
☐ SU-EAG	Tu-204-120S	64028	[CAI]
☐ SU-EAH	Tu-204-120	64023	
☐ SU-EAI	Tu-204-120	64025	[CAI]
☐ SU-EAJ	Tu-204-120S	64029	[CAI]

EGYPTAIR   MS / MSR

☐ SU-BDG	A300B4-203F	200
☐ SU-GAC	A300B4-203F	255
☐ SU-GAS	A300B4-622RF	561
☐ SU-GAY	A300B4-622RF	607
☐ SU-GBA	A320-231	0165
☐ SU-GBB	A320-231	0166
☐ SU-GBC	A320-231	0178

☐ SU-GBD	A320-231	0194	
☐ SU-GBE	A320-231	0198	
☐ SU-GBF	A320-231	0351	
☐ SU-GBG	A320-231	0366	
☐ SU-GBZ	A320-232	2070	
☐ SU-GCA	A320-232	2073	
☐ SU-GCB	A320-232	2079	
☐ SU-GCC	A320-232	2088	
☐ SU-GCD	A320-232	2094	
☐ SU-GCL	A320-231	0322	
☐ SU-GBT	A321-231	0680	
☐ SU-GBU	A321-231	0687	
☐ SU-GBV	A321-231	0715	
☐ SU-GBW	A321-231	0725	
☐ SU-GCE	A330-243	600	
☐ SU-GCF	A330-243	610	
☐ SU-GCG	A330-243	666	
☐ SU-GCH	A330-243	683	
☐ SU-GCI	A330-243	696	
☐ SU-GCJ	A330-243	709	
☐ SU-GCK	A330-243	726	
☐ SU-GDS	A330-343X	1143	♦
☐ SU-	A330-343X		o/o♦
☐ SU-	A330-343X		o/o♦
☐ SU-	A330-343X		o/o♦
☐ SU-	A330-343X		o/o♦
☐ SU-GBM	A340-212	156	
☐ SU-GBN	A340-212	159	
☐ SU-GBO	A340-212	178	
☐ SU-GBH	B737-566	25084/2019	
☐ SU-GBJ	B737-566	25352/2169	
☐ SU-GBK	B737-566	26052/2276	
☐ SU-GBL	B737-566	26051/2282	
☐ SU-GCM	B737-866/W	35558/2054	
☐ SU-GCN	B737-866/W	35559/2113	
☐ SU-GCO	B737-866/W	35561/2369	
☐ SU-GCP	B737-866/W	35560/2434	
☐ SU-GCR	B737-866/W	35562/2826	
☐ SU-GCS	B737-866/W	35563/2695	
☐ SU-GCZ	B737-866/W	35568/2795	
☐ SU-GDA	B737-866/W	35565/2999	
☐ SU-GDB	B737-866/W	35567/3017	
☐ SU-GDC	B737-866/W	35564/3040	
☐ SU-GDD	B737-866/W	35566/3061	
☐ SU-GDE	B737-866/W	35569/3043	
☐ SU-GDX	B737-866/W	40757/3409	♦
☐ SU-GDY	B737-866/W	40758/3442	♦
☐ SU-GDZ	B737-866/W	40759/2472	♦
☐ SU-GEA	B737-866/W	40760/3492	♦
☐ SU-	B737-866/W		o/o♦
☐ SU-	B737-866/W		o/o♦
☐ SU-GBP	B777-266	28423/71	
☐ SU-GBR	B777-266	28424/80	
☐ SU-GBS	B777-266	28425/85	
☐ SU-GBX	B777-266ER	32629/362	
☐ SU-GBY	B777-266ER	32630/368	
☐ SU-GDL	B777-36NER	38284/850	♦
☐ SU-GDM	B777-36NER	38285/862	♦
☐ SU-GDN	B777-36NER	38288/896	♦
☐ SU-GDO	B777-36NER	38289/907	♦
☐ SU-	B777-36NER		o/o♦

EGYPTAIR EXPRESS   MSE

☐ SU-GCT	ERJ-170LR	17000167
☐ SU-GCU	ERJ-170LR	17000169
☐ SU-GCV	ERJ-170LR	17000170
☐ SU-GCW	ERJ-170LR	17000175
☐ SU-GCX	ERJ-170LR	17000178
☐ SU-GCY	ERJ-170LR	17000185

☐	SU-GDF	ERJ-170LR	17000266
☐	SU-GDG	ERJ-170LR	17000269
☐	SU-GDH	ERJ-170LR	17000274
☐	SU-GDI	ERJ-170LR	17000276
☐	SU-GDJ	ERJ-170LR	17000282
☐	SU-GDK	ERJ-170LR	17000284

KORAL BLUE   KBR

☐	SU-KBA	A320-212	0937	
☐	SU-KBB	A319-112	3171	
☐	SU-KBC	A320-214	2123	
☐	SU-KBD	A320-214	1597	
☐	SU-KBE	A320-214	1454	♦

LOTUS AIR   TAS

☐	SU-LBG	A320-233	0743
☐	SU-LBH	A320-233	0739
☐	SU-LBI	A320-232	0667

MIDWEST AIRLINES EGYPT   MY / MWA

☐	SU-MWD	B737-86N/W	28591/233	♦
☐	SU-MWE	B737-8Q8/W	30040/1693	♦
☐	SU-MWF	B737-8Q8/W	32841/1705	♦

NESMA AIR

☐	SU-NMA	A320-232	1697	♦

NILE AIR   NIA

☐	SU-BQB	A320-232	3183
☐	SU-BQC	A320-232	3219

PETROLEUM AIR SERVICES

☐	SU-CBA	DHC-7-102	093	
☐	SU-CBB	DHC-7-102	096	[CAI]
☐	SU-CBC	DHC-7-102	097	
☐	SU-CBD	DHC-7-102	098	
☐	SU-CBE	DHC-7-102	099	
☐	SU-CBF	DHC-8Q-315	584	
☐	SU-CBG	DHC-8Q-315	585	
☐	SU-CBH	DHC-8Q-315	594	
☐	SU-CBJ	DHC-8Q-315	607	
☐	SU-CBN	DHC-8Q-315	632	

TRISTAR AIR   TSY

☐	SU-BMZ	A300B4-203F	129

SX - GREECE

AEGEAN AIRLINES   A3 / AEE

☐	SX-DGB	A320-232	4165	
☐	SX-	A320-232		o/o
☐	SX-	A320-232		o/o
☐	SX-	A320-232		o/o
☐	SX-	A320-232		o/o
☐	SX-DVG	A320-232	3033	
☐	SX-DVH	A320-232	3066	
☐	SX-DVI	A320-232	3074	
☐	SX-DVJ	A320-232	3365	
☐	SX-DVK	A320-232	3392	
☐	SX-DVL	A320-232	3423	
☐	SX-DVM	A320-232	3439	
☐	SX-DVN	A320-232	3478	
☐	SX-DVQ	A320-232	3526	
☐	SX-DVR	A320-232	3714	
☐	SX-DVS	A320-232	3709	
☐	SX-DVT	A320-232	3745	
☐	SX-DVU	A320-232	3753	

☐	SX-DVV	A320-232	3773	
☐	SX-DVW	A320-232	3785	
☐	SX-DVX	A320-232	3829	
☐	SX-DVY	A320-232	3850	
☐	SX-DGA	A321-231	3878	
☐	SX-DVO	A321-231	3462	
☐	SX-DVP	A321-231	3527	
☐	SX-DVZ	A321-231	3820	
☐	EC-KVI	ATR 72-212A	824	<SWT
☐	SX-DVA	Avro 146-RJ100	E3341	
☐	SX-DVB	Avro 146-RJ100	E3343	
☐	SX-DVC	Avro 146-RJ100	E3358	
☐	SX-DVD	Avro 146-RJ100	E3362	

AEROLAND AIRWAYS   3S / AEN

☐	SX-BVE	DHC-8-106	351

ASTRA AIRLINES   A2

☐	SX-DIX	BAe146 Srs.300	E3193
☐	SX-DIZ	BAe146 Srs.300	E3206

AVIATOR AIRWAYS   AVW

☐	SX-BSR	BAeJetstream 31	718

BLUEBIRD AIRWAYS

☐	SX-DAV	B737-4Q8	24704/1855	♦

EPSILON AVIATION   GRV

☐	SX-BMM	SA.227AC Metro III	BC-774B
☐	SX-BNN	SA.227AC Metro III	BC-771B

GAINJET

☐	SX-RFA	B757-23N/W	30232/888

HELLAS JET   HJ / HEJ

☐	SX-BVL	A320-212	0087

HELLENIC IMPERIAL AIRWAYS   IMP

☐	SX-TIB	B747-230B	23622/665	
☐	SX-TIC	B747-281B	23501/648	
☐	SX-TID	B747-281B	23502/649	
☐	SX-TIE	B747-230M	23509/663	<UVS

OLYMPIC AIR   OA / NOA

☐	SX-OAF	A319-111	3895
☐	SX-OAG	A319-112	3950
☐	SX-OAJ	A319-112	3905
☐	SX-OAN	A319-133	1727
☐	SX-OAO	A319-133	1880
☐	SX-OAH	A320-232	3316
☐	SX-OAI	A320-232	3162
☐	SX-OAM	A320-232	3990
☐	SX-OAP	A320-232	4065
☐	SX-OAQ	A320-232	3748
☐	SX-OAR	A320-232	3812
☐	SX-OAS	A320-232	4094
☐	SX-OAT	A320-232	4190
☐	SX-OAU	A320-232	4193
☐	SX-BIO	DHC-8-102	330
☐	SX-BIP	DHC-8-102	347
☐	SX-BIQ	DHC-8-102	361
☐	SX-BIR	DHC-8-102	364
☐	SX-BIW	DHC-8-102	289

☐	SX-BIT	DHC-8-402Q	4148	
☐	SX-BIU	DHC-8-402Q	4152	
☐	SX-OBA	DHC-8-402Q	4267	
☐	SX-OBB	DHC-8-402Q	4268	
☐	SX-OBC	DHC-8-402Q	4276	
☐	SX-OBD	DHC-8-402Q	4311	♦
☐	SX-OBE	DHC-8-402Q	4314	♦
☐	SX-OBF	DHC-8-402Q	4318	♦
☐	SX-OBG	DHC-8-402Q	4321	♦
☐	SX-OBH	DHC-8-402Q	4327	♦
☐	SX-DFA	A340-313X	235	[ATH]
☐	SX-DFB	A340-313X	239	[ATH]
☐	SX-DFC	A340-313X	280	[ATH]
☐	SX-DFD	A340-313X	292	[ATH]
☐	SX-BIA	ATR 42-320	169	[ATH]
☐	SX-BIB	ATR 42-320	182	[ATH]
☐	SX-BIC	ATR 42-320	197	[ATH]
☐	SX-BID	ATR 42-320	219	[ATH]
☐	SX-BIE	ATR 72-202	239	[ATH]
☐	SX-BIF	ATR 72-202	241	[ATH]
☐	SX-BIG	ATR 72-202	290	[ATH]
☐	SX-BIH	ATR 72-202	305	[ATH]
☐	SX-BII	ATR 72-202	353	[ATH]
☐	SX-BIK	ATR 72-202	350	[ATH]
☐	SX-BIL	ATR 72-202	437	[ATH]
☐	SX-BPA	ATR 42-300	033	[ATH]
☐	SX-BKA	B737-484	25313/2109	[ATH]
☐	SX-BKB	B737-484	25314/2124	[ATH]
☐	SX-BKC	B737-484	25361/2130	[ATH]
☐	SX-BKD	B737-484	25362/2142	[ATH]
☐	SX-BKE	B737-484	25417/2160	[ATH]
☐	SX-BKF	B737-484	25430/2174	[ATH]
☐	SX-BLD	B737-3M8	25071/2039	[ATH]
☐	SX-BMC	B737-42J	27143/2457	[CHR]

SKY EXPRESS — G3 / SEH

☐	SX-BLL	MD-83	49933/1837	
☐	SX-BPP	MD-83	53377/2057	
☐	SX-IDI	BAeJetstream 32	947	
☐	SX-DIA	BAeJetstream 41	41075	
☐	SX-ROD	BAeJetstream 41	41076	
☐	SX-SEB	BAeJetstream 41	41070	
☐	SX-SEC	BAeJetstream 41	41014	♦
☐	SX-SKY	BAeJetstream 31	829	♦
☐	SX-	BAeJetstream 41	41040	o/o♦

SKYWINGS AIRLINES — GSW

☐	SX-BTF	MD-83	49857/1687	
☐	SX-BTG	MD-83	49856/1675	
☐	SX-BTH	B757-29J	27204/591	
☐	SX-	A320-231	0405	o/o♦

SWIFTAIR HELLAS — MDF

☐	SX-BGU	SA.227AC Metro III	AC-615B
☐	SX-BKZ	SA.227AC Metro III	AC-694B
☐	SX-BMT	SA.227AC Metro III	AC-699B

VIKING HELLAS AIRLINES

☐	SX-SMT	A320-231	0393	♦
☐	SX-SMU	A320-231	0414	♦
☐	SX-SMS	MD-83	49631/1596	

S2 - BANGLADESH

BEST AIR — 5Q / BEA

☐	S2-AAT	HS.748 Srs.2A/351	1770
☐	S2-ABE	HS.748 Srs.2A/245	1658
☐	S2-AEE	HS.748 Srs 2A/242	1647

BIMAN BANGLADESH AIRLINES — BG / BBC

☐	S2-ADF	A310-325	700	
☐	S2-ADK	A310-325	594	
☐	S2-AFT	A310-325ET	642	♦
☐	TC-API	B737-86N/W	32732/1056	<PGT
☐	S2-AFL	B737-83N/W	28648/888	
☐	S2-AFM	B737-83N/W	28653/948	
☐	CS-TFM	B777-212ER	28513/144	<MMZ
☐	S2-AFO	B777-3E9ER		o/o♦
☐	S2-AFP	B777-3E9ER		o/o♦
☐	S2-ACO	DC-10-30	46993/263	
☐	S2-ACP	DC-10-30	46995/275	
☐	S2-ACQ	DC-10-30	47817/300	
☐	S2-ACR	DC-10-30	48317/445	
☐	S2-ACV	F.28 Fellowship 4000	11124	
☐	S2-ACW	F.28 Fellowship 4000	11148	
☐	S2-ADY	F.28 Fellowship 4000	11120	
☐	S2-ADZ	F.28 Fellowship 4000	11123	[DAC]

BISMILLAH AIRLINES — 5Z / BML

☐	S2-ADW	HS.748 Srs 2A/347	1766

EASY FLY

☐	S2-AAX	HS.748 Srs.2A/242	1767	[DAK]

GMG AIRLINES — Z5

☐	S2-AAA	DHC-8-102	245	
☐	S2-ACT	DHC-8-311	307	
☐	S2-ADM	MD-82	53147/2069	
☐	S2-ADO	MD-82	53481/2145	
☐	S2-ADP	MD-83	53044/1776	
☐	S2-ADX	DHC-8Q-311A	464	
☐	S2-AFD	B767-3Q8ER	30301/762	♦

REGENT AIRLINES — RX

☐	S2-AHA	DHC-8Q-314	521	♦
☐	S2-AHB	DHC-8Q-314	543	♦

ROYAL BENGAL AIRLINES — 4A

☐	S2-AEL	DHC-8-102A	225

UNITED AIRWAYS — 4H / UBD

☐	S2-AER	DHC-8-103	366	
☐	S2-AES	DHC-8-103	363	
☐	S2-AEH	MD-83	49937/1784	
☐	S2-AEU	MD-83	49790/1643	
☐	S2-AFF	A310-325	672	♦

ZOOM AIRWAYS — 3Z / ZAW

☐	S2-AET	L-1011-1F Tristar	193-1012

S5 - SLOVENIA

ADRIA AIRWAYS — JP / ADR

☐	S5-AAP	A319-132	4282	♦
☐	S5-AAR	A319-132	4301	♦
☐	S5-	A319-132		o/o♦
☐	S5-AAA	A320-231	0043	[LJU]
☐	S5-AAD	CRJ-200LR	7166	
☐	S5-AAE	CRJ-200LR	7170	
☐	S5-AAF	CRJ-200LR	7272	
☐	S5-AAG	CRJ-200LR	7384	

☐	S5-AAH	CRJ-200LR	7032
☐	S5-AAI	CRJ-200LR	7248
☐	S5-AAJ	CRJ-200LR	8010
☐	S5-AAK	CRJ-900ER	15128
☐	S5-AAL	CRJ-900ER	15129
☐	S5-AAN	CRJ-900ER	15207
☐	S5-AAO	CRJ-900ER	15215
☐	S5-	CRJ-1000ER	o/o♦

AURORA AIRLINES — URR

☐	S5-ACC	MD-82	48095/1055
☐	S5-ACD	MD-82	49143/1095 [IST]

SOLINAIR — SOP

☐	S5-ABS	A300B4-203F	126
☐	S5-ABV	B737-4K5SF	24128/1715 ♦
☐	S5-BAF	LET L-410UVP-E8C	912540
☐	S5-BAM	SAAB SF.340AF	340A-020
☐	S5-BAO	SAAB SF.340AF	340A-011
☐	S5-BAT	SAAB SF.340AF	340A-007

S7- SEYCHELLES

AIR SEYCHELLES — HM / SEY

☐	S7-AHM	B767-37DER	26328/637
☐	S7-ASY	B767-3Q8ER	29386/831
☐	S7-FCS	B767-306ER	28884/738
☐	S7-ILF	B767-205	23057/81
☐	S7-SEZ	B767-219ER	24150/239

S9 - SAO TOME

GOLIAF AIR — GLE

☐	S9-BOH	An-32	2108
☐	S9-BOZ	An-12A	2340803
☐	S9-DAB	DC-9-32	47313/268
☐	S9-DAF	An-12A	2340606
☐	S9-DBA	An-12AP	2400802
☐	S9-GAR	L-1011-200 Tristar	193U-1201
☐	S9-PSE	An-32	2803
☐	S9-PSO	An-12BP	5343109

TRANSAFRIK INTERNATIONAL — TFK

☐	S9-BAE	B727-31F	18903/147
☐	S9-BAG	B727-30C	19313/411 [UTN]
☐	S9-BAV	B727-223	21383/1324
☐	S9-BOC	B727-23F	18447/127 [UTN]
☐	S9-BOD	B727-25F	18968/223 [UTN]
☐	S9-BOG	B727-90C	19170/332 [UTN]
☐	S9-CAA	B727-95F	19836/494
☐	S9-PAC	B727-44C	20475/854
☐	S9-PST	B727-171C	19859/559Opf DTA
☐	S9-TAO	B727-23F	19390/350
☐	S9-BOF	L-382G-32C Hercules	4586
☐	S9-BOR	L-382E-20C Hercules	4362
☐	S9-CAV	L-382G-11C Hercules	4301
☐	S9-CAW	L-382G-13C Hercules	4300
☐	S9-NAL	L-382E-25C Hercules	4385

TRANSLIZ AVIATION

☐	S9-KHC	An-12B	347306
☐	S9-KHD	An-12B	1347908
☐	S9-KHF	An-12V	347109
☐	S9-KHL	An-12B	347401

TC - TURKEY

ACT AIRLINES — 9T / RUN

☐	TC-ACC	A300B4-203F	147
☐	TC-ACD	A300B4-203F	075
☐	TC-ACE	A300B4-203F	154
☐	TC-ACU	A300B4-203F	183
☐	TC-ACY	A300B4-203F	107
☐	TC-ACZ	A300B4-203F	105

ANADOLU JET

☐	TC-JDT	B737-4Y0	25261/2258	
☐	TC-JEU	B737-4Y0	26078/2431	
☐	TC-JEY	B737-4Y0	26086/2475	
☐	TC-JEZ	B737-4Y0	26088/2487	
☐	TC-JGA	B737-8F2/W	29785/544	♦
☐	TC-JGC	B737-8F2/W	29787/771	♦
☐	TC-JGF	B737-8F2/W	29790/1088	♦
☐	TC-JHG	B737-8GJ/W	34958/2688	
☐	TC-JHH	B737-8GJ/W	34959/2719	
☐	TC-JHI	B737-8FH/W	35092/2160	
☐	TC-JHJ	B737-86Q	30296/1647	♦
☐	TC-JKF	B737-76N/W	32684/1889	
☐	TC-JKG	B737-76N/W	34754/2172	
☐	TC-JKH	B737-76N/W	34757/2241	
☐	TC-JKI	B737-76N/W	34758/2266	
☐	TC-JKL	B737-76N/W	34753/2165	
☐	TC-JKM	B737-76N/W	34755/2187	
☐	TC-JKS	B737-73V	32419/1321	♦
☐	TC-JKT	B737-73V	32420/1341	♦

ATLASJET INTERNATIONAL — KK / KKK

☐	TC-OGI	A320-232	0640	
☐	TC-OGJ	A320-232	0676	
☐	TC-ETF	A321-231	1438	>SVA
☐	TC-ETH	A321-231	0968	
☐	TC-ETJ	A321-231	0974	
☐	TC-ETM	A321-131	0604	
☐	TC-ETN	A321-131	0614	
☐	TC-ETR	A321-211	2117	♦
☐	TC-ETV	A321-231	1950	♦
☐	TC-ETK	A330-223	358	Lst SVA
☐	TC-ETL	A330-223	364	>SVA
☐	TC-ETP	A330-223	343	♦
☐	TC-ETE	B757-2Q8	30044/954	♦
☐	TC-ETG	B757-256	26254/905	>SVA
☐	TC-OGS	B757-256	29307/924	>SVA
☐	TC-OGT	B757-256	29308/935	>SVA

BEST AIR — 5F / BST

☐	TC-TUA	MD-82	49138/1090

BORAJET

☐	TC-YAB	ATR 72-212A	588
☐	TC-YAC	ATR 72-212A	701
☐	TC-YAD	ATR 72-212A	702

CORENDON AIR — 7H / CAI

☐	TC-TJB	B737-3Q8	27633/2878	
☐	TC-TJC	B737-4Q8	25374/2562	
☐	TC-TJD	B737-4Q8	25375/2598	
☐	TC-TJE	B737-4Y0	26073/2375	
☐	TC-TJF	B737-4Y0	26078/2431	
☐	TC-TJG	B737-86J/W	29120/202	♦
☐	TC-TJH	B737-86J/W	29121/239	♦

FREEBIRD AIRLINES — FHY

☐ TC-FBE	A320-212	0132
☐ TC-FBF	A320-212	0288
☐ TC-FBH	A320-214	4207 ♦
☐ TC-FBJ	A320-232	0580
☐ TC-FBR	A320-232	2524
☐ TC-FBG	A321-231	0771
☐ TC-FBT	A321-231	0855

IZMIR AIRLINES — IZM

☐ TC-IZH	A319-132	2452
☐ TC-IZM	A319-132	2404
☐ TC-IZR	A319-132	2414
☐ TC-IZA	A320-233	2118
☐ TC-IZL	A320-233	1730

MNG CARGO AIRLINES — MB / MNB

☐ TC-MCA	A300C4-605R	755 ♦
☐ TC-MCB	A300B4-203F	304
☐ TC-MNB	A300B4-203F	292
☐ TC-MNC	A300B4-203F	277
☐ TC-MND	A300C4-203F	212
☐ TC-MNJ	A300B4-203F	123
☐ TC-MNU	A300B4-203F	047
☐ TC-MNV	A300C4-605R	758
☐ TC-MCF	B737-4K5SF	24126/1697 ♦
☐ TC-MBA	F.27 Friendship 500	10654
☐ TC-MBB	F.27 Friendship 500	10660
☐ TC-MBF	F.27 Friendship 600	10405
☐ TC-MBH	F.27 Friendship 500	10550

ONUR AIR — 8Q / OHY

☐ TC-OAA	A300B4-605R	744
☐ TC-OAB	A300B4-605R	749
☐ TC-OAG	A300B4-605R	747
☐ TC-OAH	A300B4-605R	584 >SVA
☐ TC-OAO	A300B4-605R	764
☐ TC-OAZ	A300B4-605R	603
☐ TC-ONT	A300B4-203	138
☐ TC-ONU	A300B4-203	192
☐ TC-OBD	A320-232	0455
☐ TC-OBE	A320-232	0471
☐ TC-OBH	A319-132	1492 ♦
☐ TC-OAE	A321-231	0663
☐ TC-OAF	A321-231	0668
☐ TC-OAI	A321-231	0787
☐ TC-OAK	A321-231	0954
☐ TC-OAL	A321-231	1004
☐ TC-OAN	A321-231	1421
☐ TC-OBF	A321-131	0963
☐ TC-ONJ	A321-131	0385
☐ TC-ONS	A321-131	0364
☐ TC-OCA	A330-322	072 ♦
☐ TC-OCB	A330-342	098 ♦
☐ TC-ONM	MD-88	53546/2167
☐ TC-ONN	MD-88	53547/2176
☐ TC-ONO	MD-88	53548/2180
☐ TC-ONP	MD-88	53549/2185
☐ TC-ONR	MD-88	53550/2187

PEGASUS AIRLINES — 1I / PGT

☐ TC-AAD	B737-5Q8	28201/2999
☐ TC-AAF	B737-58E	29122/2991
☐ TC-AAG	B737-5L9	29234/3068
☐ TC-APD	B737-42R	29107/2997
☐ TC-APR	B737-4Y0	24685/1859
☐ TC-AAE	B737-82R/W	35700/2435
☐ TC-AAH	B737-82R/W	35701/2496
☐ TC-AAI	B737-82R/W	35699/2712
☐ TC-AAJ	B737-82R/W	35702/2810
☐ TC-AAK	B737-8FH/W	35094/2195
☐ TC-AAL	B737-82R/W	35984/2937
☐ TC-AAN	B737-82R/W	38173/3011
☐ TC-AAO	B737-86N/W	28619/534
☐ TC-AAP	B737-86N/W	32736/1113
☐ TC-AAR	B737-86N/W	28624/585
☐ TC-AAS	B737-82R/W	40871/3212 ♦
☐ TC-AAT	B737-82R/W	40872/3227 ♦
☐ TC-AAV	B737-82R/W	40696/3285 ♦
☐ TC-AAY	B737-82R/W	40874/3316 ♦
☐ TC-AAZ	B737-82R/W	40875/3325 ♦
☐ TC-ABP	B737-82R/W	40876/3326 ♦
☐ TC-ACP	B737-82R/W	40697/3354 ♦
☐ TC-ADP	B737-82R/W	40720/3526 ♦
☐ TC-AEP	B737-82R/W	40724/3563 ♦
☐ TC-APH	B737-8S3/W	29250/792
☐ TC-API	B737-86N/W	32732/1056 >BBC
☐ TC-APJ	B737-86N/W	32735/1104
☐ TC-APU	B737-82R	29344/849
☐ TC-	B737-82R/W	o/o ♦
☐ TC-	B737-82R/W	o/o ♦
☐ TC-	B737-82R/W	o/o ♦
☐ TC-	B737-82R/W	o/o ♦

REDSTAR AVIATION

☐ TC-RSA	BAeJetstream 32EP	986

SAGA AIRLINES — SGX

☐ TC-SGA	A300B2K-3C	90 >IRM
☐ TC-SGB	A310-304	562
☐ TC-SGC	A310-304	519 >AFG
☐ TC-SGE	B737-48E	25775/2925
☐ TC-SGF	B737-83N/W	28249/1123
☐ TC-SGG	B737-83N/W	30706/929
☐ TC-SGH	B737-86J/W	28068/36
☐ TC-SGI	B737-86J/W	28069/42 >AFG
☐ TC-SGJ	A330-343	407 >THY ♦

SKY AIRLINES — SHY

☐ TC-SKJ	A320-211	0138
☐ TC-SKK	A320-211	0148
☐ TC-SKT	A320-232	1194 ♦
☐ TC-SKI	A321-231	0811
☐ TC-SKL	A321-231	1670
☐ TC-SKB	B737-430	27004/2344
☐ TC-SKD	B737-4Q8	25372/2280
☐ TC-SKE	B737-4Q8	25163/2264
☐ TC-SKF	B737-4Q8	26291/2513
☐ TC-SKG	B737-4Q8	25371/2195
☐ TC-SKH	B737-8BK	29644/2231
☐ TC-SKM	B737-49R	28882/2845
☐ TC-SKN	B737-94XER/W	36086/2910
☐ TC-SKP	B737-94XER/W	36087/2928
☐ TC-SKR	B737-83N/W	32576/875 ♦
☐ TC-SKS	B737-83N/W	32348/933 ♦
☐ TC-SKU	B737-883	30194/666 ♦

SUNEXPRESS — XQ / SXS

☐ TC-SNE	B737-8HX/W	29684/2539
☐ TC-SNF	B737-8HC/W	36529/2566
☐ TC-SNG	B737-8HC/W	36530/2622
☐ TC-SNH	B737-8FH/W	30826/1732
☐ TC-SNI	B737-8FH/W	29671/1700

	Reg	Type	c/n	Notes
☐	TC-SNJ	B737-86J/W	30827/1632	
☐	TC-SNL	B737-86N/W	34251/1817	♦
☐	TC-SNM	B737-8BK/W	33023/1682	♦
☐	TC-SNN	B737-8HC/W	40775/3250	♦
☐	TC-SNO	B737-8HC/W	40776/3273	♦
☐	TC-SNP	B737-8HC/W	40777/3320	♦
☐	TC-SNR	B737-8HC/W	40754/3352	♦
☐	TC-SNT	B737-8HC/W	40755/3400	♦
☐	TC-SNU	B737-8HC/W	40756/3457	♦
☐	TC-SUG	B737-8CX/W	32365/1209	
☐	TC-SUH	B737-8CX/W	32366/1235	
☐	TC-SUI	B737-8CX/W	32367/1253	
☐	TC-SUJ	B737-8CX/W	32368/1289	
☐	TC-SUL	B737-85F/W	28822/166	
☐	TC-SUM	B737-85F/W	28826/238	
☐	TC-SUO	B737-86Q/W	30272/824	
☐	TC-SUU	B737-86Q/W	30274/845	
☐	TC-SUV	B737-86N/W	30807/829	
☐	TC-SUY	B737-86N/W	30806/790	
☐	TC-SUZ	B737-8HX/W	29649/2515	
☐	TC-SNB	B757-2Q8/W	26271/592	
☐	TC-SNC	B757-2Q8/W	26273/597	
☐	TC-SND	B757-2Q8/W	26268/590	

TAILWIND AIRLINES — TI

	Reg	Type	c/n	Notes
☐	TC-TLA	B737-4Q8	25107/2526	
☐	TC-TLB	B737-4Q8	25108/2551	
☐	TC-TLC	B737-4Q8	25112/2638	
☐	TC-TLD	B737-4Q8	28199/2826	♦
☐	TC-TLE	B737-4Q8	27628/2858	♦

TARHAN AIR — TTH

	Reg	Type	c/n	Notes
☐	TC-TTA	MD-83	48096/1057	[IST]
☐	TC-TTB	MD-82	49144/1096	[IST]

TURKISH AIRLINES — TK / THY

	Reg	Type	c/n	Notes
☐	TC-JCT	A310-304F	502	
☐	TC-JCV	A310-304F	476	
☐	TC-JCY	A310-304F	478	
☐	TC-JCZ	A310-304F	480	
☐	TC-JLM	A319-132	2738	
☐	TC-JLN	A319-132	2739	
☐	TC-JLO	A319-132	2631	
☐	TC-JLP	A319-132	2655	
☐	TC-JLR	A319-132	3142	>BON♦
☐	TC-	A319-132		o/o♦
☐	TC-	A319-132		o/o♦
☐	TC-JLJ	A320-232	1856	
☐	TC-JLK	A320-232	1909	
☐	TC-JLL	A320-232	1956	
☐	TC-JPA	A320-232	2609	
☐	TC-JPB	A320-232	2626	
☐	TC-JPC	A320-232	2928	
☐	TC-JPD	A320-232	2934	
☐	TC-JPE	A320-232	2941	
☐	TC-JPF	A320-232	2984	
☐	TC-JPG	A320-232	3010	
☐	TC-JPH	A320-232	3185	
☐	TC-JPI	A320-232	3208	
☐	TC-JPJ	A320-232	3239	
☐	TC-JPK	A320-232	3257	
☐	TC-JPL	A320-232	3303	
☐	TC-JPM	A320-232	3341	
☐	TC-JPN	A320-232	3558	
☐	TC-JPO	A320-232	3567	
☐	TC-JPP	A320-232	3603	
☐	TC-JPR	A320-232	3654	
☐	TC-JPS	A320-232	3718	
☐	TC-JPT	A320-232	3719	
☐	TC-JPU	A320-214	3896	♦
☐	TC-JPV	A320-214	3931	♦
☐	TC-JPY	A320-214	3949	♦
☐	TC-	A320-2		o/o♦
☐	TC-	A320-2		o/o♦
☐	TC-	A320-2		o/o♦
☐	TC-	A320-2		o/o♦
☐	TC-	A320-2		o/o♦
☐	TC-	A320-2		o/o♦
☐	TC-	A320-2		o/o♦
☐	TC-	A320-2		o/o♦
☐	TC-JMC	A321-231	0806	
☐	TC-JMD	A321-231	0810	
☐	TC-JME	A321-211	1219	
☐	TC-JMF	A321-211	1233	
☐	TC-JMH	A321-231	3637	
☐	TC-JMI	A321-231	3673	
☐	TC-JMJ	A321-231	3688	
☐	TC-JMK	A321-231	3738	
☐	TC-JML	A321-231	3382	
☐	TC-JRA	A321-231	2823	
☐	TC-JRB	A321-231	2868	
☐	TC-JRC	A321-231	2999	
☐	TC-JRD	A321-231	3015	
☐	TC-JRE	A321-231	3126	
☐	TC-JRF	A321-231	3207	
☐	TC-JRG	A321-231	3283	
☐	TC-JRH	A321-231	3350	
☐	TC-JRI	A321-231	3405	
☐	TC-JRJ	A321-231	3429	
☐	TC-JRK	A321-231	3525	
☐	TC-JRL	A321-231	3539	
☐	G-WWBM	A330-243	398	<BMA
☐	TC-JDO	A330-223F	1004	
☐	TC-	A330-223F		o/o♦
☐	TC-JNA	A330-203	697	
☐	TC-JNB	A330-203	704	
☐	TC-JNC	A330-203	742	
☐	TC-JND	A330-203	754	
☐	TC-JNE	A330-203	774	
☐	TC-JNF	A330-202	463	
☐	TC-JNG	A330-202	504	
☐	TC-JNH	A330-343X	1150	♦
☐	TC-JNI	A330-343X	1160	♦
☐	TC-JNJ	A330-343X	1170	♦
☐	TC-JNK	A330-343X	1172	♦
☐	TC-	A330-343X		o/o♦
☐	TC-	A330-343X		o/o♦
☐	TC-	A330-343X		o/o♦
☐	TC-	A330-343X		o/o♦
☐	TC-	A330-343X		o/o♦
☐	TC-	A330-343X		o/o♦
☐	TC-SGJ	A330-343	407	<SGX♦
☐	TC-JDJ	A340-311	23	
☐	TC-JDK	A340-311	25	
☐	TC-JDL	A340-311	57	
☐	TC-JDM	A340-311	115	
☐	TC-JDN	A340-313X	180	
☐	TC-JIH	A340-313X	270	
☐	TC-JII	A340-313X	331	
☐	TC-JIJ	A340-313X	216	
☐	TC-JIK	A340-313X	257	
☐	TC-JDG	B737-4Y0	25181/2203	
☐	TC-JDH	B737-4Y0	25184/2227	
☐	TC-JKJ	B737-752/W	34297/1808	
☐	TC-JKK	B737-752/W	34298/1812	
☐	TC-JKN	B737-752/W	34299/1829	♦
☐	TC-JKO	B737-752/W	34300/1848	♦
☐	TC-JKR	B737-7GL/W	34760/2352	♦
☐	TC-JFC	B737-8F2/W	29765/80	
☐	TC-JFD	B737-8F2/W	29766/87	

	Reg	Type	C/N	Notes
☐	TC-JFE	B737-8F2/W	29767/95	
☐	TC-JFF	B737-8F2/W	29768/99	
☐	TC-JFG	B737-8F2/W	29769/102	
☐	TC-JFH	B737-8F2/W	29770/114	
☐	TC-JFI	B737-8F2/W	29771/228	
☐	TC-JFJ	B737-8F2/W	29772/242	
☐	TC-JFK	B737-8F2/W	29773/259	
☐	TC-JFL	B737-8F2/W	29774/269	
☐	TC-JFM	B737-8F2/W	29775/279	
☐	TC-JFN	B737-8F2/W	29776/308	
☐	TC-JFO	B737-8F2/W	29777/309	
☐	TC-JFP	B737-8F2/W	29778/349	
☐	TC-JFR	B737-8F2/W	29779/370	
☐	TC-JFT	B737-8F2/W	29780/454	
☐	TC-JFU	B737-8F2/W	29781/461	
☐	TC-JFV	B737-8F2/W	29782/490	
☐	TC-JFY	B737-8F2/W	29783/497	
☐	TC-JFZ	B737-8F2/W	29784/539	
☐	TC-JGB	B737-8F2/W	29786/566	
☐	TC-JGD	B737-8F2/W	29788/791	
☐	TC-JGG	B737-8F2/W	34405/1828	
☐	TC-JGH	B737-8F2/W	34406/1852	
☐	TC-JGI	B737-8F2/W	34407/1873	
☐	TC-JGJ	B737-8F2/W	34408/1880	
☐	TC-JGK	B737-8F2/W	34409/1924	
☐	TC-JGL	B737-8F2/W	34410/1927	
☐	TC-JGM	B737-8F2/W	34411/1944	
☐	TC-JGN	B737-8F2/W	34412/1949	
☐	TC-JGO	B737-8F2/W	34413/1972	
☐	TC-JGP	B737-8F2/W	34414/1978	
☐	TC-JGR	B737-8F2/W	34415/1988	
☐	TC-JGS	B737-8F2/W	34416/1996	
☐	TC-JGT	B737-8F2/W	34417/2009	
☐	TC-JGU	B737-8F2/W	34418/2012	
☐	TC-JGV	B737-8F2/W	34419/2021	
☐	TC-JGY	B737-8F2/W	35738/2592	
☐	TC-JGZ	B737-8F2/W	35739/2654	
☐	TC-JHA	B737-8F2/W	35740/2673	
☐	TC-JHB	B737-8F2/W	35741/2685	
☐	TC-JHC	B737-8F2/W	35742/2708	
☐	TC-JHD	B737-8F2/W	35743/2717	
☐	TC-JHE	B737-8F2/W	357442733	
☐	TC-JHF	B737-8F2/W	35745/2748	
☐	TC-	B737-8F2/W		♦
☐	TC-	B737-8F2/W		♦
☐	TC-	B737-8F2/W		♦
☐	TC-	B737-8F2/W		♦
☐	TC-	B737-8F2/W		♦
☐	TC-JJA	B777-35RER	35160/653	
☐	TC-JJB	B777-35RER	35162/666	
☐	TC-JJC	B777-35RER	35164/660	
☐	TC-JJD	B777-35RER	35159/650	
☐	TC-JJE	B777-3F2ER	40707/895	♦
☐	TC-JJF	B777-3F2ER	40708/899	♦
☐	TC-JJG	B777-3F2ER	40791/903	♦
☐	TC-JJH	B777-3F2ER	40792/906	♦
☐	TC-JJI	B777-3F2ER	40709/909	♦
☐	TC-JJJ	B777-3F2ER	40710/913	♦
☐	TC-JJK	B777-3F2ER	40711/916	o/o♦
☐	TC-JJL	B777-3F2ER	40793/919	o/o♦
☐	TC-JJM	B777-3F2ER	40794/923	o/o♦
☐	TC-	B777-3F2ER		o/o♦
☐	TC-	B777-3F2ER		o/o♦

TURKUAZ AIR　　　　　　　　TRK

☐	TC-TCE	A321-211	0666
☐	TC-TCF	A321-211	0775
☐	TC-TCG	A321-211	1905

UNSPED PAKET SERVISI　　　UNS

| ☐ | TC-UPS | SA.226TC Merlin IVA | AT-044Opf UPS |

ULS CARGO

☐	TC-ABK	A300B4-203	101	
☐	TC-AGK	A300B4-203F	117	>AHK
☐	TC-KZU	A300B4-203	173	>AHK
☐	TC-KZV	A300B4-103F	041	
☐	TC-LER	A310-304F	646	
☐	TC-SGM	A310-304F	592	
☐	TC-VEL	A310-304F	622	

TF - ICELAND

AIR ATLANTA　　　　　　　CC / ABD

☐	TF-ELF	A300B4-622RF	529	>TAY♦
☐	TF-ELK	A300B4-622RF	557Opf ETD	
☐	TF-AAA	B747-236B(SCD)	22442/526	>MAS
☐	TF-ALF	B747-428BCF	25302/884	o/o♦
☐	TF-AMD	B747-243M	23476/647	
☐	TF-AME	B747-312	23032/603	
☐	TF-AMI	B747-412(SF)	27066/940	>SVA
☐	TF-AMJ	B747-312	23030/593	
☐	TF-AMS	B747-481BCF	24920/832	Lst SVA
☐	TF-AMT	B747-481	25135/863	Lst SVA
☐	TF-AMU	B747-48EF	27603/1210	Lst SVA
☐	TF-AMV	B747-412	28022/1082	>SVA
☐	TF-ARH	B747-230M(SF)	22669/549	
☐	TF-ARJ	B747-236M	23735/674	>MAS
☐	TF-ARL	B747-230B(SF)	22671/574	
☐	TF-ARM	B747-230B(SF)	22363/490	
☐	TF-ARN	B747-2F6B(SF)	22382/498	>MAS
☐	TF-ARU	B747-344	22970/577	>SVA
☐	TF-ATI	B747-341	24107/702	[VCV]♦
☐	TF-ATJ	B747-341	24108/703	[VCV]
☐	TF-ATZ	B747-236B(SF)	24088/697	

AIR ICELAND　　　　　　　NY / FXI

☐	TF-JMM	Fokker 50	20214
☐	TF-JMN	Fokker 50	20223
☐	TF-JMO	Fokker 50	20205
☐	TF-JMR	Fokker 50	20243
☐	TF-JMS	Fokker 50	20244
☐	TF-JMT	Fokker 50	20250
☐	TF-JMA	DHC-8-106	335
☐	TF-JMB	DHC-8-106	337
☐	TF-JMC	DHC-6 Twin Otter 300	413
☐	TF-JMD	DHC-6 Twin Otter 300	475

BLUEBIRD CARGO　　　　　BF / BBD

☐	TF-BBD	B737-3Y0(SF)	24463/1701	
☐	TF-BBE	B737-36E(SF)	25256/2123	
☐	TF-BBF	B737-36E(SF)	25264/2194	
☐	TF-BBG	B737-36E(SF)	25263/2187	
☐	TF-BBH	B737-4Y0F	23865/1582	
☐	TF-TNM	B737-34S(SF)	29108/2983	♦

ERNIR AIR　　　　　　　　FEI

| ☐ | TF-ORA | BAeJetstream 32 | 925 |
| ☐ | TF-ORC | BAeJetstream 3212 | 981 |

ICEJET　　　　　　　　　ICJ

☐	TF-MIK	Do 328 Jet	3147
☐	TF-MIL	Do 328 Jet	3149
☐	TF-MIO	Do 328 Jet	3181
☐	TF-NPB	Do 328 Jet	3161

ICELANDAIR　　　　　　　FI / ICE

| ☐ | TF-CIB | B757-204 (PCF) | 26962/440 |
| ☐ | TF-FIA | B757-256/W | 29310/938 |

☐	TF-FID	B757-23A (PCF)	24567/257
☐	TF-FIE	B757-23A (PCF)	24566/255
☐	TF-FIG	B757-23APF	24456/237
☐	TF-FIH	B757-208 (PCF)	24739/273
☐	TF-FII	B757-208	24760/281 Lst GBK
☐	TF-FIJ	B757-208/W	25085/368
☐	TF-FIK	B757-2Y0	26151/472 ♦
☐	TF-FIN	B757-208/W	28989/780
☐	TF-FIO	B757-208/W	29436/859
☐	TF-FIP	B757-208/W	30423/916
☐	TF-FIR	B757-256/W	26242/593
☐	TF-FIU	B757-256/W	26243/603
☐	TF-FIV	B757-208/W	30424/956
☐	TF-FIX	B757-308/W	29434/1004
☐	TF-FIZ	B757-256/W	30052/948
☐	TF-FIB	B767-383ER	25365/395

ICELAND EXPRESS

☐	G-STRF	B737-76N/W	29885/1120
☐	G-STRN	B737-7L9/W	28007/136

TG - GUATEMALA

AVIATECA

☐	TG-TRA	ATR 42-300(QC)	312
☐	TG-TRB	ATR 42-300(QC)	317

AVCOM

☐	TG-JAY	DHC-7-102	46

DHL DE GUATEMALA — L3 / JOS

☐	TG-DHP	ATR 42-300	52

INTER — 9O / TSP

☐	TG-MYH	ATR 42-300	113 >APP

TI - COSTA RICA

SANSA REGIONAL — RZ / LRS

☐	TG-RYM	ATR 42-300	109

TACA COSTA RICA — TI / TAT

☐	TI-BCF	ERJ-190AR	19000205
☐	TI-BCG	ERJ-190AR	19000215
☐	TI-BCH	ERJ-190AR	19000221
☐	TI-BCI	ERJ-190AR	19000228

TJ - CAMEROON

CAMEROON AIRLINES — UY / UYC

☐	TJ-CAC	B767-33AER	28138/822 [YAO]
☐	TJ-CAD	B767-231ER	22564/14
☐	TJ-CCG	HS.748 Srs.2B/435	1805 [DLA]

TL - CENTRAL AFRICAN REPUBLIC

AFRICA WEST

☐	S9-BOZ	An-12A	2340803 <GLE
☐	UN-11376	An-12BK	8345805

CENTRAFRIQUE AIR EXPRESS

☐	TL-ADR	B737-268	21281/472
☐	TL-ADY	B727-223	21385/1331

LOBAYE AIRWAYS

☐	TL-ADU	B737-247	23518/1265

PRIVILEGE JET AIRLINES

☐	TL-ADW	L-1011-500 Tristar	293B-1242

TN - CONGO BRAZZAVILLE

AERO FRET BUSINESS

☐	EX-124	An-12BK	7345403
☐	TN-AHH	An-24RV	47309705

AEROSERVICE — BF / RSR

☐	ER-AZP	An-24RV	17307002 <PXA

AIR CONGO INTERNATIONAL

☐	TN-AHL	AVIC 1 MA-60	405
☐	TN-AHN	AVIC 1 MA-60	406
☐	TN-AHO	AVIC 1 MA-60	408

BRAZZA AIRWAYS

☐	TN-AHZ	An-12B	8345507

CANADIAN AIRWAYS CONGO

☐	EX-008	An-24RV	37308307

TRANSAIR CONGO — Q8 / TSG

☐	EX-041	An-24B	99901908
☐	TN-AFZ	B727-23	19839/542
☐	TN-AGK	An-12BP	402006
☐	TN-AHI	B737-247	23609/1403
☐	TN-AIN	B737-236	23172/1091
☐	ZS-XGV	F.28 Fellowship 4000	11128

TR - GABON

AIR SERVICE GABON — X7 / AGB

☐	TR-LFJ	DHC-8-311	332
☐	TR-LGC	DHC-8-102	241
☐	TR-LGR	DHC-8-102	237
☐	TR-LHF	DHC-8-102	206

AVIREX — G2 / AVX

☐	TR-LGP	F.28 Fellowship 4000	11126
☐	TR-LHG	DC-9-32	47198/302

GABON AIRLINES — GY / GBK

☐	TF-FII	B757-208	24760/281 <ICE
☐	TR-LHP	B767-222	21877/46
☐	TR-LHQ	B767-222	21878/48

NOUVELLES AIR AFFAIRES GABON — NVS

☐	TR-CLB	DHC-8Q-314	545
☐	TR-LGQ	Fokker 100	11424
☐	PH-JXK	Fokker 50	20233 <DNM

SKY GABON SA — GV

☐	C-FHNM	Convair 580F	454 Lsf NRL

SOLENTA AVIATION GABON

☐	TR-LID	An-26	47302203
☐	TR-LIE	An-26	87307504

TS - TUNISIA

KARTHAGO AIRLINES 5R / KAJ

☐ TS-IEG	B737-31S	29116/3005
☐ TS-IEJ	B737-322	24655/1814

NOUVELAIR BJ / LBT

☐ TS-INA	A320-214	1121	
☐ TS-INB	A320-214	1175	
☐ TS-INC	A320-214	1744	
☐ TS-IND	A320-212	0348	>LAA
☐ TS-INE	A320-212	0222	>LAA
☐ TS-INF	A320-212	0299	
☐ TS-ING	A320-214	4347	♦
☐ TS-INI	A320-212	0301	
☐ TS-INL	A320-212	0400	
☐ TS-INN	A320-212	0793	
☐ TS-INO	A320-214	3480	
☐ TS-	A320-214		o/o♦
☐ TS-	A320-214		o/o♦
☐ TS-IQA	A321-211	0970	
☐ TS-IQB	A321-211	0995	

SEVENAIR UG / TUI

☐ TS-LBA	ATR 42-300	245	>MTW
☐ TS-LBC	ATR 72-202	281	
☐ TS-LBD	ATR 72-202	756	
☐ TS-LBE	ATR 72-202	794	
☐ TS-ISA	CRJ-900	15091	
☐ TS-	CRJ-900		o/o

TUNISAIR TU / TAR

☐ TS-IPA	A300B4-605R	558	
☐ TS-IPB	A300B4-605R	563	
☐ TS-IPC	A300B4-605R	505	
☐ TS-IMJ	A319-114	0869	
☐ TS-IMK	A319-114	0880	
☐ TS-IMO	A319-114	1479	
☐ TS-IMQ	A319-112	3096	
☐ TS-IMB	A320-211	0119	
☐ TS-IMC	A320-211	0124	
☐ TS-IMD	A320-211	0205	
☐ TS-IME	A320-211	0123	
☐ TS-IMF	A320-211	0370	
☐ TS-IMG	A320-211	0390	
☐ TS-IMH	A320-211	0402	>MTW
☐ TS-IMI	A320-211	0511	
☐ TS-IML	A320-211	0958	
☐ TS-IMM	A320-211	0975	
☐ TS-IMN	A320-211	1187	
☐ TS-IMP	A320-211	1700	
☐ TS-IMR	A320-214	4344	♦
☐ TS-	A320-214		o/o♦
☐ TS-	A320-214		o/o♦
☐ TS-	A320-214		o/o♦
☐ TS-	A320-214		o/o♦
☐ TS-	A320-214		o/o♦
☐ TS-	A320-214		o/o♦
☐ TS-	A320-214		o/o♦
☐ TS-IEB	B737-7L9/W	28015/785	>MTW
☐ TS-IOG	B737-5H3	26639/2253	
☐ TS-IOH	B737-5H3	26640/2474	
☐ TS-IOI	B737-5H3	27257/2583	
☐ TS-IOJ	B737-5H3	27912/2701	
☐ TS-IOK	B737-6H3	29496/268	
☐ TS-IOL	B737-6H3	29497/282	
☐ TS-IOM	B737-6H3	29498/310	
☐ TS-ION	B737-6H3	29499/510	
☐ TS-IOP	B737-6H3	29500/543	
☐ TS-IOQ	B737-6H3	29501/563	
☐ TS-IOR	B737-6H3	29502/816	

TT - CHAD

AMW TCHAD MCW

☐ TT-DAE	L-1011-100 Tristar	193N-1101
☐ TT-DWE	L-1011-100 Tristar	193N-1093

MID EXPRESS TCHAD

☐ TT-DAX	B707-3K1C	20803/878

TOUMAI AIR CHAD 9D / THE

☐ OD-WOL	B737-232	23083/1008	<WLB
☐ TT-EAS	F.28 Fellowship 4000	11173	

TU - IVORY COAST

AIR INTER IVOIRE NTV

☐ TU-TDC	Fairchild FH-227B	558

AIR IVOIRE VU / VUN

☐ F-OIVU	A321-211	1017	
☐ TU-TIW	F.28 Fellowship 4000	11233	
☐ TU-TIX	F.28 Fellowship 4000	11237	
☐ TU-TSC	B737-522	25001/1948	
☐ TU-TSD	B737-522	25008/1987	
☐ TU-TSE	B737-522	25009/1999	

TY - BENIN

BENIN GOLF AIR A8 / BGL

☐ XU-RKA	B737-2H4	22061/639	<RKH
☐ XU-RKC	B737-2H4	22903/905	<RKH
☐ XU-RKG	B727-223F	19475/511	
☐ 3D-BGA	B737-2H4	21722/568	<RFC

ROYAL AIR

☐ TY-KEC	L-1011-1 Tristar	193C-1225
☐ TY-KEQ	L-1011-1 Tristar	193C-1199
☐ TY-KEU	L-1011-1 Tristar	193C-1226

TZ - MALI

ASKARI AVIATION

☐ TZ-SGI	L1011-250 Tristar	193C-1245
☐ TZ-SPA	L1011-250 Tristar	193C-1237

COMPAGNIE AERIENNE DU MALI

☐ TZ-RCA	CRJ-200ER	7392	♦
☐ TZ-RMA	MD-87	49832/1703	
☐ TZ-RMB	MD-87	49841/1751	
☐ TZ-RMK	MD-83	53463/2089	

MALI AIR TRANSPORT

☐ TZ-NBA	B727-2K5/W	21853/1640

T8A - PALAU

PACIFICFLYER PI / PFL

☐ CS-TEI	A310-304	495	<HFY♦

UK - UZBEKISTAN

AVIALEASING — EC / TWN

N5057E	An-26	6101
UK 11418	An-12B	402504
UK 12002	An-12B	402002
UK 26001	An-26B	67314402
UK 26003	An-26	7310406

QANOT SHARQ — QNT

UK 76353	Il-76TD	102314454

TAPO AVIA — 4C / CTP

UK 11807	An-12BK	346910
UK 58644	An-12BP	2340303
UK 76375	Il-76TD	1033414496
UK 76821	Il-76TD	23441200

UZBEKISTAN AIRWAYS — HY / UZB

UK 31004	A300B4-622RF	717	
UK 31005	A300B4-622RF	722	
UK 31001	A310-324	574	
UK 31002	A310-324	576	
UK 31003	A310-324	706	
UK 33011	A320-214	4371	◆
UK 33012	A320-214	4395	◆
UK 33014	A320-214	4417	◆
UK 33015	A320-214	4485	◆
UK 33016	A320-214	4492	◆
UK	A320-214	o/o	◆
UK	A320-214	o/o	◆
UK	A320-214	o/o	◆
UK 46223	An-24B	77303102	
UK 46360	An-24B	7305901	
UK 46373	An-24B	7306004	
UK 46387	An-24B	7306110	
UK 46392	An-24B	7306205	
UK 46573	An-24B	87304807	
UK 46594	An-24B	97305104	
UK 46623	An-24RV	37308710	
UK 46658	An-24RV	47309304	
UK 47274	An-24B	7306404	
UK 80001	Avro 146-RJ85	E2312	
UK 80002	Avro 146-RJ85	E2309	
UK 80003	Avro 146-RJ85	E2319	
UK 75700	B757-23P	28338/731 Opf Govt	
VP-BUB	B757-23P	30060/875	
VP-BUD	B757-23P	30061/886	
VP-BUH	B757-231	30339/896	
VP-BUI	B757-231	28487/878	
VP-BUJ	B757-231	28488/884	
UK 67000	B767-33PER	35796/958	
UK 67001	B767-33PER	28370/635	
VP-BUE	B767-3CBER	33469/904	
VP-BUF	B767-33PER	33078/928	
VP-BUZ	B767-33PER	28392/650	
UK 76351	Il-76TD	1013408240	[TAS]
UK 76358	Il-76TD	1023410339	
UK 76359	Il-76TD	1033414483	
UK 76426	Il-76TD	1043419644	
UK 76428	Il-76TD	1043419648	
UK 76449	Il-76TD	1023403058	
UK 76782	Il-76TD	93498971	
UK 76793	Il-76TD	93498951	
UK 76794	Il-76TD	93498954	[TAS]
UK 76805	Il-76TD	1003403109	
UK 76811	Il-76TD	1013407223	[TAS]
UK 76813	Il-76TD	1013408246	[TAS]
UK 76824	Il-76TD	1023410327	[TAS]
UK 86056	Il-86	51483203023	[TAS]
UK 86064	Il-86	51483203031	[TAS]
UK 86090	Il-86	51483207061	[TAS]
UK 91102	Il-114-100	109380202	
UK 91104	Il-114-100	2093800204	
UK 91105	Il-114-100	2063800205	
UK 91106	Il-114-100	2063800206	
UK 85575	Tu-154B-2	83A575	[TAS]
UK 85578	Tu-154B-2	83A578	[TAS]
UK 85600	Tu-154B-2	84A600	[TAS]
UK 85711	Tu-154M	91A887	[TAS]
UK 85764	Tu-154M	93A947	[TAS]
UK 85776	Tu-154M	93A958	[TAS]
UK 87923	Yak-40	9741455	
UK 88194	Yak-40	9621448	
UK 88217	Yak-40	9630350	

UP - KAZAKHSTAN

AEROTRANS — ATG

UN-85521	Tu-154B-2	81A521
UN-85569	Tu-154B-2	82A569

AEROTUR AIR — RAN

UP-T5407	Tu-154M	87A754

AIR ALMATY — LMY

UP-AN215	An-12BP	6344305
UP-I7601	Il-76TD	1013409295
UP-I7602	Il-76T	3427796
UP-I7603	Il-76	83414432
UP-I7633	Il-76T	93420594

AIR ASTANA — KC / KZR

P4-YAS	A319-132	3614	
P4-PAS	A320-232	2128	
P4-SAS	A320-232	2016	
P4-TAS	A320-232	2828	
P4-UAS	A320-232	2987	
P4-VAS	A320-232	3141	
P4-WAS	A320-232	3484	
P4-XAS	A320-232	3519	
P4-NAS	A321-231	1042	
P4-OAS	A321-231	1204	
P4-EAS	B757-2G5/W	29488/830	
P4-FAS	B757-2G5/W	29489/834	
P4-GAS	B757-2G5/W	28112/708	
P4-MAS	B757-28A/W	28833/782	
P4-KCA	B767-306ER	27612/647	
P4-KCB	B767-306ER	27614/661	
	ERJ-190LR	o/o	◆
	ERJ-190LR	o/o	◆
P4-HAS	Fokker 50	20198	
P4-IAS	Fokker 50	20188	
P4-JAS	Fokker 50	20195	
P4-KAS	Fokker 50	20187	
P4-LAS	Fokker 50	20193	
P4-RAS	Fokker 50	20237	

ASIA CONTINENTAL AIRLINES — CID

☐ UP-I7617	Il-76TD	013430890
☐ UP-I7618	Il-76T	013428831
☐ UP-I7627	Il-76T	0003423699

ATMA — AMA

☐ UP-AN211	An-12B	2348207
☐ UP-AN212	An-12TB	1347701
☐ UP-AN213	An-12BP	2340806
☐ UN-76499	Il-76TD	23441186

ATYRAU AIR WAYS — IP / JOL

☐ UP-T3405	Tu-134A	40150
☐ UP-T3406	Tu-134A	31218
☐ UN-65069	Tu-134A-3	49908
☐ UN-65070	Tu-134A-3	49912
☐ UP-T5406	Tu-154M	93A965

AVIA JAYNAR — SAP

☐ UP-AN401	An-24B	88901605

BEIBARS

☐ UP-I7625	Il-76TD	33446350
☐ UP-I7626	Il-76M	1013409303

BERKUT AIR — BEK

☐ UP-Y4003	Yak-40	9632048
☐ UP-Y4021	Yak-40	9411533
☐ UN-87306	Yak-40	9302229
☐ UN-88191	Yak-40	9621148
☐ UN-88260	Yak-40	9711552

BERKUT STATE AIR COMPANY — BEC

☐ UP-AN205	An-12BP	2348304
☐ UP-B6701	B767-2DXER	32954/861
☐ UP-I7604	Il-76TD	1033414485
☐ UP-I7605	Il-76TD	1033416520
☐ UP-T5401	Tu-154M	91A889
☐ UP-B5701	B757-2M6ER	23454/102
☐ UN-85464	Tu-154B-2	80A464

DETA AIR

☐ UP-DC101	DC-10-40F	47823/306
☐ UP-DC102	DC-10-40F	47855/349
☐ UP-I6206	Il-62M	3242321
☐ UP-I6207	Il-62M	1545951
☐ UP-I6209	Il-62M	3139956

EAST WING — EWZ

☐ UN-11006	An-12BP	1347909
☐ UN-11008	An-12B	4342505
☐ UN-11009	An-12B	53403408
☐ UN-11010	An-12B	53403606
☐ UN-26087	An-26	27312601
☐ UP-I7621	Il-76TD	0013434018
☐ UP-I7622	Il-76T	03426765
☐ UP-I7623	Il-76TD	033448404
☐ UP-I7624	Il-76TD	023442218
☐ UN-76497	Il-76T	043402039

EASTERN EXPRESS

☐ UN-11020	An-12	
☐ UP-AN203	An-12BK	347408
☐ UN-11021	An-12	
☐ UP-I7606	Il-76T	33446325

☐ UP-I7607	Il-76TD	33447364	
☐ UP-I7612	Il-76T	3425746	
☐ UP-I7628	Il-76TD	53460790	
☐ UP-I7629	Il-76TD	1013408257	
☐ UN-76029	Il-76TD	1013406294	

EURO-ASIA INTERNATIONAL — 5B / EAK

☐ UP-Y4026	Yak-40	9510639
☐ UP-Y4027	Yak-40K	9741856
☐ UP-Y4028	Yak-40K	9710453
☐ UP-Y4030	Yak-40	9541444

EXCELLENT GLIDE

☐ UP-Y4208	Yak-42D	

INVESTAVIA — TLG

☐ UP-I6210	Il-62M	3255333

KAZ AIR TRANS

☐ UP-B3704	B737-2H3	22624/758

KAZAIR WEST — KAW

☐ UP-T3402	Tu-134B-3	63187
☐ UP-Y4015	Yak-40K	9831958

KAZAKHMYS

☐ UP-Y4012	Yak-40K	9741755
☐ UP-Y4014	Yak-40K	9732054

KAZZINC

☐ UP-Y4006	Yak-40K	9740556
☐ UP-Y4204	Yak-42	

KHOZU AVIA — OZU

☐ UP-Y4201	Yak-42D	4520423302017
☐ UP-Y4202	Yak-42D	4520423402116
☐ UP-Y4204	Yak-42D	4520423408016

KOKSHETAU AIRLINES — KRT

☐ UN-86505	Il-62M	1748445	[ALA]
☐ UN-86506	Il-62M	1138234	[ALA]
☐ UN-87913	Yak-40	9730255	
☐ UN-88221	Yak-40	9630750	
☐ UN-88277	Yak-40	9721953	

MAKAIR — AKM

☐ UP-T5405	Tu-154M	89A823

MEGA AIRCOMPANY — MGK

☐ UP-B2701	B727-232	22045/1602
☐ UP-B2702	B727-232	21861/1554
☐ UP-B2703	B727-232	21584/1478
☐ UP-I1801	Il-18D	187010204
☐ UP-I1802	Il-18E	185008603
☐ UP-I1803	Il-18V	184006903
☐ UP-I1804	Il-18GrM	186009202
☐ UN-26517	An-26	7002

MIRAS AIR

☐ UP-AN201	An-12BP	01348007

SAMALAIR — SAV

☐ UP-T3401	Tu-134AK-3	63684	[ALA]
☐ UN-86507	Il-62M	4242654	

SAT AIRLINES SOZ

☐ UP-T3403	Tu-134A-3	62545
☐ UP-T3404	Tu-134A-3	66212
☐ UN-A3101	A310-322	399
☐ UN-65720	Tu-134B-3	62820

SAYAKHAT W7 / SAH

☐ UP-I7613	Il-76	1023412395
☐ UP-I7615	Il-76TD	1003401015
☐ UP-T5402	Tu-154M	86A726
☐ UP-T5403	Tu-154M	86A728
☐ UP-T5404	Tu-154M	86A729

SAYATAIR SYM

☐ UP-I6204	Il-62M	4255152
☐ UP-I6205	Il-62M	3357947

SCAT AIRCOMPANY DV / VSV

☐ UP-AN202	An-12BP	3341201
☐ UP-AN404	An-24B	17307303
☐ UP-AN405	An-24B	77303508
☐ UP-AN406	An-24B	77303604
☐ UP-AN407	An-24B	87305305
☐ UP-AN408	An-24B	97305608
☐ UP-AN409	An-24B	7305909
☐ UP-AN410	An-24B	7306104
☐ UP-AN411	An-24B	87304106
☐ UP-AN412	An-24B	87304309
☐ UP-AN413	An-24RV	37309305
☐ UP-AN414	An-24RV	37308305
☐ UP-AN415	An-24RV	47309505
☐ UP-AN416	An-24RV	47309604
☐ UP-AN417	An-24RV	47309910
☐ UP-AN418	An-24B	89901810
☐ UP-AN419	An-24RV	27307609
☐ UP-AN420	An-24B	7306308
☐ UP-AN421	An-24B	7306407
☐ UP-AN422	An-24B	7306504
☐ UP-AN423	An-24RV	67310509
☐ UP-AN424	An-24RV	27307509
☐ UP-AN425	An-24B	79901307
☐ UP-AN426	An-24B	17307406
☐ UP-AN601	An-26	503
☐ LY-FLB	B737-322/W	24667/1893
☐ UP-B3701	B737-230	22123/726
☐ UP-B3702	B737-277	22650/806
☐ LY-FLG	B757-204	27237/602
☐ UP-Y4203	Yak-42D	
☐ UP-Y4205	Yak-42D	
☐ UP-Y4210	Yak-42D	

SEMEYAVIA SMK

☐ UP-Y4016	Yak-40K	9810557
☐ UN-87204	Yak-40K	9810157

STARLINE KZ

☐ UP-B2704	B727-225F	22046/1604

TULPAR AIR SERVICE 2T / TUX

☐ UP-AN427	An-24B	97305001
☐ UN-46448	An-24B	87304410
☐ UN-46492	An-24RV	27305001
☐ UN-46611	An-24RV	37308608
☐ UN-26579	An-26B	13404

YUZHNAYA AIRCOMPANY UGN

☐ UN-75001	Il-18D	187009904
☐ UN-85478	Tu-154B-2	81A478

ZHETYSU AVIA JTU

☐ UP-Y4019	Yak-40K	9741855
☐ UN-87931	Yak-40	9740256

ZHEZHAIR KZH

☐ UP-Y4012	Yak-40	9742055
☐ UP-Y4013	Yak-40	9731055

UR - UKRAINE

AERO-CHARTER UKRAINE DW / UCR

☐ UR-CDW	Yak-40	9610546
☐ UR-DAP	Yak-40	9521241
☐ UR-DWC	Yak-40	9541144
☐ UR-LRZ	Yak-40K	9641851
☐ UR-88290	Yak-40K	9840459
☐ UR-DWA	An-26	47313905
☐ UR-DWB	An-26B	6207
☐ UR-DWD	An-26B	10103
☐ UR-DWF	An-12BK	8345802
☐ UR-DWG	An-12BP	8345710

AEROMOST KHARKOV HT / AHW

☐ UR-14002	An-140	36525302006

AEROSTAR UAR

☐ UR-AIS	Yak-40	9211821
☐ UR-BWH	Yak-40	9640951

AEROSVIT AIRLINES VV / AEW

☐ UR-46677	An-24RV	47309609	
☐ UR-47294	An-24RV	7306604	<URP
☐ UR-47312	An-24RV	57310403	
☐ UR-	An-148-100B		o/o♦
☐ UR-	An-148-100B		o/o♦
☐ UR-	An-148-100B		o/o♦
☐ UR-	An-148-100B		o/o♦
☐ UR-	An-148-100B		o/o♦
☐ UR-BVY	B737-2Q8	22760/852	
☐ UR-VVA	B737-3Q8	24492/1808	
☐ UR-VVE	B737-448	24521/1788	
☐ UR-VVL	B737-448	25052/2036	
☐ UR-VVM	B737-448	25736/2269	
☐ UR-VVN	B737-4Y0	24903/1978	♦
☐ UR-VVP	B737-4Q8	26290/2482	
☐ UR-VVQ	B737-5L9	29235/3076	
☐ UR-VVR	B737-3Q8	24699/1886	
☐ UR-VVS	B737-5Q8	26324/2735	
☐ UR-VVU	B737-5Q8	26323/2770	
☐ UR-AAG	B767-33AER	25532/442	♦
☐ UR-AAH	B767-33AER	25534/477	♦
☐ UR-AAJ	B767-33AER	25533/454	♦
☐ UR-DNM	B767-322ER	25280/391	♦
☐ UR-VVF	B767-383ER	24476/274	
☐ UR-VVO	B767-383ER	24475/273	
☐ UR-VVT	B767-3Q8ER	28132/692	
☐ UR-VVV	B767-33AER	25536/504	♦
☐ UR-VVW	B767-33AER	27189/521	o/o♦

AEROVIS AIRLINES VIZ

☐ UR-CBF	An-12BP	2340507

☐	UR-CBG	An-12BP	6343705
☐	UR-CCP	An-12A	2340505
☐	UR-CEX	An-12B	4342103
☐	UR-CEZ	An-12B	6344304
☐	UR-CFB	An-12BP	6343802
☐	UR-CGU	An-12BK	7345203

AIR URGA 3N / URG

☐	UR-CFU	An-24RV	7310609
☐	UR-ELC	An-24RV	57310410
☐	UR-ELK	An-24RV	57310203
☐	UR-ELL	An-24RV	67310503
☐	UR-ELM	An-24RV	67310506
☐	UR-ELN	An-24B	89901607
☐	UR-ELO	An-24RV	47309507
☐	UR-ELT	An-24RV	27307809
☐	UR-ELW	An-24RV	57310109
☐	UR-46311	An-24B	97305307
☐	UR-46464	An-24RV	27307810
☐	UR-ELB	An-26B	14005
☐	UR-ELD	An-26B	14010
☐	UR-ELE	An-26B	12108
☐	UR-ELF	An-26B	12204
☐	UR-ELG	An-26B	12902
☐	UR-ELH	An-26B	12908
☐	UR-ELP	An-26B	47313408
☐	UR-ELR	An-26B	9807

ANTONOV AIRLINES ADB

☐	UR-11315	An-12BP	4342307	
☐	UR-09307	An-22A	43481244	
☐	UR-74010	An-74T	36547030450	
☐	UR-82007	An-124-100	01005	
☐	UR-82008	An-124-100M-150	01006	
☐	UR-82009	An-124-100	01007	
☐	UR-82027	An-124-100	02288	
☐	UR-82029	An-124-100	02630	
☐	UR-82072	An-124-100	3359136	
☐	UR-82073	An-124-100	4359139	
☐	UR-82060	An-225	19530503763	

ARP 410 AIRLINES URP

☐	UR-CDY	An-24RV	47309305	
☐	UR-PWA	An-24RV	67302608	
☐	UR-47256	An-24RV	27307708	
☐	UR-47294	An-24RV	7306604	>AEW
☐	UR-47297	An-24RV	7306610	
☐	UR-BWZ	An-26B	12208	
☐	UR-CBJ	An-26B	11401	
☐	UR-26581	An-26B	57313503	

ARTEM AVIA ABA

☐	UR-26094	An-26B	12706

AS AVIAKOMPANIA

☐	UR-30036	An-30	703

AVIANT UAK

☐	UR-ZYD	An-124-100	19530502843	>MXU
☐	UR-48023	An-32B	3409	
☐	UR-48086	An-32P	2901	
☐	UR-48087	An-32B	2904	

AZOV-AVIA AZV

☐	UR-ZVB	Il-76MD	53463902
☐	UR-ZVC	Il-76TD	53463891

CHALLANGE AERO 5U / CLO

☐	UR-CLB	Yak-40K	9731555
☐	UR-ECL	Yak-40K	9932059
☐	UR-88309	Yak-40	9840859
☐	UR-88310	Yak-40	9940760

CONSTANTA AIRLINES UZA

☐	UR-ETG	Yak-40	9531143
☐	UR-FRU	Yak-40	9440737

DNEPR-AIR Z6 / UDN

☐	UR-IVK	B737-3L9	24571/1815	
☐	UR-KIV	B737-4Y0	24686/1861	
☐	UR-DNC	B737-5L9	28995/2947	
☐	UR-DND	B737-5L9	28722/2868	
☐	UR-DNH	B737-5Y0	24696/1960	
☐	UR-DNJ	B737-36Q	28659/2680	
☐	UR-DNA	ERJ-145EU	145088	
☐	UR-DNB	ERJ-145EU	145094	
☐	UR-DNE	ERJ-145EU	145357	
☐	UR-DNF	ERJ-145EU	145404	
☐	UR-DNG	ERJ-145EP	145394	
☐	UR-DNI	ERJ-145EP	145325	
☐	UR-DNK	ERJ-145EU	145039	
☐	UR-DNL	ERJ-145EU	145042	
☐	UR-DNO	ERJ-145EP	145237	
☐	UR-DNP	ERJ-145EP	145290	
☐	UR-DNQ	ERJ-145EP	145315	
☐	UR-DNV	ERJ-145LR	145738	♦
☐	UR-DNW	ERJ-145LR	145286	♦
☐	UR-DNX	ERJ-145LR	145316	♦
☐	UR-DNY	ERJ-145LR	145436	♦
☐	UR-DNZ	ERJ-145LR	145282	♦
☐	UR-DPB	ERJ-145LR	145250	♦
☐	UR-BWE	Yak-40	9530943	
☐	UR-BWF	Yak-40	9711352	
☐	UR-PIT	Yak-40	9610647	
☐	UR-42449	Yak-42D	14010180118	

DONBASSAERO 7D / UDC

☐	UR-DAA	A320-211	0085	
☐	UR-DAB	A320-231	0230	
☐	UR-DAC	A320-233	0733	
☐	UR-DAD	A320-233	0747	
☐	UR-DAE	A320-211	0285	♦
☐	UR-	A320-231	0362	o/o♦
☐	UR-DAF	A321-231	1869	♦
☐	UR-42327	Yak-42	44021610506	
☐	UR-42366	Yak-42	48140470110	
☐	UR-42372	Yak-42D	39142661010	
☐	UR-42377	Yak-42D	10144790711	
☐	UR-42381	Yak-42D	22014576	♦
☐	UR-42383	Yak-42D	20162010312	

GORLITSA AIRLINES GOR

☐	UR-BXU	An-26B-100	17311703
☐	UR-BXV	An-26B-100	12110
☐	UR-GLS	An-26B	7310109
☐	UR-YMR	An-12BK	9346302

ILYICH AVIA

☐	UR-MMK	Yak-40	9521540
☐	UR-14007	An-140-100	36525305029
☐	UR-14008	An-140-100	36525305032

ISD AVIA — ISD

☐	UR-CAR	Yak-40K	9741756
☐	UR-ISD	Yak-40	9530541

KHARKOV AVIATION PRODUCTION ASSN

☐	UR-NPO	LET L-410UVP-E	871932
☐	UR-67472	LET L-410UVP	841237

KHORS AIR — X9 / KHO

☐	UR-CBV	DC-9-51	47772/890	
☐	UR-CBY	DC-9-51	47773/891	>UKM
☐	UR-CCT	DC-9-51	47696/808	>UKM
☐	UR-BXI	MD-82	53170/2065	
☐	UR-BXL	MD-82	49512/1548	
☐	UR-BXN	MD-83	49569/1405	>IRK
☐	UR-CBN	MD-82	49490/1352	
☐	UR-CBO	MD-82	49483/1314	
☐	UR-CDN	MD-83	53520/2137	
☐	UR-CDP	MD-83	49769/1559	
☐	UR-CDR	MD-83	49949/1906	
☐	UR-CDQ	MD-82	49372/1252	>IZG
☐	UR-CEL	MD-83	49390/1269	♦
☐	UR-CHJ	MD-82	53066/1938	
☐	UR-CHK	MD-82	49188/1172	
☐	UR-CHM	MD-83	53465/2093	♦
☐	UR-CHP	MD-83	53466/2101	♦
☐	UR-CHQ	MD-83	53488/2134	♦
☐	UR-CHS	MD-83	49572/1468	>IRK
☐	UR-CHZ	MD-82	53169/2063	
☐	UR-CJC	MD-83	49986/1842	♦
☐	UR-	MD-83	53198/1847	♦

KIROVOHRADAVIA — KAD

☐	UR-87814	Yak-40	9230524

KRYM — KYM

☐	UR-46833	An-24RV	17306710	[SIP]
☐	UR-47265	An-24RV	27307807	

LIZING TEKHTRANS

☐	UR-NTA	An-148	101

LUGANSK AVIATION ENTERPRISE — LE / LHS

☐	UR-46514	An-24RV	37308410	>AEW

LVIV AIRLINES — 5V / UKW

☐	UR-42317	Yak-42	22020390505	
☐	UR-42369	Yak-42D	29141900710	
☐	UR-42403	Yak-42D	21165880813	>SAI
☐	UR-42527	Yak-42	11040903	

MERIDIAN — MEM

☐	UR-CAG	An-12BK	9346904	
☐	UR-CAH	An-12BK	8345604	
☐	UR-CAJ	An-12BK	8346106	
☐	UR-CAK	An-12BP	6343707	
☐	UR-CGV	An-12B	6344610	♦
☐	UR-CGW	An-12B	402410	
☐	UR-CHT	An-26B	77305901	
☐	UR-MDA	An-26-100	87307108	

MOTOR SICH AIRLINES — M9 / MSI

☐	UR-BXC	An-24RV	37308902
☐	UR-MSI	An-24RV	27307608

☐	UR-11316	An-12BK	9346810	
☐	UR-11819	An-12B	6344009	
☐	UR-14005	An-140	36525305021	
☐	UR-14006	An-140K	36525305025	
☐	UR-74026	An-74TK-200	36547096919	
☐	UR-87215	Yak-40	9510540	

ODESSA AIRLINES — 5K / ODS

☐	UR-87421	Yak-40	9421734
☐	UR-14001	An-140	36535391003

PODILIA AVIA — PDA

☐	UR-46397	An-24B	7306301

SEVASTOPOL AVIA — SVL

☐	UR-TMD	Il-18D	187009903

SHOVKOVLY SKLYAH — S8 / SWW

☐	UR-CAF	An-12BP	3341209
☐	UR-CBU	An-12TBK	9346308
☐	UR-CGX	An-12BP	5343510

SOUTH AIRLINES — YG / OTL

☐	UR-BZY	Tu-134A-3	6348565
☐	UR-EEE	Yak-40	9340632
☐	UR-IMX	SAAB SF.340B	340B-225

TAVREY AIRCOMPANY — T6 / TVR

☐	UR-CER	Yak-42D

UKRAINE AIR ALLIANCE — UKL

☐	UR-BXQ	Il-76TD	1023410360	>MXU
☐	UR-BXR	Il-76TD	1023411384	>MXU
☐	UR-BXS	Il-76TD	1023411368	>MXU
☐	UR-CAI	An-26B	7010	>TAC
☐	UR-CAT	Il-76TD	0053464922	
☐	UR-CID	Il-76TD	0063465956	
☐	UR-26650	An-26B	87307507	
☐	UR-48083	An-32B	3001	

UKRAINE AIR ENTERPRISE — UKN

☐	UR-YVA	An-74TK-300	36547098984
☐	UR-65556	Tu-134A-3	66372
☐	UR-65718	Tu-134A-3	63668
☐	UR-65782	Tu-134A-3	62672
☐	UR-86527	Il-62M	4037758
☐	UR-86528	Il-62M	4038111

UKRAINE FLIGHT STATE ACADEMY — UFA

☐	UR-47791	An-24B	67303004

UKRAINE INTERNATIONAL AL — PS / AUI

☐	UR-FAA	B737-3Y0(SF)	24462/1691
☐	UR-GAH	B737-32Q/W	29130/3105
☐	UR-GAJ	B737-5Y0	25192/2262
☐	UR-GAK	B737-5Y0/W	26075/2374
☐	UR-GAM	B737-4Y0	25190/2256
☐	UR-GAN	B737-36N/W	28569/2996
☐	UR-GAO	B737-4Z9	25147/2043
☐	UR-GAP	B737-4Z9	27094/2432
☐	UR-GAQ	B737-33R/W	28869/2887
☐	UR-GAS	B737-528/W	25236/2443
☐	UR-GAT	B737-528/W	25237/2464
☐	UR-GAU	B737-5Y0/W	25182/2211
☐	UR-GAV	B737-4C9	26437/2249
☐	UR-GAW	B737-5Y0/W	24898/2079
☐	UR-GAX	B737-4Y0	26066/2301

☐	UR-PSA	B737-8HX/W	29658/2970·
☐	UR-PSB	B737-8HX/W	29654/3018
☐	UR-PSC	B737-8HX/W	29662/3182 ♦
☐	UR-PSD	B737-8HX/W	29686/3259 ♦

UKRAINIAN CARGO AIRWAYS — 6Z / UKS

☐	UR-UCN	An-12BK	347604
☐	UR-UDM	An-26	909
☐	UR-UCC	Il-76MD	0083489647
☐	UR-UCO	Il-76MD	0053458749
☐	UR-UCU	Il-76MD	0073476275

UKTRANSLIZING

☐	UR-14004	An-140	3652530211

UM AIR — UF / UKM

☐	UR-CBY	DC-9-51	47773/891 <KHO
☐	UR-CCS	DC-9-51	47737/829 <KHO
☐	UR-CCT	DC-9-51	47696/808 <KHO
☐	UR-BHJ	MD-83	53184/2088 >CPN
☐	UR-CFF	MD-83	49845/1573
☐	UR-CFG	MD-82	49370/1206
☐	UR-CHN	MD-83	49938/1785 >CPN♦
☐	UR-CHY	MD-82	53171/2067

UTAIR UKRAINE — UTN

☐	UR-UTA	ATR 42-320	382
☐	UR-UTB	ATR 42-320	386
☐	UR-UTG	B737-4Q8	25377/2717 ♦

VETERAN AIRLINES — VPB

☐	UR-CBZ	An-12BP	402707
☐	UR-CDB	An-12BP	401605
☐	UR-CEM	An-12BP	3340908 >ACP
☐	UR-CEN	An-12BP	2348203
☐	UR-PAS	An-12AP	2401105Opf SDR
☐	UR-YMR	An-12BK	9346302 <GOR

VOLARE AVIATION ENTERPRISE — VRE

☐	UR-BWM	An-12BK	347004
☐	UR-76628	Il-76TD	53458741

WIND ROSE — 7W / WRC

☐	UR-WRH	A321-231	2462 ♦
☐	UR-WRI	A321-231	2682 ♦
☐	UR-WRA	An-24RV	37308709
☐	UR-WRF	ERJ-190	19000169
☐	UR-WRG	ERJ-190	19000157
☐	UR-CDI	MD-82	49279/1230
☐	UR-CDX	MD-82	53119/1956
☐	UR-CEW	MD-82	49634/1419
☐	UR-WRB	MD-82	49364/1276
☐	UR-WRE	MD-82	49278/1183

WIZZ AIR UKRAINE — WU / WUA

☐	UR-WUA	A320-232	3531
☐	UR-WUB	A319-132	3741

YAVSON

☐	UR-MAY	Yak-40	

YUZMASHAVIA — 2N / UMK

☐	UR-78785	Il-76MD	83489691
☐	UR-78786	Il-76TD	83490693
☐	UR-87951	Yak-40K	9810957

VH - AUSTRALIA

AIRNORTH REGIONAL — TL / ANO

☐	VH-ANO	ERJ-170LR	17000099
☐	VH-ANV	ERJ-170LR	17000280
☐	VH-SWO	ERJ-170LR	17000081 ♦

ALLIANCE AIRLINES — QQ / UTY

☐	VH-FKP	Fokker 50	20161
☐	VH-FKV	Fokker 50	20303
☐	VH-FKW	Fokker 50	20306
☐	VH-FKX	Fokker 50	20312
☐	VH-FKY	Fokker 50	20284
☐	VH-FKZ	Fokker 50	20286
☐	VH-FKA	Fokker 100	11345
☐	VH-FKC	Fokker 100	11349
☐	VH-FKD	Fokker 100	11357
☐	VH-FKE	Fokker 100	11358 [BNE]
☐	VH-FKF	Fokker 100	11365
☐	VH-FKG	Fokker 100	11366
☐	VH-FKJ	Fokker 100	11372
☐	VH-FKK	Fokker 100	11379
☐	VH-FKL	Fokker 100	11380
☐	VH-FWH	Fokker 100	11316
☐	VH-FWI	Fokker 100	11318
☐	VH-XWM	Fokker 100	11276 ♦
☐	VH-XWN	Fokker 100	11278 ♦
☐	VH-XWO	Fokker 100	11300 ♦
☐	VH-XWR	Fokker 100	11306 ♦
☐	VH-XWS	Fokker 100	11314 ♦
☐	VH-XWT	Fokker 100	11338 ♦

AUSTRALIAN AIR EXPRESS — XM / XME

☐	VH-NJF	BAe146 Srs.300QT	E3198Opb NJS
☐	VH-NJM	BAe146 Srs.300QT	E3194Opb NJS
☐	VH-NJV	BAe146 Srs.100QT	E1002Opb NJS
☐	VH-XMB	B737-376(SF)	23478/1251Opb EFA
☐	VH-XML	B737-376(SF)	23486/1286Opb EFA
☐	VH-XMO	B737-376(SF)	23488/1352Opb EFA
☐	VH-XMR	B737-376(SF)	23490/1390Opb EFA

COBHAM AVN SVCS AUSTRALIA — NC / NJS

☐	VH-NBK	Avro 146-RJ100	E3365 ♦
☐	VH-NBU	Avro 146-RJ100	E3243 ♦
☐	VH-NJC	BAe146 Srs.100	E1013
☐	VH-NJF	BAe146 Srs.300QT	E3198
☐	VH-NJG	BAe146 Srs.200	E2170
☐	VH-NJL	BAe146 Srs.300	E3213
☐	VH-NJM	BAe146 Srs.300QT	E3194
☐	VH-NJN	BAe146 Srs.300	E3217
☐	VH-NJP	Avro 146-RJ100	E3354
☐	VH-NJQ	Avro 146-RJ100	E3328 ♦
☐	VH-NJR	BAe146 Srs.100	E1152 [ADL]♦
☐	VH-NJT	Avro 146-RJ70A	E1228
☐	VH-NJV	BAe146 Srs.100QT	E1002
☐	VH-NJX	BAe146 Srs.100	E1003 [ADL]
☐	VH-NJY	Avro 146-RJ100	E3331
☐	VH-NJZ	BAe146 Srs.300QT	E3126 ♦
☐	VH-YAD	BAe146 Srs.200	E2097
☐	VH-YAE	BAe146 Srs.200	E2107
☐	VH-JSJ	DHC-8-103	170
☐	VH-LCL	DHC-8Q-202	492Opf RAN
☐	VH-SBJ	DHC-8Q-315	578
☐	VH-ZZA	DHC-8-202MPA	419
☐	VH-ZZB	DHC-8-202MPA	424
☐	VH-ZZC	DHC-8-202MPA	433
☐	VH-ZZE	DHC-8Q-315MPA	640
☐	VH-ZZF	DHC-8Q-315MPA	643
☐	VH-ZZG	DHC-8Q-315MPA	644
☐	VH-ZZI	DHC-8-202MPA	550

	Reg	Type	c/n	
☐	VH-ZZJ	DHC-8-202MPA	551	
☐	VH-ZZN	DHC-8-315	399	
☐	VH-ZZP	DHC-8-202	411	

EXPRESS FREIGHTERS AUSTRALIA   EFA

	Reg	Type	c/n	
☐	VH-XMB	B737-376(SF)	23478/1251	Opf XME
☐	VH-XML	B737-376(SF)	23486/1286	Opf XME
☐	VH-XMO	B737-376(SF)	23488/1352	Opf XME
☐	VH-XMR	B737-376(SF)	23490/1390	Opf XME
☐	VH-	B767-381F	33510/939	o/o♦

HEAVYLIFT CARGO AIRLINES   HN / HVY

	Reg	Type	c/n
☐	RP-C8017	B727-51C	19289/403
☐	RP-C8019	B727-227F	21249/1219
☐	RP-C8020	Short SC.5 Belfast	SH1819

JETSTAR AIRWAYS   JQ / JST

	Reg	Type	c/n	
☐	VH-JQG	A320-232	2169	
☐	VH-JQL	A320-232	2185	
☐	VH-JQW	A320-232	2423	
☐	VH-JQX	A320-232	2197	
☐	VH-	A320-232		o/o♦
☐	VH-	A320-232		o/o♦
☐	VH-	A320-232		o/o♦
☐	VH-	A320-232		o/o♦
☐	VH-VGD	A320-232	4527	♦
☐	VH-VGF	A320-232	4497	♦
☐	VH-VGH	A320-232	4495	♦
☐	VH-VGI	A320-232	4464	♦
☐	VH-VGJ	A320-232	4460	♦
☐	VH-VGN	A320-232	4434	♦
☐	VH-VGO	A320-232	4356	♦
☐	VH-VGP	A320-232	4343	♦
☐	VH-VGQ	A320-232	4303	♦
☐	VH-VGR	A320-232	4257	♦
☐	VH-VGT	A320-232	4178	
☐	VH-VGU	A320-232	4245	♦
☐	VH-VGV	A320-232	4229	♦
☐	VH-VGY	A320-232	4177	
☐	VH-VGZ	A320-232	3917	
☐	VH-VQA	A320-232	3783	
☐	VH-VQB	A320-232	3743	
☐	VH-VQC	A320-232	3668	
☐	VH-VQD	A320-232	3547	
☐	VH-VQE	A320-232	3495	
☐	VH-VQF	A320-232	3474	
☐	VH-VQG	A320-232	2787	
☐	VH-VQH	A320-232	2766	
☐	VH-VQI	A320-232	2717	
☐	VH-VQJ	A320-232	2703	
☐	VH-VQK	A320-232	2651	
☐	VH-VQL	A320-232	2642	
☐	VH-VQM	A320-232	2608	
☐	VH-VQN	A320-232	2600	
☐	VH-VQO	A320-232	2587	
☐	VH-VQP	A320-232	2573	
☐	VH-VQQ	A320-232	2537	
☐	VH-VQR	A320-232	2526	
☐	VH-VQS	A320-232	2515	
☐	VH-VQT	A320-232	2475	
☐	VH-VQU	A320-232	2455	
☐	VH-VQV	A320-232	2338	
☐	VH-VQW	A320-232	2329	
☐	VH-VQX	A320-232	2322	
☐	VH-VQY	A320-232	2299	
☐	VH-VQZ	A320-232	2292	
☐	VH-VWT	A321-231	3717	
☐	VH-VWU	A321-231	3948	
☐	VH-VWW	A321-231	3916	
☐	VH-VWX	A321-231	3899	
☐	VH-VWY	A321-231	1408	
☐	VH-VWZ	A321-231	1195	

	Reg	Type	c/n
☐	VH-EBA	A330-202	508
☐	VH-EBB	A330-202	522
☐	VH-EBC	A330-202	506
☐	VH-EBD	A330-202	513
☐	VH-EBE	A330-202	842
☐	VH-EBF	A330-202	853
☐	VH-EBK	A330-202	945

MAROOMBA AIRLINES

	Reg	Type	c/n
☐	VH-QQA	DHC-8-102	005
☐	VH-QQB	DHC-8-102	004

NETWORK AVIATION AUSTRALIA

	Reg	Type	c/n
☐	VH-NHF	Fokker 100	11398
☐	VH-NHO	Fokker 100	11312
☐	VH-NHP	Fokker 100	11399

NORFOLK AIR

	Reg	Type	c/n
☐	VH-NLK	B737-33A	23635/1436

PEL-AIR   QWA

	Reg	Type	c/n
☐	VH-EKT	SAAB SF.340AF	340A-085
☐	VH-KDB	SAAB SF.340AF	340A-008
☐	VH-KDK	SAAB SF.340AF	340A-016

PIONAIR AUSTRALIA

	Reg	Type	c/n
☐	VH-PDW	Convair 580F	86
☐	VH-PDX	Convair 580F	126

QANTAS AIRWAYS   QF / QFA

	Reg	Type	c/n	
☐	VH-EBG	A330-203	887	
☐	VH-EBH	A330-203	892	
☐	VH-EBI	A330-203	898	
☐	VH-EBJ	A330-203	940	
☐	VH-EBL	A330-203	976	
☐	VH-EBM	A330-203	1061	
☐	VH-EBN	A330-203	1094	♦
☐	VH-EBO	A330-203	1169	♦
☐	VH-EBP	A330-203	1174	♦
☐	VH-QPA	A330-303	553	
☐	VH-QPB	A330-303	558	
☐	VH-QPC	A330-303	564	
☐	VH-QPD	A330-303	574	
☐	VH-QPE	A330-303	593	
☐	VH-QPF	A330-303	595	
☐	VH-QPG	A330-303	603	
☐	VH-QPH	A330-303	695	
☐	VH-QPI	A330-303	705	
☐	VH-QPJ	A330-303	712	
☐	VH-OQA	A380-842	014	
☐	VH-OQB	A380-842	015	
☐	VH-OQC	A380-842	022	
☐	VH-OQD	A380-842	026	
☐	VH-OQE	A380-842	027	
☐	VH-OQF	A380-842	029	
☐	VH-OQG	A380-842	047	♦
☐	VH-OQH	A380-842	050	♦
☐	VH-OQI	A380-842	055	♦
☐	VH-OQJ	A380-842	062	o/o♦
☐	VH-OQK	A380-842	063	o/o♦
☐	VH-OQL	A380-842	074	o/o♦
☐	VH-OQM	A380-842	091	o/o♦
☐	VH-TJE	B737-476	24430/1820	
☐	VH-TJF	B737-476	24431/1863	
☐	VH-TJG	B737-476	24432/1879	
☐	VH-TJH	B737-476	24433/1881	
☐	VH-TJI	B737-476	24434/1912	
☐	VH-TJJ	B737-476	24435/1959	
☐	VH-TJK	B737-476	24436/1998	

☐ VH-TJL	B737-476	24437/2162	
☐ VH-TJM	B737-476	24438/2171	
☐ VH-TJO	B737-476	24440/2324	
☐ VH-TJR	B737-476	24443/2398	
☐ VH-TJS	B737-476	24444/2454	
☐ VH-TJT	B737-476	24445/2539	
☐ VH-TJU	B737-476	24446/2569	
☐ VH-TJW	B737-4L7	26961/2517	
☐ VH-TJX	B737-476	28150/2773	
☐ VH-TJY	B737-476	28151/2785	
☐ VH-VXA	B737-838/W	29551/1042	
☐ VH-VXB	B737-838/W	30101/1045	
☐ VH-VXC	B737-838/W	30897/1049	
☐ VH-VXD	B737-838/W	29552/1063	
☐ VH-VXE	B737-838/W	30899/1071	
☐ VH-VXF	B737-838/W	29553/1096	
☐ VH-VXG	B737-838/W	30901/1102	
☐ VH-VXH	B737-838/W	33478/1137	
☐ VH-VXI	B737-838/W	33479/1141	
☐ VH-VXJ	B737-838/W	33480/1157	
☐ VH-VXK	B737-838/W	33481/1160	
☐ VH-VXL	B737-838/W	33482/1172	
☐ VH-VXM	B737-838/W	33483/1177	
☐ VH-VXN	B737-838/W	33484/1180	
☐ VH-VXO	B737-838/W	33485/1183	
☐ VH-VXP	B737-838/W	33722/1324	
☐ VH-VXQ	B737-838/W	33723/1335	
☐ VH-VXR	B737-838/W	33724/1340	
☐ VH-VXS	B737-838/W	33725/1352	
☐ VH-VXT	B737-838/W	33760/1412	
☐ VH-VXU	B737-838/W	33761/1420	
☐ VH-VYA	B737-838/W	33762/1532	
☐ VH-VYB	B737-838/W	33763/1534	
☐ VH-VYC	B737-838/W	33991/1612	
☐ VH-VYD	B737-838/W	33992/1706	
☐ VH-VYE	B737-838/W	33993/1712	
☐ VH-VYF	B737-838/W	33994/1727	
☐ VH-VYG	B737-838/W	33995/1736	
☐ VH-VYH	B737-838/W	34180/1815	
☐ VH-VYI	B737-838/W	34181/1840	
☐ VH-VYJ	B737-838/W	34182/1842	
☐ VH-VYK	B737-838/W	34183/1846	
☐ VH-VYL	B737-838/W	34184/1854	
☐ VH-VZA	B737-838/W	34195/2502	
☐ VH-VZB	B737-838/W	34196/2623	
☐ VH-VZC	B737-838/W	34197/2648	
☐ VH-VZD	B737-838/W	34198/2659	
☐ VH-VZE	B737-838/W	34199/2661	
☐ VH-OEB	B747-48E	25778/983	
☐ VH-OEC	B747-4H6	24836/808	[VCV]
☐ VH-OED	B747-4H6	25126/858	[VCV]
☐ VH-OEE	B747-438ER	32909/1308	
☐ VH-OEF	B747-438ER	32910/1313	
☐ VH-OEG	B747-438ER	32911/1320	
☐ VH-OEH	B747-438ER	32912/1321	
☐ VH-OEI	B747-438ER	32913/1330	
☐ VH-OEJ	B747-438ER	32914/1331	
☐ VH-OJA	B747-438	24354/731	
☐ VH-OJB	B747-438	24373/746	
☐ VH-OJC	B747-438	24406/751	
☐ VH-OJD	B747-438	24481/764	
☐ VH-OJE	B747-438	24482/765	
☐ VH-OJF	B747-438	24483/781	
☐ VH-OJG	B747-438	24779/801	
☐ VH-OJH	B747-438	24806/807	
☐ VH-OJI	B747-438	24887/826	
☐ VH-OJJ	B747-438	24974/835	
☐ VH-OJK	B747-438	25067/857	[VCV]
☐ VH-OJL	B747-438	25151/865	
☐ VH-OJM	B747-438	25245/875	
☐ VH-OJN	B747-438	25315/883	
☐ VH-OJO	B747-438	25544/894	
☐ VH-OJP	B747-438	25545/916	
☐ VH-OJQ	B747-438	25546/924	

☐ VH-OJR	B747-438	25547/936	
☐ VH-OJS	B747-438	25564/1230	
☐ VH-OJT	B747-438	25565/1233	
☐ VH-OJU	B747-438	25566/1239	
☐ VH-OGB	B767-338ER	24316/242	
☐ VH-OGC	B767-338ER	24317/246	[VCV]♦
☐ VH-OGD	B767-338ER	24407/247	[VCV]
☐ VH-OGE	B767-338ER	24531/278	
☐ VH-OGF	B767-338ER	24853/319	
☐ VH-OGG	B767-338ER	24929/343	
☐ VH-OGH	B767-338ER	24930/344	
☐ VH-OGI	B767-338ER	25246/387	
☐ VH-OGJ	B767-338ER	25274/396	
☐ VH-OGK	B767-338ER	25316/397	
☐ VH-OGL	B767-338ER	25363/402	
☐ VH-OGM	B767-338ER	25575/451	
☐ VH-OGN	B767-338ER	25576/549	
☐ VH-OGO	B767-338ER	25577/550	
☐ VH-OGP	B767-338ER	28153/615	
☐ VH-OGQ	B767-338ER	28154/623	
☐ VH-OGR	B767-338ER	28724/662	
☐ VH-OGS	B767-338ER	28725/664	
☐ VH-OGT	B767-338ER	29117/710	
☐ VH-OGU	B767-338ER	29118/713	
☐ VH-OGV	B767-338ER	30186/796	
☐ VH-ZXA	B767-336ER	24337/288	
☐ VH-ZXB	B767-336ER	24338/293	
☐ VH-ZXC	B767-336ER	24339/298	
☐ VH-ZXD	B767-336ER	24342/363	
☐ VH-ZXE	B767-336ER	24343/364	
☐ VH-ZXF	B767-336ER	25203/365	
☐ VH-ZXG	B767-336ER	25443/419	

QANTASLINK — QF / QFA

☐ VH-NXD	B717-23S	55062/5031	
☐ VH-NXE	B717-23S	55063/5034	
☐ VH-NXG	B717-2K9	55057/5020	
☐ VH-NXH	B717-2K9	55055/5014	
☐ VH-NXI	B717-2K9	55054/5013	
☐ VH-NXK	B717-231	55092/5077	
☐ VH-NXL	B717-231	55093/5083	
☐ VH-NXM	B717-231	55094/5084	
☐ VH-NXN	B717-231	55095/5087	
☐ VH-NXO	B717-231	55096/5093	
☐ VH-NXQ	B717-231	55097/5095	
☐ VH-SBB	DHC-8Q-315	539	
☐ VH-SBG	DHC-8Q-315	575	
☐ VH-SBI	DHC-8Q-315	605	
☐ VH-SBT	DHC-8Q-315	580	
☐ VH-SBV	DHC-8Q-315	595	
☐ VH-SBW	DHC-8Q-315	599	
☐ VH-SCE	DHC-8Q-315	602	
☐ VH-SDA	DHC-8Q-202	482	
☐ VH-SDE	DHC-8Q-202	453	
☐ VH-TQD	DHC-8Q-315	598	
☐ VH-TQE	DHC-8Q-315	596	
☐ VH-TQG	DHC-8-201	430	
☐ VH-TQH	DHC-8Q-315	597	
☐ VH-TQK	DHC-8Q-315	600	
☐ VH-TQL	DHC-8Q-315	603	
☐ VH-TQM	DHC-8Q-315	604	
☐ VH-TQS	DHC-8-202	418	
☐ VH-TQX	DHC-8-202	439	
☐ VH-TQY	DHC-8Q-315	552	
☐ VH-TQZ	DHC-8Q-315	555	
☐ VH-LQB	DHC-8-402Q	4343	♦
☐ VH-	DHC-8-402Q		o/o♦
☐ VH-QOA	DHC-8-402Q	4112	
☐ VH-QOB	DHC-8-402Q	4116	
☐ VH-QOC	DHC-8-402Q	4117	
☐ VH-QOD	DHC-8-402Q	4123	
☐ VH-QOE	DHC-8-402Q	4125	

☐	VH-QOF	DHC-8-402Q	4128
☐	VH-QOH	DHC-8-402Q	4132
☐	VH-QOI	DHC-8-402Q	4189
☐	VH-QOJ	DHC-8-402Q	4192
☐	VH-QOK	DHC-8-402Q	4215
☐	VH-QOM	DHC-8-402Q	4217
☐	VH-QON	DHC-8-402Q	4218
☐	VH-QOP	DHC-8-402Q	4238
☐	VH-QOR	DHC-8-402Q	4241
☐	VH-QOS	DHC-8-402Q	4263
☐	VH-QOT	DHC-8-402Q	4269
☐	VH-QOU	DHC-8-402Q	4275
☐	VH-QOV	DHC-8-402Q	4277
☐	VH-QOW	DHC-8-402Q	4285
☐	VH-QOX	DHC-8-402Q	4287
☐	VH-QOY	DHC-8-402Q	4288

REX - REGIONAL EXPRESS ZL / RXA

☐	VH-EKD	SAAB SF.340A	340A-155
☐	VH-EKH	SAAB SF.340B	340B-369
☐	VH-EKX	SAAB SF.340B	340B-257
☐	VH-JRX	SAAB SF.340B	340B-186
☐	VH-KDQ	SAAB SF.340B	340B-325
☐	VH-KDV	SAAB SF.340B	340B-322
☐	VH-KRX	SAAB SF.340B	340B-290
☐	VH-NRX	SAAB SF.340B	340B-291
☐	VH-OLL	SAAB SF.340B	340B-175
☐	VH-OLM	SAAB SF.340B	340B-205
☐	VH-ORX	SAAB SF.340B	340B-293
☐	VH-PRX	SAAB SF.340B	340B-303
☐	VH-RXE	SAAB SF.340B	340B-275
☐	VH-RXN	SAAB SF.340B	340B-279
☐	VH-RXQ	SAAB SF.340B	340B-200
☐	VH-RXS	SAAB SF.340B	340B-285
☐	VH-RXX	SAAB SF.340B	340B-209
☐	VH-SBA	SAAB SF.340B	340B-311
☐	VH-TRX	SAAB SF.340B	340B-287
☐	VH-XRX	SAAB SF.340B	340B-179
☐	VH-YRX	SAAB SF.340B	340B-178
☐	VH-ZLA	SAAB SF.340B	340B-371
☐	VH-ZLC	SAAB SF.340B	340B-373
☐	VH-ZLF	SAAB SF.340B	340B-374
☐	VH-ZLG	SAAB SF.340B	340B-375
☐	VH-ZLH	SAAB SF.340B	340B-376
☐	VH-ZLJ	SAAB SF.340B	340B-380
☐	VH-ZLK	SAAB SF.340B	340B-381
☐	VH-ZLO	SAAB SF.340B	340B-382
☐	VH-ZLQ	SAAB SF.340B	340B-370
☐	VH-ZLR	SAAB SF.340B	340B-229
☐	VH-ZLS	SAAB SF.340B	340B-383
☐	VH-ZLV	SAAB SF.340B	340B-386
☐	VH-ZLW	SAAB SF.340B	340B-387
☐	VH-ZLX	SAAB SF.340B	340B-182
☐	VH-ZRB	SAAB SF.340B	340B-389
☐	VH-ZRC	SAAB SF.340B	340B-390
☐	VH-ZRE	SAAB SF.340B	340B-391
☐	VH-ZRH	SAAB SF.340B	340B-392
☐	VH-ZRI	SAAB SF.340B	340B-394
☐	VH-ZRJ	SAAB SF.340B	340B-396
☐	VH-ZRK	SAAB SF.340B	340B-397
☐	VH-ZRL	SAAB SF.340B	340B-398
☐	VH-ZRM	SAAB SF.340B	340B-400	♦
☐	VH-ZRN	SAAB SF.340B	340B-393
☐	VH-ZRY	SAAB SF.340B	340B-401
☐	VH-ZRZ	SAAB SF.340B	340B-388

SKIPPERS AVIATION

☐	VH-XFP	DHC-8-102A	346
☐	VH-XFQ	DHC-8-106	306
☐	VH-XFT	DHC-8-102	052
☐	VH-XFU	DHC-8-102	151
☐	VH-XFV	DHC-8-314A	350
☐	VH-XFW	DHC-8-314A	356

☐	VH-XFX	DHC-8-314A	313
☐	VH-XFZ	DHC-8-314A	365

SKYTRANS REGIONAL

☐	VH-QQA	DHC-8-102	005	
☐	VH-QQB	DHC-8-102	004	
☐	VH-QQC	DHC-8-102	008	
☐	VH-QQD	DHC-8-102	041	
☐	VH-QQE	DHC-8-102	173	
☐	VH-QQF	DHC-8-102	014	
☐	VH-QQG	DHC-8-102	036	
☐	VH-QQH	DHC-8-102A	380	
☐	VH-QQI	DHC-8-102	067	
☐	VH-QQJ	DHC-8-102	392	
☐	VH-QQK	DHC-8-102	326	♦
☐	VH-QQL	DHC-8-102A	388	♦

SKYWEST AIRLINES XR / OZW

☐	VH-FNP	A320-231	0429	♦
☐	VH-FNA	Fokker 50	20106	
☐	VH-FNB	Fokker 50	20107	
☐	VH-FND	Fokker 50	20129	
☐	VH-FNE	Fokker 50	20212	
☐	VH-FNF	Fokker 50	20200	
☐	VH-FNH	Fokker 50	20113	
☐	VH-FNI	Fokker 50	20114	
☐	VH-FSL	Fokker 50	20249	o/o
☐	VH-FNC	Fokker 100	11334	
☐	VH-FNJ	Fokker 100	11489	
☐	VH-FNN	Fokker 100	11326	
☐	VH-FNR	Fokker 100	11488	
☐	VH-FNT	Fokker 100	11461	
☐	VH-FNU	Fokker 100	11373	
☐	VH-FNY	Fokker 100	11484	
☐	VH-FSQ	Fokker 100	11450	
☐	VH-FSW	Fokker 100	11391	

STRATEGIC AIRLINES VC

☐	F-GSTR	A320-212	0436	
☐	F-GSTS	A320-212	0420	
☐	LX-STA	A320-212	0446	♦
☐	VH-YQA	A320-212	0190	
☐	VH-YQB	A320-211	0279	♦
☐	VH-YQC	A320-211	0395	♦
☐	VH-SSA	A330-223	324	

TASMAN CARGO AIRLINES HJ / AXF

☐	VH-DHE	B727-2J4F	22080/1598	
☐	G-BMRJ	B757-236(SF)	24268/214	<DHK♦

TIGER AIRWAYS TT

☐	VH-VNB	A320-232	2906	
☐	VH-VNC	A320-232	3275	
☐	VH-VND	A320-232	3296	
☐	VH-VNF	A320-232	3332	
☐	VH-VNG	A320-232	3674	
☐	VH-VNH	A320-232	3734	
☐	VH-VNJ	A320-232	2982	
☐	VH-VNK	A320-232	3986	
☐	VH-VNO	A320-232	4053	
☐	VH-VNP	A320-232	2952	♦
☐	VH-	A320-232		o/o♦
☐	VH-	A320-232		o/o♦
☐	VH-	A320-232		o/o♦

TOLL PRIORITY TFR

☐	VH-TOQ	ATR 42-300F	79
☐	VH-TOX	ATR 42-300F	24

☐ ZK-TLA	B737-3B7(SF)	23383/1425
☐ ZK-TLC	B737-3B7(SF)	23705/1497
☐ ZK-TLD	B737-3B7(SF)	23706/1499

V AUSTRALIA

☐ VH-VOZ	B777-3ZGER	35302/745	
☐ VH-VPD	B777-3ZGER	37938/756	
☐ VH-VPE	B777-3ZGER	37939/764	
☐ VH-VPF	B777-3ZGER	37940/801	
☐ VH-VPH	B777-3ZGER	37943/898	♦

VIRGIN BLUE AIRLINES   DJ / VOZ

☐ VH-XFA	A330-243	365	♦
☐ VH-	A330-243	372	♦
☐ VH-VBA	B737-7Q8/W	28238/817	
☐ VH-VBB	B737-7Q8/W	28240/832	
☐ VH-VBC	B737-7Q8	30638/858	
☐ VH-VBD	B737-7Q8/W	30707/975	
☐ VH-VBF	B737-7Q8/W	30630/1032	
☐ VH-VBH	B737-7Q8/W	30641/1080	
☐ VH-VBI	B737-7Q8/W	30644/1107	
☐ VH-VBJ	B737-7Q8/W	30647/1159	
☐ VH-VBK	B737-7Q8/W	30648/1171	
☐ VH-VBL	B737-7Q8/W	30633/1220	
☐ VH-VBM	B737-76N/W	32734/1090	
☐ VH-VBN	B737-76N/W	33005/1134	
☐ VH-VBO	B737-76N/W	33418/1226	
☐ VH-VBP	B737-7BX/W	30743/922	
☐ VH-VBQ	B737-7BX/W	30744/989	
☐ VH-VBR	B737-7BX/W	30745/1027	
☐ VH-VBU	B737-7BK/W	30288/1322	
☐ VH-VBV	B737-7BK/W	33015/1384	
☐ VH-VBY	B737-7FE/W	34323/1751	
☐ VH-VBZ	B737-7FE/W	34322/1777	
☐ VH-BZG	B737-8FE/W	37822/3355	♦
☐ VH-VOA	B737-8BK/W	30620/991	
☐ VH-VOB	B737-8BK/W	30622/1108	
☐ VH-VOC	B737-8BK/W	30623/1136	
☐ VH-VOD	B737-8BK/W	30624/1193	
☐ VH-VOK	B737-8FE/W	33758/1359	
☐ VH-VOL	B737-8FE/W	33759/1364	
☐ VH-VOM	B737-8FE/W	33794/1373	
☐ VH-VON	B737-8FE/W	33795/1375	
☐ VH-VOQ	B737-8FE/W	33798/1391	
☐ VH-VOS	B737-8FE/W	33800/1483	
☐ VH-VOT	B737-8FE/W	33801/1504	
☐ VH-VOU	B737-8Q8/W	30665/1436	
☐ VH-VOV	B737-82R/W	30658/1325	
☐ VH-VOW	B737-8Q8/W	32798/1470	
☐ VH-VOX	B737-8BK/W	33017/1446	
☐ VH-VUA	B737-8FE/W	33997/1559	
☐ VH-VUC	B737-8FE/W	34014/1582	
☐ VH-VUE	B737-8FE/W	34167/1676	
☐ VH-VUF	B737-8FE/W	34168/1697	
☐ VH-VUG	B737-8FE/W	34438/1948	
☐ VH-VUI	B737-8FE/W	34441/2015	
☐ VH-VUJ	B737-8FE/W	34443/2056	
☐ VH-VUK	B737-8FE/W	36602/2353	
☐ VH-VUL	B737-8FE/W	36603/2356	
☐ VH-VUM	B737-8BK/W	29675/2414	>PBN
☐ VH-VUN	B737-8BK/W	29676/2432	>PBN
☐ VH-VUR	B737-8FE/W	36606/3059	
☐ VH-VUS	B737-8FE/W	36607/3082	
☐ VH-VUT	B737-8FE/W	36608/3132	
☐ VH-VUU	B737-8FE/W	36609/3232	♦
☐ VH-VUV	B737-8FE/W	37821/3288	♦
☐ VH-VUW	B737-8KG/W	39449/3398	♦
☐ VH-VUX	B737-8FE/W	37823/3415	♦
☐ VH-VUY	B737-8KG/W	39450/3494	♦
☐ VH-VUZ	B737-8FE/W	39921/3536	♦
☐ VH-	B737-8	o/o	♦
☐ VH-	B737-8	o/o	♦

☐ VH-	B737-8	o/o	♦
☐ VH-	B737-8	o/o	♦
☐ VH-	B737-8	o/o	♦
☐ VH-	B737-8	o/o	♦
☐ VH-	B737-8	o/o	♦
☐ VH-	B737-8	o/o	♦
☐ VH-ZHA	ERJ-170LR	17000180	
☐ VH-ZHB	ERJ-170LR	17000187	
☐ VH-ZHC	ERJ-170LR	17000191	
☐ VH-ZHD	ERJ-170LR	17000227	
☐ VH-ZHE	ERJ-170LR	17000247	
☐ VH-ZHF	ERJ-170LR	17000255	
☐ VH-ZPA	ERJ-190AR	19000148	
☐ VH-ZPB	ERJ-190AR	19000162	
☐ VH-ZPC	ERJ-190AR	19000170	
☐ VH-ZPD	ERJ-190AR	19000176	
☐ VH-ZPE	ERJ-190AR	19000187	
☐ VH-ZPF	ERJ-190AR	19000193	
☐ VH-ZPG	ERJ-190AR	19000195	
☐ VH-ZPH	ERJ-190AR	19000199	
☐ VH-ZPI	ERJ-190AR	19000202	
☐ VH-ZPJ	ERJ-190AR	19000209	
☐ VH-ZPK	ERJ-190AR	19000218	
☐ VH-ZPL	ERJ-190AR	19000220	
☐ VH-ZPM	ERJ-190AR	19000262	
☐ VH-ZPN	ERJ-190AR	19000312	
☐ VH-ZPO	ERJ-190AR	19000321	
☐ VH-	ERJ-190AR	o/o	♦
☐ VH-	ERJ-190AR	o/o	♦
☐ VH-	ERJ-190AR	o/o	♦

VN - VIETNAM

AIR MEKONG

☐ VN-A801	CRJ-900	15102	♦
☐ VN-A802	CRJ-900	15103	♦
☐ VN-A803	CRJ-900	15110	♦
☐ VN-A804	CRJ-900	15112	♦

JETSTAR PACIFIC AIRLINES   BL / PIC

☐ VN-A189	B737-43Q	28490/2830	
☐ VN-A190	B737-4H6	27383/2657	
☐ VN-A191	B737-4H6	27306/2685	
☐ VN-A192	B737-4Q8	26289/2486	
☐ VN-A195	A320-232	0990	
☐ VN-A198	A320-232	4459	♦

VIETNAM AIRLINES   VN / HVN

☐ VN-A301	A320-214	0590	
☐ VN-A302	A320-214	0594	
☐ VN-A303	A320-214	0601	
☐ VN-A304	A320-214	0605	
☐ VN-A305	A320-214	0607	
☐ VN-A306	A320-214	0611	
☐ VN-A307	A320-214	0617	
☐ VN-A308	A320-214	0619	
☐ VN-A311	A320-214	0648	
☐ VN-A322	A321-231	4311	♦
☐ VN-A344	A321-231	2255	
☐ VN-A345	A321-231	2261	
☐ VN-A347	A321-231	2267	
☐ VN-A348	A321-231	2303	
☐ VN-A349	A321-231	2480	
☐ VN-A350	A321-231	2974	
☐ VN-A351	A321-231	3005	>VAV
☐ VN-A352	A321-231	3013	
☐ VN-A353	A321-231	3022	
☐ VN-A354	A321-231	3198	
☐ VN-A356	A321-231	3315	
☐ VN-A357	A321-231	3355	
☐ VN-A358	A321-231	3600	

	Reg	Type	c/n	
☐	VN-A359	A321-231	3737	
☐	VN-A360	A321-231	3862	
☐	VN-A361	A321-231	3964	
☐	VN-A362	A321-231	3966	
☐	VN-A363	A321-231	4136	
☐	VN-A365	A321-231	4213	♦
☐	VN-A366	A321-231	4277	♦
☐	VN-A367	A321-231	4315	♦
☐	VN-	A321-231		o/o♦
☐	VN-	A321-231		o/o♦
☐	VN-A368	A330-322	087	
☐	VN-A369	A330-223	255	
☐	VN-A370	A330-223	262	
☐	VN-A371	A330-223	275	
☐	VN-A372	A330-223	294	
☐	VN-A374	A330-223	299	
☐	VN-A375	A330-223	366	
☐	VN-A376	A330-223	943	♦
☐	VN-A377	A330-223	962	♦
☐	VN-A378	A330-223	1019	♦
☐	VN-B210	ATR 72-212A	678	
☐	VN-B212	ATR 72-212A	685	>VAV
☐	VN-B214	ATR 72-212A	688	>VAV
☐	VN-B216	ATR 72-212A	450	
☐	VN-B218	ATR 72-212A	877	
☐	VN-B219	ATR 72-212A	886	
☐	VN-B220	ATR 72-212A	890	
☐	VN-B221	ATR 72-212A	892	
☐	VN-B223	ATR 72-212A	896	
☐	VN-B225	ATR 72-212A	897	
☐	VN-B227	ATR 72-212A	899	>VAV♦
☐	VN-B231	ATR 72-212A	906	>VAV♦
☐	VN-B233	ATR 72-212A	912	♦
☐	VN-B236	ATR 72-212A	914	♦
☐	VN-B237	ATR 72-212A	925	♦
☐	VN-B239	ATR 72-212A	927	♦
☐	VN-B240	ATR 72-212A	939	♦
☐	VN-A141	B777-2Q8ER	28688/436	
☐	VN-A142	B777-2Q8ER	32701/443	
☐	VN-A143	B777-26KER	33502/450	
☐	VN-A144	B777-26KER	33503/453	
☐	VN-A145	B777-26KER	33504/491	
☐	VN-A146	B777-26KER	33505/486	
☐	VN-A147	B777-2Q8ER	27607/135	
☐	VN-A149	B777-2Q8ER	32716/518	
☐	VN-A150	B777-2Q8ER	32717/541	
☐	VN-A151	B777-2Q8ER	27608/164	
☐	VN-A502	Fokker 70	11580	
☐	VN-A504	Fokker 70	11585	

VP-C CAYMAN ISLANDS

CAYMAN AIRWAYS KX / CAY

	Reg	Type	c/n	
☐	VP-CAY	B737-3Q8	26286/2424	
☐	VP-CKW	B737-36E	26322/2769	
☐	VP-CKX	B737-236	23162/1056	
☐	VP-CKY	B737-3Q8	26282/2355	
☐	VP-CKZ	B737-36E	27626/2792	
☐	VP-CYB	B737-2S2C	21929/608	[MZJ]

VT - INDIA

AIR INDIA AI / AIC

	Reg	Type	c/n
☐	VT-AIB	A310-324	680
☐	VT-EJG	A310-304	406
☐	VT-EJH	A310-304F	407
☐	VT-EJI	A310-304F	413
☐	VT-EJJ	A310-304	428
☐	VT-EJK	A310-304	429
☐	VT-EJL	A310-304	392

	Reg	Type	c/n	
☐	VT-EQS	A310-304F	538	
☐	VT-EQT	A310-304F	544	
☐	VT-SCA	A319-112	2593	
☐	VT-SCB	A319-112	2624	
☐	VT-SCC	A319-112	2629	
☐	VT-SCD	A319-112	1668	
☐	VT-SCE	A319-112	1718	
☐	VT-SCF	A319-112	2907	
☐	VT-SCG	A319-112	3271	
☐	VT-SCH	A319-112	3288	
☐	VT-SCI	A319-112	3300	
☐	VT-SCJ	A319-112	3305	
☐	VT-SCK	A319-112	3344	
☐	VT-SCL	A319-112	3551	
☐	VT-SCM	A319-112	3620	
☐	VT-SCN	A319-112	3687	
☐	VT-SCO	A319-112	3822	
☐	VT-SCP	A319-112	3874	
☐	VT-SCQ	A319-112	3918	
☐	VT-SCR	A319-112	3970	
☐	VT-SCS	A319-112	4020	
☐	VT-SCT	A319-112	4029	
☐	VT-SCU	A319-112	4052	
☐	VT-SCV	A319-112	4089	
☐	VT-SCW	A319-112	4121	
☐	VT-SCX	A319-112	4164	
☐	VT-EDC	A320-214	4201	♦
☐	VT-EDD	A320-214	4212	♦
☐	VT-EDF	A320-214	4237	♦
☐	VT-EPB	A320-231	0045	
☐	VT-EPC	A320-231	0046	
☐	VT-EPD	A320-231	0047	
☐	VT-EPE	A320-231	0048	
☐	VT-EPF	A320-231	0049	
☐	VT-EPG	A320-231	0050	
☐	VT-EPH	A320-231	0051	
☐	VT-EPI	A320-231	0056	
☐	VT-EPJ	A320-231	0057	
☐	VT-EPL	A320-231	0074	
☐	VT-EPM	A320-231	0075	
☐	VT-EPO	A320-231	0080	
☐	VT-EPQ	A320-231	0090	
☐	VT-EPR	A320-231	0095	
☐	VT-EPS	A320-231	0096	
☐	VT-ESA	A320-231	0396	
☐	VT-ESB	A320-231	0398	
☐	VT-ESC	A320-231	0416	
☐	VT-ESD	A320-231	0423	
☐	VT-ESE	A320-231	0431	
☐	VT-ESF	A320-231	0432	
☐	VT-ESG	A320-231	0451	
☐	VT-ESH	A320-231	0469	
☐	VT-ESI	A320-231	0486	
☐	VT-ESJ	A320-231	0490	
☐	VT-ESK	A320-231	0492	
☐	VT-ESL	A320-231	0499	
☐	VT-EVO	A320-231	0247	
☐	VT-EVP	A320-231	0257	
☐	VT-EVQ	A320-231	0327	
☐	VT-EVR	A320-231	0336	
☐	VT-EVS	A320-231	0308	
☐	VT-EVT	A320-231	0314	
☐	VT-EYB	A320-231	0386	
☐	VT-EYL	A320-231	0480	
☐	VT-PPA	A321-211	3130	
☐	VT-PPB	A321-211	3146	
☐	VT-PPD	A321-211	3212	
☐	VT-PPE	A321-211	3326	
☐	VT-PPF	A321-211	3340	
☐	VT-PPG	A321-211	3367	
☐	VT-PPH	A321-211	3498	
☐	VT-PPI	A321-211	3557	
☐	VT-PPJ	A321-211	3573	

☐ VT-PPK	A321-211	3619	
☐ VT-PPL	A321-211	3752	
☐ VT-PPM	A321-211	3792	
☐ VT-PPN	A321-211	3955	
☐ VT-PPO	A321-211	4002	
☐ VT-PPQ	A321-211	4009	
☐ VT-PPT	A321-211	4078	
☐ VT-PPU	A321-211	4096	
☐ VT-PPV	A321-211	4138	
☐ VT-PPW	A321-211	4155	
☐ VT-PPX	A321-211	4280	♦
☐ VT-IWA	A330-223	353	
☐ VT-IWB	A330-223	362	
☐ VT-EPW	B747-337M	24159/711	
☐ VT-ESN	B747-437	27164/1003	
☐ VT-ESO	B747-437	27165/1009	
☐ VT-ESP	B747-437	27214/1034	
☐ VT-EVA	B747-437	28094/1089	
☐ VT-EVB	B747-437	28095/1093	
☐ VT-AIL	B777-222ER	26935/88	
☐ VT-AIR	B777-222	26917/8	
☐ VT-ALA	B777-237LR	36300/610	
☐ VT-ALB	B777-237LR	36301/621	
☐ VT-ALC	B777-237LR	36302/629	
☐ VT-ALD	B777-237LR	36303/663	
☐ VT-ALE	B777-237LR	36304/698	
☐ VT-ALF	B777-237LR	36305/793	
☐ VT-ALG	B777-237LR	36306/800	
☐ VT-ALH	B777-237LR	36307/805	
☐ VT-ALJ	B777-337ER	36308/643	
☐ VT-ALK	B777-337ER	36309/652	
☐ VT-ALL	B777-337ER	36310/656	
☐ VT-ALM	B777-337ER	36311/713	
☐ VT-ALN	B777-337ER	36312/719	
☐ VT-ALO	B777-337ER	36313/798	
☐ VT-ALP	B777-337ER	36314/804	
☐ VT-ALQ	B777-337ER	36315/809	
☐ VT-ALR	B777-337ER	36316/814	
☐ VT-ALS	B777-337ER	36317/864	♦
☐ VT-ALT	B777-337ER	36318/871	♦
☐ VT-ALU	B777-337ER	36319/880	♦
☐ VT-ANA	B787-837	36273/25	o/o♦
☐ VT-ANC	B787-837	36274/28	o/o♦
☐ VT-AND	B787-837	36278/29	o/o♦
☐ VT-ANE	B787-837	26280/30	o/o♦
☐ VT-	B787-837		o/o♦
☐ VT-	B787-837		o/o♦

AIR INDIA EXPRESS — AI / AXB

☐ VT-AXC	B737-8BK	33024/1688
☐ VT-AXD	B737-8Q8/W	30696/1892
☐ VT-AXE	B737-8Q8/W	29368/1910
☐ VT-AXF	B737-8Q8/W	29369/1939
☐ VT-AXG	B737-8Q8/W	30701/1946
☐ VT-AXH	B737-8HG/W	36323/2108
☐ VT-AXI	B737-8HG/W	36324/2132
☐ VT-AXJ	B737-8HG/W	36325/2142
☐ VT-AXM	B737-8HG/W	36326/2148
☐ VT-AXN	B737-8HG/W	36327/2154
☐ VT-AXP	B737-8HG/W	36328/2177
☐ VT-AXQ	B737-8HG/W	36329/2258
☐ VT-AXR	B737-8HG/W	36330/2317
☐ VT-AXT	B737-8HG/W	36331/2324
☐ VT-AXU	B737-8HG/W	36332/2381
☐ VT-AXW	B737-8HG/W	36334/2612
☐ VT-AXX	B737-8HG/W	36335/2672
☐ VT-AXZ	B737-8HG/W	36336/2782
☐ VT-AYA	B737-8HG/W	36337/2861
☐ VT-AYB	B737-8HG/W	36338/2962
☐ VT-AYC	B737-8HG/W	36339/3039

AIR INDIA REGIONAL

☐ VT-ABA	ATR 42-320	390
☐ VT-ABB	ATR 42-320	392
☐ VT-ABC	ATR 42-320	315
☐ VT-ABD	ATR 42-320	356
☐ VT-ABE	ATR 42-320	333
☐ VT-ABF	ATR 42-320	351
☐ VT-ABO	ATR 42-320	406

ALLIANCE AIR — CD / LLR

☐ VT-EGE	B737-2A8	22281/679	[DEL]
☐ VT-EGF	B737-2A8F	22282/681	
☐ VT-EGG	B737-2A8F	22283/689	
☐ VT-EGH	B737-2A8	22284/739	
☐ VT-EGI	B737-2A8F	22285/798	
☐ VT-EGJ	B737-2A8F	22286/799	
☐ VT-EGM	B737-2A8C	22473/747	
☐ VT-EHE	B737-2A8	22860/899	
☐ VT-EHF	B737-2A8	22861/902	[DEL]
☐ VT-EHG	B737-2A8	22862/903	[DEL]
☐ VT-EHH	B737-2A8F	22863/907	
☐ VT-RJB	CRJ-700	10217	
☐ VT-RJC	CRJ-700	10052	
☐ VT-RJD	CRJ-700	10048	
☐ VT-RJE	CRJ-700	10029	

BLUE DART AVIATION — BZ / BDA

☐ VT-BDG	B737-2K9F	22415/702
☐ VT-BDH	B737-25C	24236/1585
☐ VT-BDI	B737-2T4F	23272/1093
☐ VT-BDJ	B757-236(SF)	24102/179
☐ VT-BDK	B757-236(SF)	24267/211
☐ VT-BDM	B757-23N(SF)	27598/692
☐ VT-BDN	B757-25CF	25898/475

DECCAN CARGO

☐ VT-AIN	A310-324F	684
☐ VT-AIO	A310-324F	693
☐ VT-AIP	A310-324F	697

GO AIR — G8 / GOW

☐ VT-WAC	A320-233	1482	
☐ VT-WAE	A320-214	3256	
☐ VT-WAF	A320-214	3306	
☐ VT-WAG	A320-214	3597	
☐ VT-WAH	A320-214	3616	
☐ VT-WAI	A320-214	3798	
☐ VT-WAJ	A320-214	3827	
☐ VT-WAK	A320-214	3900	
☐ VT-WAL	A320-214	3915	
☐ VT-WAM	A320-214	4399	♦
☐ VT-WAN	A320-214	4438	♦

INDIGO AIRLINES — 6E / IGO

☐ VT-IGH	A320-232	4008	
☐ VT-IGI	A320-232	4113	
☐ VT-IGJ	A320-232	4156	
☐ VT-IGK	A320-232	4216	♦
☐ VT-IGL	A320-232	4312	♦
☐ VT-IGS	A320-232	4328	♦
☐ VT-IGT	A320-232	4384	♦
☐ VT-IGU	A320-232	4488	♦
☐ VT-IGV	A320-232	4481	♦
☐ VT-IGW	A320-232	4506	♦
☐ VT-IGX	A320-232	4518	♦
☐ VT-IGY	A320-232	4535	♦
☐ VT-IGZ	A320-232	4552	♦
☐ VT-INA	A320-232	2844	

Reg	Type	c/n	
VT-INB	A320-232	2863	
VT-INC	A320-232	2883	
VT-IND	A320-232	2911	
VT-INE	A320-232	2958	
VT-INF	A320-232	2990	
VT-INI	A320-232	3086	
VT-INJ	A320-232	3159	
VT-INK	A320-232	3192	
VT-INL	A320-232	3227	
VT-INO	A320-232	3335	
VT-INP	A320-232	3357	
VT-INQ	A320-232	3414	
VT-INR	A320-232	3453	
VT-INS	A320-232	3457	
VT-INT	A320-232	3497	
VT-INU	A320-232	3541	
VT-INV	A320-232	3618	
VT-INX	A320-232	3782	
VT-INY	A320-232	3863	
VT-INZ	A320-232	3943	
VT-	A320-232		o/o♦
VT-	A320-232		o/o♦
VT-	A320-232		o/o♦
VT-	A320-232		o/o♦
VT-	A320-232		o/o♦
VT-	A320-232		o/o♦
VT-	A320-232		o/o♦
VT-	A320-232		o/o♦
VT-	A320-232		o/o♦
VT-	A320-232		o/o♦
VT-	A320-232		o/o♦
VT-	A320-232		o/o♦

JAGSON Airlines

VT-JJC	Avro 146-RJ85	E2299	♦

JET AIRWAYS — 9W / JAI

VT-JWD	A330-243	751	
VT-JWE	A330-243	807	
VT-JWF	A330-202	825	
VT-JWG	A330-202	831	
VT-JWH	A330-202	882	
VT-JWJ	A330-202	885	
VT-JWK	A330-202	888	
VT-JWL	A330-202	901	
VT-JWM	A330-202	923	
VT-JWN	A330-202	932	
VT-JWP	A330-202	947	
VT-JWQ	A330-202	956	
VT-JCA	ATR 72-212A	572	
VT-JCB	ATR 72-212A	575	
VT-JCC	ATR 72-212A	593	
VT-JCD	ATR 72-212A	636	
VT-JCF	ATR 72-212A	674	<SFR
VT-JCG	ATR 72-212A	679	<SFR
VT-JCH	ATR 72-212A	681	<SFR
VT-JCJ	ATR 72-212A	771	
VT-JCK	ATR 72-212A	775	
VT-JCL	ATR 72-212A	791	
VT-JCM	ATR 72-212A	793	
VT-JCN	ATR 72-212A	825	
VT-JCP	ATR 72-212A	841	
VT-JCQ	ATR 72-212A	843	
VT-JCR	ATR 72-212A	919	♦
VT-JCS	ATR 72-212A	920	♦
VT-JCT	ATR 72-212A	924	♦
VT-JCU	ATR 72-212A	928	♦
VT-JCV	ATR 72-212A	932	♦
VT-JCW	ATR 72-212A	933	♦
VT-JBB	B737-8HX/W	36846/2368	
VT-JBC	B737-8HX/W	36847/2388	
VT-JBD	B737-85R/W	35099/2439	
VT-JBE	B737-85R/W	35106/2530	
VT-JBF	B737-85R/W	35082/2550	
VT-JBG	B737-85R/W	35083/2535	
VT-JBH	B737-85R/W	35289/2811	
VT-JBJ	B737-85R/W	36551/2974	
VT-JBK	B737-85R/W	36553/3074	
VT-JBL	B737-85R/W	35651/3000	
VT-JBM	B737-86N/W	36817/3055	
VT-JBN	B737-86N/W	36818/3087	
VT-JBP	B737-86N/W	36819/3101	
VT-JBR	B737-85R/W	36695/3281	♦
VT-JBQ	B737-85R/W	36694/3264	♦
VT-JBS	B737-85R/W	36698/3433	♦
VT-JGA	B737-85R	30410/1228	
VT-JGB	B737-75R/W	30411/1282	
VT-JGC	B737-95R	30412/1314	
VT-JGD	B737-95R	33740/1350	
VT-JGE	B737-83N/W	32663/1608	
VT-JGF	B737-8FH/W	29639/1643	
VT-JGG	B737-8FH/W	29668/1686	
VT-JGH	B737-83N/W	32577/973	
VT-JGJ	B737-83N/W	32578/998	
VT-JGK	B737-83N/W	32579/1002	
VT-JGL	B737-76N/W	32738/1392	
VT-JGM	B737-83N/W	32614/1201	
VT-JGN	B737-83N/W	32616/1212	
VT-JGP	B737-85R/W	34798/1920	
VT-JGQ	B737-85R/W	34797/2007	
VT-JGR	B737-85R/W	34799/2044	
VT-JGS	B737-85R/W	34800/2085	
VT-JGT	B737-85R/W	34801/2125	
VT-JGU	B737-85R/W	34802/2170	
VT-JGV	B737-85R/W	34803/2209	
VT-JGW	B737-85R/W	34804/2297	
VT-JGX	B737-75R/W	34805/2360	
VT-JGY	B737-75R/W	34806/2404	
VT-JGZ	B737-76N/W	35218/2342	
VT-JLE	B737-8AS/W	33555/1426	♦
VT-JLF	B737-8AS/W	33556/1428	♦
VT-JNF	B737-71Q	29044/152	
VT-JNG	B737-71Q	29045/169	
VT-JNH	B737-71Q	29046/181	
VT-JNJ	B737-85R	29038/297	
VT-JNL	B737-85R	29039/326	
VT-JNM	B737-85R	29040/465	
VT-JNN	B737-85R	29041/489	
VT-JNR	B737-85R	30403/749	
VT-JNS	B737-73A	28498/775	
VT-JNU	B737-75R	30404/835	
VT-JNV	B737-75R	30405/927	
VT-JNW	B737-75R	30406/1016	
VT-JNX	B737-85R	30407/1073	
VT-JNY	B737-85R	30408/1146	
VT-JNZ	B737-85R	30409/1185	
VT-	B737-75R		o/o
VT-	B737-8AL		o/o
VT-	B737-8AL		o/o
VT-JEA	B777-35RER	35157/627	
VT-JEB	B777-35RER	35158/637	
VT-JEG	B777-35RER	35163/675	
VT-JEH	B777-35RER	35166/678	
VT-JEJ	B777-35RER	35161/693	
VT-JEK	B777-35RER	35165/696	

JETLITE — S2 / RSH

VT-JLA	B737-7Q8	30037/1449	
VT-JLB	B737-7Q8	28250/1142	
VT-JLC	B737-71Q	29043/138	♦
VT-SIJ	B737-81Q	29049/424	
VT-SIK	B737-81Q	29050/444	
VT-SIU	B737-7K9	28090/205	
VT-SIV	B737-7K9	28091/223	[DEL]
VT-SIZ	B737-7BK	33025/1707	

☐	VT-SJA	B737-7BK	33026/1715
☐	VT-SJE	B737-7Q8	30727/1005
☐	VT-SJF	B737-86N	28610/449
☐	VT-SJG	B737-8Q8/W	30694/1863
☐	VT-SJH	B737-8Q8/W	30695/1891
☐	VT-SJI	B737-8K9/W	34399/2030
☐	VT-SJJ	B737-8K9/W	34400/2053
☐	VT-SAL	CRJ-200ER	7224
☐	VT-SAQ	CRJ-200ER	7345
☐	VT-SAR	CRJ-200ER	7393

KINGFISHER AIRLINES — IT / KFR

☐	VT-VJK	A330-223	874
☐	VT-VJL	A330-223	891
☐	VT-VJN	A330-223	927
☐	VT-VJO	A330-223	939
☐	VT-VJP	A330-223	946

KINGFISHER DECCAN — IT / KFR

☐	VT-KFH	A319-131	2621	[DEL]
☐	VT-KFI	A319-131	2634	
☐	VT-KFJ	A319-131	2664	
☐	VT-VJM	A319-133X	2650	
☐	VT-ADR	A320-232	2922	
☐	VT-ADU	A320-232	2874	
☐	VT-ADV	A320-232	2366	
☐	VT-ADW	A320-232	2376	
☐	VT-DKR	A320-232	2731	
☐	VT-DKS	A320-232	2747	
☐	VT-DKT	A320-232	2753	
☐	VT-DKU	A320-232	2676	
☐	VT-DKV	A320-232	2645	[BOM]
☐	VT-DNZ	A320-232	3012	
☐	VT-KFA	A320-232	2413	
☐	VT-KFB	A320-232	2443	
☐	VT-KFC	A320-232	2496	
☐	VT-KFD	A320-232	2502	
☐	VT-KFE	A320-232	2522	
☐	VT-KFF	A320-232	2531	
☐	VT-KFG	A320-232	2576	
☐	VT-KFK	A320-232	2670	
☐	VT-KFL	A320-232	2817	
☐	VT-KFM	A320-232	2856	
☐	VT-KFT	A320-232	3089	
☐	VT-KFV	A320-232	3105	
☐	VT-KFX	A320-232	3270	
☐	VT-	A320-232		o/o
☐	VT-	A320-232		o/o
☐	VT-	A320-232		o/o
☐	VT-	A320-232		o/o
☐	VT-	A320-232		o/o
☐	VT-KFN	A321-231	2916	[BOM]
☐	VT-KFP	A321-231	2919	
☐	VT-KFQ	A321-231	2927	
☐	VT-KFR	A321-231	2933	
☐	VT-KFS	A321-231	3034	
☐	VT-KFW	A321-231	3120	
☐	VT-KFY	A321-231	3302	
☐	VT-KFZ	A321-231	3322	
☐	VT-ADJ	ATR 42-500	612	
☐	VT-ADK	ATR 42-500	613	
☐	VT-ADN	ATR 42-500	576	<OMA
☐	VT-DKA	ATR 72-212A	718	
☐	VT-DKB	ATR 72-212A	720	
☐	VT-DKD	ATR 72-212A	725	
☐	VT-DKE	ATR 72-212A	723	
☐	VT-DKH	ATR 72-212A	739	
☐	VT-DKI	ATR 72-212A	732	
☐	VT-DKJ	ATR 72-212A	733	
☐	VT-DKK	ATR 72-212A	740	
☐	VT-KAA	ATR 72-212A	699	

☐	VT-KAB	ATR 72-212A	728
☐	VT-KAD	ATR 72-212A	730
☐	VT-KAE	ATR 72-212A	737
☐	VT-KAF	ATR 72-212A	738
☐	VT-KAG	ATR 72-212A	743
☐	VT-KAH	ATR 72-212A	746
☐	VT-KAI	ATR 72-212A	750
☐	VT-KAJ	ATR 72-212A	754
☐	VT-KAK	ATR 72-212A	758
☐	VT-KAL	ATR 72-212A	759
☐	VT-KAM	ATR 72-212A	762
☐	VT-KAN	ATR 72-212A	767
☐	VT-KAO	ATR 72-212A	772
☐	VT-KAP	ATR 72-212A	776
☐	VT-KAQ	ATR 72-212A	777
☐	VT-KAR	ATR 72-212A	782

MDLR AIRLINES

☐	VT-MDL	Avro 146-RJ70	E1229
☐	VT-MDM	Avro 146-RJ70	E1230
☐	VT-MDN	Avro 146-RJ70	E1252

SPICEJET — SG / SEJ

☐	VT-SGE	B737-86N/W	32693/1951	
☐	VT-SGF	B737-8GJ/W	36367/3218	♦
☐	VT-SGG	B737-8GJ/W	36368/3310	♦
☐	VT-SGH	B737-8GJ/W	36369/3363	♦
☐	VT-SGI	B737-8GJ/W	37361/3506	♦
☐	VT-SGJ	B737-86J/W	29641/1654	♦
☐	VT-SGK	B737-8BK/W	33019/1502	♦
☐	VT-SGL	B737-8AS/W	29925/588	♦
☐	VT-SGO	B737-8AS/W	29926/722	♦
☐	VT-SGQ	B737-8GJ/W	37365/3539	♦
☐	VT-SPE	B737-86N	28621/570	
☐	VT-SPF	B737-8GJ/W	34896/1861	
☐	VT-SPH	B737-83N/W	30660/1330	
☐	VT-SPJ	B737-8GJ/W	34897/2069	
☐	VT-SPK	B737-8GJ/W	34898/2104	
☐	VT-SPL	B737-8GJ/W	34899/2128	
☐	VT-SPM	B737-8GJ/W	34900/2167	
☐	VT-SPO	B737-86N/W	35216/2321	
☐	VT-SPP	B737-86N/W	35217/2359	
☐	VT-SPQ	B737-8GJ/W	34903/2335	
☐	VT-SPR	B737-8GJ/W	34904/2347	
☐	VT-SPS	B737-8GJ/W	34905/2392	
☐	VT-SPW	B737-86N/W	32672/1932	
☐	VT-	B737-8GJ/W		o/o♦
☐	VT-	B737-8GJ/W		o/o♦
☐	VT-SGB	B737-9GJER/W	34956/2608	
☐	VT-SGC	B737-9GJER/W	34957/2639	
☐	VT-SGD	B737-9GJER/W	34961/2744	
☐	VT-SPT	B737-9GJER/W	34952/2426	
☐	VT-SPU	B737-9GJER/W	34953/2466	
☐	VT-	B737-9GJER/W		o/o♦
☐	VT-	DHC-8-402Q		o/o♦
☐	VT-	DHC-8-402Q		o/o♦
☐	VT-	DHC-8-402Q		o/o♦
☐	VT-	DHC-8-402Q		o/o♦
☐	VT-	DHC-8-402Q		o/o♦
☐	VT-	DHC-8-402Q		o/o♦

STAR AVIATION

☐	VT-SMC	ERJ-170LR	17000279

V2 - ANTIGUA

LIAT - THE CARIBBEAN AIRLINE — LI / LIA

☐	V2-LCY	DHC-8-110	35	[ANU]
☐	V2-LDQ	DHC-8-102	113	
☐	V2-LDU	DHC-8-103	270	
☐	V2-LEF	DHC-8-103	144	

☐	V2-LES	DHC-8-311B	412
☐	V2-LET	DHC-8-311B	416
☐	V2-LEU	DHC-8-311	408
☐	V2-LFF	DHC-8-314	410
☐	V2-LFM	DHC-8-311A	267
☐	V2-LFU	DHC-8-311	250
☐	V2-LFV	DHC-8-311A	283
☐	V2-LGA	DHC-8-311A	232
☐	V2-LGB	DHC-8-311A	266
☐	V2-LGC	DHC-8-311	298
☐	V2-LGG	DHC-8-311A	404
☐	V2-LGH	DHC-8-311	242
☐	V2-LGI	DHC-8-311A	325
☐	V2-LGN	DHC-8-311A	230

V5 - NAMIBIA

AIR NAMIBIA   SW / NMB

☐	V5-NME	A340-311	51
☐	V5-NMF	A340-311	47
☐	V5-NDI	B737-528	25228/2170
☐	V5-TNP	B737-528	25229/2180

V8 - BRUNEI

ROYAL BRUNEI AIRLINES   BI / RBA

☐	V8-RBP	A319-132	2023	
☐	V8-RBR	A319-132	2032	
☐	V8-RBS	A320-232	2135	
☐	V8-RBT	A320-232	2139	
☐	V8-RBF	B767-33AER	25530/414	
☐	V8-BLA	B777-212ER	30871/378	◆
☐	V8-BLB	B777-212ER	30872/398	◆
☐	V8-BLC	B777-212ER	28524/350	◆
☐	V8-BLD	B777-212ER	28525/353	◆
☐	V8-BLE	B777-212ER	28526/355	◆
☐	V8-BLF	B777-212ER	30869/366	◆

XA -MEXICO

AEROCEDROS

☐	XA-RYV	Convair 440-0	474
☐	XA-TFY	Convair 440-0	472
☐	XA-TFZ	Convair 440-94	439

AERODAN

☐	XA-YYS	NAMC YS-11A	2071

AEROLINEAS REGIONALES   RCQ

☐	XA-RCB	B737-2T4C	23066

AEROMAR AIRLINES   VW / TAO

☐	XA-SJJ	ATR 42-320	39	
☐	XA-SYH	ATR 42-320	62	
☐	XA-TAH	ATR 42-500	471	
☐	XA-TAI	ATR 42-500	474	
☐	XA-TIC	ATR 42-320	58	
☐	XA-TKJ	ATR 42-500	561	
☐	XA-TLN	ATR 42-500	564	
☐	XA-TPR	ATR 42-500	586	
☐	XA-TPS	ATR 42-500	594	
☐	XA-TRI	ATR 42-500	607	
☐	XA-TRJ	ATR 42-500	608	
☐	XA-UAU	ATR 42-500	462	
☐	XA-UAV	ATR 42-500	476	
☐	XA-UFA	ATR 42-500	412	
☐	XA-UOZ	CRJ-200ER	7544	◆
☐	XA-UPA	CRJ-200ER	7545	◆

AEROMEXICO   AM / AMX

☐	EI-DRD	B737-752/W	35117/2122	
☐	EI-DRE	B737-752/W	35787/2111	
☐	N432AM	B737-73V	32423/1433	◆
☐	N784XA	B737-752/W	33784/1393	
☐	N788XA	B737-752/W	33788/1439	
☐	N842AM	B737-752/W	32842/1814	
☐	N850AM	B737-752/W	33786/1403	
☐	N851AM	B737-752/W	29363/1417	
☐	N852AM	B737-752/W	33787/1421	
☐	N853AM	B737-752/W	33791/1557	
☐	N855AM	B737-752/W	33792/1571	
☐	N857AM	B737-752/W	33793/1597	
☐	N904AM	B737-752/W	28262/1565	
☐	N906AM	B737-752/W	29356/1586	
☐	N908AM	B737-752/W	30038/1601	
☐	N997AM	B737-76Q/W	30283/1156	
☐	XA-AAM	B737-752/W	33783/1381	
☐	XA-AGM	B737-752/W	35786/2098	
☐	XA-CAM	B737-752/W	35785/1398	
☐	XA-CTG	B737-752/W	35123/2374	
☐	XA-CYM	B737-752/W	35124/2456	
☐	XA-GMV	B737-752/W	35118/2151	
☐	XA-GOL	B737-752/W	35785/2011	
☐	XA-HAM	B737-752/W	33789/1524	
☐	XA-MAH	B737-752/W	35122/2348	
☐	XA-NAM	B737-752/W	33790/1533	
☐	XA-PAM	B737-752/W	34293/1747	
☐	XA-QAM	B737-752/W	34294/1761	
☐	XA-VAM	B737-752/W	34295/1765	
☐	XA-	B737-752/W		o/o
☐	XA-	B737-752/W		o/o
☐	XA-	B737-752/W		o/o
☐	EI-DRA	B737-852/W	35114/2037	
☐	EI-DRB	B737-852/W	35115/2070	
☐	EI-DRC	B737-852/W	35116/2081	
☐	N359AM	B737-8CX/W	32359/1041	◆
☐	XA-JOY	B737-852/W	35121/2327	
☐	XA-MIA	B737-852/W	35119/2273	
☐	XA-ZAM	B737-852/W	35120/2290	
☐	XA-AMX	B767-25DER	24733/261	◆
☐	XA-APB	B767-3Q8ER	27618/727	
☐	XA-JBC	B767-284ER	24762/307	
☐	XA-MAT	B767-3Y0ER	24947/351	
☐	XA-OAM	B767-2B1ER	26471/511	
☐	XA-TOJ	B767-283ER	24727/301	
☐	N745AM	B777-2Q8ER	32718/554	
☐	N746AM	B777-2Q8ER	32719/562	
☐	N774AM	B777-2Q8ER	28689/365	
☐	N776AM	B777-2Q8	28692/373	
☐	XA-TPM	MD-87	49671/1463	[MEX]

AEROMEXICO CONNECT   5D / SLI

☐	XA-ACA	ERJ-145LR	145144	
☐	XA-ACB	ERJ-145LR	145221	◆
☐	XA-ALI	ERJ-145LR	145795	
☐	XA-BLI	ERJ-145LR	145798	
☐	XA-CLI	ERJ-145LR	14500803	
☐	XA-DLI	ERJ-145LR	14500852	
☐	XA-ELI	ERJ-145LR	14500861	
☐	XA-FLI	ERJ-145MP	145203	
☐	XA-GAC	ERJ-145MP	145406	
☐	XA-GLI	ERJ-145MP	145444	
☐	XA-HLI	ERJ-145MP	145337	
☐	XA-ILI	ERJ-145LU	145564	
☐	XA-JLI	ERJ-145MP	145426	
☐	XA-KAC	ERJ-145MP	145322	
☐	XA-KLI	ERJ-145MP	145440	
☐	XA-LLI	ERJ-145ER	145060	
☐	XA-MLI	ERJ-145ER	145065	
☐	XA-NLI	ERJ-145ER	145083	

☐	XA-OLI	ERJ-145ER	145089
☐	XA-PAC	ERJ-145LR	145498
☐	XA-PLI	ERJ-145ER	145090
☐	XA-QAC	ERJ-145LR	145510
☐	XA-QLI	ERJ-145LU	145588
☐	XA-RAC	ERJ-145LR	145313
☐	XA-RLI	ERJ-145LU	145559
☐	XA-SLI	ERJ-145LU	145580
☐	XA-TAK	ERJ-145LR	145475
☐	XA-TLI	ERJ-145LU	145601
☐	XA-ULI	ERJ-145LU	145570
☐	XA-VAC	ERJ-145LR	145232
☐	XA-VLI	ERJ-145LU	145574
☐	XA-WAC	ERJ-145LR	145255
☐	XA-WLI	ERJ-145LU	145434
☐	XA-XAC	ERJ-145LR	145128
☐	XA-XLI	ERJ-145LU	145456
☐	XA-YAC	ERJ-145LR	145168
☐	XA-YLI	ERJ-145LR	145400
☐	XA-ZAC	ERJ-145LR	145199
☐	XA-ZLI	ERJ-145LU	145420
☐	XA-AAC	ERJ-190LR	19000121
☐	XA-BAC	ERJ-190LR	19000129
☐	XA-CAC	ERJ-190LR	19000135
☐	XA-EAC	ERJ-190LR	19000145
☐	XA-FAC	ERJ-190LR	19000234
☐	XA-IAC	ERJ-190LR	19000238
☐	XA-JAC	ERJ-190LR	19000248
☐	XA-	ERJ-190LR	o/o♦
☐	XA-	ERJ-190LR	o/o♦
☐	XA-	ERJ-190LR	o/o♦
☐	XA-	ERJ-190LR	o/o♦
☐	XA-	ERJ-190LR	o/o♦
☐	XA-	ERJ-190LR	o/o♦

AEROMEXICO TRAVEL

☐	XA-TXC	MD-87	49389/1333
☐	N583MD	MD-83	49659/1438
☐	N838AM	MD-83	49397/1331
☐	N848SH	MD-83	49848/1592 ♦

AERONAVES TSM

☐	XA-TYF	Convair 600F	101
☐	XA-	Convair 640	332 ♦
☐	XA-UOG	DC-9-33RC	47194/324 ♦

AEROPOSTAL · PCG

☐	XA-TXS	DC-8-63CF	46054/453

AEROUNION · 6R / TNO

☐	XA-FPP	A300B4-203F	247 ♦
☐	XA-LRL	A300B4-203F	210 ♦
☐	XA-MRC	A300B4-203F	227 ♦
☐	XA-TVU	A300B4-203F	074
☐	XA-TWQ	A300B4-203F	045

ESTAFETA CARGA AEREA · E7 / ESF

☐	XA-AJA	B737-3Y0(SF)	23747/1363
☐	XA-ECA	B737-3M8(SF)	24024/1689
☐	XA-EMX	B737-375F	23707/1388
☐	XA-ESA	CRJ-100ER	7085
☐	XA-GGB	B737-3M8(SF)	24023/1675
☐	XA-SPO	CRJ-100ER	7088
☐	XA-TWP	B737-229C	21738/576

FLYMEX

☐	XA-AAS	Do 328 Jet	3127
☐	XA-FAS	Do 328 Jet	3125

GLOBAL AIR · DMJ

☐	XA-TWR	B737-2H4	21812/611 >VCV
☐	XA-UBB	B737-291	21750/574 >CUB
☐	XA-UMQ	B737-29Q3	24103/1565
☐	XA-UNG	B737-3L9	26441/2550 ♦
☐	XA-UNW	B737-3T0	23458/1244 ♦

INTERJET · 4O / INJ

☐	XA-ABC	A320-214	3690
☐	XA-ACO	A320-214	1322
☐	XA-ALM	A320-214	1308
☐	XA-IJA	A320-214	1244
☐	XA-IJT	A320-214	1132
☐	XA-ILY	A320-214	3123 ♦
☐	XA-INJ	A320-214	1162
☐	XA-JCV	A320-214	3514
☐	XA-MLR	A320-214	2227
☐	XA-MTY	A320-214	1179
☐	XA-MXM	A320-214	3286
☐	XA-MYR	A320-214	3021 ♦
☐	XA-SOB	A320-214	2189 ♦
☐	XA-TLC	A320-214	3312
☐	XA-UHE	A320-214	3149
☐	XA-VAI	A320-214	3160
☐	XA-VFI	A320-214	1780 ♦
☐	XA-VIP	A320-214	3304 ♦
☐	XA-VTA	A320-214	1259
☐	XA-XII	A320-214	3508
☐	XA-ZIH	A320-214	3667
☐	XA-	A320-214	o/o♦
☐	XA-	A320-214	o/o♦
☐	XA-	A320-214	o/o♦
☐	XA-	A320-214	o/o♦
☐	XA-	A320-214	o/o♦
☐	XA-	A320-214	o/o♦

MAGNICHARTERS · GMT

☐	XA-MAA	B737-377	23655/1274
☐	XA-MAB	B737-301	23232/1169
☐	XA-MAC	B737-2C3	21014/397
☐	XA-MAD	B737-277	22652/831
☐	XA-MAE	B737-277	22648/789
☐	XA-MAF	B737-2K9	22505/815
☐	XA-MAI	B737-322	24537/1774
☐	XA-UNA	B737-322	24248/1636 ♦
☐	XA-UNL	B737-322	24532/1754 ♦

MAS AIR CARGO · MY / MAA

☐	N314LA	B767-316ERF	32573/848 <LCO
☐	N420LA	B767-316ERF	34627/948 <LCO

MAYAIR · MYI

☐	XA-MYI	Short SD.3-60	SH3602

MEXICANA · MX / MXA

☐	XA-MXR	A320-231	0252
☐	XA-MXS	A320-231	0259
☐	XA-MXT	A320-231	0260
☐	XA-MXU	A320-231	0275
☐	XA-MXV	A320-231	0276
☐	XA-MXW	A320-231	0296
☐	XA-MXX	A320-231	0320
☐	XA-MXY	A320-231	0321
☐	XA-MXZ	A320-231	0353
☐	XA-UMN	A320-231	0261

NOVA AIR · M4

☐	XA-OCI	B737-217	22257/756 [MEX]
☐	XA-OHC	B737-291	21640/536

REPUBLICAIR			RBC
☐ XA-RBC	B737-277	22647/785	[MEX]
☐ XA-RBD	B737-277	22649/801	

VIVA AEROBUS			VIV
☐ XA-TAR	B737-301	23259/1132	
☐ XA-UGL	B737-3B7	22958/1137	
☐ XA-VIA	B737-3B7	23856/1501	
☐ XA-VIB	B737-3B7	23378/1339	
☐ XA-VIF	B737-301	23552/1382	
☐ XA-VIH	B737-301	23554/1408	
☐ XA-VIJ	B737-3Y0	24677/1837	♦
☐ XA-VIK	B737-3L9	26442/2277	♦
☐ XA-VIL	B737-33A	25010/2008	♦
☐ XA-VIM	B737-33A	25032/2014	♦
☐ XA-VIV	B737-301	23560/1463	
☐ XA-VIX	B737-3B7	23312/1162	
☐ XA-VIY	B737-3B7	22959/1140	

VOLARIS			V4 / VOI
☐ N473TA	A319-132	1140	
☐ N474TA	A319-132	1159	
☐ N501VL	A319-133	2979	
☐ N502VL	A319-132	3463	
☐ N503VL	A319-132	3491	
☐ N504VL	A319-132	3590	
☐ XA-VOA	A319-132	2771	
☐ XA-VOB	A319-133	2780	
☐ XA-VOC	A319-132	2997	
☐ XA-VOD	A319-133	3045	
☐ XA-VOE	A319-133	3069	
☐ XA-VOF	A319-133	3077	
☐ XA-VOG	A319-133	3175	
☐ XA-VOH	A319-133	3253	
☐ XA-VOI	A319-132	2657	
☐ XA-VOJ	A319-133	3279	
☐ XA-VOK	A319-133	3450	
☐ XA-VOL	A319-132	2666	
☐ XA-VOO	A319-133	3705	
☐ XA-VOP	A319-133	4403	♦
☐ XA-VOQ	A319-133	4422	♦
☐ XA-VOR	A319-132	2296	♦
☐ XA-VOS	A319-132	3252	♦
☐ XA-VOT	A319-132	3317	♦
☐ XA-	A319-112	3589	o/o♦
☐ XA-	A319-132		o/o♦
☐ XA-	A319-132		o/o♦
☐ XA-VOM	A320-233	3624	
☐ XA-VON	A320-232	3672	
☐ XA-	A320-232		o/o♦
☐ XA-	A320-232		o/o♦

XT - BURKINA FASO

AIR BURKINA			2J / VBW
☐ XT-ABC	MD-87	49834/1714	
☐ XT-ABD	MD-87	49839/1739	
☐ XT-ABF	MD-83	53464/2091	
☐ XT-FZP	F.28 Fellowship 4000	11185	

XU - CAMBODIA

CAMBODIA ANGKOR AIR			K6 / VAV
☐ VN-A351	A321-231	3005	Lsf HVN
☐ VN-B212	ATR 72-212A	685	<HVN
☐ VN-B214	ATR 72-212A	688	<HVN
☐ VN-B227	ATR 72-212A	899	<HVN♦
☐ VN-B231	ATR 72-212A	906	<HVN♦

IMTREC AVIATION			IMT
☐ RDPL-34155	Il-76T	73411338	
☐ RDPL-34158	An-32	402437	
☐ XU-315	An-12BP	2400702	

PMT AIR			PMT
☐ XU-U4B	B737-281	20450/262	
☐ XU-U4E	MD-83	49395/1286	[JKT]
☐ XU-U4H	B727-200		

PRESIDENT AIRLINES			TO / PSD
☐ XU-335	An-24B	99902009	
☐ XU-881	F.27 Friendship 100	10168	[PNH]
☐ XU-888	F.28 Fellowship 1000	11012	[PNH]

ROYAL KHMER AIRLINES			RK / RKH
☐ XU-RKA	B737-2H4	22061/639	
☐ XU-RKB	B737-2H4	22674/827	
☐ XU-RKC	B737-2H4	22903/905	
☐ XU-RKF	B727-223F	19494/661	
☐ XU-RKH	B737-232	23105/1068	
☐ XU-RKJ	B727-223	20989/1144	
☐ XU-RKK	B737-2H4	23054/969	>IAW

ROYAL PHNOM PENH AIRWAYS			RL / PPW
☐ XU-070	AVIC 1 Y-7-100C	9706	
☐ XU-071	AVIC 1 Y-7-100C	8708	
☐ XU-072	AVIC 1 Y-7-100C	8705	

XY - MYANMAR

AIR BAGAN			W9 / JAB
☐ XY-AGC	Fokker 100	11327	>MMA
☐ XY-AGD	A310-222	419	
☐ XY-AGE	A310-222	320	
☐ XY-AGF	Fokker 100	11282	
☐ XY-AIA	ATR 72-212	422	
☐ XY-AIC	ATR 42-320	159	
☐ XY-AID	ATR 42-300	152	
☐ XY-AIE	ATR 72-212	458	
☐ XY-AIH	ATR 72-212	469	
☐ XY-AIS	ATR 72-212A	626	♦

AIR MANDALAY			6T
☐ XY-AEY	ATR 72-212	393	
☐ XY-AIJ	ATR 42-320	268	
☐ XY-AIR	ATR 72-212	467	♦

MYANMAR AIRWAYS			UB / UBA
☐ XY-ADZ	F.27 Friendship 600	10574	
☐ XY-AEQ	F.27 Friendship 400	10294	[RGN]
☐ XY-AEW	F.27 Friendship 600	10352	[RGN]
☐ XY-AEZ	ATR 72-212	475	
☐ XY-AGA	F.28 Fellowship 4000	11232	
☐ XY-AGB	F.28 Fellowship 4000	11184	
☐ XY-AGH	F.28 Fellowship 4000	11161	♦
☐ XY-AIB	ATR 42-320	178	
☐ XY-AIF	ATR 72-212A	765	
☐ XY-AIG	ATR 72-212A	781	

MYANMAR AIRWAYS INL			8M / MMA
☐ XY-AGC	Fokker 100	11327	<JAB
☐ XY-AGG	A320-231	0114	
☐ XY-AGI	A320-231	0113	

YANGON AIRLINES — HK

☐	XY-AIM	ATR 72-212	479 ♦
☐	XY-AIN	ATR 72-212	481 ♦

YA - AFGHANISTAN

ARIANA AFGHAN AIRLINES — FG / AFG

☐	TC-SGC	A310-304	519	<SGX
☐	TC-SGI	B737-86J/W	28069/42	<SGX
☐	YA-BAB	A300B4-203	180	
☐	YA-BAC	A300B4-203	190	[FRA]
☐	YA-CAQ	A310-304	496	
☐	YA-CAV	A310-304ER	497	
☐	YA-DAL	An-24RV	57310409	
☐	YA-DAM	An-24RV	57310404	
☐	YA-FAM	B727-223	21088/1255	
☐	YA-FAN	B727-227F	21245/1202	
☐	YA-FAS	B727-223	21388/1345	
☐	YA-FAT	B727-221/W	22542/1799	
☐	YA-FAY	B727-228	22289/1719	

KABULAIR

☐	YA-KAC	An-12BP	5343204
☐	YA-KAD	An-12BP	6343810
☐	YA-KAN	Il-76TD	43449468

KAM AIR — RQ / KMF

☐	EY-87963	Yak-40K	9831058	<TJK
☐	YA-GAD	B727-243	22702/1814	
☐	YA-KAM	B767-222	21879/49	
☐	YA-KMB	An-26B	17311802	
☐	YA-KMC	An-24RV	37309008	
☐	YA-KMF	MD-82	49704/1490	
☐	YA-KMG	MD-83	49567/1367	♦
☐	YA-VIB	DC-8-63AF	46034/434	♦
☐	YA-VIC	DC-8-63F	46035/438	♦

PAMIR AIR — NR / PIR

☐	YA-PIB	B737-4Y0	26077/2425
☐	YA-PID	B737-4Y0	26085/2468
☐	YA-PIR	B737-232	23077/996
☐	EY-538	B737-4Y0	23980/1667

SAFI AIRWAYS

☐	YA-AQS	B767-2J6ER	23745/156	
☐	YA-HSB	B737-3J6	23303/1237	
☐	YA-SFL	B737-3J6	23302/1224	
☐	YA-TTB	A340-311	015	
☐	YA-TTC	A320-212	0671	♦

YI - IRAQ

AZMAR AIRLINES

☐	C5-JDZ	DC-9-31	48145/1042
☐	C5-LPS	DC-9-31	48146/1044

IRAQI AIRWAYS — IA / IAW

☐	YI-APW	B737-2B7	22885/966	
☐	YI-APY	B737-201	22274/682	
☐	YI-APZ	B737-201	22354/736	
☐	YI-AQK	B737-7BD/W	33935/2315	
☐	YI-AQL	B737-7BD/W	35789/2201	
☐	YI-AQN	B737-322	24717/1930	o/o♦
☐	YI-AQO	B737-322	24673/1920	
☐	EY-537	B737-4B7	24550/1793	♦
☐	XU-RKK	B737-2H4	23054/969	<RKH
☐	9L-LEL	B727-247	21483/1350	

☐	YI-AQA	CRJ-900NG	15189
☐	YI-AQB	CRJ-900NG	15202
☐	YI-AQC	CRJ-900NG	15213
☐	YI-AQD	CRJ-900NG	15220

YJ - VANUATU

AIR VANUATU — NF / AVN

☐	YJ-AV1	B737-8Q8/W	30734/2477
☐	YJ-AV4	AVIC II Y-12 II	028
☐	YJ-AV5	AVIC II Y-12 II	029
☐	YJ-AV6	AVIC II Y-12 II	032
☐	YJ-AV72	ATR 72-212A	876

YK - SYRIA

CHAM WINGS AIRLINES

☐	SU-BOZ	MD-83	53192/2155	<AMV

SYRIANAIR — RB / SYR

☐	YK-AKA	A320-232	0886	
☐	YK-AKB	A320-232	0918	
☐	YK-AKC	A320-232	1032	
☐	YK-AKD	A320-232	1076	
☐	YK-AKE	A320-232	1085	
☐	YK-AKF	A320-232	1117	
☐	YK-ANA	An-24B	87304203	
☐	YK-ANC	An-26	3007	
☐	YK-AND	An-26	3008	
☐	YK-ANE	An-26	3103	
☐	YK-ANF	An-26	3104	
☐	YK-ANG	An-26B	10907	
☐	YK-ANH	An-26B	11406	
☐	YK-AVA	ATR 72-212A	836	♦
☐	YK-AVB	ATR 72-212A	845	♦
☐	YK-AGA	B727-294	21203/1188	[DAM]
☐	YK-AGB	B727-294	21204/1194	[DAM]
☐	YK-AGC	B727-294	21205/1198	[DAM]
☐	YK-AGD	B727-269	22360/1670	[DAM]
☐	YK-AGE	B727-269	22361/1716	[DAM]
☐	YK-AGF	B727-269	22763/1788	[DAM]
☐	YK-AHA	B747SP-94	21174/284	[DAM]
☐	YK-AHB	B747SP-94	21175/290	[DAM]
☐	YK-ATA	Il-76TD	93421613	
☐	YK-ATB	Il-76T	93421619	
☐	YK-ATC	Il-76T	13431911	
☐	YK-ATD	Il-76T	13431915	
☐	YK-AYA	Tu-134B-3	63992	
☐	YK-AYB	Tu-134B-3	63994	
☐	YK-AYE	Tu-134B-3	66187	
☐	YK-AYF	Tu-134B-3	63190	
☐	YK-AQA	Yak-40	9341932	
☐	YK-AQB	Yak-40	9530443	
☐	YK-AQD	Yak-40	9830158	
☐	YK-AQE	Yak-40K	9830258	
☐	YK-AQF	Yak-40	9931859	
☐	YK-AQG	Yak-40K	9941959	

YL - LATVIA

AIR BALTIC — BT / BTI

☐	YL-BBD	B737-53S	29075/3101	
☐	YL-BBE	B737-53S	29073/3083	
☐	YL-BBF	B737-548/W	24878/1939	
☐	YL-BBG	B737-548/W	24919/1970	♦
☐	YL-BBH	B737-548/W	24968/1975	

☐ YL-BBI	B737-33A/W	27454/2703	
☐ YL-BBJ	B737-36Q/W	30333/3117	
☐ YL-BBK	B737-33V/W	29332/3072	
☐ YL-BBL	B737-33V/W	29334/3089	
☐ YL-BBM	B737-522	26680/2366	
☐ YL-BBN	B737-522	26683/2368	
☐ YL-BBP	B737-522	26688/2404	
☐ YL-BBQ	B737-522	26691/2408	
☐ YL-BBR	B737-31S	29266/3092	
☐ YL-BBS	B737-31S	29267/3093	
☐ YL-BBX	B737-36Q/W	30334/3120	
☐ YL-BBY	B737-36Q/W	30335/3129	
☐ YL-BDB	B757-256/W	26251/897	
☐ YL-BDC	B757-256/W	26253/902	
☐ YL-BAE	DHC-8-402Q	4289	
☐ YL-BAF	DHC-8-402Q	4293	
☐ YL-BAH	DHC-8-402Q	4296	
☐ YL-BAI	DHC-8-402Q	4302	◆
☐ YL-BAJ	DHC-8-402Q	4309	◆
☐ YL-BAQ	DHC-8-402Q	4313	◆
☐ YL-BAX	DHC-8-402Q	4324	◆
☐ YL-BAY	DHC-8-402Q	4331	◆
☐ LY-BAO	Fokker 50	20189	
☐ LY-BAV	Fokker 50	20190	
☐ LY-BAZ	Fokker 50	20153	
☐ YL-BAA	Fokker 50	20120	
☐ YL-BAC	Fokker 50	20216	
☐ YL-BAR	Fokker 50	20149	
☐ YL-BAS	Fokker 50	20162	
☐ YL-BAT	Fokker 50	20163	
☐ YL-BAU	Fokker 50	20126	
☐ YL-BAW	Fokker 50	20148	

INVERSIJA — INV

☐ YL-LAK	Il-76T	3424707
☐ YL-LAL	Il-76T	13433984

KS AVIA — KSA

☐ YL-KSA	An-74-200	36547098957
☐ YL-KSB	An-74	36547136013

RAF-AVIA — MTL

☐ YL-RAA	An-26B	97311206	
☐ YL-RAB	An-26B	7310508	
☐ YL-RAC	An-26	7309903	
☐ YL-RAD	An-26B	47313909	
☐ YL-RAE	An-26B	57314004	
☐ YL-RAF	An-74TK-100	36547095905	<CBI
☐ YL-RAG	SAAB SF.340A	340A-052	
☐ YL-RAH	SAAB SF.340A	340A-081	

SMARTLYNX — 6Y / ART

☐ YL-BBC	A320-211	0142	
☐ YL-BCB	A320-211	0726	
☐ YL-LCA	A320-211	0333	◆
☐ YL-LCB	A320-211	0384	◆
☐ YL-LCC	A320-211	0310	
☐ YL-LCD	A320-211	0359	
☐ YL-LCE	A320-211	0311	
☐ YL-LCG	A320-211	0283	◆
☐ YL-LCH	A320-212	0914	◆
☐ YL-LCY	B767-3Y0ER	24952/357	>BBR
☐ YL-LCZ	B767-3Y0ER	25000/386	>BBR

YN - NICARAGUA

AIR CHARTER CARGO

☐ YN-CGA	An-32	3007

LA COSTENA

☐ YN-CHG	ATR 42-320	323	◆
☐ YN-CGG	Short SD.3-60	SH3612	<APP

YR - ROMANIA

BLUE AIR — 0B / JOR

☐ YR-BAC	B737-377	23653/1260	<AWK
☐ YR-BAE	B737-4Y0	28723/2886	
☐ YR-BAF	B737-322F	24453/1730	
☐ YR-BAG	B737-5L9	24778/1816	
☐ YR-BAH	B737-505	24274/2035	◆
☐ YR-BAI	B737-4Y0	24314/1680	◆
☐ YR-BAJ	B737-430	27005/2359	◆
☐ YR-BAK	B737-430	27003/2328	◆
☐ YR-DAA	SAAB 340A	340A-116	
☐ YR-DAB	SAAB 340A	340A-137	

CARPATAIR — V3 / KRP

☐ YR-KMA	Fokker 70	11564	
☐ YR-KMB	Fokker 70	11565	
☐ YR-KMC	Fokker 70	11569	◆
☐ YR-FKA	Fokker 100	11340	◆
☐ YR-FKB	Fokker 100	11369	
☐ YR-SBA	SAAB 2000	2000-038	<SWR
☐ YR-SBB	SAAB 2000	2000-026	<SWR
☐ YR-SBC	SAAB 2000	2000-039	<SWR
☐ YR-SBD	SAAB 2000	2000-004	<SWR
☐ YR-SBE	SAAB 2000	2000-041	<SWR
☐ YR-SBI	SAAB 2000	2000-052	
☐ YR-SBJ	SAAB 2000	2000-018	<SWR
☐ YR-SBK	SAAB 2000	2000-033	<SWR
☐ YR-SBL	SAAB 2000	2000-013	
☐ YR-SBM	SAAB 2000	2000-014	
☐ YR-SBN	SAAB 2000	2000-044	
☐ YR-VGP	SAAB SF.340B	340B-228	

JETRAN INTERNATIONAL AIRWAYS — MDJ

☐ YR-MDJ	MD-81	48053/986
☐ YR-MDK	MD-82	49139/1090
☐ YR-MDL	MD-82	48079/1016
☐ YR-MDR	MD-82	48097/1059
☐ YR-MDS	MD-82	48098/1060
☐ YR-MDT	MD-82	49570/1440
☐ YR-OTN	MD-82	49119/1070

MEDALLION AIR

☐ YR-HBA	MD-82	49937/1784

MIA AIRLINES — JLA

☐ YR-HRS	BAC One-Eleven 488GH	259
☐ YR-MIA	BAC One-Eleven 492GM	260

ROMAVIA — WQ / RMV

☐ EX-115	Il-18	187009904
☐ YR-ABB	B707-3K1C	20804/883

TAROM — RO / ROT

☐ YR-LCA	A310-325	636
☐ YR-LCB	A310-325	644
☐ YR-ASA	A318-111	2931
☐ YR-ASB	A318-111	2955
☐ YR-ASC	A318-111	3220
☐ YR-ASD	A318-111	3225
☐ YR-ATA	ATR 42-500	566
☐ YR-ATB	ATR 42-500	569

☐	YR-ATC	ATR 42-500	589	
☐	YR-ATD	ATR 42-500	591	
☐	YR-ATE	ATR 42-500	596	
☐	YR-ATF	ATR 42-500	599	
☐	YR-ATG	ATR 42-500	605	
☐	YR-ATH	ATR 72-212A	861	
☐	YR-ATI	ATR 72-212A	867	
☐	YR-BGA	B737-38J	27179/2524	
☐	YR-BGB	B737-38J	27180/2529	
☐	YR-BGD	B737-38J	27182/2663	
☐	YR-BGE	B737-38J	27395/2671	
☐	YR-BGF	B737-78J	28440/795	
☐	YR-BGG	B737-78J	28442/827	
☐	YR-BGH	B737-78J	28438/1394	
☐	YR-BGI	B737-78J/W	28439/1419	♦
☐	YR-BGP	B737-86J/W	37740/2638	
☐	YR-BGR	B737-86J/W	37741/2686	
☐	YR-BGS	B737-8GJ/W	37360/2783	

YS - EL SALVADOR

TACA INTERNATIONAL AIRLINES — TA / TAI

☐	N471TA	A319-132	1066	>TPU
☐	N472TA	A319-132	1113	>TPU
☐	N476TA	A319-132	1934	
☐	N477TA	A319-132	1952	
☐	N478TA	A319-132	2339	
☐	N479TA	A319-132	2444	
☐	N480TA	A319-132	3057	
☐	N520TA	A319-132	3248	
☐	N521TA	A319-132	3276	
☐	N990TA	A319-112	1598	♦
☐		A319-132		o/o♦
☐		A319-132		o/o♦
☐		A319-132		o/o♦
☐	EI-TAB	A320-233	1624	
☐	EI-TAD	A320-233	1334	
☐	EI-TAG	A320-233	2791	
☐	N490TA	A320-232	2282	
☐	N491TA	A320-233	2301	
☐	N492TA	A320-233	2434	
☐	N493TA	A320-233	2917	
☐	N494TA	A320-233	3042	
☐	N495TA	A320-233	3103	
☐	N496TA	A320-233	3113	
☐	N497TA	A320-233	3378	
☐	N498TA	A320-233	3418	
☐	N499TA	A320-233	3510	
☐	N680TA	A320-233	3538	
☐	N681TA	A320-233	3577	
☐	N682TA	A320-233	3581	
☐		A320-233		o/o♦
☐		A320-233		o/o♦
☐		A320-233		o/o♦
☐	N564TA	A321-231	2862	
☐	N566TA	A321-231	2553	
☐	N567TA	A321-231	2610	
☐	N568TA	A321-231	2687	
☐	N570TA	A321-231	3869	
☐	N982TA	ERJ-190AR	19000259	
☐	N983TA	ERJ-190AR	19000265	
☐	N984TA	ERJ-190AR	19000273	
☐	N985TA	ERJ-190AR	19000287	
☐	N986TA	ERJ-190AR	19000360	♦
☐	N987TA	ERJ-190AR	19000393	♦
☐	N988TA	ERJ-190AR	19000399	♦

YU - SERBIA

AVIOGENEX — AGX

☐	YU-ANP	B737-2K3	23912/1401	

JAT AIRWAYS — JU / JAT

☐	YU-ALN	ATR 72-202	180
☐	YU-ALO	ATR 72-202	186
☐	YU-ALP	ATR 72-202	189
☐	YU-ALS	ATR 72-202	140
☐	YU-AND	B737-3H9	23329/1134
☐	YU-ANF	B737-3H9	23330/1136
☐	YU-ANH	B737-3H9	23415/1171
☐	YU-ANI	B737-3H9	23416/1175
☐	YU-ANJ	B737-3H9	23714/1305
☐	YU-ANK	B737-3H9	23715/1310
☐	YU-ANL	B737-3H9	23716/1321
☐	YU-ANV	B737-3H9	24140/1524
☐	YU-ANW	B737-3H9	24141/1526
☐	YU-AON	B737-3Q4	24208/1490

KOSMAS AIR CARGO — KMG

☐	YU-AMI	Il-76MD	93499982

UNITED INTENATIONAL AIRLINES — UIL

☐	YU-UIA	An-12	2348007

YV - VENEZUELA

AECA

☐	YV211T	DC-3	10201
☐	YV214T	DC-6	

AERO EJECUTIVOS — VEJ

☐	YV1854	DC-3	6135
☐	YV201T	DC-3	11775
☐	YV212T	DC-6B	44419/491
☐	YV-426C	DC-3	4093
☐	YV-440C	DC-3	2201

AEROSPOSTAL — VH / LAV

☐	YV1120	DC-9-51	47705/842	
☐	YV1121	DC-9-51	47719/845	
☐	YV1122	DC-9-51	47703/841	
☐	YV1123	DC-9-32	47727/848	
☐	YV1124	DC-9-32	47721/847	
☐	YV1126	DC-9-51	47782/893	
☐	YV1127	DC-9-34CF	47752/872	
☐	YV135T	DC-9-51	47712/815	
☐	YV136T	DC-9-51	47738/830	
☐	YV137T	DC-9-51	47771/883	
☐	YV138T	DC-9-51	47656/783	
☐	YV139T	DC-9-51	47695/806	
☐	YV140T	DC-9-51	47694/805	
☐	YV141T	DC-9-32	47535/610	
☐	YV142T	DC-9-32	45847/394	
☐	YV143T	DC-9-32	47539/637	
☐	YV148T	DC-9-51	47713/820	
☐	N120DL	B767-332	23279/154	<RYN
☐	(YV1327)	MD-82	49103/1083	[MIA]
☐	YV130T	MD-83	49822/1539	[CCS]
☐	YV-40C	B727-231	21632/1462	[CCS]

ASAP CHARTER

☐	YV1404	Yak-40	9441137

ASERCA AIRLINES — R7 / OCA

☐	YV116T	DC-9-31	45867/283
☐	YV117T	DC-9-31	47272/390
☐	YV119T	DC-9-31	47271/389
☐	YV122T	DC-9-31	45875/365

☐	YV125T	DC-9-31	47157/322	
☐	YV241T	DC-9-31	48118/942	
☐	YV244T	DC-9-31	48141/1030	
☐	YV298T	DC-9-31	48147/1048	
☐	YV367T	DC-9-32	47128/210	
☐	YV368T	DC-9-32	47518/614	
☐	YV371T	DC-9-32	47235/436	
☐	YV372T	DC-9-32	47575/680	
☐	YV1492	DC-9-31	45864/130	
☐	YV1663	DC-9-31	48144/1039	
☐	YV1879	DC-9-31	48139/1024	
☐	YV1921	DC-9-31	48154/1046	
☐	YV1922	DC-9-31	48138/1021	
☐	YV2220	DC-9-31	48155/1050	♦
☐	YV2249	DC-9-31	48120/949	
☐	YV2431	DC-9-31	48119/943	
☐	YV2434	DC-9-31	47473/598	
☐	YV2444	DC-9-32	47282/446	
☐	YV2445	DC-9-32	47479/605	
☐	YV-714C	DC-9-31	47007/87	
☐	YV-718C	DC-9-31	47187/282	
☐	YV-720C	DC-9-31	45837/103	
☐	YV	DC-9-32	47129/225	
☐	YV	DC-9-31	47249/297	[ROW]
☐	YV	DC-9-31	47343/460	[ROW]

AVIOR AIRLINES — 9V / ROI

☐	YV1360	B737-201	21665/534
☐	YV1361	B737-2H4	22286/878
☐	YV187T	B737-2H4	22964/933
☐	YV234T	B737-2H4	21970/613
☐	YV340T	B737-232	23079/1003
☐	YV342T	B737-232	23090/1020
☐	YV343T	B737-232	23101/1041
☐	YV399T	B737-2Y5	24031/1523

CIACA AIRLINES

| ☐ | YV-1070CP | Yak-40 | 9412032 |

CONVIASA — V0 / VCV

☐	YV1005	ATR 42-320	491	
☐	YV1008	ATR 42-320	346	
☐	YV1009	ATR 42-320	487	
☐	YV1850	ATR 72-201	276	
☐	YV2421	ATR 72-212	482	
☐	YV2422	ATR 72-212	486	
☐	XA-TWR	B737-2H4	21812/611	<DMJ
☐	YV1000	DHC-7-102	68	
☐	YV1003	DHC-7-102	103	
☐	YV1004	A340-211	31	
☐	YV1007	B737-322	23949/1493	
☐	YV2556	B737-3G7	24712/1869	
☐	YV2557	B737-3G7	24633/1809	
☐	YV2558	B737-232	23096/1028	
☐	YV2559	B737-232	23097/1029	
☐	YV101T	B737-291	21747/555	
☐	YV206T	B737-205	21184/440	
☐	YV398T	B737-25A	23789/1392	
☐	YV1115	CRJ-702NG	10271	
☐	YV2088	CRJ-702NG	10274	
☐	YV2115	CRJ-702NG	10275	
☐	YV	Il-96-300	74392302014	o/o
☐	YV	Il-96-300	74392302011	o/o

LASER — QL / LER

☐	YV1240	MD-81	49907/1734	[CCS]
☐	YV1243	MD-81	49908/1749	[CCS]
☐	YV1382	DC-9-14	45745/32	
☐	YV166T	DC-9-32	45789/217	[CCS]
☐	YV167T	DC-9-32	47281/427	

| ☐ | YV331T | DC-9-31 | 48157/1054 |
| ☐ | YV332T | DC-9-31 | 48158/1056 |

LINEA AEREA IAACA — KG / BNX

| ☐ | YV1929 | ATR 72-212 | 492 |

LINEA TURISTICA AEREOTUY — LD / TUY

☐	YV1184	DHC-7-102	30	
☐	YV1185	DHC-7-102	5	
☐	YV382T	ATR 42-320	110	
☐	YV383T	ATR 42-320	206	
☐	YV-640C	DHC-7-102	17	[CCS]

ORIENTAL

| ☐ | YV-594C | Yak-40 | 9841159 |
| ☐ | YV-1072C | Yak-40 | 9841059 |

RAINBOW AIR — TZR

| ☐ | EX-024 | An-26B | 11901 |

RUTACA — RUC

☐	YV1381	B737-2S3	21774/563	
☐	YV169T	B737-2S3	21776/577	
☐	YV369T	B737-230	22113/649	
☐	YV379T	B737-230	22115/694	
☐	YV380T	B737-230	22127/745	
☐	YV390T	B737-230	22128/752	
☐	YV396T	B737-236	23225/1102	♦

SANTA BARBARA AIRLINES — S3 / BBR

☐	YV1421	ATR 42-320	300	
☐	YV1422	ATR 42-320	340	
☐	YV1423	ATR 42-320	360	
☐	YV1424	ATR 42-320	368	
☐	YV2314	ATR 42-300	038	
☐	YV288T	B757-21B	24402/233	
☐	YV304T	B757-21B	24714/262	
☐	YV2242	B757-236	24119/167	
☐	YV2243	B757-236	24118/163	
☐	YV	B757-236	24370/218	o/o♦
☐	YV	B757-236	24371/225	o/o♦
☐	YV-1056C	B727-2D3	22269/1701	
☐	YL-LCY	B767-3Y0ER	24952/357	<LTC
☐	YL-LCZ	B767-3Y0ER	25000/386	<LTC
☐	YV153T	MD-82	49486/1317	o/o
☐	YV348T	MD-82	49120/1071	♦

SOLAR CARGO — OLC

| ☐ | YV1402 | An-26 | 87307207 | <CUB |
| ☐ | YV1403 | An-26 | 17309810 | |

VENESCAR INTERNATIONAL — V4 / VEC

☐	YV2308	ATR 42-300F	61	302
☐	YV2309	B727-31F	20114/712	
☐	YV149T	B727-35F	19167/325	402
☐	YV155T	B727-223F	20992/1187	408
☐	YV	B727-227F	21996/1571	

VENEZOLANA — VNE

☐	YV191T	MD-83	49392/1272	
☐	YV260T	B737-200		
☐	YV268T	B737-232	23099/1035	
☐	YV287T	B737-217	22728/911	>CUB
☐	YV295T	B737-217	21717/581	
☐	YV296T	B737-2T5	22024/641	
☐	YV302T	B737-2T5	23087/1013	
☐	YV341T	B737-232	23089/1019	

Z - ZIMBABWE

AIR ZIMBABWE — UM / AZW

☐ Z-WPA	B737-2N0	23677/1313
☐ Z-WPB	B737-2N0	23678/1405
☐ Z-WPC	B737-2N0	23679/1415
☐ Z-WPD	BAe146 Srs.200	E2065
☐ Z-WPE	B767-2N0ER	24713/287
☐ Z-WPF	B767-2N0ER	24867/333
☐ Z-WPJ	CAIC MA60	302
☐ Z-WPK	CAIC MA60	303
☐ Z-WPL	CAIC MA60	304

AVIENT AVIATION — Z3 / SMJ

☐ Z-ALS	DC-10-30F	46976/254
☐ Z-ALT	DC-10-30F	47818/305
☐ Z-ARL	DC-10-30CF	47907/157
☐ Z-AVT	DC-10-30F	46590/266
☐ Z-BVT	MD-11BCF	48410/495

SKY RELIEF

☐ 9Q-CSR	DHC-5 Buffalo	7
☐ 5Y-SRE	DHC-5 Buffalo	9

ZA - ALBANIA

ALBANIAN AIRLINES — LV / LBC

☐ OM-ASE	B737-306	23545/1343
☐ ZA-MAK	BAe146 Srs.100	E1085
☐ ZA-MAL	BAe146 Srs.200	E2054
☐ ZA-MEV	BAe146 Srs.300	E3197

BELLEAIR — LZ / LBY

☐ F-ORAA	ATR 72-212A	879	
☐ F-ORAD	A320-233	0558	
☐ F-ORAE	A320-233	0561	
☐ F-ORAF	A319-132	2335	
☐ F-ORAG	A319-132	1098	♦
☐ LZ-ATR	ATR 42-300	151	<HMS
☐ ZA-ARD	MD-82	49104/1085	

STAR AIRWAYS

☐ ZA-	A320-211	0112	o/o♦
☐ ZA-RED	A320-231	0415	[MPL]♦

ZK - NEW ZEALAND

AIR CHATHAMS — CV / CVA

☐ ZK-CIB	Convair 580	327A	
☐ ZK-CID	Convair 580F	385	[PMR]
☐ ZK-CIE	Convair 580	399	
☐ ZK-CIF	Convair 580	381	>FAJ

AIR FREIGHT NZ

☐ ZK-FTA	Convair 580	168
☐ ZK-KFH	Convair 580	42
☐ ZK-KFJ	Convair 580	114
☐ ZK-KFL	Convair 580	372
☐ ZK-KFS	Convair 5800	277

AIR NATIONAL

☐ ZK-ECO	BAe146 Srs.200	E2130

AIR NEW ZEALAND — NZ / ANZ

☐ ZK-OAB	A320-232	4553	♦

☐ ZK-OJA	A320-232	2085	
☐ ZK-OJB	A320-232	2090	
☐ ZK-OJC	A320-232	2112	
☐ ZK-OJD	A320-232	2130	
☐ ZK-OJE	A320-232	2148	
☐ ZK-OJF	A320-232	2153	
☐ ZK-OJG	A320-232	2173	
☐ ZK-OJH	A320-232	2257	
☐ ZK-OJI	A320-232	2297	
☐ ZK-OJM	A320-232	2533	
☐ ZK-OJN	A320-232	2594	
☐ ZK-OJO	A320-232	2663	
☐ ZK-	A320-232		o/o♦
☐ ZK-	A320-232		o/o♦
☐ ZK-	A320-232		o/o♦
☐ ZK-NGD	B737-3U3	28732/2966	
☐ ZK-NGE	B737-3U3	28733/2969	
☐ ZK-NGF	B737-3U3	28734/2974	
☐ ZK-NGG	B737-319	25606/3123	
☐ ZK-NGH	B737-319	25607/3126	
☐ ZK-NGI	B737-319	25608/3128	
☐ ZK-NGJ	B737-319	25609/3130	
☐ ZK-NGK	B737-3K2	26318/2731	
☐ ZK-NGM	B737-3K2	28085/2722	
☐ ZK-NGO	B737-37Q	28548/2961	
☐ ZK-NGP	B737-33A	27459/3007	
☐ ZK-NGR	B737-33A	27460/3021	
☐ ZK-SJB	B737-33R	28868/2881	
☐ ZK-SJC	B737-3U3	28738/2988	
☐ ZK-SJE	B737-3K2	27635/2721	
☐ ZK-NBT	B747-419	24855/815	[AKL]
☐ ZK-NBU	B747-419	25605/933	
☐ ZK-NBV	B747-419	26910/1180	
☐ ZK-NBW	B747-419	29375/1228	
☐ ZK-SUH	B747-419	24896/855	
☐ ZK-SUI	B747-441	24957/971	
☐ ZK-SUJ	B747-4F6	27602/1161	
☐ ZK-NCG	B767-319ER/W	26912/509	
☐ ZK-NCI	B767-319ER/W	26913/558	
☐ ZK-NCJ	B767-319ER/W	26915/574	
☐ ZK-NCK	B767-319ER/W	26971/663	
☐ ZK-NCL	B767-319ER/W	28745/677	
☐ ZK-OKA	B777-219ER	29404/534	
☐ ZK-OKB	B777-219ER	34376/537	
☐ ZK-OKC	B777-219ER	34377/546	
☐ ZK-OKD	B777-219ER	29401/550	
☐ ZK-OKE	B777-219ER	32712/564	
☐ ZK-OKF	B777-219ER	34378/575	
☐ ZK-OKG	B777-219ER	29403/591	
☐ ZK-OKH	B777-219ER	34379/605	
☐ ZK-OKM	B777-319ER	38405/902	♦
☐ ZK-OKN	B777-319ER	38406/911	o/o♦
☐ ZK-OKO	B777-319ER	38407/921	o/o♦
☐ ZK-	B777-319ER		o/o♦

AIR NEW ZEALAND LINK — NZ / NZA

☐ ZK-MCA	ATR 72-212A	597
☐ ZK-MCB	ATR 72-212A	598
☐ ZK-MCC	ATR 72-212A	714
☐ ZK-MCF	ATR 72-212A	600
☐ ZK-MCJ	ATR 72-212A	624
☐ ZK-MCO	ATR 72-212A	628
☐ ZK-MCP	ATR 72-212A	630
☐ ZK-MCU	ATR 72-212A	632
☐ ZK-MCW	ATR 72-212A	646
☐ ZK-MCX	ATR 72-212A	687
☐ ZK-MCY	ATR 72-212A	703
☐ ZK-NEA	DHC-8Q-311	611
☐ ZK-NEB	DHC-8Q-311	615
☐ ZK-NEC	DHC-8Q-311	616
☐ ZK-NED	DHC-8Q-311	617

☐	ZK-NEE	DHC-8Q-311	618	
☐	ZK-NEF	DHC-8Q-311	620	
☐	ZK-NEG	DHC-8Q-311	621	
☐	ZK-NEH	DHC-8Q-311	623	
☐	ZK-NEJ	DHC-8Q-311	625	
☐	ZK-NEK	DHC-8Q-311	629	
☐	ZK-NEM	DHC-8Q-311	630	
☐	ZK-NEO	DHC-8Q-311	633	
☐	ZK-NEP	DHC-8Q-311	634	
☐	ZK-NEQ	DHC-8Q-311	636	
☐	ZK-NER	DHC-8Q-311	639	
☐	ZK-NES	DHC-8Q-311	641	
☐	ZK-NET	DHC-8Q-311	642	
☐	ZK-NEU	DHC-8Q-311	647	
☐	ZK-NEW	DHC-8Q-311	648	
☐	ZK-NEZ	DHC-8Q-311	654	
☐	ZK-NFA	DHC-8Q-311	659	
☐	ZK-NFB	DHC-8Q-311	670	
☐	ZK-NFI	DHC-8Q-311	671	

AIRWORK NEW ZEALAND   AWK

☐	ZK-NAO	F.27 Friendship 500	10364	
☐	ZK-NQC	B737-219C	22994/928	
☐	ZK-PAX	F.27 Friendship 500	10596	
☐	ZK-POH	F.27 Friendship 500	10680	
☐	ZK-TLA	B737-3B7(SF)	23383/1425	
☐	ZK-TLC	B737-3B7(SF)	23705/1497	
☐	ZK-TLD	B737-3B7(SF)	23706/1499	
☐	ZK-TLE	B737-3S1(SF)	24834/1896	o/o♦

JETCONNECT   QNZ

☐	ZK-JTP	B737-476	24441/2363	
☐	ZK-JTQ	B737-476	24442/2371	
☐	ZK-JTR	B737-476	24439/2265	
☐	ZK-JTS	B737-476	28152/2829	
☐	ZK-ZQA	B737-838/W	34200/2989	
☐	ZK-ZQB	B737-838/W	34201/3006	
☐	ZK-ZQC	B737-838/W	34202/3048	
☐	ZK-ZQD	B737-838/W	34203/3515	♦
☐	ZK-ZQE	B737-838/W	34185/3542	o/o♦
☐	ZK-ZQF	B737-838/W	34204/3552	o/o♦
☐	ZK-	B737-838/W		o/o♦

PACIFIC BLUE   DJ / PBN

☐	VH-VUM	B737-8BK/W	29675/2414	<VOZ
☐	VH-VUN	B737-8BK/W	29676/2432	<VOZ
☐	ZK-PBA	B737-8FE/W	33796/1377	<VOZ
☐	ZK-PBB	B737-8FE/W	33797/1389	<VOZ
☐	ZK-PBD	B737-8FE/W	33996/1551	<VOZ
☐	ZK-PBF	B737-8FE/W	33799/1462	<VOZ
☐	ZK-PBG	B737-8FE/W	34015/1594	<VOZ
☐	ZK-PBI	B737-8FE/W	34440/2003	<VOZ
☐	ZK-PBJ	B737-8FE/W	34013/1573	<VOZ
☐	ZK-PBK	B737-8FE/W	36604/2650	<VOZ
☐	ZK-PBL	B737-8FE/W	36605/2710	<VOZ♦
☐	ZK-PBM	B737-8FE/W	36601/2525	<VOZ

VINCENT AVIATION

☐	ZK-VAC	DHC-8-102	60	

ZP - PARAGUAY

REGIONAL PARAGUAYA

☐	ZP-CAH	B737-230	22121/720	
☐	ZP-CAJ	B737-230	22124/727	
☐	ZP-CAQ	B737-201	20211/141	

SOL DEL PARAGUAY

☐	ZP-CAL	Fokker 100	11341	♦

ZS - SOUTH AFRICA

AIRLINK   4Z / LNK

☐	ZS-ASW	Avro 146-RJ85	E2313	<SFR
☐	ZS-ASX	Avro 146-RJ85	E2314	<SFR
☐	ZS-ASY	Avro 146-RJ85	E2316	<SFR
☐	ZS-ASZ	Avro 146-RJ85	E2318	<SFR
☐	ZS-SSH	Avro 146-RJ85	E2285	♦
☐	ZS-SSI	Avro 146-RJ85	E2383	♦
☐	ZS-SSJ	Avro 146-RJ85	E2385	♦
☐	ZS-SSK	Avro 146-RJ85	E2251	♦
☐	ZS-NRE	BAeJetstream 41	41048	
☐	ZS-NRF	BAeJetstream 41	41050	
☐	ZS-NRG	BAeJetstream 41	41051	
☐	ZS-NRH	BAeJetstream 41	41054	
☐	ZS-NRI	BAeJetstream 41	41061	
☐	ZS-NRJ	BAeJetstream 41	41062	
☐	ZS-NRK	BAeJetstream 41	41065	>SZL
☐	ZS-NRL	BAeJetstream 41	41068	
☐	ZS-OEX	BAeJetstream 41	41103	
☐	ZS-OMF	BAeJetstream 41	41034	
☐	ZS-OMS	BAeJetstream 41	41035	
☐	ZS-OMY	BAeJetstream 41	41036	
☐	ZS-OMZ	BAeJetstream 41	41037	
☐	ZS-OTM	ERJ-135LR	145485	
☐	ZS-OTN	ERJ-135LR	145491	
☐	ZS-OUV	ERJ-135LR	145493	
☐	ZS-SJW	ERJ-135LR	145423	
☐	ZS-SJX	ERJ-135LR	145428	
☐	ZS-SNV	ERJ-135LR	145551	♦
☐	ZS-SNW	ERJ-135LR	145720	♦
☐	ZS-SNX	ERJ-135LR	145620	
☐	ZS-SNZ	ERJ-135LR	145725	
☐	ZS-	ERJ-170LR		o/o♦
☐	ZS-	ERJ-170LR		o/o♦

AIRQUARIUS AVIATION   AQU

☐	ZS-SOR	BAe146 Srs.300	E3155	♦
☐	ZS-GAV	B737-2L9	22735/825	
☐	ZS-DRF	F.28 Fellowship 4000	11239	
☐	ZS-JES	F.28 Fellowship 4000	11236	
☐	ZS-SKA	Fokker 70	11559	♦
☐	ZS-XGW	F.28 Fellowship 4000	11130	

ALLEGIANCE AIR

☐	ZS-AAX	BAe146 Srs.200	E2092	♦
☐	ZS-AAY	BAe146 Srs.200	E2044	♦
☐	ZS-AAZ	BAe146 Srs.200	E2039	♦
☐	ZS-PZY	BAe146 Srs.200	E2051	♦
☐	ZS-SDX	BAe146 Srs.200	E2046	♦

BIONIC AIR

☐	ZS-PVU	B737-2Q8C	21959/610	
☐	ZS-SMO	BAe146 Srs.300	E3169	

BRANSON AIR

☐	ZS-KIS	B737-291	22743/909	

COMAIR   MN / CAW

☐	ZS-NNH	B737-236	21797/653	
☐	ZS-OAA	B737-4L7	26960/2483	
☐	ZS-OAF	B737-4S3	25116/2061	
☐	ZS-OAG	B737-4H6	27168/2435	
☐	ZS-OAH	B737-33A	24460/1831	
☐	ZS-OAI	B737-33A	24030/1654	
☐	ZS-OAM	B737-4S3	24164/1702	
☐	ZS-OAO	B737-4S3	24163/1700	

☐ ZS-OAP	B737-4S3	24167/1736	
☐ ZS-OAV	B737-4H6	27086/2426	
☐ ZS-OKB	B737-376	23477/1225	
☐ ZS-OKC	B737-376	23484/1270	
☐ ZS-OKG	B737-376	23483/1264	
☐ ZS-OKH	B737-376	23479/1259	
☐ ZS-OKI	B737-376	23489/1356	
☐ ZS-OKJ	B737-376	23487/1306	
☐ ZS-OKK	B737-376	23485/1277	
☐ ZS-OLA	B737-236	23163/1058	
☐ ZS-OLB	B737-236	23167/1074	
☐ ZS-OTF	B737-436	25305/2147	<SFR
☐ ZS-OTG	B737-436	25840/2197	<SFR
☐ ZS-OTH	B737-436	25841/2222	<SFR
☐ ZS-ZWO	B737-8K2/W	28373/51	
☐ ZS-ZWP	B737-86N/W	28612/455	
☐ ZS-ZWQ	B737-8K2/W	28374/57	♦

DODSON INTERNATIONAL CHARTER

☐ ZS-OJJ	AMI Turbo DC-3TP	16213/32961
☐ ZS-OJK	AMI Turbo DC-3TP	14165/25610
☐ ZS-OJL	AMI Turbo DC-3TP	16565/33313
☐ ZS-OJM	AMI Turbo DC-3TP	14101/25546

EGOLI AIR

☐ ZS-PSO	An-32B	2808

EXECUTIVE AEROSPACE · EAS

☐ ZS-AGB	HS.748 Srs.2B/501	1807	[JNB]
☐ ZS-LSO	HS.748 Srs.2B/FAA	1783	
☐ ZS-NNW	HS.748 Srs.2B/378	1785	[DUR]
☐ ZS-NWW	HS.748 Srs.2B/378	1786	[JNB]
☐ ZS-PLO	HS.748 Srs.2B/378	1797	
☐ ZS-TPW	HS.748 Srs.2B/378	1784	[JNB]

IMPERIAL AIR CARGO

☐ ZS-IAB	Boeing 737-210C	20917/344	♦
☐ ZS-IAC	B727-227F	21247/1217	<SFR
☐ ZS-SMG	B737-3Y0F	23499/1242	
☐ ZS-SMJ	B737-3Y0F	23500/1243	♦

INTER AIR · D6 / ILN

☐ ZS-IJB	B767-266ERM	23180/99	♦
☐ ZS-IJI	B707-323C	19517/614	
☐ ZS-IJJ	B737-2H7C	20591/309	
☐ ZS-IJK	B727-61	19176/290	
☐ ZS-IJN	F.28Fellowship 4000	11118	
☐ ZS-SIH	B737-244	22587/835	
☐ ZS-SIM	B737-244	22828/881	
☐ 3D-ITC	B727-2F2	21260/1222	

INTERLINK AIRLINES · ID / ITK

☐ ZS-OLC	B737-230	22119/714
☐ ZS-SIC	B737-244F	22582/805
☐ ZS-SIN	B737-236	21802/670
☐ ZS-SIP	B737-230	22116/701

MANGO · JEJ

☐ ZS-SJG	B737-8BG/W	32353/711	<SAA
☐ ZS-SJH	B737-8BG/W	32354/725	<SAA
☐ ZS-SJK	B737-8BG/W	32355/807	<SAA
☐ ZS-SJL	B737-8BG/W	32356/819	<SAA

1TIME AIRLINE · 1T / RNX

☐ ZS-ANX	DC-9-15	45799/69	[JNB]
☐ ZS-NNN	DC-9-32	47516/630	
☐ ZS-NRA	DC-9-32	47430/609	[JNB]
☐ ZS-NRB	DC-9-32	47468/611	[JNB]
☐ ZS-OBK	MD-82	49115/1135	<SFR

☐ ZS-OPZ	MD-83	49617/1464	<SFR
☐ ZS-SIG	B737-244	22586/829	<SFR
☐ ZS-SKB	MD-83	49966/2047	
☐ ZS-TRD	MD-82	48022/1079	
☐ ZS-TRE	MD-82	49387/1288	
☐ ZS-TRF	MD-82	49440/1304	
☐ ZS-TRG	MD-87	49830/1684	
☐ ZS-TRH	MD-87	49831/1688	
☐ ZS-TRI	MD-83	49707/1487	

PHOEBUS APOLLO AVIATION · PHB

☐ ZS-DIW	DC-3	11991
☐ ZS-PAI	C-54E	27319
☐ S9-KAZ	DC-9-32	47368/505

ROVOS AIR · VOS

☐ ZS-ARV	Convair 340-67	228
☐ ZS-AUA	DC-4	42934
☐ ZS-BRV	Convair 340-67	215
☐ ZS-CRV	DC-3	13331

SAFAIR · FA / SFR

☐ ZS-ASW	Avro 146-RJ85	E2313	>LNK
☐ ZS-ASX	Avro 146-RJ85	E2314	>LNK
☐ ZS-ASY	Avro 146-RJ85	E2316	>LNK
☐ ZS-ASZ	Avro 146-RJ85	E2318	>LNK
☐ ZS-IAC	B727-227F	21247/1217	
☐ ZS-PDL	B727-281F	20466/865	
☐ ZS-OTF	B737-436	25305/2147	>CAW
☐ ZS-OTG	B737-436	25840/2197	>CAW
☐ ZS-OTH	B737-436	25841/2222	>CAW
☐ ZS-SGX	B737-2T5	22396/730	
☐ ZS-SID	B737-244F	22583/809	>SAA
☐ ZS-SIF	B737-244F	22585/828	>SAA
☐ ZS-SIG	B737-244	22586/829	>RNX
☐ ZS-SII	B737-244	22588/836	[JNB]
☐ ZS-SIK	B737-244	22590/854	
☐ ZS-SIL	B737-244	22591/859	
☐ ZS-SIM	B737-244	22828/881	>ILN
☐ ZS-SIT	B737-236	21790/599	
☐ ZS-SPU	B737-3S3	24059/1517	♦
☐ ZS-JIZ	L-382G-35C Hercules	4695	
☐ ZS-ORA	L-382G-7C Hercules	4208	
☐ ZS-ORB	L-382G-14C Hercules	4248	
☐ ZS-ORC	L-382G-23C Hercules	4388	
☐ ZS-RSC	L-382G-28C Hercules	4475	
☐ ZS-RSF	L-382G-31C Hercules	4562	
☐ ZS-RSG	L-382G-31C Hercules	4565	
☐ ZS-RSI	L-382G-31C Hercules	4600	>FAB
☐ ZS-OBF	MD-82	48019/1001	[JNB]
☐ ZS-OBG	MD-82	48020/1045	[ROW]
☐ ZS-OBK	MD-82	49115/1135	>RNX
☐ ZS-OPX	MD-83	53012/1736	>RNX
☐ ZS-OPZ	MD-83	49617/1464	>RNX

SKY ONE AIR

☐ ZS-PWM	F.28 Fellowship 000	11045

SKYHAUL · HAU

☐ ZS-SKG	Convair 580	25
☐ ZS-SKI	Convair 580	186
☐ ZS-SKK	Convair 580	135
☐ ZS-SKL	Convair 580	458

SOLENTA AVIATION

☐ TR-LII	An-26		
☐ ZS-ATR	ATR 42-300F	060	Opf DHL

☐	ZS-LUC	ATR 42-320	032	
☐	ZS-OVP	ATR 42-300F	088Opf DHL	
☐	ZS-OVR	ATR 42-300F	116Opf DHL	
☐	ZS-OVS	ATR 42-300F	075Opf DHL	
☐	ZS-XCC	ATR 42-500	528	♦

SOUTH AFRICAN AIRLINES — SA / SAA

☐	ZS-SFD	A319-131	2268	
☐	ZS-SFE	A319-131	2281	
☐	ZS-SFF	A319-131	2308	
☐	ZS-SFG	A319-131	2326	
☐	ZS-SFH	A319-131	2355	
☐	ZS-SFI	A319-131	2375	
☐	ZS-SFJ	A319-131	2379	
☐	ZS-SFK	A319-131	2418	
☐	ZS-SFL	A319-131	2438	
☐	ZS-SFM	A319-131	2469	
☐	ZS-SFN	A319-131	2501	
☐	ZS-	A330-243		o/o♦
☐	ZS-SXW	A330-243	1236	o/o♦
☐	ZS-SXX	A330-243	1223	o/o♦
☐	ZS-SXY	A330-243	1210	o/o♦
☐	ZS-SXZ	A330-243	1191	♦
☐	ZS-SLA	A340-212	008	
☐	ZS-SLB	A340-212	011	
☐	ZS-SLC	A340-212	018	
☐	ZS-SLD	A340-212	019	
☐	ZS-SLE	A340-212	021	
☐	ZS-SLF	A340-212	006	
☐	ZS-SNA	A340-642	410	
☐	ZS-SNB	A340-642	417	
☐	ZS-SNC	A340-642	426	
☐	ZS-SND	A340-642	531	
☐	ZS-SNE	A340-642	534	
☐	ZS-SNF	A340-642	547	
☐	ZS-SNG	A340-642	557	
☐	ZS-SNH	A340-642	626	
☐	ZS-SNI	A340-642	630	
☐	ZS-SXA	A340-313E	544	
☐	ZS-SXB	A340-313E	582	
☐	ZS-SXC	A340-313E	590	
☐	ZS-SXD	A340-313E	643	
☐	ZS-SXE	A340-313E	646	
☐	ZS-SXF	A340-313E	651	
☐	ZS-SXG	A340-313X	378	♦
☐	ZS-SXH	A340-313X	197	♦
☐	ZS-SBA	B737-3Y0F	26070/2349	
☐	ZS-SBB	B737-3Y0F	26072/2369	
☐	ZS-SID	B737-244F	22583/809	<SFR
☐	ZS-SIF	B737-244F	22585/828	<SFR
☐	ZS-SJA	B737-8S3/W	29248/561	
☐	ZS-SJB	B737-8S3/W	29249/653	
☐	ZS-SJC	B737-85F/W	28828/565	
☐	ZS-SJD	B737-85F/W	28829/582	
☐	ZS-SJE	B737-85F/W	28830/669	
☐	ZS-SJF	B737-85F/W	30006/688	
☐	ZS-SJG	B737-8BG/W	32353/711	
☐	ZS-SJH	B737-8BG/W	32354/725	
☐	ZS-SJI	B737-85F/W	30007/746	
☐	ZS-SJJ	B737-85F/W	30567/761	
☐	ZS-SJK	B737-8BG/W	32355/807	
☐	ZS-SJL	B737-8BG/W	32356/819	
☐	ZS-SJM	B737-85F/W	30476/789	
☐	ZS-SJN	B737-85F/W	30569/850	
☐	ZS-SJO	B737-8BG/W	32357/918	
☐	ZS-SJP	B737-8BG/W	32358/955	
☐	ZS-SJR	B737-844/W	32631/1176	
☐	ZS-SJS	B737-844/W	32632/1205	
☐	ZS-SJT	B737-844/W	32633/1225	
☐	ZS-SJU	B737-844/W	32634/1383	
☐	ZS-SJV	B737-844/W	32635/1407	

☐	ZS-SAZ	B747-444	29119/1187

SOUTH AFRICAN EXPRESS AW — XZ / EXY

☐	ZS-NBA	CRJ-200ER	7702	♦
☐	ZS-NMC	CRJ-200ER	7225	
☐	ZS-NMD	CRJ-200ER	7233	
☐	ZS-NME	CRJ-200ER	7240	
☐	ZS-NMF	CRJ-200ER	7287	
☐	ZS-NMG	CRJ-200ER	7772	
☐	ZS-NMH	CRJ-200ER	7787	
☐	ZS-NMI	CRJ-200ER	7153	
☐	ZS-NMJ	CRJ-200ER	7161	
☐	ZS-NMK	CRJ-200ER	7198	
☐	ZS-NML	CRJ-200ER	7201	
☐	ZS-NMM	CRJ-200ER	7234	
☐	ZS-NMN	CRJ-200ER	7237	
☐	ZS-NBD	CRJ-701	10033	♦
☐	ZS-NLT	CRJ-701	10024	
☐	ZS-NLV	CRJ-701	10010	
☐	ZS-	CRJ-701ER	10028	♦
☐	ZS-	CRJ-701ER	10039	♦

☐	ZS-NLW	DHC-8-315	338	301
☐	ZS-NLX	DHC-8-315	348	302
☐	ZS-NLY	DHC-8-315	352	303
☐	ZS-NLZ	DHC-8-315	354	304
☐	ZS-NMA	DHC-8-315	358	305
☐	ZS-NMB	DHC-8-315	368	306
☐	ZS-NMO	DHC-8-402Q	4122	
☐	ZS-NMP	DHC-8-315B	420	307
☐	ZS-NMS	DHC-8-402Q	4127	

STAR AIR CARGO

☐	ZS-PUI	B737-2B7	22890/986	>AML
☐	ZS-SFX	B737-2B7	22889/983	
☐	ZS-SHL	B737-247	23520/1329	
☐	ZS-SKW	B737-219	23474/1199	
☐	ZS-SMD	B737-219	23472/1194	

STARS AWAY AVIATION — STX

☐	ZS-DBH	DC-9-33F	47384/543
☐	ZS-DBL	HS.748 Srs.2B/287 LFD	1737
☐	9G-MKV	HS.748 Srs.2B/287 LFD	1736

Z3 - MACEDONIA

MAT MACEDONIAN AIRLINES — IN / MAK

☐	N237MA	B737-529	25249/2145

SKYWING INTERNATIONAL — GSW

☐	Z3-AAJ	B737-33A/W	23827/1444	
☐	Z3-AAN	B737-382	24365/1695	♦

STAR AIRLINES

☐	Z3-CAA	B747-2U3B (SCD)	22769/562
☐	Z3-CAB	B747-256B(SF)	24071/699

3B - MAURITIUS

AIR MAURITIUS — MK / MAU

☐	3B-NBF	A319-112	1592
☐	3B-NBH	A319-112	1936
☐	3B-NBL	A330-202	1057
☐	3B-NBM	A330-202	883
☐	3B-NAU	A340-312	076
☐	3B-NAY	A340-313X	152
☐	3B-NBD	A340-313X	194
☐	3B-NBE	A340-313X	268

☐ 3B-NBI	A340-313E	793	
☐ 3B-NBJ	A340-313E	800	
☐ 3B-NBG	ATR 72-212A	690	
☐ 3B-NBK	ATR 72-212A	595	<CIM
☐ 3B-NBN	ATR 72-212A	921	♦

3C - EQUATORIAL GUINEA

CEIBA INTERNATIONAL

☐ TC-MND	A300C4-203F	212
☐ 3C-LLG	ATR 42-300	335
☐ 3C-LLH	ATR 42-300	671
☐ 3C-LLI	ATR 72-212A	790
☐ 3C-LLM	ATR 72-212A	810

GEASA — GEA

☐ RA-87956	Yak-40K	9821757

GENERAL WORK AVIACION

☐ 3C-GWA	F.28 Fellowship 4000	11240
☐ 3C-GWB	F.28 Fellowship 4000	11156
☐ 3C-GWC	F.28 Fellowship 4000	11238

GETRA — GET

☐ 3C-LLF	F.28 Fellowship 1000	11073

GUINEA EQUATORIAL AIRLINES — RGE

☐ 3C-LGF	Il-76MD	73479386

STAR EQUATORIAL AIRLINES

☐ 3C-LLN	B737-260	23915/1583

UTAGE — UTG

☐ ER-AZB	An-24RV	27307507
☐ ZS-OKT	EMB.120RT	120254

3D - SWAZILAND

AERO AFRICA — RFC

☐ 3D-AAJ	B737-222	19075/97
☐ 3D-AVC	B727-251	21155/1169
☐ 3D-BGA	B737-2H4	21722/568
☐ 3D-ITC	B727-2F2	21260/1222
☐ 3D-JJM	B727-231	20053/713
☐ 3D-ZZM	B737-2H7C	20590/304

3X - GUINEA

AIR GUINEA EXPRESS — 2U / GIP

☐ 3X-GCB	B737-2R6C	22627/779 [PGF]

EXIM TRADING

☐ 3X-GEM	An-12BK	347005

GUINEE AIR CARGO

☐ 3X-GEE	HS.748 Srs.2A	1602

4K - AZERBAIJAN

AZAL CARGO — AHC

☐ 4K-AZ16	Il-76TD	1023412411
☐ 4K-AZ26	Il-76TD	1033416525
☐ 4K-26584	An-26B	13509 [BAK]

AZERBAIJAN AIRLINES — J2 / AHY

☐ 4K-AZ01	A319-115X	2487	
☐ 4K-AZ03	A319-111	2516	
☐ 4K-AZ04	A319-111	2588	
☐ 4K-AZ05	A319-111	2788	
☐ 4K-AZ54	A320-211	0331	
☐ 4K-AZ77	A320-214	2846	
☐ 4K-AZ78	A320-214	2853	♦
☐ 4K-AZ79	A320-214	2865	♦
☐ 4K-AZ80	A320-214	2991	♦
☐ 4K-AZ52	ATR 42-500	667	
☐ 4K-AZ53	ATR 42-500	689	
☐ 4K-AZ64	ATR 72-212A	761	
☐ 4K-AZ65	ATR 72-212A	789	
☐ 4K-AZ66	ATR 72-212A	799	
☐ 4K-AZ67	ATR 72-212A	818	
☐ VP-BBR	B757-22L	29305/894	
☐ VP-BBS	B757-22L	30834/947	
☐ 4K-AZ38	B757-256	26246/620	
☐ 4K-AZ43	B757-2M6	23453/100	
☐ 4K-	B767-3		o/o♦
☐ 4K-	B767-3		o/o♦
☐ 4K-AZ49	An-140-100	36525307041	
☐ 4K-AZ712	Tu-134B-3	63515	
☐ 4K-AZ713	Tu-134B-3	63520	
☐ 4K-AZ714	Tu-134B-3	63527	
☐ 4K-AZ10	Tu-154M	98A1013	
☐ 4K-AZ729	Tu-154M	92A911	
☐ 4K-AZ734	Tu-154M	92A916	
☐ 4K-AZ738	Tu-154M	92A921	

IMAIR — IK / ITX

☐ 4K-AZ17	Tu-154M	85A718
☐ 4K-85732	Tu-154M	92A914

SILKWAY AIRLINES — ZP / AZQ

☐ 4K-AZ23	An-12BK	8345605	
☐ 4K-AZ808	ATR 42-500	673	
☐ 4K-800	B747-4R7F	29729/1189	♦
☐ 4K-AZ19	Il-76TD	53460820	
☐ 4K-AZ31	Il-76TD	1013405184	
☐ 4K-AZ40	Il-76TD	1043419632	
☐ 4K-AZ41	Il-76TD	1093420673	
☐ 4K-AZ55	Il-76TD	2053420680	
☐ 4K-AZ70	Il-76TD	2093421717	
☐ 4K-AZ100	Il-76TD-90VD	2073421208	
☐ 4K-AZ101	Il-76TD-90VD	2083421716	

SKYWIND — AZH

☐ 4K-AZ32	An-12B	5343006
☐ 4K-AZ37	An-12BK	347506
☐ 4K-AZ57	An-26B	9504
☐ 4K-78129	Il-76MD	83489683
☐ 4K-78130	Il-76MD	43454611

TURBANAIR — 3T / URN

☐ 4K-727	Tu-154M	86A727

4L - GEORGIA

AIR BATUMI

☐ 4L-BTM	B737-33A	23628/1304	o/o♦

AIR SIRIN

☐ 4L-AFL	An-26B	17310610
☐ 4L-AFS	An-26	97308608

AIR VICTORY

☐ 4L-HUS	An-12BP	6343708
☐ 4L-IRA	An-12B	9346510
☐ 4L-VAL	An-12BP	9346807
☐ 4L-VPI	An-12B	8345510

AIRZENA - GEORGIAN AIRWAYS — A9 / TGZ

☐ 4L-TGA	B737-5Q8	28055/3024	
☐ 4L-TGI	B737-505	26336/2805	♦
☐ 4L-TGR	B737-59D	24694/1834	
☐ 4L-TGT	B737-4Q8	26306/2653	
☐ 4L-GAE	CRJ-200ER	7070	
☐ 4L-GAF	Challenger 850	8046	
☐ 4L-GAL	CRJ-200ER	7076	
☐ 4L-TGB	CRJ-200LR	7442	♦
☐ 4L-TGG	CRJ-200LR	7386	
☐ 4L-TGS	CRJ-200LR	7373	
☐ 4L-TGN	Yak-40	9611246	

EUREX

☐ 4L-KMK	Boeing 747-281F	23139/608

EUROLINE

☐ 4L-AJA	B737-5C9	26439/2444	♦

GLOBAL GEORGIAN AIRWAYS — GGZ

☐ 4L-12008	An-12BP	5343103

SAKAVIA SERVICE — AZG

☐ 4L-GLG	An-24RV	27308005
☐ 4L-GLM	Il-76T	93418543
☐ 4L-GLN	An-12BK	9346704
☐ 4L-GLR	Il-76T	13432955
☐ 4L-GLX	Il-76TD	33448390

SKY GEORGIA — QB / GFG

☐ 4L-GNL	DC-9-51	48134/980	
☐ 4L-GNN	DC-9-51	47657/787	
☐ 4L-SKD	Il-76TD	1023410344	♦
☐ 4L-SKY	Il-76TD	0053464934	

TBILAVIAMSHENI — L6 / VNZ

☐ 4L-AAK	Yak-40	9531043

TRANSAVIA SERVICE — 5I / FNV

☐ 4L-FAS	An-72-100	36572020358
☐ 4L-NAS	An-72	36572020362
☐ 4L-VAS	An-12BK	7345201

TRADE LINKS AVIATION

☐ 4L-TAS	An-24B	89901506

VIP-AVIA — VPV

☐ 4L-VIP	Yak-40	9320129

4O - MONTENEGRO

MONTENEGRO AIRLINES — YM / MGX

☐ 4O-AOA	ERJ-195LR	19000180
☐ 4O-AOB	ERJ-195LR	19000283	
☐ 4O-AOC	ERJ-195LR	19000358	♦
☐ 4O-AOK	Fokker 100	11272	
☐ 4O-AOL	Fokker 100	11268	
☐ 4O-AOM	Fokker 100	11321	
☐ 4O-AOP	Fokker 100	11332	
☐ 4O-AOT	Fokker 100	11350	

4R - SRI LANKA

AERO LANKA AIRLINES — QL / RNL

☐ 4R-SER	HS.748 Srs.2B/426	1799

EXPO AIR — 8D / EXV

☐ 4R-EXD	Il-18GrM	187009802	<RMV
☐ 4R-EXJ	DC-8-63CF	46049/479	

MIHIN LANKA — MJ / MLR

☐ 4R-MLA	F.27 Friendship 500RF	10642	<EXV
☐ 4R-MRA	F.27 Friendship 500RF	10631	
☐ 4R-MRB	A320-232	0977	
☐ 4R-MRC	A321-231	3106	♦

SRILANKAN — UL / ALK

☐ 4R-ABB	A320-231	0406	
☐ 4R-ABC	A320-231	0304	
☐ 4R-ABE	A320-231	0169	
☐ 4R-ABG	A320-232	2908	
☐ 4R-ABH	A320-232	2914	
☐ 4R-ABJ	A320-232	2564	
☐ 4R-ABK	A320-214	2584	♦
☐ 4R-ALA	A330-243	303	
☐ 4R-ALB	A330-243	306	
☐ 4R-ALC	A330-243	311	
☐ 4R-ALD	A330-243	313	
☐ 4R-ALG	A330-243	404	♦
☐ 4R-ADA	A340-311	032	
☐ 4R-ADB	A340-311	033	
☐ 4R-ADC	A340-311	034	
☐ 4R-ADE	A340-313X	367	
☐ 4R-ADF	A340-313X	374	
☐ 4R-	A340-313X	381	o/o♦

4X - ISRAEL

ARKIA ISRAELI AIRLINES — IZ / AIZ

☐ 4X-AVT	ATR 72-212A	894	
☐ 4X-AVU	ATR 72-212A	587	
☐ 4X-AVW	ATR 72-212A	583	
☐ 4X-AVX	ATR 72-212A	656	
☐ 4X-AVZ	ATR 72-212A	577	
☐ 4X-BAU	B757-3E7	30178/906	
☐ 4X-BAW	B757-3E7	30179/912	
☐ 4X-AHM	DHC-7-102	73	[SDV]
☐ 4X-EMA	ERJ-195LR	19000172	

CARGO AIR LINES — 5C / ICL

☐ 4X-ICL	B747-271C	21964/416	<GTI
☐ 4X-ICM	B747-271C	21965/438	<GTI
☐ 4X-ICO	B747-230F	23348/625	♦

ELAL ISRAEL AIRLINES — LY / ELY

☐ 4X-EKA	B737-858	29957/204	801
☐ 4X-EKB	B737-858	29958/249	802
☐ 4X-EKC	B737-858	29959/314	803
☐ 4X-EKD	B737-758	29960/327	701

☐ 4X-EKE	B737-758	29961/442	702
☐ 4X-EKF	B737-8HX	29638/2766	804
☐ 4X-EKH	B737-85P/W	35485/2871	807
☐ 4X-EKI	B737-86N	28587/192	812
☐ 4X-EKJ	B737-85P/W	35486/2908	
☐ 4X-EKL	B737-85P/W	35487/2941	
☐ 4X-EKO	B737-86Q/W	30287/1308	
☐ 4X-EKP	B737-8Q8/W	30639/935	
☐ 4X-EKS	B737-8Q8/W	36433/2702	
☐ 4X-EKT	B737-8BK/W	33030/1968	♦
☐ 4X-AXF	B747-258C	21594/327	405
☐ 4X-AXK	B747-245F	22150/476	
☐ 4X-AXL	B747-245F	22151/478	
☐ 4X-AXM	B747-2B5B(SF)	22485/513	
☐ 4X-ELA	B747-458	26055/1027	201
☐ 4X-ELB	B747-458	26056/1032	202
☐ 4X-ELC	B747-458	27915/1062	203
☐ 4X-ELD	B747-458	29328/1215	204
☐ 4X-ELE	B747-412	26551/1045	
☐ 4X-ELF	B747-412F	26563/1036	♦
☐ 4X-EBM	B757-258	23918/156	502
☐ 4X-EBS	B757-258ER	24884/325	504
☐ 4X-EBT	B757-258ER	25036/356	505
☐ 4X-EBU	B757-258	26053/529	506
☐ 4X-EBV	B757-258	26054/547	507
☐ 4X-EAA	B767-258	22972/62	601
☐ 4X-EAC	B767-258ER	22974/86	603
☐ 4X-EAD	B767-258ER	22975/89	604
☐ 4X-EAE	B767-27EER	24832/316	605
☐ 4X-EAF	B767-27EER	24854/326	606
☐ 4X-EAJ	B767-330ER	25208/381	635
☐ 4X-EAP	B767-3Y0ER	24953/405	
☐ 4X-EAR	B767-352ER	26262/583	
☐ 4X-ECA	B777-258ER	30831/319	101
☐ 4X-ECB	B777-258ER	30832/325	102
☐ 4X-ECC	B777-258ER	30833/335	103
☐ 4X-ECD	B777-258ER	33169/405	104
☐ 4X-ECE	B777-258ER	36083/648	105
☐ 4X-ECF	B777-258ER	36084/655	106

ISRAIR — 6H / ISR

☐ 4X-ABF	A320-232	4354	♦
☐ 4X-ABG	A320-232	4413	♦
☐ 4X-ABH	A320-211	0426	♦
☐ 4X-	A320-232		o/o♦
☐ 4X-ATM	ATR 42-320	069	
☐ 4X-ATN	ATR 42-320	053	
☐ 4X-ATO	ATR 42-320	064	

5A - LIBYA

AFRIQIYAH AIRWAYS — 8U / AAW

☐ 5A-IAY	A300B4-620	354	<NVJ
☐ 5A-ONC	A319-111	3615	
☐ 5A-OND	A319-111	3657	
☐ 5A-ONI	A319-111	4004	
☐ S5-AAA	A320-231	0043	<ADR
☐ 5A-ONA	A320-214	3224	
☐ 5A-ONB	A320-214	3236	
☐ 5A-ONJ	A320-214	4203	♦
☐ 5A-ONK	A320-214	4330	♦
☐ 5A-ONL	A320-214	4489	♦
☐ 5A-ONM	A320-214	4521	♦
☐ 5A-	A320-214		o/o♦
☐ 5A-	A320-214		o/o♦
☐ 5A-ONF	A330-202	999	
☐ 5A-ONH	A330-202	1043	
☐ 5A-ONE	A340-213	151	

AIR LIBYA — 7Q / TLR

☐ 5A-	An-140		o/o
☐ 5A-	An-140		o/o
☐ 5A-	An-140		o/o
☐ 5A-	An-140		o/o
☐ 5A-	An-140		o/o
☐ 5A-DKQ	BAe146 Srs.300	E3191	
☐ 5A-DKV	B727-2D6	22374/1711	
☐ 5A-DKX	B727-2D6	22765/1801	[BEN]
☐ 5A-DKY	B737-2D6	22766/853	
☐ EX-87664	Yak-40	9240825	<AAP
☐ 4L-AVP	Yak-40	9640152	
☐ 5A-DKG	Yak-40	9640152	
☐ 5A-DKI	Yak-40	9331229	
☐ 5A-DKJ	Yak-40K	9720853	
☐ 5A-DKK	Yak-40	9420235	
☐ 5A-DKM	Yak-40KD	9841659	

AIR ONE NINE — N6 / ONR

☐ ZS-GAR	DC-9-32	47132/229
☐ 3D-MRL	DC-9-32	47102/198

ALLEBIA AIR CARGO

☐ 5A-DSH	An-72	36572020337

BURAQ AIR — UZ / BRQ

☐ J2-KCG	DC-10-15	48258/346	
☐ 5A-DMG	B737-8GK/W	34948/2074	
☐ 5A-DMH	B737-8GK/W	34949/2106	
☐ 5A-DMN	B727-228	22287/1710	[TIP]
☐ 5A-DMO	B727-2F2	20983/1088	[TIP]
☐ 5A-DMP	B727-2F2	20981/1086	[TIP]
☐ 5A-DMU	B737-2D6	21212/459	[TIP]
☐ 5A-DMV	B737-2D6	21286/482	[TIP]
☐ 5A-DNA	Il-76TD	23439140	
☐ 5A-MAB	B737-406	24857/1902	
☐ 5A-MAC	B737-4B6	26531/2453	♦

GLOBALAIR — GAK

☐ 5A-DQA	Il-76TD	1003405167
☐ 5A-DQB	Il-86	51483208069

KALLAT EL SAKER AIR — KES

☐ XT-BRK	L-1011-500 Tristar	293B-1243
☐ XT-DMK	B747-238B	21316/309
☐ XT-DMS	B747-238B	20009/147
☐ XT-RAD	L-1011-500 Tristar	193H-1246

LIBYAN AIR CARGO — LCR

☐ 5A-DOA	An-26B	12306
☐ 5A-DOB	An-26B	12307
☐ 5A-DOC	An-26B	12308
☐ 5A-DOD	An-26B	12406
☐ 5A-DOE	An-26B	13003
☐ 5A-DOF	An-26B	13007
☐ 5A-DOG	An-26-100	13008
☐ 5A-DOH	An-26B	13202
☐ 5A-DON	An-26B	13009
☐ 5A-DOU	An-26B-100	13201T
☐ 5A-DOV	An-26B-100	13109T
☐ 5A-DOW	An-26B	11808
☐ 5A-DOZ	An-26B-100	
☐ 5A-DRC	An-32P	703
☐ 5A-DRD	An-32P	1306
☐ 5A-DRF	An-32P	3602
☐ 5A-	An-72	

☐ 5A-	An-72		
☐ 5A-	An-72		
☐ 5A-	An-72		
☐ 5A-DKL	An-124-100	19530502761	
☐ 5A-DKN	An-124-100	19530502792	
☐ 5A-DKS	Il-76TD	1033418584	
☐ 5A-DLL	Il-76	93493799	
☐ 5A-DNC	Il-76TD	23437084	
☐ 5A-DND	Il-76TD	33445299	
☐ 5A-DNE	Il-76T	13432952	
☐ 5A-DNG	Il-76TD	13432961	
☐ 5A-DNH	Il-76TD	33446356	
☐ 5A-DNI	Il-76T	13430878	[FJR]
☐ 5A-DNJ	Il-76T	13430869	[DME]
☐ 5A-DNK	Il-76T	13430882	
☐ 5A-DNO	Il-76T	43451509	
☐ 5A-DNQ	Il-76TD	43454641	
☐ 5A-DNT	Il-76TD	23439141	
☐ 5A-DNU	Il-76TD	43454651	
☐ 5A-DNV	Il-76TD	43454645	
☐ 5A-DRR	Il-76M	83415469	
☐ 5A-DRS	Il-76M	1033414474	
☐ 5A-DRT	Il-76TD	1003403063	
☐ 5A-DZZ	Il-76M	93416501	
☐ 5A-DJQ	L-382G-40C Hercules	4798	
☐ 5A-DJR	L-382E-15C Hercules	4302	
☐ 5A-DOM	L-382G-62C Hercules	4992	
☐ 5A-DOO	L-382G-64C Hercules	5000	

LIBYAN AIRLINES — LN / LAA

☐ 5A-DLY	A300B4-622R	601	
☐ 5A-DLZ	A300B4-622R	616	
☐ 5A-LAH	A320-214	4405	♦
☐ 5A-LAI	A320-214	4450	♦
☐ 5A-LAJ	A320-214	4490	♦
☐ 5A-LAK	A320-214	4526	♦
☐ 5A-	A320-214		o/o♦
☐ 5A-	A320-214		o/o♦
☐ 5A-	A320-214		o/o♦
☐ 5A-	A320-214		o/o♦
☐ TS-IND	A320-212	0348	<LBT
☐ TS-INE	A320-212	0222	<LBT
☐ 5A-	A330-2		o/o♦
☐ 5A-LAF	ATR 42-500	691	
☐ 5A-LAG	ATR 42-500	802	
☐ 5A-DIB	B727-2L5	21051/1109	[TIP]
☐ 5A-DIC	B727-2L5	21052/1110	[TIP]
☐ 5A-DID	B727-2L5	21229/1213	[TIP]
☐ 5A-DIE	B727-2L5	21230/1215	[TIP]
☐ 5A-DIF	B727-2L5	21332/1257	[TIP]
☐ 5A-DIH	B727-2L5	21539/1371	
☐ 5A-DII	B727-2L5	21540/1386	
☐ 5A-LAA	CRJ-900	15120	
☐ 5A-LAB	CRJ-900	15121	
☐ 5A-LAC	CRJ-900	15122	
☐ 5A-LAD	CRJ-900	15214	
☐ 5A-LAE	CRJ-900	15216	
☐ 5A-LAL	CRJ-900	15256	♦
☐ 5A-LAM	CRJ-900	15257	♦
☐ 5A-LAN	CRJ-900	15258	♦
☐ 5A-DCT	DHC-6 Twin Otter 300	627	
☐ 5A-DCV	DHC-6 Twin Otter 300	637	
☐ 5A-DCX	DHC-6 Twin Otter 300	641	
☐ 5A-DCZ	DHC-6 Twin Otter 300	645	
☐ 5A-DDB	DHC-6 Twin Otter 300	653	
☐ 5A-DDE	DHC-6 Twin Otter 300	677	
☐ 5A-DHY	DHC-6 Twin Otter 300	661	
☐ 5A-DJG	DHC-6 Twin Otter 300	744	
☐ 5A-DJH	DHC-6 Twin Otter 300	747	
☐ 5A-DJI	DHC-6 Twin Otter 300	757	
☐ 5A-DJJ	DHC-6 Twin Otter 300	769	
☐ 5A-DLV	F.28 Fellowship 4000	11200	
☐ 5A-DLW	F.28 Fellowship 4000	11194	
☐ 5A-DTG	F.28 Fellowship 4000	11139	
☐ 5A-DTH	F.28 Fellowship 4000	11140	

LIBAVIA

☐ 5A-DMX	A300C4-203F	83	Mersin

PETRO AIR

☐ 5A-AGR	DHC-8-315	601	
☐ 5A-PAA	ERJ-170LR	17000275	♦

5B - CYPRUS

CYPRUS AIRWAYS — CY / CYP

☐ 5B-DBO	A319-112	1729	
☐ 5B-DBP	A319-112	1768	
☐ 5B-DCF	A319-132	2718	
☐ 5B-DBA	A320-231	0180	
☐ 5B-DBB	A320-231	0256	
☐ 5B-DBC	A320-231	0295	
☐ 5B-DCG	A320-232	4197	♦
☐ 5B-DCH	A320-232	2359	♦
☐ 5B-DCJ	A320-232	2108	♦
☐ 5B-DCK	A320-232	2275	♦
☐ 5B-DBS	A330-243	505	
☐ 5B-DBT	A330-243	526	

5H - TANZANIA

AIR TANZANIA — TC / ATC

☐ 5H-MWF	DHC-8-311	474	
☐ 5H-MWG	DHC-8-311	462	

PRECISIONAIR — PW / PRF

☐ 5H-PAA	ATR 42-320	308	
☐ 5H-PAG	ATR 42-320	384	
☐ 5H-PWF	ATR 42-500	819	♦
☐ 5H-PWA	ATR 72-212A	780	
☐ 5H-PWB	ATR 72-212A	834	
☐ 5H-PWC	ATR 72-212A	866	
☐ 5H-PWD	ATR 72-212A	880	
☐ 5H-PWE	ATR 72-212A	815	♦
☐ 5H-PWG	ATR 72-212A	923	♦

REGIONAL AIR SERVICES — REG

☐ 5H-BMP	DHC-7-102	80	

5N - NIGERIA

AERO CONTACTORS — AJ / NIG

☐ 5N-BIZ	B737-4B7	24558/1845	
☐ 5N-BJA	B737-4B7	24873/1931	
☐ 5N-BKQ	B737-522	26695/2423	
☐ 5N-BKR	B737-522	26699/2485	
☐ 5N-BLC	B737-522	26692/2421	
☐ 5N-BLD	B737-522	26675/2345	
☐ 5N-BLE	B737-522	26672/2343	
☐ 5N-BLG	B737-522	25387/2179	o/o
☐ 5N-BIA	DHC-8Q-315	608	
☐ 5N-BIB	DHC-8Q-315	609	
☐ 5N-BJO	DHC-8Q-311	534	

AFRIJET AIRLINES — 6F / FRJ

☐	5N-	ATR 72-500	o/o♦
☐	5N-	ATR 72-500	o/o♦
☐	5N-	ATR 72-500	o/o♦
☐	5N-BCC	Fairchild FH-227D	575 [LOS]
☐	5N-BKO	MD-83	49855/1728
☐	5N-FRJ	Fairchild F-27J	126

AIR MIDWEST

☐	5N-PVA	B737-5H6	27354/2637

AIR NIGERIA — VK / VGN

☐	5N-VNC	B737-33V	29338/3114
☐	5N-VND	B737-33V	29337/3113
☐	5N-VNE	B737-33V	29340/3121
☐	5N-VNF	B737-33V	29341/3125
☐	5N-VNG	B737-33V	29342/3127
☐	5N-VNJ	B737-36N	28558/2876
☐	5N-VNK	B737-33A	27469/2864 ♦
☐	5N-VNL	B737-33A	27910/2873 ♦
☐	5N-VNH	ERJ-190AR	19000210
☐	5N-VNI	ERJ-190AR	19000226

ALLIED AIR CARGO — AJK

☐	5N-BJN	B727-221F	22540/1796
☐	5N-BMQ	B727-2Q6F	21971/1540
☐	5N-JNR	B727-217F	21056/1122 [MIA]♦
☐	5N-RKY	B727-217F	21055/1117

ARIKAIR — W3 / ARA

☐	5N-EIA	A330-223	1002 ♦
☐	CS-TFW	A340-542	910
☐	CS-TFX	A340-542	912
☐	5N-MJA	B737-322	24454/1750
☐	5N-MJB	B737-322	24360/1692
☐	5N-MJC	B737-7BD/W	33932/2234
☐	5N-MJD	B737-7BD/W	36073/2248
☐	5N-MJE	B737-7GL/W	34761/2401
☐	5N-MJF	B737-7GL/W	34762/2427
☐	5N-MJG	B737-7BD/W	33944/2576
☐	5N-MJH	B737-7BD/W	36719/2589
☐	5N-MJI	B737-76N/W	28640/799
☐	5N-MJJ	B737-76N/W	28641/809
☐	5N-MJK	B737-76N/W	30830/855
☐	5N-MJN	B737-86N/W	35638/2789
☐	5N-MJO	B737-86N/W	35640/2819
☐	5N-MJP	B737-8JE/W	38970/3030
☐	5N-MJQ	B737-8JE/W	38971/3065
☐	5N-	B737-8JE/W	o/o♦
☐	5N-	B737-8JE/W	o/o♦
☐	5N-	B737-8JE/W	o/o♦
☐	5N-	B737-8JE/W	o/o♦
☐	5N-	B737-8JE/W	o/o♦
☐	5N-	B777-3	o/o♦
☐	5N-	B777-3	o/o♦
☐	5N-	B777-3	o/o♦
☐	5N-	B777-3	o/o♦
☐	5N-JEA	CRJ-900ER	15058
☐	5N-JEB	CRJ-900ER	15059
☐	5N-JEC	CRJ-900ER	15054
☐	5N-JED	CRJ-900ER	15114
☐	5N-BKU	DHC-8-402Q	4207
☐	5N-BKV	DHC-8-402Q	4219
☐	5N-BKW	DHC-8-402Q	4262 ♦
☐	5N-	DHC-8-402Q	o/o♦
☐	5N-	DHC-8-402Q	o/o♦
☐	5N-	DHC-8-402Q	o/o♦

ASSOCIATED AIR CARGO

☐	UR-PAS	An-12AP	2401105opb VPB
☐	5N-BBL	Short SD.3-60	SH3637
☐	5N-BHV	B727-227F	21364/1261
☐	5N-BJX	B727-225F	20627/947

AXIOM AIR

☐	5N-BMA	B737-3Q4(SF)	24209/1492

BELLVIEW AIRLINES — B3 / BLV

☐	F-GHXK	B737-2A1	21599/514 [LOS]
☐	F-GHXL	B737-2S3	21775/570
☐	5N-BFM	B737-2L9	22733/812
☐	5N-BFX	B737-291	23024/965 [LOS]

BRISTOW HELICOPTERS (NIGERIA) — BHN

☐	5N-SPM	Do 328 Jet	3141
☐	5N-SPN	Do 328 Jet	3151 [OBF]

CHANCHANGI AIRLINES

☐	5N-BMB	B737-3J6	25079/2016
☐	5N-BMC	B737-3Z0	25089/2027

DANA — DAV

☐	5N-DOX	Do328-110	3073
☐	5N-DOY	Do328-110	3089
☐	5N-IEP	Do328-110	3026
☐	5N-SAG	Do328-110	3016

DANA AIR

☐	5N-JAI	MD-83	53016/1850
☐	5N-RAM	MD-83	53019/1784
☐	5N-SAI	MD-83	53018/1779
☐	5N-SRI	MD-83	53020/1789

EAS AIRLINES — EXW

☐	5N-DOZ	Do328-110	3031

FREEDOM AIR SERVICES — FFF

☐	5N-BCY	B727-235	19461/538

IRS AIRLINES — LVB

☐	5N-AKR	B727-223A	20984/1121
☐	5N-BJM	ERJ-145LR	14500984
☐	5N-CEO	Fokker 100	11295 [WOE]
☐	5N-COO	Fokker 100	11297
☐	5N-HIR	Fokker 100	11498
☐	5N-SIK	Fokker 100	11286 ♦
☐	5N-SMR	Fokker 100	11291 ♦
☐	5N-NCZ	F.28 Fellowship 4000	11241
☐	5N-SSZ	F.28 Fellowship 4000	11190

KABO AIR — N2 / QNK

☐	5N-DKB	B747-251B	23548/644
☐	5N-EEE	B747-243B	19732/134 [MZJ]
☐	5N-JRM	B747-251B	23549/651
☐	5N-MAD	B747-251B	23547/642
☐	5N-OOO	B747-136	20952/246
☐	5N-PDP	B747-238B	20842/238
☐	5N-PPP	B747-238B	20921/241
☐	5N-RRR	B747-136	19765/109
☐	5N-LLL	B727-224	20654 [ADD]

MAXAIR

☐ 5N-BMG	B747-346	23638/658
☐ 5N-DBM	B747-346	23968/693
☐ 5N-DDK	B747-346	23967/692
☐ 5N-MBB	B747-346	24018/694

OVERLAND AIRWAYS OJ / OLA

☐ 5N-BCR	ATR 42-300	031	
☐ 5N-BCS	ATR 42-300	025	
☐ 5N-BND	ATR 42-300	363	♦

PREMIUM AIR SHUTTLE EMI

☐ 5N-BOS	Yak-40	9341431

TRANSKY AIRLINES

☐ 5N-TSA	B737-2H4	23110/1017

5R - MADAGASCAR

AIR MADAGASCAR MD / MDG

☐ 5R-MJG	ATR 42-500	649
☐ 5R-MVT	ATR 42-320	044
☐ 5R-MJT	ATR 42-320	221
☐ 5R-MJE	ATR 72-212A	694
☐ 5R-MJF	ATR 72-212A	698
☐ 5R-MFH	B737-3Q8	26305/2651
☐ 5R-MFI	B737-3Q8	26301/2623
☐ 5R-MRM	B737-3Z9	24081/1515
☐ 5R-MFG	B767-383ER	25088/359
☐ 5R-MFJ	B767-3Y0ER	26200/450

5T - MAURITANIA

MAURITANIA AIRWAYS YD / MTW

☐ TS-IMH	A320-211	0402	<TAR
☐ TS-LBA	ATR 42-300	245	<TUI
☐ TS-IEB	B737-7L9/W	28015/785	<TAR
☐ 5T-CLB	B737-55S	28469/2849	♦
☐ 5T-CLB	B737-55S	28470/2861	♦

5V - TOGO

ASKY AIRLINES SKK

☐ ET-ANG	B737-7K9/W	34401/2216	<ETH♦
☐ ET-ANH	B737-7K9/W	34402/2270	<ETH♦
☐ ET-AOK	B737-790/W	33012/1206	<ETH♦
☐ ET-ANW	DHC-8-402Q	4320	<ETH♦

5X - UGANDA

AIR UGANDA U7 / UGB

☐ 5X-UGA	MD-87	49840/1745	
☐ 5X-UGB	MD-87	49837/1730	
☐ 5X-UGC	MD-87	49838/1733	
☐ 5X-UGD	CRJ-100ER	7162	
☐ 5X-UGE	CRJ-200ER	7356	♦

EAST AFRICAN AIRLINES QU / UGX

☐ 5X-EAA	B737-291	22741/871

5Y - KENYA

AFRICAN EXPRESS AIRWAYS XU / AXK

☐ 5Y-AXB	B727-231	19565/603
☐ 5Y-AXD	DC-9-32	47088/180
☐ 5Y-AXE	B727-256	21611/1382
☐ 5Y-AXF	DC-9-32	47093/237
☐ 5Y-AXL	MD-82	49204/1179
☐ 5Y-AXN	MD-82	49207/1189
☐ 5Y-AXO	MD-82	49206/1188

AIRKENYA P2 / XAK

☐ 5Y-BMJ	DHC-7-102	83
☐ 5Y-BPD	DHC-7-102	32
☐ 5Y-BTZ	DHC-8-102	203

ALS

☐ 5Y-BVO	DHC-8-102	7	
☐ 5Y-BXH	DHC-8-102	205	
☐ 5Y-BXI	DHC-8-102	376	
☐ 5Y-BXU	DHC-8-102	344	♦
☐ 5Y-PRV	DHC-8-102	185	
☐ 5Y-STN	DHC-8-102	179	
☐ 5Y-BVY	ERJ-135LR	145599	
☐ 5Y-BVZ	ERJ-135LR	145661	

ASTRAL AVIATION 8V / ACP

☐ 5Y-SAN	DC-9-34CF	47706/821
☐ S9-DBQ	An-12BP	

BLUEBIRD AVIATION BBZ

☐ 5Y-VVN	DHC-8-102	62	
☐ 5Y-VVP	DHC-8-106	339	
☐ 5Y-VVR	DHC-8-102	204	
☐ 5Y-VVS	DHC-8-102A	349	
☐ 5Y-VVT	DHC-8-102A	362	
☐ 5Y-VVW	DHC-8-402Q	4011	
☐ 5Y-VVX	DHC-8-402Q	4018	
☐ 5Y-VVY	DHC-8-402Q	4009	♦
☐ 5Y-VVF	Fokker 50	20136	
☐ 5Y-VVG	Fokker 50	20137	
☐ 5Y-VVH	Fokker 50	20203	
☐ 5Y-VVJ	Fokker 50	20133	
☐ 5Y-VVK	Fokker 50	20213	

DELTA CONNECTION Z9 / DCP

☐ 5Y-JAP	B737-229C	20915/401	<EAF

EAST AFRICAN EXPRESS B5 / EXZ

☐ 5Y-EEE	F.28 Fellowship 4000	11229
☐ 5Y-XXA	DC-9-14	45725/19
☐ 5Y-XXB	DC-9-14	45711/4

FLY540 5H / FFV

☐ 5Y-BUN	ATR 42-320	205	
☐ 5Y-BUT	ATR 42-320	240	
☐ 5Y-BUZ	DHC-8-102	253	
☐ 5Y-BVD	ATR 42-320	115	
☐ 5Y-	DHC-8-102	114	
☐ 5Y-	ATR 72-212A		o/o♦
☐ 5Y-	ATR 72-212A		o/o♦
☐ 5Y-	ATR 72-212A		o/o♦
☐ 5Y-	ATR 72-212A		o/o♦
☐ 5Y-	ATR 72-212A		o/o♦
☐ 5X-FFD	F.27 Friendship 500CRF	10530
☐ 5X-FFN	F.27 Friendship 500CRF	10531

JETLINK EXPRESS — J0 / JLX

	Reg	Type	Serial	
☐	5Y-JLA	F.28Fellowship 4000	11093	
☐	5Y-JLB	CRJ-200	7006	
☐	5Y-JLC	CRJ-200	7183	
☐	5Y-JLD	CRJ-200	7197	
☐	5Y-JLE	CRJ-200	7016	
☐	5Y-JLG	CRJ-200	7126	♦
☐	5Y-JLH	CRJ-200	7113	

KENYA AIRWAYS — KQ / KQA

	Reg	Type	Serial	
☐	5Y-KQA	B737-3U8	28746/2863	
☐	5Y-KQB	B737-3U8	28747/2884	
☐	5Y-KQC	B737-3U8	29088/3034	
☐	5Y-KQD	B737-3U8	29750/3095	
☐	5Y-KQJ	B737-248	21714/565	[NBO]
☐	5Y-KQK	B737-248	21715/579	[NBO]
☐	5Y-KYN	B737-306	28720/2957	♦
☐	5Y-KQE	B737-76N/W	30133/877	
☐	5Y-KQF	B737-76N/W	30136/1145	
☐	5Y-KQG	B737-7U8/W	32371/1242	
☐	5Y-KQH	B737-7U8/W	32372/1327	
☐	5Y-KYB	B737-8AL/W	35070/2115	
☐	5Y-KYC	B737-8AL/W	35071/2138	
☐	5Y-KYD	B737-86N/W	35632/2690	
☐	5Y-KYE	B737-86N/W	35286/2757	
☐	5Y-KYF	B737-86N/W	35637/2803	
☐	5Y-KQX	B767-36NER	30854/844	
☐	5Y-KQY	B767-36NER	30841/841	
☐	5Y-KQZ	B767-36NER	30853/837	
☐	5Y-KYW	B767-319ER	30586/808	♦
☐	5Y-KYX	B767-3P6ER	24484/260	
☐	5Y-KYY	B767-3Q8ER	29383/747	
☐	5Y-KQS	B777-2U8ER	33683/522	
☐	5Y-KQT	B777-2U8ER	33682/514	
☐	5Y-KQU	B777-2U8ER	33681/479	
☐	5Y-KYZ	B777-2U8ER	36124/614	
☐	5Y-KYG	ERJ-170LR	17000141	♦
☐	5Y-KYH	ERJ-170LR	17000230	
☐	5Y-KYJ	ERJ-170LR	17000128	
☐	5Y-KYK	ERJ-170LR	17000111	
☐	5Y-KYL	ERJ-170LR	17000146	♦
☐	5Y-KYP	ERJ-190AR	19000398	♦
☐	5Y-	ERJ-190AR		o/o♦

KNIGHT AVIATION

	Reg	Type	Serial	
☐	5Y-SRJ	F.27 Friendship 500F	10372	

SAFARI LINKS

	Reg	Type	Serial	
☐	5Y-SLD	DHC-8-102	331	

748 AIR SERVICES — IHO

	Reg	Type	Serial	
☐	5Y-BSX	HS.780 Andover C.1	Set 20	
☐	3C-KKC	HS.780 Andover C.1	Set 18	
☐	5Y-HAJ	HS.748 Srs.2B/371LFD	1776	
☐	5Y-BVQ	HS.748 Srs.2B/399LFD	1778	
☐	5Y-JGM	DHC-8-102A	287	
☐	5Y-IHO	DHC-8-106	268	

TRIDENT AVIATION

	Reg	Type	Serial	
☐	5Y-MEG	DHC-5D Buffalo	62	
☐	5Y-OPL	DHC-5D Buffalo	84A	
☐	5Y-TAJ	DHC-5E Buffalo	108	
☐	5Y-TEL	DHC-5D Buffalo	68	
☐	5Y-BTP	DHC-8-102	104	
☐	5Y-BWG	DHC-8Q-311	406	
☐	5Y-DAC	DHC-8-102	251	

	Reg	Type	Serial	
☐	5Y-ENA	DHC-8-102	297	
☐	5Y-GRS	DHC-8-102	355	
☐	5Y-MOC	DHC-8-311	374	
☐	5Y-PTA	DHC-8-315	397	

6O - SOMALIA

JUBBA AIRWAYS — 6J / JUB

	Reg	Type	Serial	
☐	5Y-BXG	B737-247	23519/1299	

MUDAN AIRLINES — MDN

	Reg	Type	Serial	
☐	ER-46711	An-24B	99902109	

6V - SENEGAL

AIR SENEGAL INTERNATIONAL — V7 / SNG

	Reg	Type	Serial	
☐	6V-AHL	DHC-8-315	556	[MST]

ASECNA — XKX

	Reg	Type	Serial	
☐	6V-AFW	ATR 42-300	117	

SENEGAL AIRLINES — SGG

	Reg	Type	Serial	
☐	6V-AIH	A320-214	0799	♦
☐	6V-AII	A320-214	0879	♦

TURBOT AIR CARGO — TAC

	Reg	Type	Serial	
☐	UR-CAI	An-26B	7010	<UKL
☐	UR-MDA	An-26	7108	<MEM

6Y - JAMAICA

AIR JAMAICA — JM / AJM

	Reg	Type	Serial	
☐	6Y-JAD	A319-112	3331	201
☐	6Y-JAI	A320-214	0628	628
☐	6Y-JMF	A320-214	1213	632
☐	6Y-JMG	A320-214	1390	634
☐	6Y-JMJ	A320-214	1751	
☐	6Y-JMH	A321-211	1503	515

7O- YEMEN

FELIX AIRWAYS

	Reg	Type	Serial	
☐	7O-FAA	CRJ-702NG	10267	
☐	7O-FAB	CRJ-702NG	10268	
☐	7O-	CRJ-702NG		o/o♦
☐	7O-	CRJ-702NG		o/o♦
☐	7O-	CRJ-702NG		o/o♦
☐	7O-	CRJ-702NG		o/o♦
☐	7O-	CRJ-702NG		o/o♦
☐	7O-	CRJ-702NG		o/o♦
☐	7O-FAI	CRJ-200ER	7307	
☐	7O-FAJ	CRJ-200ER	7308	

YEMENIA — IY / IYE

	Reg	Type	Serial	
☐	7O-ADR	A310-324ET	568	
☐	7O-ADV	A310-325	702	
☐	7O-ADW	A310-325	704	
☐	7O-	A320-232		o/o♦
☐	7O-	A320-232		o/o♦
☐	7O-	A320-232		o/o♦
☐	7O-	A320-232		o/o♦
☐	7O-ADP	A330-243	625	

☐	7O-ADT	A330-243	632
☐	7O-ADX	A330-243	627 ♦
☐	7O-ACV	B727-2N8	21844/1518
☐	7O-ACY	B727-2N8	21847/1557
☐	7O-ADA	B727-2N8	21842/1512
☐	7O-ADM	B737-8Q8/W	28252/1195
☐	7O-ADN	B737-8Q8/W	30661/1186
☐	7O-ADQ	B737-8Q8/W	30730/2399
☐	7O-YMN	B747SP-27	21786/413
☐	7O-ADS	DHC-8-102	280
☐	7O-ADU	DHC-8-102A	327
☐	7O-ADY	DHC-8-103	333
☐	7O-ADF	Il-76TD	1033418578
☐	7O-ADG	Il-76TD	1023412402
☐	7O-ADD	L-382C-86D Hercules	4827
☐	7O-ADE	L-382C-86D Hercules	4825

7Q - MALAWI

AIR MALAWI — QM / AML

☐	ZS-PUI	B737-2B7	22890/986
☐	7Q-YKP	B737-33A	25056/2045 [JNB]
☐	7Q-YKQ	ATR 42-320	236
☐	7Q-YKW	B737-522	25384/2149 [JNB]
☐	7Q-YKX	B737-2K9	23405/1178

7T - ALGERIA

AIR ALGERIE — AH / DAH

☐	7T-VJC	A310-203	291
☐	7T-VJD	A310-203	293
☐	7T-VJV	A330-202	644
☐	7T-VJW	A330-202	647
☐	7T-VJX	A330-202	650
☐	7T-VJY	A330-202	653
☐	7T-VJZ	A330-202	667
☐	7T-VUI	ATR 72-212A	644
☐	7T-VUJ	ATR 72-212A	648
☐	7T-VUK	ATR 72-212A	652
☐	7T-VUL	ATR 72-212A	672
☐	7T-VUM	ATR 72-212A	677
☐	7T-VUN	ATR 72-212A	684
☐	7T-VUO	ATR 72-212A	901 ♦
☐	7T-VUP	ATR 72-212A	903 ♦
☐	7T-VUQ	ATR 72-212A	909 ♦
☐	7T-VUS	ATR 72-212A	913 ♦
☐	7T-VVQ	ATR 72-212A	676
☐	7T-VVR	ATR 72-212A	683
☐	7T-VEA	B727-2D6	20472/850
☐	7T-VEB	B727-2D6	20473/855
☐	7T-VEI	B727-2D6	21053/1111
☐	7T-VEM	B727-2D6	21210/1204
☐	7T-VEP	B727-2D6	21284/1233
☐	7T-VET	B727-2D6	22372/1662
☐	7T-VEU	B727-2D6	22373/1664
☐	7T-VEV	B727-2D6	22374/1711
☐	7T-VEW	B727-2D6	22375/1723
☐	7T-VEX	B727-2D6	22765/1801
☐	TC-SKD	B737-4Q8	25372/2280 <SHY
☐	7T-VED	B737-2D6C	20850/311
☐	7T-VEF	B737-2D6	20759/332
☐	7T-VEG	B737-2D6	20884/361
☐	7T-VEJ	B737-2D6	21063/407
☐	7T-VEK	B737-2D6	21064/409
☐	7T-VEL	B737-2D6	21065/416
☐	7T-VEQ	B737-2D6	21285/473

☐	7T-VJQ	B737-6D6	30209/1115
☐	7T-VJR	B737-6D6	30545/1131
☐	7T-VJS	B737-6D6	30210/1150
☐	7T-VJT	B737-6D6	30546/1152
☐	7T-VJU	B737-6D6	30211/1164
☐	7T-VJJ	B737-8D6	30202/610
☐	7T-VJK	B737-8D6	30203/640
☐	7T-VJL	B737-8D6	30204/652
☐	7T-VJM	B737-8D6	30205/691
☐	7T-VJN	B737-8D6	30206/751
☐	7T-VJO	B737-8D6	30207/868
☐	7T-VJP	B737-8D6	30208/896
☐	7T-VKA	B737-8D6/W	34164/1748
☐	7T-VKB	B737-8D6/W	34165/1768
☐	7T-VKC	B737-8D6/W	34166/1773
☐	7T-VKD	B737-8D6/W	40858/3406 ♦
☐	7T-VKE	B737-8D6/W	40859/3446 ♦
☐	7T-VKF	B737-8D6/W	40860/3471 ♦
☐	7T-	B737-8D6/W	o/o♦
☐	7T-	B737-8D6/W	o/o♦
☐	7T-	B737-8D6/W	o/o♦
☐	7T-VJG	B767-3D6ER	24766/310
☐	7T-VJH	B767-3D6ER	24767/323
☐	7T-VJI	B767-3D6ER	24768/332
☐	7T-VHL	L-382-51D Hercules	4886

TASSILI AIRLINES — SF / DTH

☐	7T-	B737-8	o/o♦
☐	7T-	B737-8	o/o♦
☐	7T-	B737-8	o/o♦
☐	7T-	B737-8	o/o♦
☐	7T-VCL	DHC-8Q-402	4167
☐	7T-VCM	DHC-8Q-402	4169
☐	7T-VCN	DHC-8Q-402	4173
☐	7T-VCO	DHC-8Q-402	4178
☐	7T-VCP	DHC-8-202	661
☐	7T-VCQ	DHC-8-202	664
☐	7T-VCR	DHC-8-202	665
☐	7T-VCS	DHC-8-202	666

8P - BARBADOS

REDJET

☐	8P-IGA	MD-82	49469/1410 ♦
☐	8P-IGB	MD-82	49471/1418 ♦

8Q - MALDIVES

ISLAND AVIATION SERVICES — Q2

☐	8Q-AMD	DHC-8-202	429
☐	8Q-IAO	DHC-8Q-314	544
☐	8Q-IAP	DHC-8Q-315	491
☐	8Q-IAQ	DHC-8-202	542

MEGA MALDIVES AIRLINES

☐	8Q-MEG	B767-3P6ER	24496/270 ♦

TRANS MALDIVIAN AIRWAYS — TMW

☐	8Q-ATM	ATR 42-320	194
☐	8Q-ATN	ATR 42-300	96

9A - CROATIA

CROATIA AIRLINES — OU / CTN

☐	9A-CTG	A319-112	0767
☐	9A-CTH	A319-112	0833

☐	9A-CTI	A319-112	1029
☐	9A-CTL	A319-112	1252
☐	9A-CTF	A320-212	0258
☐	9A-CTJ	A320-214	1009
☐	9A-CTK	A320-214	1237

☐	9A-CQA	DHC-8-402Q	4205
☐	9A-CQB	DHC-8-402Q	4211
☐	9A-CQC	DHC-8-402Q	4258
☐	9A-CQD	DHC-8-402Q	4260
☐	9A-CQE	DHC-8-402Q	4300
☐	9A-CQF	DHC-8-402Q	4301

DUBROVNIK AIRLINE — DBK

☐	9A-CDA	MD-83	49602/1435
☐	9A-CDC	MD-82	49112/1068
☐	9A-CDD	MD-82	49113/1069
☐	9A-CDE	MD-82	48066/1019

TRADE AIR — TDR

☐	9A-BTB	LET L-410UVP-E3	902506
☐	9A-BTC	LET L-410UVP-E3	902507
☐	9A-BTD	Fokker 100	11407
☐	9A-BTE	Fokker 100	11416

9G - GHANA

AEROGEM AIRLINES — GCK

| ☐ | 9G-OAL | B707-324C | 19350/537 |

ANTRAK AIR GHANA — O4 / ABV

☐	EX-132	B737-2Q8	21687/554	
☐	9G-AAB	ATR 42-300	41	
☐	9G-ANT	ATR 42-300	86	
☐	9G-NAN	DC-9-51	47732/861	[ACC]
☐	9G-NIN	DC-9-51	47746/864	[SCC]

JOHNSONS AIR — JON

☐	9G-FAB	DC-8-63F	46121/500	
☐	9G-LIL	DC-8-63AF	46147/549	>RSE
☐	9G-PEL	DC-8F-62	46085/481	
☐	9G-RAC	DC-8-63PF	46093/496	
☐	9G-SIM	DC-8-63CF	46061/480	
☐	9G-TOP	DC-8-63CF	46151/540	

MERIDIAN AIRWAYS — ACE

☐	TZ-MHI	L-1011-100 Tristar	193B-1221
☐	9G-AED	DC-8-62AF	46162/555
☐	9G-AXA	DC-8-63F	46113/521
☐	9G-AXB	DC-8-63PF	46097/503
☐	9G-AXC	DC-8-63F	45999/377
☐	9G-AXD	DC-8-63F	45927/327
☐	9G-AXE	DC-8-63F	46041/439

SOBELAIR

| ☐ | 9G-AIR | F.27 Friendship 100 | 10266 |
| ☐ | 9G-SOB | F.27 Friendship 100 | 10287 |

9H - MALTA

AIR MALTA — KM / AMC

☐	9H-AEG	A319-112	2113
☐	9H-AEH	A319-112	2122
☐	9H-AEJ	A319-112	2186
☐	9H-AEL	A319-112	2332
☐	9H-AEM	A319-112	2382

| ☐ | 9H-AEF | A320-214 | 2142 |
| ☐ | 9H-AEK | A320-214 | 2291 |

☐	9H-AEN	A320-214	2665
☐	9H-AEO	A320-214	2768
☐	9H-AEP	A320-214	3056
☐	9H-AEQ	A320-214	3068

EFLY — LEF

| ☐ | 9H-ELE | BAe146 Srs.300 | E3209 |

MEDAVIA — MDM

☐	9H-AET	Do328-110	3117	
☐	9H-AEW	DHC-8-102	222	
☐	9H-AEY	DHC-8-315	508	
☐	9H-AFD	DHC-8Q-315	458	>ATW♦

9J - ZAMBIA

ZAMBEZI AIRLINES

☐	9J-ZJA	B737-5Y0	26101/2544	
☐	9J-ZJB	B737-5Y0	26100/2538	
☐	9J-ZJC	B737-53S	29074/3086	♦

ZAMBIAN AIRWAYS — Q3 / MBN

| ☐ | 9J-JOY | B737-244 | 22584/821 | [JNB] |

9K - KUWAIT

GRYPHON AIRWAYS

| ☐ | ZS-GAT | DC-9-32 | 47797/913 |
| ☐ | ZS-GAU | DC-9-32 | 47798/914 |

JAZEERA AIRWAYS — J9 / JZR

☐	9K-CAA	A320-214	2569
☐	9K-CAC	A320-214	2792
☐	9K-CAD	A320-214	2822
☐	9K-CAI	A320-214	3919
☐	9K-CAJ	A320-214	3939
☐	9K-CAK	A320-214	4162

KUWAIT AIRWAYS — KU / KAC

☐	9K-AHI	A300C4-620	344Opf Govt
☐	9K-AMA	A300B4-605R	673
☐	9K-AMB	A300B4-605R	694
☐	9K-AMC	A300B4-605R	699
☐	9K-AMD	A300B4-605R	719
☐	9K-AME	A300B4-605R	721

☐	9K-ALA	A310-308	647
☐	9K-ALB	A310-308	649
☐	9K-ALC	A310-308	663
☐	9K-ALD	A310-308	648Opf Govt

☐	9K-AKA	A320-212	0181
☐	9K-AKB	A320-212	0182
☐	9K-AKC	A320-212	0195
☐	9K-AKD	A320-212	2046

☐	9K-ANA	A340-313	089
☐	9K-ANB	A340-313	090
☐	9K-ANC	A340-313	101
☐	9K-AND	A340-313	104

☐	9K-ADE	B747-469M	27338/1046Opf Govt
☐	9K-AOA	B777-269ER	28743/125
☐	9K-AOB	B777-269ER	28744/145

LOADAIR CARGO

| ☐ | 9K-DAA | B747-4HQERF | 37303/1416 | o/o |
| ☐ | 9K-DAB | B747-4HQERF | 37304/1419 | o/o |

WATANIYA AIRWAYS

☐	9K-EAA	A320-214	3739
☐	9K-EAB	A320-214	3791
☐	9K-EAC	A320-214	3907
☐	9K-EAD	A320-214	4049
☐	9K-EAE	A320-214	4235	♦
☐	9K-EAF	A320-214	4304	♦
☐	9K-EAG	A320-214	4411	♦

9L - SIERRA LEONE

AIR RUM   RUM

☐	C5-GAE	B727-51	19124/347
☐	9L-LDV	L-1011-1 Tristar	193C-1200
☐	9L-LFB	L-1011-1 Tristar	193P-1156

9M - MALAYSIA

AIRASIA   AK / AXM

☐	9M-AFA	A320-214	2612
☐	9M-AFB	A320-214	2633
☐	9M-AFC	A320-214	2656
☐	9M-AFD	A320-214	2683
☐	9M-AFE	A320-214	2699
☐	9M-AFF	A320-214	2760
☐	9M-AFG	A320-216	2816
☐	9M-AFH	A320-216	2826
☐	9M-AFI	A320-216	2842
☐	9M-AFJ	A320-216	2881
☐	9M-AFK	A320-216	2885
☐	9M-AFL	A320-216	2926
☐	9M-AFM	A320-216	2944
☐	9M-AFN	A320-216	2956
☐	9M-AFO	A320-216	2989
☐	9M-AFP	A320-216	3000
☐	9M-AFQ	A320-216	3018
☐	9M-AFR	A320-216	3064
☐	9M-AFS	A320-216	3117
☐	9M-AFT	A320-216	3140
☐	9M-AFU	A320-216	3154
☐	9M-AFV	A320-216	3173
☐	9M-AFW	A320-216	3404
☐	9M-AFY	A320-216	3194
☐	9M-AFZ	A320-216	3201
☐	9M-AHA	A320-216	3223
☐	9M-AHB	A320-216	3232
☐	9M-AHC	A320-216	3261
☐	9M-AHD	A320-216	3291
☐	9M-AHE	A320-216	3327
☐	9M-AHF	A320-216	3353
☐	9M-AHG	A320-216	3370
☐	9M-AHH	A320-216	3427
☐	9M-AHI	A320-216	3448
☐	9M-AHJ	A320-216	3477
☐	9M-AHK	A320-216	3486
☐	9M-AHL	A320-216	3521
☐	9M-AHM	A320-216	3536
☐	9M-AHN	A320-216	3549
☐	9M-AHO	A320-216	3568
☐	9M-AHP	A320-216	3582
☐	9M-AHQ	A320-216	3628
☐	9M-AHR	A320-216	3701
☐	9M-AHS	A320-216	3776
☐	9M-AHT	A320-216	3997
☐	9M-AHU	A320-216	4070
☐	9M-AHV	A320-216	4079
☐	9M-AHW	A320-216	4098
☐	9M-AHX	A320-216	4263	♦
☐	9M-AHY	A320-216	4293	♦
☐	9M-AHZ	A320-216	4361	♦
☐	9M-AQA	A320-216	4404	♦

☐	9M-AQB	A320-216	4458	♦
☐	9M-	A320-216		o/o ♦
☐	9M-	A320-216		o/o ♦
☐	9M-	A320-216		o/o ♦
☐	9M-	A320-216		o/o ♦
☐	9M-	A320-216		o/o ♦
☐	9M-	A320-216		o/o ♦
☐	9M-	A320-216		o/o ♦
☐	9M-	A320-216		o/o ♦

AIR ASIA X   D7 / XAX

☐	9M-XAA	A330-301	054	
☐	9M-XXA	A330-343E	952	
☐	9M-XXB	A330-343E	974	
☐	9M-XXC	A330-343E	1048	
☐	9M-XXD	A330-343E	1066	
☐	9M-XXE	A330-343E	1075	♦
☐	9M-XXF	A330-343E	1126	♦
☐	9M-XXG	A330-343E	1131	♦
☐	9M-XXH	A330-343E	1165	♦
☐	9M-	A330-343E		o/o ♦
☐	9M-	A330-343E		o/o ♦
☐	9M-	A330-343E		o/o ♦
☐	9M-	A330-343E		o/o ♦
☐	9M-	A330-343E		o/o ♦
☐	9M-	A330-343E		o/o ♦
☐	9M-XAB	A340-313X	273	
☐	9M-XAC	A340-313X	278	

BERJAYA AIR CHARTER   J8 / BVT

☐	9M-TAG	ATR 72-212A	858	
☐	9M-TAQ	ATR 72-212A	875	♦
☐	9M-TAH	DHC-7-110	109	
☐	9M-TAK	DHC-7-110	110	
☐	9M-TAL	DHC-7-110	112	

FIREFLY   7E / FFM

☐	9M-FYA	ATR 72-212A	812	
☐	9M-FYB	ATR 72-212A	814	
☐	9M-FYC	ATR 72-212A	821	
☐	9M-FYD	ATR 72-212A	830	
☐	9M-FYE	ATR 72-212A	840	
☐	9M-ГYF	ATR 72-212A	860	
☐	9M-FYG	ATR 72-212A	868	
☐	9M-FYH	ATR 72-212A	934	♦
☐	9M-FYI	ATR 72-212A	935	♦
☐	9M-FYJ	ATR 72-212A	941	♦
☐	9M-FFA	B737-8Q8/W	30702/1953	♦
☐	9M-FFB	B737-8Q8/W	30703/1964	♦
☐	9M-FZA	B737-430	27001/2316	♦
☐	9M-MGI	Fokker 50	20175	[SZB]

HERITAGE AIR

☐	RP-C5525	BAe146 Srs.200	E2031	♦

MALAYSIA AIRLINES   MH / MAS

☐	9M-MKA	A330-322	067
☐	9M-MKC	A330-322	069
☐	9M-MKD	A330-322	073
☐	9M-MKE	A330-322	077
☐	9M-MKF	A330-322	100
☐	9M-MKG	A330-322	107
☐	9M-MKH	A330-322	110
☐	9M-MKI	A330-322	116
☐	9M-MKJ	A330-322	119
☐	9M-MKS	A330-322	143
☐	9M-MKV	A330-223	296
☐	9M-MKW	A330-223	300

	Reg	Type	c/n	Notes
☐	9M-MKX	A330-223	290	
☐	9M-	A330-322		o/o♦
☐	9M-	A330-322		o/o♦
☐	9M-	A330-322		o/o♦
☐	9M-	A330-322		o/o♦
☐	9M-	A330-322		o/o♦
☐	9M-	A330-223F		o/o♦
☐	9M-	A330-223F		o/o♦
☐	9M-MMA	B737-4H6	26443/2272	
☐	9M-MMB	B737-4H6	26444/2308	
☐	9M-MMC	B737-4H6	26453/2332	
☐	9M-MMD	B737-4H6	26464/2340	
☐	9M-MME	B737-4H6	26465/2362	
☐	9M-MMF	B737-4H6	26466/2372	
☐	9M-MMG	B737-4H6	26467/2378	
☐	9M-MMH	B737-4H6	27084/2391	
☐	9M-MMI	B737-4H6	27096/2395	
☐	9M-MMJ	B737-4H6	27097/2399	
☐	9M-MMK	B737-4H6	27083/2403	
☐	9M-MML	B737-4H6	27085/2407	
☐	9M-MMM	B737-4H6	27166/2410	
☐	9M-MMN	B737-4H6	27167/2419	
☐	9M-MMQ	B737-4H6	27087/2441	
☐	9M-MMR	B737-4H6	26468/2445	
☐	9M-MMS	B737-4H6	27169/2450	
☐	9M-MMT	B737-4H6	27170/2462	
☐	9M-MMU	B737-4H6	26447/2479	
☐	9M-MMV	B737-4H6	26449/2491	
☐	9M-MMW	B737-4H6	26451/2496	
☐	9M-MMX	B737-4H6	26452/2501	
☐	9M-MMY	B737-4H6	26455/2507	>UBA
☐	9M-MMZ	B737-4H6	26457/2521	
☐	9M-MQA	B737-4H6	26458/2525	
☐	9M-MQB	B737-4H6	26459/2530	
☐	9M-MQC	B737-4H6	26460/2533	
☐	9M-MQD	B737-4H6	26461/2536	
☐	9M-MQE	B737-4H6	26462/2542	
☐	9M-MQF	B737-4H6	26463/2560	
☐	9M-MQG	B737-4H6	27190/2568	
☐	9M-MQI	B737-4H6	27353/2632	
☐	9M-MQK	B737-4H6	27384/2673	
☐	9M-MQN	B737-4H6	27673/2852	
☐	9M-MQO	B737-4H6	27674/2877	
☐	9M-MQP	B737-46J	28038/2794	
☐	9M-MQQ	B737-4Y0	24915/2055	
☐	9M-MLC	B737-8Q8/W	32690/2250	
☐	9M-MLD	B737-8GQ/W	35793/2428	♦
☐	9M-MLE	B737-8FH/W	35105/2501	♦
☐	9M-MLF	B737-8FZ/W	29657/3335	♦
☐	9M-MLG	B737-8FZ/W	31779/3395	♦
☐	9M-MLH	B737-8FZ/W	31723/3435	♦
☐	9M-MLI	B737-8FZ/W	31793/3503	♦
☐	9M-MLJ	B737-8FZ/W	39319/3564	o/o♦
☐	9M-MLK	B737-8FZ/W		o/o♦
☐	9M-MXA	B737-8FH6W	40128/3421	♦
☐	9M-MXB	B737-8FH6W	40129/3458	♦
☐	9M-MXC	B737-8FH6W	40130/3495	♦
☐	9M-	B737-8FH6W		o/o♦
☐	9M-	B737-8FH6W		o/o♦
☐	9M-	B737-8FH6W		o/o♦
☐	TF-AAA	B747-236B (SCD)	22442/526	<ABD
☐	TF-AAB	B747-236B (SCD)	22304/502	
☐	TF-ARJ	B747-236M	23735/674opb ABD	
☐	TF-ARN	B747-2F6B(SF)	22382/498opb ABD	
☐	9M-MPB	B747-4H6	25699/965	
☐	9M-MPF	B747-4H6	27043/1017	
☐	9M-MPH	B747-4H6	27044/1041	
☐	9M-MPK	B747-4H6	28427/1147	
☐	9M-MPL	B747-4H6	28428/1150	
☐	9M-MPM	B747-4H6	28435/1152	
☐	9M-MPN	B747-4H6	28432/1247	
☐	9M-MPO	B747-4H6	28433/1290	
☐	9M-MPP	B747-4H6	29900/1296	

	Reg	Type	c/n	Notes
☐	9M-MPQ	B747-4H6	29901/1301	
☐	9M-MPR	B747-4H6F	28434/1371	
☐	9M-MPS	B747-4H6F	29902/1374	
☐	9M-MRA	B777-2H6ER	28408/64	
☐	9M-MRB	B777-2H6ER	28409/74	
☐	9M-MRC	B777-2H6ER	28410/78	
☐	9M-MRD	B777-2H6ER	28411/84	
☐	9M-MRE	B777-2H6ER	28412/115	
☐	9M-MRF	B777-2H6ER	28413/128	
☐	9M-MRG	B777-2H6ER	28414/140	
☐	9M-MRH	B777-2H6ER	28415/151	
☐	9M-MRI	B777-2H6ER	28416/155	
☐	9M-MRJ	B777-2H6ER	28417/222	
☐	9M-MRK	B777-2H6ER	28418/231	
☐	9M-MRL	B777-2H6ER	29065/329	
☐	9M-MRM	B777-2H6ER	29066/336	
☐	9M-MRN	B777-2H6ER	28419/394	
☐	9M-MRO	B777-2H6ER	28420/404	
☐	9M-MRP	B777-2H6ER	28421/496	
☐	9M-MRQ	B777-2H6ER	28422/498	

MASWINGS

	Reg	Type	c/n	Notes
☐	9M-MWA	ATR 72-212A	817	
☐	9M-MWB	ATR 72-212A	856	
☐	9M-MWC	ATR 72-212A	863	
☐	9M-MWD	ATR 72-212A	873	
☐	9M-MWE	ATR 72-212A	885	
☐	9M-MWF	ATR 72-212A	889	
☐	9M-MWG	ATR 72-212A	895	
☐	9M-MWH	ATR 72-212A	900	
☐	9M-MWI	ATR 72-212A	904	♦
☐	9M-MWJ	ATR 72-212A	910	♦
☐	9M-MGA	Fokker 50	20150	
☐	9M-MGB	Fokker 50	20156	
☐	9M-MGD	Fokker 50	20164	
☐	9M-MGE	Fokker 50	20166	
☐	9M-MGF	Fokker 50	20167	
☐	9M-MGG	Fokker 50	20170	[SZB]
☐	9M-MGJ	Fokker 50	20204	[SZB]

NEPTUNE AIR

	Reg	Type	c/n	Notes
☐	9M-NEA	B737-210C	21822/605	
☐	9M-NEP	B727-277F	22641/1753	

PERFECT AVIATION

	Reg	Type	c/n	Notes
☐	N854AA	B727-223F	20995/1192	

TRANSMILE AIR SERVICES   TH / TSE

	Reg	Type	c/n	Notes
☐	9M-TGB	B727-2F2F/W	22998/1810	
☐	9M-TGE	B727-247F	21697/1471	♦
☐	9M-TGF	B727-247F	21698/1474	
☐	9M-TGG	B727-247F	21699/1485	
☐	9M-TGH	B727-247F	21701/1493	
☐	9M-TGL	B727-225F	21856/1537	
☐	9M-TGM	B727-225F	22549/1737	
☐	9M-PML	B737-275C	21116/427	
☐	9M-PMM	B737-205C	20458/278	[KUL]
☐	9M-PMP	B737-248C	20220/215	
☐	9M-PMQ	B737-230C	20254/230	
☐	9M-PMW	B737-209F	24197/1581	♦
☐	9M-PMZ	B737-209	23796/1420	♦
☐	9M-TGP	MD-11F	48444/459	[KUL]
☐	9M-TGQ	MD-11F	48446/463	[KUL]
☐	9M-TGR	MD-11F	48485/502	[KUL]
☐	9M-TGS	MD-11F	48486/509	[KUL]

9N - NEPAL

BUDDHA AIR — BHA

☐	9N-AIM	ATR 42-320	388
☐	9N-AIN	ATR 42-320	403
☐	9N-AIT	ATR 42-320	409
☐	9N-AJO	ATR 72-212A	535	♦

NEPAL AIRLINES — RA / RNA

☐	9N-ACA	B757-2F8	23850/142
☐	9N-ACB	B757-2F8C	23863/182

9Q - CONGO KINSHASA

AEROLIFT SERVICES

☐	9Q-CJU	An-32	1408

AFRICA ONE

☐	9Q-CAF	An-32	1703

AIR BOYOMA

☐	UR-ELH	An-26B	12908	<URG

AIR KASAI

☐	9Q-CFD	An-26B	12901
☐	9Q-CFL	An-26B	14003
☐	9Q-CFM	An-26b	07310405
☐	9Q-CFP	An-26	07310605

AIR TROPIQUES

☐	9Q-CLN	F.27 Friendship 100	10152

ALAJNIHAH AIR TRANSPORT

☐	9Q-CGV	Il-76TD	33449441

ATO - AIR TRANSPORT OFFICE

☐	9Q-CTO	L-188A Electra	1073
☐	9Q-CVK	HS.780 Andover E.3	Set 17

BRAVO AIR CONGO

☐	TN-AHQ	DC-9-32	48126/951	
☐	9Q-CDO	DC-9-32	48125/947	[FIH]
☐	9Q-CDT	DC-9-32	48128/964	
☐	9Q-CVT	DC-9-32	48127/961	[FIH]

CAA - COMPAIGNIE AFRICAINE D'AVIATION

☐	9Q-CSB	A320-212	0438	♦
☐	9Q-CAB	Fokker 50	20276	♦
☐	9Q-CBD	Fokker 50	20270	♦
☐	9Q-CJB	Fokker 50	20196	♦
☐	9Q-CIB	MD-82	49394/1285	

CETRACA AIR SERVICE

☐	9Q-CKO	An-26	5210
☐	9Q-CKT	An-26B	12001

CO-ZA AIRWAYS

☐	9Q-CML	An-26	7408

ESPACE AVIATION

☐	9Q-CTA	DC-8-54F	45802/247

ETRAM AIR WING

☐	4K-48136	An-32B	3103	
☐	D2-FDZ	B707-399C	19415/601	
☐	N56FA	DC-8-54F	45663/189	[LAD]

FILAIR

☐	9Q-CTR	An-24RV	77310802

GALAXY KAVATSI AVIATION

☐	9Q-CVE	An-26	5301

HEWA BORA AIRWAYS — EO / ALX

☐	9Q-CBW	B707-329C	20200/828	
☐	9Q-CKK	B707-366C	20761/867	
☐	9Q-CKR	B707-351C	19411/540	
☐	9Q-CWB	B707-3B4C	20259/822	
☐	S9-DBM	B727-22/W	18323/136	
☐	S9-ROI	B727-30/W	18933/185	
☐	9Q-CHD	B727-232	22494/1749	[FIH]
☐	9Q-CHE	B727-232	21310/1298	
☐	9Q-CHF	B727-232	22677/1785	
☐	9Q-CHG	B727-232	21586/1488	
☐	9Q-CHK	B727-29F/W	19401/419	
☐	9Q-CRG	B727-30	18361/28	[FIH]
☐	9Q-CRS	B727-214	19687/573	
☐	9Q-CWA	B727-227	20775/998	[FIH]
☐	9Q-CKZ	B737-293	19309/47	
☐	S9-TOP	B767-266ER	23178/97	
☐	S9-TOA	MD-82	49176/1120	
☐	S9-TOB	MD-82	49178/1122	
☐	9Q-CHL	DC-8F-55	45820/246	
☐	9Q-CHC	L-1011-500 Tristar	193H-1209	[FIH]

ITAB

☐	9Q-CON	BAC One-Eleven 537GF	261
☐	9Q-CSJ	BAC One-Eleven 201AC	13
☐	9Q-CVC	HS.780 Andover C Mk.1	Set 29
☐	9Q-CYB	HS.780 Andover C Mk.1	Set 22

LIGNES AERIENNES CONGOLAISE — LCG

☐	9Q-CSV	B737-281	20276/231

MALIFT AIR — MLC

☐	9Q-CMD	An-32B	2210	[SHJ]
☐	9Q-CMK	An-24RV	47309902	
☐	9Q-CMS	An-26	4206	

MANGO MAT AIRLINES

☐	S9-PSK	An-12BK	8345807
☐	9Q-CVM	An-12B	8345503

SERVICE AIR

☐	9Q-	Boeing 727-2S2F	22930/1824
☐	9Q-CVS	Boeing 727-2S2F	22924/1818

SOFT TRANS AIR

☐	9Q-CYN	An-26	67304001

STAG

☐	9Q-CFB	An-26B	56312909

232

SUCCESS AIRLINES

☐	9Q-CJI	An-26	6004

TMK AIR COMMUTER

☐	9Q-CWP	DHC-8-102	105	♦

TOLAZ AVIATION GROUP

☐	9Q-CGM	An-26B	6401

TRANSAIR CARGO SERVICE

☐	3X-GEP	DC-8-62F	45921/322	
☐	9Q-CJH	DC-8-62F	46023/407	[JNB]
☐	9Q-CJL	DC-8-62F	45909/307	
☐	9Q-CMP	B727-22C	19892/640	
☐	9Q-CYS	NAMC YS-11A	2051	

WIMBI DIRA AIRWAYS — 9C / WDA

☐	9Q-CWD	B727-231F	19562/576
☐	9Q-CWE	DC-9-32	47701/822
☐	9Q-CWG	B707-323C	19587/686
☐	9Q-CWH	DC-9-32	47744/837
☐	9Q-	DC-9-32	47090/190
☐	S9-	DC-9-34CF	47707/823

9V - SINGAPORE

JETSTAR ASIA AIRWAYS — 3K / JSA

☐	9V-JSA	A320-232	2316	
☐	9V-JSB	A320-232	2356	
☐	9V-JSC	A320-232	2395	
☐	9V-JSD	A320-232	2401	
☐	9V-JSF	A320-232	2453	
☐	9V-JSG	A320-232	2457	
☐	9V-JSH	A320-232	2604	
☐	9V-JSI	A320-232	4443	♦
☐	9V-	A320-232		o/o♦
☐	9V-	A320-232		o/o♦

JETT 8 AIRLINES CARGO — JEC

☐	9V-JEB	B747-281F	23350/623

SILKAIR — MI / SLK

☐	9V-SBC	A319-132	1228	
☐	9V-SBD	A319-132	1698	
☐	9V-SBE	A319-132	2568	
☐	9V-SBF	A319-132	3104	
☐	9V-SBG	A319-132	4215	♦
☐	9V-SBH	A319-132	4259	♦
☐	9V-SBI	A319-132		o/o
☐	9V-SBJ	A319-132		o/o
☐	9V-SLB	A320-232	0899	
☐	9V-SLC	A320-232	0969	
☐	9V-SLD	A320-232	1422	
☐	9V-SLE	A320-232	1561	
☐	9V-SLF	A320-232	2058	
☐	9V-SLG	A320-233	2252	
☐	9V-SLH	A320-233	2517	
☐	9V-SLI	A320-233	2775	
☐	9V-SLJ	A320-233	3570	
☐	9V-SLK	A320-233	3821	
☐	9V-SLL	A320-232	4118	
☐	9V-SLM	A320-232	4457	♦
☐	9V-	A320-232		o/o♦
☐	9V-	A320-232		o/o♦
☐	9V-	A320-232		o/o♦

SINGAPORE AIRLINES — SQ / SIA

☐	9V-STA	A330-343E	978	
☐	9V-STB	A330-343E	983	
☐	9V-STC	A330-343E	986	
☐	9V-STD	A330-343E	997	
☐	9V-STE	A330-343E	1006	
☐	9V-STF	A330-343E	1010	
☐	9V-STG	A330-343E	1012	
☐	9V-STH	A330-343E	1015	
☐	9V-STI	A330-343E	1085	
☐	9V-STJ	A330-343E	1098	♦
☐	9V-STK	A330-343E	1099	♦
☐	9V-STL	A330-343E	1105	♦
☐	9V-STM	A330-343E	1107	♦
☐	9V-STN	A330-343E	1124	♦
☐	9V-STO	A330-343E	1132	♦
☐	9V-STP	A330-343E	1146	♦
☐	9V-STQ	A330-343E	1149	♦
☐	9V-STR	A330-343E	1156	♦
☐	9V-STS	A330-343E	1157	♦
☐	9V-SGA	A340-541	492	
☐	9V-SGB	A340-541	499	
☐	9V-SGC	A340-541	478	
☐	9V-SGD	A340-541	560	
☐	9V-SGE	A340-541	563	
☐	9V-SKA	A380-841	003	
☐	9V-SKB	A380-841	005	
☐	9V-SKC	A380-841	006	
☐	9V-SKD	A380-841	008	
☐	9V-SKE	A380-841	010	
☐	9V-SKF	A380-841	012	
☐	9V-SKG	A380-841	019	
☐	9V-SKH	A380-841	021	
☐	9V-SKI	A380-841	034	
☐	9V-SKJ	A380-841	045	
☐	9V-SKK	A380-841	051	♦
☐	9V-SKL	A380-841	058	o/o♦
☐	9V-SKM	A380-841	065	o/o♦
☐	9V-SKN	A380-841	071	o/o♦
☐	9V-SKO	A380-841	076	o/o♦
☐	9V-SKP	A380-841	079	o/o♦
☐	9V-SMU	B747-412	27068/1000	
☐	9V-SPA	B747-412	26550/1040	
☐	9V-SPE	B747-412	26554/1070	
☐	9V-SPJ	B747-412	26556/1084	
☐	9V-SPM	B747-412	29950/1241	[VCV]
☐	9V-SPN	B747-412	28031/1266	[VCV]
☐	9V-SPO	B747-412	28028/1270	
☐	9V-SPP	B747-412	28029/1276	
☐	9V-SPQ	B747-412	28025/1289	
☐	9V-SQA	B777-212ER	28507/67	
☐	9V-SQB	B777-212ER	28508/83	
☐	9V-SQC	B777-212ER	28509/86	
☐	9V-SQD	B777-212ER	28510/90	
☐	9V-SQF	B777-212ER	28512/126	
☐	9V-SQG	B777-212ER	28518/226	
☐	9V-SQH	B777-212ER	28519/237	
☐	9V-SQI	B777-212ER	28530/390	
☐	9V-SQJ	B777-212ER	30875/406	
☐	9V-SQK	B777-212ER	33368/428	
☐	9V-SQL	B777-212ER	33370/451	
☐	9V-SQM	B777-212ER	33372/485	
☐	9V-SQN	B777-212ER	33373/487	
☐	9V-SRD	B777-212ER	28514/153	
☐	9V-SRE	B777-212ER	28523/239	
☐	9V-SRF	B777-212ER	28521/330	
☐	9V-SRG	B777-212ER	28522/337	
☐	9V-SRH	B777-212ER	30866/343	
☐	9V-SRI	B777-212ER	30867/348	
☐	9V-SRJ	B777-212ER	28527/372	
☐	9V-SRK	B777-212ER	28529/389	

	Reg	Type	C/N
☐	9V-SRL	B777-212ER	32334/409
☐	9V-SRM	B777-212ER	32320/438
☐	9V-SRN	B777-212ER	32318/441
☐	9V-SRO	B777-212ER	32321/447
☐	9V-SRP	B777-212ER	33369/448
☐	9V-SRQ	B777-212ER	33371/449
☐	9V-SVE	B777-212ER	30870/374
☐	9V-SVH	B777-212ER	28532/407
☐	9V-SVI	B777-212ER	32316/412
☐	9V-SVJ	B777-212ER	32335/415
☐	9V-SVK	B777-212ER	28520/419
☐	9V-SVL	B777-212ER	32336/422
☐	9V-SVM	B777-212ER	30874/430
☐	9V-SVN	B777-212ER	30873/431
☐	9V-SVO	B777-212ER	28533/471
☐	9V-SWA	B777-312ER	34568/586 [VCV]
☐	9V-SWB	B777-312ER	33377/592
☐	9V-SWD	B777-312ER	34569/600
☐	9V-SWE	B777-312ER	34570/602
☐	9V-SWF	B777-312ER	34571/603
☐	9V-SWG	B777-312ER	34572/604
☐	9V-SWH	B777-312ER	34573/615
☐	9V-SWI	B777-312ER	34574/618
☐	9V-SWJ	B777-312ER	34575/623
☐	9V-SWK	B777-312ER	34576/644
☐	9V-SWL	B777-312ER	34577/673
☐	9V-SWM	B777-312ER	34578/701
☐	9V-SWN	B777-312ER	34579/703
☐	9V-SWO	B777-312ER	34580/708
☐	9V-SWP	B777-312ER	34581/710
☐	9V-SWQ	B777-312ER	34582/716
☐	9V-SWR	B777-312ER	34583/722
☐	9V-SWS	B777-312ER	34584/729
☐	9V-SWT	B777-312ER	34585/759
☐	9V-SYA	B777-312	28515/180
☐	9V-SYB	B777-312	28516/184
☐	9V-SYC	B777-312	28517/188
☐	9V-SYD	B777-312	28534/192
☐	9V-SYE	B777-312	28531/244
☐	9V-SYF	B777-312	30868/360
☐	9V-SYG	B777-312	28528/364
☐	9V-SYH	B777-312	32317/420
☐	9V-SYI	B777-312	32327/484
☐	9V-SYJ	B777-312	33374/503
☐	9V-SYK	B777-312	33375/505
☐	9V-SYL	B777-312	33376/515

SINGAPORE AIRLINES CARGO — SQ / SQC

	Reg	Type	C/N	
☐	9V-SFC	B747-412F	26560/1052	
☐	9V-SFD	B747-412F	26553/1069	
☐	9V-SFF	B747-412F	28026/1105	
☐	9V-SFG	B747-412F	26558/1173	
☐	9V-SFJ	B747-412F	26559/1285	
☐	9V-SFK	B747-412F	28030/1298	
☐	9V-SFL	B747-412F	32897/1322	[VCV]
☐	9V-SFM	B747-412F	32898/1333	
☐	9V-SFN	B747-412F	32899/1342	
☐	9V-SFO	B747-412F	32900/1349	
☐	9V-SFP	B747-412F	32902/1364	>/3.
☐	9V-SFQ	B747-412F	32901/1369	

TIGER AIRWAYS — TR / TGW

	Reg	Type	C/N	
☐	9V-TAB	A320-232	2195	
☐	9V-TAC	A320-232	2331	
☐	9V-TAD	A320-232	2340	
☐	9V-TAE	A320-232	2724	
☐	9V-TAF	A320-232	2728	
☐	9V-TAM	A320-232	4181	
☐	9V-TAN	A320-232	4210	♦
☐	9V-TAO	A320-232	4421	♦
☐	9V-TAP	A320-232	4445	♦
☐	9V-TAQ	A320-232	4469	♦
☐	9V-TAR	A320-232	4491	♦
☐	9V-TAS	A320-232	4493	♦
☐	9V-TAT	A320-232	4532	♦
☐	9V-TAU	A320-232	4561	♦
☐	9V-	A320-232		o/o ♦
☐	9V-	A320-232		o/o ♦
☐	9V-	A320-232		o/o ♦
☐	9V-	A320-232		o/o ♦
☐	9V-	A320-232		o/o ♦
☐	9V-	A320-232		o/o ♦
☐	9V-TRA	A319-132	3757	
☐	9V-TRB	A319-132	3801	

VALUAIR — VF / VLU

	Reg	Type	C/N	
☐	9V-VLE	A320-232	2156	♦
☐	9V-VLF	A320-232	2164	♦

9XR - RWANDA

RWANDAIR EXPRESS — WB / RWD

	Reg	Type	C/N	
☐	9XR-WA	CRJ-200LR	7439	
☐	9XR-WB	CRJ-200LR	7449	
☐	9XR-WD	B737-55D	27416/2389	♦
☐	9XR-WE	B737-55D	27417/2392	♦
☐	ET-ALX	DHC-8-202	475	<TNW
☐	7Q-YKW	B737-522	25384/2149	

SILVERBACK CARGO FREIGHTERS — VRB

	Reg	Type	C/N
☐	9XR-SC	DC-8-62F	46068/463
☐	9XR-SD	DC-8-62F	45956/376

9Y - TRINIDAD & TOBAGO

CARIBBEAN AIRLINES — BW / BWA

	Reg	Type	C/N	
☐	9Y-ANU	B737-8Q8/W	28235/697	
☐	9Y-BGI	B737-8Q8/W	28232/547	
☐	9Y-GEO	B737-8Q8/W	28225/433	
☐	9Y-JMA	B737-8Q8/W	30645/1129	♦
☐	9Y-KIN	B737-8Q8/W	28234/680	
☐	9Y-PBM	B737-8BK/W	29635/2326	
☐	9Y-POS	B737-8Q8/W	28230/506	
☐	9Y-SLU	B737-83N/W	28246/1081	
☐	9Y-TAB	B737-8Q8/W	28233/598	
☐	9Y-TJR	B737-8K2/W	37160/2880	
☐	9Y-WIL	DHC-8Q-311	489	
☐	9Y-WIN	DHC-8Q-311	499	
☐	9Y-WIP	DHC-8Q-311	538	
☐	9Y-WIT	DHC-8Q-311	487	
☐	9Y-WIZ	DHC-8Q-311	557	

Corporate & VIP aircraft

Registration	Type	Serial
A4O-AA	A320-232	2566
A4O-OMN	B747-430	32445/1292
A4O-SO	B747-SP27	21785/405
A6-AAB	Avro RJ100	E3387
A6-AAM	A318 Elite	1599
A6-AIN	B737 BBJ1	29268/280
A6-AJA	Legacy 600	14501089
A6-AJB	Legacy 600	14501098
A6-AJC	A318 Elite	3985
A6-AJH	Lineage 1000	19000140
A6-AJI	Lineage 1000	19000261
A6-ALN	B777-2ANER	29953/252
A6-ARK	Lineage 1000	19000109
A6-AUH	B737 BBJ2	33473/1196
A6-BNH	Challenger 850	8069
A6-COM	B747-433M	25074/862
A6-DAS	B737 BBJ1	29858/530
A6-DFR	B737 BBJ1	30884/747
A6-DLM	A320-232	2403
A6-DPW	Legacy 600	14500955
A6-ESH	A319CJ	0910
A6-FLL	Legacy 600	14501051
A6-FLO	Legacy 600	14501096
A6-HEH	B737 BBJ2	32825/1602
A6-HHS	Lineage 1000	19000296
A6-HMS	A320-232	3379
A6-HRM	B747-422	26903/1171
A6-HRS	B737 BBJ1	29251/150
A6-KAH	Lineage 1000	19000236
A6-LIW	Avro RJ70	E1267
A6-MAZ	Legacy 600	14500978
A6-MMM	B747-422	26906/1185
A6-MRM	B737 BBJ2	32450/787
A6-MRS	B737 BBJ2	35238/1966
A6-NKL	Legacy 600	14500944
A6-NLA	Legacy 600	14501075
A6-PJE	Legacy 600	14500972
A6-RJ1	Avro RJ85	E2323
A6-RJ2	Avro RJ85	E2325
A6-RJX	B737 BBJ1	29865/241
A6-RJY	B737 BBJ1	29857/445
A6-RJZ	B737 BBJ1	29269/432
A6-SSV	Legacy 600	14501041
A6-SUN	Legacy 600	14501001
A6-UAE	B747-48EM	28551/1131
A6-UGH	Legacy 600	14500993
A6-VVV	Legacy 600	14501075
A6-YAS	B747-4F6	28961/1174
A7-AAG	A320-232	927
A7-AAH	A340-313X	528
A7-AFE	A310-308	667
A7-HHH	A340-541	495
A7-HHJ	A319CJ	1335
A7-HHK	A340-211	026
A7-HHM	A330-202	605
A7-HJJ	A330-202	487
A7-MBK	A320-232	4170
A9C-AWL	Avro RJ100	E3386
A9C-BA	B727-2M7/W RE	21824/1595
A9C-BDF	Avro RJ85	E2390
A9C-DAA	B737-268	22050/622
A9C-HAK	B747-SPZ5	23610/676
A9C-HMK	B747-4P8	33684/1324
A9C-HWR	Avro RJ85	E2306
A9C-MTC	Legacy 600	14500975
B-4005	Challenger 800	7138
B-4006	Challenger 800	7149
B-4007	Challenger 800	7180
B-4010	Challenger 800	7189
B-4011	Challenger 800	7193
B-4012	Yak-42D	4520424914375
B-4013	Yak-42D	45204249144##
B-4028	Tu154M	967
B-4060	Challenger 870	10164
B-4061	Challenger 870	10183
B-4062	Challenger 870	10187
B-4063	Challenger 870	10204
B-4064	Challenger 870	10206
B-4138	Tu154M	712
B-4701	Challenger 800	7639
B-4702	Challenger 800	7455
B-5266	B737 BBJ1	29866/408
B-6178	A319-133X	3548
B-6186	A318 Elite	3333
B-6188	A318 Elite	3617
B-6411	A318 Elite	3886
B-7695	CRJ200ER	7268
B-7697	Challenger 850	8089
B-LEX	B737 BBJ1	34683/1859
C-FPHS	B737-53A	24970/1977
C-FWEZ	Challenger 850	8092
C-GCPW	Do328 Jet	3129
C-GDTD	Challenger 850	8067
C-GSLL	Challenger 850	8103
C-GSUA	Challenger 890	15182
C-GSUM	Challenger 890	15158
C-GSUW	Challenger 850	8047
CN-MBP	Legacy 600	14501117
CN-MVI	B737 BBJ2	37545/2696
CP-2634	BAe-146-200	E2096
CS-TFU	A319CJ	2440
CS-TLU	A319CJ	1256
D-AAIJ	Challenger 850	8065
D-AANN	Challenger 850	8073
D-ACBN	A319CJ	3243
D-ACRN	CRJ200LR	7486
D-ADCP	Legacy 600	14501067
D-ADCQ	Legacy 650	14501134
D-ADNA	A319CJ	1053
D-AHAD	A319CJ	3632
D-AKAT	Legacy 600	14501038
D-ALEY	A319CJ	3513
D-ARTN	Legacy 600	14500941
D-ATRI	Challenger 850	8081
D-AVIB	Legacy 600	14501109
D-BGAS	Do328 Jet	3139
D-BJET	Do328 Jet	3207
D-CATZ	Do328-100	3090
D-CPWF	Do328-100	3112
D2-MAN	B707-321B	20025/780
D2-TPR	B707-3J6B	20715/870
EC-IIR	Legacy 600	145540
EC-KHT	Legacy 600	14500863
EI-EEZ	Challenger 850	8085
EK-42470	Yak-42D	4520424116677
EK-RA01	A319-132	0913
EP-AGA	B737-286	21317/483
EP-AGB	A321-231	1202
EP-AJD	B707-320C	20832/886
EP-AJE	B707-368C	21396/928
EW-001PA	B737 BBJ2	33079/1075
EW-301PJ	Challenger 850	8057
EW-85815	Tu154M	1010
EW-88187	Yak-40	9620748
G-CGSE	Legacy 600	14500995
G-CJMD	Legacy 600	14500994
G-CMAF	Legacy 600	14501011
G-GJMB	Challenger 850	8055
G-HUBY	Legacy 600	14500854
G-IGWT	Challenger 850	8078
G-IRSH	Legacy 600	14501048
G-LALE	Legacy 600	14501017
G-LEGC	Legacy 600	14501025
G-NMAK	A319CJ	2550
G-NOAH	A319CJ	3826
G-OFOA	BAe-146-100	E1006
G-OFOM	BAe-146-100	E1144
G-OGSK	Legacy 600	14501074

	Reg	Type	Serial
☐	G-PGRP	Legacy 600	14501102
☐	G-RAJJ	BAe-146-200	E2108
☐	G-RBNB	Lineage 1000	19000203
☐	G-RBNS	Legacy 650	14501121
☐	G-RHMS	Legacy 600	14501072
☐	G-RUBE	Legacy 600	14501100
☐	G-SHAL	Challenger 850	8066
☐	G-SHSI	Legacy 600	14501114
☐	G-SUGA	Legacy 650	14501128
☐	G-SYLJ	Legacy 600	14500937
☐	G-THFC	Legacy 600	14500954
☐	G-WCCI	Legacy 600	145505
☐	HB-AEU	Do328 Jet	Envoy 3
☐	HB-IDJ	Challenger 800	7136
☐	HB-IEE	B757-23A/W	24527/249
☐	HB-JED	Legacy 600	145644
☐	HB-JEL	Legacy 600	14500933
☐	HB-JJA	B737 BBJ1	34303/1758
☐	HL7227	B737 BBJ1	35977/2047
☐	HL7465	B747-4B5	26412/1284
☐	HL7759	B737 BBJ1	35990/2107
☐	HL7787	B737 BBJ1	36852/2475
☐	HL8222	B737 BBJ1	37660/2997
☐	HP-1A	Legacy 600	14501066
☐	HS-CMV	B737-4Z6	27906/2698
☐	HS-TYQ	A310-324	591
☐	HS-TYR	A319CJ	1908
☐	HS-TYS	B737-8Z6/W	35478/1955
☐	HZ-A2	A320-214	3164
☐	HZ-A4	A319-112	1494
☐	HZ-AB3	B727-2U5 RE	22362/1657
☐	HZ-AIF	B747-SP68	22503/529
☐	HZ-AIJ	B747-SP68	22750/560
☐	HZ-AJ3	A320-214	0764
☐	HZ-HM1A	B747-3G1	23070/592
☐	HZ-HM1B	B747-SP68	21652/329
☐	HZ-HMS2	A340-213	204
☐	HZ-MF1	B737 BBJ1	33405/1204
☐	HZ-MF2	B737 BBJ1	33499/1217
☐	HZ-MIS	B737-2K5	22600/816
☐	HZ-NSA	A310-304	431
☐	HZ-SKI	B727-212 RE	21460/1340
☐	HZ-TAA	B737 BBJ1	29188/217
☐	HZ-WBT7	B747-4J6	25880/926
☐	HZ-XY7	A320-214	2165
☐	JY-CMC	Legacy 650	14501126
☐	JY-KME	Legacy 600	14501055
☐	J2-KBA	B727-191	19394/418
☐	J2-KBE	B767-216ER	23624/144
☐	LX-GJC	A318 Elite	3100
☐	LX-NVB	Legacy 600	14501002
☐	LX-RLG	Legacy 600	14500967
☐	LZ-AOB	A319-112	3188
☐	LZ-TIM	Avro RJ70	E1258
☐	M-AKAK	Legacy 600	14500970
☐	M-ANTA	Challenger 850	8094
☐	M-DSCL	Legacy 600	14500851
☐	M-ESGR	Legacy 600	14501016
☐	M-ETIS	B727-2X8 RE	22687/1784
☐	M-FAHD	B727-176 RE	19254/298
☐	M-FZMH	Challenger 850	8068
☐	M-ISLA	Challenger 850	8080
☐	M-KPCO	Legacy 600	14500973
☐	M-NATH	Legacy 600	14501021
☐	M-OLEG	Legacy 600	14500991
☐	M-RCCG	Legacy 600	14501113
☐	M-SBAH	Lineage 1000	19000225
☐	M-TAKE	Challenger 850	8079
☐	M-URUS	B737 BBJ1	34622/1785
☐	M-YBBJ	B737 BBJ1	36027/2068
☐	M-YNJC	Legacy 600	14500961
☐	N1RL	Challenger 870	10004
☐	N2TS	B737 BBJ1	29102/101
☐	N6GD	Legacy 600	14500983
☐	N10SV	Legacy 600	14500974
☐	N25AZ	B727-130	18370/134
☐	N28CG	Do328-100	3024
☐	N30MP	B727-121	18998/239
☐	N37NY	B737-4YO	23976/1651
☐	N38CG	Do328-100	3034
☐	N43PR	B737 BBJ1	28581/126
☐	N44KS	SAAB 340A	050
☐	N50TC	B737 BBJ1	29024/131
☐	N53NA	Legacy 600	145770
☐	N57TT	Do328 Jet	3205
☐	N63AG	Legacy 600	14501061
☐	N73HK	B737-2S9	21957/618
☐	N88WR	B737 BBJ1	29441/111
☐	N88ZL	B707-330B	18928/457
☐	N89FE	Legacy 600	14501058
☐	N89LD	ERJ-135SE	145648
☐	N90R	B737 BBJ1	32775/889
☐	N92SR	B737 BBJ1	37111/2595
☐	N108MS	B737 BBJ1	33102/1111
☐	N111VM	B737 BBJ1	36090/2196
☐	N114M	BAe-146-100	E1068
☐	N117LM	Do328 Jet	3167
☐	N124LS	Legacy 600	14500948
☐	N131BC	Do328 Jet	3168
☐	N135BC	Challenger 800	7075
☐	N135SK	Legacy 600	14500989
☐	N135SL	Legacy 600	145711
☐	N138DE	ERJ-145LR	145129
☐	N155MW	CRJ200LR	7021
☐	N162WC	B737 BBJ1	30329/384
☐	N164RJ	B737 BBJ1	30328/377
☐	N168CF	MD-87	49670/1453
☐	N169KT	B727-269	22359/1652
☐	N226HY	Legacy 600	14501014
☐	N227WE	Legacy 600	14501018
☐	N287KB	MD-87	49768/1595
☐	N307UE	Jetstream 41	41021
☐	N311AG	B727-117 RE	20512/858
☐	N315TS	B737 BBJ1	30772/554
☐	N325JF	ERJ-135SE	145499
☐	N325SV	SAAB 340A	072
☐	N328WW	Do328 Jet	3116
☐	N357TE	Legacy 600	14501079
☐	N359SK	Do328 Jet	3202
☐	N370BC	B737-205	23468/1262
☐	N371BC	B737 BBJ2	32971/996
☐	N373RB	Legacy 600	14500957
☐	N386CH	ERJ-135SE	145467
☐	N388LS	L-1011 TriStar-500	1249
☐	N406FJ	Do328 Jet	3156
☐	N410TJ	Jetstream 41	41038
☐	N413JG	B737-2Q8	23148/1059
☐	N431BC	SAAB 340B	260
☐	N444HE	B737-39A/W	23800/1409
☐	N451DJ	Legacy 600	145789
☐	N486TM	ERJ-135SE	145364
☐	N494TG	Legacy 600	145678
☐	N500DE	ERJ-145EP	145084
☐	N500LS	B737 BBJ1	29054/143
☐	N500PR	Challenger 800	7846
☐	N500VP	B737-2H4	22062/640
☐	N501LS	Challenger 800	7584
☐	N502MG	B727-191	19391309
☐	N503JT	Legacy 600	14501032
☐	N508RH	SAAB 2000	027
☐	N509RH	SAAB 2000	030
☐	N511RH	SAAB 2000	020
☐	N515JT	Legacy 600	14500950
☐	N519JG	SAAB 2000	017
☐	N529DB	Challenger 800	7152
☐	N541BC	SAAB 340A	029
☐	N580ML	Legacy 600	14500990
☐	N600YC	Legacy 600	14501069
☐	N601LS	Challenger 800	7008
☐	N605WG	Legacy 600	14500980

☐	N606DH	B727-130	18365/52
☐	N615PA	B727-243	21266/1227
☐	N615PG	Legacy 600	14501004
☐	N617WA	Legacy 600	14500884
☐	N632RF	SAAB 340A	042
☐	N642AG	Legacy 600	145642
☐	N673BF	B767-238ER	23402/133
☐	N676TC	Legacy 600	145699
☐	N678RC	Legacy 600	14501064
☐	N680AS	Jetstream 41	41030
☐	N697BJ	DC-9-32	47799/918
☐	N698SS	B727-223	21369/1275
☐	N702DR	Legacy 600	14500925
☐	N702RS	SAAB 340B	233
☐	N703RS	SAAB 340B	252
☐	N707JT	B707-138B	18740/388
☐	N711WM	Challenger 800	7140
☐	N720MM	B737 BBJ1	33010/1037
☐	N724CL	B727-151	19121/264
☐	N724YS	B727-281 RE	21474/1378
☐	N727AH	B727-121	19261/422
☐	N727DL	SAAB 340A	036
☐	N727NK	B727-212	21945/1502
☐	N727VJ	B727-144	19318/348
☐	N728PH	Legacy 600	14500985
☐	N730BH	Legacy 600	145730
☐	N731VA	B737-33A	27456/2749
☐	N733PA	B737-205	23466/1236
☐	N733TW	B737-2H4	22732/877
☐	N736BP	B737-205	23465/1226
☐	N737AG	B737 BBJ1	30496/301
☐	N737CC	B737 BBJ1	29135/206
☐	N737ER	B737 BBJ1	30754/516
☐	N737L	B737 BBJ1	30751/401
☐	N737M	B737 BBJ2	33361/1124
☐	N737WH	B737 BBJ1	29142/167
☐	N742PB	B737 BBJ1	29200/234
☐	N747A	B747-SP27	21992/447
☐	N757LL	B757-23N/W	27972/694
☐	N757MA	B757-24Q	28463/739
☐	N757SS	B757-236	22176/14
☐	N767A	B767-2AXER	33685/903
☐	N767KS	B767-24QER	28270/629
☐	N767MW	B767-277	22694/32
☐	N770BB	B757-2J4/W	25220/387
☐	N777AS	B777-24QER	29271/174
☐	N787WH	B737-2V6	22431/803
☐	N796BA	B737 BBJ1	30327/356
☐	N800AK	B727-123QX RE	20045/596
☐	N800KS	B737 BBJ1	30782/586
☐	N801DM	B757-256/W	26240/561
☐	N804CE	Do328 Jet	3184
☐	N804MS	B767-3P6ER	27255/525
☐	N806D	Legacy 600	14501095
☐	N809TD	Legacy 600	14500809
☐	N818HR	Legacy 600	14501105
☐	N821MW	Do328 Jet	3160
☐	N827TV	Legacy 600	14500971
☐	N829RN	ERJ-135SE	145361
☐	N835BA	B737 BBJ1	30572/491
☐	N836BA	B737 BBJ1	30756/569
☐	N865LS	Legacy 600	14501080
☐	N870DC	Challenger 870 NG	10314
☐	N880DF	DC-9-32	47635/754
☐	N880DP	MD-83	49504/1363
☐	N888AU	CRJ200 Phoenix	7211
☐	N888GY	CRJ200 ExecLiner	7471
☐	N888ML	Legacy 600	14500818
☐	N888TY	B737 BBJ1	29749/456
☐	N888WU	CRJ200 ExecLiner	7481
☐	N888YF	B737 BBJ1	33036/1060
☐	N889NC	B737 BBJ1	30070/244
☐	N898JS	Legacy 600	14501071
☐	N900DP	Legacy 600	14500903
☐	N900EM	Legacy 600	14500976

☐	N902WG	B737-2H6	22620/822
☐	N904FL	Legacy 600	145780
☐	N905FL	Legacy 600	145775
☐	N908JE	B727-131	20115/735
☐	N909LX	Legacy 600	14500942
☐	N909TT	Legacy 600	14501044
☐	N910LX	Legacy 600	14500952
☐	N912JC	Legacy 600	14501015
☐	N912NB	B737-2H4	22675/839
☐	N913LX	Legacy 600	14501007
☐	N920DS	B737 BBJ1	28579/312
☐	N924AK	Legacy 600	14501034
☐	N925FL	Legacy 600	14500825
☐	N926FM	ERJ-135SE	145466
☐	N939AJ	Legacy 600	14500939
☐	N948AL	ERJ-135SE	145450
☐	N966JS	Legacy 600	14500966
☐	N983JC	ERJ-135LR	14500977
☐	N999BW	One-Eleven-419EP	120
☐	N1023C	ERJ-135SE	145550
☐	N1757	B757-23A/W	24923/332
☐	N2767	B767-238ER	23896/183
☐	N3618F	A319CJ	2748
☐	N7600K	B737 BBJ1	32628/953
☐	N8767	B737 BBJ1	32807/926
☐	N8860	DC-9-15	45797/51
☐	N79711	B737 BBJ1	30547/423
☐	OD-AMR	CRJ200ER	7255
☐	OD-TAL	CRJ200 ExecLiner	7086
☐	OE-HMS	Do328 Jet	3121
☐	OE-HRJ	Do328 Jet	3206
☐	OE-HTJ	Do328 Jet	3114
☐	OE-IBK	Legacy 600	14501110
☐	OE-IBR	Legacy 600	14500960
☐	OE-IDB	Legacy 600	14500999
☐	OE-IDH	Legacy 600	14501026
☐	OE-IIB	Fokker 100	11403
☐	OE-IIC	Fokker 100	11406
☐	OE-IID	Fokker 100	11368
☐	OE-IKG	Challenger 850	8063
☐	OE-ILI	Challenger 850	8048
☐	OE-ILV	Challenger 850	8082
☐	OE-ILX	B737 BBJ2	32777/882
☐	OE-ILY	Challenger 850	8076
☐	OE-ILZ	Challenger 850	8086
☐	OE-IRK	Legacy 600	14500916
☐	OE-ISA	Challenger 850	8043
☐	OE-LGS	A319CJ	3046
☐	OH-SPB	Challenger 850	8056
☐	OK-GGG	Legacy 600	14500986
☐	OK-JNT	Legacy 600	14501087
☐	OK-KKG	Legacy 600	14500873
☐	OK-ROM	Legacy 600	14501039
☐	OK-SLN	Legacy 600	145796
☐	OK-SUN	Legacy 600	14500963
☐	OM-BYE	Yak-40	9440338
☐	OM-BYL	Yak-40	9940560
☐	OM-BYR	Tu154M	1012
☐	OO-ELI	Do328-100	3060
☐	OY-NAD	Challenger 850	8052
☐	OY-VEG	Challenger 850	8075
☐	OY-VGA	Challenger 850	8077
☐	P-618	IL62M	2546624
☐	PH-AAG	CRJ200 Hemisphere	7763
☐	PH-EVY	Do328-100	3095
☐	PH-KBX	Fokker 70	11547
☐	PK-DHK	Legacy 600	14501046
☐	PK-OME	Legacy 600	145516
☐	PK-OSP	BAe-146-100	E1124
☐	PK-PJJ	Avro RJ85	E2239
☐	PK-RJG	Legacy 600	14500969
☐	PK-RJW	Legacy 600	14501106
☐	PK-RSS	Legacy 600	14501020
☐	PP-VVA	ERJ-135LR	145702
☐	PP-VVV	Legacy 600	14501099

☐ PR-AVX	Legacy 600	14501037
☐ PR-BBS	B737 BBJ1	32575/861
☐ PR-BEB	Legacy 600	14501035
☐ PR-DPF	ERJ-145EP	145127
☐ PR-JDJ	Legacy 650	14501131
☐ PR-LTC	Legacy 600	14501091
☐ PR-NIO	Legacy 600	14501012
☐ PR-ODF	Legacy 600	14501054
☐ PR-ORE	Legacy 600	145625
☐ PR-PFN	ERJ-145LR	145002
☐ PR-RIO	Legacy 600	145717
☐ PT-SCR	Legacy 600	14500946
☐ PT-SKW	Legacy 600	14501006
☐ PT-SPM	ERJ-145EP	145114
☐ P4-AEG	Legacy 600	14501111
☐ P4-AFK	B737 BBJ1	36493/2211
☐ P4-ARL	A319CJ	2192
☐ P4-ASL	B737 BBJ1	29791/336
☐ P4-AST	Challenger 850	8054
☐ P4-FLY	B727-122	19148/473
☐ P4-FSH	B747-SP31	21963/441
☐ P4-GAZ	CRJ200 Renaissance	7159
☐ P4-GJL	Challenger 850	8053
☐ P4-IVM	Legacy 600	145686
☐ P4-KAZ	B737 BBJ1	32774/853
☐ P4-LIG	B737 BBJ1	37592/2752
☐ P4-MES	B767-33AER	33425/909
☐ P4-MIS	A319CJ	3133
☐ P4-MIV	Legacy 600	14501031
☐ P4-MSG	Legacy 600	14500913
☐ P4-NGK	B737 BBJ1	37583/2869
☐ P4-PAM	Legacy 600	14500982
☐ P4-SIS	Legacy 600	145586
☐ P4-SMS	Legacy 650	14501123
☐ P4-SVM	Legacy 600	14501060
☐ P4-VIP	CRJ200 Renaissance	7158
☐ P4-VNL	A319CJ	2921
☐ P4-VVP	Legacy 600	145549
☐ RA-42330	Yak-42D	4520422505122
☐ RA-42344	Yak-42D	4520422708295
☐ RA-42365	Yak-42D	4520424811447
☐ RA-42368	Yak-42D	4520422914166
☐ RA-42402	Yak-42D	4520422116583
☐ RA-42411	Yak-42D	4520421219043
☐ RA-42412	Yak-42D	4520422219055
☐ RA-42415	Yak-42D	4520422219089
☐ RA-42423	Yak-42D	4520424216606
☐ RA-42424	Yak-42D-100	4520421502016
☐ RA-42427	Yak-42D	4520422305016
☐ RA-42438	Yak-42D	4520423609018
☐ RA-42440	Yak-42D	4520424210018
☐ RA-42441	Yak-42D	4520421402018
☐ RA-42442	Yak-42D	4520421402019
☐ RA-42445	Yak-42D	4520424116669
☐ RA-42451	Yak-42D	4520422708018
☐ RA-64010	Tu-204-300	1450743164010
☐ RA-64517	Tu-204-214	41709017
☐ RA-64520	Tu-204-214	####020
☐ RA-65079	Tu134A	60054
☐ RA-65124	Tu134A	60560
☐ RA-65127	Tu134A	60627
☐ RA-65132	Tu134A	60639
☐ RA-65550	Tu134A	66200
☐ RA-65557	Tu134A	66380
☐ RA-65559	Tu134A	49909
☐ RA-65570	Tu134A	66550
☐ RA-65574	Tu-134B	64748
☐ RA-65576	Tu-134B	63285
☐ RA-65604	Tu134A	62561
☐ RA-65608	Tu134A	38040
☐ RA-65692	Tu-134B	63215
☐ RA-65700	Tu-134B	64783
☐ RA-65719	Tu134A	63637
☐ RA-65721	Tu134A	66130
☐ RA-65722	Tu134A	66420
☐ RA-65723	Tu134A	66440
☐ RA-65724	Tu134A	66445
☐ RA-65727	Tu-134B	64820
☐ RA-65737	Tu-134B	64195
☐ RA-65747	Tu-134B	64715
☐ RA-65756	Tu134A	62179
☐ RA-65790	Tu134A	63100
☐ RA-65798	Tu134A	63179
☐ RA-65805	Tu-134B	64775
☐ RA-65830	Tu134A	12093
☐ RA-65903	Tu134A	63750
☐ RA-65908	Tu134A	63870
☐ RA-65917	Tu134A	63991
☐ RA-65926	Tu134A	66101
☐ RA-65927	Tu134A	66198
☐ RA-65930	Tu134A	66500
☐ RA-65932	Tu134A	66405
☐ RA-65934	Tu134A	66143
☐ RA-65941	Tu134A	60642
☐ RA-65945	Tu-134B	64010
☐ RA-65965	Tu134A	2351803
☐ RA-65978	Tu134A	63357
☐ RA-65979	Tu134A	63158
☐ RA-65984	Tu134A	63400
☐ RA-67218	Challenger 850	8074
☐ RA-67219	Challenger 850	8090
☐ RA-67220	Challenger 850	8091
☐ RA-85001	Tu154M	820
☐ RA-85019	Tu154M	1019
☐ RA-85084	Tu154M	1004
☐ RA-85155	Tu154M	1000
☐ RA-85360	Tu-154B	360
☐ RA-85510	Tu-154B	510
☐ RA-85565	Tu-154B	565
☐ RA-85614	Tu154M	723
☐ RA-85686	Tu154M	854
☐ RA-85712	Tu154M	888
☐ RA-86467	IL62M	3749733
☐ RA-86468	IL62M	4749857
☐ RA-86539	IL62M	2344615
☐ RA-86540	IL62M	3546548
☐ RA-86551	IL62M	4547315
☐ RA-86559	IL62M	2153258
☐ RA-86561	IL62M	4154842
☐ RA-86579	IL62M	2951636
☐ RA-86583	IL62M	1356851
☐ RA-87203	Yak-40	9741456
☐ RA-87216	Yak-40	9510440
☐ RA-87224	Yak-40K	9841459
☐ RA-87226	Yak-40K	9841259
☐ RA-87227	Yak-40K	9841559
☐ RA-87253	Yak-40	9321026
☐ RA-87280	Yak-40	9322025
☐ RA-87286	Yak-40	9310128
☐ RA-87342	Yak-40	9511139
☐ RA-87353	Yak-40	9330231
☐ RA-87397	Yak-40	9410933
☐ RA-87429	Yak-40	9420535
☐ RA-87447	Yak-40	9430436
☐ RA-87496	Yak-40	9541945
☐ RA-87499	Yak-40	9610246
☐ RA-87503	Yak-40	9520240
☐ RA-87517	Yak-40	9521940
☐ RA-87524	Yak-40	9520641
☐ RA-87535	Yak-40	9521941
☐ RA-87569	Yak-40D	9220222
☐ RA-87655	Yak-40	9211820
☐ RA-87669	Yak-40	9021760
☐ RA-87807	Yak-40D	9231723
☐ RA-87828	Yak-40	9242024
☐ RA-87900	Yak-40K	9720254
☐ RA-87908	Yak-40	9721354
☐ RA-87938	Yak-40K	9710153
☐ RA-87953	Yak-40K	9811157
☐ RA-87966	Yak-40	9820958

Registration	Type	Serial
RA-87968	Yak-40	9841258
RA-87969	Yak-40	9831358
RA-87971	Yak-40	9831558
RA-87977	Yak-40	9321128
RA-87983	Yak-40	9540644
RA-88227	Yak-40K	9641550
RA-88240	Yak-40	9641151
RA-88293	Yak-40	9510138
RA-88294	Yak-40	9331029
RA-88295	Yak-40	9331329
RA-88296	Yak-40	9421634
RA-88297	Yak-40	9530142
RA-88298	Yak-40K	9930160
RA-88306	Yak-40K	9640651
RA-88308	Yak-40	9230224
RA-96012	Il-96-300	74393201009
RA-96016	Il-96-300	74393202010
RA-96018	Il-96-300	74393202018
RA-96019	Il-96-300	74393202019
RF-88301	Yak-40K	9641251
RP-C6226	Challenger 850	8088
SE-DJG	Legacy 600	14501042
SP-LIG	ERJ175LR	17000283
SP-LIH	ERJ175LR	17000288
ST-PRA	IL62M	2357711
SU-GGG	A340-212	061
SX-CDK	Legacy 600	14500998
SX-DGM	Legacy 600	14501023
SX-IFA	MD-83	49809/1843
SX-MTF	B737-329	23774/1443
SX-RFA	B757-23N/W	30232/888
S5-ABL	Legacy 600	14501008
S5-ALA	Legacy 600	14501029
TC-ANA	A319CJ	1002
TJ-ALG	F.28-4000	11227
TS-IOO	B737 BBJ1	29149/348
TT-ABC	MD-87	49888/1692
TT-ABD	B737 BBJ1	29136/225
TZ-BSA	One-Eleven-492GM	260
TZ-BSB	One-Eleven-401AK	086
TZ-BSC	One-Eleven-488GH	259
TZ-MBA	B727-2K5	21853/640
TZ-TAC	B707-3L6B	21049/896
UK-67000	B767-3P6ER	35796/958
UK-75700	B757-23P	28338/731
UK-80001	Avro RJ85	E2312
UN-65683	Tu134A	62199
UN-85464	Tu-154B	464
UN-87213	Yak-40K	9641050
UN-87488	Yak-40	9441638
UN-87533	Yak-40	9541741
UN-87816	Yak-40	9230724
UP-42721	Yak-42D	4520423310017
UP-87850	Yak-40	9441738
UP-A2001	A320-214	3199
UP-A3001	A330-243	863
UP-B5701	B757-2M6	23454/102
UP-B6701	B767-2DXER	32945/861
UP-BA111	One-Eleven-401AK	078
UP-C8502	Challenger 850	8049
UP-C8503	Challenger 850	8093
UP-CL001	Challenger 870 NG	10289
UP-T3402	Tu-134B	63187
UP-T3409	Tu-134B	62820
UP-Y4015	Yak-40	9530842
UP-Y4025	Yak-40K	9831958
UP-Y4201	Yak-42D	4520423302017
UP-Y4202	Yak-42D	4520423402116
UR-65556	Tu134A	66372
UR-65718	Tu134A	63668
UR-86527	IL62M	4037758
UR-86528	IL62M	4038111
UR-87215	Yak-40	9510540
UR-87964	Yak-40	9820758
UR-88310	Yak-40	9940760
UR-ABA	A319CJ	3260
UR-AER	Do328 Jet	3176
UR-BWF	Yak-40	9711352
UR-CAR	Yak-40K	9741756
UR-CDW	Yak-40	9610546
UR-CLH	Yak-40	9530642
UR-DAP	Yak-40	9521241
UR-DWC	Yak-40	9541144
UR-ECL	Yak-40K	9932059
UR-ETG	Yak-40	9531143
UR-FRU	Yak-40	9440737
UR-ICD	Challenger 850	8072
UR-LRZ	Yak-40K	9641851
UR-OAM	Challenger 850	8084
UR-PVS	Yak-40	9331430
UR-RUS	CRJ200LR	7990
UR-UAS	Yak-40	9420835
UR-WOG	Do328 Jet	3118
VH-LEF	Challenger 850	8060
VH-VHD	A319CJ	1999
VH-VLT	Legacy 600	14501107
VP-BAJ	B727-130 RE	18936/249
VP-BAP	B727-121	19260/412
VP-BAT	B747-SP21	21648/367
VP-BBJ	B737 BBJ1	29273/146
VP-BBW	B737 BBJ1	30076/179
VP-BCC	Challenger 800	7717
VP-BCL	Challenger 870	10247
VP-BDJ	B727-123	20046/605
VP-BED	A319CJ	3073
VP-BEL	B737 BBJ1	29139/189
VP-BEX	A319CJ	2706
VP-BEY	A319CJ	2675
VP-BFT	B737 BBJ1	36714/2340
VP-BHM	DC-8-62	46111/491
VP-BHN	B737 BBJ2	32438/779
VP-BIF	B727-1H2 RE	20533/869
VP-BIZ	B737 BBJ1	34477/1825
VP-BJJ	B737 BBJ1	30330/415
VP-BKS	B767-3P6ER	27254/522
VP-BLK	B747-SP31	21961/415
VP-BNZ	B737 BBJ1	35959/2029
VP-BPZ	B727-117 RE	20327/797
VP-BRM	B737 BBJ1	28976/158
VP-BRT	B737 BBJ1	32970/988
VP-BSD	Challenger 850	8051
VP-BVJ	Challenger 850	8071
VP-BWR	B737 BBJ1	29317/265
VP-BYA	B737 BBJ1	29972/642
VP-BZL	B737 BBJ2	32915/969
VP-CAN	A319-112)	1886
VP-CBA	B737-2W8	22628820
VP-CBB	B737 BBJ2	32806/912
VP-CBH	MD-82	53577/2189
VP-CCJ	A319CJ	2421
VP-CFA	Legacy 600	145637
VP-CHP	Legacy 600	14500802
VP-CIE	A319CJ	1589
VP-CJD	Do328 Jet	3221
VP-CJN	B727-176	20371/822
VP-CKH	A318 Elite	3530
VP-CKS	A318 Elite	3238
VP-CLL	Legacy 600	14501052
VP-CLR	B737 BBJ1	34865/1865
VP-CME	B767-231EM	22567/30
VP-CMK	Legacy 600	14501083
VP-CML	B727-2Y4	22968/1815
VP-CNI	MD-87	49767/1587
VP-CON	Challenger 850	8083
VP-CPA	B737 BBJ1	30031/251
VP-CSK	B737 BBJ2	34620/1803
VP-CSS	A320-232	3402
VP-CTF	MD-87	49777/1634
VP-CUP	Legacy 600	145555
VP-CVX	A319CJ	1212

	Reg	Type	Serial	Code
☐	VP-CZY	B727-2P1 RE	21595/1406	
☐	VQ-BDD	A318 Elite	3751	
☐	VQ-BFP	Legacy 600	14501049	
☐	VQ-BFQ	Legacy 600	14501062	
☐	VQ-BLU	Legacy 600	14501086	
☐	VQ-BMS	B747-SP21	21649/373	
☐	VQ-BOS	B737-8GQ/W	35792/2351	
☐	VT-ARE	CRJ200 ExecLiner	7163	
☐	VT-BSF	Legacy 600	14500901	
☐	VT-CKP	Legacy 600	14501094	
☐	VT-IAH	A319CJ	2837	
☐	VT-IBP	Challenger 850	8070	
☐	VT-KML	Challenger 800	7351	
☐	VT-VJM	A319CJ	2650	
☐	V8-ALI	B747-430	26426/910	
☐	V8-BKH	A340-212	046	
☐	V8-MHB	B767-27GER	25537/517	
☐	XA-AYJ	Lineage 1000	19000243	
☐	XC-FAD	B727-114	18912/169	
☐	XC-LJG	B737-322	24361/1694	
☐	XC-LLS	Do328 Jet	3197	
☐	XC-UJB	B737-33A	24095/1737	
☐	XC-UJM	B757-225/W	22690/151	
☐	XT-BFA	B727-282 RE	22430/1715	
☐	YI-APX	A300B4-203	239	
☐	YK-AQB	Yak-40	9530443	
☐	YK-AYA	Tu-134B	63992	
☐	YK-AYB	Tu-134B	63994	
☐	YR-ANJ	BAe-146-200	E2079	
☐	ZS-IJA	B737-201	22751/857	
☐	ZS-IOC	Do328 Jet	3219	
☐	ZS-JSM	Jetstream 41	41052	
☐	ZS-MNT	DC-9-15	45740/62	
☐	ZS-NOM	Jetstream 41	41047	
☐	ZS-PVX	B727-2N6 RE	22825/1805	
☐	ZS-RSA	B737 BBJ1	32627/826	
☐	ZS-SOF	B767-259ER	24835/321	
☐	3C-EGE	B737 BBJ1	33367/1189	
☐	3C-QQH	ERJ-145EP	145076	
☐	4K-65496	Tu134A	63468	
☐	4K-85729	Tu154M	911	
☐	4K-8888	B727-251	22543/1700	
☐	4K-AZ01	A319CJ	2487	
☐	4L-GAF	Challenger 850	8046	
☐	5A-DSO	F.28-2000	11110	
☐	5A-UAD	Challenger 850	8087	
☐	5H-CCM	F.28-3000	11137	
☐	5N-FGT	B737 BBJ1	34260/1746	
☐	5N-RSG	Legacy 600	14500891	
☐	5R-MRM	737-3Z8	24081/1515	
☐	5U-BAG	737-2N9C	21499/513	
☐	5V-TAI	F.28-1000	11079	
☐	6V-AEF	727-2M1/W RE	21091/1134	
☐	7T-VPP	A340-540	917	
☐	9H-AFK	A319CJ	2592	
☐	9H-AFL	A318 Elite	3363	
☐	9H-AFM	A318 Elite	2910	
☐	9H-AFT	A318 Elite	4169	
☐	9H-AFU	Challenger 800	7176	
☐	9H-BBJ	B737 BBJ1	30791/623	
☐	9H-SNA	A319CJ	3356	
☐	9K-GEA	A319CJ	3957	
☐	9M-NAA	A319CJ	2949	
☐	J-757	A310-304	473	(AP)
☐	OB2	Do328-100	3083	(A2)
☐	554	A320-210	3723	(A4O)
☐	555	A320-210	4117	(A4O)
☐	3701	B737-8AR/W	30139/428	(B)
☐	921	737-58N	28866/2929	(CC)
☐	985	767-3YOER	26205/474	(CC)
☐	10+21	A310-304	498	(D)
☐	10+22	A310-304	499	(D)
☐	15+01	A319CJ	3897	(D)
☐	15+02	A319CJ	4060	(D)
☐	98+47	A340-311	274	(D)
☐	T-501	Legacy 600	14500981	(D2)
☐	T.22-1	A310-304	550	(EC)
☐	F-RAJA	A340-211	075	(F)
☐	F-RARF	A330-223	240	(F)
☐	ZE700	BAe-146-100	E1021	(G)
☐	ZE701	BAe-146-100	E1029	(G)
☐	FAE-051	Legacy 600	14501082	(HC)
☐	FAE-620	B727-230	21620/1419	(HC)
☐	FAE-691	B727-134	19691/487	(HC)
☐	FAC0001	B737 BBJ1	29272/323	(HK)
☐	FAC0002	F.28-1000	11992	(HK)
☐	FAC1041	F.28-3000C	11162	(HK)
☐	85101	737-3Z8	23152/1073	(HL)
☐	1084	ERJ-135LR	14501084	(HS)
☐	1124	ERJ-135LR	14501124	(HS)
☐	HZ-101	B737 BBJ1	32805/940	(HZ)
☐	HZ-102	B737 BBJ2	32451/836	(HZ)
☐	MM62174	A319CJ	1157	(I)
☐	MM62209	A319CJ	1795	(I)
☐	MM62243	A319CJ	2507	(I)
☐	20-1101	B747-47C	24730/816	(JA)
☐	20-1102	B747-47C	24731/839	(JA)
☐	T-01	B757-23A	25487/470	(LV)
☐	T-02	F.28-4000	11203	(LV)
☐	T-03	F.28-1000	11028	(LV)
☐	T-50	F.28-1000	11048	(LV)
☐	01-0015	B737 BBJ1	32916/979	(N)
☐	01-0040	B737 BBJ1	29971/684	(N)
☐	01-0041	B737 BBJ1	33080/1089	(N)
☐	02-0042	B737 BBJ1	33500/1223	(N)
☐	02-0201	B737 BBJ1	30755/545	(N)
☐	02-0202	B737 BBJ1	30753/481	(N)
☐	02-0203	B737 BBJ1	33434/1211	(N)
☐	05-0730	B737 BBJ1	34807/1908	(N)
☐	05-0932	B737 BBJ1	34808/2008	(N)
☐	05-4613	B737 BBJ1	34809/2141	(N)
☐	82-8000	747-2G4B	23824/679	(N)
☐	92-9000	747-2G4B	23825/685	(N)
☐	98-0001	757-2GW/W	29025/783	(N)
☐	98-0002	757-2GW/W	29026/787	(N)
☐	99-0003	757-2GW/W	29027/824	(N)
☐	99-0004	757-2GW/W	29028/829	(N)
☐	FAP-350	B737-244	19707/82	(OB)
☐	FAP-352	B737-282	23042/967	(OB)
☐	FAP356	B737-528	27426/2739	(OB)
☐	2801	A319CJ	2801	(OK)
☐	3085	A319CJ	3085	(OK)
☐	CE-01	ERJ-135ER	145449	(OO)
☐	CE-02	ERJ-135LR	145480	(OO)
☐	CE-03	ERJ-145LR	145526	(OO)
☐	CE-04	ERJ-145LR	145548	(OO)
☐	A-2801	F.28-1000	11042	(PK)
☐	2101	A319CJ	2263	(PP)
☐	2112	ERJ-135LR	14501077	(PP)
☐	2113	ERJ-135LR	14501125	(PP)
☐	2115	B737-2N3	21165/441	(PP)
☐	2116	B737-2N3	21166/445	(PP)
☐	2524	ERJ-145EP	145034	(PP)
☐	2560	ERJ-135LR	145600	(PP)
☐	2561	ERJ-135LR	145608	(PP)
☐	2580	Legacy 600	145412	(PP)
☐	2581	Legacy 600	145462	(PP)
☐	2582	Legacy 600	145495	(PP)
☐	2583	Legacy 600	145528	(PP)
☐	2584	Legacy 600	14500997	(PP)
☐	2585	Legacy 600	14501078	(PP)
☐	2590	ERJ-190LR	19000214	(PP)
☐	2591	ERJ-190LR	19000277	(PP)
☐	102	Tu154M	862	(SP)
☐	209	ERJ-135ER	145209	(SX)
☐	484	Legacy 600	145484	(SX)
☐	A36-001	B737 BBJ1	30829/738	(VH)
☐	A36-002	B737 BBJ1	30790/613	(VH)
☐	K2412	B737-2A8	23036/977	(VT)
☐	K2413	B737-2A8	23037/982	(VT)

☐ K3186	B737-2A8	20484/275	(VT)
☐ K-3187	B737-2A8	20483/273	(VT)
☐ K3601	Legacy 600	14500867	(VT)
☐ K3602	Legacy 600	14500880	(VT)
☐ K3603	Legacy 600	14500910	(VT)
☐ K3604	Legacy 600	14500919	(VT)
☐ K-5012	B737 BBJ1	36106/2118	(VT)
☐ K-5013	B737 BBJ1	36107/2325	(VT)
☐ K-5014	B737 BBJ1	36108/2425	(VT)
☐ 0001	A319CJ	1468	(YV)
☐ 0207	B737-2N1	21167/442	(YV)
☐ KAF308	Fokker 70	11557	(5Y)
☐ G-530	F.28-3000	11125	(9G)
☐ M28-01	F.28-1000	11088	(9M)
☐ M53-01	B737 BBJ1	29274/397	(9M)

Would you like to know more about airline fleets?

Air-Britain's **Airline Fleets 2011** lists the full fleets of almost 2,800 operators in 200 countries including most small twins and commercially-used singles and helicopters. The airline two-and three-letter codes are given together with bases and airport codes. C/ns, most recent previous identity, fleet numbers, aircraft names, non-standard colour schemes and lease details are also included. Aircraft in non-airline use, full indices of all airline codes, operators and major airports also contribute to this valuable reference.

Indispensible for the serious airline enthusiast, this A5 hardback book runs to 720 pages for 2011, costing £26 to non-members and £19.95 to Air-Britain members.

Did you know that there are other Quick Reference titles available?

Business Jets and Turboprops 2011 (BizQR) lists all such aircraft currently in service by registration or military serial, with c/ns. Known reservations are also included. In A5 softback format with 160 pages at £8.95 to non-members, or £6.95 to members.

UK, IoM and Ireland Civil Registers 2011 (UKQR) includes registrations and types of all currently registered G-, M-, and EI- aircraft together with a list of foreign-registered aircraft based in the UK. Also featured are current military serials, a military/civil registration decode, base index and museums listing. Expected 192 pages A5 softback, £8.95 to non-members or £6.95 to members.

European Registers Handbook 2011 is a mixed-media publication with current civil registers of 45 countries (not UK) in QR registration/type format in an A5 softback book of over 500 pages together with a fully searchable CD giving full c/ns, identities and additional information, plus photographs from 2010 events. Available May.

Other annual hardback publications are:

The Civil Aircraft Registers of United Kingdom, Ireland and Isle of Man, 2011. This larger-format of over 650 pages gives full type, c/n, previous identities, date regd, owners, bases and airworthiness details of all current aircraft and many additional reference features. Available April.

Business Jets International 2011 contains full production lists of every type, past and present, in c/n order together with a 77,000-entry regn/c/n index. Available May.

Air-Britain membership offers many advantages, not least reduced prices on all our publications as shown above. There is one 160-page monthly magazine *Air-Britain News*, and a choice of three A4 quarterlies *Aviation World, Aeromilitaria* and *Archive*, together with access to exclusive websites, an information service and travel. Full details may be found on www.air-britain.co.uk or write to Air-Britain, 1 Rose Cottages, 179 Penn Road, Hazlemere, High Wycombe, Bucks HP15 7NE for a free information pack.